ISADORA

A Sensational Life

Peter Kurth

LITTLE, BROWN AND COMPANY

A *Little, Brown* Book

First published in the United States of America by Little, Brown in 2001
First published in Great Britain by Little, Brown in 2002

Copyright © 2001 Peter Kurth

The moral right of the author has been asserted.

Excerpts from *My Life* by Isadora Duncan, copyright © 1927
by Boni & Liveright, Inc. Reissued in a Liveright paperback edition 1995.
Copyright renewed 1955 by Liveright Publishing Corporation.
Excerpts from Mabel Dodge Luhan's *Movers and Shakers*
and her January 1915 letter to Gertrude Stein reprinted with
the permission of Yale University, which holds the copyright.
'Heroism Plus Heroics: Difficulties in Worshipping Isadora Duncan'
quoted courtesy of Lilly Library, Indiana University, Bloomington, IN.

A CIP catalogue record for this book
is available from the British Library.

ISBN 0 316 85435 2

Printed and bound in Great Britain
by Clays Ltd, St Ives plc

Little, Brown
An imprint of
Time Warner Books UK
Brettenham House
Lancaster Place
London WC2E 7EN

www.TimeWarnerBooks.co.uk

ISADORA

Also by Peter Kurth

ANASTASIA
The Riddle of Anna Anderson

AMERICAN CASSANDRA
The Life of Dorothy Thompson

TSAR
The Lost World of Nicholas
and Alexandra

For John Hannah

ad Duncanum gloriam

Contents

Preface   ix

PART I
THE HAPPIER AGE OF GOLD: 1877–1904
3

1. A Baby Bolshevik   5
2. "I Dreamed of a Different Dance"   20
3. Flying Eastward   34
4. London   55
5. Paris   68
6. Germany   92
7. Myth   109

PART II
TWIN SOULS: 1904–1907
127

8. Teddy and Topsy   129
9. "Your Isadora"   147
10. Their Own Sweet Will   165
11. Maternity   184
12. Breaking Stones   200

PART III
PASSION AND THE STORM: 1907–1914
217

13. Pim and Pure Pleasure   219
14. Daughter of Prometheus   236

15. To Love in a Certain Way   255
16. One Great Cry   283
17. The Rock of Niobe   303

PART IV

DECRESCENDO: 1914–1921

321

18. Dionysion 1915   323
19. South America   340
20. "I Tell You She Drives 'Em Mad"   356
21. Sunk in Sorrow, Tossed in Joy   372
22. The Bad Fairy   390

PART V

RUSSIA: 1921–1924

409

23. Comrade Duncan   411
24. Wayward Child   428
25. "How Russian! How Russian!"   441
26. Just a Wee Bit Eccentric   464
27. Genius and Kaputt   481

PART VI

"SANS LIMITES": 1924–1927

497

28. Love and Ideals   499
29. Seraphita   517
30. The Ride to Glory   536

Epilogue   555
Sources and Acknowledgments   559
Abbreviations   563
Notes   565
Index   629

Preface

In those moments where beauty and emotion fuse and climax, something of the immortal floats about the dancer. She wanders in a divine ray, in a mist where all works of art circle in unison with her.

These words about Isadora Duncan, written in 1913 by French composer Reynaldo Hahn,[1] have guided me over the ten years since I began to study her life for a proposed biography. A friend gave me the idea almost casually over lunch, when I found myself (as I always do) thrashing between projects. My first book was a biography of Anna Anderson, the Anastasia claimant, a woman of huge notoriety and no particular substance beyond the question of her identity. My second was the life of journalist Dorothy Thompson, in which the equation was reversed: here was a woman of power, achievement, and depth who nevertheless had been completely forgotten by the time I wrote about her. She had no lasting fame at all. Now I wanted a subject both popular and material, and from the same era — the first part of the twentieth century — which I hoped would keep at least one of my books from consuming a decade of my life.

Alas, as Isadora said, "no flower of art ever fully bloomed save it was nourished by tears of agony."[2] I knew nothing about Isadora when I started — nothing, that is, beyond what most people know: that she was a dancer, a "modern" dancer, and that she died famously, when her long silk scarf (in fact, a shawl with trailing fringes) caught in the wheel of the car she was riding in and strangled her. While still in my teens, about 1970, I had seen Ken Russell's mischievous film for the BBC, *Isadora Duncan: The Biggest Dancer in the World*, starring Vivian Pickles, and took away an impression of Isadora as one of the world's great flakes, an impression still easily gained by the proliferation of her name and features on T-shirts, joke cards, and kitsch — always dancing, always ridiculous, and always with her fatal scarf. Only after I began reading seriously about Isadora did I dare to watch Vanessa

Redgrave in Karel Reisz's 1968 romance, *Isadora* — originally released as *The Loves of Isadora* — and only when I saw Redgrave playing Isadora onstage in London, in Martin Sherman's enchanting play *When She Danced*, did I decide to go ahead with the book. By then I'd come to understand Isadora differently. I remember thinking it was lucky that Martin's play was closing, because if too many more people saw Vanessa as Isadora — live, in the flesh — I wouldn't need to write a word.

This is not a "dance book." Isadora needs rescuing from dancers — more particularly, from dance scholars, whose ideas on her impact and contribution to the art rise frequently to a brilliance of their own but who speak in a language she didn't know, about a subject she dismissed out of hand. "I hate dancing," Isadora once said. "I am an *expressioniste* of beauty. I use my body as my medium, just as the writer uses his words. Do not call me a dancer."[3] Much was made in her own time of the bridge she appeared to build between the decadent Old World and the dynamic New — how she arrived on the scene in 1900 "like a glorious bounding Minerva," in Janet Flanner's phrase, "fusing Zeitgeists" and delivering "an electric shock" to the world of art.[4]

"Art meant Isadora," said John Dos Passos. "Art was whatever Isadora did."[5] At the beginning I didn't know which scared me more — the prospect of learning about "dance," a field as foreign to me as physics or stock-car racing, or Isadora's larger and, I believe, more important role as "Muse of Modernism," the title of a 1998 Duncan exhibition at the Georgia Museum of Art. Books and monographs can be and have been written about every aspect of her stupendous career, from her valiant attempt to establish a school in Moscow after the Russian Revolution to her epochal impact on feminism and fashion, her ideas on education and the theater, her world-famous love life, and her immortal gift, not just to dancers and actors but to graphic artists like Abraham Walkowitz, who produced more than eight thousand paintings and drawings of Isadora and sold them in initially for a nickel apiece on the sidewalks of New York. "I have done more Isadora Duncans than I have hair on my head," Walkowitz confessed. "She had no laws. She created."[6] And inspired. "Her example and fame have evoked a very rash of 'classical dancing' schools," wrote Irish American poet Shaemas O'Sheel, "and have made the lawns of every women's college and girls' school the scene of amazing antics by bare-legged females clad in 'three yards of cheesecloth.' And precisely these results constitute the most striking proof that genius is the golden and priceless thing in the arts, and that nothing else matters very much."[7]

To list the many friends, guides, scholars, and librarians who helped me along the Duncan road is beyond the scope of this preface; a complete list of sources and acknowledgments follows at the back of the book. It was my good fortune when I started out to know George Seldes, the great American reporter, foreign correspondent, and truth teller, who saw Isadora dance in Pittsburgh in 1909 and remembered the occasion with a reverence bordering on adoration. At his house in Vermont, I asked George to tell me what she had looked like "when she danced," but he said only, "No, no, you had to see it! You had to be there! What a woman!" I knew right there that his last three words held the key to the case. With Isadora, I discovered, the question wasn't whether I could learn enough but whether I could be enough. It wasn't detachment, but surrender. "Her dancing has, in the strangest way, the quality of a remembering," said American stage designer Robert Edmond Jones. "It seems to remind us of a beauty we have always known. It tells us of a sublime order and harmony of which we are a part, if we can only recall it. . . . She has given back to us something that once was ours. More than this, she has said to us again and again, in the trancelike exaltations of the evening: *You told me this. Do you remember? Do you remember?*"[8]

JULY 2001

To seek in nature the fairest forms and to find the movement which expresses the soul in these forms — this is the art of the dancer. . . . My inspiration has been drawn from trees, from waves, from clouds, from the sympathies that exist between passion and the storm.

—Isadora Duncan

What is great in man is that he is a bridge and not an end: what can be loved in man is that he is an overture and a going under. I love those who do not know how to live, except by going under, for they are those who cross over. I love the great despisers because they are the great reverers, the arrows of longing for the other shore.

—Friedrich Nietzsche

All truly sacred truths are rich in comedy.

—George Bernard Shaw

ISADORA

Part I

THE HAPPIER AGE

OF GOLD

(1877–1904)

See, garlanded and gracious,

From realms serene and spacious,

A grave and ancient rapture she has brought our

troubled times.

Bearer of mystic treasures,

With magic in her measures,

She comes, her light steps lyric, and her white feet

shod in rhymes.

— Shaemas O'Sheel, "Isadora"

1

A Baby Bolshevik

First, her name.

"I am called Isadora," she wrote. "That means Child of Isis — or *Gift* of Isis."[1] Properly, it should have been *Isidora* (the feminine of Isidore), but the name was hers, given at baptism and not invented later in an effort to seem exotic. Among Isadora's books was a biography of Girolamo Savonarola, the fifteenth-century reformer and heretic, bearing an inscription: "To Isadora Duncan from her mother, also Isadora."[2] The name had entered the family through an "ultra-Catholic" aunt with a devotion to Saint Isidore of Seville, "the most learned man of the Middle Ages," according to *The Catholic Encyclopedia,* and the patron saint of students and scholars. In 1946 Isadora's brother Augustin confirmed that "her full name was Angela Isadora Duncan, the initials spelling 'AID.' Our mother said that meant she was going to be an aid to the family, and she was."[3]

She was born in San Francisco on May 26, 1877, "under the star of Aphrodite," as she told it, the daughter of "wind and wave and the winged flight of bird and bee."[4] Isadora's earliest memory was of being tossed from the window of a building in flames; later, when her children had drowned and her father, whom she barely knew, died in a shipwreck off the coast of England, she compared the Duncan run of misfortune to the sorrows of the House of Atreus.

"The gods sell their gifts dearly," Isadora warned. "For every joy there is a corresponding agony. For what they give of Fame, Wealth, Love, they extract Blood and Tears and grinding Sorrow. I am continually surrounded by flames." Whether the fire she described as her first conscious experience ever really took place is a matter for academics to determine. Facts were not Isadora's concern. The records of her childhood, like the house she was born in on the corner of Geary and Taylor Streets in San Francisco, were lost in the earthquake of 1906: "Always fire and water and sudden fearful death."[5]

Isadora was the child of American pioneers, the "Argonauts" of 1848–49 who opened the way to California and turned San Francisco, a forlorn collection of hovels and tents on the site of a Spanish mission, into a shimmering city known the world over for its forward spirit. No stories needed inventing to add a touch of glamour to the gold rush, but invented they were, not least by Isadora. At the end of her life, seeking to explain the genesis of her art, she put it down to a love of legend:

> It has often made me smile — but somewhat ironically — when people have called my dancing "Greek." For I myself count its origin in the stories which my Irish grandmother often told us of crossing the plains with grandfather in '49 in a covered wagon — she 18, he 21 — and how her first child was born in such a wagon during a famous battle with the redskins, and how, when the Indians were finally defeated, my grandfather put his head in at the door of the wagon, with a smoking gun in his hand, to greet his newborn child.

That none of this was true, Isadora may have known. Her mother, Mary Dora Gray, the *last* child of the grandparents she describes, was born in St. Louis, a full year before the Gray family headed for San Francisco — by ship, through Panama, "the rich man's route." There were no prairies, no covered wagons, no "redskins." Still, said Isadora:

> My grandmother, thinking of Ireland, used often to sing the Irish songs and dance the Irish jigs, only I fancy that into these Irish jigs had crept some of the heroic spirit of the pioneer and the battle with the redskins — probably some of the gestures of the redskins themselves — and, again, a bit of "Yankee Doodle" when grandfather, Colonel Thomas Gray, came marching home from the Civil War.
> All this grandmother danced in the Irish jig, and I learned it from her and put it into my own aspiration of Young America, and finally

my great spiritual realization of life from the lines of Walt Whitman. And that is the origin of the so-called Greek dance with which I have flooded the world.[6]

Isadora's maternal grandfather, Thomas Gray, was indeed a veteran of the Civil War and, before that, the Black Hawk War, in which he had been friendly with Abraham Lincoln. A native of Cloghan, King's County (now County Offaly), Ireland, Gray came to the United States as a teenager in 1819, settling first in Baltimore and later in Ohio, Illinois, and Missouri. An 1880 census in San Francisco lists Colonel Gray as a sea captain, the operator of the first commercial ferry service between Oakland and San Francisco and a three-time delegate to the California state legislature. Gray's wife, Maggie Gorman, was "a Spanish type of beauty"[7] (not uncommon among the Irish), and together they had eight children, including three daughters in addition to Isadora's mother: Ellen, Elizabeth, and Augusta, still living at home in her early thirties, whom Isadora remembered as a "remarkably talented" woman.

"She often visited us and would have performances of private theatricals," Isadora wrote. "She was very beautiful, with black eyes and coal black hair, and I remember her dressed in black velvet 'shorts' as Hamlet. She had a beautiful voice and might have had a great career as a singer had it not been that everything relating to the theatre was looked upon by her father and mother as pertaining to the Devil."[8] The specter of the devil was undoubtedly strong in Isadora's imagination. Once, she asked her mother's sisters to tell her something about her father, and the answer came back, "Your father was a demon who ruined your mother's life." After that, said Isadora, "I always imagined him as a demon in a picture book, with horns and a tail, and when other children at school spoke of their fathers, I kept silent."[9]

Isadora's father was Joseph Charles Duncan, a man of cheerful temperament and high ambition, "full of push and pluck," a poet, a ladies' man, and a luckless entrepreneur, "one of the most daring bank-wreckers that ever flitted above the financial horizons of the Golden Gate."[10] Reports agree that Duncan's "arc of oscillation was wide" and that even repeated failures and scandals failed to quell his brazen spirit. Isadora's brother Raymond confirmed with pride: "My father knew General Grant. . . . He said he never knew if or when he was beaten, so he just kept on going."[11]

Born in Philadelphia in 1819, Joseph Duncan was effectively of the same generation as Isadora's grandfather, Colonel Gray, and his early life reflects the same pioneer spirit and continual migration: from Philadelphia to Maryland, New York, Illinois, New Orleans, and, finally, San Francisco. Joseph Duncan's father, Joseph Moulder Duncan, had been a teacher, a professor of belles lettres at Washington College in Chestertown, Maryland. In 1827 the first of the family fires broke out and the college burned to the ground. A local newspaper reported that the Duncans' loss was more severe than any other: they were "deprived of nearly every article of property [they] possessed. Mr. Duncan has been in an instant, as it were, stripped of his all and left in a destitute situation, with a wife and two small children."[12] The pattern of disaster would assert itself inexorably in the years ahead.

From Maryland, the Duncan family moved to New York — Manhattan — where bad luck followed them: fire, "Asian cholera," and the financial panic of 1837, when the New York economy collapsed and an estimated 100,000 people fled the city. Shortly afterward, Isadora's father set off for Indiana and Illinois with his younger brother and partner, William Lorenzo, where they busied themselves "buying up produce and horses and hogs, shipping out stocks to St. Louis and the then rapidly developing city of Chicago."[13] But the scent of belles lettres was still strong in the air. In Bloomington, Illinois, Duncan edited what was described as the first literary magazine in that state, *The Prairie Flower,* "containing original tales, poetry, sketches of the west, illustrations of history, letters from the east, biographical sketches, anecdotes and literature in general."[14] Within a year, the magazine failed. About the same time, Duncan contracted his first marriage, to Elmira Hill, a Virginian, who bore him four children, Isadora's half sisters and brothers: Caroline, Harriet, William, and Joseph. Society notes in the Bloomington newspaper reveal that in 1846 Duncan attended temperance meetings, though whether as a thumper or a penitent, it's impossible to say.

Duncan landed in California in September 1850, at almost the same moment Colonel Gray got there. Fifty thousand people arrived in San Francisco in 1849 alone; two years later the city already rivaled Boston and New York in foreign trade. "There evolved a democracy of happy greed," writes historian Tom Cole. "Distances were so great and the city's needs so unpredictable that Eastern merchants were simply filling up boats with whatever they thought might sell in San Francisco and sending them off with a prayer." In the absence of warehouses, goods were kept, when not on the streets, in the holds of ships, which also served as hotels, banks, business offices, brothels, drunk tanks, "and, in the case of the *Euphemia,* [as] a much-needed jail and refuge for lunatics."[15] San Francisco was a city of freebooters, thieves, soldiers, "pols," vigilantes, snake-oil salesmen, and Emperor Norton — a British-born forty-niner who, having lost everything in a bid to control San Francisco's rice trade, declared himself "Emperor of the United States and Protector of Mexico" in 1859. Norton printed his own money, abolished Congress, fired Abraham Lincoln, outlawed the Democratic and Republican Parties, and dropped dead on California Street in 1880, when Isadora was three, one of many extravagant characters who gave San Francisco its legacy of outrageousness.

"I have seen purer liquors, better seegars, finer tobacco, truer guns and pistols, larger dirks and bowie knives, and prettier cortezans, here in San Francisco than in any place I have ever visited," said a satisfied migrant, "and it is my unbiased opinion that California can and does furnish the best bad things that are obtainable in America."[16] On reaching the city, Joseph Duncan helped organize a lottery, in which he subsequently lost $225,000. Because money was locally printed, however, and because everyone around him was in the same boat, the failure had no effect on his ambition. Fifteen years later Mark Twain arrived in San Francisco and found "a wild, free, disorderly, grotesque society" still gripped by gambling fever:

> Stocks went on rising, speculation went mad; bankers, merchants, lawyers, doctors, mechanics, laborers, even the very washerwomen and servant girls, were putting up their earnings on silver stocks, and every sun that rose in the morning went down on paupers enriched and rich men beggared. What a gambling carnival it was! . . . And then — all of a sudden, out went the bottom and everything and everybody went to ruin and destruction! The wreck was complete. The bubble left scarcely a microscopic moisture behind it.[17]

In the course of his career, Joseph Duncan would edit three newspapers, the *Morning Globe,* the *Evening Globe,* and the *Mirror,* as well as a treacly Sunday supplement drenched in contented wisdom, the *California Home Journal.* Earlier, when one of his printing presses burned, he emerged as proprietor of the "Chinese Sales Room" on the wharf in San Francisco, selling "Bandas and Pongees, Mantillas and Mantelets, Silks Embroidered by Patient Hindoos, Work-boxes of Bombay, Scented Sandalwood, Grotesque Carriages from Japan, etc., etc." As an "art importer," Duncan made buying trips to Europe, and once — while also listed on San Francisco's delinquent tax list — he negotiated the sale of rare miniatures of George and Martha Washington to the tsar of Russia.

In 1856 J. C. Duncan & Co. auctioned the jewelry of Lola Montez, the Irish-born adventuress and "Spanish dancer," who may have been Duncan's lover — he would have been one among many. Montez's career as an international beauty, author, dancer, huckster, courtesan, philosopher, and Bavarian countess had taken her from Limerick through the courts of Europe to Munich, where she seduced King Ludwig I of Bavaria and helped bring down the monarchy in 1848. Later she settled in Grass Valley, near Sacramento. "The international bad girl of the mid-Victorians," Montez had also been the mistress of Franz Liszt and Alexandre Dumas and was known across Europe as La Grande Horizontale.[18]

While the most notorious, Montez wasn't the first or last of Joseph Duncan's needy female clients. By the 1860s, as founder of the San Francisco Art Association, he was "the admitted authority on all matters appertaining to art on the Pacific Coast" — a grand and onerous claim not forgotten by his daughter.[19] Duncan's poems appeared in magazines and handsome anthologies (one of them edited by his friend Bret Harte), and he was the first to publish the work of Ina Donna Coolbrith, red-haired niece of Mormon prophet Joseph Smith and the woman who became California's first poet laureate. Before she died in 1928, Coolbrith would acknowledge Duncan as the love of her life, "so gentle, so great an idealist and so fine a poet."[20] His "art spirit" and splashing personality remained a source of pride to Isadora, even when scandal and bankruptcy had ruined her family on Duncan's account.

Isadora's parents were married when her father was past fifty and her mother, Mary Dora Gray, not quite twenty-one. Duncan's union with Elmira Hill had dissolved along the way;[21] their children were grown, and it couldn't have been happy for the Gray family — Catholic, with notions about the devil — to see their daughter and sister married to an Episcopal speculator, poet, and bon vivant thirty years her senior. Nothing is recorded of the Duncans' meeting or courtship, only that the wedding was performed on January 21, 1871, at the home of the bride's father and that Mary Dora "was a forerunner of the feminists, boldly printing her first name on calling cards and wearing low-cut dresses, much to [her] father's chagrin."[22]

Of the four children of Joseph Duncan's second marriage, Mary Elizabeth was born first, in November 1871. Augustin followed in

1873, Raymond in 1875, and Isadora, last, in 1877. That year, on October 13, she was baptized at Old Saint Mary's Church on California Street, just five days after the worst disaster of her father's career — the collapse of the Pioneer Land and Loan Bank, popularly known as "Duncan's Bank," which Duncan had founded after two decades of auctioneering, publishing, and "homestead enterprises." In her autobiography, Isadora fudges dates and improves the tale, but she hardly exaggerates the atmosphere of storm that attended her first months of life.

"The character of a child is already plain, even in its mother's womb," she wrote. "Before I was born my mother was in great agony of spirit and in a tragic situation. She could take no food except iced oysters and iced champagne. If people ask me when I began to dance I reply, 'In my mother's womb, probably as a result of the oysters and champagne — the food of Aphrodite.'"[23] All her life, she insisted that her father's disappearance had coincided with her birth, that she was "born in America in the city of San Francisco on the day when a revolution broke out there," as she declared in a speech in Russia in 1924: "The revolution, of course, was a 'golden' one; it was the 'golden' day when all the banks in San Francisco went bankrupt. Furious crowds raged in the streets." A mob had stormed the Duncans' house on Geary Street, crying, "Hang Duncan!" and menacing the family with torches and pikes.[24] If Isadora invented these stories, she was telling them already as a little girl; her mother, reputedly in labor in the midst of the riots, "expected a monster."

"This child that will be born will surely not be normal," Mrs. Duncan predicted. "And in fact," wrote Isadora, "from the moment I was born it seemed that I began to agitate my arms and legs in such a fury that my mother cried, 'You see I was quite right; the child is a maniac!'"[25] It would be another three years before her parents were divorced, but their separation was fact by the time Isadora was baptized. Mrs. Duncan said later that "if her four children had not been [born] so close together," if Duncan hadn't had so many "woman friends" or had refrained from melting down the table silver and pawning her jewelry, their marriage "might have succeeded."[26]

The collapse of Duncan's bank, while described in San Francisco newspapers as "a swindle of more than ordinary magnitude,"[27] was part of a larger and drastic reorganization of the city's finances and enterprise, a period of crushing reversals that attended the closing of the silver mines and the conversion of the local economy to less speculative pursuits. Most of the Pioneer's customers were workingmen and -women — "laborers and servant girls predominating" — who, beginning in 1874, had entrusted their savings to Duncan in return for "the highest rate of interest ever paid by a like concern."[28] Duncan was chief stockholder in his own company, its "projector" and organizer, but he was assisted in business by one of his sons; his brother, William Lorenzo; a son-in-law, Benjamin Le Warne; and his new wife's father, Colonel Gray, who became the Pioneer's nominal president.

At its peak, the Pioneer Bank had some three thousand depositors. The five-story building that rose to house it on the southeast corner of Montgomery and California Streets was the work of architect William Patton and an ornament of the city, "visited by every stranger" in San Francisco. Duncan himself was hailed in the newspapers as "the poor man's friend," a family man, a Sunday-school teacher, "the disinterested financier of modern times."[29]

By 1877, however, as one San Francisco bank after another shut its doors, Duncan found himself trapped in the larger crisis of the time. He panicked, recklessly speculating in stocks and raising shares to stay afloat. When the Pioneer's vaults were opened, most of them were empty; an employee testified later that the bank had never had more than $8,000 cash on hand. On October 8 the Pioneer shut down, and "by noon the town was ripe for lynching."[30] A crowd gathered in Montgomery Street, clamoring for Duncan's head. Later Duncan insisted that he had done all he could to rescue the bank, that he had "not intended to defraud anyone" and had "transferred no property" to himself or anyone in his family.[31] In the meantime, prudently, he went into hiding.

DAINTY DUNCAN, read the headline in the *Oakland Tribune* on October 10: HIS DASTARDLY DOINGS. DUNCAN'S DEPRAVITY GROWS GREATER EVERY HOUR. Suddenly, the poor man's friend was an "oily old hypocrite," "addicted to drink," "about as pious as the average polite thief of the last half of the nineteenth century," according to a vituperative essay in the *San Francisco Chronicle*.[32] "The wildest excitement" prevailed in the city. Ships were searched and attics combed. Until Duncan was finally apprehended in a rooming house on Kearny Street, four months later, San Francisco police chief Captain John Kirkpatrick bore the weight of public outrage. That Duncan was captured in a house right next door to Kirkpatrick's did nothing to salvage the reputation of the police: he had been hiding there for weeks, "in a bureau with a makeshift bed." A Captain Isaiah Lees was the hero of the hour, who quietly knocked on the door of Duncan's hideout and threatened "to blow off the top of his head" if he tried to escape.

Duncan was arraigned on sixteen charges of forgery and one of felony (for "false swearing"). An investigation revealed that, for much of his hiding, he had walked around San Francisco disguised as a woman. A search of the Kearny Street cupboard produced "a chemise with a lace border, a skirt with suitable bustle attached, . . . a wig of woman's chestnut hair, a cute black velvet hat with a pretty bunch of violets on the crown, and a thick brown veil." Apparently, Duncan hoped "to board an outgoing vessel and make good his escape" while disguised as a prostitute. "I am wrecked," he confessed, "financially, physically and mentally."[33]

Over the next few years, Duncan was brought to trial four times. Three juries split, and the fourth voted for acquittal on a technicality, by order of the judge.[34] It was no secret in San Francisco that Duncan still had powerful friends and that many of them, including his father-in-law, Colonel Gray, were significantly mixed up in the business of the doomed Pioneer. Duncan's crime seemed larger than most, however, since it wasn't the rich whose lives had been disrupted in the crash, but the working poor. Newspapers spoke of "ruin on all sides. Men and women prostrated by the wiping out of their life's work became despondent and in many instances reckless. Lives were blighted and shattered. Models of sobriety became drunkards, and men and women of unquestioned morality turned into outlaws against society."[35]

The date of Joseph Duncan's divorce from Mary Dora Gray is no longer known (a casualty, again, of the San Francisco earthquake). More than a banking scandal moved Isadora's mother to such a drastic solution: at the height of the crisis, she had discovered "perfumed letters" in Duncan's office, signed by another woman and outlining plans for escape from the maelstrom. It was a betrayal Mary Dora never forgave. Her divorce was probably final by 1880. Duncan stayed in the Bay Area for three more years, operating as "a broker" on Montgomery Street, until, finally, he went south to the boomtown of Los Angeles. There he remarried — the sister of the wife of one of his grown sons — and began a new career in real estate.

"When the boom in real estate came along he was in the forefront of the speculators," the *San Francisco Examiner* reported. "He bought and sold property day and night. At one stage of the boom he was reputed to be worth easily $250,000 in cash. . . . But a second time he overreached himself, and when the bottom dropped out of the boom

Duncan was practically a pauper." On October 14, 1898, with his third wife, Mary, and their twelve-year-old daughter, Rosa, he was sailing from London to New York on the S.S. *Mohegan* when it crashed on Manacle Rocks near Falmouth, in Cornwall: "There had been a dance aboard the *Mohegan* that night and the crew were tipsy."[36] More than a hundred people died in the disaster, "and a few hours after the wreck the waves, with strange caprice," laid the bodies of the Duncan family "one after the other on the shingled beach of St. Keverne."[37] Joseph Duncan was seventy-nine.

Later, with utmost seriousness, Isadora Duncan insisted that her "first idea" of movement, of the dance, came from "the rhythm of the waves," that she was "born by the sea," and that all the great events of her life had taken place by the sea.[38] Her mother, meantime, shamed and outraged, gave advice to both of her daughters. "Don't trust men," said Mrs. Duncan. "Don't marry them."[39]

In her autobiography, apart from mentioning his poetic soul and the "tremendous impact" his absence would have on her life, Isadora describes her father only once:

> When I was seven years old, we were living in two very bare rooms on the third floor [in Oakland], and one day I heard the front door bell ring, and, on going out into the hall to answer it, I saw a very good-looking gentleman in a top hat, who said:
>
> "Can you direct me to Mrs. Duncan's apartment?"
>
> "I am Mrs. Duncan's little girl," I replied.
>
> "Is this my Princess Pug?" said the strange gentleman. (That had been his name for me when I was a baby.)
>
> And suddenly he took me in his arms and covered me with tears and kisses. I was very much astonished at this proceeding, and asked him who he was. To which he replied with tears, "I am your father."

"Delighted," Isadora rushed inside to tell the family:

> "There is a man there who says he is my father."
>
> My mother rose, very white and agitated, and, going into the next room, locked the door behind her. One of my brothers hid under the bed and the other retired to a cupboard, while my sister had a violent fit of hysterics.
>
> "Tell him to go away, tell him to go away," they cried.

Isadora went back to the hall, "much amazed," but managed to summon her finest manner. "The family are rather indisposed," she declared, "and cannot receive to-day." Then her father took her by the hand and led her to an ice-cream parlor, where he "stuffed [her] with ice-cream and cakes." She remained in a state of "bewildered enchantment" for as long as the idyll lasted, but at home she found her family "in a terribly depressed condition."

"He is a perfectly charming man," said Isadora, "and he is coming tomorrow to give me more ice-cream." But he didn't: "The family refused to see him, and after a time he returned to his other family at Los Angeles." All her childhood, Isadora wrote, was passed in "the black shadow of this mysterious father of whom no one would speak, and the terrible word divorce was imprinted on the sensitive plate of my mind. As I could not ask anyone for the explanation of these things, I tried to reason them out for myself."[40] The task seemed more urgent in light of her mother's constant warnings — apparently, Mrs. Duncan never scrupled to tell her children that if they met their father, he would kidnap them.[41] By the time she reached her teens, a winsome, sturdy girl with light brown hair and gray-blue eyes, Isadora had already decided that marriage was "a pretty low-down proposition," resolving then and there "to fight against marriage and for the emancipation of women, and for the right of every woman to have a child or children as it pleased her, and to uphold her right and her virtue."[42] The "Christian education," Isadora concluded, "does not know how to teach children Nietzsche's superb phrase: 'Be hard!' Only from an early age some spirit kept whispering to me, 'Be hard.'"[43]

Isadora was "a joy" to her family from the moment of her birth, according to her brother Augustin, "a lovely child, sweet and kind. She was docile as a girl, too."[44] Like her mother, she was called Dora, sometimes Dorita, and quickly lived up to the prophecy that she would be an aid to her family in distress. After her divorce, Mrs. Duncan moved with her children to Oakland, where, at different times over the next dozen years, they lived in a succession of walk-ups, rooming houses, hotels, and cold-water flats — on Fourth Street, Eighth Street, Tenth Street, Sunpath Avenue, and, briefly, on a rented farm in the Napa Valley, where they "hid out . . . miles from anywhere," and Mary Dora nursed her wounds.[45]

"Although she was an educated woman," Isadora remarked, "she was barely able to earn a bit of bread for herself and her children by giving music lessons. Her earnings were small and not enough to feed us. Whenever I remember my childhood, I see before me an empty house. With my mother at her lessons, we children sat by ourselves, generally hungry, and in winters generally cold."[46] A friend remembered Mrs. Duncan as "a very critical and outspoken woman" with an aversion to "grown-ups."[47] She preferred the company of children to any other and was incapable of managing money. Florence Treadwell, Isadora's best childhood friend and schoolmate in Oakland, ventured that the Duncans were by nature improvident: "They either had abundance or nothing. There was no frugality; no thrift. . . . They were governed by impulse. On getting a little money they would go to the city and have a big French dinner with wine. On one meal would be spent money that could, if spent judiciously, have fed them the following week."[48]

Oakland in the 1880s was a pleasant, tree-lined community of about fifteen thousand people, connected to San Francisco only by ferryboat and prized for its less turbulent weather and the illusion it gave of country living. Florence Treadwell remembered Oakland as "a great meadow with generously distributed groups of magnificent old oak trees . . . dairy farms, cool, shady canyons, and homes with palm trees and windmills."[49] Later, when they knew each other as expatriates in Paris, Raymond Duncan confessed to Gertrude Stein that he and Isadora had often stolen apples from her father's orchard. The Steins, who moved to Oakland in 1880, "had ten acres where they had every kind of fruit tree growing, and they had cows and dogs and horses and hay making, and the sun in the summer dry and baking, and the wind in the autumn and in the winter the rain beating and then in the springtime the hedge of roses to fence all these joys in."[50]

In fact, Oakland was a railroad town, the western terminus of the transcontinental railway. When times were good, as they sometimes were, Mrs. Duncan employed servants. A Chinese cook is mentioned, along with a nurse, Mary Ward, whom the Duncans teased for her Catholic faith.

"If God created man," the children cried, "who created God?" They were raised in an atmosphere of aggressive freethinking and hedonism, their mother having "revolted violently to definite atheism" and broken with the Catholic Church at the time of her divorce.[51] Mrs. Duncan became a disciple of Robert Ingersoll, the Great Agnostic, whose anticlerical maxims included the advice "with soap, baptism is a good thing" and "many people think they have religion when they are merely troubled with dyspepsia." More important, Isadora found in Ingersoll's writings the thread of her own life's philosophy: "Art in its highest forms increases passion, gives tone and color and zest to life. . . . It is careless of conduct and consequence. For a moment, the chain of cause and effect seems broken; the soul is free. . . . Under the influence of art the walls expand, the roof rises, and it becomes a temple."[52]

While teaching music in Oakland, Isadora's mother also earned money by knitting mittens, hats, and scarves, which she sold to local shops and stores and which figure prominently in Isadora's catalog of formative experiences. Later, she recalled her childhood as "a perpetual state of terror . . . a continual changing of address from one lodging or small cottage to another." But the youngest Duncan was also "the most courageous," in her own account, the winning child who went to the butcher and the baker to beg for credit when the last coins were spent. One day she found her mother weeping on the bed. Mrs. Duncan had failed to sell her knitting, and Isadora gave way to revolt. If her brother remembered her as docile, she grew out of it quickly enough:

> I decided I would sell these things for Mother and at a good price. I put on one of the little red knitted capes and caps, and with the rest in a basket I set forth. From house to house I peddled my wares. Some people were kind, others rude. On the whole I had success, but it was the first awakening in my childish breast of the monstrous injustice of the world. And that little red knitted cap that my mother had made was the cap of a baby Bolshevik.[53]

Isadora raised a memorable ruckus at Oakland's Cole Elementary School one Christmas in the 1880s, when her teacher gave out candy with the words "See, children, what Santa Claus has brought you."

"I don't believe you," Isadora piped up; "there is no such thing as Santa Claus."

"Candies are only for little girls who believe in Santa Claus," the teacher replied.

"Then I don't want your candy," said Isadora.

She was called to the front of the class and ordered to sit on the floor. Instead, she turned to her classmates and made "the first of [her] famous speeches."

"I don't believe lies," Isadora cried. "My mother told me she is too poor to be Santa Claus; it is only the rich mothers who can pretend to be Santa Claus and give presents." The teacher grabbed her by the shoulders and tried to force her to her knees, "but I stiffened my legs and held on to her, and she only succeeded in hitting my heels against the parquet."

"There is no Santa Claus! There is no Santa Claus," Isadora chanted. She was sent to a corner and finally home, still shouting, "There is no Santa Claus."

"Wasn't I right?" she asked her mother. "There is no Santa Claus, is there?"

"There is no Santa Claus," Mrs. Duncan replied, "and there is no God, only your own spirit to help you."[54]

In fact, there was more. There was music, and there was art — art with a capital A. For the length of Isadora's childhood, wherever the Duncans lived, a copy of Botticelli's *Primavera* hung conspicuously over the bookcase. "It came to me what a wonderful movement there was in that picture," Isadora wrote, "and how each figure through that movement told the story of its new life. And then as Mother played Mendelssohn's Spring Song, as if by the impulse of a gentle wind, the daisies in the grass would sway and the figures in the picture would move."[55] At night, Mrs. Duncan read aloud from Shakespeare, Browning, Shelley, Keats, Dickens, Thackeray, Burns, and Whitman, whose "Song of Myself" would become Isadora's religion. "I am the spiritual daughter of Walt Whitman," she declared:

> *I celebrate myself, and sing myself,*
> *And what I assume you shall assume,*
> *For every atom belonging to me as good belongs to you.*
> . . . .
> *Creeds and schools in abeyance,*
> *Retiring back a while sufficed at what they are, but never forgotten,*
> *I harbor for good or bad, I permit to speak at every hazard,*
> *Nature without check with original energy.*

Notwithstanding the continual hunt for money, poetry and music came first in the lives of the Duncans. For hours Mrs. Duncan sat at the piano, playing "Beethoven, Schubert, Mozart, Schumann." Isadora remembered these evenings as enchanted idylls and said that her "real education" was gained while lying on the rug at her mother's feet. Her formal schooling proved "absolutely useless." No one could learn "with an empty stomach, or cold feet in wet shoes"; Isadora's teachers had revealed "a brutal incomprehension of children."

"I remember that in the classroom I was either considered amazingly intelligent and at the head of my class, or quite hopelessly stupid and at the bottom of the class," Isadora wrote. "It all depended on a trick of memory, and whether I had taken the trouble to memorise the subject we were given to learn. And I really had not the slightest idea what it was about." She was a clock-watcher, waiting impatiently to leave school each day for Oakland's public library, where she, like "Gerty" Stein, was taken under the wing of the librarian, Ina Coolbrith, the Poet of the Pacific, whom Isadora's father had published and loved. Legend maintained that when Coolbrith's mother fled Mormon polygamy in 1851 and headed for California, haunted all the way by visions of the Donner Party, Jim Beckwourth had lifted ten-year-old Ina into his saddle for the last day's ride, so she could be "the first white child" to see the promised land. "There, little girl," Beckwourth said, "there is California! There is your kingdom!" It having been conquered already, Stein and Isadora would both turn their backs on it. "The dominant note of my childhood was the constant spirit of revolt against the narrowness of the society in which we lived," Isadora wrote, "and a growing desire to fly eastward to something I imagined might be broader." At the age of ten (so she said), she quit school.[56]

"I informed my mother that it was useless for me to go to school any more," she wrote, "as it was only a waste of time when I could be making money, which I considered far more important. I put my hair on the top of my head and said that I was sixteen. As I was very tall for my age every one believed me."[57] Her mother wasn't in the habit of contradicting her — or, indeed, restricting her movements at all. "Fortunately she was blissfully unconscious," said Isadora. "I say fortunately for me, for it is certainly to this wild, untrammelled life of my childhood that I owe the inspiration of the dance I created, which was but the expression of freedom. I was never subjected to the continual 'don'ts' which it seems to me make children's lives a misery."[58] To the dismay of her staid relations, Isadora swung carelessly on a backyard trapeze, hanging by her heels, or ran away alone "into the woods" or to the deserted beach below the Cliff House in San Francisco.

"And there I danced," she wrote. "I felt even then that my shoes and my clothes only hindered me. My heavy shoes were like chains; my clothes were my prison. So I took everything off. And without any eyes watching me, entirely alone, I danced, naked by the sea. And it seemed to me as if the sea and all the trees were dancing with me."[59]

2

"I Dreamed of a Different Dance"

The birth of Duncan dance — arguably, of everything now called modern dance — was a natural phenomenon, according to Isadora, not an invention but a rediscovery of the classical principles of beauty, motion, and form. "I was possessed by the dream of Promethean creation," she wrote, "that, at my call, might spring from the Earth, descend from the Heavens, such dancing figures as the world had never seen."[1] Isadora's reference to Prometheus was neither casual nor likely to be misunderstood by her contemporaries. They all knew their Greeks, knew, too, that the characteristics of Prometheus, the Titan who stole fire from Mount Olympus and gave it to the world, were boldness, freethinking, and dedication to mankind. Isadora described herself frankly as "an egotist and a person of one idea,"[2] who at the age of six "collected half a dozen babies of the neighbourhood — all of them too young to walk," lined them up in a row on the floor, and taught them to "wave their arms" in preconscious ecstasy.[3] She would give dance to the people as Prometheus gave fire — on her own authority, having wrested her treasure from its jealous guardians and brought it fresh to a new awakening.

"The true dance is an expression of serenity," Isadora reflected; "it is controlled by the profound rhythm of human emotion. . . . The Greeks understood the continuing beauty of a movement that mounted, that spread, that ended with a promise of rebirth. The Dance — it is the rhythm of all that dies in order to live again; it is the eternal rising of the sun."[4] Through the years, in essays, letters, and speeches from the stage, she pointed to a wide array of influences as the spurs to her creative vision: the sea, the wind, the music her mother played at the piano, Botticelli's *Primavera,* Shelley's "Sensitive-Plant," "the opening of flowers," "the flight of bees," and "the free glad gold of the oranges and the California poppy." Always, it was Nature that moved Isadora — beauty, simplicity, and unbroken rhythm.[5]

From the waving of poppies to "the poetry of motion" and straight to the steps of the Parthenon was a distance traveled lightly and swiftly in Isadora's mind. In origin, at least, her life's devotion to classical Greece could be traced to the American search for cultural legitimacy and the romantic idea that "ancient" and "beautiful" were one and the same. A century of Hellenism had already done its work before Isadora saw the Elgin Marbles, the Nike of Samothrace, the caryatids, and Tanagra figurines. "I did not invent my dance," she repeated, "it existed before me, but it lay dormant. I merely discovered and awakened it."[6]

The Greece of the Duncans was the Greece of the Romantics, of Byron, Shelley, and Keats, the high-minded vision of classical antiquity popularized by eighteenth-century scholar Johann Winckelmann and made stunningly real in Isadora's childhood by Heinrich Schliemann, the German businessman and publicity wizard credited with the discovery of "the gold of Troy." Schliemann's excavations in Asia Minor in the 1870s and 1880s were the most thrilling archaeological find of the nineteenth century, giving substance and new authority to the idea of ancient Greece as a lost Utopia, a vanished world of gods and heroes, simplicity, sublimity, "harmony," and wisdom. Greece, in this sense, was wholly conceptual, open to the creative imagination and not concerned with the shards and minutiae of historical inquiry. In Emerson's words, "Our love of the antique is not love of the old, but love of the natural."

To citizens of the young American republic, particularly, the Greek archetype held a strong appeal. To be "Greek" in Victorian America was to be pure, clean, simple, virtuous, serious of purpose, and devoted to the humanist principles of science, literature, philosophy, and art. Neither was there anything elitist about the American passion for antiquity: Greece was for everybody, as evidenced by the huge proliferation in the United States of Greek architecture, Greek

theaters, Greek societies and games, "Grecian" aspects in leisure and
dress, and a "Greek" conception of individual liberty. In California,
where the climate and coastline struck residents and visitors alike as a
replica of the "free Hellenic shore,"[7] the ideal took root and flourished
in an explosion of classical images, from the Greek Theater at Berkeley and, later, the Temple of the Wings, to the early crop of Californian
whole-grain personalities, wandering the coast in cheesecloth and
sandals, disdaining "convention," preaching the healthy properties of
sunlight and air, nuts and fruits, and affirming their right to live and
love as they pleased. In this respect, Isadora's dance reflected an established Californian trend.[8]

A worship of the classics, however, couldn't by itself confer re-
spectability on dancing. "What was it that made men at that time exclaim, 'I would rather see my daughter dead than on the stage?'"
Isadora wondered.[9] Since the Reformation, at least, dancing was held
to be "the vilest vice of all" among Puritans and bluestockings, "an animal affair," "unwise, inexpedient, and, consequently, sinful."[10] For
centuries, the word *dancer* was virtually synonymous with the word
prostitute, while a ballerina, the only sort of dancer in Isadora's childhood with a potential claim to art, was an extravagant sight — "with
jewels in her pompadour," as the *New York Times'* John Martin described her, "a coquettish smile on her lips, her torso encased in
whalebone, an aura of tulle ruffles about her thighs, her shapely legs
encased in fleshings, and box-tied pink slippers upon her feet."[11] It
was against this creature, specifically, in favor of the antique ideal, that
Isadora rebelled.

"The real American type can never be a ballet dancer," she wrote
in her 1927 broadside, "I See America Dancing." "The legs are too
long, the body too supple, and the spirit too free for this school of affected grace and toe-walking. It is noteworthy that all great ballet
dancers have been very short women with small frames. A tall finely
made woman could never dance the ballet. The type which expresses
America at its finest could never dance the ballet. With the wildest
turn of the imagination, you cannot picture the Goddess of Liberty
dancing the ballet." Isadora took the title of her essay from Whitman's
"I hear America singing" and called upon American composers to
write music that would express the poet's ecstatic vision. "Long-
legged strong boys and girls will dance to this music," she predicted,
"in a striking upward tremendous mounting, powerful mounting
above the pyramids of Egypt, beyond the Parthenon of Greece, an ex-

pression of Beauty and Strength such as no civilization has ever known. That will be America dancing."[12] Wherever her career might take her, and no matter how great her disappointments, Isadora always returned to the Greek ideal. "To express what is the most moral, healthful and beautiful in art," she declared, "this is the mission of the dancer, and to this I dedicate my life." She wrote in 1903:

> The Greeks in all their painting, sculpture, architecture, literature, dance and tragedy evolved their movements from the movement of nature, as we plainly see expressed in all representations of the Greek gods, who, being no other than the representatives of natural forces, are always designed in a pose expressing the concentration and evolution of those forces. That is why the art of the Greeks is not a national or characteristic art but has been and will be the art of humanity for all time.
>
> Therefore dancing naked upon the earth I naturally fall into Greek positions, for Greek positions are only earth positions.[13]

Her early efforts to teach movement to the babies of Oakland had amused her mother, Isadora recalled, especially when Mrs. Duncan asked her what she was doing and Isadora replied "that it was my school of the dance."[14] In her autobiography, *My Life,* she gave the impression that her art was sui generis, springing from nowhere — or, more pertinently in the cultural circumstances, arriving like Athena, fully armed from the head of Zeus. "One explains the dance better by dancing than by publishing commentaries and treatises," Isadora believed. "An art should be able to do without all that."[15] Once, she went so far as to say that if she could describe what she was doing, she wouldn't need to do it; that her dances were the flower of a deeper, poetic inspiration; and that her technique as it evolved — Duncan technique — was a means to an end, "a shell," the machine that carried the soul's desire. It was the *machine,* Isadora emphasized, not the motor: "My art is an expression of life. My dancing is of the imagination and spirit, not of the body. When my body moves it is because my spirit moves it."[16]

Any formal training Isadora received in the art of the dance was, by all stretches of professional definition, eclectic and incomplete. "I had three great Masters, the three great precursors of the Dance in our century — Beethoven, Nietzsche and Wagner," she said.[17] This was a metaphor, obviously, not an evasion. No dance "system" guided her endeavors until, in concert with her family, she developed one of her own. Her girlhood friend in Oakland, Florence Treadwell, remembered that Isadora had "practiced movement" from her earliest child-hood. At the beginning, "she was painful to behold. Everything she did was studied, whether she sat down, rose, walked, it appeared to be stilted, overdone, affected, and looked cruder than a slow-motion movie. She was never off-guard in a single gesture or motion." Only gradually did Isadora's movements become second nature to her body, and her dance evolve from studied poses into a seamless integration of patterns, steps, and gestures, all based on ordinary physical activities: walking, running, skipping, turning, leaping, kneeling, reclining, and so on. Before long, Augustin Duncan could tell the Treadwells defini-tively, "Isadora knows exactly how she's going to look when she takes a pose. We think we know, but Isadora never makes a mistake."[18]

The most conspicuous feature of Duncan dance is that it permits no acrobatics, no "dancing tricks," as Isadora called them. "The great and the only principle on which I feel myself justified in leaning is a constant, absolute and universal unity between form and movement," she wrote, "a rhythmic unity which runs through all the manifesta-tions of nature."[19] When she spoke of "natural" movements, she meant those movements that "a normal body" could perform without special training. Training followed in the Duncan method — intense and rigorous training — but the principle remained, automatically excluding contortionism, exaggerated leaps and bends, fouettés, arabesques, tours de force, and "toe walking."[20]

In line with her vision of a seamless dance, Isadora never dis-cussed her work in theatrical or choreographic terms. When dancing, she warned, the body itself should be forgotten: "It is only an instru-ment, harmonized and well appropriated," trained to move by con-stant exercise and repetition but drawing on its own impulses and inspiration "to express also the sentiments and thoughts of the soul."[21] This was her practice from the start. Every Duncan dancer would be her own choreographer.

"We always danced," Augustin disclosed. "We took it up as a pro-fession when we were children. We taught dancing. It was largely so-ciety dancing and what we used to call 'fancy' dancing then. But Isadora taught her own ideas from the beginning."[22] In My Life she tells the story of an early visit to "a famous ballet teacher in San Fran-cisco," whose instruction left her cold: "When the teacher told me to stand on my toes I asked him why, and when he replied, 'Because it is beautiful,' I said that it was ugly and against nature, and after the third lesson I left his class, never to return."[23] She would go back to ballet in the future — she studied "every kind of dancing," Augustin said[24] — but her dance education entirely lacked the years-long, drill-sergeant chastisement of the barre. "I never was an acrobat," Isadora confirmed, "even in my youth."[25] In a short autobiographical sketch, written about 1905, she left a chronology of events:

> Danced first as a small child — Studied from age of four years — Began to teach "a new system of body culture and dancing" at age 11 years.
> Taught from the age of 11 years to 16 years — classes always growing — gave performances appearing both alone and with pupils — dancing singly and in chorus — and also the pupils danced and mimed small scenes — of mimodramas accompanied by Poems. The dancing of these pupils was considered wholly remarkable and as something quite opposed to the dancing of the time — Press of that time wrote expressing admiration for this New Dance.
> At age 14 [sic] made a tour of Principal Theaters of California — immense enthusiasm all along the route —
> Danced alone — & also in Combined dances with two brothers and sister.[26]

In 1892, when Isadora was fifteen, she and her sister Elizabeth were already listed in the Oakland city directory as dancing teachers: "DUNCAN, Miss A. Dora and Miss May E."[27] (Dora and May were family nicknames Isadora and Elizabeth would shortly discard.) San Francisco writer Charles Caldwell Dobie remembered the first time he saw Isadora: "She was not thrilling an audience at that time with her grace and fire. She was prosaically teaching a line of self-conscious girls and reluctant boys the steps of the polka"[28] — although she did it, even then, in vaguely Grecian attire, a white robe tied with a sash, and struck at least one of her early pupils as "a spirit from another world."[29]

The Duncans had been dance students themselves since at least 1885, when their mother first arranged for their own private lessons. Mrs. Duncan, herself listed in the city directories as a "pianiste," played for her children, while a Professor Jay Massborn, "a San Francisco dance instructor," taught them the popular dances of the day: the waltz and the schottische, the polka, the mazurka, the galop, and so forth. Raymond Duncan remembered Massborn as "a hot-tempered maestro" who wore "an outdated sort of cassock" and quit his classes with the Duncans after an argument with Isadora's mother about her piano tempos.[30] In what would prove to be typical fashion, the family carried on alone, with Elizabeth as their designated choreographer. "Dancing is all for use," Elizabeth would insist: "It isn't jigging around, it's coping with life."[31] In 1891 the Duncan children founded a "school of the arts," and four years later, just before they left San Francisco for good, the whole family, including Mrs. Duncan, was ensconced in the professional registers under the heading "Teacher, dancing."

Isadora made her public dance debut in 1890, at the First Unitarian Church in Oakland, where her friend Florence and the Treadwell family attended services. All of the Duncans appeared alongside her. A year earlier she had taken part in an Oakland civic parade, a "Great Charity festival" with "350 Participants" and "9 Floats," concluding with "a *Menuet de la Cour de Louis XIV.*"[32] Elizabeth taught dancing at Oakland's Shell Academy for Girls. "This, however, was not very satisfying," she remembered, "and we soon recognized the necessity of coming up with a more vital approach. . . . We went our own ways in order to pursue our impulses and dreams."[33] In 1893, when Isadora and her siblings embarked on their tour of the "Principal Theaters of California," they did so with a confidence that seems extraordinary.[34]

The Duncan traveling program was a mixture of scenes from Shakespeare, melodrama, comedy, and burlesque, with dancing, singing, and some high-toned "Poems" thrown in — a regular variety act, and the kind of thing Californians were well used to seeing. San Francisco had always been a theater town. From the moment the first gold nugget was panned at Sutter's Mill, the actors had descended. Along with a swarm of itinerant companies came the greatest names of the nineteenth-century theater: Helena Modjeska and Sarah Bernhardt, Oscar Wilde (in his capacity as a lecturer), Henry Irving and Ellen Terry, Lillie Langtry, Edwin Forrest, Edwin Booth, James O'Neill and his Monte Cristo Company, Maude Adams, Fanny Davenport, and Laura Keene (known in theater circles as "the Duchess," who had played at Ford's Theater in Washington on the night that Lincoln was shot). Shakespeare was the hands-down favorite among theatergoers in Isadora's youth, but the most popular performer of all was Little Lotta Crabtree, first of the American child superstars, a California girl discovered and trained by her neighbor in Grass Valley, Lola Montez.[35]

It was a heady legacy, undoubtedly, for another local girl in the next generation. When Isadora began dancing, she could scarcely have known where her gift would take her. None of the Duncans could. "We are none of us alike in our family," said Isadora.[36] Augustin — Gus — was the self-described conservative of the group, "not concerned in the innovations";[37] he would go on to be one of America's most distinguished actors and a founding director of the Theatre Guild. Elizabeth, in contrast to her burgeoning younger sister, was a "tiny" person, "with a bright, bird-like face and a little-girl voice."[38] After a childhood accident or illness, Elizabeth became lame in one leg, and her own brilliant career as a dance teacher and theorist of movement, not to mention the ups and downs in her relations with Isadora, can be appreciated only with this handicap in mind.[39] For Raymond, there is no single description that suits: he would carve out a place in social history no less original, though less celebrated, than Isadora's.[40]

All their lives the Duncans remained "clannish and self-sufficient"[41] — they called themselves, and thought of themselves, as Clan Duncan — and there seems also to have been, at least in the case of the brothers, an effort to overcome the shame they felt about their father's notoriety. Augustin, in particular, who was briefly engaged to Florence Treadwell, had a "secret ambition to clear his father's name."

"The family . . . never seemed to realize that their father had been [legally] absolved from the taint of criminal interest," Florence pointed out. "They were apparently haunted by a fear of knowing the worst, but there was no worst to be known."[42] On the contrary: in 1893, either before or as a result of their California tour, Joseph Duncan reappeared in his children's lives, flush from his Los Angeles real-estate dealings, and presented them with a house in San Francisco on the corner of Sutter and Van Ness — the "Castle" mansion, a "handsome house with large dancing rooms and open fireplaces. . . . On the grounds there were a tennis court, a windmill, and a barn."[43] This barn became a theater, as another in Oakland already had, and for the next two years, until their father lost his fourth fortune and the house was repossessed, the Duncans lived in splendor. (What Mrs. Duncan thought about any of this is not on record.)

While living at the Castle mansion in 1895, the youngest Duncan first appeared on the city lists under the name she would make famous: Isadora. That she was spotted from the beginning as the star of the family is not in dispute; the Duncans affirmed it themselves.[44] She was wholly proficient in the "fancy" dancing she taught to other children (and which Elizabeth, after the departure of Professor Massborn, had taught to her), but she "dreamed of a different dance. I did not know just what it would be, but I was feeling out towards an invisible world into which I divined I might enter if I found the key."[45]

At the age of eleven, according to Augustin, Isadora "arranged a little tableau entertainment for children that will be history some day," posing her pupils with bows and arrows and reading aloud from Longfellow: "I shot an arrow in the air / It fell to earth I know not where." This was "the true beginning," Augustin thought;[46] it was also, on the surface, unoriginal. Children's pageants and *tableaux vivants* (what Isadora called "mimodramas"), set to music and invariably accompanied by the most solemn reading of poetry, were so common at the end of the nineteenth century, so much a fixture of American life, as to have already become the object of satire and derision.

"The town's gone mad over the living pictures," wrote a reporter for the *San Francisco Chronicle* in 1894. "Every church that ever struggled to pay off a mortgage has had 'em time and again."[47] It was Isadora's condensation of the trend that ultimately set her apart from her contemporaries. As early as 1898 she stated her aim "to blend together a poem, a melody and a dance, so that you will not listen to the music, see the dance or hear the poem, but will live in the scene and the thought that all are expressing."[48] One of her first performances — given at the age of five and unhappily set to a recitation of "Ten Little Niggers" — "failed," Isadora recalled, because, instead of "representing" the action, she had employed "little nigger dolls" as props, sticking them one by one into her pockets as the poem counted down: "And then there were none."

"Now I see," said Isadora, "I shouldn't have had the dolls. One must have the symbols and not the real thing. . . . Better an artistic failure than an inartistic success."[49] Looking to explain the development of her art, an army of dance historians has been at pains to demonstrate her indebtedness to François Delsarte, the French professor of music and oratory, whose blueprint for movement and dramatic self-expression was the rage in Isadora's childhood. "Delsarte" was a democratic household craze, part of a general movement toward dress reform and "physical culture" that occupied all classes of American society at the end of the nineteenth century. A vogue for "rhythmic gymnastics" had already swept the nation (Isadora and Elizabeth both studied gymnastics in Oakland);[50] during the 1890s cycling, swimming, golf, and tennis were all at the height of fashion. For women, in particular, crushed by corsets and wearing mutton sleeves as big as balloons, a healthy, flexible body was beginning to look like a good thing.[51] In the march to woman suffrage, no aspiring American woman was without her copy of Delsarte — more exactly, *The Delsarte System of Expression,* by Genevieve Stebbins, an American elocution teacher, who never met the master but became the most effective popularizer of what was quickly called "Delsartean science."

Delsarte himself, "a poor orphan," began his career as a student of voice at the Paris Conservatoire, where the rigorous system of instruction wrecked his vocal chords. In the wake of this catastrophe, he turned first to the study of human anatomy and from there to a fascination with people under stress. Delsarte worked briefly in a madhouse, "to gain knowledge of the behavior of all ages, temperaments and castes, noting how they reacted to emotions of every sort." At night he wandered the parks of Paris, and later turned up at "mine disasters," to watch the rescue squads, the survivors, and the victims' families and friends: "Attitudes, gestures, tones of voice and manners of speech, in normal and abnormal circumstances, were observed and categorized. Reactions to birth and death, to joy and sorrow, and to every imaginable human emotion, were catalogued."[52]

Delsarte's observations about human nature and his crystallized "rules of emotional expression" were intended initially only for singers and actors. He would never have mentioned dancers in the same breath with the great musicians and tragedians who passed through his studio in Paris (among them Georges Bizet, Jenny Lind, and the divine Mademoiselle Rachel). The actor Steele MacKaye was apparently the only American to study in person with Delsarte and had planned to bring him to the United States when Delsarte suddenly died in 1871 (a victim, it is thought, of the Paris Commune). But his system crossed the ocean with MacKaye, and after Genevieve Stebbins published her book about Delsarte in 1885, it crossed the American continent, where "emotive expression" and "classical statue posing" became a kind of parlor game, the hula hoop of the 1890s and the particular province of dreamy teenagers, young couples in love, and restless, middle-class matrons. George Bernard Shaw ventured to say that Delsarte had founded a "quack religion."[53] His name was even used as a verb — "to delsarte."

That Isadora "knew Delsarte" and his principles can be taken for granted, despite her later, ungenerous denials. In the 1920s she reportedly told a friend that she "didn't know what it was all about" — it was much like her experience of elementary school, in that sense.[54] Florence Treadwell remembered that Isadora, having seen Elizabeth practice Delsarte gestures, "ridiculed" her movements,[55] but there is no doubt she absorbed the message of Delsarte's work — specifically, the connection between the body and the "inner man." Millicent Dillon, dual biographer of Isadora Duncan and Mary Cassatt, observes that Delsarte's widely quoted and codified "laws" — "to each spiritual function responds a function of the body," for example, and "there is nothing more horrible, or deplorable, than a gesture without meaning or purpose" — were central to Isadora's work. Dillon writes:

> Even Delsarte's wording about the nature of art was to become part of Isadora's language about dance. He spoke of art as "divine in its principles, divine in its essence, divine in its action, divine in its end." He considered gesture to be the "direct agent of the soul." Speaking of how he obtained his most important results, he described how he surrendered his will to become a "passive subject" that "obeyed an inner inspiration coming from whence I know not, and urging me on to results I had not aimed at." Of his power to concentrate, he said during a lecture, "I simply withdraw my vital force into the reservoir at the base of the brain."[56]

The specifically Delsartean combination of spirituality and science unquestionably held a strong appeal for Isadora — this with the notion, emphasized by Genevieve Stebbins and quickly circling the globe, that a woman's body was not a thing to be repressed. In an interview in 1898, Isadora hailed Delsarte as "the master of all principles of flexibility, and lightness of the body," and added that he "should receive universal thanks for the bonds he has removed from our constrained members."[57] Stebbins herself was photographed in Grecian robes; on her lecture tours, she invoked the spirit of Isis, the Graeco-Egyptian goddess of motherhood, birth, life, and death, adding a mystical aura to her physical demonstrations that was precisely in tune with the late-Victorian pulse.

"Isis is the Goddess of Birth," Isadora wrote in 1905. "Isis will always protect me because I have her name."[58] It was a household name in Isadora's childhood. The Russian spiritualist Helena Blavatsky had published her sensational *Isis Unveiled* in 1877, the year of Isadora's birth. That Isis was "a great magician" and the patroness of seafarers must also have spoken directly to the young dancer's soul: "I, Isis, am all that has been born, that is, or shall be, no mortal man hath ever me unveiled."[59] This was the era of the table-rappers, of theosophy and

Christian Science, but it was also the era of Darwin, whose *On the Origin of Species,* far from curtailing the wilder flights of spiritualist thought, instead gave birth to the most unscientific developments in popular culture. The revision of thinking necessary to embrace the theory of natural selection had reversed the order of the world — nothing less — demolishing "a multitude of dogmatic barriers by a single stroke," in the words of Darwin's cousin, eugenicist Francis Galton, in "a spirit of rebellion against all ancient authorities whose positive and unauthenticated statements were contradicted by modern science." Where the church once ruled (or the family, or the law), the organism now was king, striving to fulfill its particular destiny in its particular way, randomly, freed from the restrictions of hierarchical structure and governed by nothing but its own impulses.

"The chief result of [my] Inquiries has been to elicit the religious significance of the doctrine of evolution," Galton continued. "It suggests an alteration in our mental attitude, and imposes a new moral duty."[60] The combined effect of a reordered cosmos and rapid industrialization, according to Alfred Kazin, left nineteenth-century Americans "standing suddenly, as it were, between one society and another, one moral order and another. . . . The sense of impending change became almost oppressive in its vividness."[61] Embracing this new view of existence, far more significantly than any study of Delsarte, Isadora was exactly a child of her time. In daily life as well as in culture, the emphasis was increasingly on the *I* — but an *I* of glorious dimension and nobility of spirit, moving "onward and upward forever."[62]

Small wonder, then, that Isadora scoffed at the "inane coquetry" of the dancing she saw in Californian theaters and music halls. "I have a will of my own," she wrote, "and my will is to free the art of dancing from unnatural contortions . . . and lead it back to natural movements."[63] The crippling of dancers' bodies alone seemed to Isadora a violation past redeeming. Of anyone who liked or admired the European ballet, "for historical or choreographic or whatever other reasons," she argued that "they see no farther than the skirts and tricots. But look — under the tricots are dancing deformed muscles. Look still farther — underneath the muscles are deformed bones. A deformed skeleton is dancing before you. . . . The ballet condemns itself by enforcing the deformation of the beautiful woman's body! No historical, no choreographic reasons can prevail against that!"[64]

Of course, the ballet when Isadora encountered it was not the coherent dance form it later became, still less a matter for aesthetic study or dance criticism. There *were* no dance critics in the nineteenth century, as there were no proper ballet companies outside Russia, Italy, or France. When a well-known dancer came to San Francisco on tour, she was normally supported by a corps of locally and badly trained girls and was as likely to offer leg lifts and can-can as anything resembling a swan. The preeminent ballerina at the end of the century was the Italian Marie Bonfanti, famous in America for her role in *The Black Crook,* a five-hour spectacle-extravaganza combining "the Revel of Sirens," "Comely Female Forms," devils, demons, Wagnerian grottoes, and some astonishing (for the period) pyrotechnic effects, which Isadora probably saw when it was revived in San Francisco in 1893. *The Black Crook* was the absolute model for theatrical dancing as she encountered it growing up, in a series of *Green Monsters, Magic Trumpets, Red Gnomes, Trips to the Moon,* and perennial favorites modeled on the British "pantos" — *Sinbad, Aladdin, Bluebeard,* and so on.[65]

In the ballroom, meantime, things were changing but not improving, so far as Isadora could tell. The waltz, whose "wild fury" when it first appeared about the time of the French Revolution seemed to herald the collapse of civilization, had given way to the polka, which in turn had accelerated into the galop. As they were commonly practiced, Isadora loathed these dances, declaring of the waltz, for example, that it was "an expression of sickly sentimentality and romance which our youth has grown out of."[66] Generally, ballroom dancing left her "amazed at the great restraint shown by the dancers, who, clasped in one another's arms, and moving to the most lascivious music, still continue to behave in the most orthodox manner."[67] Sharp distinctions were made between dance in the theater and dance in society, where propriety ruled with an iron fist. "Skirt" dancing was the crossover form, combining easy steps with a continual rustling and shaking of crinolines that allowed respectable girls to kick up their heels — but *not* lift their legs — at cotillions and balls.[68] Again, Isadora was in full accord with her hero, Whitman, who earlier in the century had called for "the entire redemption of woman out of these incredible holds and webs of silliness, millinery, and every kind of dyspeptic depletion."[69]

"No," wrote Isadora, "the dance was once the most noble of all arts; and it shall be again. From the great depths to which it has fallen, it shall be raised."[70] Her dance as it emerged would be Greek in spirit, classical in its simplicity, and wholly American in its vision of freedom.

*   *   *

When Isadora left San Francisco, at the age of eighteen, it was because the city proved "inhospitable" to her ideas. "They don't understand Isadora," her mother complained: "They just don't understand!"[71] Mrs. Duncan went with her to an audition, where Isadora danced "in a little white tunic" for an uncomprehending road-company producer, who declared, "This sort of thing is no good for a theatre. It's more for a church. I advise you to take your little girl home." Disappointed, "but not convinced," Isadora took this rejection as the last straw.

"I made other plans for leaving," she wrote cryptically. "I called the family to a council, and in an hour's harangue made clear to them all the reasons why life in San Francisco was impossible." Mrs. Duncan, "somewhat dazed" by Isadora's speech, was nevertheless ready to follow her where their fortunes took them. They left San Francisco for Chicago in June 1895, with nothing but "a small trunk, some old-fashioned jewellry . . . and twenty-five dollars."[72] Elizabeth, Augustin, and Raymond would join them later. A visitor to the Castle mansion, just after the Duncans' eviction, noticed that "the hardwood mantels all over the house had been chopped away. Had this been the work of vandals," he wondered, "or had there been grievous need of firewood in a household always on the verge of penury?"[73] Isadora would return only twice to her native town: the first time, briefly, the following year, and not again until 1917. "As a little pilgrim I left this kind land of my birth," she wrote. "The train sped me Eastward . . . over the Great Rocky Mountains across the vast Prairies. . . . A long journey it was, and I arrived with no fortune. But gold I had."[74]

3
Flying Eastward

Isadora chose Chicago to launch her career because, in 1895, it was widely regarded as the most progressive city on the American map. Chicago was the City of Big Shoulders, rebuilt after the fire of 1871 and a world-ranking center of industry, commerce, transportation, and the arts. In 1893 the city defeated its eastern rivals, Philadelphia, Washington, and New York, to become host to the largest world's fair yet seen on American shores, the World's Columbian Exposition — a massive display of American enterprise, mandated by an act of Congress to commemorate the 400th anniversary of the voyage of Christopher Columbus, where textiles, furniture, and industrial machinery shared space with telephones, typewriters, shotguns, boxcars, addressographs, refrigerators, toys, a ten-ton block of Canadian cheese, and a model of the Venus de Milo made out of fifteen hundred pounds of chocolate.[1]

The theme of the Columbian exposition was larger even than the range of its products. *Advancement* was the word on everyone's lips; the upward movement was fully in swing. Not Matter, But Mind, read the motto of the fair: Not Things, But Men. And women: a women's department and "Board of Lady Managers" both found their voices at the Chicago fair. During the six months of its operation, from May to October 1893, more than 20 million visitors wandered through the White City in Jackson Park. When Isadora arrived, the exposition was over and the tourists were gone, but the evidence remained of progress and promise, a shimmering vision of what *might* be for an American of vitality and goodwill.

Isadora had left California with a letter of introduction to the Chicago Press Club from its San Francisco equivalent. This, with her "little white tunic" and her small wad of cash, was all she had to advance her in a strange town. According to her report, she walked into the Press Club and declared outright, "I have brought you a revelation from California. I have discovered the true movement of man. This movement, drawing its inspiration from nature and going up through the evolution of the psychology of modern thought, is the true revelation of the Dance."[2] Many have doubted that Isadora, at eighteen, could have been so bold, but no evidence exists to contradict the tales she told about her miserable summer in the Windy City.[3] With the closing of the world's fair, all nobility and refinement of feeling seemed to have vanished from Chicago. "Loving Chicago," said Nelson Algren later, was "like loving a woman with a broken nose."

"Some of the journalists joked," Isadora remembered, "some were interested to the point of asking for a demonstration. I remember . . . posing before this group of half-cynical spectators, endeavoring to show them the movement of the ideal of a human being. No one was interested, no one believed."[4] Soon her cash was gone, and her grandmother's heirlooms didn't bring in very much: "The inevitable happened. We could not pay our room rent and all our baggage was kept, and one day we found ourselves on the street without a penny." Isadora's description of these days, with its rueful flavor of hopes in the dust, is a classic of American stage-door narratives.

> I still had a little real lace collar around the neck of my dress, and . . . I walked hours and hours in the broiling sun, endeavouring to sell that lace collar. Finally . . . I succeeded. . . . It was a very beautiful piece of Irish lace, and brought me enough money to pay for a room. With the money which was left I had the idea of buying a box of tomatoes, and for a week we lived on those tomatoes — without bread or salt. My poor mother became so weak that she could not sit up any longer. I used to start out early every morning endeavouring to interview managers, but finally I decided to take any sort of work I could find and I applied to an employment bureau.
> "What can you do?" said the woman at the counter.
> "Anything," I answered.
> "Well, you look as if you could do nothing!"[5]

She went at length to a music hall, a dreaded concept in her mind, but whether she did so of her own volition — "in desperation," as she said — or because she was referred there isn't clear. After she was famous, the *Chicago Tribune* reported that her contacts at the Press Club had helped Isadora "up the ladder" — specifically, Ike Fleming, a thirty-year veteran of Chicago's newspaper scene, and an unnamed "fairy godmother," a North Shore woman "versed in 'thought prose' and the adaptation of motion to music," who arranged an audition for Isadora at the Masonic Temple Roof Garden, Chicago's leading variety house, atop the tallest building in the city.[6] She danced Mendelssohn's "Spring Song" for the Roof Garden's manager, Charles Fair, who watched her with his hat on and a cigar in his mouth and said, "Well, you're very pretty and graceful. And if you would change all that and do something with some pep in it, I'd engage you."

Isadora asked Fair what he thought a dance with "pep" might be: "I thought of my poor mother fainting at home on the last of the tomatoes."

"Well, not the sort of thing you do. Something with skirts and frills and kicks. Now you might do the Greek thing first, and then change to the frills and kicks, and it might be an interesting turn."

"But where was I to get the frills?" Isadora wondered. She had run out of money and it was brutally hot, "regular Chicago weather"; she "wandered along the street" and finally found herself at Marshall Field's, already one of the largest stores in the city:

> I went in and asked to see the manager, and I was shown into the office, where I found a young man sitting behind a desk. He had a kindly expression, and I explained to him that I must have a skirt with frills by the next morning, and that if he would give me credit I could easily pay him from the engagement. I do not know what inspired this young man to comply with my request, but he did so. Years afterwards I met him [again] in the person of the multi-millionaire, Mr. Gordon Selfridge. I bought stuff: white stuff and red stuff for petticoats, and lace frills. And with my bundle under my arm I went home, to find my mother at the last gasp. But she bravely sat up in bed and made my costume. She worked all night and by morning had the last frill sewn on. With this costume I returned to the roof-garden manager. The orchestra was ready for the trial.
>
> "What's your music?" he said.
>
> I hadn't thought of this, but I said, "The Washington Post," which was then popular. The music started up and I did my best to give that

manager a peppery dance, improvising as I went on. He was simply delighted, took the cigar out of his mouth, and said:

"That's fine! You can come on to-morrow night, and I'll have a special announcement."[7]

Isadora danced at the Roof Garden not only in frills, but as "the California Faun" — either "Isadora" was considered too highbrow for the venue or her ideals had melted in the Chicago sun. The experience "disgusted" her, and after three weeks, she quit the scene. She was finished "trying to amuse the public" and turned up next in "bohemia," the word used — it wasn't a place — to describe any collection of artists, writers, and cultural leftists who happened to band together. Chicago had a noisy bohemian presence and a number of bohemian clubs, at one of which — *the* Bohemian Club — Isadora found friends. More helpfully, she found plates of sandwiches and mugs of beer, without which, she said, she and her mother might have starved: "And I suspected many a Bohemian, like ourselves, would have had nothing to eat at all, if it had not been for the sandwiches and beer he found at the club, and which were mostly provided by the generosity of Amber."[8]

Amber was Martha Everts Holden, a journalist known throughout the Midwest under her bohemian nickname. It was Amber who organized the Bohemian Club and it was Amber who paid the bills; the club died when she did, in 1896.[9] Isadora met "the most extraordinary people" at Amber's makeshift salon and remembered her voice calling out, "like a man's: 'All good Bohemians rally round! All good Bohemians rally round!'"

"And each time she called the Bohemians to rally round," wrote Isadora, "they lifted their beer mugs and responded with cheers and songs. In the midst of this I came on with my religious dance. The Bohemians were nonplussed. They didn't know what to make of it."[10] Years later Isadora confessed to dancing on a billiard table for Amber's guests; there are further references in Chicago newspapers to a performance for "an aggregation of artists, writers, actors, musicians, and other bright lights of the circles of achievement."[11] Generally, however, she found no more understanding among Chicago's artists than she had among its theater managers: "The general conclusion . . . was that the young woman had an idea, but that clairvoyancy was required to understand it."[12]

The bohemians had only one aesthetic in common, Isadora discovered: "They were all without a cent." She was conscious of her position in the group as a fresh face — indeed, a very fresh face, with creamy skin, a turned-up nose that begged to be described as lilting, a long, supple neck, and cascades of soft brown hair. "She's as sweet as one of them beech nut hams," said Chicago meatpacker Phil Armour, who saw her not long after at a private concert.[13] That she was escorted everywhere by her mother, now risen to her feet, must only have added to Isadora's allure.

At the Bohemian Club, Isadora met Ivan Miroski, a Polish immigrant "with a great shock of red, curling hair, a red beard, and piercing blue eyes. He generally sat in a corner and smoked a pipe and looked on at the *divertissements* of the Bohemians with a slightly ironical smile." Miroski took Isadora and her mother for picnics in Jackson Park, which he and Isadora followed with "long walks" and "tête-à-têtes," while Mrs. Duncan snoozed under a tree.

"My mother evidently had no premonitions and allowed us to be alone a great deal," said Isadora. Before long, she and Miroski were in love — "madly, insanely in love." When he kissed her and asked her to marry him, however, her answer was evasive. It would be better to get married after she had "made a fortune," she explained. By that time, she had her eyes on New York.[14]

Isadora's "big break" came when she won an audition with Augustin Daly, the most important producer on Broadway and, to her mind, "the most art-loving and aesthetic" of a crass, commercial breed. As a girl, she had undoubtedly seen Daly's troupe perform in San Francisco. In the summer of 1895, Daly passed through Chicago on tour with his company and its reigning star (and Daly's mistress), Ada Rehan. Isadora stood for days outside the door of the theater, "sending in my name over and over again with the petition to see Augustin Daly. I was told that he was much too busy and that I must see his under-manager. But this I refused, saying that I must see Augustin Daly himself on a very important matter."[15] Her account of their meeting, when it took place, mentions nothing about dancing for Daly, only that she "harangued" him with a speech: "I told him that I had the germ of a great idea, a revolutionary idea, which would awaken the world to an intimacy with the art of dancing."[16] Something in her manner must have struck the right note, because Daly offered her "a little part in a pantomime" if she could reach New York by October and if she "suited" when she got there. To friends in San Francisco, Isadora sent a quick appeal for money: TRIUMPHANT ENGAGEMENT. AUGUSTIN

DALY. MUST REACH NEW YORK FIRST OCTOBER. WIRE A HUNDRED DOLLARS FOR FARE. The cash arrived, "and with it Elizabeth and . . . Augustin, who, inspired by the telegram, had decided that our fortunes were made."

There remained only the task of saying good-bye to Miroski. He was "desperate with grief," Isadora reported, but "we swore eternal love." Before leaving, she even encouraged him in his goal of marriage. "Not that I believed in marriage," she wrote, "but at that time I thought it would be necessary to please my mother. I had not yet fully taken up the cudgels for free love for which I did battle later."[17]

When Isadora described her engagement with Augustin Daly as triumphant, she was not exaggerating, nor would she have needed to justify the claim to any of her contemporaries. At that time, Daly's was the leading theater company in the United States, frequently compared with the Comédie-Française and the nearest thing America ever saw to a national school of acting. For a newcomer to the commercial theater, to be hired by Daly was roughly equivalent to being knighted. There was no place higher to go: "You had stature in your profession and outside it, too. . . . Every critic saw you; every person of distinction . . . felt it a duty to attend a performance at Daly's."[18]

Daly's was one of the last American stock companies, a stock house being an autonomous production body with its own theater and a permanent corps of actors, who played dozens of roles each year and hundreds in the course of their careers. Essentially, these parts were all the same, rigidly cast according to type — leading man and leading lady, ingenue, shrew, buffoon. The members of a nineteenth-century stock company were, in many ways, equivalent to the cast of a TV sitcom, recurring every week and trapped forever in the roles for which they were hired. Isadora recalled her experience with Daly as "two years in a Company of Marionettes, pulled by the hand of a master."[19] A ferocious enemy of the star system (with Miss Rehan's exception), Daly had an old notion about actors: that they were *actors*, not public personalities; that they were "part of the illusion of the theatre"; and that their opinions were of no use to anyone. "I want my company kept at a level," Daly said. "I put them all in a line, and then I watch, and if one head begins to bob up above the others, I give it a crack and send it down again."[20]

Isadora's first role with the Daly company was also her largest and the only one in which she was billed, when at all, as something other than "Miss Duncan."[21] She had been hired to join the cast of *Miss Pyg-*

malion, which Daly imported from Paris along with its author and star, Jane May, the leading female mime of the era. Isadora hated pantomime. "Movement is lyrical and emotional expression," she protested, "which can have nothing to do with words." But in pantomime, "people substitute gestures for words, so that it is neither the art of the dancer nor that of the actor, but falls between the two in hopeless sterility. . . . When I was told that I must point . . . to say YOU, press my heart to say LOVE, and then violently hit myself on the chest to say ME, it all seemed to be too ridiculous." Jane May reduced her to tears in rehearsal, when she summoned Daly and declared that Isadora, in the role of Cléopâtre, "had no talent whatever and could not possibly carry the part." Daly patted Isadora on the shoulder and replied, "You see, she is very expressive when she cries. She'll learn."[22]

She did. In the practice of the time, actors weren't paid until after a play had opened; thus, for six weeks the Duncans lived hand-to-mouth in their usual condition of penury. Having been evicted immediately from "a terrible boarding-house" on Sixth Avenue, the family wound up next on 189th Street, in Washington Heights, from which distance Isadora walked to her rehearsals downtown.

"I used to run on dirt, skip on pavement, and walk on wood," she remembered, "to make the way seem shorter. I had all sorts of systems for that. I didn't eat lunch because I had no money, so I used to hide in the stage box during the lunch hour and sleep from exhaustion, then start rehearsing again in the afternoon without any food." By the time *Miss Pygmalion* opened in November, she was near collapse, appearing in her New York debut in "a Directoire costume of blue silk, a blonde wig, and a big straw hat. Alas for the revolution of art which I had come to give the world!"[23] She wasn't the only one who greeted *Miss Pygmalion* with a real lack of enthusiasm. The *New York Times* disdained its "excess of gesticulation" and "endless employment of archaic symbolism. . . . Manifestly . . . it carries with it no illusion of life, and it does not stir the emotions."[24] As Isadora said, "If you want to speak, why don't you speak? Why all this effort to make gestures as in a deaf and dumb asylum?"[25]

After three weeks in New York, *Miss Pygmalion* went out on the road — exactly where, Isadora didn't specify. Her account dwells on hardships and "weary miles," but she was also without her mother for the first time, and a new kind of problem presented itself. Daly's touring players were responsible for their own lodging and board. "My limit was fifty cents a day, everything included," Isadora wrote. As a result, she often found herself in "strange neighbourhoods," where men, "mostly drunk," tried to push their way into her room: "I was terrified and, dragging the heavy wardrobe across the room, barricaded the door with it. Even then I did not dare to go to sleep, but sat up on guard all night."[26]

There is nothing to suggest that Isadora, at this stage of her life, was anything but the romantic virgin she said she was. At night she read books. She wrote letters to Ivan Miroski. The one thing she enjoyed about the tour was the opportunity it finally gave her to witness, in Jane May, the absolute value of discipline in art: "She called a rehearsal every day, and nothing ever suited her." Later Isadora would admit that she "could not help but admire the extraordinary and vibrant expression of this pantomime actress. If she had not been imprisoned in the false and vapid form of pantomime, she might have been a great dancer."[27]

For Daly, *Miss Pygmalion* was a failure — not a big one, but another debit in what proved to be the decline in his enterprise. Other producers were making themselves known on Broadway, producers without their "own" companies, as Daly complained, without their own theaters, holding open auditions for actors and mounting single productions, not repertory, in the hope of a long run. Daly abhorred the new way of doing things. In an interview he remarked that "too many fine things" were being offered to the public — and "I don't wonder," he added, "that some object to paying $2 a seat for what are really one-dollar performances."[28]

"I am sending out a company with *Midsummer Night's Dream*," Daly told Isadora when she got back from her tour. "If you like, you might dance in the fairy scene."[29] *A Midsummer Night's Dream* was a Daly warhorse, first produced in 1888 and revived as needed over the years. Nothing about it was pleasing to critics, only to audiences, who thrilled to the "shadow and smoke," the blinking lights of the fairies' wands, "the falling of the mists . . . the midnight revels of the fays and goblins." Daly further offended purists by borrowing incidental music from Weber's *Oberon* and the inevitable Mendelssohn, whose "Wedding March," inserted at the end of the fifth act, was a showstopper.[30]

Isadora had hoped that Daly would give her free rein when he cast her as the First Fairy in *A Midsummer Night's Dream*. She, too, chose Mendelssohn to accompany her steps, dancing solo "in the wood scene before the entrance of Titania and Oberon." In vain, she begged

Daly not to make her wear a pair of tinsel wings — she could "express" them herself, she said. But Daly insisted, and on opening night Isadora danced in a flashy combination of glitter, gauze, and papier-mâché. She was glad to be dancing at all.

"Here, at last," she wrote, "I was alone on a great stage with a great public before me, and I could dance. And I did dance — so well that the public broke into spontaneous applause. I had made what they call a hit." Backstage, however, Daly was furious. "This isn't a music hall!" he shouted. A head in his company had bobbed above the others: for the length of the tour, Daly dimmed the lights in Isadora's scene. She "danced in the dark. Nobody could see anything on the stage but a white fluttering thing."[31]

In the circumstances of her employment, it couldn't have been satisfying for Isadora to pass through San Francisco in May 1896, where local papers spoke of her respectfully and affectionately but where critics shared her judgment that the fairies in A Midsummer Night's Dream seemed "unusually mortal."[32] The Daly company crossed the country with three or four of its repertory standards: Dream, Twelfth Night (in which Isadora also danced), The Countess Gucki, and A School for Scandal, stopping, among other places, in Boston, Washington, Pittsburgh, Philadelphia, Atlanta, New Orleans, Omaha, and Chicago. Here Isadora renewed her romance with Ivan Miroski and gave "salon" recitals in private homes. Nine months with the Daly company had already convinced her that she and commerce couldn't mix. She was "extremely unhappy" and went back to New York, giving Miroski her promise that she would marry him. If she was serious, she was saved from herself when Augustin˙ "made enquiries" and learned that Miroski already had a wife in London. Isadora's mother, who knew about these things, forbade her to see him again, and she didn't. In 1898 Miroski volunteered for service in the Spanish-American War. He got as far as Florida, where he died of typhus in boot camp.

The loss of Miroski was "a terrible shock" to Isadora. She had few friends in the Daly company — "they regarded me as queer" — and turned up for rehearsals with a copy of Marcus Aurelius's Meditations in her hand: "I tried to adopt a Stoic philosophy to alleviate the constant misery which I felt."[33] Over the next twelve months, she would appear in Much Ado About Nothing, The Geisha, and Meg Merrilies, or the Witch of Ellangowan (based on Sir Walter Scott's novel Guy Mannering), but she had developed "a perfect nausea for the theatre: the continual repetition of the same words and the same gestures, night

after night, and the caprices, the way of looking at life."[34] *The Geisha,*
in particular, in which Isadora played a singing teahouse attendant,
deeply offended her sensibilities. The *New York Times* thought it
"pretty good fun," adding that "only a dull person or a hopeless in-
valid could fail to be amused."[35] But for Isadora it was another nail in
the coffin of her hopes. One day Daly found her crying backstage, and
as she poured her heart out to him, he slipped his hand down the back
of her dress. She was "angry" at the gesture but not deterred from her
point.

"What's the good of having me here," she cried, "with my genius,
when you make no use of me?"

"H'm!" said Daly, and left the room.[36] Isadora never saw him again;
a few days later she quit the company. It remained an irritation to her
that Daly never lived to see her genius fulfilled. He died of a heart attack in Paris in 1899.

Isadora returned to solo performance. She had made contacts in
the theater and emerged in New York almost immediately as a "choreographic philosopher," the herald of a new way of dancing and a fad
among the "swell set."[37] In *My Life,* she recounts that her family took
a studio in Carnegie Hall, where they slept on mattresses and Elizabeth opened a dancing school. Augustin joined an acting road company and was "seldom at home," while Raymond, newly arrived from
California and thinking of their father, "ventured into journalism." As
always, the Duncans lived day to day: they could afford to keep their
studio only by renting it out. Isadora rehearsed her dances at night, after Elizabeth's students had left and her "poor mother" was pressed
into service at the piano.[38] She had begun to study the operas of
Gluck, whose effort to coordinate the elements of music and drama
would greatly influence her work, but mainly she was still partial to
Mendelssohn, Strauss waltzes, and other melodies that can only be
described as sentimental and appealing directly to the middlebrow.

"I was laughed at, discouraged and disheartened at first by this
one and that, but will cherish, also, some precious encouragement
which gave me confidence," Isadora told a reporter ten years later: "In
New York a great virtuoso composer, Ethelbert Nevin, was, they told
me, indignant to learn that I danced to some of his most beautiful
pieces, written for the piano."[39] Nevin was the American composer of
"The Rosary," "Narcissus," and "Mighty Lak' a Rose," graceful, sugar-
sweet pieces that America took fervently to its heart. "Narcissus by

Nevin" was heard everywhere in parlors and at graduation exercises, while "The Rosary," in particular, became a favorite among opera divas, "a solitary tall lily in a garden rather given to marigolds and zinnias," as critic Mark Sullivan said:

> The hours I spent with thee, dear heart,
> Are as a string of pearls to me;
> I count them over, every one apart,
> My Rosary, my Rosary.*

In 1898 the thirty-five-year-old Ethelbert Nevin had just returned to the United States from Europe, "broken in health" — Isadora's references to a "dreadful disease" and "the terrible malady which caused his early death" would suggest he had tuberculosis. Nevin, too, kept a studio at Carnegie Hall, where one day, according to Isadora, he burst wild-eyed into her room and shouted, "I hear you are dancing to my music! I forbid it, I forbid it! It isn't dance music, my music. Nobody shall dance it." She took him by the hand and led him to a chair:

> "Sit there," I said, "and I will dance to your music. If you don't like it, I swear I will never dance it again."
> Then I danced his "Narcissus" for him. I had found in the melody the imagining of that youth Narcissus who stood by the brook until he fell in love with his own image, and in the end pined away and turned into a flower. This I danced for Nevin. The last note had hardly died away when he jumped up from the chair, rushed towards me, and threw his arms around me. He looked at me and his eyes were filled with tears.
> "You are an angel," he said. "You are a *divinatrice*. Those very movements I saw when I was composing the music."[40]

Thus it was that "Miss Isadore Duncan" first performed at Carnegie Hall, on March 24, 1898, in collaboration with Nevin and other musicians, singers, and actors. Nevin played solos, while Isadora "illustrated very gracefully three dances" from his *Water Scenes:* "Narcissus," "Ophelia," and the "Water Nymphs." [41] That same season, she appeared in a series of "Lenten matinees" at the old Lyceum Theatre on Fourth Avenue. An article in *The Director* reported that her dancing had "created a deep enthusiasm among the cultured people of [New York], and the manner in which they are heralded by the press as the arrival of a new creation in art has aroused a general and wide-

---

* Words by Robert Cameron Rogers.

spread interest."[42] As early as February 1898, the *New York Herald* had spotlighted Isadora's "delightful entertainments" in private salons, declaring that she "revived the graceful art of the Poetic Greeks . . . through the tripping of her feet, the swaying of her body, the expression of her sympathetic face."[43] She also began to lecture on dance, telling an audience at Carnegie Hall that after "ten years' study," she had come to "certain conclusions." Dance wasn't "dancing," she ventured to say, but "movement expressive of thought." It was "still undeveloped," but it wouldn't be for long.[44]

"If the dance is not to come to life again as an art," Isadora concluded, "then far better that its name should rest in the dust of antiquity. . . . I am not at all interested in reforming anything. I am deeply interested in the question: Is the dance a sister art or no; and if so, how shall it be brought to life as an art?"[45] To audiences who had never before considered dance to be anything but entertainment — at best, a diversion; at worst, an erotic display — her words sounded majestic, if not completely deluded. Hereafter, a speech at the end of her concerts became a staple of Duncan performance. Said dance writer Walter Terry: "At this comparatively tender age Isadora began to talk, and she never stopped talking for the rest of her life."[46]

What she neglected to do, then or later, was acknowledge the degree of dance training she had received as a member of Augustin Daly's company. Omitted from Isadora's autobiography is any mention of her first trip to England, in the summer of 1897, when she accompanied the Daly troupe on a British tour and, "prettily costumed, bearing garlands of flowers," performed in *As You Like It* at Stratford-on-Avon (specifically, as one of the "Persons in the Train of Hymen").[47] The British sojourn coincided with the Diamond Jubilee celebrations of Queen Victoria, and during it Daly sent Isadora to study with Katti Lanner, a former pupil of the Romantic ballerina Fanny Elssler and now director of ballet at the Empire Theatre in London. Dance historians are unnecessarily suspicious of Isadora's silence on this matter: her opinion of the ballet is established fact, and she couldn't have regarded lessons with Lanner as any kind of feather in her cap. Lanner was an important dancer in her own right, "known for her mime and her natural musicality,"[48] but the Empire was a music hall, where jugglers and magicians shared the bill with performing dogs and where prostitution flourished openly in the balconies (all of London's music halls were notorious pick-up sites.)[49]

In New York, while still under contract to Daly, Isadora had studied regularly with Daly's dance master, Carl Marwig, and also took classes with Marie Bonfanti, of *Black Crook* fame, to whose ballet studio in Union Square Daly dispatched her for training.[50] Accounts differ as to whether, when she began her career, she covered her legs with flesh-colored stockings or was already baring them on the stage — presumably the latter, because simulated flesh was nothing new in the theater, and some forty horrified matrons walked out of a Duncan concert in 1899 at the sight of her "unobscured limbs."

"Whenever in the dance her feet stepped far apart," a New York paper reported, "one of her legs came forward, right out of that sedate drapery, and was on transitory view full length and skin-colored. . . . Miss Duncan, it may be added, had no idea of the trouble she was about to create."[51] Her "little white tunic" was scarcely less revealing than she let on. Falling to just below her knees, it was gathered at the breast and tied at the waist, with loose, dangling sleeves that allowed Isadora's arms complete freedom of movement. She wore other costumes as it suited her, including a long gown of some "dark drapery," slashed at the front, and "a species of surgical bandage of gauze and satin of the hue of raspberry ice, with streamers of various lengths, which floated merrily or mournfully as the dancer illustrated the bridal of Helene or the burial of Adonis."[52]

In a series of photographs taken in New York by Jacob Schloss, Isadora wears what looks very much like a ballet costume (although without the ludicrous, duck-like effect at the hips). In these well-known pictures, published widely in American newspapers before Isadora left the country, she appears in a variety of lilting and languorous poses, her arms outstretched, her back gracefully arched, her face turned sometimes piously, sometimes sensually toward the camera. There is no suggestion of virtuosity, only of mood: the lengthy exposure required by photography of the time prohibited motion altogether. For that — for an idea of what Isadora actually looked like "as she bounded and whirled in ecstatic frenzy" — there are only published reviews.

"In her rendering of the song 'Spirit of Spring,'" wrote the *New York Herald*, "to which one of Strauss' waltzes is played as an accompaniment, the dancer bounds on the stage with uplifted hands and face, the incarnation of the joyous spring breaking the icy fetters of winter. To the sensuous waltz music she springs hither and thither, scattering the seeds as she goes, plucking the budding flowers, breathing the life-giving air, exhaling a joyousness of nature which is wondrous in its grace and beauty." In Nevin's "Narcissus," Isadora was "first startled, then charmed" as she portrayed the Greek youth meeting his own gaze in the water:

> Becoming more and more enamored, the dancer leans forward, seemingly viewing herself from side to side, sending kisses to the liquid image, stepping across the shallow brook and still finding the figure reflected from its surface. . . . The first start, the gradually growing conceit, the turning and bending, the ecstasy of delight at finding himself so beautiful are all most convincingly enacted.

Another of Isadora's early pieces, *A Dance of Wandering,* was set to a melody by Ignaz Paderewski. She appeared as "a spirit roaming through the forests, bewildered by the strangeness of her surroundings, trembling at every sound, the rustle of the leaves, the sighing of the winds."[53] The *New York Times* described her movements as "extremely graceful" and noted, in a physical particular, that they were "more of the body and arms than the legs."[54] Nor was dancing the only feature of Isadora's early concerts. Poetry was read, in the Delsartean mode, either by Augustin, Elizabeth, or Raymond (mistakenly identified in one report as Isadora's "diaphanous younger brother," a joke that stuck in the Duncan family). At salon recitals, Mrs. Duncan sat at the piano, "a large mama in a blue gown," whose presence on the scene did much to reassure the "well-dressed, well-fed, well-corseted, well-bred" women who made up Isadora's audience at this time. The *New York Post* described one of her Lenten matinees:

> The immense Lyceum stage was denuded of everything save hangings of cold grey and, at one side, a grand piano. The pianist played the C-Minor Prelude of Chopin . . . and then, at the first bars of a Mazurka, the audience became conscious of a presence. . . . She looked slight at first, diminished by the perpendicularity of the great hangings; but, when she began her rhythmic glidings, she seemed to loom larger until the house forgot everything but the gracious undulating figure before it. People are apt to imagine Chopin all hues of melancholy. But Miss Duncan is an interpreter, and the gentle gaiety of her demeanor [proved] in demonstration how wrong the cant acceptation of the composer is. . . . There was nothing arbitrary about the evolutions which she associated with the music, nothing accidental. Miss Duncan was not merely filling out the music with a Terpsichorean accompaniment: she was realizing the music.[55]

In the summer of 1898, Isadora entertained Newport at a *fête champêtre* on the lawn of Beechwood, the estate of Mrs. William Back-house Astor Jr. ("*the* Mrs. Astor," as she insisted on being known). Winter saw another series of Lyceum matinees, during which Isadora danced to quatrains from *The Rubáiyát of Omar Khayyám*. The *Rubáiyát* had long been a favorite of the Duncans. Indeed, it might have been written especially for them, with its ironic ruminations on the nature of existence and its gather-ye-rosebuds advice ("Ah take the Cash, and let the Credit go!"). Although Isadora worked primarily from the popular FitzGerald translation, in March 1899 she joined forces with the actor Justin Huntly McCarthy, author of the hit play *If I Were King*, in McCarthy's prose adaptation of the *Rubáiyát*, their program billed as "An Afternoon with Omar Khayyam, the Astronomer-Poet of Persia."[56] McCarthy lectured on the life of Omar, the eleventh-century poet, mathematician, and "tentmaker," while Isadora emerged to a reading of the text — "a slip of a girl," unrestrained by the "vestimentary conditions" normally imposed on dancers.

"It was no fault of McCarthy's that certain society women of New York got up and left the theatre," a critic observed. "Mr. McCarthy was properly garbed and conducted himself in every respect as an elocutionist and a gentleman should." Isadora's dancing, by contrast, was unabashedly "sensual," expressive of Omar Khayyám's well-known passion for wine, women, and song. After the concert, opinion was divided as to the state of her morals — "there was much recrimination and acrimony on both sides" — while a critic advised her to "enlarge her present repertoire or arrange a new one" for the sake of her career.[57] Still, said another, "her rendering of that mad, sad and pessimistic song of Persia was remarkable. None but an unusual artist could have so expressed in gesture the following lines:

> *O love, would you and I with Him conspire*
> *To grasp this sorry scheme of things entire;*
> *Would not we shatter it to bits — and then*
> *Re-mould it nearer to the Heart's desire?*[58]

Isadora was less controversial in salon performances — in Chicago, where she traveled with her *Rubáiyát* at the invitation of Mrs. Arend Van Vlissingen, and at Newport, where she was warred over by hostesses and had her first taste of a world of wealth and privilege she would later conquer completely. Already the New York papers had dubbed her "Society's Favorite Dancer" — "society," as always, consisting exclusively of women: Mrs. Arthur Dodge, Mrs. Whitelaw Reid, Mrs. Frederick W. Vanderbilt, Mrs. Bolton Hall. At Newport "the" Mrs. Astor was Isadora's first patroness. Her cottage on Bellevue Avenue had the largest ballroom in town, and her lawns were famous for their tubs of aloes and greenhouses filled with "delicious grapes."[59]

"Mrs. Astor represented to America what a Queen did to England," Isadora wrote. "The people who came into her presence were more awed and frightened than if they had approached royalty. But to me she was very affable."[60] Newport in the 1890s has been described as "a social Mansard, a republican Versailles," where hostesses routinely set aside $300,000 for a season's entertainment and where the walks and avenues "bristled with chateaux." Elsewhere in America, a depression held sway: "Business was at a standstill. Industries had shut down. Millions of workers were unemployed." William Jennings Bryan spoke for the rising tide of populism when he included among the legitimate duties of government "the putting of rings in the noses of hogs," but at Newport, for all its social pretension and exclusivity, money was the thing that really counted. "Not to have wealth would [be] to have only a straw crown in a madhouse," said one Newport dowager. "Diamond tiaras [are] not empty symbols."[61]

In 1898 the reign of Mrs. Astor was drawing to a close, to be replaced by a kind of politburo, "the Great Triumvirate," "the Newport Board of Social Strategy," comprised of Mrs. O. H. P. Belmont and her hilarious neighbors Mrs. Hermann Oelrichs and Mrs. Stuyvesant Fish. All three vied to present Isadora at their parties. Mrs. Belmont was "Queen of the Firsters," determined to outshine her rivals even if it meant running naked through the streets. Tessie Oelrichs was the daughter of a U.S. senator, an Irish immigrant who had made a fortune in the California gold rush — presumably, she and Isadora had a lot to talk about. Born in a miner's shack, Mrs. Oelrichs was obsessed with cleanliness, washing and polishing her own marble floors. "When I die," she exclaimed, "bury me with a cake of Sapolio in one hand and a scrubbing-brush in the other. They are my symbols."

But of all Newport's grandes dames, Mamie Fish set the most original tone — a new tone of experiment and irreverence that left the Four Hundred sputtering in their Louis XV seats. "Many women will rise up to fill my place," Mrs. Astor predicted, before senility overtook her, "but I hope my influence will be felt in one thing, and that is, in discountenancing the undignified methods employed by certain women to attract a following." Through Mrs. Fish and her "social director," Harry Lehr, a "cult of the cockeyed" was born in Newport. Artists were suddenly welcome there, poets, actresses, and even a monkey, whom Mrs. Fish once dressed in a tuxedo and introduced to her guests as a visiting prince. Newport was never known for its grasp on culture or serious conversation — an unwritten law among the Four Hundred held that nothing like a pause should ever occur at the dinner table — but no one was ready for Mrs. Fish, who greeted her guests at Crossways with a brisk "Howdy-do, howdy-do. Make yourselves at home," then added, sotto voce: "And believe me, there is no one who wishes you were there more than I do." Barely literate, unconcerned with any but sartorial and gastronomic tradition, Mrs. Fish took real pleasure in shocking her guests, declaring that she would have anyone to dinner who could hold a fork and that "no, no," she had never described Mrs. Belmont as looking like a frog: "A toad, my pet, a *toad!*"[62]

Such were the women on whom Isadora pinned her hopes. She remained "very proud" of a photograph taken on the lawn of Marble House in 1898, showing "all the famous old millionaires sitting in a row," herself dancing, her mother at the piano, and Elizabeth "doing the recitations,"[63] but she lost the picture later in Russia; in any case, she remained bitter about the stinginess of her patrons.

"These ladies were so economical of their *cachets* that we hardly made enough to pay the trip and our board," Isadora complained. "Also, although they looked upon my dancing and thought it very charming, they hadn't any of them the slightest understanding of what I was doing. . . . They had no art sense whatever."[64] She recalled a continual "gurgle" at Newport — "How perfectly sweet! How very pretty!" — and would have appreciated Newport resident Edith Wharton's subsequent regret that she had not seen Isadora dance early on, when she first had the chance.

"Only two kinds of dancing were familiar to that generation," Wharton wrote, "waltzing in the ballroom and pirouetting on the stage. I hated pirouetting, and did not go [when invited to see Isadora perform]. Those who did smiled, and said they supposed their hostess had asked the young woman to dance out of charity — as I daresay she did. Nobody had ever seen anything like it; you couldn't call it dancing, they said." Only later, in Paris, did Wharton catch up with Isadora and behold the dance she "had always dreamed of, a flowing of movement into movement, an endless interweaving of motion and music, satisfying every sense as a flower does, or a phrase of Mozart's."

Ultimately, Wharton would compare Isadora to Marcel Proust, a name "destined, like hers, to fly through our imaginations on a shower of spring blossoms."[65] In New York she was working on an "all-Greek" program, the last performance the Duncans would give together in America, danced and declaimed to Andrew Lang's translation of the "Idylls" and titled *The Happier Age of Gold*.

The Duncans' decision to leave America in 1899, like their decision to leave California four years earlier, was born of discontent and their search for a more productive atmosphere in which to work. England was on the family's mind, partly on account of Isadora's recent trip there and partly because Joseph Duncan had just died in the wreck of the *Mohegan*. A reverse voyage, some defiance of the seas, must have appealed to the family's sense of adventure.[66] Mainly, they were frustrated and increasingly bored in New York.

"I dreamed of London," Isadora wrote, "and the writers and painters one might meet there — George Meredith, Henry James, Watts, Swinburne, Burne-Jones, Whistler. . . . These were magic names, and, to speak the truth, in all my experience of New York I had found no intelligent sympathy or help for my ideas."[67] While not strictly the case, she needed bigger heads, broader venues, and, especially, larger audiences if her work was to mature. No commercial theater in the United States could afford to employ her as a solo artist — Isadora's programs, at this stage, would not have filled the halls — and she refused to join the parade of talents that made up a variety show or musical revue. Her sense of mission struck many as ridiculous, and she was so absolutist in her vision of dance and dancers as to be a figure of fun in the press.

"Miss Duncan holds forth at such ultra-fashionable places as the Waldorf-Astoria, Sherry's and Carnegie Lyceum," said a report in *Broadway Magazine*. "She spurns Broadway with a large, deep, thick spurn, that almost makes us ashamed of having anything to do with the thoroughfare. She is very, very classic, and is horribly, dreadfully afraid of becoming anything but absolutely and painfully refined. It can thus be seen that Miss Duncan occupies a rather unique position among American dancers. Long may she retain it." Beneath two Schloss portraits of Isadora were the captions, "How I love my friends, the Vanderbilts" and "Isn't Mrs. Highoppe kind to throw those flowers!"[68] Another critic, describing Isadora's last American concert in April 1899, ridiculed her "writhings and painful leaps and hops," along with her "audience of tortured souls," adding at the end of his review that Isadora meant to take her work to London: "Miss Duncan is fully determined on this reckless course, which is sad, considering we are at peace with England at present."[69]

A series of fresh calamities drove the Duncans to their goal. There was a crisis in the family when Augustin, touring America in the part of Romeo, fell in love with his Juliet, a sixteen-year-old actress named Sarah Whiteford. They were married on the road and, by the time they returned to New York, they were already expecting a baby. Said Isadora: "This was taken as an act of treason. For some reason that I could never understand, my mother was furious. She acted in much the same way as she had done on the first visit from my father, which I have already described. She went into another room and slammed the door. Elizabeth took refuge in silence and Raymond became hysterical. I was the only one who felt any sympathy."[70]

In 1899 the Duncans had moved from Carnegie Hall to the Windsor Hotel, on Fifth Avenue between Forty-sixth and Forty-seventh Streets, an address that better reflected their now solid connections with "society" and where Elizabeth conducted "Children's Classes for Cultivation of Movement and the Dance." That the classes were Elizabeth's and not her own, Isadora never denied, although she also gave lessons there and was inevitably remembered more vividly than her sister. A woman who studied with the Duncans in London recalled that complicated steps and "tours de forces were rigorously excluded" in the curriculum and that Elizabeth "made me realize how movement must invade my whole being, from the poise of the head through the poise of the body, running like a current down the limbs, even to the tips of the fingers."[71] Elizabeth's school never lacked for pupils, but two rooms at the Windsor Hotel cost ninety dollars a week, a fortune for the Duncans, and their bank account, as always, "showed a deficit."

"The Windsor was a gloomy hotel," Isadora remembered, "and we found very little joy in living there and trying to meet these heavy expenses. One night my sister and I were sitting by the fire, wondering how we were going to find the necessary cash to foot the bill. Suddenly I exclaimed: 'The only thing that can save us is for the hotel to burn down!'" It was the kind of prescience she always claimed for herself. On March 17, 1899, St. Patrick's Day, she went to a neighbor to ask for a loan — "a very rich old lady who lived on the third floor" and who turned her down while complaining about the service, saying, "I have stayed in this hotel for many years, but if they don't give me better coffee, I am going to leave."

"She did leave that afternoon," Isadora remarked, "when the whole hotel went up in flames, and she was burned to a crisp!"[72] The Windsor fire started when a guest tossed a lit match out the second-floor parlor window and it accidentally ignited the curtains. In less than an hour, the building was destroyed, the flames spreading with lightning speed from the ground floor to the top while, outside, thousands of people stood happily watching the St. Patrick's Day parade. "The Irish Volunteers had just gone past," wrote the *New York Times,* when the hotel manager tore from the building, crying, "Fire! Fire! The Windsor's afire!" It was some time before the crowd realized what was happening: "Women turned pale and screamed, little ones shrank back sobbing, and men felt sweat break out on their brows as the heads of panic-stricken people protruded from the hotel windows, turning now toward the flames and now toward the sidewalk, and calling for help in tones that made the hearers sick."[73]

Inside, Elizabeth and Isadora were giving lessons (luckily, also on the parlor floor). With them were Mrs. Duncan and about "thirty tots," each with a maid or nanny in tow. "The little ones were arrayed in flimsy tarlatan dresses and white satin slippers," the *Times* continued, "and were merrily engaged in performing *pas seuls,* when an unwonted noise in the street happened to attract the attention of Mrs. Duncan." In fact, Mrs. Duncan was at the piano when she saw bodies flying past the window. At first she thought that "her eyesight was playing her a trick," until one of the maids opened the door to the hallway and "a puff of smoke" entered the room:

> The girl closed the door with a slam, and then coolly walking over to the dancing teacher, whispered to her that the hotel was on fire. Then Mrs. Duncan realized what she had seen from the window, and that there was no time to be lost. There was no outcry or excitement, but quickly as the maids and teachers could work, the tots, now aroused to a sense that something was wrong, were bundled into their wraps.
>
> "Now, children," said Mrs. Duncan in the bravest voice she could muster, "the lesson is over. Take hold of hands, and do not on any account let go of each other." The maids were ranged on either side of the little procession, and Mrs. Duncan bravely opened the door and pushed the children out into the hall. They whimpered as the smoke assailed them, but their little hearts were steeled by the words of encouragement from their teacher as she led the file down the stairs and

to the doors, where the little ones were snatched up by willing hands and borne to places of safety. And after it was all over, Mrs. Duncan says, nobody fainted, but the adults appreciated the trial that they had been through.[74]

"This is fate," said Isadora, doubtless thinking about other fires and earlier disasters that had left the Duncans without a stitch. The *New York Herald* interviewed her in the wake of the blaze: "She said mournfully that she had saved only the dress she wore, a house gown of dark brown material with flaring Elizabethan collar. All of her costumes and those of her sister were lost as well as the bric-a-brac which they highly prized." Isadora added, in words unusual for her: "I knelt and thanked God."[75] Almost immediately, she scheduled a series of benefit concerts, one of them at Delmonico's restaurant, "Given in Aid of Miss Isadora Duncan and Other Sufferers of the Windsor Hotel Fire," with the goal of replacing her wardrobe and raising money for the Duncans' trip to England. Thus, over the next six weeks, when she wasn't dancing, she was begging, taking tea with the wives of millionaires and imploring them to help her reach London.

"In the heat of pressing my suit I became quite faint and fell over sideways," Isadora remarked. "My tears fell into the chocolate and on to the toast," but at length she had her clothes and about three hundred dollars — "not even enough for second-class tickets on an ordinary steamer." It was Isadora whose ambition would fuel the British enterprise, but "little" brother Raymond who had "the bright idea" of sailing to London on a cattle boat, with Mrs. Duncan cooking for the crew.[76] The clan left together, without Augustin and his wife, in May 1899.

4

London

The Duncans sailed to England on a freighter, accompanied by the lowing of cattle and a supply of "hot toddies," generously provided by the captain of their ship. "I believe that it was this trip which was the great influence in making Raymond a vegetarian," Isadora wrote, "for the sight of a couple of hundred poor struggling beasts in the hold, on their way to London from the plains of the Middle West, goring each other with their horns and moaning in the most piteous way, night and day, made a deep impression on us." The family was reluctant to sail under the name of Duncan; they called themselves O'Gorman, after Mrs. Duncan's mother, and took first names to suit. Thus, Isadora became Maggie O'Gorman and flirted with the first mate, "up in the lookout."[1]

"Sure, Maggie O'Gorman," he said, "I'd make a good husband to you if you would allow it." She described the voyage as "a very happy time" and remarked that when she and her family arrived in London they were "in a state of perfect ecstasy," taking a room near Marble Arch and behaving "exactly like tourists," "spending hours in Westminster Abbey, the British Museum, the South Kensington Museum [now the Victoria & Albert], the Tower of London, visiting Kew Gardens, Richmond Park, and Hampton Court." Soon enough, however, their money ran out, and their landlady did what their landladies always did: one afternoon, having heard "a most interesting lecture on the Venus and Adonis of Correggio," the Duncans arrived home to find the door locked and themselves in the lurch, with "no money, no friends," and no place to stay.

"We tried two or three hotels," Isadora remembered, "but they were adamant upon the necessity of payment in advance, in default of luggage. We tried two or three lodging-houses, but all the landladies acted in the same heartless manner. Finally we were reduced to a bench in the Green Park, but even then an enormous policeman appeared and told us to move on." According to Isadora, the Duncans spent three nights on the street, subsisting on penny buns and coffee and reading aloud from Winckelmann's *Journey to Athens,* before turning up one early morning at Claridge's, where Isadora accosted the staff:

> I informed the night porter, who was half asleep, that we had just come on the night train, that our luggage would come on from Liverpool, to give us rooms in the meantime, and to order breakfast to be sent up to us, consisting of coffee, buckwheat cakes, and other American delicacies.
>
> All that day we slept in luxurious beds. Now and then I telephoned down to the porter to complain bitterly that our luggage had not arrived.
>
> "It is quite impossible for us to go out without a change of clothes," I said, and that night we dined in our rooms.
>
> At dawn of the next day, judging that the ruse had reached its limit, we walked out exactly as we had walked in, but this time without waking the night porter![2]

In fact, Isadora was not without contacts in London — society women, for the most part, who had seen her dance on her first trip to England. It took her no time at all to conquer London salons, though it led inevitably to the same frustration and hardened her heart still further against the philistines. Sitting one morning in the graveyard of St. Luke's, on Sydney Street in Chelsea, her eyes fell on an open newspaper, where she saw the name of "a certain lady" with a house in Grosvenor Square. She returned a few hours later with an engagement for the weekend and a check for ten pounds. Raymond, interrupted in the middle of "a discourse on the platonic idea of the soul," insisted that the family rent a studio, "for we must never again subject ourselves to the insults of these low, common lodging-house women."[3]

The Duncans found a place in Manresa Road, not far from that section of Chelsea known mysteriously as World's End. Having bought food, Isadora repaired to Liberty's, where she emerged with "a few yards of veiling" to enhance her costumes, still meager after the Windsor fire: in the future, she would use only Liberty silk in her dances. Now, too, she removed her slippers, once and for all, and replaced them with sandals, "very high laced gold sandals," in the Grecian mode. Her stockings were off, but her audiences in London never seemed to notice.

"The English are such an extremely polite people," Isadora wrote sourly, "that no one even thought of remarking upon the originality of my costume and, alas! neither did they comment upon the originality of my dancing. Everyone said, 'How pretty,' 'Awfully jolly,' 'Thank you so much,' or something of the sort — but that was all." With Chelsea as her base, she moved from great house to great house, one day "dancing before Royalty, or in the garden at Lady Lowther's, and the next with nothing to eat. For sometimes I was paid," she remembered, "more often I was not." At the home of a Mrs. Ronald, Isadora danced for the Prince of Wales, the future King Edward VII. The prince admired her performance but neglected to give her a tip, and when one of her hostesses, after a charity benefit, "held up a huge bag filled with golden sovereigns and said: 'Look at the mint of money you have made for our Blind Girls' Home!'"[4] Isadora was driven nearly to distraction.

It was an unlucky beginning. "There were long days when we had not even the courage to go out," Isadora wrote, "but sat in the studio wrapped in blankets, playing chequers on an improvised chequerboard with pieces of cardboard. . . . There were days, in fact, when we no longer had the courage to get up in the morning, but slept all day." In September 1899 Elizabeth returned to New York to reopen her dancing school, pledging to send money in the future. The clan saw her off from Victoria Station, "and we three who were left behind," said Isadora, "returned to the studio, where we spent some days of absolute depression."[5]

In the first disappointment of their British migration, only one thing lifted the Duncans' spirits: they were "crazy with enthusiasm" about the British Museum, "where Raymond made sketches of all the Greek vases and bas-reliefs," Isadora wrote, "and I tried to express them to whatever music seemed . . . in harmony with the rhythms of the feet and Dionysiac set of the head, and the tossing of the thyrsis

[sic]" — the ornamented staff, sacred to Dionysus, carried by his bacchantes at their ritual orgies. Isadora's girlhood dream of Greece now became her active study. In her dances, she no longer sought to "copy" the poses and postures of the ancient world but to live them, "to steep [herself] in the spirit underlying them . . . to discover the secret of the ecstasy in them," and to put herself in touch "with the feelings that their gestures symbolized." In Greek painting, sculpture, and Tanagra figurines, she detected a perfect awareness of the body's natural capacities and, especially, a consciousness of the sequence of movement — "ever-varying, natural, unending sequences," as she wrote in 1903, in her most famous essay, "The Dance of the Future":

> People have thought that so long as one danced in rhythm the form and design did not matter; but no, one must perfectly correspond to the other. The Greeks understood this very well. There is a statuette that shows a dancing cupid. It is a child's dance. The movements of the plump little feet and arms are perfectly suited to its form. The sole of the foot rests flat on the ground, a position which might be ugly in a more developed person, but is natural in a child trying to keep its balance. One of the legs is half raised; if it were outstretched it would irritate us, because the movement would be unnatural. There is also a statue of a satyr in a dance that is quite different from that of the cupid. His movements are those of a ripe and muscular man. They are in perfect harmony with the structure of his body.[6]

Isadora had begun to absorb this idea when, dancing impromptu with Raymond in the park at Kensington Square, she met Mrs. Patrick Campbell, the actress, whose cheerful intervention in the life of the Duncans proved unusually fortuitous. In 1899 "Mrs. Pat" was at the height of her stage popularity, the bewitching star for whom George Bernard Shaw later wrote the part of Eliza Doolittle in *Pygmalion*. A longtime stage partner of Johnston Forbes-Robertson, the great Shakespearean, Mrs. Campbell was famous for her "modern" views and eccentric humor. More than that, she was fashionable and enjoyed easy access to the brightest minds and toniest drawing rooms in London.[7]

"Where on earth did you people come from?" she asked Raymond and Isadora as they danced among the rhododendrons.

"Not from the earth at all," Isadora replied, "but from the moon."

"Well, whether from the earth or the moon, you are very sweet; won't you come and see me?" They followed the actress home and into "the epoch of a change of fortune," as Isadora put it. Through

Mrs. Campbell, she was introduced to George and Sibell Wyndham, noted socialites and cultural celebrities, in whose Park Lane salon were entertained "all the artistic and literary people in London." Among them was Edward Charles Hallé, son of the German musician and founder of Britain's Hallé Orchestra, himself a painter and a member of the Royal Academy. Hallé was fifty-three when he met Isadora, a bachelor who lived with his sister on Milner Street and had "one of the most beautiful heads" Isadora had ever seen: "Deep-set eyes under a prominent forehead, a classical nose and a delicate mouth, a tall, slender figure with a slight stoop, grey hair parted in the middle and waving over his ears, and a singularly sweet expression."[8] As a painter, Hallé specialized in portraits.

"Charles Hallé was certainly an artist," said his friend Wolford Graham Robertson, the painter, playwright, and costume designer, whose *Time Was* provides an entertaining portrait of the artistic world of late-Victorian England:

> He loved art truly and well and served her faithfully, yet he never found his proper mode of self-expression. What he ought to have done I do not know; what he should not have done was apparent to all — he should never have attempted to paint. . . . His appearance was romantic, contrasting oddly with his impish sense of humor, and his most fascinating accomplishment to me was the narrating of screamingly comic and slightly Rabelaisian stories with a look of brooding melancholy in his great dark eyes that would have done credit to Manfred or the Corsair.[9]

As a young man, Hallé had joined in the "Secession" from the Royal Academy, a decisive artistic walkout, nominally provoked by the Academy's antiquated method of hanging pictures but, in fact, reflecting a discontent among painters in their quest for truth and life in art. The result was the founding, in 1877, of the Grosvenor Gallery in London, an intrepid *contre-salon* where "tasteful" display became the main concern and exhibitions by such legendary artists as Edward Burne-Jones and Lawrence Alma-Tadema made it, effectively, the center of a revived Pre-Raphaelite movement. Isadora arrived in London just too late to meet Burne-Jones, who died in 1898. But Hallé had known him — Hallé knew everyone — and Isadora now met Alma-Tadema, George F. Watts, William Holman Hunt (in 1848, one of the original founders of the Pre-Raphaelite Brotherhood), and John Singer Sargent, society's portraitist, whose recommendation opened many doors. It was an anxious time for painters, as word of evil trends wafted over London from the Continent. "In France there were known to be men who called themselves 'Impressionists' and painted decadent rubbish," said one of Watts's biographers, "and there could be little doubt that, all over the world, art was 'going to the dogs.'"[10]

How this affected the world of dance is unclear, since dance barely existed in England outside the music hall. The only dancer on the London stage who might be said to have been Isadora's precursor was Kate Vaughan, a skirt dancer, famous for her portrayal of Morgiana in *Ali Baba and the Forty Thieves*. Graham Robertson took the view that Vaughan "never really existed. She was a floating mist, a drifting moonlit cloud, a phantom of melody and rhythm. . . . To imagine Kate Vaughan eating her dinner, or putting on her boots, or blowing her nose was an obvious impossibility"[11] — this in contrast to Isadora, who not only ate her dinner but ate it heartily and was quickly developing a taste for champagne. The attempt to squeeze her into the Pre-Raphaelite mold was only partly successful. From these months in London, Isadora herself dated the war in her soul between Apollo and Dionysus — the one representing all that was pure, structured, and harmonious in art, the other seeking to create art through a willful abandonment to frenzy: inspiration, passion, destruction, and desire.

"It is possible to dance in two ways," Isadora explained: "One can throw oneself into the spirit of the dance, and dance the thing itself: Dionysus. Or one can contemplate the spirit of the dance — and dance as one who relates a story: Apollo."[12] Her performance on March 17, 1900, at the New Gallery in Regent Street, where Hallé was a director, was shaped by strictly Apollonian forces and guided by a committee of patronage breathtaking in the weight of its names: Henry James, Holman Hunt, Alma-Tadema, Andrew Lang, and two grand-nieces of Queen Victoria, the Countesses Valda and Feodora Gleichen. Presiding as "immediate patroness" was the queen's daughter Helena, Princess Christian of Schleswig-Holstein, who watched Isadora in the bemused company of her niece, Victoria of Wales. The British royal family was little known for its art appreciation, though its members undoubtedly felt at home in the overstuffed, self-consciously florid atmosphere of the New Gallery, where potted palms, colored marbles, and "vaguely Hispano-Moorish" tiles made it look like "an Aladdin's Palace sprung up in the night."[13] Isadora danced around a fountain in the central court. As music critic for the *Times* of London, John Fuller-Maitland pronounced her "a success," while regretting the presence of an orchestra that "on more than one occasion rendered the reading inaudible."[14]

A stint with Frank Benson's Shakespeare company in February had already reintroduced Isadora to British theater audiences. At Stratford-on-Avon, she appeared in Benson's production of *Henry V* in a "most picturesque and rather heretical representation of the French camp at Agincourt," where she danced, "lightly clad," for the pleasure of the Dauphin and his knights. Later, for the last time, she turned up in *A Midsummer Night's Dream*, billed only as "Fairy" and with "a good many lines to speak."[15] Her colleagues in the Benson company remembered her as "contentious" and "not very popular,"[16] but Isadora had a different explanation: her work was "too spiritual for their gross, materialistic comprehension."[17]

By the end of 1900, Isadora had largely eliminated the spoken word from her repertory. Credit for this decision is normally given to Fuller-Maitland, who told her, after her first New Gallery concert, "that it would be an improvement" if she abandoned her Persian odes and springtime lyrics in favor of "good music."[18] She was moving away from a dance that told something — a story or a poem — toward a dance that *rendered* it. Virtually all of her early champions in London were painters, more or less of the Pre-Raphaelite school, with a passion for antiquity that matched her own and an almost cabalistic devotion to the past: legends, myths, allegories of all sorts. Under the influence of the Pre-Raphaelites and their successors — Holman Hunt, William Richmond, Watts, and Alma-Tadema — Isadora began to work on a new suite of dances, which she kept in her repertory for many years and which, over time, dispensed entirely with conventional narrative techniques.

"She appears as the 'Angel with a Viol' out of the [fifteenth-century] painting by [Giovanni] Ambrogio di Predis," said German writer Karl Federn, who later introduced Isadora to the works of Nietzsche and saw the dances she composed in London when they had been considerably refined. "A long violet garment worn over greyish veils floats down to her bare feet. In her hair, which hangs loosely to her shoulders, she wears a crown of white and red roses. And the *Quattrocento* comes alive again before us with all its innocence and deep religious feeling."[19] It is reported that in her *Angel with a Viol* Isadora never moved her feet, but conveyed the blessings and the bowing of the angel solely with her torso, face, and arms. Now, too, in fulfillment of a long-standing dream, she brought to life the figures in Botticelli's *Pri-*

mavera — not just one of them, but all of them: Venus, Chloris, Flora, Zephyr, Mercury, Cupid, and the dancing Graces, Aglaia, Thalia, and Euphrosyne. The *Primavera* was a favorite of the Pre-Raphaelites, committed as they were to metaphor, moral themes, and anything that showed the human form in an idealized, classical setting. While taking all the parts, as it were, in Botticelli's allegory of spring, Isadora wore the costume of the goddess Flora, the central figure in the painting, pregnant, smiling, "born" out of Chloris through the breath of Zephyr in a symbol of pure fecundity.

"The robe appears to consist of several gauze slips worn one over another," a London critic reported. "The upper one has angel sleeves and is dim, pale green in color, painted here and there with delicate flowers. . . . Very Botticelli-like is the long, dark hair crowned with roses, and falling in curls to the waist. Ropes of roses wind about her body and the feet are shod in gold sandals."[20] Apart from the title, *Primavera*, Isadora's clothes were the only indication of the source of her dance, which she set to the tune of a sixteenth-century Venetian lute song. Dance historian Elizabeth Kendall writes keenly about this stage of Isadora's development:

> London programs show that as early as 1900 she was finding those essential motions which formed her language, which she would fit together differently in each dance, and which she would also use as the basis of her teaching. . . . In Renaissance art she experienced a new dimension and she began to show the movements of several figures within a space. She added to her language those gestures of surprise or suspended motion one sees in Renaissance canvases — the effects of figures on each other. One of the clearest signals she took is the stylization of "I am being pursued" — a nymph pursued by a satyr, a Diana chased by Acteon, Ariadne surprised by Bacchus. . . . The gesture of this appears again and again in Duncan dances: the dancer in a sideways lunge, her hands fending off the pursuer as she looks back over her shoulder. The pursuer is seen in the same dances (mimed also by the solo dancer): he lunges forward and reaches out toward the imaginary pursued. Gestures like these existed in Delsarte too; but Duncan's versions were broader — they were no longer gestures but motions because they led to other motions. Their purpose was not to transmit a mimed message but to show an action. It is extraordinary that a young dancer decided that by herself she could offer an audience not just the pantomimic intentions of one figure but the flow of question-response among several figures inside the formal space of a painting-frame or a stage.[21]

Before leaving New York, Isadora had told reporters that she intended to "put herself under her old dancing teacher" when she got to London.[22] Undoubtedly, this was Katti Lanner, mistress of the Empire Ballet, and there is evidence that Isadora did turn up at the Empire sometime in 1900, looking for a job. If so, she must have needed the money, because otherwise she was firmly embarked on her course. A journalist wrote:

> Her exits are as lovely and mysterious as her entrances. After the quivering, gleaming, daring gestures and swift flights, it suddenly all ceases, but very slowly; the last picture is held for a space, recalling the profound phrases of [Belgian violinist Eugène] Ysaye and Paderewski as they cease to play, and then, inconceivably, quietly, she again becomes as immobile as the statues she emulates, and with scarcely perceptible footsteps steals behind the curtains. . . . At times, if the music be sad, morbid, ironical, she moves and gestures in sad and mystic fashion . . . ; at others, when the harmonies are full of that revolt, bitterness, intense nervous suffering which so tortured the soul of Chopin, she runs madly across the stage, with an almost fearful monotony, with arms outstretched at tension behind her. Her hair blows down in disorder, and on her face one sees the marks of an eternity of grief and doom. If Chopin caught the music of our souls and "gave it cry," so does Isadora Duncan give it tangible flesh, withal a silent life.[23]

Within a short time, Isadora's art had progressed so far that when she stepped onto a naked stage, spectators imagined they could see meadows and flowers, "hear the waves break against the shore and surmise the approach in the distance of a fleet of ancient ships with billowing sails." From Pre-Raphaelite gowns, she switched back to a simple gauze tunic, "her hair tied into a knot," for her performance of *Pan and Echo*.

"We ask ourselves," Karl Federn wrote: "Can this possibly be the same creature?" The legend of Orpheus was about to enter Isadora's repertory and would seal her transformation: "In a heavily draped Greek attire, she mourns to music of Gluck over the death of Eurydice, in rhythmic, measured, ceremonious grief that mounts and mounts until she sinks to the ground in despair. And then she appears again — this time the scene is darker, wrapped in somber shadows, and her gown is colorless and floating, and her movements are rapid and ghostlike: the shadows of the underworld."[24] Skeptics would insist that Isadora's talents were essentially mimic, while no less a critic of dance than Russian André Levinson, stuck with sugarplums and rows of prancing fairies, complained that there was "something bucolic" about her: "There is no tragedy. No eroticism. There is no real femininity in her essence. . . . And this is why this artist-androgyne can be at once Orpheus and Eurydice, Narcissus and Daphne, Pan and Echo."[25] In time, Levinson would realize that he had been caught short in the face of a stupendous innovation, and would understand what Isadora herself only slowly came to realize: that when she danced these stories, her favored myths, she was neither the narrator nor the characters, but "the soul of the music" itself — "a rôle reserved by the Greeks," she observed, "for the Chorus."[26]

In May 1900 Isadora danced again for the Prince of Wales — "Tum-Tum" himself, who would be king of England in just eight months. A review in *The Lady* provided a neat summary of her London experiences, not neglecting to admonish those society women who, earlier, had failed to reward her with "any great enthusiasm: Miss Duncan's dancing was either too unusual, or dancing in a garden too bold a departure. But the whirligig of Time has his revenges, and when Miss Duncan danced the other day in the 'Teraph' at the Court Theatre [in Sloan Square, now the Royal Court], she achieved a triumph . . . and is now talked about all over London."[27] Two more concerts followed at the New Gallery in July. At the third, with the help of early-music advocate Arnold Dolmetsch, Isadora unveiled her "Italian Renaissance" program — the strains of Lully, Monteverdi, and "old Italian songs" accompanied her steps. "I can still hear in memory the soft swish of her bare feet on the marble pavement," wrote a woman who saw her in London. "I remember a recurrent passage . . . when she raised her arm above her thrown-back head, in a fluid rippling gesture, as though crushing invisible grapes into her mouth from a high-flung vine. I thought I saw those grapes."[28] Another remarked, "She had genius in her arms and hands alone."[29]

Missing at all three of Isadora's New Gallery recitals was her brother Raymond, whose "California diction" apparently disconcerted British audiences and whose services were no longer needed when Isadora discarded readings from her repertory. Soon Raymond left for Paris with his own ambitions and more than a little pique. It was not just his exclusion from Isadora's concerts that chafed at Raymond — he was still given credit on her programs for his "arrangement" — but the undisguised shift in her allegiances. London newspapers reported that Isadora could be found almost every day at the British Museum, but they neglected to say that she went there with Charles Hallé or Alma-Tadema, whom she later acknowledged as her "guide" to Greek art. Always protective of their sister and star, the Duncans were positively alarmed when Isadora began to flirt with her admirers — distinguished men, it might be said, much older than she, with important names and reputations and undoubted stature in the world. For her mother, especially, the spectacle of Isadora's infatuation with the fiftyish Hallé must have reminded her of her own youthful attachment to Joseph Duncan; when Isadora also struck up a friendship with Scottish poet Douglas Ainslie, "descended from a line of Stewarts" and with soft and "dreamy eyes," Mrs. Duncan never left her side. Isadora wrote:

> Every evening at dusk [Ainslie] appeared at the studio with three or four volumes under his arm, and read to me the poems of Swinburne, Keats, Browning, Rosetti, and Oscar Wilde. He loved reading aloud and I adored listening to him. My poor mother, who deemed that it was absolutely necessary to act as chaperon on these occasions . . . could not understand the Oxford manner of reciting poetry, and after an hour or so, especially of William Morris, she used to fall asleep, at which moment the young poet would lean forward and kiss me lightly on the cheek.[30]

In fact, Ainslie was forty-four, "young" only in comparison with the rest of Isadora's suitors. Between Ainslie and Hallé (who disliked each other) she "desired no other friends. Ordinary young men bored me exceedingly," she wrote, and her attitude toward them "was so superior that they were completely frozen." Isadora's correspondence with Ainslie reflects a nicety she would lose:

> I have been leading a most orderly and charming existence in our little Kensington House, doing every thing except going to the Parish Church that a demure Kensington Maiden should — If you come you will find me in white dress and a blue sash sitting in a pink parlor pouring tea. . . . Town is quite horrid now — except the British Museum — When I can no longer stand the low ceilings in this crackerbox of a house I go there, where I find everything I want — or everything I ought to want, which isn't the same thing.[31]

As it happened, Isadora still carried a torch for Ivan Miroski, her "bohemian" suitor from Chicago, who had died in Florida on his way to war. In London, without telling her family, she located Miroski's widow and went to see her in Hammersmith, arriving in a "Kate Greenaway dress, . . . a big straw hat on my head, and my hair in curls on my shoulders." Not unconsciously, she was the very picture of chastity. However:

> Her welcome was not very cordial. I tried to explain who I was.
> "I know," she said, "you are Isadora; Ivan spoke to me about you."
> "I am so sorry," I faltered. "He never spoke to me about you in any of his letters."
> "No," she said, "he would not, but I was to have gone out to him and now — he is dead."
> She said this with such an expression of voice that I began to cry. Then she began to cry, too, and with that it was as though we had always been friends.

They sat together most of the afternoon, reminiscing about Ivan and gazing at his pictures, which his widow had festooned with black crepe and arranged in her bedroom as a shrine to the fallen. Isadora rode home that day "on the tops of 'buses," weeping for Ivan and his "poor little wife," but exulting in her own "sense of power," her mounting "contempt for people who were failures, or who spent their whole lives waiting for things."[32] She was working hard in her studio, and at night she sometimes went with Hallé to the theater, where she saw Ellen Terry in *Cymbeline,* Henry Irving in *The Bells,* and Eleonora Duse as *The Second Mrs. Tanqueray.* As a young girl, Terry had been married to Watts, the aged painter, now doting on Isadora, walking her through his garden and telling her about his life and art: "I think he makes me believe that 84 is quite the best age." A bolder spirit entered her relations with men, and when Douglas Ainslie went off to Paris, she sent him a note to wish him "Good Morning" when he got there.

"Not for a long week will you think of me but will see many wonderful Things and people and think beautiful Thoughts," Isadora wrote. "I remaining here will lose you Seven days and Nights . . . only being happy in remembering the precious minutes you cared to spend with me — and wishing also that — what am I wishing?" She signed her letters "Terpsichore" and crafted a poem to express "all the love and longing" Ainslie had aroused: "The kiss you gave my fingertips / Was envied by my amorous lips." Managing her emotions was "quite a task," and she was devastated when Ainslie, one way or another, rejected her advances and sent her "back meekly repentant in sack cloth and ashes to [her] particular Good Angels." It wasn't the last time Isadora Duncan would frighten a man.

"Ideas are eternally satisfactory," she pronounced, "always there to welcome one, if one comes in the right spirit. People, on the contrary, are most unsatisfactory and cause pain." From Paris, Raymond sent telegrams extolling the joys of *la vie de bohème* and imploring Isadora not to waste her time on Anglo-Saxons. "I realize in my philosophy that a desire for the unattainable is perhaps the happiest of states," she finally confessed to Ainslie. For the moment, Apollo had won the war:

> I think your note helped me to that. I was holding the Thyrsus wand in the right hand and needed a little extra height on the left side. Any way I regained the poise with new harmony, and . . . am once more happy and in my own element. I have been dancing Greek friezes — all afternoon Impersonal little friezes — of figures that have kept the same attitude for years and years — intent on their own meaning of grass and flowers and earth — with an exquisite aloofness from human things.[33]

At the end of the summer, she left for Paris.

5

Paris

To Isadora, France seemed "like a garden," a fresh, bountiful country fixed in perpetual springtime. She offered no explanation for her decision to leave England in 1900, except to say that Raymond had wanted it and that he was much changed when she arrived in Paris.

"He had let his hair grow long over his ears," Isadora wrote, "and wore a turned-down collar and a flowing tie. . . . He took us to his lodging, where we met a little midinette running down the stairs, and he regaled us on a bottle of red wine." A *midinette*, specifically, is a serving girl who goes home at noon (*à midi*). This one didn't. Apparently, she was Raymond's lover, because Isadora writes that he shortly "gave [her] up and devoted himself to me,"[1] a remark that makes sense only if Raymond's relations with the girl went beyond the dishes and dusting. Hitherto, Isadora's thoughts had rarely strayed far from the holiness of art. In Paris they were distracted from the outset by the pull of her senses, a powerful eroticism she had never before experienced and did nothing to turn aside. She "yearned," "burned," "ached," "longed" — she was determined to lose her virginity.

"Let those judge me who can," Isadora wrote later, "but rather blame Nature or God, that He has made this one moment to be worth more, and more desirable, than all else in the universe that we, who know, can experience."[2] It would be two more years before she experienced it herself, and then not in Paris but in Budapest, where Gypsy music and the perfume of lilacs sent her into a frank delirium and sealed her commitment to sexual love. Isadora recalled her first awareness of her body "as something other than an instrument to express the sacred harmony of music.

"My breasts," she wrote, "which until then had been hardly perceptible, began to swell softly and astonish me with charming and embarrassing sensations. My hips, which had been like a boy's, took on another undulation, and through my whole being I felt one great surging, longing, unmistakable urge, so that I could no longer sleep at night, but tossed and turned in feverish, painful unrest."[3] While waiting for the event, dreaming of "another expression" in her relations with men, Isadora resembled no one so much as Voltaire's Candide — eager to learn, anxious to please, and disillusioned at every turn.

The first days in Paris passed as usual for the Duncans, in a glad reunion and a hunt for a studio. Raymond worked in Paris at unspecified "printing-related enterprises,"[4] which explains how they soon found themselves in a cheap apartment over a printing press, where "terrific earthquakes" shook the walls at night "and the whole [building] seemed to jump into the air and then fall flat." Not to be deterred from the pleasures of Paris, Isadora "proposed that it sounded like the sea and that we should pretend we were at the seaside." In the mornings, she and Raymond rose early and danced through the Luxembourg Gardens on their way to the Louvre.

"We spent so much time in the Greek vase room that the guardian became suspicious," Isadora wrote, "and when I explained in pantomime that I had only come there to dance, he decided that he had to do with harmless lunatics, so he let us alone." The Louvre was her paradise, and for years afterward she met people who remembered seeing her there with Raymond, in her white dress and Liberty hat — "two bizarre figures," Isadora recalled, crying to each other across the room, "Look, here is Dionysus!" or, "Here's Medea killing her children!"[5]

From the Louvre, Isadora moved to the Carnavalet, the Musée de Cluny, the Bibliothèque Nationale, and later, after she made some headway with the French language, to the library of the Paris Opéra, where the staff "took an affectionate interest" and provided her with "every work ever written on dancing"[6] (a claim that might be greeted skeptically had there been a great deal to read on the subject). Isadora took pages of notes from her researches, and within a short time she graduated to Rousseau and Descartes, whose ideas on the division of the soul and the body she pondered with interest before rejecting them as irrelevant to her concerns. The rationalist Descartes, somehow, had located the soul in a gland at the base of the brain, but to Isadora assertion was all — she confessed to being full of "deep convictions and naive daring" at the time: "I burned with apostolic fire for my art. . . . I wanted to make over life, down to its least details of costume, of morals, of way of living."[7]

Isadora came to Paris at the right time for big ideas, during the Universal Exposition of 1900. Chicago's world's fair had celebrated American achievement; France's aimed to mirror the whole globe, on 270 acres in the center of Paris. According to bulletins from the French government, the exposition was designed to "synthesize the nineteenth century" while delivering the world confidently into the hands of the twentieth. The result was a predictable nightmare of mixed conceptions, with a Palace of Electricity and a Pavilion of Russian Alcohol vying for space with a Javanese temple, a reconstruction of medieval Nuremberg, and a newfangled *trottoir roulant,* advertised as "the sidewalk of the future," which carried visitors through the fairgrounds suspended some twenty feet in the air. Of the structures that still exist in Paris from the 1900 jamboree, the Pont Alexandre III and the domes and portals of the Grand Palais best exemplify its schizophrenic style, an impossible blending of girders, cherubs, and mock minarets.[8]

Isadora found two attractions at the fair that thrilled her, the first in the small, art nouveau theater built for Loie Fuller, the American-born "Fairy of Light," whose solo dances at the Folies-Bergère in the 1890s altered theater history and gave their creator a cultural stature in France unequaled by any other foreign performer. "La Loïe" worked in the tradition of the skirt dancers, which is to say that she rustled and swayed more than she danced, swathed in yards of silk and billowing veils, her costumes manipulated in sweeps and circles by means of concealed sticks and the hidden play of mirrors, gels, and colored lights. The wonders of electricity were the most popular attraction at the Paris exposition, and Loie Fuller in 1900 was the world's high priestess of electrical effects. She didn't "burn," said a critic: she "oozed brightness." She was "flame itself." When Marie and Pierre Curie, great friends of Fuller's, isolated radium in 1898, Fuller opened her own laboratory and began to experiment with "fluorescent salts," adding a "Radium Dance" to her repertory. Long before, in the American West, she had worked in rodeo and carnivals as a side-kick of Buffalo Bill and would become the bosom friend of Europe's most original queen, Marie of Romania. Her autobiography, published in 1908, contained a forward by Anatole France.

Fuller's better-known dances — *La Danse du Feu, The Butterfly, La Danse Blanche,* and *The "Milles Baisers" Waltz* — called for her to blossom from a pudgy, "badly dressed girl with a Kalmuck face" (as Marie Curie described her) into a huge and gaudy flower, "a sort of giant calyx with her bust as the pistil." She could do orchids, seaflowers, spiral lilies, metallic snakes, sparkling gems — "all the magic of Merlin," Isadora wrote: "What an extraordinary genius! No imitator of Loie Fuller has ever been able even to hint at her genius! . . . Unbelievable. Not to be repeated."[9] Fuller's lasting contribution to dance was to demonstrate, as Isadora would, "that a single person dancing on the stage could create an image capable of gripping and moving a huge audience" for as long as her strength and her vogue held out.[10]

Isadora didn't see Fuller perform until the following year, in Berlin. At the Paris exposition, the Théâtre Loïe Fuller was given over to the Japanese company of Kawakami Otojiro and his wife, Sada Yacco, protégés of Fuller's, whose work came to Isadora as a pure revelation. It was rare enough to see a Japanese production of *The Merchant of Venice,* stranger still to see a No troupe with a female star. Trained as a geisha, Sada Yacco was the only woman in the Otojiro company, ostracized in her own country for appearing on the stage at all and, further, for mixing styles, blurring the lines between East and West by slashing her most enduring vehicle, *The Geisha and the Knight,* from fourteen hours down to two, in order to suit the capacities of Western audiences. Critics found Yacco's acting "entrancing," "curiously natural," with "odd marionette movements of the arms" and "a wild 'electric' grace, something of a wave or a tiger by Hokusai." Isadora, noting her movements exactly, saw in Yacco what she considered a perfect blend of emotion and control, a "wondrous art" she returned to see again and again over the course of the year.

Not far from Fuller's theater, in the place de l'Alma, was the Rodin Pavilion, where more than 150 of the sculptor's works, in plaster, bronze, and stone, were assembled from different collections. In 1900 Auguste Rodin was acknowledged as the greatest living sculptor in the world, but the Paris exposition marked the first time his works had been seen together in one place. He had had to fund and build the pavilion himself, so timid were the exposition's organizers about the commercial value of modern art (at the Grand Palais, a simultaneous retrospective of nineteenth-century French painting excluded the impressionists). Isadora walked through Rodin's pavilion into "a new world," mesmerized by *Balzac* and *The Gates of Hell,* while "vulgar people" jostled to get a look at the figures and wondered, "Where is his head?" or "Where is her arm?" There was no limit to cultural obtuseness, Isadora feared, taking the opportunity to "apostrophize" the crowd.

"Don't you know that this is not the thing itself, but a symbol," she cried, "a conception of the ideal of life?"[11] Rodin's own commentary on his work might have come from Isadora's mouth. "I have always endeavored to express the inner feelings by the mobility of the muscles," the sculptor said. "I obey nature in everything, and I never pretend to command her," just as Isadora saved her harshest criticism of the academic ballet for its pretended defiance of gravity. Rodin cast his statues from life, unlike most sculptors at the time, and left them marked with the "hollows and lumps" of their bronzing, "visual evidence of the passage of the medium itself from one state to another."[12] A year later, when she visited Rodin in his studio, Isadora noticed that "he murmured the names of his statues" while he worked: "He ran his hands over them and caressed them. I remember thinking that beneath his hands the marble seemed to flow like molten lead."[13] She was all the more impressed with Rodin because she had found very little to inspire her even in Paris. Isadora was "bitterly disappointed" by a performance of "Greek Dancing" at the Paris Opéra, for example: it was only "modified Ballet in white gowns," she scoffed, "not in acme Greek."

"I thought I might find some teacher, some help there," Isadora wrote to Douglas Ainslie in London, "but it was all stupid, vanity and vexation — They do not dance for love — They do not dance for the Gods."[14] When Charles Hallé, a native Parisian who arrived to escort Isadora through the 1900 exposition, returned to London, he left her in the care of his nephew, Charles Noufflard, who introduced her, in turn, to two of his friends, "a pretty youth called Jacques Beaugnies" and the writer André Beaunier, a friend of Proust's and later the author of *Petrarch* and *Simonde.* Noufflard, Beaunier, and Beaugnies were Isadora's "three cavaliers," the momentary focus of her sexual longings and her ticket to Paris society. She was amazed at the ease with which she slipped into the salons of the Belle Epoque, "a little, uneducated American girl," as she coyly put it, who "in some mysterious manner had found the key [to] . . . the hearts and minds of the intellectual and artistic élite."[15] American newspaper correspondents in Paris made no bones about it: Isadora Duncan, "the lithe-limbed Hebe," had conquered "the city of fads."

HEROINE OF THE WINDSOR FIRE TAKES THE FRENCH BY STORM, read a headline in the *New York World*.[16] Isadora's success was all but instantaneous: "The very best people in Paris have taken her up, and she has appeared in the most impenetrable drawing-rooms of the Faubourg St-Germain."[17] Through Jacques Beaugnies, Isadora was presented at the salon of his mother, Meg de Saint-Marceaux, where she danced to Chopin with Maurice Ravel at the piano and was "quite overcome" by the kindness of the crowd.

"Quel ravissement!" the audience cried. *"Quelle jolie enfant! Bravo, bravo, comme elle est exquise!"* Mme. de Saint-Marceaux's Friday night musical salons were famous for their guest lists; newcomers might meet anyone from Paul Verlaine and Claude Debussy to the British composer Ethel Smyth and a young French writer called Colette.[18] Gabriel Fauré, Edmond de Goncourt, Paul Claudel, François Mauriac, André Maurois, Man Ray, and Princess Marthe Bibesco all mixed in this milieu, along with a weight of noble names that left Isadora's girlhood friends in Oakland agog: "Princess Dominique Radziwill, Princess Auguste de Croy, the Marquise and Mlle. de Montesquiou," etc. One night, after a concert, she found herself swept up in the arms of Messager, the composer, who kissed her on both cheeks — and her mouth, she added — and asked, *"Quel est ton nom, petite fille?"*

"Isadora."

"But do you have a nickname?" Messager asked.

"When I was a little girl they called me Dorita."

"Oh, Dorita, tu es adorable!"[19] Her awkward French alone had won her some hearts, at a time when a number of hostesses in the Paris *gratin* were American women: Anna Gould de Castellane, daughter of the American railway magnate Jay Gould; Clara Ward de Caraman-Chimay, from Detroit; and Winaretta and Isabelle Singer, who were Princess de Polignac and Duchess Decazes, respectively. (The duchess's daughter, the beauteous Daisy Fellowes, a granddaughter of Isaac Merritt Singer, crossed herself whenever she saw an advertisement for sewing machines.)[20]

From Meg de Saint-Marceaux's musical evenings, it was a short leap for Isadora to the salon of Elisabeth Greffulhe, Paris's "reigning Society Queen," one of the models for Proust's Duchesse de Guermantes, later a patron of Diaghilev's Ballets Russes, and a founder of France's Comité International du Patronage Artistique. Isadora wasn't sure that Countess Greffulhe's rose-choked drawing room showed her dancing to its best advantage. She remembered "an overcrowded salon full of marvelously dressed and bejewelled women" and "a front row of *jeunesse dorée*, whose noses just reached the end of the stage and were almost brushed by my dancing toes." Neither could she tell if the countess's interest in her was entirely "artistic."

"The Countess hailed me as a renaissance of Greek Art," Isadora wrote, "but she was rather under the influence of the *Aphrodite* of Pierre de Louÿs and his *Chanson de Bilitis,* whereas I had the expression of a Doric column and the Parthenon pediments as seen in the cold light of the British Museum." Isadora had read the *Chansons de Bilitis,* along with the poems of Sappho, but their lesbian sensibility went right over her head — "which proves that there is no necessity to censor the literature of the young," she wrote: "What one has not experienced, one will never understand in print."[21] Love between women caused barely a ripple in Paris society. "With ingenuous grace," Isadora stood in the salon of the Duchess d'Uzès and declared, "When I am rich, I shall rebuild the Temple of Paestum and open a college of priestesses, a school of the dance. I shall teach an army of young girls, who will renounce, as I have done, every other sensation, every other career. The dance is a religion and should have its worshippers." American papers reported that she had "shocked society,"[22] but she hadn't — even in Paris, world capital of art, Isadora felt misunderstood.

She was flirting like mad with everyone around her, and especially with André Beaunier — among her three cavaliers, the one she preferred. Beaunier wasn't blond, "tall and pleasant" like Charles Noufflard, or "good-looking" like Jacques Beaugnies. "He was pale and round-faced and wore glasses," Isadora sighed, "but what a mind! I was always a '*cerebrale,*' and, although people will not believe it, my love-affairs of the head . . . were as interesting to me as those of the heart." She had no intention of stopping in either realm: she meant to see Beaunier in bed.

"My mother could not understand my enthusiasm for this man," Isadora remarked, with considerable finesse, "who was not her *beau idéal* of what a lover should be." She had to get her mother out of the house when Beaunier came to call, books and magazines tucked under his arm, wearing convex spectacles that completely obscured his eyes. By now, Isadora read and spoke French "fairly easily"[23] (although she never lost a strong "Britannic" accent, according to French friends, and "continually mixed her tenses");[24] Beaunier was the man who introduced her to French literature, to Molière, Flaubert, de Maupassant, and Maeterlinck, whose *Pelléas et Mélisande* had enough thwarted love in it to satisfy the most cynical mind. With Beaunier, Isadora rode buses around the city and gazed at Notre Dame in the moonlight. "He knew every figure of the facade," she remembered, "and could tell me the history of every stone," but, as she later wrote to Gordon Craig, he "never, never ————."[25] Beaunier's stricken reaction to the death of Oscar Wilde in 1900 might have given her a clue to his affinity.

"He came to me white and trembling in a terrible state of depression," Isadora recalled. "I had read and heard vaguely about Oscar Wilde but knew very little about him." Pertinently, Isadora didn't know that Wilde had been imprisoned in England for sodomy and that the love that dare not speak its name was prudent in Paris, too — at least when it came to walks in the moonlight with American girls, and despite the fact that homosexual acts weren't illegal in France, alone among European nations. When Isadora asked Beaunier how Wilde came to die alone, in a miserable hotel room near the Ecole des Beaux-Arts, "he blushed to the roots of his hair and refused to answer."

"You are my only confidante," Beaunier said, telling Isadora nothing more about himself and leaving her with "the strange impression that some uncanny calamity had befallen the world." Once, walking in the woods at Meudon, they sat down at a crossroads and gave names to the various paths. They called the right-hand one "Fortune," the left, "Peace," and the road ahead, "Immortality."

"Where are we sitting?" Isadora asked.

"Love," Beaunier replied.

"Then I prefer to remain here."

"We can't remain here," Beaunier snapped, and scuttled off "very fast down the road."

"But why, but why, why do you leave me?" Isadora cried. A bottle of champagne and a carefully planned meal did nothing to melt the ice when, one night, she "plotted to send Mother and Raymond to the Opera" and resolved outright to seduce Beaunier. She wore her dancing tunic and wreathed her hair in roses, but neither limbs nor wine nor flowers had any effect on her fellow *cérébrale,* and she was left weeping bitterly in the soup.

"When you recollect that at that time I was young and remarkably pretty," Isadora reflected, "it's difficult to find an explanation of this episode, and indeed I have never found one."[26] She was equally un-witting when she opened her doors to Winaretta Singer, the American sewing-machine heiress, whose "implacable lesbianism" was the stuff of legend.[27] Born in Yonkers, the twentieth child of Isaac Singer, "Princess Winnie" had been married off, first, to the Prince de Scey-Montbéliard, whom she attacked with an umbrella on their wedding night and threatened to kill if he came anywhere near her. "I have sel-dom seen a woman sit so firmly," said the writer and diplomat Harold Nicolson. "There was determination in every line of her bum."[28] Win-nie's second union with Prince Edmond de Polignac was a "marriage of reason" and a perfect match — the prince, too, was homosexual. Both prince and princess were gifted pianists; in addition, Winaretta was a painter of such skill that her works were sometimes mistaken for Manet's. She appeared unannounced at Isadora's studio, looking like "a Roman emperor" and "bearing portents of coming events."

"I am the Princess de Polignac," said Winaretta, flat out, inviting Isadora to dance and leaving two thousand francs at the door when she left.[29] Along with her taste for young women, generosity was among Princess Winnie's most celebrated traits. Not content to pre-sent Isadora to her own circle of friends, the princess arranged a series of subscription concerts that brought a range of notables to Isadora's studio in rue de la Gaité: Gustave Fauré, Octave Mirbeau, Georges Clemenceau, and Rodin, whose fascination with dancers was equaled only by Isadora's reverence for his genius. She pursued Rodin "like Psyche seeking the God Pan," and when he came one day to watch her dance — just the two of them, alone in her studio — he was less in-terested in Isadora's theories than in her body. She remembered:

> He gazed at me with lowered lids, his eyes blazing, and then, with the same expression that he had before his works, he came toward me. He ran his hands over my neck, breast, stroked my arms and ran his hands over my hips, my bare legs and feet. He began to knead my whole body as if it were clay, while from him emanated [a] heat that scorched and melted me. My whole desire was to yield to him my en-tire being and, indeed, I would have done so if it had not been that my absurd upbringing caused me to become frightened, and I withdrew, threw my dress over my tunic, and sent him away bewildered. What a pity! How often I have regretted this childish miscomprehension

which lost to me the divine chance of giving my virginity to the Great God Pan, the mighty Rodin. Surely Art and all Life would have been richer thereby![30]

She was beginning to get impatient, with herself and all the men around her. Isadora's warmest friendship at this time was with the painter Eugène Carrière, who lived with his wife and children in Montmartre and whom Isadora revered as "my model." Carrière was Rodin's closest friend in Paris, hard to classify as a painter because — like Rodin, like Isadora — he adhered to no school. His canvases were known for their mystery, opaqueness, and distinctive atmosphere of shadow and fog; diarist Edmond de Goncourt, commenting on Carrière, remarked that "he does not paint the portrait of a face, but the portrait of a smile." He was also universally liked, a man of whom no evil word seems ever to have been spoken.[31]

"He had the strongest spiritual presence I have ever felt," said Isadora, who worshiped the memory of Carrière to the end of her life. "When coming into his presence I felt as I imagine I would have felt had I met the Christ. I was filled with such awe. I wanted to fall on my knees, and would have done it had not the timidity and reserve of my nature held me back." Plainly, she was out of control, tossed from passion to passion and mode to mode, so that actress Lotte Yorska, who met Isadora at Carrière's, remarked that "except for Lillian Gish, I have never seen an American girl look so shy."[32] At the Comédie-Française, Isadora burst into tears during a performance of *Oedipus Rex,* "weeping," "swaying," "fainting," as she watched tragedian Jean Mounet-Sully rend his garments and rip out his eyes "in the final moment of superb anguish."

"Thenceforth," Isadora wrote, "I knew my way." Apollo was overthrown. In an exalted frame of mind, she went one night to a raffish hotel with Hallé's nephew, Charles Noufflard, where they secured a room under fictitious names and Noufflard proved "as enterprising as André [Beaunier] was backwards in embraces and kisses."

"I found myself in his arms," Isadora wrote, "submerged in a storm of caresses, my heart pounding, every nerve bathed in pleasure," until Noufflard surmised that she was a virgin and leaped from the bed, crying, "'Oh — why didn't you tell me? What a crime I was about to commit — No, no, you must remain pure. Dress, dress at once!'"

"And, deaf to my laments," said Isadora, "he put my coat around

me and hurried me to a cab." She had ample time in the future to reflect on the "too religious and awe-inspiring effect" she produced in
men, and went back with a vengeance to her work.[33]

In 1901 the Duncans moved from rue de la Gaité to an apartment
at 45, avenue de Villiers, in the eighth *arrondissement,* where Raymond painted columns on the walls and put rolls of tinfoil on the gas
jets to simulate the light of ancient torches. At the piano, Mrs. Duncan
pounded out preludes, waltzes, mazurkas, and the entire score of
Gluck's *Orfeo ed Euridice.* When Isadora asked her to stop the music,
she did, looking on with some trepidation as her daughter worked out
an essential theory of the dance.

"I spent long days and nights in the studio," Isadora wrote, in
what is probably the most quoted passage of her autobiography, "seeking that dance which might be the divine expression of the human
spirit through the medium of the body's movement. For hours I would
stand quite still, my two hands folded between my breasts, covering
the solar plexus. My mother often became alarmed to see me remain
for such long intervals quite motionless as if in a trance — but I was
seeking, and finally discovered, the central spring of all movement,
the crater of motor power, the unity from which all diversities of movement are born."[34] It was the *impulse* to movement Isadora had found,
the driving concept of modern dance: "Motion is motivated by emotion, and must be expressed with the instrument of the entire human
body."[35] That this was just the beginning, the crystallization of everything she had worked toward till now, does not detract from the significance of the moment. By fixing the urge to move in the solar plexus,
the region of the heart and visceral organs, Isadora was concerned
with the dancer's need to return to an "original" condition, a primal
state of awakened response, from which a specific technique might flow,
"like the petals of a flower."

"I have often tried to explain to artists this first basic theory of my
Art," Isadora wrote, conceding that the idea was "difficult" to understand in instructional terms. On the stage, in motion, her theory of a
"central spring" translated most noticeably into an ecstatic lifting of the
chest, a continual upward striving. All Duncan dances are propelled not
by the legs but by the torso, in contrast to ballet technique, in which
movement extends outward from the spine, and arms, legs, head, and
neck serve essentially as extensions, giving the impression of "an artic-

ulated puppet," in Isadora's phrase, "an artificial mechanical movement not worthy of the soul. I, on the contrary, sought the source of the spiritual expression to flow into the channels of the body, filling it with vibrating light — the centrifugal force reflecting the spirit's vision."[36]

What Isadora describes is the same process of "preparedness" and "recall" that emerged a decade later from the Moscow Art Theatre, under the direction of Konstantin Stanislavsky, the system known to the world as Method acting. All art begins, in this view, not with technique but with truth — indeed, with personal truth — which can be nourished and, with practice, summoned at will. Any dance technique, properly learned, would respond to this imperative, Isadora believed, but not the other way around. Truth must come first, and technique after; as Isadora said, "Life is the root, and art is the flower"[37] — the definition of modern art.

"She insisted that the dancer's body be regarded simply as an instrument for the expression of emotional concepts, and not as a performing machine," wrote John Martin, the first dance critic of the *New York Times* and for years doyen of American dance writers: "[Her] uncovering of the substance of the dance as expressional movement is one of the monumental achievements in the history of the arts."[38] Martin went on:

> What she was primarily concerned with can only be called basic dance — not a trade or a profession or even an art to begin with, but a biological function. . . . If the individual becomes aware of the world in which he lives through its direct effect upon his nerves and muscles, nature's fundamental perceptive mechanism, he has won his freedom from the arbitrary thou-shalts and shalt-nots which established social cults and creeds put upon him the moment he is old enough to be dominated. Only when he has developed the power to touch life at first hand does he begin to be aware of his inherent selfhood, and until he has become thus aware he cannot develop his true bent or resist the forces that would conventionalize him into a mass product. This was and is a colossal concept, not only affecting the dance but virtually adding another dimension to life. [39]

Throughout her career, Isadora would rely on music to "start the motor in [her] soul," as she called it later in conversation with Stanislavsky. But she envisioned a day when dance would be propelled solely from the inside, independent of external stimuli:

Imagine then a dancer, who, after long study, prayer and inspiration, has attained such a degree of understanding that his body is simply the luminous manifestation of his soul; whose body dances in accordance with a music heard inwardly, in an expression of something out of another, a profounder world. This is the truly creative dancer, natural but not imitative, speaking in movement out of himself and out of something greater than all selves.[40]

In Paris, where she began to give dancing lessons, Isadora instructed her pupils in words that became her credo: "Listen to the music with *your soul*. Now, while listening, do you not feel an inner self awakening deep within you — that it is by its strength that your head is lifted, that your arms are raised, that you are walking slowly toward the light?"[41] These weren't just airy thoughts. No dancer in the future could afford to ignore them, and no dance could succeed without surrendering to their truth.[42] Modern dance would "vary greatly from this simple beginning," Martin concluded, "but in all its manifestations it is still essentially Isadora's technique rationalized, stripped of its Victorian romanticism and mysticism, and broadened by contacts with the advancing times and the multiplicity of creative forces which they have produced. We no longer speak of 'the will to beauty,' but we build our art on the same inner impulse."[43]

There was no shortage of girls in Paris eager to study with Isadora, at a time when "the idyll was her element" and she stood poised on the brink of international fame. She had not yet appeared in Paris theaters and wouldn't for another two years, when triumphs in Vienna, Budapest, Munich, and Berlin gave her unchallenged access to commercial houses. Most of her performances at this time took place in her own studio, before invited audiences picked for their discrimination or their status in society. A printed invitation survives from the period, dated December 12, 1901: *"Miss Duncan will dance to the sound of harp and flute in her Studio next Thursday Evening and if you feel that seeing this small person dancing against the waves of an overpowering destiny is of ten francs benefit to you — why come along!"*[44] She was already known for her sense of humor, arriving one night for a party at the American embassy dressed as Cleopatra and carrying a shiny dagger. "[She] looked willing and ready to use it," a guest recalled, "if the expression on her face . . . meant anything." At a reception held in the Palais de l'Elysée by French president Emile Loubet, Isadora's dancing earned a "tremendous and touching" ovation.[45] American millionaire

Harry Thaw, later notorious for the murder of architect Stanford White, met her in the summer of 1901 and told her that "he could be happy with her anywhere, because he knew he had his millions to help them through almost any wilderness they might happen to come across." Thaw reminded Isadora pointedly of the famous quatrain in *The Rubáiyát:*

> *A Book of Verses underneath the Bough,*
> *A Jug of Wine, a Loaf of Bread — and Thou*
> *Beside me singing in the Wilderness —*
> *O, Wilderness, were Paradise now.*

But Isadora had "her own ideas," according to press reports: "Mr. Thaw and his millions are out of the race, for he has gone from her presence with these words ringing in his ears: 'Not for a million. Not on any account!' . . . The poetry of motion has not disturbed the mental equilibrium of Miss Duncan an atom."[46] In the classroom, she dressed severely, in black, with a high lace collar and rhinestone bows, charging five dollars a lesson, three days a week.

"One did not realize the striking handsomeness of her features or the glorious beauty of her body until, freed from conventional apparel, she donned the classic robes of the dance," said one of Isadora's pupils, Princess der Ling, teenage daughter of the Chinese ambassador to France. "Neither then, nor at any later time did she appear a significant figure in ordinary dress. . . . 'I do not live in ordinary dress,' I once heard her say. 'I cover my body because the law demands it. . . . Silly, the law!'" Her studio in Paris was "a barn-like place," with a long, bare stage at the end:

Her classes were growing by leaps and bounds. . . . After a time so many pupils clamored for lessons that she had to divide them up into three classes, tripling her labors, which were already beyond the capabilities of anyone else I could have named. . . . The class would be lined up like soldiers. Isadora would tell them carefully, almost spelling out her lessons, exactly what to do, and just where each movement fitted in with the music. . . . Fat girls, thin girls, tall girls, stubby girls; girls with knees, girls with calves, girls with neither knees nor calves! It seemed to me, watching, that none of them did correctly anything that Isadora told them, and that no two of them did the same thing. It must have seemed that way to Duncan, too, for at the very first movement she would say: "Stop! . . . The arms must be exactly so, the curve of the limbs exactly so, the expression of the face, the curve of the neck, the position of the head . . . exactly so."

Along with Isadora, Princess der Ling never forgot "that patient mother of hers, who endlessly thumped at the piano. . . . *Thump! Thump! Thumpety-thump!* . . . I might have appreciated her martyr-dom more if only she hadn't insisted on kissing us when we met!"[47] Mrs. Duncan was in the habit of kissing any child she saw, snatching babies from their mothers' arms and cooing, "Oh, you darling! What is your name?"

"Is this your baby?" she asked Mary Desti, an American from Chicago.[48] Mary had come to France to study voice on the heels of what she called "a disastrous runaway marriage," with her two-year-old son, Preston, in tow. She was "scarcely more than a child" herself, by her own, guileless description, a stranger in Paris, "without a maid or a nurse," dreaming of a career on the stage. Mary met Mrs. Duncan at the office of Donald Downey, who specialized in finding apartments for Americans in Paris.

"Why, Mary, you darling, I am going to take you both right home to Isadora," Mrs. Duncan said. They bundled into a cab and drove to avenue de Villiers, where Mrs. Duncan "threw open the door with a great flourish," crying, "Isadora, Isadora, look what I have brought you, Mary and her baby!"

Without a word, Mary remembered, Isadora and Raymond "both came forward, clasping me in their arms and dancing around in a cir-cle as though I were some person they had been waiting for." Mrs. Duncan shot to the piano, plunked the baby on the seat, and "gaily played some marvelous dance tunes," while Isadora, Mary, and Ray-mond whirled about the room in a ring. "Here began the friendship which lasted all the rest of our lives," Mary wrote, doubting that her "poor stumbling pen" could do justice to the tale:

> How [to] describe Isadora? Had I been ushered into Paradise and given over to my guardian angel, I could not have been more uplifted. Isadora was in her little dancing tunic, a colorless gauze of some sort, draped softly about her slender, ethereal form; her exquisite little head poised on her swan-like throat and tilted to one side like a bird, as though the weight of her auburn curls caused it to droop; a little retroussé nose that gave just the slightest human touch, otherwise I should have thrown myself on my knees before her, believing I was worshipping a celestial being.[49]

At twenty-nine, with one marriage already behind her and many more to come, Mary Desti was cast for life in the romantic mode. Desti wasn't her real name. It was Dempsey, which she had altered, according to her son, with the explanation that it was "a misnomer, bestowed upon the family in error by the vulgar Irish varlets attending her ancestor, a distinguished Italian prince. . . . What these uneducated flunkies were trying to say was 'd'Este,' only they couldn't pronounce it."[50] Having brought Mary and the Duncans together, it was Preston, the baby, who sealed their friendship when he fell ill with pneumonia in 1901 and nearly died. Mrs. Duncan nursed him with a bottle of champagne, which she spooned into his mouth every hour on the hour and appeared to regard, like Thomas de Quincey, as a panacea for all human woes.

They were all drinking a lot, if their own and other testimony can be taken as a guide. As early as 1902, Isadora was seen nipping at a bottle of Moët et Chandon before dancing; her dressing rooms were invariably stocked with wine, and, according to Mary, she danced barefoot before Georges Clemenceau at a recital in Paris because she had spilled a glass of Hunter's rye on her sandals.

"We began to giggle and laugh," Mary remembered, "until try as we would, we could not get the sandals on. . . . This was the first time that Isadora Duncan ever danced barefoot in her life and it created such a sensation, everyone raving over the beauty of her feet, that she adopted this forever."[51] True or not, Mary's story is articulate of the madcap existence Isadora was already leading. These were the "banquet years" in a Paris still reeling from the multiple traumas of the fin de siècle. "Put in oversimplified terms," writes Vincent Cronin, "Parisians from 1880 to the end of the century went to parties in order to forget such matters as the defeat by Prussia, political scandals, the Dreyfus affair; from 1900 they went to parties to celebrate."[52] For a while Isadora and Mary lived together in an apartment in rue d'Antin, near the Grand Palais, sending Mrs. Duncan and the baby to Giverny, where they occasionally went themselves on the weekends.

"I remember one Easter Sunday when we climbed high in the hills and sat all day and listened to Isadora read Shakespeare and Shelley," Mary reported. "Here was nothing but beauty and innocence. . . . At this time Isadora knew nothing of love or lovers and I don't think the question of sex was ever mentioned between us."[53] Isadora was courted by all kinds of men, nonetheless, among them an American painter, Joe Smith, who "drove her mad" with his piano renditions of

"Swanee River," and a French count, unnamed, who sent her roses every day, which she promptly dropped out the studio window to the courtyard: "The janitor found the box, with Miss Duncan's name on it, and the well meaning old fellow brought the flowers back to her . . . watching in astonishment as they made another flight, far faster and more furious than the first one, out the window again."[54] It was a happy, tipsy time, ended only when Mary herself left Paris to marry "an old sweetheart" in America, stockbroker Solomon Sturges. In 1902 she went back to Chicago with Preston, where the boy was adopted by his stepfather and became known to a later generation, in another art form, as Preston Sturges, master director of American screwball comedies.

Only a few months separated Isadora from the final leap to fame. Sometime in the winter of 1902, Raymond Duncan left Paris in the company of Emma Nevada, the American soprano, for whom he would act as "advance agent" on a concert tour in the United States that also included cellist Pablo Casals. It had been a frustrating time for Raymond, as he watched the rise of his sister's star while busying himself with ingenious but still profitless occupations. "At this time Raymond invented his famous sandals, having discovered that all shoes were obnoxious," Isadora wrote. He was "very clever with his pencil" and took photographs of Isadora in the nude that were published anonymously as "Greek silhouettes." Raymond was well on his way to a messianic philosophy of holistic living when he met Mme. Nevada — "the Western nightingale," who "sang like an enchantress" and swept him off his feet.[55]

"I noticed that little violet-scented notes were often poked under the door in the early morning hours, followed by the surreptitious disappearance of Raymond," Isadora wrote. "As he was not in the habit of taking walks before breakfast, I put two and two together, and gathered my conclusions." She was happy to conspire with the infatuated pair, still under Mrs. Duncan's watchful eye, in exchange for the favors Nevada provided — first among them, a meeting with Loie Fuller, the "marvelous," the "incomparable," the dancing flower of the Folies-Bergère.

Nevada brought Fuller to Isadora's studio, where Isadora danced for her and tried to explain her ideas, "as I did for everyone," she said, "and would have done for the plumber had he come in."[56] In her own account of their meeting, Fuller recalled that Isadora "gave promise of great things" and that she had offered to "keep her" by inviting her on a tour of Germany, with her own troupe and the Otojiro company, including Sada Yacco. Isadora was thrilled to accept, and so was Mrs. Duncan, having been assured that Loie Fuller was "a good woman,"[57] and that her name had "never been connected with any scandal."[58]

In fact, this was not the case. In the early 1890s, while still in America, Fuller made headlines as the plaintiff in an ugly divorce action, in which it was revealed that her husband, a nephew of President Rutherford B. Hayes, was a bigamist — "indeed, a trigamist"[59] — and, furthermore, a pornographer, and in which accusations of "unnatural practices" streamed from both sides. Born in an Illinois barroom in 1862, Loie — it was short for Mary Louise — had already enjoyed a colorful career in vaudeville before she began to experiment with her costumes and lights, in a New York production of *Quack, M.D.* Here she found the "dancing" technique that propelled her to stardom — a whirling, spinning, incandescent floor show that left audiences gasping and poets, painters, and fashion designers straining to capture its effects. Fuller was called the Queen of Art Nouveau, but above all things, she was a producer, the complete *régisseur,* who supervised her own performances and guarded her theatrical secrets with a jealousy bordering on paranoia: "Even her dresses were made in secret." Like Isadora, Fuller lived with her mother, though she traveled with a troupe of young women — officially, her students[60] — who appeared sporadically in her productions and "to whom she was attached with extraordinary affection." It was the first thing Isadora noticed when she joined the company in Berlin:

> I arrived in Berlin at the Hotel Bristol, where, in a magnificent apartment, I found Loie Fuller surrounded by her entourage. A dozen or so beautiful girls were grouped about her, alternately stroking her hands and kissing her. In my rather simple upbringing, although my mother certainly loved us all, she rarely caressed us, and so I was completely taken aback. . . . *I sat aloof, hearing strangely for the first time such phrases as "my pretty; my dove; my darling; little one; sweetest; honey; dearest; darling," which seemed the coin of their intercourse.* * Here was an atmosphere of such warmth as I had never met before.[61]

Before leaving Paris, Isadora said good-bye to André Beaunier and thought she could detect "a glint of anguish behind his spectacles." She hadn't been long on the road before she wished with all her heart that

---

* The passage in italics was excised from English-language editions of *My Life.*

she had brought her mother. (Mrs. Duncan, "ill" with something, stayed in Paris.) Among the "brightly colored butterflies" in Fuller's entourage were the ballerina Rita Sacchetto; a French chorine and "child of nature" called Orchidée; Gertrud von Axen, "known for her waltzes"; and a dark young woman in a black suit, who circled around the others "like some scarab of ancient Egypt" and was undoubtedly Gabrielle Bloch, Loie Fuller's primary companion for many years. Isadora herself became ill upon arriving in Berlin and was unable to dance. She followed the Fuller company to Leipzig, Munich, and Vienna, dazzled by a "luxurious life of champagne dinners and palatial hotel suites," but increasingly dismayed by the ardent attentions of the troupe.

"Loie Fuller's generosity was unbounded," Isadora reported — she was all but swept away by her patron's "marvellous ephemeral art," only stopping to wonder how it was possible for Fuller to dance at all: "She seemed to be suffering from terrible pains in the spine, for which her lovely entourage brought ice bags from time to time and placed them between her back and the back of the chair. 'Just another ice bag, darling,' she would say; 'it seems to make the pain go.'"[62] The exertion required for Fuller to perform, pushing and twisting the hidden sticks that left her "whirling on her own axis like a corkscrew or a spinning top," threatened to paralyze her arms. Her program of solo dances rarely lasted more than half an hour, and she normally had to be carried from the stage when they were finished. In press interviews, Fuller lamented that she wasn't happy as a star, that she longed "to be a mother" and look after her "brood," and it was this euphemistic version of her private life that Isadora took for granted.

For her part, Fuller remembered Isadora as a mystic and a visionary, an arrogant "artist-dancer" who walked around in a gray Empire robe and "a man's hat with a flying veil" and made an "absurd" impression on everyone around her. "She was as talented as she was eccentric," Fuller recalled, "and her present appearance was normal, I may say, compared with what she wanted to do, for she was always saying she intended to take nearly all her clothes off and dance in the streets. Of course I attributed this extreme condition of mind to the fact that she must be a genius."[63]

In Vienna, Fuller took steps to present Isadora to "the great public," inviting journalists, artists, and theater managers to a private concert under the high patronage of Paulina Metternich, "the most powerful woman at the Court of Austria," as Fuller described her, whose seal of approval was cultural law in the reaches of the Hapsburg empire.[64] It was the nightmare of Fuller's life — in her memoirs, she titled the chapter on Isadora, simply, "An Experience."[65] Having gathered not just Princess Metternich but the press, "the literary and artistic world" (including Gustav Klimt), and the American and British ambassadors to Vienna, Fuller sat with the others in the drawing room of the Hotel Bristol one late afternoon while the clock ticked away and Isadora left them waiting for what seemed an eternity.

"I found her with her feet in warm water, in the act of dressing her hair," wrote Fuller, who had gone to Isadora's room to see what the matter was. "I begged her to hurry, explaining that she ran the risk through her negligence of offending a public which might definitely launch her." Since Isadora had only recently danced for the president of France, she may have felt she had time to spare. When she finally entered, "calm, indifferent, and careless of whatever interest these people might have of her," there was a moment of stunned silence.

"Was I blind?" Fuller wondered. "She seemed to have no clothing on to speak of. . . . She appeared to me nude, or nearly so, so slight were the gauzes that covered her form."

> She took her place near the orchestra [Fuller continues], and while they played a prelude of Chopin she stood there motionless, her eyes cast down and her arms hanging listlessly at her side. Then she danced.
>
> Oh! how I loved it! To me it was the most beautiful thing in the world. I forgot the woman and all her faults, her silly fancies and absurd manners and dress. I only saw the dancer and loved her for the joy she gave me.
>
> She finished. No one spoke. My heart beat fast. I went to the Princess. She spoke to me softly. "Why does she dance so insufficiently clothed?"[66]

The word spread quickly through Vienna: a "barefoot dancer," a "naked nymph." Inevitably, Isadora rose to stardom everywhere in Europe only when she was seen to be flying in the face of common morality.[67] At no time in her career was she entirely naked under her tissues of gauze and silk. Her breasts were free, but her groin was covered and her tunics were strapped securely to her shoulders and waist by means of elastics. Loie Fuller, grasping at straws, told Princess Metternich that Isadora's nudity was "accidental."

"I forgot to tell you how amiable our artiste is," Fuller said. "Her baggage has not yet arrived, but rather than disappoint us here today she has consented to appear in her practicing costume."[68] If the princess was fooled, the public wasn't, and Fuller found herself pushed aside as Isadora rode the crest of affronted sensibilities and took the German world by storm. Not long after, at the Karl Theater in Vienna, she stopped the show when an Austrian cavalry officer shouted from his box, "How disgusting!" Isadora retired to her dressing room and refused to continue until the offended warrior had left, taking "every officer in the playhouse" with him.⁶⁹ The occasional plea from timid souls that she wear a shift beneath her tunic met with the same refusal: she would dance her own way, or not at all.

"My dancing is for the élite," Isadora told the impresario Sándor Grosz, "for the artists, sculptors, painters, musicians, but not for the general public."⁷⁰ It was Grosz who persuaded her to sign a contract for a tour of Hungary, although Fuller took credit for the matter and "could not, would not" believe it when Isadora set off for Budapest without a word of thanks or good-bye. Mrs. Duncan had arrived from Paris, in Fuller's account, with her eye on the future and a nose for gold. "I had two guests instead of one," Fuller complained, attributing to Isadora's mother an un-Duncan-like remark: "Now that she has set you on your feet, you don't need her anymore. I wouldn't think of going back again."

"This was particularly cruel," Fuller wrote, "because I had just lost over a hundred thousand francs through a . . . manager having failed to pay me for my Japanese." Otojiro's company comprised more than thirty people, who cost Fuller "more than ninety of another nationality would have done, for apart from everything that I was obliged to do to entertain them, I had . . . to attach to each train . . . an enormous car laden with Japanese delicacies, rice, salted fish, mushrooms and preserved turnips. . . . I tried for a long time to get my money back by transporting my Nipponese and their viands up and down the earth, but, weary of the struggle, I finally assembled another troupe."⁷¹ Fuller was on the verge of bankruptcy when Isadora bolted and left her with a lasting resentment. Years later, at a party in Brussels, she heard that Isadora had denied ever knowing her.

Isadora's version of the story is completely different, detailed in her autobiography with an exquisite sense of comedy and notable chiefly for what it doesn't say. "By this time," she wrote, "in spite of my admiration for the art of Loie Fuller, I began to ask myself why I had left my mother alone in Paris, and what I was doing in this troupe of beautiful but demented ladies."⁷² She arrived in Budapest in the middle of March and rehearsed for a month before opening at the Urania Theatre on April 19, 1902, the first of twenty sold-out performances from which, ever after, she could date her status as a legend. Isadora's new manager, Grosz, couldn't have been more adept at building anticipation for her debut, inviting his friends and colleagues to her rehearsals and encouraging them to talk and write about her: Isadora was already known in Budapest as "the Little Dancer Poetess" before the public saw her.[73] Possibly in response to the storm in Vienna, Grosz's agents told of her "angelic face" and "touching modesty," while Isadora herself rhapsodized about the Hungarian spring, "the river," "the hills," "the lilacs," the food, and a particular Hungarian "of god-like features" and bedroom eyes — Oszkár Beregi, the man who became her first lover and transformed her from "the chaste nymph that I was into a wild and careless bacchante."

Beregi was a leading actor of the Hungarian National Theater. Isadora never mentioned his name in her autobiography, content to remember him through a rapturous mist as "Romeo . . . my Romeo." They had met at a party in her honor, she recalled,

> over a glass of golden Tokay . . . two large black eyes that burned and glowed into mine with such ardent adoration and Hungarian passion that in one look was all the meaning of the spring in Budapest. He was tall, of magnificent proportions, a head covered with luxuriant curls, black, with purple lights in them. Indeed, he might have posed for the David of [Michelangelo]. . . . From our first look every power of attraction we possessed rushed from us in mad embrace. From that first gaze we were already in each other's arms, and no power on earth could have prevented this.[74]

Beregi remembered the same occasion in terms more subtly dramatic. "It was spring," he wrote simply, "and I was twenty-six years old." Hoping to practice his English, he had brought flowers for Isadora, the "exotic foreign dancer," whose appearance on the streets of Budapest literally stopped traffic:

> At the end of the dim, shabby corridor a Renoir painting was suddenly coming to life and floated toward the door, dangling her hat on a band on her arm; she was accompanied by a refined, white-haired lady in a long, grey dress, a few steps behind her. I was standing stiffly in the doorway. I had never before seen a woman move in so free a manner. She was already standing in front of me, and without realizing what I was saying, the words left my lips in English, as I proffered her the flowers: "This is for you . . ."[75]

That day, Isadora wore a dress of light blue crepe, in the Empire style. "Her neck was soft, long, white, and without jewelry," said Beregi. "Her hair was light brown, and her eyes . . . her eyes were like those of a fawn: warm, radiant, and innocent. She was smiling."

"Let's look for a book," Isadora suddenly said, walking toward the shelves of her host's apartment. "Our hands touched," Beregi wrote. He invited her to see him that night in *Julius Caesar:* "I am Mark Antony. Of course, you are familiar with the piece. . . ."

"Of course," Isadora answered brightly: "We study Shakespeare in school."[76] Then she ran to Mrs. Duncan: "Mother, this gentleman has invited us to the theatre for tonight, we are going . . . we are going."[77] Soon Beregi was reading poetry at her concerts — not the mood-enhancing stanzas that once inspired her steps, but great, sonorous lines from Ovid and Horace, backed by the chorus of the Hungarian Royal Opera and interspersed between her dances.

For her Budapest debut, Isadora included her *Primavera* and *Angel with a Viol,* along with her newer, mythic pieces: *Orpheus, Pan and Echo, Bacchus and Ariadne, Alcestis' Farewell.* To these, over the course of her run, she added five works of Chopin, a "song of the gypsies," and Liszt's *Rakoczy March,* which she performed in a scarlet tunic as a *Hymn to the Heroes of Hungary.* Before her opening, in rehearsal, she also improvised a dance to Strauss's *Blue Danube* waltz, "carried away by the enticing music," but refused to add it to her repertoire.

"By Heaven! You should have seen her wide eyes fill with tears of indignation," said the actress Mari Jászai, whom Grosz had brought to see Isadora that day. "In tears she told us: 'Why should I tread the pioneer's thorny path in order to perform a commonplace, profane dance before a cultured audience? — the kind of dance I've known since I was four? If that were my purpose, I'd go into vaudeville . . . and make a lot of money.'"[78] Nevertheless, at the end of her second night in Budapest, as she bowed to thunderous applause, hats and roses raining onto the stage, Isadora quietly signaled the orchestra to strike up the waltz. "With a leap of joy, like one arisen from some hiding place in the rocks," she began to move, rocking and swaying in a dance "so humanly jubilant," "with such a musical joy of life," that the crowd erupted in shouts and cheers. "The whole audience sprang to their feet in such a delirium of enthusiasm," Isadora wrote, "that I had to repeat the waltz many times before they would behave less like mad people."[79]

"When she danced the *Blue Danube,*" said a woman who saw it later, "her simple waltzing forward and back, like the oncoming and receding waves of the shore, had such an ecstasy of rhythm that audiences became frenzied with the contagion of it. . . . She was, in the true sense of the word, inspired, gathering within herself forces beyond the boundaries of her own or any personality, and sending them forth so that we all felt them, and were exalted by a vision of unknown worlds."[80]

In the fullness of success, Isadora rode through Budapest in an open carriage and, at night, while her mother slept, surrendered to her "Romeo," knowing, for the first time, "the unsurpassed joy of waking at dawn to find my hair tangled in his black scented curls, and to feel his arms around me." In a notebook she had bought in Paris, where she kept her thoughts and theories of the dance, Beregi inscribed words she might have read as the highest expression of her life: *The sun, sunshine, my soul, I am, yours.*[81]

6

Germany

In 1902 Oszkár Beregi wasn't yet the most famous actor in Hungary, but he would be, going on to a career in theater and films that spanned six decades and took him from European stages to London, New York, and Los Angeles, where he died in 1965 at the age of ninety. Among Isadora's biographers, Beregi is consistently ill-served, caricatured as a wild Hungarian and "handsome *jeune premier*" who took her virginity and then left her to her own devices when his passion died. Certainly, this is the impression Isadora gave in *My Life*.[1] But Beregi's reminiscences of Isadora are wholly adoring — she, in describing their love affair, used the occasion mainly to meditate on the nature of her passions.

"It was then, and has always been, the experience of my temperament that, no matter how violent the sensation or passion, the brain worked at the same time with a lightning and luxurious rapidity," Isadora wrote. "I have, therefore, never, in the slang sense, lost my head; on the contrary, the more acute the pleasure of the senses, the more vivid the thought."[2] She was conscious of Beregi's smooth technique and suspected he was talking rubbish when he told her that he had "changed his interpretation of the part of Romeo" in response to meeting her.

"Your face is like a flower," Beregi moaned. "You are my flower.

My flower — my flower."[3] Isadora was desperate for "some soporific to dull the incessant unwanted commentary" in her head. She found it in a complete surrender to the physical, recalling the cry of her brain when compunction gave up the ghost: "Yes. I admit all else in life, including your art, is as vapour and nonsense to the glory of this moment, and, for this moment, willingly I abdicate to dissolution, destruction, death." Having rejected Cartesian distinctions of soul and body, Isadora now added another, more romantic and dangerous component to her conception of Apollo and Dionysus — a war between love and art, as she experienced it, a battle of the senses and the mind.

"How I envy those natures which can give themselves entirely to the voluptuousness of the moment," Isadora wrote, "without fear of the critic who sits aloft and separates and insists upon interjecting his view, when least wanted, to the coupled senses beneath."[4] In her memoirs, she describes the moment of her seduction as frankly as the time would allow, and a bit more:

> One evening, after his theatre and mine, we went into the salon quite unknown to my mother, who thought I was safe asleep. At first Romeo was happy just reciting his rôles, or speaking of his art and the theatre, and I was quite happy listening to him, but gradually I noticed that he seemed troubled, and at times quite upset and speechless. He clenched his hands and appeared to feel quite ill, and at such times I noticed that his beautiful face became quite congested, his eyes inflamed, his lips swollen, and he bit them till the blood came.

The next lines of Isadora's narrative were censored for publication in English; the offending passages are in italics:

> I myself felt ill and dizzy, while an irresistible longing to press him closer and closer surged in me, until, losing all control and falling into a fury, he carried me *to the couch.* Frightened, *ravished with ecstasy,* the realisation *of sex* was made clear to me. I confess my first impressions were a horrible fright, *and terrible pain which seemed to resemble the pain of having many teeth pulled at once,* but a great pity for what he seemed to be suffering prevented me from running away from what was at first sheer *mutilation* and torture.
>
> That morning at dawn we left the hotel together, and taking a belated two-horse carriage, which we found in the street, we drove miles out, into the country. We stopped at a peasant's hut, where the wife gave us a room with an old-fashioned four-poster bed. *Then, what was to me at that time, a ghastly, suffering experience continued, amidst my*

martyr's groans and cries. All that day we remained in the country, Romeo frequently hushing my cries and drying my tears.

I'm afraid I gave the public a very bad performance that evening, for I felt quite *crippled.* When, however, I met Romeo afterwards in the salon, he was in such a state of joy and elation that I felt repaid for all my suffering, and only desired to recommence, especially as he assured me tenderly *that the pain would soon cease,* that I would finally know what Heaven was on earth. A prophecy which was soon fulfilled.[5]

Beregi's memoir of these days differs from Isadora's in tone and detail. "Do you like my little dances . . . ?" she had asked him on her opening night. "Do you like my little dances . . . ?" Her success was "frantic," Beregi wrote. Isadora was "unspeakably happy."

> We were again at the Hotel Royal, in the drawing room of their suite, the mother drunk with success, her daughter, and myself, drunk no less. Dinner was served, white wine, red wine, champagne, up to three waiters bustled around us. Mr. Grosz, the impresario, appeared. He brought money. He took it out of his briefcase and, sorting out the bank notes, he counted them onto the large table. Isadora ran there, grabbed a handful of the paper and metal coins, held them up high and let them drop back. She said laughingly:
>
> "Money, money, money, you are nothing, nothing, money is nothing . . ."

They made no attempt to hide their delight with each other, according to Beregi, or the nature of their relationship. Soon they left Budapest for Fiume (Rijeka), on the Adriatic coast, where they went to meet Elizabeth Duncan, summoned by her mother in high dudgeon when Mrs. Duncan realized what had happened.[6] The lovers got no farther than a country village called Somogyszob:

> "What a sweet little place it looks to be, and what a funny name it has," said Isadora as we looked out of the [train] window. . . . "Don't you want to spend a night here . . . ?" And, amidst ecstatic bursts of laughter, we were already standing down on the platform with our luggage, like two irresponsible teenagers, and waved our hands, flourishing our handkerchiefs, at the train as it left the station. . . . Dusk was falling. . . . The good woman sent us for a walk and, while we walked through the small village, she cooked a wonderful chicken paprikash in our honor. She also lit a fire in the fireplace because of the cool spring night.

I was lying on my bed with open eyes. Isadora put out the candle and began to dance. It was a marvellous dance. The shadow of her splendid young body was bending to and fro in the golden field of the wall illuminated by the light of the fire, music was furnished by the crackling of the logs, and the crackling sparks served as *pizzicati*. There, at Somogyszob, were our real nuptials. There, we did not have to be afraid of the door being opened on us, or of the dawn. She was lying beside me, she went to sleep in my arms, smiling and exhausted. We did not even notice, and we had played away three unforgettable days.[7]

"Oh, Mary, Mary, why didn't you tell me?" Isadora cried when she next met up with Mary Desti, now Mrs. Sturges: "Why didn't you tell me?"

"Tell you what?"

"Why didn't you tell me what love was? . . . Oh, you needn't blush, I know all about it. It is the most wonderful thing in the world. . . . Now I know the meaning of things, music, dancing, everything seems different since the revelation of love. I was born for love."[8] Isadora said nothing at the time to reveal her misgivings, if indeed she had any. In Budapest she prepared a speech for reporters in her journal, writing that she had "known many springs but never such a one" and that her heart was filled with the beauty of the lilacs — "one radiance of purple blinding to the eyes, exhaling a perfume so wonderful. . . . Could I dance the happiness of one little tree in this Garden. . . . They are like a madness. . . . I should like to go back to California and dance them for my people — a little message of the love & loveliness I find here." When she shortly embarked on a tour of the provinces, she went alone, bravely: "I feel something of the youth and strength of this country creeping into my spirit. This country has much to teach. I must not go until I learn all."[9]

Isadora's tour took her through the provincial capitals of Central Europe, from Budapest to Bratislava, Pécs, Timişoara, and Oldenburg, ranging along the Danube into stretches of what are now Romania and the Czech Republic. Her concerts normally sold out within hours of being announced, although tickets cost more than twice the price commanded by the National Theater. A note of skepticism crept into the general elation, notably in small towns, where Isadora's high prices were apt to be resented. (In Debrecen, specifically, it was wondered if "a terrible crime against Hungarian art" had been committed in the heat of the moment.)[10] Otherwise, for Isadora, it was all roses, ovations, and cheers. "In each [town Sándor] Grosz had a victoria waiting with white horses," she wrote, "and filled with white flowers, and I, dressed all in white . . . was conducted through the town like some visiting goddess from another world."

Isadora got back to Budapest and began giving orders. Great as her triumphs in the country were, she had pined the whole time for Beregi and gave no quarter now to the protests of her family. Isadora told Mary Desti that her mother and Elizabeth had both been "furious" with her.[11] She found their presence "unbearable" and dispatched them on "a little trip to the Tyrol,"[12] giving in fully to the strength of her passions and appearing around Budapest as Beregi's mistress: "I no longer recked of the possible ruin of my Art, the despair of my mother, or the ruin and loss of the world in general. . . . And naturally, just as the flight is high, so the crash of awakening is terrible." Beregi himself was "stunned by the vehemence of her emotions."

"Darling, I want a child," Isadora said. "I want a child so much. A cow can have a calf, a cat can have kittens . . . why couldn't I have babies . . . why couldn't I?"[13] It wasn't long before she felt "some strange change" in her lover.

At parties, she saw the "curious smiles" of Beregi's friends and attributed his unmistakable air of abstraction to the fact that he played Marc Antony, as well as Romeo, several times a week. "Was it that [his] artistic, intense temperament was so influenced by this change of rôle?" Isadora wondered. At her performances, she kept him front and center, even including him in a hastily put together version of *Pygmalion and Galatea,* the scene set, according to program notes, "in Pygmalion's bedroom." It failed.

"No one could take Beregi's Pygmalion seriously," a critic wrote. "His declamation was sloppy. The same applies to the verses accompanying the other dances, which Beregi recited. . . . Word and dance were in constant controversy." To what extent Beregi felt unmanned by Isadora's success can only be surmised: "The public who entirely filled the theatre — both on Saturday and on Sunday — was very much pleased with the performance, so that they even forgave the repulsive affectations of Mr. Oszkár Beregi for the sake of Miss Duncan."[14] It couldn't have been easy to be seen around town with a goddess. "Like the eruption of a volcano," Beregi recalled, "her words, her laughter, and her promises gushed forth ardently. The greater and more ardent her flood of words became, the more I grew silent and coming to my senses."

"Oscar," Isadora cried, "the world belongs to us! . . . You want me to stay here? . . . Oscar, this beautiful little country of yours, what can it give to me . . . when the world is waiting for me with banners, decked out in flags?" Beregi answered that if she wanted children, if she wanted a family, she would "have to be the wife of a member of the Hungarian National Theatre."[15] As Isadora put it, her lover's "passionate interest" now transferred from "his Juliet" to "the Roman populace."

"One day, during a long stroll in the country, sitting by the side of a haystack, he finally asked me if I did not think I should do better to continue my career and leave him to his," she recalled. "These were not his exact words, but that was his meaning. I still remember the haystack and the field before us, and the cold chill that struck my breast. That afternoon I signed a contract with [Sándor Grosz] for Vienna and Berlin, and all the cities of Germany." She had stayed in Hungary for five months and left it a different person, "born for love," as she correctly surmised, but aware already of the special agony that goes with abandonment, in every sense of the word. Isadora sat in a private box at the National Theater a final time before she left, fighting back tears as she watched Beregi on the stage and feeling as if she had "eaten bushels of broken glass."[16]

The rumor arose and persisted for years that Isadora was pregnant when she left Budapest. A photograph was supposed to exist, showing her in a "pleated and ample skirt" that couldn't hide her condition.[17] In *My Life*, Isadora says that she "fell ill" when she reached Vienna "and was placed by [Grosz] in a clinic," where she stayed for several weeks "in utter prostration and horrible suffering." The journey from Budapest was the saddest in her experience: "All joy seemed suddenly to have left the universe. . . . I was languid and sad, refusing to be interested either in the beautiful country or the kind friends about me."[18] And, indeed, she was pregnant, as Beregi's memoir confirms.

Three months of silence. Then a telegram arrived from Vienna. It notified me that she was lying ill in a private hospital. After my evening performance I impatiently jumped on a train; by morning I was in Vienna and had myself taken directly to her. The nurse had spruced Isadora up, and she was sitting in her bed like somebody who was not even ill. But her smile, carefree at other times, looked now as if it were sorrowful. I was standing beside her bed. The nurse left us alone; I kissed her tenderly and laid her back on her pillows. She was just looking with those unforgettable, fawn-like eyes, saying nothing, just looking. Finally, in a scarcely audible voice, she only said:

"No baby . . ."

I could not say a word. Neither did she say anything. We were just holding each other's hands.

"I fell on the stairs of the Grand Hotel. I had a bad fall. They brought me here."

"How . . . ?"

"I fell . . . because you weren't holding my hand. . . ."[19]

In September 1902 Isadora went with Grosz and his wife to Franzensbad (Františkovy Lázně), in the hills of Bohemia, a spa noted for its expertise in the treatment of women's "complaints." Pregnancy and the loss of a child seem odd omissions from *My Life,* famous before anything for its frankness, but Isadora's collapse was only the first in what became a series of vaguely defined breakdowns, described as "neurasthenic" in her autobiography. The combined effect of a giant success, a miscarriage, and a broken love affair had left her in a sort of stupor. In Franzensbad, she wrote, she forgot that her "name had become magic in the country" and was taken off-guard one night, dining with Grosz and his wife, when a crowd gathered outside her hotel and actually broke the glass window of the restaurant in order to get a look at her.

A lack of money got Isadora dancing again, and dancing took her out of her depression. "Fortunately for me, probably," she wrote, "the expensive doctors and nurses had exhausted the bank account." Grosz arranged a tour of the spas Franzensbad, Marienbad (Mariánské Lázně, and Carlsbad (Karlovy Vary). "So one day I opened my trunk again, and took out my dancing tunics."

> I remember bursting into tears, kissing my little red dress in which I danced all my Revolutionary dances, and swearing never to desert Art for love again. . . . Probably skeptics will find this hard to believe, but it is the very truth that from the experience of Budapest, for years after, my entire emotional reaction had such a revolution that I really believed I had finished with that phase, and in the future would only give myself to my Art. . . . After that brutal awakening my senses slept; nor did I desire of them anything at all. . . . I remember that I already thought about life like a man who has been to the wars with good intentions and who has been terribly wounded, and who, on reflection, says: "Why should I not teach a gospel that will spare others such mutilation?"[20]

In Vienna, Isadora was reconciled with her mother and Elizabeth, "who were delighted to see me again alone," she reported, "although they found me changed and saddened." Here, too, in a willed effort to transform her experience, she began to explore the legend of Iphigenia, the daughter of the House of Atreus sacrificed by her father, Agamemnon, at the start of the Trojan War. With music from the two operas of Gluck, *Iphigenia in Aulis* and *Iphigenia in Tauris,* Isadora would fashion her most successful and enduring dance-drama — the story, it might be said, of the ultimate abandoned woman. After a trip with Elizabeth to the Croatian resort of Opatija, on the Adriatic, she moved to Munich, once again confident of her direction.[21]

If she had known what kind of reception awaited her in the Bavarian capital, she might have gone there sooner. In Munich the German "cult of Isadora" was born, a national craze that took her beyond success and notoriety into the realms of literature, philosophy, feminism, and even science, where she appeared — and eagerly presented herself — as the realization of Darwin's dream, the "Dancer of the Future," whose coming proclaimed the triumph of beauty and the liberation of women in the final perfection of the race. It was never necessary for Isadora to exaggerate the rapturous acclaim the Germans gave her; her notices, as she told a friend, were "no mere prosaic criticisms" but "poetic dithyrambs."[22] First in Germany and later in France, the name *Isadora* came to symbolize women's freedom, beauty, and the birth of a new world of art.

At the turn of the new year, 1903, American newspapers reported that Isadora's dancing had "divided Germany"; that a theater would be built in her honor in Berlin; that the kaiser had wept on seeing her perform — not true — and that the Austrian emperor, Franz Josef, had begged her to come back to Vienna: "I will make you the court dancer at the Hofburg Theatre. You can name your own terms, and you will be a law unto yourself. . . . Do not refuse this chance to brighten the declining years of a lonesome old man." Isadora dismissed the story with a quick, "How absurd! I have never danced for the emperor of Germany, although I expect to. I did dance for the emperor of Austria, and he was very kind and complimentary." Siegfried Wagner, son of the composer, hurried from Bayreuth to see her perform, while tickets for her concerts at the Künstlerhaus in Munich, where she made her debut on November 15, 1902, were sold out "without any sensational advertising, no pictures on billboards or in the store windows . . . merely here and there a modest poster giving date of performance and program."[23]

The Munich Künstlerhaus (House of Artists) was the central shrine of the *Jugendstil*, the German expression of art nouveau and a movement as strictly ordered as any other aspect of German national life. Isadora had had a hard time gaining entry to the tabernacle, despite Grosz's efforts and the enthusiasm of most artists on the scene. Here it was a question of the relationship of dancing to art. When Isadora arrived in Munich, the Belgian Cléo de Mérode, "the greatest beauty of her time," famous for her liaisons with royalty, held forth at another theater, charging catchpenny prices for her sexually suggestive "exotic" dances. It was not just to make money that Grosz set a top price of three marks for Isadora, unheard of at the time for a dancer. The idea was to take her out of the realm of entertainment and into the realm of art.

Isadora's debut at the Künstlerhaus, when she finally made it, "was the greatest artistic event and sensation that the town had experienced in many years." She did not overstate the case. Her performances became front-page news in the German press, and she was obliged to schedule six additional concerts in Munich. At the university, the winter semester had begun and the students were festive. They "went fairly crazy," Isadora remembered, "singing their student songs and leaping with lighted torches on either side" of her carriage when she left the theater at night. "Often, for hours, they would group themselves outside the hotel window and sing, until I threw them my flowers and handkerchiefs." An article in the satirical weekly *Simplicissimus* reported complaints about the noise around Isadora's hotel, the Bayerischer Hof. "Sober people" were scandalized, but it made no difference to her: "I also learnt to drink the good Munich beer; and the recent shock to my senses was somewhat calmed."[24] According to the *St. Louis Sunday Gazette:*

> The most talked of American girl now in Europe is Isadore [sic] Duncan, the California dancer — she of the bare and twinkling feet that have either scandalized or delighted so many thousands of spectators.
>
> Daily verbal battles are fought by the two factions. . . . The second says she is only a fad, that favoritism (in a strictly proper sense, mind you) is responsible for her success, and that it will be ephemeral.
>
> Meantime, the demure little maiden is quietly raking in the shekels, getting higher prices for her unaided performances than are commanded by a Wagner opera. . . . This pale, slender American girl . . .

who, while undeniably pretty, would herself be the first to ridicule any attempt to exploit her as a second Helen of Troy, sets whole communities by the ears. . . . What is the secret of it all? That is the burning question of the day.[25]

Photographs taken of Isadora in Munich at this time give only clues to the beauty of her movement. It was left to artists to render that, among them, Fritz von Kaulbach, whose pastel portrait of Isadora dancing later graced the cover of *Jugend,* showing more clearly than any photograph of the time how her body was aligned in motion, how coherent her movements were, and how lovely their effect. "Her grace is indisputable," St. Louis was assured. "Never an abrupt movement, never a sharp angle."[26]

Before leaving Munich for Berlin, Isadora gave a closed lecture to Künstlerhaus members, thanking them "in her charming English-German" for their wisdom in judging her dancing "not with their eyes, but with their fine imaginations." She was crowned with a wreath of laurel when she left the hall, blithely discoursing with learned professors about "the relation of music to the will."[27] Isadora had been reading Schopenhauer in German and was "carried away" by his thoughts on music as the purest of the arts. When she got to Berlin she made a speech to the press — "Every creature is its own creation," as Schopenhauer said.

"I come to Berlin to learn," Isadora began. "I come as an eager and thirsty Pilgrim to drink from the Great fountain Head of German Knowledge and science. I come as a wistful weakling to be made strong by contact with men and women who have been cradled in the Birthplace of such Giants as von Humboldt, Goethe and Kant."[28] She hadn't liked Berlin when she saw it first with the Loie Fuller company in 1902, finding in its outsize imperial architecture an all too "Nordic" sensibility: "These columns are not the Doric columns which should soar into the skies of Olympian blue. These are the Germanic, pedantic, archaeological professors' conception of Greece." Now, she was reading Kant's *Critique of Pure Reason* over a glass of milk at bedtime, entirely under the sway of the Teutonic *Geist* — "*der Heiligthum des Gedankes,*" as she called it ("the holiness of thought").[29] Isadora would make her Berlin debut at Kroll's New Royal Opera House in January 1903, but even before that, she addressed an audience of "white beards and gold spectacles" in what amounted to a closed session of the Prussian Academy of the Arts.

"I can still see her," said the writer Max Osborn, "draped in her loose, almost baroque, pale violet gown, as if wafted in the room on a breath of roses."[30] Select performances followed for architects, sculptors, conductors, museum directors, and a variety of art and music critics, whose response to Isadora's dancing is described as "diverse,"[31] but whose influence with the public was not so great that they could keep her from becoming the leading attraction in Berlin. "It is not in the rapidly whirling skirts of a fandango or the sand-scattering buck-and-wing dance . . . that Miss Duncan has made her great hit," wrote a newspaper in her hometown, San Francisco. "Berlin could not afford to risk her staid artistic reputation on anything so frivolous. Nothing less than Greek dances, Roman posturings and the most classic of gyrations satisfy the endeavors of Miss Duncan, and whether or not the archaeologists would admit the correctness of her dancing and her costumes, she has pleased the crowds immensely and her success is beyond question."[32] At her first concert, having danced solo for more than two hours, she delivered "encore after encore," until the audience rushed the footlights.

"Hundreds of young students actually climbed upon the stage," Isadora remembered, "until I was in danger of being crushed to death by too much adoration." That night and for many following, the students escorted her home, unhitching the horses from her carriage in the Romantic tradition and pulling her bodily down Unter den Linden to her hotel.[33] Within weeks, she was commanding prices "as high as those of Coquelin and Mme. Bernhardt," according to a story in the *San Francisco Call,* and was said to be charging up to $750 a night for private recitals.[34] Legends were born about the healing properties of her dance, to the point that invalids were brought to the theater on litters and cots to see her. She was photographed and written about as a species of priestess, mystical and transcendent, "so deeply lost in [her] concentration of the Greek art that she is no longer able to return to our sophisticated world."[35]

It was Isadora's good fortune to have reached Berlin at a time when the image of the "new woman" was rampant in Germany; the issue of women's emancipation had broadened out from the central question of political enfranchisement into every aspect of modern life: legal, moral, social, and sexual. "Does the recognition of Beauty as the highest Idea belong wholly to the province of Man's Intellect?" Isadora wondered. "Or do you think that a woman might also attain to a knowledge of the highest beauty?"[36] She was not a feminist in any organized or political sense;[37] but just as she rejected marriage as oppressive and unnecessary, so she denied that a dancer needed men to direct her, train her, guide her, clothe her, shape her body, and assign her roles that trivialized her utterly and left her powerless and expendable against the next generation of nymphs. Isadora's Berlin speeches can be read only in the light of a changing social reality, a vision of women's dignity and freedom that had little to do with aesthetics and everything to do with power. With boldness born of ecstatic conviction, she didn't hesitate to link the advancement of women to evolutionary theory, finding in an age of mystical scientism all the support she needed for her dancer's call to arms.[38] In March 1903 Isadora was invited to address the Berlin Press Club with a speech, "The Dance of the Future," her most famous essay and the guiding manifesto of modern dance:

> I am asked to speak upon the "Dance of the Future" — yet how is it possible? In fifty years I may have something to say. Besides, I have always found it indiscreet for me to speak of my dance. The people who are in sympathy with me understand what I am trying to do better than myself, the people who are not in sympathy, understand better than I why they are not.[39]

She was up to the job, of course, not intimidated by either the splendor of her mission or the hisses of her critics. Along with Darwin, Isadora had been reading Nietzsche, "the dancing philosopher," whose *Thus Spake Zarathustra* joined her bedside library, carried with her everywhere in English translation and scarred with her annotations. It was not alone Nietzsche's pronouncements on the dance that captured Isadora's imagination — "Only in the dance do I know how to tell the parable of the highest things" — but his concept of the superman and the doctrine of eternal return. In *The Birth of Tragedy from the Spirit of Music,* his first book (1872), Nietzsche examined Greek art as the confluence of Dionysian and Apollonian forces — on one hand, "the will," and on the other, "representation" — "an art in which life is contained but not destroyed, and in which the terrible and the irrational exist side by side with the serene." The superman was the hoped-for realization of the classical ideal, the man who had "surpassed" himself, "organized the chaos of his passions, given style to his character, and become creative."[40] Not since Whitman had Isadora found a spiritual mentor more suited to her own concerns.

The whole emphasis of her "Dance of the Future" was on "development," upward movement, and self-actualization, with a specifically Nietzschean attention to the body and the earth. She continued:

> The movement of waves, of winds, of the earth is ever the same in lasting harmony. We do not stand on the beach and inquire of the ocean what was its movement in the past and what will be its movement in the future. We realize that the movement peculiar to its nature is eternal to its nature. The movement of the free animals and birds remains always in correspondence to their nature, the necessities and wants of that nature, and its correspondence to earth nature. It is only when you put free animals under false restrictions that they lose the power of moving in harmony with nature, and adopt a movement expressive of the restrictions placed about them.
>
> So it has been with civilized man. The movements of the savage, who lived in freedom in constant touch with Nature, were unrestricted, natural and beautiful. Only the movements of the naked body can be perfectly natural. Man, arrived at the end of civilization, will have to return to nakedness, *not to the unconscious nakedness of the savage, but to the conscious and acknowledged nakedness of the mature Man,* whose body will be the harmonious expression of his spiritual being [emphasis added].

Isadora went on to attack the ballet, which she described more provocatively than ever as "an expression of degeneration, of living death," an endless succession of stops and starts, leaps and bends, demonstrating only too obviously that the human body cannot fly. "All the movements of our modern ballet school are sterile," said Isadora, "because they are unnatural: their purpose is to create the delusion that the law of gravitation does not exist for them." She returned to her premise — "The movements of the human body must correspond to its form. . . . All movements must have within them the seeds from which will evolve all other movements" — and declared again that she was ready to found a school. It would not be a school of dance, said Isadora, but a "school of life . . . a theatre where a hundred little girls shall be trained in my art, which they, in their turn, will better. In this school I shall not teach the children to imitate my movements, but to make their own. I shall not force them to study certain definite movements; I shall help them to develop those movements which are natural to them." If the school Isadora had in mind sounded like a temple or a convent, it was just as she intended. "For art which is not religious," she concluded, "is not art, is mere merchandise."

These flowers before me contain the dream of a dance; it could be named "The light falling on white flowers." A dance that would be a subtle translation of the light and the whiteness. So pure, so strong, that people would say: it is a soul we see moving, a soul that has reached the light and found the whiteness. . . .

The dancer of the future will be one whose body and soul have grown so harmoniously together that the natural language of that soul will have become the movement of the body. The dancer will not belong to a nation but to all humanity. She will not dance in the form of nymph, nor fairy, nor coquette, but in the form of woman in her greatest and purest expression. She will realize the mission of woman's body and the holiness of all its parts. She will dance the changing life of nature, showing how each part is transformed into the other. From all parts of her body shall shine radiant intelligence, bringing to the world the message of the thoughts and aspirations of thousands of women. She shall dance the freedom of woman. . . .

Oh, she is coming, the dancer of the future: the free spirit . . . more glorious than any woman who has yet been; more beautiful than the Egyptian, than the Greek, the early Italian, than all women of past centuries — the highest intelligence in the freest body![41]

Isadora's speech would send balletomanes into fits, opening the gates, as her critics believed, to an orgy of self-expression and a swarm of dilettantes. Her school was already functioning by the time the academic ballet, specifically in Russia, could launch a counterattack. Later in 1903 "The Dance of the Future" was published as a pamphlet, amid a storm of publicity and "much sympathy," according to Isadora: "The journals write about it as seriously as if I were a Member of Parliament."[42] She had caused "a barefoot fad" among German women and remained "politely indifferent" to the attentions of men.

"There was a candor on her brow," said a woman who knew her, "a purity one seldom sees. The fire she knew how to release in her blood, traveling along her body, burned her clean and clear. No one could look so chaste and new as Isadora, washed in her own fine energy."[43] It was little known even to her friends that she suffered from stage fright; that the arms of a dresser or maid held her at the waist before she stepped on stage through her dusky blue curtains, which she carried from theater to theater, along with a carpet for her feet.[44] As her career progressed, Isadora's curtains grew larger and taller, until they finally seemed to disappear in the shadows above the stage. A student described the lit effect: "Horizon blue — the sky at dusk —

the blue of the sea — the blue vert of the forests and mountains from afar — the blue of night — endless space — infinity. . . . They suggested everything — shadow and light — all depth and all heights."[45] In theater circles, Isadora's "famous blue curtains" became as widely talked about as her naked feet, for they eluded "scenery" and opened her performance entirely to the imagination of the audience. This was new: the Duncan stage was tabula rasa, the only background Isadora ever willingly used.

In the spring of 1903, Isadora went back to Paris, where she hoped to repeat her Berlin success. For the moment, she was rich — "There was in the bank a sum which seemed to me inexhaustible" — and she could afford to rent the Théâtre Sarah Bernhardt in the place du Châtelet.[46] It was a mistake: the Sarah Bernhardt was one of the largest theaters in the city, and Isadora had no commercial reputation in France as yet. The artists and writers who praised her work during her studio days were no less admiring now, but a vital ingredient was missing in the form of popular enthusiasm. It would take more than a triumph in Germany to impress the French. According to writer Georges Maurevert, "She made no hit and no profit."[47]

On the eve of her opening, Isadora went with her brother Raymond to the Ecole des Beaux-Arts and gave free tickets to the art students there, knowing or guessing that her name alone would not be enough to fill the hall. Raymond had recently returned to France from the United States, hoping to resume his position as Isadora's impresario, a role she was happy to have him fill, in the absence of her regular manager, Grosz. Whether Grosz had balked at the Paris experiment for financial reasons or because Isadora was rather too loudly intent on "destiny" cannot now be determined. She was the despair of all her managers, then and later, and remembered that she had left Berlin to the sound of Grosz's "entreaties and lamentations," having refused his suggestion that she embark on a tour of Germany to magnify her success.

"I felt that I was only at the gateway of the study of my Art," Isadora protested: "I wanted to study, continue my researches, create a dance and movements which then did not exist, and the dream of my school, which had haunted all my childhood, became stronger and stronger."[48] In Paris she was reunited with all her family, including Augustin; his wife, Sarah; and their three-year-old daughter, Temple (so named, presumably, in honor of the Duncans' overriding passion for antiquity). For the next year, as if in reaction to the unaccustomed torrent of "shekels," Isadora remained tightly bound to the clan. Before her opening in Paris, Raymond even came to blows with her orchestra conductor, who happened also to be composing original music for Isadora's dancing of the legend of Pan and Echo. The offended maestro stormed off, taking his musicians and sheet music with him.

Alarmed, Isadora sought help from Arnold Dolmetsch, who had collaborated with her earlier in London and now worked "far into the night" to provide new accompaniment for the piece. At the last minute, however, she balked, saying that Dolmetsch's music might "put her out" — bravely, she danced *Pan and Echo* without music at all.

"The airy flights of the nymph in her diaphanous draperies and floral garlands were effective and charming, despite the absence of music," Dolmetsch's wife remembered. "But when (still thus attired) she suddenly assumed a sinister frown, and twiddling her fingers to suggest the manipulation of a wood instrument, broke into uncouth gambols, a ripple of incredulous laughter ran through the audience."[49] When a dancer from the Paris Opéra rose and hooted, Isadora complained about "payoffs" to the press, which generally gave her good reviews. Jean d'Udine joined her in attacking "our modern choreographic art, in which a small leg, like a small mouth, is, forsooth, 'more distinguished.'" A quick trip to the Louvre, the critic suggested, would easily "justify Miss Duncan. All these beautiful remains of antiquity show us . . . that, when passion rises or pales, the body has a right to leap or to throw itself brusquely to the ground."[50] At her last performance, on June 13, Isadora conceded the difficulties she was having, telling her audience in her curtain speech that she had tried to do her best: "I thank you all for having understood me. . . . And I danced the last dance better than the first ones because I felt in sympathy with you. And so I thank you. I thank you." Her work was still in development — "very little, very little, an indication, as you say. But I am happy if I have made you feel that sculpture and dancing are sister arts — are they not?"[51]

Isadora was amply supported on that score two weeks later, when she went to Vélizy to pay homage to Rodin. At sixty-three, Rodin had just been inducted into the French Legion of Honor; the retrospective of his work at the exposition of 1900 had had the desired effect of solidifying his popular reputation as the greatest sculptor the world had seen since Michelangelo. At Vélizy, where his friends and students rented a restaurant for their celebration, Rodin's headless *St. John the Baptist Preaching* stood on a column in the garden, while his pupil and assistant, Emile-Antoine Bourdelle, led the company in toasts.

"Is it the torso of St. John?" asked Bourdelle. "Is it the torso of Bacchus? Is it the torso of the prudent Ulysses? Is it the torso of Theseus? Perhaps. What difference does the name make?" What Isadora wanted to show in dance, sculptors had begun to take for granted. "It is indestructible flesh made through your spirit," Bourdelle went on; "it is an indefatigable torso born of your knowing; it is the human torso, it is sublime life, it is art."[52]

When he finished his speech, Bourdelle joined Norwegian painter Fritz Thaulow in a fiddle on the lawn. "Somebody said the lovely dancer must dance," wrote Kathleen Bruce, herself a sculptor, who had met Isadora on the train from Paris that morning. Isadora danced and fell at Rodin's feet, whereupon he took her hand and pressed it in Kathleen's. "My children, you two artists should understand each other," he said.[53] In a letter to a friend, Rodin described Isadora as "sister of the breezes,"[54] the first of many tributes that she excerpted and printed in her program notes: "It may be said of Isadora Duncan that she attains sculpture and emotion effortlessly. . . . Suppleness, emotion, these high qualities, the soul of the dance, are her complete and sovereign art."[55] Later, Rodin regretted that he never made drawings of Isadora from life, in motion. Always fascinated with dancers, he believed "that any attempt to seize one moment alone in progression was fatal to the illusion of movement" and sketched her only from memory or in repose.[56] For her part, Isadora remained timid in the presence of the master. "He is too great for me," she said, in a rare acknowledgment that such a thing might be possible. "As soon as he appears I feel like a nymph before a centaur . . . before the very force of nature."[57]

At the end of her season at the Sarah Bernhardt, Isadora left Paris suddenly, having suffered the embarrassment of a French bailiff arriving to collect a debt while she gave a dinner in her hotel suite. "Miss Duncan is the newest toy with which the petulant, spoiled, capricious child, Paris, amuses itself," wrote society correspondent Helen Ten Broeck.[58] For once, she declined to speak with reporters: "The truth is Miss Duncan doesn't give a damn."[59] A tour of German cities kept her busy into the fall; then she turned back to her family and let her career hang fire. She had "her own ideas" about what she needed and would see them fulfilled.

7
Myth

In the autumn of 1903, Isadora left for Greece on "a spiritual pilgrimage"[1] with the Duncans and Kathleen Bruce, Rodin's young protégée, whom she had met at Vélizy. Neither Isadora nor Kathleen mentioned the other in her published account of the journey. Isadora wrote only about her family, while Kathleen, the orphaned daughter of a canon of York, whose mother was born in Greece, said that she "knew some folk who were going, dancing vagabonds like myself," and joined them there.[2] Raymond Duncan persuaded the party to abandon Western clothing for the trip. He had had an epiphany on holiday in Normandy, when he invited a hired valet to join him for a swim and the man refused, saying: "I can't. I'm in livery."

"That was an eye-opener," said Raymond. "I learned what clothes do to and for a man. I had a smart Bond Street wardrobe and I turned them all over to . . . the valet. I bought some thick white linen and cut a hole for my head to slip through. They wouldn't let me on the beach. I said to myself, if people are so blind that they can't see the man, only his clothes, I intend to live long enough to show them the man."[3] By the time they got to Athens, the Duncans were all attired in the tunic, chlamys, and peplum of the ancient Greeks, to the amusement of the population and the fascination of the press.

"We had decided that even the Directoire dresses which I wore, and Raymond's knickerbockers, open collars, and flowing ties, were degenerate garments," Isadora reported. "To me it seemed sacrilege to touch the stones of Grecian temples with the high-heeled shoes of a decadent civilization; to sweep with the silk petticoat of the twentieth century the sacred marbles of the Acropolis."[4] For the rest of his life, Raymond never again wore anything but Greek robes and sandals of his own design. Elizabeth settled into "soft draperies and glove-like shoes," while Isadora, for years to come, "always dressed like an antique statue."[5] Of the four Duncan siblings, only Augustin had some doubts about the wardrobe, adopting the Greek style awkwardly for the trip to Athens.

The Duncans started out in Italy, where they sailed from Brindisi to the island of Levkás, the ancient site of Ithaca and, according to legend, the place where the poet Sappho threw herself from the rocks to her death. Here they hired a fishing smack to take them on what was conceived as a re-creation of the voyage of Ulysses, with Raymond giving directions to the boat's owner in a mixture of pantomime and ancient Greek. "The fisherman didn't seem to understand much about Ulysses," Isadora wrote, "but the sight of many drachmas encouraged him to set sail, although he was loath to go far, and pointed many times to the sky, saying, 'Boom, Boom,' . . . to inform us that the sea was treacherous." When they landed at Karvasaras, they promptly kissed the ground.

"The inhabitants all came down to the beach to greet us," Isadora recalled, "and the first landing of Christopher Columbus in America could not have caused more astonishment." The Duncans moved from village to village, hugging the natives, dancing in squares, and falling to their knees in prayer: "Salute, O Olympian Zeus! And Apollo! And Aphrodite! Prepare, O ye Muses, to dance again!" At night, they slept in bug-infested inns, and in daylight they walked, sweeping the road ahead of them with branches of laurel, while Mrs. Duncan rode on a two-horse cart.

"We sped along on the light wings of youthful feet," wrote Isadora, "often leaping and bounding before the carriage, accompanying our steps with shouts and songs of joy. . . . Often our emotions were so violent that we could only find expression in tearful embraces." From Karvasaras, they moved to Agrinion and Missolonghi, where Lord Byron had died in 1824, during the war for Greek independence, and where they paused "with full hearts and tearful eyes" to honor his memory. But at Patras they got impatient and boarded a train, arriving in Athens late at night and barely sleeping before they climbed the Acropolis at dawn. Beholding the Parthenon, it seemed to Isadora that she had been "born for the first time in that long breath and first gaze of pure beauty." She wrote:

> The sun was rising from behind Mount Pentelicus, revealing her marvellous clearness and the splendour of her marble sides sparkling in the sunlight. We mounted the last step of the Propylæa and gazed on the Temple shining in the morning light. With one accord we remained silent. We separated slightly from one another; for here was Beauty too sacred for words. It struck strange terror into our hearts. No cries or embraces now. We each found our vantage-point of worship and remained for hours in an ecstasy of meditation which left us all weak and shaken.

A few days later, from her suite at the Hotel Angleterre, Isadora declared her mission to the press. She was reclined on a sofa, her feet shod in sandals, a fillet in her hair: she had "a wondrous figure," a reporter wrote, "slim but rounded. There was a finely shaped head with a coil of glorious hair setting against the back of the neck, two arms exquisitely molded — the very classic simplicity of the costume only made the wearer the more beautiful, the more graceful."

"Ah, you cannot imagine how ineffably happy I am in beautiful Athens," Isadora began. "I came here to realize my life's dream; to be in a place sacred to the imperishable traditions of Greek art and Greek culture; to steep myself to the lips in the mysteries." She would stay through the end of the year, she continued; after a season in Berlin, she would come back to Athens permanently: "I pass my day in the Acropolis and at different museums, inhaling inspiration and completing my education. . . . I am still dazzled. My dance at present is to lift my hands to the sky, to feel the glorious sunshine and to thank the gods that I am here." When someone asked if she was cold in her ancient garb, she answered, "Cold! Who could be conscious of such things amid these surroundings? . . . *Cold?*" All the same, wrote the *New York World,* "some warm woolen undergarments would probably do away with the risk she is now taking of leaving her bones here as well as her heart."[6]

The Duncans refused to live as tourists in Greece; while keeping a suite at the Angleterre, they spent most nights camping outdoors, on one or another of the hills that overlook Athens. There were excursions from the city: to Colonus, where Isadora paused to be pho-

tographed beside Plato's olive tree, and Eleusis, thirteen miles from
Athens, where the Duncans "substituted dancing for walking," in an
effort "to propitiate the gods."[7] Often, they gathered in the ruined theater of Dionysus at the foot of the Acropolis, where Isadora danced for
the empty stone benches. "Just the same there were forty thousand
Greeks there to see me dance the old dances," she told the *World,*
whose reporter must have looked surprised. "I mean, you see, the
spirits of those who lived in those glorious times."[8]

Looking back in her autobiography, Isadora summarized the
Greek adventure as "really curious," writing in the tone of quivering
disbelief that follows an orgy or excess: "We decided that the Clan
Duncan should remain in Athens eternally, and there build a temple
that should be characteristic of us. . . . Not only that, but, as Hamlet
says, we vowed, too, that there would be no more marriages. 'Let
those who are married remain married,' etc." This instruction was
aimed specifically at Augustin, who had confessed that he missed his
wife and daughter: "We considered this a great weakness on his part,
but consented — as he was already married and had a child — that
there was nothing for us to do but send for them." Not to be bent or
broken were the new rules for living that Raymond, in particular, imposed on the clan, a purely American blend of utopian vision and
Spartan self-denial. Isadora recalled:

> We accepted Augustin's wife with ill-concealed reservation. But
> for our own part, we drew up a plan in a copy-book, which was to ex-
> clude all but the Clan Duncan, and therein we set down the rules for
> our lives. . . . We did this somewhat on the same plan as Plato in his
> *Republic.* It was decreed to rise at sunrise. We were to greet the rising
> sun with joyous songs and dances. Afterwards we were to refresh our-
> selves with a modest bowl of goat's milk. The mornings were to be de-
> voted to teaching the inhabitants to dance and sing. They must be
> made to celebrate the Greek gods and to give up their terrible modern
> costumes. Then, after our light lunch of green vegetables — for we
> had decided to give up meat and become vegetarians — the after-
> noons were to be spent in meditation, and the evenings given over to
> pagan ceremonies with appropriate music.

Raymond found a whole collection of "inhabitants" on the slopes
of Mount Hymettos, the cool, forested pinnacle that faces the Acropolis, five miles to the east. The Duncans were walking in search of land
to buy, when they saw "a rise in the ground." Dramatically, Raymond

dropped his staff and said, "Look, we are on the same level as the Acropolis!" The land the Duncans bought, a "barren hillock" in the forest, looked directly at the east portal of the Parthenon and had been known since ancient times as Kopanos.[9]

"But there were difficulties with this place," Isadora wrote. "First, no one knew to whom the land belonged. It was so far from Athens, and frequented only by shepherds tending their flocks and goats." Persistent inquiries led to five shepherd families, who had never before considered their land to be of any value but were happy to sell it to the outlandish Americans who tracked them down. "They asked a sum entirely out of proportion," Isadora noted. "Nevertheless the Clan Duncan was determined to buy this site. . . . We invited the five families to a banquet where we had lamb on the spit, and other kinds of tempting food. We also served much *raki* — the cognac of the country." That night a contract was drawn up, the inhabitants signed, and Kopanos belonged to the Duncans.

They were serious about building a temple — part theater, part tabernacle — and insisted that it could be constructed only from the stone of Mount Pentelicus, whose quarries had yielded the rock that built the Parthenon in the fifth century B.C. Modestly enough, Raymond settled for "the red stone which is found at the base of the mountain" rather than the pure white marble farther in; he produced designs modeled on the palace of Agamemnon at Mycenae, and construction began at once under his direction.

"From then on," said Isadora, "each day could be seen a long procession of carts, carrying these red stones; winding their torturous way from Pentelicus to Kopanos." She paid for everything herself, out of her earnings from Vienna and Berlin — it would be some time before she realized that her bank account was drying up. Kopanos itself had no access to water. Wells were dug, but without result. "Nothing daunted," Raymond soldiered on, ordering that the walls of the building be made two feet thick, to conform with Agamemnon's original. When the cornerstone was laid, an Orthodox priest came to bless the project. None of the Duncans had "a churchy turn of mind," Isadora wrote, "goodness knows," but they wanted to get along with their neighbors, who joined them in celebration when the priest slit the throat of a "black cock" and wet the cornerstone with its blood:

> Then followed prayer and incantation. He blessed all the stones of
> the house and, asking us our names, he uttered a prayer in which we

frequently heard the names *Isadora Duncan* (my mother), *Augustin,
Raymond, Elizabeth,* and *Little Isadora* (myself). . . . Great barrels of
wine and *raki* were opened. A roaring bonfire was set ablaze on the
hill, and we, together with our neighbours, the peasantry, danced and
drank and made merry all through the night.

So much for a modest bowl of goat's milk. Kathleen Bruce, who
camped with the Duncans at Kopanos, remembered "days of apparent
indolence, seeding time, and nights, too, of character! Sleeping out of
doors undoubtedly adds to the interest of life." Five months passed
"like a dream in the night."

> There were days when we rode bareback on ponies on the lovely
> beach beyond Phaleron, riding into the sea and falling off by intent
> into the water. Native riders, stripped, would come down to water
> their horses in groups of eight or ten, looking for all the world like the
> Parthenon frieze, glorious in pose and a marvel of color, their red-
> bronzed limbs against the blue sea. . . . They age very quickly these
> peasants, but the sixteen- or seventeen-year-old boys, many of them
> married, were as beautiful human beings as could be found.[10]

The Greek dream "burst like a glorious bubble" at the end of
1903, even as Kopanos was being built and Raymond dug up relics to
prove that it had once been the site of an ancient village. Raymond
never tired of his investigations and had become friendly with the
Greek poet Angelos Sikelianos and his sister, Penelope, a beautiful,
redheaded girl steeped in history and art who, either on the spot or
shortly thereafter, became Raymond's wife. Isadora may have been
bored by this time; she was certainly going broke. She described a moment of sad revelation, as she ascended the "sacred hill" of the Acropolis and realized that "we were not, nor ever could be, other than
moderns. . . . I was, after all, but a Scotch-Irish-American." The spectacle of her family on Kopanos had already attracted "the fashionable
people of Athens" and even the king, George I, who rode out to the
site one morning with his whole entourage.

"We remained unimpressed," Isadora noted. "For we were living
under the reign of other kings, Agamemnon, Menelaus, and Priam."
She danced for the Greek royal family at a performance in the city but
preferred to hobnob with students, who paraded in front of her hotel,
thronged her carriage when she drove through Athens, "and ac-
claimed our Hellenic tunics." When the Duncans soon boarded a train

for Vienna, leaving Raymond behind to finish the house, Isadora draped herself in the Greek flag and left the station to the strains of the national anthem. She had seen what she came to see in Greece and learned what she wanted to know. In "The Parthenon," an essay written just before she left, she explains the secret the ancients had taught her: "These columns which seem so straight and still are not really straight, each one is curving gently from the base to the height, each one is in flowing movements, never resting, and the movement of each is in harmony with the others. And as I thought this my arms rose slowly toward the Temple and I leaned forward — and then I knew I had found my dance, and it was a Prayer."[11]

Comedy followed comedy on Isadora's return to Europe, as if in counterpoint to the solemnity of her Greek fugue. She returned to Vienna with a chorus of ten boys and a "Byzantine schoolmaster," an Orthodox seminarian she had hired to direct and train the boys in a performance of Aeschylus's *Suppliants,* the text set to Byzantine church music.[12] The Duncans had heard the Greek boys singing on a moonlit night in the theater of Dionysus and were so transported by the "unearthly quality" of their voices that they held a contest, nightly competitions, to form an international touring company out of a collection of street urchins.

The Suppliants is the story of Danaus, who flees from Egypt with his fifty daughters when his brother, Aegyptus, usurps the throne. Aegyptus sends his own fifty sons in pursuit, with the order that they abduct and "marry" the Danaids. On the communal wedding night, the brides murder all but one of the incestuous cousins. This was the grim drama Isadora brought back to Europe after five months in Athens with her family, eerily sung by the Greek boys and danced, alone, by her.

"As there were fifty 'daughters of Danaus,'" Isadora wrote, "I found it very difficult to express, in my slight figure, the emotions of fifty maidens all at once, but I had the feeling of multiple oneness, and did my best." She was fascinated by the role of the chorus in Greek tragedy and was looking for ways to "indicate" it in her dancing. But the crowds in Vienna proved indifferent to her experiments and only demanded that she dance *The Blue Danube.* "We must revive the beauty of the chorus," Isadora called from the stage: "But still the audience shouted: 'Nein. Mach nicht. Tanze. Tanze die Schöne Blaue Donau. Tanze noch einmal.' And they applauded over and over again."[13]

From Vienna, "laden with new gold," Isadora went with her boys and their professor to Berlin, where audiences proved equally unresponsive to her innovations and *The Blue Danube* again saved the day. "In the meantime," she wrote,

> the little Greek boys themselves were feeling the effects of their unaccustomed environment. I had received several complaints from our worthy hotel proprietor of their bad manners and the violence of their tempers. It seems that they asked continually for black bread, black ripe olives, and raw onions, and, when these condiments were not in their daily menu, they became enraged with the waiters — going so far as to throw beefsteaks at their heads and attack them with knives.

Eventually, Isadora moved her turbulent wards into her Berlin apartment, where she set them up in the parlor on cots. "The climax . . . came when the police authorities informed us that our Greek boys were surreptitiously escaping from the window at night," she confessed, "frequenting cheap cafés and making the acquaintance of the lowest specimens of their compatriots which the city held." Worse, the boys' voices had begun to change, and their singing became "more and more off any key whatever. One could no longer excuse it on the ground that it was Byzantine. It was simply a fearful bad noise." One morning, therefore, Isadora and Elizabeth took the boys shopping, bought them new clothes, and packed them all on a train to Athens, with one-way tickets in their hands.[14] British birth-control activist Marie Stopes saw Isadora that spring in Munich, after she reverted to her more popular repertory: "The audience cheered, clapped, waved handkerchiefs in wild excitement." Leaving the theater, Stopes "was swept up with the crowd that followed Isadora to the station, where railway officials had to shovel students off the steps of her departing train."[15]

Isadora's manager had again asked her to tour Europe, hoping to capitalize on her celebrity and to ward off imitators, of whom there were suddenly a number to contend with. In Germany the French dancer Madeleine enjoyed a vogue, dancing "stories, philosophies, poems, and history" while reputedly in a hypnotic trance. "Learned persons were invited upon the platform to pinch Mlle. Madeleine's calves," according to reports, "and convince themselves of her unconscious state in every way possible."[16] Grosz urged Isadora to think less about the Greeks and more about her career.

"He continually bombarded me with entreaties to travel," she recalled, "and continually came in, wailing with anguish, showing me newspapers which told how, in London and elsewhere, copies of my curtains, my costumes, and my dances were being . . . turned into certain success and hailed as original. But even this had no effect on me."[17] Instead, she went back to Paris, where in May she unveiled her interpretation of Beethoven's Seventh Symphony, the work Richard Wagner called "the Apotheosis of Dance," which would become Isadora's own most controversial creation. She had tried it out first in Munich and Berlin, where even her adoring students were shocked by her audacity in attempting to "interpret" Beethoven. *Jugend* had published a cartoon of Isadora stomping merrily on Beethoven's head, over the caption *"Lerne leiden, ohne zu klagen!"* (Learn to suffer without complaining!).[18] But in Paris she scored a hit, dancing three of the symphony's four movements before "an immense crowd" at the Trocadéro, in a Beethoven program that also included selections from the *Moonlight* and *Pathétique* sonatas.

"For the third time a great artist has passed through Paris," wrote critic Louis Laloy, "and this time Paris understood."[19] The pale reception Isadora had won the year before was forgotten, in a swell of cheers, "unending acclamations," and her own rousing speeches from the stage. At the Trocadéro, she danced under the baton of Edouard Colonne and the Colonne Orchestra, considered the finest in Paris. Composer Gustave Charpentier observed in the *Mercure de France:* "With all the refinement of her being, her leaps, her languors, the tremblings of nakedness beneath her veils, she has created a new vocabulary, an ensemble of metaphors capable of speaking in the most immediate and musical of languages."[20]

From the stage, heaped in roses, Isadora explained how hard she had worked over the previous year: "But it is still not enough. The Art of the Dance is a very great thing and what I am doing is only the beginning. It is like a little girl making her first steps. I hope to do better next year; and I hope above all to teach young pupils who will outstep me and realize all that I foresee."[21] At her second concert, she was so overwhelmed by the enthusiasm of the audience that she began to cry and couldn't speak — a novelty for her. A third "Beethoven Evening" was added to the schedule to meet demand. And still Isadora refused to tour, permanently ending Grosz's hopes by announcing that she would spend the summer at the Wagner festival in Bayreuth, where she had agreed to choreograph the Bacchanal and dance the part of the First Grace in a revived production of *Tannhäuser.*

For Isadora, Bayreuth marked a serious departure.[22] It required her not only to study some of the most difficult music ever written for the stage but also to dance in concert with the enemy — a classically trained corps de ballet. *Tannhäuser* was Wagner's most popular opera but hadn't been seen in Bayreuth since 1891, when, according to critic Paul Busching, "the presentation of the Bacchanal proved to be an outstanding test for the stage art of Bayreuth" — in other words, a flop.[23] Isadora accepted the challenge to rework the Bacchanal even before she went to Greece, when Wagner's son, Siegfried, called on her in Berlin. Later she received a written invitation from the composer's widow, Cosima Wagner, who since his death in 1883 had taken command at Bayreuth and run the festival single-handed as a vast, commercial shrine to her husband's genius.

In explaining her decision to dance at Bayreuth, Isadora later told a friend "that it was very simple — she was young, passionately involved in her studies, and eager to meet . . . great musicians, artists and scholars."[24] That she might also turn Bayreuth on its head was probably not far from her thoughts. She had no way of knowing that the Wagners' invitation would prove more formal than substantial; that the new production of *Tannhäuser* wouldn't otherwise change by so much as a hair from the 1891 version; or that Cosima Wagner was "afraid of abstractions," having once instructed a singer at Bayreuth who wanted to discuss his concept of his part, "My dear friend, we have no 'concepts' in Bayreuth. Phrase according to sense, pronounce each word distinctly, observe the indicated rhythm exactly! Then you've done your part; everything else is contained in the work itself."[25] Cosima's grandson Wolfgang Wagner explained: "She was . . . wholly un-Wagnerian in her insistence on preserving productions unchanged, and thereby building up an inviolable tradition which nothing and no one could challenge. She did not consider it her function to create anything new or trend-setting."[26]

Of the *Tannhäuser* Bacchanal, when she came to study it, Isadora observed correctly that it "expresses all the frenzy of voluptuous longing of a *cerebrale*" — that is to say, of the composer himself: "The closed grotto of the satyrs and the nymphs . . . was the closed grotto of Wagner's mind, exasperated by the continual longing for a sensual outlet which he could find only within his own imagination."[27] In Cosima Wagner's hands, *Tannhäuser* remained a black-and-white tale of the war between the physical and the spiritual, between the desires of the body and the call of love, honor, religion, and duty. Isadora's stamp on the 1904 revival came first after the overture, as Tannhäuser, the thirteenth-century poet and minnesinger, lies dreaming of Venus and sexual pleasure. In keeping with her foremost preoccupation, it was her intention to "indicate," rather than depict, the scene in Tannhäuser's mind.

She descended on Bayreuth in full antique regalia, riding through the fairy-tale Bavarian town in an open carriage, waving at crowds, and providing "a most extraordinary sight," according to Christian Ebersberger, *Hausverwalter* — a kind of glorified janitor — at Villa Wahnfried, Wagner's last home and resting place, which Cosima preserved in a state of inviolability, exactly as Wagner left it. "Great and small alike crowded around the carriage to see Miss Duncan," Ebersberger recalled. "And I must admit that I could not see enough; I could not get my fill of this beautiful figure which suddenly appeared before me." On arrival, Isadora agreed to dance for the Wagner family. She was late for her recital. When the guests became restless, Cosima sent Ebersberger upstairs to find out what was wrong.

"Without the faintest idea of what I was to find in the room, I walked in to give my message," Ebersberger reported. "As I entered I saw Miss Duncan dressed only in Eve's costume" — that is, naked — "while the maid was trying to cover her with a scarf."[28] Isadora's reputation for nudity was the talk of Bayreuth, where the most sensational items on offer, in the normal run of things, were Richard Wagner stickpins, beer mugs, wallets, and teacups bearing the image of Tristan and Isolde.[29] Isadora played her image to the hilt, rejecting Cosima's plea on the opening night of *Tannhäuser* that she wear a white chemise under the filmy gauze of her costume and answering straight-faced, when Cosima asked her whether all American women dressed as she did, "Oh, no, some wear feathers."[30]

"I have never met a woman who impressed me with such high intellectual fervour as Cosima Wagner," Isadora wrote later, "with her tall, stately carriage, her beautiful eyes, a nose perhaps too prominent for femininity, and a forehead which radiated intelligence."[31] Now sixty-seven, the daughter of Franz Liszt and French Countess Marie d'Agoult, Cosima had been born out of wedlock and had created a scandal of her own in 1870, when she divorced her husband, the conductor Hans von Bülow, to marry Wagner, amid a storm of publicity and near universal condemnation. They had met nine years before — as it happened, during the Paris production of *Tannhäuser* — and had two children before their union was regulated. For a time Cosima Wagner was among the most notorious women in Europe, and nothing about her starchy Victorian widowhood prevented her from judging Isadora shrewdly, artist to artist.

"While she thinks about the music, she is not musical," Cosima noted, "and does not dance rhythmically. . . . She belittles the importance of the right costume and surely her figure needs a flattering costume. Nevertheless, contradictions, stubbornness, limitations notwithstanding, we have a personality before us of true artistic importance."[32] On the day they met, Cosima guided Isadora through Villa Wahnfried and led her to Wagner's grave, the central stop for any pilgrim in her circle. As the summer wore on, Isadora, too, was submerged in the sound of Wagner, attending rehearsals not just for *Tannhäuser* but for all the productions at Bayreuth that season, until she found herself "in a constant state of intoxication. . . . My mind was saturated with these legends, and my being was vibrating with the waves of Wagner's melody. I reached that state where all the outward world seemed cold, shadowy, and unreal, and the only reality for me was what took place in the theatre."[33]

Joining Isadora in Bayreuth was Mary Desti Sturges, who, tiring of life in Chicago as a businessman's wife, secured an agreement from her husband that she could spend six months of every year in Europe with their son, Preston. "I don't remember getting there," Preston Sturges would write, "but one day in the very early spring of 1904 Mother and I arrived at Isadora's apartment in Berlin. Mrs. Duncan was there and so was lovely Temple Duncan, Isadora's niece, a few months older than I and my first and desperate sweetheart."[34] Dressing Mary in clothes identical to hers — "loose flowing garments, blue shawls and white capes, with bare feet and gold sandals" — Isadora left Preston and Temple with her mother and took Mary to Bayreuth as her companion. To strangers meeting them for the first time, they looked so much alike that many thought they were sisters. "Isadora, I thought you were one, but you are two," said Cosima Wagner, to Isadora's annoyance.[35]

"Early each morning we drove in a funny little, old-fashioned one-hoss shay, miles up to what Isadora always called the Little Red Barn on the hill," Mary remembered. "This was the famous Wagner theatre. Here we met other devotees and soon scattered through the dark theatre in groups of twos or threes or fours." Ordinarily, no one apart from musicians and performers was allowed in the *Festspielhaus* during rehearsals, but "I was there because Isadora and I were never separated," Mary wrote, "I watching her performance and occasionally dancing her part with the two German ballet dancers while she watched with Frau Wagner from the auditorium." Again, casually, Cosima turned to Isadora and remarked, "*Wie schön,* but how she resembles you!"

"Isadora flew on the stage," Mary recalled, "shaking me by the two shoulders: 'Don't ever do it again,' she cried. 'Never, never.'" On the drive home, she was still upset: "It's awful, even the very expression of my eyes. No, I will never teach anyone again. They only succeed in making an imitation of me."[36] Mary was the most devoted of Isadora's women friends and always would be, but she roused more hilarity than respect as she tried to keep up with the star, "bringing with her wherever she went more noise and disorder than harmony and peace."[37] In Bayreuth, Mary met composers, philosophers, singers, musicians, "toy royalty," and other personalities and imagined herself at the end of the season to be on intimate terms with them all. "My mother was in no sense a liar," Preston Sturges declared, "nor even intentionally unacquainted with the truth. . . . She was, however, endowed with such a rich and powerful imagination that anything she had said three times, she believed firmly. Often, twice was enough."[38]

In Bayreuth, Isadora took a lease on Philipsruhe — Philip's Rest — a stone house in the Hermitage gardens, built by "Mad Ludwig" of Bavaria, Ludwig II, Richard Wagner's royal patron. She went a bit mad herself, as the summer progressed, and she found herself fixated on Cosima Wagner's son-in-law, historian Heinrich Thode. Since the end of her affair with Oszkár Beregi, Isadora had lived "chastely," as she wrote, "relapsing, in a curious manner, to the state in which I was as a virgin."[39] Her passion for Thode would also remain sexless, another platonic, "luminous" attachment to which she attached the word *cérébrale.* Thode's wife, Daniela, was the coldest, if not the strangest, of Cosima Wagner's daughters, and her marriage to Thode had been grim.[40] At Bayreuth, Thode was working on a book about Saint Francis of Assisi, which he read to Isadora, chapter by chapter, as he also read to her the entire *Divine Comedy* of Dante and portions of his earlier biography of Michelangelo.

"He was like a man in a dream," Isadora sighed, "and regarded me with eyes filled with prayer and light." Gordon Craig, who met Thode with Isadora the following year in Berlin, remembered him as "a delightful man, brimming full of fun — a writer and a keen enjoyer of music & drawings & dancing & jolly books."[41] But to Isadora, Thode was all soul and sensitivity, the pure receptor of the erotic longing roused in her, at least in part, by her effort to "indicate" carnality on the stage. She wrote:

> As I returned his gaze, suddenly I was uplifted and, with him, tra-versed heavenly spheres or paths of shining light. . . . The feeling of delight through all my nerves became so poignant that the slightest touch of his arm sent such thrills of ecstasy through me that I turned sick and faint, with the sweet, gnawing, painful pleasure. It revolved in my head like a thousand whirls of myriad lights. It throbbed in my throat with such joy that I wanted to cry out. Often I felt his slight hand pressed over my lips to silence the sighs and little groans that I could not control. It was as if every nerve in my body arrived at that climax of love which is generally limited to the instant; and hummed with such insistence that I hardly knew whether it was utter joy or horrible suffering. My soul partook of both, and I longed to cry out with Amfortas, to shriek with Kundry.[42]

Adding to Isadora's turmoil that summer was the presence of Beregi, who had traveled from Budapest to see her and found her not indifferent to his charm. She made no mention of this visit in her ac-count of the Wagner festival; Mary reported that she had kept Beregi at bay, but a photograph from the Wagner archives, taken in the gar-den at Philipsruhe, shows the two of them kissing passionately.

"Isadora was incapable of hurting anyone," wrote Mary, "and would suffer any inconvenience herself rather than hurt another. (I have known her to go away from home for several weeks because of some unsympathetic guest whom she had not the heart to send away.) So she had given Romeo hospitality, insisting, however, that he must live up in the Hermitage gardens in a private hotel,"[43] where she also installed her mother, Temple Duncan, and Preston Sturges when they came down from Berlin, decking them all out in Greek garb and sub-jecting them, as Preston recalled, "to a mandatory dose of exposure to great minds. . . . Bayreuth was aswarm with musicians, artists, vaga-bonds, painters, tramps and scholars. We were probably lucky not to be housed in a tree." Preston, too, once wandered into Isadora's bed-room and found her stark naked before the mirror.

"A *lady*," he said, "wouldn't stand around in front of a gentleman without any clothes on at all!"

"A *gentleman*," Isadora answered, "wouldn't come crashing into a lady's room without knocking!" She doted on Preston, as she did on all children, and made a point of showing him off to her guests. "Temple and I sat on the lap of Ernst Haeckel," Preston remembered, "who discovered the invisible organisms in seawater and looked like Father Time. We also graced the lap of Frau Cosima, and the tenor Burgstahler's lap, and Humperdinck's lap, and Frau Thode's lap, and the laps of the King and Queen of Württemberg. . . . [We] came pretty close to being professional lap-sitters that summer of 1904."[44] This in itself was a flagrant display of modern thinking about children in Wilhelmine Germany, where pragmatism and militarism warred eternally with mysticism and the search for the "one soul" of Schiller's — and Beethoven's — "Ode to Joy."

Of all Isadora's provocative attachments, in this regard, her friendship with Ernst Haeckel, the German biologist and philosopher, provoked the most comment in Bayreuth. Isadora had read translations of Haeckel's work in London and kept a copy of his treatise *The Riddle of the Universe* on her bedside table, along with his *Natural History of Creation,* in which Haeckel outlines his theories of *Naturphilosophie* and "monism." This was the term he coined to express his concept of the unity of matter and, more darkly, "the literal transfer of the laws of biology to the social realm."[45] As a scientist, Haeckel was Darwinian; as a philosopher, he had questions about the theory of natural selection, with its insistence on randomness, preferring to see a plan of "progressive perfection" at work in the universe. Haeckel was responsible for the notorious dictum, later exploited by the Nazis, that "politics is applied biology" and that natural equality never exists among organisms, species, or races. In 1904 he was already a German folk hero, revered despite his attacks on Christianity, bourgeois morality, and the concept of immortality — Heaven — which he declared outright to be "ludicrous."[46]

With thousands of others in Germany, Isadora sent Haeckel her best wishes on his seventieth birthday, celebrated in 1904 almost as a sacred event. His work had brought her "religion and understanding," she wrote, "which counts for more than life." When Haeckel replied in a friendly way, they began to correspond — Isadora opened her letters with "Dear Master" and signed them, "All my love, Isadora Duncan."[47] At the end of August, Haeckel arrived as her guest at Bayreuth, where she paraded him through the town with a huge and beaming pride:

> He possessed a magnificent, athletic figure, with a white beard and white hair. He wore strange, baggy clothes, and carried a carpet

bag. We had never met, but we recognised each other at once. I was immediately enfolded in his great arms, and found my face buried in his beard. His whole being gave forth a fine perfume of health and strength and intelligence, if one can speak of the perfume of intelligence. . . . That afternoon, before the astonished audience, I promenaded during the entr'acte, in my Greek tunic, bare legs and bare feet, hand-in-hand with Ernst Haeckel, his white head towering above the multitude.[48]

Haeckel's visit caused Isadora some awkwardness with Cosima Wagner, who, art or no art, was staunchly Catholic and scandalized by the atheist philosopher's presence at her shrine. "Oh, Herr Professor," Isadora said to her friend, "you looked today like a god!"

"Why look, who is here!" Haeckel answered. "My goddess!"[49] Gods and goddesses were never lightly invoked at Villa Wahnfried. It didn't help that Isadora's Bacchanal, for all the publicity it got, fell flat, in both her own and Cosima's estimation. Writing in *Die Musik,* Busching described it as "fundamentally unsuccessful, a half-hearted intermezzo," emphasizing that "Duncan danced delightfully, but she danced among ballerinas. Her dance was therefore not in the right frame." The contrast between Isadora's "athletic, liberal movement" and the "shackled dislocation" of "Parisian" ballet dancers proved more repellent than enlightening, Busching thought. (Cosima used the so-called Paris score of *Tannhäuser,* rather than the original, Dresden version, always a sore point in Germany.) Busching praised Isadora's revisionist impulse and predicted that what she had danced as "a single Grace . . . should and will be danced by all who take part in the Bacchanal in the future, at least in Bayreuth"[50] For opera lovers, she was simply a bomb. "As for Miss Duncan," wrote Robert Sand, "she was indeed the one before whom the amorous couples take flight. Venus was forgotten the moment [she] entered."[51] According to Isadora, the Berlin corps de ballet scattered tacks on her carpet, hoping to cut her feet while she danced.

"So here I was," she wrote, "a perfect pagan to all, fighting the Philistines."[52] She stayed in Bayreuth into September, creating "a hullabaloo" among festival patrons and earning a reputation for debauchery by receiving her guests while lying on a sofa. "[Philipsruhe] contained many couches and cushions," Isadora explained, "rose-coloured lamps and no chairs. It was looked upon by some as a Temple of Iniquity. . . . The village people considered it a veritable witches' house, and described our innocent revels as 'terrible orgies.'"[53] At lunch with Cosima and other guests, Isadora committed the final heresy by saying that "the Master's mistakes were as great as his genius," specifically, that Wagner's concept of *Musik-Drama,* the unifying vision of music and action that transformed the face of opera, was "nonsense. . . . It is impossible to mix in any way, one with the other. *Musik-Drama kann nie sein* [Music-Drama can never be]." She would think harder about it later, but the damage was done.

"I had uttered such blasphemy that nothing further was possible," Isadora confessed. "I gazed innocently around me, to meet expressive visages of absolute consternation." Whether this particular unburdening of opinion was the cause, or whether she had simply worn out her welcome through her relentless self-display, she was not invited back to Bayreuth.[54]

In October 1904 Isadora began a new tour of German cities, at the same time taking the lease on a large apartment in Berlin, at 11 Hardenbergstrasse, where she was joined by all the members of her family except Raymond, who stayed in Greece. That fall she also purchased a house in the forest suburb of Grunewald, a splendid, three-story mansion that would be the site of her first school. She returned to Budapest for a short engagement and danced in Warsaw for the first time, but still she pined for Heinrich Thode, for "the keenest pleasure and intensity of love." "I left Bayreuth," Isadora wrote,

> but I carried a potent poison in my blood. I had heard the call of the sirens. The yearning pain, the haunted remorse, the sorrowful sacrifice, the theme of Love calling Death — all were hereafter to obliterate for ever the clear vision of Doric columns and the reasoning wisdom of Socrates. . . . The spiritual ecstasy with which [Thode] had inspired me in Bayreuth gradually gave place to an exasperated state of uncontrollable desire.[55]

In this condition, Isadora met Gordon Craig, possibly the most influential Western stage designer of the twentieth century. "Here stood before me brilliant youth, beauty, genius," she wrote, "and, all inflamed with sudden love, I flew into his arms with all the magnetic willingness of a temperament which had for two years lain dormant." The shift in her desire from Thode to Craig was accomplished without a pause for breath, the difference being that Craig responded lustily to her advances: "Here I found an answering temperament, worthy of my metal. In him I met the flesh of my flesh, the blood of my blood. . . . This was not a young man making love to a girl. This was the meeting of twin souls." That Craig was married; that he had a second, common-law wife in England; and that his "answering temperament" outstripped her own were of no concern to Isadora at the time.

"I do not know how other women remember their lovers," she wrote: "But I always see him, at that first night in the studio, when his white, lithe, gleaming body emerged from the chrysalis of clothes and shone upon my dazzled eyes in all his splendour. . . . Hardly were my eyes ravished by his beauty than I was drawn toward him, entwined, melted. As flame meets flame, we burned in one bright fire."⁵⁶ In Craig, she found the man she was looking for — "& being armed by the Gods," Craig observed, "she soon made everyone understand that all would be as she wished."⁵⁷

Part II

TWIN SOULS

(1904-1907)

All things have only an imaginary existence — Man is man. . . .

For the remembering of an act — "I went with her

through those lighted streets and we

bought our supper from three or four shops" —

is greater than the act itself. . . .

Beyond wonder wonderful — that seemed and seems

as I see those shops — that street —

the lights, it becomes again so wonderful

that I turn sick with pain of gazing — It is gone

by — that glimpse.

— Edward Gordon Craig ("Berlin, October 26, 1908, passing
through Hardenbergstrasse over the bridge in the train")

8

Teddy and Topsy

"Isadora — Isadora Isadora," wrote Craig. "Where is the man or woman on earth who will rival me in my right & my joy in repeating that name? It becomes like a new element. Earth, Air, Fire, Water, Isadora — & all the four are summed up in the fifth." Rereading her letters in 1917, ten years after their affair ended, Craig stopped with the first one, "because I do not want to die suddenly — Love like Poison does not kill if taken [in] little bits."[1] Isadora, for her part, remarked about Craig, "There are joys so complete, so all perfect, that one should not survive them. Ah, why did not my burning soul find exit that night, and fly, like Blake's angel, through the clouds of our earth to another sphere?"[2]

The night Isadora speaks about wasn't the night she met Craig, but the night they consummated their union on the floor of Craig's studio in Berlin. In her autobiography, she garbles facts, placing her meeting with Craig in 1905 instead of 1904, and at a theater where she was dancing rather than at a reception in her own apartment. "It was in Berlin in 1904 that I first saw her," Craig remembered: "I am not quite certain of the date."[3] On December 13, in a letter to his friend and patron, Count Harry Kessler, he extolled, "Be nice about Isadora D. Indeed *Indeed* she is the only dancer existing!"[4] But she isn't mentioned in Craig's daybook until the fifteenth, with the simple

notation: "Isadora Duncan." There comes, two days later, the lone entry: "God Almighty."[5] It is right to let Isadora tell the story first:

> One night . . . I was dancing in Berlin. Although as a rule I never
> notice the audience when I am dancing — they always seem to me
> like some great god representing Humanity — this evening I was
> aware of some personality sitting in the front row. Not that I looked, or
> saw, who it was, but I was psychically aware of its presence, and, when
> the performance was over, there came into my loge a beautiful being.
> But he was very angry.
>
> "You are marvellous!" he exclaimed. "You are wonderful! But why
> have you stolen my ideas? Where did you get my scenery?"
>
> "What are you talking about? These are my own blue curtains. I
> invented them when I was five years old, and I have danced before
> them ever since!"
>
> "No! They are my *décors* and my ideas! But you are the being I
> imagined in them. You are the living realisation of all my dreams."
>
> "But who are you?"
>
> Then came from his mouth these wonderful words:
>
> "I am the son of Ellen Terry."
>
> Ellen Terry, my most perfect ideal of woman! Ellen Terry . . . !
>
> "Why, you must come home and have supper with us," said my
> unsuspecting mother. "Since you take such an interest in Isadora's art,
> you must come home to supper with us."
>
> And Craig came home to supper.[6]

Indeed, to his consternation, Gordon Craig was the son of Ellen
Terry, the "sweetheart of England" and great actress of the British
stage.[7] Craig was born at Stevenage, in Hertfordshire, in 1872, the second child of Terry and architect Edward William Godwin. Called Edward after his father, he was nicknamed Teddy, and later, Ted, but for
years his surname remained unsettled. Ellen Terry had eloped with
Godwin after her separation from painter G. F. Watts; they never married. Neither Ted nor his elder sister, Edy (short for Edith), had a family name until, together, they chose Craig, after a barren island off the
coast of Scotland, Aisla Craig, that had intrigued them as children. In
1888, at the age of sixteen, Craig was finally christened: Edward Henry
Gordon Craig (Henry for his godfather and Ellen Terry's acting partner, Sir Henry Irving, and Gordon for his godmother, Lady Gordon).[8]

He was "a born actor," according to his mother, who called him
"the feather of England" when he was a baby because he was so light

to hold.[9] An irrepressible sense of humor was among Ellen Terry's finest qualities. In a commonplace book she kept by her bed, she inscribed words she had read in a Christmas sermon and chose to live by: "If your morals make you dreary, depend upon it, they are wrong."[10] With her golden hair, rose complexion, and rich, liquid voice, trained to perfection in the works of Shakespeare, Terry was the picture of Victorian womanhood — "the loveliest of all young actresses," as J. M. Barrie called her, "the dearest of all old ones."[11] In a career spanning nearly seventy years, she played every role available to an actress of her stature and bestrode them all with her easy, laughing personality, to the point that critics didn't dare attack her for fear of offending England. Terry was more than an actress, said Craig: "She spread herself out and encompassed the stage, the stalls, the pit, gallery, and somehow the air."[12]

At the time of Craig's birth, Ellen Terry wasn't yet a star. That came later, after Godwin abruptly left her and she returned to the stage to support her family. Her first great success was as Olivia in an adaptation of *The Vicar of Wakefield*, but she reached her highest peaks in partnership with Henry Irving, whose Lyceum Company she joined in 1878. With Irving, Terry played almost all of Shakespeare's heroines and toured America eight times. She disliked most of her characters, complaining about Desdemona's "passivity," for example, and insisting that Lady Macbeth was misunderstood: "Her strength is all nervous force; her ambition is all for her husband" — in itself, a venerable Victorian trait. "Be damned *charming!*" Terry told herself when she rehearsed *Macbeth*. The public even forgave her renegade union with Godwin, in view of the fact that she had been "devoted" to him.

After Godwin left her, Craig never saw or heard from him again. Terry was married a second time in 1877, to the actor Charles Wardell (known professionally as Charles Kelly), but Craig's father was the love of her life: she kept Godwin's photograph in her handbag, inscribed with the words "'Tis better to have loved and lost, than never to have loved at all." Wardell was a drinker, and Terry's second marriage, like her first to Watts, quickly failed. "I gave him three-quarters of what I earned," she remembered, "and prayed him to go."[13]

Thus, Craig "fell into the hands of a house of women," as he complained in *Ellen Terry and Her Secret Self,* the strange, angry little book that prompted Terry's friend George Bernard Shaw to exclaim: "Oh, bother Gordon Craig! The baby is squalling again . . . and nobody will

whack it because it is Ellen Terry's baby. Well, let it squall."[14] By all evidence, Terry was as devoted to her children as she was to the stage,
even if, as Craig believed, "no one is less suited than a busy actress to
cope with her children properly. . . . Until I found friends to help me
as I wanted to be helped, I count my development as nil. I was born
sleepy-fat, fair-haired and fast asleep — a gourmand, a sensualist, a
conceited lump and a dreamer."[15] The story is told of Craig's sister
smacking him on the head with a spoon when he cried as a child, in-
structing him to "Be a woman!" For Craig, all his life, women would
be a "damned" source of inspiration, pleasure, and menace; always fled,
and always pursued; to be feared and avoided, "beaten," and possessed.

"You must *influence* the girls," Craig declared, "& the more you
beat them spiritually (or physically for that matter) the more they will
understand — & *obey*."[16] *Genius* was the word Isadora would use to
glide over statements like these. Like Isadora, Craig idolized the memory of his missing father, and by means of similar, distant reports. According to Oscar Wilde, Godwin was "one of the most artistic spirits
of the century in England," who, apart from practicing architecture,
had designed costumes for Terry, wrote widely about the theater, and
argued for an end to the cramped, "realistic" stage sets of the Victorian
era, with their painted backdrops, potted plants, and jumble of ugly
furniture. In an article for *The British Architect* in 1878, Godwin called
for "the abolition of footlights," a vision his son would realize later in
his "kinetic" stage — "a near-abstraction of spaces and planes, with
elevations disposed in curves and angles in a way that evoked . . . the
essence of the work being played."[17]

In 1885, when he was thirteen, Craig joined Terry in America,
where she was appearing in Chicago with the Irving company and
where he made his own stage debut in a melodrama, adapted from
Thomas Hood's *Dream of Eugene Aram*. Sent next to boarding school
in Heidelberg, he was soon expelled for his "very ill-disciplined nature" and "impulsive temper";[18] at seventeen, he joined the Irving
company himself, intending, as everyone thought, to be an actor.
Craig worshiped Irving, calling him "master" and not concealing his
belief that he had found a father. That Irving may also have been
Terry's lover no doubt complicated the attachment. It was customary
for junior company members to tour the provinces in summer; Craig
was given leading roles, playing Romeo, Petruchio, Hamlet, and Macbeth, but it wasn't long before he concluded that he would never live
up to the example his mother and Irving had set. He turned instead to

drawing, learning to make woodblocks, bookplates, posters, illustrations, and stage designs.

In these, as in all matters, Craig was self-taught, moving from passion to passion and form to form with the ease of one to the manner born. Soon he emerged as a radical, determined to destroy everything Ellen Terry held dear about the theater. "Ted caught socialism long ago," she wrote to Bernard Shaw. "I allow him £500 each year so that he may be laid hold on by his whims and fancies whilst he is very young (he's a baby) and get it all over very soon."[19] Max Beerbohm left a sketch of Craig in his diary about this time: "Playing piano — leaping up — throwing back hair — flowing cloak. German student — Heidelberg — one expected sabre cuts — Unearthly — The Young Bacchus — His amours, almost mythological . . . pure type of artist — *Genius*."[20]

As Isadora did about dance, Craig believed that the theater, by the time he found it, had been lost to artifice, "enslaved by acting, music, literature, painting and costume designing." The modern stage director, he argued, "should work not for statement but suggestion, and should appeal primarily to the eye by color and mass and movement, the words and other things being allowed to help out with the meaning."[21] Before he was through, Craig would argue for the elimination of actors from the stage, to be replaced by what he called the *Übermarionette,* or super-puppet, a "supremely beautiful creature — something like a Greek statue," that could be controlled and manipulated entirely by the director in the interest of the work.[22]

"Art arrives only by design," Craig observed in 1908. "To make any art it is clear we may work only in those materials with which we can calculate. Man is not one of those materials."[23] To his friend Martin Shaw, the genial, Cockney organist, composer, and musicologist who helped him mount his first productions in London, he wrote that "actors must cease to *speak* and must *move* only, if they want to restore the art to its old place. Acting is Action — Dance the poetry of Action."[24] After meeting Isadora, Craig declared that "she was the first and only true dancer" he had ever seen, "except for some Negroes in a street in Genoa and some in a barn near York."[25] To say that she inspired him and gave wing to his ideas is only to state what he confessed himself.

"Inspiration is given out by the thousand volt per second from Miss D.," Craig wrote to Martin Shaw. "And I am alive again (as artist) through her."[26] Duncan scholar Ann Daly makes the point: "They shared a primary belief in 'Nature,' in suggestion over realism, in the grandeur of simplicity, in the unity of mise-en-scène, in movement, proportion, and the Greek ideal. They believed in art as revelation."[27] Plainly implicit in Craig's actorless theater was a rejection of his mother, nor could he ever bring himself to admit that Isadora's success was anything but "a divine accident." On seeing her dance in Berlin, he felt "a mixture of overwhelming admiration and furious resentment," according to his son and biographer, Edward A. Craig, "admiration for what had been to him the greatest artistic experience in his life, resentment that this revelation should come from a woman." In Craig's own family, at least, there was no confusion about this: "Through [Isadora's] art he was to discover the final ingredient necessary to the formula that was to be the basis of all his future ideas for the theatre."[28]

Given the importance Craig assumed in her life, Isadora devotes surprisingly few words to him in her autobiography, and most of these are about the conflicts that finally drove them apart. That Craig was "one of the most extraordinary geniuses of our epoch" she never failed to say, "a creature like Shelley, made of fire and lightning," "the inspirer of the whole trend of the modern theatre." But for every rapturous exclamation over Craig's body, mind, and art, Isadora reserved more for his jealousy, arrogance, and violent temper. She quotes his endless refrain — "My work. My work!" — and remembers him telling her that "all women are damned nuisances, and you are a damned nuisance, interfering with my work. My work! My work!" Suffice it to say that she wrote with hindsight, after the bitterest experiences, and her published account bears no resemblance to the worshipful letters she sent Craig throughout their affair. In *My Life,* Isadora appeared to be settling scores:

> Craig was tall, willowy, with a face recalling that of his wonderful mother, but even more delicate in features. In spite of his height, there was something feminine about him, especially about the mouth, which was sensitive and thin-lipped. The golden curls of his boyhood pictures — Ellen Terry's golden-haired little boy, so familiar to London audiences — were somewhat darkened. His eyes, very near-sighted, flashed a steely fire behind his glasses. He gave one the impression of delicacy, a certain almost womanly weakness. Only his hands, with their broad-tipped fingers and simian square thumbs, bespoke strength. He always laughingly referred to them as murderous thumbs — "Good to choke you with, my dear!" . . .
>
> His love was young, fresh, and strong, and he had neither the nerves nor nature of a voluptuary, but preferred to turn from love-

making before satiety set in, and to translate the fiery energy of his
youth to the magic of his Art. . . .

One never spent a dull moment with him. No, he was always either in the throes of highest delight or the other extreme — in those
moods which suddenly followed after, when the whole sky seemed to
turn black, and a sudden apprehension filled all the air. One's breath
was slowly pumped from the body, and nothing was left anywhere but
the blackness of anguish. . . .

It was my fate to inspire the great love of this genius; and it was
my fate to endeavour to reconcile the continuing of my own career
with his love. Impossible combination! After the first few weeks of wild,
impassioned love-making, jealousy, that green-eyed serpent, possessed
him; *and I may say that I was a martyr to his difficult moods and caprices.
He was jealous of my family, jealous of my School, jealous even of my
ideas*. . . . And yet Gordon Craig appreciates my Art as no one else has
ever appreciated it. But his *amour propre,* his jealousy as an artist, would
not allow him to admit that any woman could really be an artist.[29]

Consider how Isadora writes these passages: in stark, dramatic
images and intense awareness of the physical world. The breath leaves
her body; the sky turns black. This is the essence of her remembrance — as distinct from Craig, who wrote constantly and compulsively about Isadora and never stopped revising his depiction of her.
In the end, Craig had nearly sixty years to reflect on what she had
meant to him. He told one of his sons that "from the beginning,"
Isadora was associated in his mind with death. And later: "Isadora was
the only woman I knew, Bobby, who was not a tame cat, and whose ardor matched my own."[30] Her era—and her character, too, no doubt —
ensured that she would lose her heart to a man who resented her
achievements; Craig had an idea about the divine right of artists that
made her own look pale. "Art may not be for Art's sake," he wrote,
"but the artist is certainly for the artist's sake. That is to say, he is selfish to the core."[31] No one who knew Craig had any doubt about that.

"If one or another person exhilarated him to the extent that it
helped him with an idea, he would consume that person, then discard
their shattered and disillusioned remains," writes Edward Craig, "in
the same way that other creative artists consume spirits and toss the
empty bottle into the dustbin. And in this respect he was particularly

---

*Italicized portion excised from English editions.

ruthless with women. . . . When he was working on some idea, anything irrelevant to that idea would not be tolerated. 'Get rid of that
chattering fool; she's getting in the way of my thoughts.'"[32] That the
fools in Craig's life were so frequently female says more about his own
lack of confidence than about the legion of women he seduced and
abandoned over half a century. Along with his talent went a rampant
sexuality that became the wonder of Europe.

Craig was married for the first and only time in 1893, to May Gibson, who was pregnant with their fourth child, five years later, when
he left her for another woman. This was Jess Dorynne, "a beautiful
young actress with a far-away look in her eyes," whom he also abandoned — also during a pregnancy. "The last thing he wanted at that
time was any feeling of responsibility," says Edward Craig. "He was
twenty-eight, with a superbly flowering imagination, but with a very
immature approach to life."[33] In 1902 Craig met Elena Meo, a deeply
religious British violinist of Italian descent who feared for her soul
when they fell in love and ran away together, but remained loyal to
Craig for the rest of her life, as Craig did to her — if a constant return
to Elena's embrace from other affairs can be counted as loyalty.

When Craig met Isadora, Elena was already pregnant with their
third child — Edward Craig, who brought the known total of Craig's off-
spring, at that time, to eight — and counted on his promise to marry her
as soon as his wife had secured a divorce. He never did. Commenting on
his overactive sexuality in his autobiography, *Index to the Story of My
Days,* Craig blames it on his missing father — the same explanation routinely trotted out by biographers and critics to account for Isadora's. "It
distressed me," Craig wrote. "Those sudden attacks bewildered me, and
much later on I saw some relation between sex and creative ability in my
work. . . . It is a huge power which, properly guided, lends its strength
to the creative artist — this is very certain. What else it assists I cannot
say — but wrongly dealt with it damages those who attempt to crush it.
It is not a thing to quarrel with — you must make friends with it."[34] In
this, Craig was more enlightened and more cynical than Isadora, who, as
yet, imagined her sexual passions to be at war with her creativity. "There
is too much feminine in my composition," she told Craig, "that's it —
a silly mixture."[35] Sir Bernard Miles, founding director of the Mermaid
Theatre in London, left a stinging portrait of Craig's personality:

> He remained mother's spoilt baby boy to the last, huge poseur and
> more than a bit of a bounder — the wide-brimmed hat, the cloak, the

mischievous twinkle as much as to say, "Ah, if they only knew what I know." Superb wood engraver, devilish handsome . . . selfish, suspicious, greedy, envious, crafty, ruthless. But could be very charming and gay and was always physically beautiful. . . . By no means such a great innovator as he pretended — tied to the picture-frame with hoops of steel as if he had never seen a Greek or Roman theatre. So the three-dimensional always eluded him — making pictures, never creating spaces. . . .

Craig was a man you would never have cared to leave your seventeen-year-old daughter with for more than three minutes, and then you would only just get back in time! . . . He told me the secret of getting a secretary on the cheap — "Never pay more than five pounds a week and as soon as possible put them in the family way. Then they have to stay for a while at least!" Also with a twinkle claimed to be one of the original members of the Four Fs Club, which I had never heard of but which he explained as "Find 'em, Fool 'em, Fuck 'em and Forget 'em." But only occasionally unbuttoned like that — usually pseudo-prudish and respectable! . . . An education to be with and as you can guess vastly entertaining. . . . I suppose he would have to be called a genius — but, but, but, but, but . . . !³⁶

Before meeting Isadora, between 1899 and 1902, Craig had designed six stage productions in London, three of them — *Dido and Aeneas, Acis and Galatea,* and *The Mask of Love* — in collaboration with Martin Shaw and their jointly founded Purcell Operatic Society. Later, Craig mounted Ibsen's *Vikings* and Shakespeare's *Much Ado About Nothing* in the West End. All were funded by his mother, who cheerfully pulled strings to advance his career.³⁷ "He is a donkey," said Ellen Terry, "but he's a *white* one."³⁸ By 1904 Terry was half retired, having purchased a farmhouse in Kent, where she expressed the wish to live out her days "as a dear old Frump in an armchair."³⁹ She was, as usual, joking. But Craig was never satisfied.

"I am full of a lot of feelings that I cannot express," he wrote to Martin Shaw. "Doesn't one ache to achieve a tremendous something or other and then at the end it looks like so much rubbish. One *is* so much more than one can do — and so much less than one can dream."⁴⁰ Craig's experiences in the commercial theater soon convinced him that there was no room for his ideas in England. "If I am engaged to produce anything," he wrote from London in 1903, "I am always ready to do so [provided] . . . I assume entire control of the production (play, PLAY ACTORS etc) & that absolute power is given me, beyond which there is no appeal."[41] Few impresarios were willing to grant such rights to anyone; indeed, when Craig arrived in Germany in the summer of 1904, the result was the same as at home. Through the patronage of Count Harry Kessler, who had seen and admired his work in London, Craig was invited by the director of the Lessing Theatre in Berlin, Dr. Otto Brahm, to design a production of Thomas Otway's *Venice Preserved*, in a new translation by Hugo von Hofmannsthal. He had submitted only two drawings when he concluded that Brahm didn't understand his ideas. There was a quarrel about a door: Brahm wanted one, Craig didn't.

"There is a way in and a way out," said Craig, pointing to his designs.

"Yes," said Brahm, "but I see no door handle or lock. You cannot have a door without a handle."[42] It was enough to send Craig back to his tent, threatening lawsuits and sulking like Achilles. "A clean clear dear fresh theatre," he proclaimed: "That is my aim."[43] After a trip to Weimar to stay with Count Kessler — "Anglophile, Francophile, half-Irish German diplomat and amateur of the arts"[44] — he returned to Berlin and the first major exhibit of his designs and woodcuts, which Kessler had arranged for him at the Friedmann and Weber Gallery. Kessler provided an introduction for the catalog, "a fine essay on Craig's ideals for the theatre of the future," writes Edward Craig, "an essay which did much to establish him as a man of genius in the minds of the art critics and the more advanced members of the theatrical profession in Europe."[45] At the same time, Craig's reputation as a martinet and a prima donna took hold in many minds.

"Can you bind down the sea by a contract?" he thundered. "Neither can you bind the artist by one. . . . And this is the only defense the artist shall bring: that he is part of nature, that he obeys the laws of nature, and stands or falls with nature; and that if mankind is an enemy to nature, if mankind has conquered nature . . . then mankind has also conquered the artist."[46] Both nature and mankind would be welcome to Craig only as ideas. In December he met Isadora, "and over the next two years," his son observes, "they were bound together in a fitful dream of adventure, love, art, and disillusionment, from which only one of them would escape unscarred."[47]

"I had heard that there was a sort of governess who had taken to dancing in an artistic manner — at whom some people laughed, while others crowded in the thousands to see her dance — the name Isadora

Duncan." Thus Craig opened the section on Isadora in *Index to the Story of My Days*. He had been with Count Kessler in Weimar:

She and I met in December 1904 — in Berlin. She took quite a liking to me and I thought she wasn't such a bad sort of governess after all. She was dancing in the city, but I hadn't seen her dance yet. She didn't impress me as anything especially learned: a governess generally says "Hic, haec, hoc" before half an hour has gone by, but Isadora said none of these things. So I took it that Weimar was just a bit stupid, and I asked Isadora how she did.

She said, "I'm all right — how are you?" "I'm fine," I said. She then asserted that I was her *"lieber Mann"* — her dear husband. She began singing this to all and sundry — the room was full of the sundry. She then called for her coach, like poor Ophelia, and said to me, "Hi! you come along . . . you, *mein lieber Mann*." And down we went, down the spacious staircase leading to the vast hall which conducted to the street.

A coach awaited us. We got in and after saying "To Potsdam," we leant back in the spacious coach and began to sing. We were not drunk; we had not touched wine or any stuff out of bottles — we were, I grieve to say, only happy.

If I do not make a great mistake, the happiness of Genius is an intense and awful delusion, born of the imagination. Both this girl and I were held to possess genius and we agreed we would not be party to any silly delusion like that — "No, no — *nothing serious* — look at all the serious faces!" We were galloping past hundreds of them, all really serious people — grave, grieved, some tied hand and foot, others clothed in gloomy dark raiment. *"Schnell — schnell nach Potsdam."* . . .

So this governess and I were off to Potsdam — and almost got there, too. We started late and said to the coachman "Don't hurry," so it was quite early as we neared the Palace where Voltaire and Frederick talked. But Frederick [the Great] and Voltaire never talked as much as we did — we talked sort of three-ply, if you can guess what I mean. We said a lot of words and looked a thousand more. . . .

The journey to Potsdam took quite a time — about forty-eight hours,* and most of the hours were dark. We began to count the hours after twelve had struck. Every hour, it seems, counted in Germany differently from hours in Holland or the Azores. In Prussia in 1904 an hour had 700 minutes if it was a *good hour.*[48]

---

*Potsdam is a nearby suburb of Berlin.

In *My Life,* Isadora condenses the same drive to Potsdam into two short paragraphs:

> I, like one hypnotised, allowed [Craig] to put my cape over my little white tunic. He took my hand; we flew down the stairs to the street. Then he hailed a taxi and said, in his best German, "Meine Frau und mich, wir wollen nach Potsdam gehen." [My wife and I want to go to Potsdam.]
>
> Several taxis refused to take us, but finally we found one, and off we went to Potsdam. At dawn we arrived. We stopped at a little hotel that was just opening its doors, and we drank coffee. Then, as the sun was getting high in the heavens, we started back for Berlin.[49]

Craig left another, less whimsical account of his affair with Isadora in a notebook he called *Book Topsy,*[50] after the nickname he gave her when they became lovers. There is some dispute over the origin of this giddy endearment, whether "Topsy" was taken from the slave girl in *Uncle Tom's Cabin* — who insists she was never born but just "growed" — or whether it was a laughing reference to Topsy Sinden, a popular skirt dancer in London music halls in the 1890s and 1910s.[51] The first explanation is presumably correct, reflecting Isadora's self-taught status and her insistence that she hadn't "invented" her dance but only rediscovered what "existed before." A mutual friend introduced her to Craig — Elise de Brouckère, daughter of a Belgian senator, whose sister, Jeanne, was a member of Craig's operatic society in London. In *Book Topsy,* Craig begins with first impressions:

> ISADORA. A woman of brains & beauty — not a little woman, nor a huge one — but the right size —
>
> The expression on her face changes & seems to me to be at times the faces of very many women I have known. . . . Each day I suddenly recognize a familiar face in hers — or a familiar voice — It's queer.
>
> I think she is really Aphrodite, which accounts for it. She is the calmest thing I have ever seen in a woman.
>
> I see her one afternoon at her flat in Hardenbergstrasse, Berlin. . . . I entered the room with my eyeglasses off — so I could not see very well — I was introduced first to her sister Elizabeth — then to her — & her mother & so on — then to Sarah her sister-in-law. And Sarah's daughter, Temple, & Sarah's husband-lover Augustin Duncan. . . .
>
> Owing to my short sight (when without glasses) at first I took Elizabeth for the famous dancer I had heard about & was struck by her strangely harsh accent — I felt puzzled but told myself at once

that often it is the small & insignificant women who are remarkable. "What sort of dance can she put up" thought I — & then I came to Isadora. Augustin Duncan I took to at once as most people did owing to his personal charm — Isadora talks a lot of nonsense that 1st day — shows me gods — & pictures & all . . . A book with dancing figures — She was in fine spun robes — simple & lovely. (All this time I have not seen her dance, & I find she is a nice Greekish lady by art & a fine American girl by nature, and I am sure I shall be bored by her dancing.) She then talks on & on about the way she likes her theatre to be shaped — curving her arms to describe something. (This curving the arms was a movement of embracing an immense ball.) She at once suggests the amateur-hypnotic lady & I should distrust her if she were not beautiful & Beauty is the only thing we can entirely trust. This reference to her beauty is rather strange, for in features she was not beautiful, but in *movement* she made up for [its] lack. . . .[52]

Craig dreaded the prospect of seeing Isadora dance, fearing she would be merely ridiculous. She had invited him to a *Chopin Abend*. On his program, he noted the "Mazurka A flat op 17, no 4" and wrote next to it: "Faultless." And again, the "Mazurka H [sic] flat op 33, no 4 — amazing — it is so beautiful."[53] Later Craig made a quick sketch of the stage as he remembered it: "Grand piano wooden greek columns about 5½ feet high . . . nice dark grey curtains, same height hung between each pilaster all very modest and useful."[54] This concert swept him away:

> She was speaking in her own language . . . and so she came to move as no one had ever seen anyone move before. . . . No one would ever be able to report truly, yet no one present had a moment's doubt. Only this can we say — that she was telling to the air the very things we longed to hear, and till she came we had never dreamed we should hear; and now we heard them, and this sent us all into an unusual state of joy, and I . . . I sat still and speechless.[55]

After her performance, as Isadora remembered, "Craig came home to supper." He wrote:

> The next thing she does is to ———— no, I will not write it — but I remember it, and how she discovers (bless her) that I am just an ordinary gentleman — for her anyhow!!!
> All the people at table are good souls & poor bodied persons (except for Augustin) — she has a good soul & a good body — is young

in both, fresh in both, & while everyone talks a lot of lies we 2 go on talking either frank rubbish or all sorts of truth. She had the blessed sense of humor.

Anyhow we know that we know each other. She does not deceive me — much: & she can read me with ease. I flatter her — I say "It is flattering the Greeks of 2000 years ago to say she is like a Greek dancer." She says "now that *is* nice" — yet knows it's only a nice speech & yet feels & knows that I mean it.

And what is more I *do* & I *did* mean it. Because she is genius, & better than her it would be impossible to be. Then after supper they all dance waltzes — she sits & won't dance except alone — the waist business not appearing to fit her.

So she sits with me & her old literary friend [Karl Federn][56] & we talk.

Near the time when I go she gives me a picture of herself & writes on it "with Love Isadora."

A regular hussy of a girl, one would say if one thought about it — but that only proves that to think is often a mistake — and leads to error. She can write so because she knows I read it well. No — put it differently — say she always signs her photographs so — & by the manner in which the "with love" is taken, she judges the man: perhaps so: but all the same he\she knew what she was writing.

The next day Isadora arrived at Craig's gallery exhibition: "60 drawings were shown on the walls, 13 of them sketches of English Landscapes. Some 31 were scenes & costume designs."[57] Over the next year, Count Kessler would introduce Craig to painters, producers, architects, and gallery owners all over Germany, and he would dazzle most of them: he arrived in Berlin "a handsome Hamlet, with blond hair flowing beneath a black, broad-brimmed hat. . . . Before long Craig's new ideas permeated a generation of rising European designers . . . and, in America, Robert Edmond Jones, Norman Bel Geddes and . . . Lee Simonson."[58] *Book Topsy* continues:

All in white she walks round with me & looks at each drawing — curiously interested or bored, I don't know which — nor do I care but I guess she is feeling things — that is something — the rest feel nothing and talk a lot. She goes away — I took her to the door & I can still see her look as the large door closed slowly she with her eyes on me to the last, I my eyes on her — this moment has often returned to me . . . this farewell after meeting in our particular land — and I go to write her a letter in the café. . . . I tell her I must write a line — Just to speak — not because I have anything to say — I tell her I am just amazed! I ask her to come *once* more & see my *studio* drawings. She is *white* before my drawings which are so black. It was I remember a letter of love if ever a letter held love in it. I cannot post it, it is too late: I go round to her house — rush upstairs, leave it & tear off again.

Next morning (as agreed) 4 of us (Augustin, Sarah, Isadora & I) (we are 2) are to meet to drive out.

The 3 others call for me in carriage & 2 jolly horses. I join them — everyone is in such good spirits & they laugh so much they almost drown my spirits. I am stupidly thinking often of my letter which seems so foolish now these others are near us . . . & now that she & I are so near. . . .

We visit her new school [in Grunewald]. The lilies (painted) on the walls revolt me — The others approve of it *all*. I find it all ugly except her. We lunch & laugh. Then we dance along by the trees & generally behave like 6 & 7 year old children. We salute passing strangers who seem quite happy to see us happy — Then we return — we have tea — & she tells me the fairy tale of Psyche — it breaks off like all fairy tales & as all the others go I have to go too.[59]

The myth of Psyche and her lover, Eros, has as its theme the inability of the loved one to be named or possessed. Psyche is "visited" each night by Eros, but when she once lights a lamp to see his face, a drop of hot oil falls on his shoulder and he vanishes. Psyche wanders high and low, searching for her lover, only to become a slave to Aphrodite, Eros's jealous mother, who sets her a number of grueling tasks and treats her with scorn and contempt. At length, Eros and Psyche are reunited and she becomes immortal. Telling this tale over tea, Isadora signaled not just her desire for Craig but her multiplied yearning for sexual love, a "waiting temperament" to which she would, indeed, become a slave.

They didn't have much time to waste. Isadora was scheduled to dance in St. Petersburg on December 26, her first trip to Russia. Craig's studio, at 11 Siegmundshof in Berlin, was a third-floor walkup, "an immense place with the traditional skylight on one side," as Edward Craig describes it, "and on the other, a kind of mezzanine-gallery, or balcony, reached by a flight of stairs."[60] Craig remembered the place being "empty — except for books & sketches — no carpets — no armchairs. A very tall studio with 2 windows facing south I think — for I recall the great sun of morning."[61] He wrote:

At 4 she arrives — away we drive for an hour in her carriage. Then tea. Then carriage dismissed — Then supper — then we sleep together on our balcony. *17 December — our marriage night on the floor of the dear studio.* I tell her I am going to marry in about 4 months time — she does not believe in marriage —

We talk a lot before we make our bed on the wooden floor. All good or silly talk — all unnecessary, as is proved.

Our bed was 2 carpets on which [we put] a fur cloak (hers) with my overcoat as pillow & 2 blankets and a sheet as covering —

We do not sleep much all night, it is too lovely to have her there —

18th Dec. In the morning — we sit in the sun . . . sit there . . . talk a little . . . but look . . . sit still — kiss & rest contentish.[62]

Kiss was Craig's euphemism for sex; he and Isadora used it in the sense that the French use the word *baiser,* interchangeably with its common meaning. But it meant more to her than it did to him. In a 1943 addendum to *Book Topsy,* Craig returned to the hours that led up to their "marriage night," when Isadora had escaped from her family and they drove to Craig's studio in a blaze of lit shops and Christmas decorations: "I can see them now! — & I can hear her now, talking, talking, — not saying much — but the heart talking millions to the minute — & I can hear the wheels of our carriage . . . & forget as I forgot then all but just that hugging arm — that great friendly heart."[63]

The next day, exhausted, Isadora and Craig returned to the Duncans' apartment at about five in the afternoon, "she dressed in the bed and I'm the pillow." Craig wrote:

We walk along happy & as she says "It's wonderful how independent & free virtue can be & feel" & we laugh for that's *just it.*

Since we were born to lie holding each other, the scriptures of nature are only being fulfilled.

At her house is a reception. About 50 to 80 people. We enter: she slips in and bathes.

The Reception happens. She like a queen — cold — cool — lovely — everyone else excited & struggling to have 2 minutes conversation with her —

By 6:30 everyone is gone & we dance into each other's arms.

Everyone very chilly towards us in the house. Mothers, sisters, cousins & aunts. Only Sarah is alive. The rest dead.

Then she goes out in the evening to another Reception. . . . I was going — but can't stand the fussy people all around us.

She goes alone — writes to me in evening after she gets back.[64]

At home, as she feared, Isadora faced an angry clan. Her "Aunt Lizzie" Lightner, Mrs. Duncan's sister, had arrived in Berlin and would remain a fixture there, first in the city and later at the school in Grunewald, where Isadora would welcome her first students in a few weeks' time. She was carrying a lot, not just her dancing, the school, and now Craig but the fury and resentment of her mother, who saw Craig's arrival on the scene as her last opportunity to save Isadora from sexual predators. When, on December 19, Isadora once again disappeared with Craig, Mrs. Duncan called the police. A notice went out to the newspapers — "wisely," Isadora thought — "to the effect that Miss Isadora Duncan had been taken seriously ill with tonsilitis" and that her performances would be canceled until further notice. According to Isadora, when she next saw Craig, Mrs. Duncan greeted him with the words "Vile seducer, leave the house!"[65]

"She didn't *know* me," Craig wrote, "but she had seen that Isadora & I were really in love with each other — & that was enough for her: she was out after for my scalp."[66] In the first letter she is known to have sent to Craig after they became lovers, Isadora confirmed, "You were quite right — it was a sort of Blasphemy to go among a lot of people . . . it was Horrid."[67] Craig wrote: "December 19, 20, 21, 22, 1904. — Our perfect time. . . . In those nights she gives herself to me & reserves nothing."[68]

Before leaving Berlin for Russia, swirling with love and exhaustion both, Isadora wrote again to Craig. "Thank you Thank you Thank you for making me Happy," she said, "whole Complete I love you love you love you & I Hope we'll have a dear sweet lovely Baby — & I'm happy forever."[69]

A second note read simply: "Isadora loves *you* loves you." On the back of it Craig wrote: "Home here at 5 o'clock — good God — & find myself saying 'if only she were here.' She is not here — she is rushing through space, away from me — Oh, you *dear* one."[70] He composed the first part of *Book Topsy* while Isadora was in Russia:

Do I love her?
Does she love me?

I do not know or want to know. We love to be together. We love to hear each other, see each other, & to kiss & to lie arms round each other.

Is that love? I do not know.

She says she loves me. What does that mean from her? I do not know. She tells me about her life & whom she has loved (?) before. Laughs & laughs & laughs — we always laugh (courage & fear is in this laughter) but always seem to know what a laugh means.[71]

A third letter arrived from Isadora before she boarded her train that night. It was this one that Craig read again in 1917 and put down for fear of "dying suddenly."

Dearest Sweetest Spirit

You will never know how beautiful you are. Only I know that. You will never know what an immense Joy *Giver* you are. All that joy is with me. You have given joy & love unspeakable. What shall I give you in return — All all that I have in my power to give & that is not enough — but perhaps you will find a cold empty corner for it. . . .

We were born in the same star and we came in its rays to earth, & for a little I was in your heart & then I wandered far away & now I am back. That is our History.

No one could ever understand it — but us.

Good night.

I am your love if you will have me — if not —

but I am

Your Isadora[72]

9

"Your Isadora"

"I'm being borne away away away," Isadora wrote to Craig from the train to St. Petersburg. "The clouds are flying past — Am I transformed to a grey bird flying always North — I think so — or am I just Your Isadora who loves you Yes you."[1]

She was on her way to a triumph of an epochal nature; her two performances in St. Petersburg at the end of 1904 gave the Russian ballet "a shock from which it could never recover,"[2] as reported by Sergei Diaghilev, the aesthete-impresario who, four years later, in collaboration with choreographer Michel Fokine and the finest Russian dancers and designers, would create the Ballets Russes. Nowhere had ballet reached such a level of artistry and sophistication as in Russia, and nowhere did it rule more inflexibly in a glittering display of technical proficiency. The Ballet Russes were themselves a rebellion against the state-sponsored dance of imperial Russia, taking shape for the first time during a 1905 strike at the Maryinsky Theatre and the first ballets of any kind that could legitimately be called modern. "And we owe it all to the inspiration of an American girl," Diaghilev supposedly said. "If Isadora Duncan had never come to Russia, probably there would be no Diaghilev ballet. She pointed the way and we followed."[3]

The true extent of Isadora's influence on the Ballets Russes, and specifically on Fokine's choreography, remains a matter of cantankerous debate. The arguers come in two camps: balletomanes, who can't bring themselves to imagine that an "untrained" dancer with "no technique" could upset two centuries of codified tradition; and Duncan disciples, who affirm that Isadora's influence on ballet was direct and indelible and ask that she be recognized as the inspiration for its dramatic rebirth in the twentieth century. The battle can be understood at all only in the knowledge that when Isadora came to Russia, ballet had deteriorated almost completely into a parody of itself.

Clouding the issue, as if on cue, are Isadora's account of her Russian journey in *My Life,* where she combines the experiences of several trips into one, and the conflicting statements of Fokine and Diaghilev, who praised her when she first appeared but ultimately sought to disassociate themselves from her and from each other. In 1926, long after Fokine had left the Ballets Russes, Diaghilev confirmed that they had watched Isadora together when she first danced in St. Petersburg: "Fokine was mad about her, and Duncan's influence on him was the initial basis of his entire creation."[4] The same point is made in *Dancing in Petersburg,* the autobiography of Mathilde Kschessinska, *prima ballerina assoluta* of the Maryinsky Theatre, who had already seen Isadora dance in Vienna and had come home with enthusiastic reports. "The appearance of Isadora in St. Petersburg made an enormous impression on the young dancer and future *maître de ballet* M. M. Fokine," Kschessinska wrote baldly, "who at once began to cut out new paths for classical ballet."[5]

Fokine himself was "seared [to] the soul" by his colleagues' remarks. He did nothing to minimize Isadora's influence on his artistic vision, saying that "she reproduced in her dancing the whole range of human emotion" and that she was "the greatest American gift to the art."[6] But Fokine's work was his own, as he rightly contended, and the dispute about Isadora degenerates into a useless tit for tat. It is fact that after she went to Russia, nothing was the same in ballet; simultaneously, it goes without saying that the men who remade the ballet in Russia were looking for a way to do it before they saw her in performance. "With Miss Duncan's technical limitations or virtuosity they were not concerned," wrote a critic of the time. "What she brought them was the vision of the ballet now known to the world as Russian."[7]

Isadora had arrived in Russia at a time of climactic upheaval. Only days after her return to Berlin, in January 1905, revolution broke out in St. Petersburg, culminating in Bloody Sunday and the massacre of scores of peaceful protesters outside the Winter Palace. When she returned to the city with Craig at the beginning of February, Isadora saw firsthand the effects of the failed uprising, later blending both of her trips into a ghostly narration that left out Craig completely.[8] "Here I was," she wrote, "in the black dawn of Russia, quite alone, on the way to the hotel, when suddenly I beheld a sight equal in ghastliness to any in the imagination of Edgar Allan Poe."

> It was a long procession that I saw from a distance. Black and mournful it came. There were men laden and bent under their loads — coffins — one after another. The coachman slowed his horse to a walk, and bent and crossed himself. I looked on in the indistinct dawn, filled with horror. I asked him what this was. Although I knew no Russian, he managed to convey to me that these were the workmen shot down before the Winter Palace the day before — the fatal January 5, 1905 — because, unarmed, they had come to ask the Tsar for help in their distress — for bread for their wives and children. I told the coachman to stop. The tears ran down my face and were frozen on my cheeks as this sad, endless procession passed me. . . . If I had never seen it, all my life would have been different.[9]

Did she see it? In 1905 Russia was still on the "old," or Julian, calendar, thirteen days behind the West. Clearly, Isadora never arrived in St. Petersburg the day after Bloody Sunday, which took place on January 9/22, not January 5/18, as she asserts. When she got back to Russia, however, on January 19/February 2, Bloody Sunday was fresh in the memory; hurried burials, always held at dawn as she describes, may still have been conducted for victims who had survived the shooting and died later of their wounds. Neither were the dead of Bloody Sunday the only martyrs of the 1905 revolution.[10] "There," wrote Isadora, "before this seemingly endless procession, this tragedy, I vowed myself and my forces to the service of the people and the down-trodden. Ah, how small and useless now seemed all my personal love desires and sufferings! How useless even my Art, unless it could help this."[11]

Isadora mentions nothing about the downtrodden in her letters to Craig from Russia. She mentions little but her longing for him. "I am passing a river," she wrote from the train to St. Petersburg. "I don't know the name but the flowing waters are quite *black* & the banks covered with snow make the most amazing contrast — stretching off in great desolate fields with here & there a black forest patch — It might be the river Styx."[12] The train stopped several times along the way, and she "walked up & down looking out over the waste & felt just like Napoleon."[13] She arrived in St. Petersburg on Christmas morning and went to the Hotel Europe off Nevsky Prospect. The staff took her first to the bridal suite, but she "stoutly refused to stay in it" alone.

"This is no place for a person with a nice cheerful disposition like me," Isadora wrote, "it looks like those parlors in the Novels where they plot things. . . . It would be an awfully good sort of place to indulge any disposition to suicide."[14] She was still rattled from her journey: "All night long the train has been not flying over but going pim de pim over Great fields of snow — vast plains of snow — Great bare Countries covered with snow . . . and over all this the Moon shining — & across the window always a Golden shower of sparks — from the locomotive — it was quite worth seeing and I lay there looking out on it all & thinking of you — of you you dearest sweetest best darling."[15] At the hotel, she took a bath and went to bed, writing Craig again later in the afternoon:

> I have been asleep ever since — dreadful lots of people came but I was quite savage & frightened my little maid out of her Wits — telling her to make 'em go away at once — Then I closed my eyes — & such a Wonderful thing happened — I could *feel you breathing*. You sweet You dear — it's almost too nice to write about but I could. After that they woke me up and I had to come & see awful people who talked at me. They've all gone thank the Gods. . . .
>
> O *you* you darling — I've just got your telegram — You Sweetheart — I love you I adore you — I am nothing without you. . . . I think the best thing to do with St. Petersburg is to forget it — and pretend I'm not here. I'll not see it — I swear I won't — Darling — Sweetest Love — I shut my eyes think of it and heard your Breathing — but when I awoke I was alone — alone alone —
>
> It's Horrible. It's Ghastly. If I could only sleep till the 30 [when she was scheduled to go back to Berlin].
>
> Your Isadora
>
> You Darling — I love you — Know what that means — Am I Yours —[16]

Isadora made her Petersburg debut on the night of December 13/26 at the Hall of Nobles, directly opposite the Hotel Europe. The invitation had come from the Society for the Prevention of Cruelty to Children, under the patronage of Nicholas II's sister, Grand Duchess

Olga Alexandrovna. Before leaving Berlin, Isadora had announced the opening of her school at Grunewald and advertised exactly what she was looking for: "Physically and mentally fit, graceful girls under the age of ten, wishing to be educated in the art of Dance. . . . In the selection of pupils, no national or social discrimination will be made. The school is democratic and international. Fatherless and motherless children, as well as children of uncertain origin, are also welcome."[17] She was famous in Petersburg already as a personality, if not a dancer, before she got there.

"Miss Duncan does not recognize the ballet," wrote the *Petersburg Gazette*. "However, we advised her to go tomorrow to the Maryinsky Theatre."[18] Few in St. Petersburg were prepared to admit that Isadora's opposition to ballet could be anything but eccentric, even if many agreed that the Russian Romantic ballet, under the direction of Frenchman Marius Petipa, had reached its zenith a decade before and died there, "buried in its own greatness," in the words of dance historian Walter Sorell, with Petipa's classic productions of *Don Quixote, La Bayadère,* and Tchaikovsky's *Sleeping Beauty* and *Swan Lake.* "He perfected the pas de deux," Sorell observes, "believing in dancing for the sake of dancing and in virtuosity heightened to a spectacle. He could never choreograph satisfactorily for the male dancer, who appeared in his ballets mainly as the cavalier supporting the lady in her adagios."[19] Russian ballets were long, normally composed in four or five acts; there was little attempt to integrate the separate dance pieces, and no concession to the requirements of dramatic action, the showstopping star turns being left always to the prima ballerina and her interchangeable male partners.

"It must also be admitted that the cultural level of the Russian ballet was not high," Prince Peter Lieven wrote in his history of the Ballets Russes; "ballerinas and male dancers were not educated people, their interests were all limited, and they were not interested in art outside the narrow sphere of their concerns."[20] Isadora, by contrast, spoke of nothing but Art in the high sense. Since 1903 Russians had been reading about her, when she was first described in newspapers as the *amerikanskaya bozonzhka,* translatable as the "American barefoot dancer." This was one of several variations and diminutives applied to Isadora in Russia, with reference to her naked feet and her association with Nature. Before she appeared in St. Petersburg, she was considered to be more of an exalted health reformer or missionary than a dancer, alternately called *Kneippistka,* after a popular fad involving "barefoot walking" and hydrocures, and *boznozhka* — again, a reference to her feet, and a term that finally entered the Russian language to describe the style of her dancing.[21]

At Isadora's first performance, velvet rugs were laid in a path from her dressing room to the stage. In the imperial box, the aunt and uncle of Nicholas II, Grand Duke Vladimir Alexandrovitch and Grand Duchess Maria Pavlovna, the foremost art patrons of the Romanov family, sat with their son, Grand Duke Boris. "No one knew what to expect," wrote a young dancer who saw Isadora that night. "Every kind of rumor and talk had preceded her arrival. . . . Rumor had it that an almost nude woman would dance barefooted."[22] If there were many in the audience who had come only for that reason, others hoped for a sensation of a different kind. The Hall of Nobles was filled to capacity, not only with art patrons, courtiers, and socialites but with painters, poets, musicians, and writers. Fokine was there, with Diaghilev, artists Alexandre Benois and Léon Bakst, the symbolist Andrei Bely, and a host of mocking balletomanes, who came "to see La Duncan dance some kind of virginal cancan" but left in a different mood altogether, alternately astonished and outraged.

A review in the *Petersburg Gazette,* signed pseudonymously by theater critic Nicolai Georgievitch Shebuyev, testifies to the impact of Isadora's performance. She danced her Chopin program, against a blue backdrop, a grand piano her only accompaniment: "On the stage, a thick rug. . . . At the sides, cigar-like poplars and fragments of classical columns, to take one to Rome or to Greece, to the days of ancient Attica." Shebuyev's critique is one of the few that describe Isadora's dances individually, in detail:

> A rosy light shone out at the rear of the stage on the left, and pale violet tones began to gleam on the blue backdrop. The sound of Chopin's Mazurka (B-major, op. 7, no. 1) made one's nerves tingle, and onto the stage there entered a sylph. A bit of pink-blue gauze mistily enveloped her slender waist, and veiled yet revealed her bare feet. She is not at all beautiful, but her face is . . . exotic . . . and on it, with equal expressiveness, joy, sorrow, a tear, a smile, are fleetingly born and quickly die.
>
> She emerged and swam like an Undine, swaying in time with the beat, waving her hands with the beat, smiling, diving with the beat — and suddenly she flew up like a bird and soared carefree, joyful, chirping soundlessly — no: tunefully, rather — for her dancing merged into a single chord with Chopin's Mazurka. And then she floated down

again from the sky — touched the cold surface of the river — shuddered — and swam again, green and graceful, proud of her cold, nymphlike beauty. And dived again — and once again froze, her arms stretched forward at the finale.

That was all.

But on analyzing what at first glimpse seems little, one finds much.

First, the marvelous plastic sensibility. Her body is as though bewitched by the music. It is as though you yourself were bathing in the music. Then, the expressive hands. Have you ever heard of mimicry by hands? . . . And yet Duncan's hands are as expressive as her face. And the legs? For after all, it was the legs, the bare feet, that were supposed to be the sensation of the evening. It was considered very dull not to make witty remarks about the "Kneippist" ballerina, and one lost count of how often one overheard Briusov's line: *"O, cover thy pale legs!"* Actually, the legs play the least important role in these dances. Here *everything* dances: waist, arms, neck, head — *and* legs. Duncan's bare legs and bare feet are like those of a rustic vagabond: they are innocent: this is not a *nudité* that arouses sinful thoughts, but rather a kind of corporeal nudity.[23]

On this point, Russian critics all agreed with Shebuyev. "I have almost forgotten to say something about Duncan's bare legs," wrote one. "Indeed it was these legs that everyone had been waiting for. And — what do you think? A complete disappointment they were. Just imagine: ordinary women's legs, strong and graceful, but devoid of any alluring perfections."[24] Valerian Svetlov, who became one of "Duncanism's" fiercest critics in Russia, remarked with relief, "There is nothing here to shock the moral sense. . . . Only a thoroughly corrupted member of our present bourgeois society will see this nudity of the revived classical statue as a violation of the laws of decency or morality."[25] Shebuyev went on:

For the Mazurka in A-flat (op. 17, no. 4) there came onstage a figure severe and sorrowful, looking intently upward, all her being yearning for heaven while her hands seemed to beg, trying to seize something. Then suddenly her eyes flashed with Bacchic ecstasy — the flame died — there was another flash — then once again a look of severity and prayer. . . .

With the Mazurka in A-flat (op. 33, no. 4) she danced an entire tragedy. As she entered, consternation was on her face — the face of a bewitched Trilby; in her dancing, fear, tears, horror alternated with a morbid, decadent, compulsive *Presto*. And when, with this tragic look in her eyes, she approached the footlights and rose on her toes, she seemed to grow taller — majestic, fateful. This number moved the audience more than any of those preceding it.

The last of the Mazurkas was that in A-sharp major (op. 24, no. 3), lacelike, woven of soft, catlike, stealthy leaps; and there was a sort of caressing languor in her swaying movements that was at once feminine and maidenly.

Even more interesting are the four Preludes (op. 28, nos. 4, 7, 20, 6). To the first of them she listens, standing at the piano. . . . To the second . . . she stretched with the utmost grace, and thawed. The third was a funeral dance: the wailing woman, shattered by grief, now seeks forgetfulness in dancing, now is tormented by memories, and, at the end, falls to the ground exhausted. There is no dance for the fourth Prelude — only a mood, the mood of autumnal leaves and autumnal tears, autumnal beauty and sadness.

The best number of all, however, was the Polonaise in A-sharp major, op. 53. This was the dance of Diana. In a short red gauze tunic, her legs bare, she leaps, gambols in a round, shoots from a bow; there are occasional flashes of something animal. . . .

Duncan has no ballet technique; she does not aim at *fouettés* and *cabrioles*. But there is so much sculpture in her, so much color and simplicity, that she fully deserves the capacity audience which she is already assured for next Thursday.[26]

Isadora's second performance at the Hall of Nobles brought doubters among the critics — "Attentive copying still cannot substitute for creativity and talent!" — but they were in the minority; her novelty, if nothing else, seemed to silence dissenters. Fokine himself explained what she showed the Russian ballet: "that all the primitive, plain, natural movements — a simple step, run, turn on both feet, small jump on one foot — are far better than all the richness of ballet technique, if to this technique must be sacrificed grace, expressiveness, and beauty."[27] In Fokine's future work, Isadora's figure was plainly seen: in his first, "Greek" ballets, *Acis and Galatea, Eunice,* and *Chopiniana,* better known as *Les Sylphides,* and in the motions and gestures of all his dancers. Under Fokine, "the foot broke out of its traditional hemisphere," liberated from toe shoes, when necessary, and free to rise or grip the stage. Arms, torso, neck, head, and hands all came to life under Fokine's direction — famously, in *The Dying Swan,* which he choreographed for Anna Pavlova in 1905 — giving fluidity, emotion, and a revived romanticism to the clockwork mo-

tions of the past.[28] Beauty was the aim, and expression the means —
the essence of "Duncanism," remade for ballet.

"In spite of the shortness of my visit, I had left a considerable impression," Isadora noted. "There were many quarrels for and against
my ideals; and one duel was actually fought between a fanatic *bal-
letoman* and a Duncan enthusiast. It was from that epoch that the Russian ballet began to annex the music of Chopin and Schumann and
wear Greek costumes; some ballet dancers even going so far as to take
off their shoes and stockings."[29] Her wry observation conceals her
own disappointment in her St. Petersburg performances. "The yellow
dog and the gas man liked it," she wrote to Craig after the first night,
"and so apparently did all the Kings & Queens in the audience —
(It was full of Imperial Loges and Kings and things like that)." But
her muscles were "quite Capoot," and she couldn't "dance worth a
Cent!!!!!!" Isadora drew a weeping face at the bottom of her letter.
"This is how I feel about a 'great success,'" she said. "These is tears."[30]

At her second concert, on December 16/29, where she offered her
Dance Idylls, Isadora played to an even larger crowd, "having yielded
considerable sums in favor of the Society for the Prevention of Cruelty
to Children," as the *Petersburg Gazette* reported: "Gentle elegy and
bacchic dancing equally charmed the spectators: there was not a single crude gesture, not a single exaggeration. . . . The barefoot dancer
was presented with several gorgeous baskets of flowers and many
bouquets. The farewell curtains lasted for a long time, and the applauding public would not go away."[31] After twenty curtain calls,
Isadora finally asked for a candle from the wings. "What's Russian for
good-night?" she said: "And carrying her lighted candle, she went out
in the sudden darkness [wishing] them *'Dobroi Nochie.'*"[32]

At home, Craig was sketching and writing, among other things, a
letter to Isadora that he never sent, where he inscribed a quatrain from
the *Arabian Nights:*

> *She came appareled in a vest of blue,*
> *That mocked the skies and shamed their azure hue;*
> *I thought thus clad she burst upon my sight,*
> *Like summer moonshine on a wintry night.*

"I always recall Isadora moving when I repeat [those] words,"
Craig wrote later, "she burst upon my sight like summer moonshine

on a wintry night."[33] Another letter did reach her in Russia, reassuring her a great deal and moving her to reflect on fate: "How did it Come — it was like a sudden Thunderclap & then all was changed." She found St. Petersburg "very fine, covered with snow & the air like Champagne,"[34] but said nothing about her meeting with Kschessinska, Russia's first ballerina, or the evening she spent at dinner with Anna Pavlova, Bakst, Benois, and Diaghilev. Kschessinska had been the mistress of Nicholas II before his marriage and now lived openly with his cousin, Grand Duke Andrei Vladimirovitch, by whom she also had a child. It was a tradition — practically a requirement — for Russian ballerinas to be kept by Romanov and other princes, and Kschessinska's salon was one of the finest in St. Petersburg. When she invited Isadora to see her dance at the Maryinsky, Isadora was both generous and "astounded." Onstage, Kschessinska seemed "more like a lovely bird or butterfly than a human being." It was the same with Pavlova, whom Isadora saw in a "ravishing" production of *Giselle* and who invited her the next day to watch her exercise at the barre.

"She seemed to be made of steel and elastic," Isadora wrote. "Her beautiful face took on the stern lines of a martyr. She never stopped for one moment. The whole tendency of this training seems to be to separate the gymnastic movements of the body completely from the mind." At the Maryinsky school, Isadora saw "all the little pupils standing in rows. . . . They stood on the tips of their toes for hours, like so many victims of a cruel and unnecessary Inquisition. The great, bare dancing-rooms . . . were like a torture chamber."[35] She made no secret of her opinions at supper with Pavlova and the others. Benois described the evening in an article for *Slovo:*

> In her opinion, the only thing that matters is beauty, the pursuit of beauty in order to make all life beautiful. In the presence of beauty even suffering has no terrors, even death does not frighten, beauty illumines everything, it is mankind's best comforter. In answer to a question asked by a writer who was present, "But what are we to do about ugliness, since it exists in the world?" Miss Duncan, still aglow after her impassioned speech, replied without hesitation, *"Il faut la tuer, la laideur! Il faut la tuer!"* [We must kill ugliness! It must be killed!]

She went on to outline her main objections to the ballet, fearless in the circumstances: "The ballet in its present form is incontestably an 18th century legacy. With a few exceptions, [it] . . . represents an overcoming of difficulties, an acrobatism, some sort of complicated and excruciating mechanism." Benois was mainly impressed by what he considered Isadora's naïveté. Like his colleagues, he couldn't think of dance *except* as ballet:

> Today Duncan keeps dreaming about her school, about the "new" ballet. For the time being, she takes only girls, because she realizes that she, a woman alone, could not cope with rambunctious boys; but she hopes that in seven or eight years male dancers, too, will be found, and then she will be in a position to come forward as a new ballet mistress. In this connection she made the following remark concerning male dancers in her awkward French: *"Si un homme pouvait danser bien, cet homme serait un dieu!"* [Any man who could dance well would be a god!][36]

The only man on Isadora's mind as she waited to leave St. Petersburg was Craig. "I think that as an inspiration for a Dancer *you* are not a Success," she wrote. "You give me only one inspiration and that is to run away from all Publics and the like and rush to you — & then *die* or what ever."[37] She began sending him telegrams. SOON SATURDAY NIGHT, she cabled. And the next day: TOMORROW LOVE.[38] She left Russia on December 30 and wrote to Craig when she finally crossed the German border:

> Darling — This darned old train is 3 hours 3 centuries 3 eternities late late late — We will arrive about ten and the secretary & the maid will *yank* me up to Hardenberg Strasse — but I will slip away as soon as I can & come to No. 11. . . . Darling I've come back Back Back from the Land of Snow & Ice — I think I discovered the North Pole. . . . The only thing that has kept me . . . half alive is your sweet picture — and now I will see you you You — Imagine since yesterday Early morning in this train — Years & centuries *coming to you.*[39]

Their reunion was predictably unbridled; after that, Isadora needed to mollify her family. On the back of a photograph taken of them in Berlin before she went to Russia, Craig had penciled the words "Two villains," an obvious reference to the Duncans' wrath. Isadora was already supporting him, as his letters to England make clear. "I'm not making a penny but living like a Duke," Craig confessed. And again, when he went with Isadora to Russia in February: "As you may guess, I am not paying my own hotel bills & haven't a sou in the world — but am damned if I'll starve or sit on a stool & wait for things."[40]

For the next two years, Isadora would pay not just for Craig and his dreams for the theater but for her mother and aunt, her brother Augustin (whom she had recently named as her business manager), her sister, her household staff, the musicians and conductors who accompanied her on tour, and the whole expense of her new school at Grunewald, where she would employ professors, governesses, cooks, maids, and instructors in various fields. For better or worse, she was the Duncans' sole source of income, and some hostility to Craig might be assumed for that reason. "We eat about 1:30 — don't be late,"[41] Isadora wrote; she introduced him only slowly to the clan. They never lived together — that is, Isadora kept her address. She had "a strong sense of Duty," said Craig. "She loved the family very much. Released . . . and off we went whenever we could. But she always did as most of us do, took the easiest way and the most pleasant."[42]

Apart from Isadora's mother, Craig identified Elizabeth as his main adversary in the Duncan household, calling her "une 'être dangereuse' de Balzac. Anyhow an enemy by intention or through folly."[43] At Isadora's new school, Elizabeth would be director and chief of operations: she was a strong and unavoidable presence in Isadora's life. Craig thought she was jealous of Isadora, as a dancer and a woman. Isadora answered that "Elizabeth had her own ideas, but she did not make them public."[44] She only disliked Craig and feared, for good reason or otherwise, that he would leave Isadora in the dust.

Worst for Isadora was the unhappiness of Mrs. Duncan, whose "temper became most uneven" as her daughter's successes mounted. "For the first time since our voyage abroad, she began to express a longing for America," Isadora wrote, "and said how much better everything was there — the food, and so forth. . . . I think that this turning of her character was probably due to the habitual state of virtue in which my mother had lived, for so many years devoting herself only to her children . . . sentimental and virtuous, she could only suffer and weep."[45] Nor were Mrs. Duncan's the only humors in the house. Augustin's marriage to Sarah Whiteford was falling apart. Soon Raymond would return to Paris with his wife, Penelope, having "gone completely Greek," according to Gertrude Stein, who knew the Duncans from Oakland and whose apartment on rue de Fleurus wasn't far from Raymond's new atelier. From Athens, Raymond had continued to send Isadora bills for work on Agamemnon's palace at Kopanos — "and all the time my Brother my wise little Brother boy is singing to his goats on the hill side while his little Greek girl plays on the flute," Isadora grumbled.[46] According to Stein, she "lost interest in him, she found the girl too modern a Greek. At any rate Raymond was at this time without any money at all and his wife was enceinte."[47] In November 1905 Raymond and Penelope's child was born, a son they named Menalkas, "after the shepherd boy in Theocritus,"[48] and the financial pressure on Isadora grew accordingly.

Isadora was back in Berlin for less than a week before she started touring again. "Her physical and mental stamina were astonishing," Karl Federn remembered. "She could practice the whole day, dance for two hours at night on the stage, go directly from the theatre to the train station, take a train to St. Petersburg, and, while her secretary, accompanist, and chambermaid went directly to bed on arrival, appear again in the theatre and carry on merrily till morning at a champagne supper."[49] On January 5 she was in Cologne with Craig, where they wrote bantering dialogue on stationery from the Dom Hotel. "I've drunk enough here God knows," said Isadora.

"But God will never tell," said Craig.[50] They had fun with the dialogue form, which Craig would use to effect that year in his first published book, *The Art of the Theatre,* the pioneering treatise that secured his reputation as a theater revolutionary and, at the same time, turned him toward writing when he wasn't making pictures and designs.[51] "This book seems to me to contain . . . the bomb for an immense explosion of all things which exist as we know them in the theatre," Isadora wrote later, while Craig looked over her shoulder. "An upheaval so general and so deadly . . . it presents to our mind's eye the entire theatres of the world suddenly heaved sky high in the air, [with] pieces of the buildings, shreds of their scenes, tatters of their costumes . . . yea heads of their actors shooting through the air in one wild, chaotic bang!"[52] The playful, one-upping tone of their conversation is captured in another document, dated January 15, which they wrote in the train from Berlin to Dresden. Craig's remarks are clever and offhanded, Isadora's heartfelt and brash, in keeping with what Craig called her "American 'push.'" He wrote: "We both spoke the same language — hers the American brand, mine the English. . . . The Star Spangles were all over her, & her speech was modelled on Daniel Webster."[53] In these early days, he made no secret of his infatuation.

"My dear lad," Craig wrote to Martin Shaw in England, "artist or not — this is a marvelous being — beauty — nature & *brain.* I don't like brainy women but brains, intelligence, is a rare and lovely thing. If you could see *one* dance you would understand how wonderful it is. . . . I have seldom been so moved by anything. It's a great, a rare gift brought to perfection by 18 years of persistent labor — & we may all agree to worship such things."[54] In Hamburg, where they spent the last week of January 1905, they complained about the bed — "too big," said Isadora — and auditioned dozens of young girls for the new Duncan school. "Here she invited people to bring their girl children and she would make dancers of them," Craig wrote. "She made speeches about this at the end of her performances — told them where to bring the children — to the Hamburger Hof [Hotel]: between eleven and twelve."[55]

The Duncan school had opened officially on December 1, but none of the pupils, with the exception of Isadora's six-year-old niece, Temple, would arrive before the middle of January. Whether her recent visit to the torture chambers of Russian ballet persuaded her to hurry or whether the time was simply right for her to act, she got the school running within a month of her return from Russia.[56] An article published in newspapers across Germany described the gabled, Swiss-style villa where the children would live:

> The building is a three-story structure with a large basement and top floor. All the rooms are spacious and airy and the many windows allow free access of sunlight and fresh air. On the walls in every room are representations of antique art, and in the dormitories hang Donatello's terra cottas depicting children at play as well as Della Robbia's colorful Madonnas. There are large copies of dancing figures on friezes in the schoolroom, and on a long shelf in the music room is a lovely collection of Tanagra figurines. All these works of art are supposed to give the children a sense and appreciation of beauty, which in turn will influence their dancing, according to Miss Duncan. . . .
>
> This free, non-profit dance school, founded by Isadora Duncan and entirely supported by her financially, is not a philanthropic institution in the ordinary sense but an enterprise dedicated to the promotion of health and beauty in mankind. Both physically and spiritually the children will here receive an education providing them with the highest intelligence in the healthiest body.[57]

From the stage, nightly after her performances, Isadora conducted her search. "I am going to give these beings a finer life," she told her audiences, "a higher education, so that later in their turn they can spread joy and beauty about them like a glow over this sad earth."[58] In Dresden, where she danced three times that January, she went hunting for girls in her Greek attire and returned to Berlin with three of them: Marta, a seven-year-old, whose surname is lost; Elisabeth Milker —

Lisa — also seven; and Theresa Kruger, nearly ten and already stage-struck, the youngest child of a Prussian cavalry officer, who had died when she was a baby. That winter Theresa appeared with her sister in a Christmas pantomime, *The Sea King's Daughter.* "I was dancing the part of the Pearl," she remembered, "trying to outshine the Coral, the Shell, and the Phosphorescent Fish," when Isadora, "like a white angel," took her seat in the proscenium loge. Theresa recalled:

> I wore a headband with a large pearl in the center, that shook as I turned my head from side to side — which I was supposed to do slowly. As I did this, for some reason, I became amused in a child-like way, and began to move my head faster — in a sharp, one-two count — which seemed to me to be more appropriate for the music. Carried away with the motion, I found myself almost under the proscenium loge, near the "white angel," who was smiling so sweetly at me. I forgot my dance completely! All I could do was stand there and shake first one foot and then the other. . . .
>
> I did this repeatedly, because I was so enthralled by the apparition in the box. My sister came over and whispered, "If you do that again, the dance master will not have us in his group — never mind who is in the box!" "But," I said, "if she is not an angel, then she is Penelope" — whose statue my sister and I had often seen in the royal gardens of the [Dresden] museum.

The next morning, unannounced, Isadora turned up at the Krugers' door, still dressed in her Greek robes. "Possibly not since Christ had anyone been seen walking around in such clothes," said Theresa; "and here it was the dead of winter, with five feet of snow on the ground." Isadora came straight to the point, telling Frau Kruger that she wanted Theresa for her school and asking them all to her next performance. "The huge audience in the theatre was spellbound," Theresa wrote, "and my mother, realizing the beauty of it, said to me, 'My dear child, do you want to learn to dance like that?' When I said, softly, 'Yes,' she replied, 'It means you will have to leave us.'" Two days later Theresa did, arriving with the other girls at the Hotel Bellevue in Dresden: "Gordon Craig opened the door and, seeing us, said, 'Isadora, your children are here!'"[59]

By the end of April 1905, Isadora had collected eighteen pupils, ranging in age from four to twelve. Most were German girls, but two were from Brussels, one from Warsaw, and a fourth, Anna Denzler, had been born in Zurich and carried Swiss citizenship. Anna remembered turning up at her audition in Berlin "looking like a disaster . . . disheveled and sweaty" from her long train ride; all her life, she believed she was chosen only on the strength of her "winning smile."[60] It wasn't dancing skill Isadora looked for in her pupils — just the opposite. She wanted minds and raw material, untrained bodies. Only one of the girls, Susanna, had had any serious ballet training, in Hamburg. She became the bully of the school.[61]

"Do you think that by sending your girl to a ballet school you will help her to dance?" Craig wrote. "You won't — you will hinder her. What must she do, then? Why, what Isadora did — learn what it is to move: to step, to walk, to run; few people can do these things. First the thought — then the head — then the hands and feet a little — just move, and *look around, watch all which moves.*"[62] In Hamburg six-year-old Irma Erich-Grimme was practically dragged to an audition with Isadora by her overworked mother, the widow of a grocer, who had already tried to place her in drama school, without success. They were late getting to the hotel and almost turned away. Only after Irma's mother pleaded for admittance were they ushered into Isadora's suite, still filled with dozens of children and their parents. Irma wrote:

> On entering the famous dancer's room, I felt a pleasant sensation of warmth and the fragrance of numerous vases and baskets of fresh flowers. The instant she stepped forward to greet me, in bare feet and ankle-length white tunic, I had eyes only for her. With childish pleasure I noticed the white ribbon she wore in her light brown hair. I had never seen anyone so lovely and angelic-looking or anyone dressed in that way. Beside mother's long black dress made in the Victorian fashion, Isadora's simple attire gave her the appearance of a creature from another planet. I fell completely under the charm of her sweet smile when she bent down to take my hand while I curtsied.
>
> In a soft voice, speaking in halting German, she told mother that the tryout was over. Mother once again made her excuses, and Isadora must have relented, for she told her to remove my clothes quickly so she could have a look at me. Mother knelt down and promptly started to undress me, right there in front of all those people. It happened so quickly I didn't have time to be scared. In her haste to comply with Isadora's request, mother had difficulty with the many hooks and buttons that encumbered even children's clothing in those days.
>
> After she had removed the black stockings, the high-buttoned shoes, and the last petticoat, I stood exposed in a cotton camisole and a pair of lace-edged underpants, from which dangled long black garters. I felt terribly ashamed when, thus accoutered, I was made to

stand alone in the center of the room. But not for long. The lovely vision in the Greek tunic returned and asked my name.

"Come and stand here in front of me, Irma, and do exactly as I do."

The soft strains of Schumann's *Träumerei* came floating to my ears as Isadora Duncan slowly began to raise her bare arms to the music. She watched me closely as I imitated her gesture and then, after a while, she seemed no longer to pay attention to me. A faraway look had come into her eyes as, lost in the music, she raised her beautiful arms and with a swaying motion of her body moved them from side to side like the branches of a tree put in motion by the wind. . . .

A nod to the musician at the upright piano, and the tempo changed to a lighter rhythm, an allegretto. She swiftly changed the mood and darted away, skipping gracefully around the room. All eyes, I was fascinated watching her circle about me like a bird. She reminded me of the sea gulls I had often observed skimming across the big lake directly in front of the hotel. Uncertain what to do next, I remained where I was. Still dancing, she beckoned to me and called out gaily, "Follow me! Follow me!"

Her radiant personality was contagious. I lost my self-consciousness and bravely skipped after her, trying my best to do exactly as she did. I undulated my little arms in emulation of her for all I was worth. But, in that absurd déshabille with the long black garters flapping against my legs at every step, I must have looked comical. I heard her laugh when she stopped abruptly and said, "That is enough. Go and put on your things."[63]

Crestfallen, Irma dressed while Isadora walked in a circle among the waiting children: "I shall take you and you, and you and you. . . ." Irma and her mother were already leaving when Isadora bent down to talk to Craig, who sat sketching the proceedings. "Take her," he said quietly, pointing to Irma. "She has the eyes."

"And that is how I became Isadora Duncan's pupil," Irma wrote. "Was it hazard or destiny — who can tell?"[64] Five girls from Hamburg left with Isadora for Berlin the next morning, already decked out in tunic, sandals, and "a little hooded woolen cape," as Irma remembered. "I distinctly recall the sense of freedom I experienced in those light and simple clothes, which were the distinctive Duncan uniform and which would henceforth set us apart from other people." In Berlin, they joined Isadora in a carriage for the drive to Grunewald. "To my childish imagination she represented the legendary Fairy Queen in her coach," said Irma, "carrying me and my companions off to her enchanted castle in the forest."

The wonder continued when they arrived at the villa. "Never was I so surprised as when the door opened and there right in front of me stood the seminude statue of a Greek Amazon on the pedestal, her head nearly touching the ceiling!" Irma recalled. "We all gaped with astonishment. When I recovered from my initial shock, I turned to look for an explanation from the beautiful lady who had brought us here. But the Fairy Queen had vanished — coach and all." At that moment, Elizabeth came in. Irma wrote:

> Over to one side some sliding doors opened a crack, and out peered a small monkey-like face, brown and wrinkled. This face stared at us for a minute; then the doors opened wider, and a small woman stepped out. Outlandishly attired in a long red Chinese coat embroidered all over with flowers and parrots, this strange apparition mysteriously approached, limping slightly. She slowly circled around the little group, huddled close together for protection. She kept her hands hidden Chinese-fashion in her voluminous sleeves.
>
> We did not know what to make of it. Who was this?
>
> Without a kind word of greeting to the pathetic little group in her house, this odd creature poked her funny face into each one of our faces for a silent scrutiny and then disappeared as mysteriously as she had come, closing the sliding doors behind her.
>
> I suddenly longed for the comforting arms of my mother. The others must have had similar reactions, for Erika — the youngest, a mere tyke of four — suddenly burst into loud, heartrending wails. We all were about to join her when, luckily, two nursemaids appeared.
>
> "Ah! here they are, our little Hamburgers!" they exclaimed. With pleasant grins lighting up their young faces, they said, "Welcome to the Duncan School!" and in a cheerful, lively manner hustled us off.

That night, having been given a number and a bed, Irma felt lonely and afraid: "All the fresh impressions and strange sights that had crowded these last three days tumbled through my mind. The pine-scented air of the nearby forest filled the room with fragrance. Through the open window I could hear the distant rumble of the *Rundbahn* passing by." She missed her mother and, having seen Elizabeth, she missed Isadora.

"I began to fear I would never see her again," wrote Irma, "when I noticed a shadowy vision tiptoeing silently from bed to bed, bending over each child. At last she reached me. It was the Fairy Queen! She placed a cookie between my lips and kissed me. 'Good night, darling, sleep well,' she murmured, and was gone."[65]

10

Their Own Sweet Will

The Isadora Duncan School of Dance was housed in a yellow stucco villa on Trabenerstrasse in Grunewald — at the time, still part of the ancient forest that ringed Berlin to the south. Since the 1880s, when the first of its suburban mansions were built, Grunewald had been an art colony and stamping-ground for the rich and nature-conscious, savored for its primordial atmosphere and whimsical, gingerbread train station, designed by Karl Cornelius to evoke the tales of the Brothers Grimm. Isadora chose the site for both its secluded character and the proximity of like minds: Engelbert Humperdinck, composer of the children's operas *Hänsel und Gretel* and *Königskinder,* also lived on Trabenerstrasse and urged her to buy the house next door to his. The new building, number sixteen, "was just passing from the workmen's hands" when Isadora snapped it up, unfurnished, and "set about to make of our villa a real children's Paradise."[1]

From the start, the education of children through the medium of dance had been central to Isadora's mission. As early as 1898, she had told the *New York Herald:* "In the practicing of dancing, or its exercise, the child is also obtaining the foundation of all other studies. The child is obtaining a knowledge of itself."[2] That the self was worth knowing, and that knowledge would lead children to natural expression, was Isadora's first and inflexible principle; in essays and interviews, she also made plain that her purpose was not to train dancers for the stage. "What I want is a *school of life*," she wrote, "for man's greatest riches are in his soul, his imagination. . . . When asked for the pedagogic program of my school, I reply: 'Let us first teach little children to breathe, to vibrate, to feel, and to become one with the general harmony and movement of nature. Let us first produce a beautiful human being, a dancing child.'"[3]

The Duncan school, named for Isadora but conceived as a family enterprise, with Elizabeth in charge, predated Maria Montessori's "child-directed" learning centers by nearly three years. In Germany anxiety about public education had risen to high pitch in the nineteenth century, as democratic reformers, visionaries, and mystics, under the general influence of Rousseau and Kant, battled with a centralized, Prussian state system of instruction that dated back to Frederick the Great. All over Europe, children were emerging from the unseen, unheard corners of the Victorian age, suddenly imagined as something other than workers, property, or drains on society. Kant, Rousseau, Darwin, Spencer, Whitman, Nietzsche, Robert Ingersoll, and Friedrich Froebel, founder of the German kindergarten movement, all influenced Isadora's thinking about childhood education, a great, utopian soufflé, combining academics with "nature awareness," music, dance, gymnastics, and a dose of *Peter Pan* — first published in England that same year, 1904.[4]

Having secured a villa, Isadora and Elizabeth next bought "forty little beds, each covered with white muslin curtains, drawn back with blue ribbons." Blue and white became the colors of the school, reflected in everything from the children's uniforms and dancing costumes to the bas-reliefs with which the Duncans decorated the halls and dormitories. Everywhere in the house, the image of happy children looked down on the students, "paintings of children dancing on Greek vases, tiny figures from Tanagra and Bœtia, the group of Donatello's dancing children . . . and the dancing children of Gainsborough."[5] It wasn't just sentiment that dictated the style; the profusion of cherubs and nymphs served a specific educational purpose. Isadora wrote:

> All these figures have a certain fraternity in the naïve grace of their
> form and their movements, as if the children of all ages met each other
> and joined their hands across the centuries, and the real children of
> my school, moving and dancing in the midst of these forms, would
> surely grow to resemble them, to reflect unconsciously, in their move-

ments and their faces, a little of the joy and the same childlike grace. It would be the first step toward their becoming beautiful, the first step toward the new art of the dance.

I also placed in my school the figures of young girls dancing, running, jumping . . . exquisite images in terra cotta, with flying veils and flowing garments. . . . They represented the future ideal to attain, and the pupils of my school, learning to feel an intimate love for these forms, would grow each day to resemble them, and would become each day a little more imbued with the secret of this harmony.[6]

For the students, life with the Duncans was unlike anything they had known.[7] With only a few exceptions, the girls came from "disadvantaged" backgrounds, where, as in Isadora's case, the fathers were absent or deceased and the mothers were the breadwinners. The children's impoverished condition undoubtedly made it easier for Isadora to win their hearts and minds — and those of their families — from the first day. Irma could hardly believe her eyes when she saw the canopied bed she would sleep in at Grunewald — a *Himmelbett,* associated in her mind "always with children of the rich."[8] Early on, the Duncans rejected the idea of accepting day students, basing their judgment on Rousseau's theory that the student must live with his tutor at all times, free from outside influence and "preferably in a pastoral place." Their goal was to make the children fit and aware, even before they learned to dance.

Every morning before breakfast, the girls exercised at a ballet barre, working primarily on their elevation. Twice weekly, they received instruction from a Swedish gymnastics teacher, performing handstands, somersaults, push-ups, and a variety of leaps and kicks to teach them balance, coordination, and endurance. Dance was only one of the subjects taught, and then just twice a week, on Wednesdays and Saturdays, from four to six in the afternoon. There were four hours of general schoolwork in the morning, provided by state-certified teachers. The children learned history, literature, mathematics, natural science, drawing, singing, languages, and music. Two governesses, Fräulein Lippach and Fräulein Konegen, supervised their every activity, from the moment they rose at 6:30 A.M. till they went to bed at night, after a meal of bread and milk, "carrots or Brussels sprouts, beans, and cold cooked cabbage." The girls were "supposed to be vegetarians," according to Isabelle Branche, a student from Brussels: "We had meat only once a week."[9] They were taught to sew and to knit and were armed with sketchbooks when they went outdoors.

"Few of us had any knowledge of drawing or any ability," Theresa Kruger said. "Then it seemed a joke. Now I understand that sketching was just a ruse to get us to concentrate on natural movement. Trees and grasses bending in the wind carry a message for every dancer. If she is observant, and even if she isn't, the rhythm and pulse of nature are bound to affect her"[10] — as clean a summation of Isadora's educational theory as any she offered herself. She was "no teacher in the ordinary sense," Theresa advised. "Isadora taught by inspiring. She danced or indicated by a gesture. She believed that art should be caught on the wings of genius. . . . The spark within you must turn into flame."[11] Their lessons and exercises were all designed to prepare the girls for the moment of revelation. "The body must then be forgotten," Isadora said. "Each one, while forming part of a whole . . . will preserve a creative individuality. And all the parts together will compose a unified harmony that will bring a new birth to the world: will make live again the flaming beauty of the dramatic Chorus, the Chorus of tragedy, the eternal hymn of the struggle between man and Destiny."[12]

In the three years of its existence at Grunewald, the Duncan school never had more than twenty students in residence, despite Isadora's optimistic purchase of forty beds and her dream of training "thousands of young dancing maidens." Of the original pupils, six would emerge as stars: Anna, Theresa, Irma, Lisa, Gretel, and Erika. They were the future "Isadorables," so named in 1909 by French poet Fernand Divoire. A few of the girls left the school within weeks, to be replaced by new recruits, whom Isadora picked up on the road. Visits from parents and families were restricted, in order to keep the girls' minds focused entirely on their new environment; for infractions or laziness, they were denied their twice-weekly dancing lesson. Most of them later blamed Elizabeth for their sufferings as children, believing that if Isadora had supervised daily operations at the school, all would have been light, love, and joy. But Isadora was away on tour most of the time, dancing to support her dependents and leaving the girls, as they saw it, at Elizabeth's mercy. They were all afraid of her, including her niece, Temple, whose kinship with Isadora earned her a special admiration in the class.

"Elizabeth was very different [from Isadora]," Anna confirmed. "Very strict and cold, disciplined. Whenever we heard her coming, we ran away. . . . She was a strange individual. Isadora was just the opposite, very outgoing. . . . I remember she often said, 'Don't grow up —

like Peter Pan, you must not grow up!'"[13] Elizabeth's lameness kept her from a dancing career but not from teaching the girls the same dances she had taught Isadora as a child — "polkas, mazurkas, gavottes, the Duncan waltz with its upward lilt."[14] As a teacher, she was everything that Isadora wasn't: meticulous, organized, systematic, and even more convinced, if possible, that dance should be a part of life. The children called her "Tante Miss" — Auntie Miss — having assumed, when they were first introduced to "Miss Duncan," that *Miss* was Elizabeth's given name. Isadora would have none of it. "Now that you are my pupils," she told the girls, "you may call me Isadora, or darling Isadora, but never, never call me Auntie!"[15] Elizabeth had developed what can only be called a Teutonic streak.

"It seems strange that a woman suffering from a defect, which made one leg shorter than the other, should have been put in charge of our basic dance instruction," Irma wrote. "As we grew up, we learned to accept with equanimity Isadora's unpredictable nature. But for a long time I puzzled, trying to figure out how Isadora expected us to learn to dance from her lame sister."[16] During her lessons, Elizabeth rarely rose to demonstrate. "She sat on a Greek bench" and tapped out her instructions with a stick, using her hands to explain the more intricate patterns and not concealing her disappointment when the girls fell short of the mark.

"Touch the hills!" Elizabeth cried. "Reach out your fingers until you can touch the hills. . . . Up! Up! Don't stay down on the *ground* when you can go so *high! UP!*" She had "a sharp tongue and she never spared it," according to Mabel Dodge, the American socialite and salon hostess who became one of Elizabeth's closest friends. "With a dry giggle she pronounced sarcastic judgments on awkward poses or heavy treads. No one *dared* to be clumsy anywhere near Elizabeth. It was a crime."[17] Irma reported bitterly that in all the time they spent with her, Elizabeth never once "offered an endearment or a gentle pat on the cheek to any of her pupils."[18] Anna, however, as many did, thought that Irma judged Elizabeth unfairly: "We lived like princesses, don't forget. . . . Although Elizabeth did not have the same human warmth and affection for us, she nevertheless did have a very deep understanding and appreciation of her sister's art. And though she hardly ever showed us a step, she did draw out of us little children the artistic quality needed to perform Isadora's abstract art of the dance."[19]

It was the image of Isadora, the promise of her company and guidance, that sustained the girls at Grunewald through the long weeks and months under Elizabeth's tutelage. Naturally enough, for children removed abruptly from their homes and plunged into a new way of life, a deep, mystical bond formed between them and the woman they regarded as "a goddess" — a bond made stronger, not weaker, by Isadora's frequent absences from the school. The children worshiped Isadora. "She was love personified," Anna said. Theresa called her "my 'angel in white.' . . . I always had the impression that she had been sent to me from on high. When she greeted us with her quiet musical voice, she instantly gave us the effect of having been dipped in warm radiant sunshine."[20] For the girls, one dance lesson with Isadora was worth twenty with Elizabeth, nor did Elizabeth misinterpret their enthusiasm. "If these girls are to become artists," she later declared, "there is only one person who can do it, and that is my sister. If they are to become dancers, only Isadora can accomplish that."[21]

"Unfortunately," wrote Irma, Isadora "turned out to be a very impatient teacher. Her method consisted of demonstrating the sequence of a dance perfectly executed by herself. Then, without demonstrating it step by step, she expected her pupils to understand immediately and repeat it."[22] Theresa agreed: "She had no method, no theory, no pedantic arrangements of steps, and not the slightest pedagogical idea."[23] Isadora taught the children their first words of English by reading aloud from Keats: " 'Beauty is Truth, Truth Beauty, — that is all / Ye know on earth, and all ye need to know.' That is the motto of our school, and I want each and every one to learn these words by heart."[24]

Germans quickly became fascinated with the lives of the *Duncan-Kinder* (or *Duncaninchen,* as they were also called: Duncan rabbits). The girls felt themselves part of a great experiment and learned quickly that living with genius carries a price. Irma remembered "shocked expressions among the local population, especially women," when they went for walks, clad only in their tunics, capes, and sandals: "Pitying exclamations like, 'Oh, you poor, poor, little children! Why, you must be freezing to death with so little on!' . . . Approaching our innocent governess with threatening gestures and looks, they shouted after her, 'It's cruelty, that's what it is! We ought to get the police after you. Cruel! Cruel! Cruel!' " Sometimes the girls were pelted with stones, "like the Christian martyrs of old," while boys of the neighborhood preferred to attack them with dung from the street. "We often panicked," Irma confessed, "despite heroic efforts on the part of our chaperones to fend off these wild hordes of insult-screaming juveniles. . . . But a novel idea was on the march and nothing could stop its progress."[25]

In June 1905, encouraged by the progress of the children, Isadora embarked on a subscription drive to raise money for an addition to the school, which she hoped to build on an empty lot nearby in anticipation of taking twenty-five more students — "and so also that in five or six years time the School may become a Self supporting Institution," as she wrote to King Ferdinand of Bulgaria, in an appeal for support. Isadora and the king had met at Bayreuth. "This is a difficult thing for me to do alone," she said. "Capital and all costs I have given from money made solely from my dancing Self. The Building I am paying for in installments — food clothes music etc. cost me more than 2000 marks a month."[26] Later, a "Society for the Support and Maintenance of the Dance School of Isadora Duncan," weighted with illustrious names, was formed under Elizabeth's guidance. Money came from artists, sculptors, musicians, and prominent women of Berlin, among them Giulietta Mendelssohn, of the banking family, Princess Heinrich VII of Reuss, Victoria of Saxe-Meiningen, and some ladies-in-waiting to Empress Augusta. But even this was "not enough," and for that reason, on July 20, 1905, Isadora allowed the girls to perform in public for the first time, unbilled, in a benefit concert to aid the school at Kroll's Opera House in Berlin.

"Isadora gave us new silk tunics in pastel shades of blue, pink, and yellow to wear for the occasion," Irma wrote, "making us discard the cheesecloth ones entirely. Also we had small wreaths of rosebuds for our hair. . . . The excitement of that moment can never be repeated."[27] Gordon Craig sat in the audience and pronounced the afternoon "a wild success," remembering how Isadora, "after dancing her own dances, called her little pupils to come with her and please the public with their little leapings and runnings. As they did — and with her leading them the whole troupe became irresistibly lovely."[28] German critics were fulsome in their praise as, over the next several years, the girls began to perform regularly around the country. Max Osborn saw them at the end of October when they danced at the Theater des Westens in Berlin:

> When the curtain went up, a winning little child with her dark hair combed over her ears, a narrow fillet of gold on her head, a dainty frock of gauze over her white undergarments, and bare legs and feet,

which tripped lightly and daintily over the carpet, flitted into the room to the strains of a melody by Schumann. This was Temple Duncan, a niece of Miss Isadora Duncan. She was quickly followed by a second and a third elf-like figure, as daintily and airily clad as the first, until, gradually, the whole stage was filled with a score of similar figures. They flitted past and played a game of touch like iridescent butterflies with variegated wings; they curtseyed and bowed — then leaped and danced like sprites . . . ran hither and thither, flinging about their slender little legs under their short-skirted frocks. . . . They mirrored the notes of the music by unstudied movements full of the most delightful rhythm, making one feel as though every trill and harmony had turned into flesh and blood. . . .

For the most part all the [dances] were carried out with marvelous accuracy, as though learned by rote, but often the severity of the figures relaxed and the little ones skipped about at their own sweet will. This had a special charm and even a special interest of its own, for it showed clearly how well they had learned to move. Indeed, it must be admitted that there was a general absence of anything like stiltedness or affectation. The whole thing was like some voluntary game played by gay and frolicsome children, but directed by someone who could enter lovingly into a child's idiosyncrasies and capacity for expression.[29]

In most German cities, the response was the same: warm reviews for the children and appreciation, if not endorsement, of Isadora's ideas. How much of the school's initial success derived from her fame is a moot question. In Berlin, after the girls' debut, the *Tägliche Rundschau* pronounced it "lucky" that education in Germany had progressed so far "that we can remain serious when an American, who can't even speak German, declares herself capable of giving German children a proper education."[30] From that point of view, Elizabeth was always better suited to it. A Berlin reporter, visiting the school the following year, remarked that "any possible traces of skepticism or desire to scoff" were dispelled by the girls' dancing: "It matters not whether these little Duncan children are marching solemnly round after the manner of the antique chorus, or are hopping merrily in pantomimic games — their every movement seems to be inspired by the very Spirit of Music."[31] Between 1905 and 1909, when Isadora moved permanently to Paris, the girls would perform more than seventy times, with and without her, in Germany, Holland, Switzerland, Russia, Finland, England, and France. "To have stood on the same stage with Her," Anna declared, "performing Her dances and bringing joy and solace to so many . . . to have had the wonderful and privileged experience of a life of culture and adventure with Her . . . this wonderful woman and creative artist . . . our *Maestra*."[32] Theresa, who suffered badly at first from the separation from her family, "had only one desire" after a year with Isadora: "To become a great artist. . . . There was no alternative."[33] And Irma described the thrill they all felt when they heard the sound of applause at Kroll's, descending on them

> with the suddenness of a thunderclap. . . . Isadora quickly whispered to us to dance toward her, one by one, from the opposite corner of the stage. We did so, and as each child skipped up she handed her a pink rose. With the flowers in our hands, we then circled about her as she posed in the center of the stage, arms outstretched as if to embrace us all in a loving, maternal gesture. Happy, laughing children danced a rondo about her, a real '*Rosenringel Reigen*,' and in that ecstatic group was one who wished this happy dance would never, never stop.[34]

At the beginning of February 1905, Isadora returned to Russia with Craig, dancing in St. Petersburg, Moscow, and Kiev in quick succession. The second Russian journey wasn't the triumph the first had been. In the five weeks since her appearance in St. Petersburg, Isadora's work had been widely attacked in the Russian press, especially in Russian musical journals. On February 3, in Petersburg, she offered an "all-Beethoven" evening — the same program she had danced so successfully in Paris at the Trocadéro — and left the Russian musical establishment in a rage.

It bears noting that until Isadora established the precedent, the music of great composers was rarely associated with theatrical dance. In Paris, Loie Fuller had sometimes performed to the music of Chopin, but her dazzling electric floor show was so unique, so far removed from actual dancing, that it has to be regarded as an isolated construction, making no revisionist claims on music. Chopin wrote music in dance form — waltzes, mazurkas, polonaises, and so on; while many thought that Isadora "went too far," even then, by dancing to his music, a case could be made for it on purely structural grounds. This wasn't true of Beethoven — or of most of the music she employed over time. Her use of concert music as the foundation of her work — "pure" music, written only to be played and heard — was radical, offensive, and even sacrilegious to traditionalists.

Critics inveighed especially against Isadora's "perverted use" of

Beethoven's Seventh Symphony, a monumental work she explored
and developed for years, in full knowledge that what she was doing
was controversial and never wholly a success. That most dramatic of
Russian composers, Nikolai Rimsky-Korsakov, denounced her for
"foisting [herself] unbidden upon music . . . tacking her art onto musical compositions . . . whose authors do not at all need her company,
and never reckoned on it."[35] Rimsky-Korsakov's ouster as head of the
St. Petersburg Conservatory in 1905 was almost simultaneous with
Isadora's second trip to Russia; in 1907 he pronounced Scriabin "half-
mad" when he heard "a piano reduction of his *Poème de l'extase*" —
French music of any kind brought the composer's "long, admonitory
finger [wagging] in the air."[36] When asked what she intended to add
or convey by dancing musical works that were artistic creations in
themselves — works like the Seventh Symphony, known to audiences
the world over — Isadora answered, *"Der Geist der Musik"*[37] ("the
spirit of the music"), which she envisioned as serving the same function as the chorus in Greek tragedy. Music was the original creative
force, she argued, preexisting and independent, "the great, impersonal, eternal and divine well-spring" of *all* art: poetry, drama, painting, sculpture — and dance.[38]

"This is the highest aim and object of dancing," Isadora wrote:
"To take its legitimate place in tragedy with music and poetry, to be
the intermediary between the tragedy and the audience."[39] If her point
was better served by her interpretations of the narrative operas of
Gluck — *Orpheo* and *Iphigénie* — she also thought it applied to symphonic works.

"It's this music question," Isadora wrote to Craig the following
year. "I must settle *once* for all — antique? Early Italian? Gluck? Modern? or None?"[40] The problem would preoccupy her more and more as
her art matured. "This question of the *music* must be fixed," she wrote
again to Craig, "or it will be the complete *ruin* of me as an artist and
eventually financial also — as finances generally fall apart when art
falls in spite of all one can say to the contrary. . . . I *must have* a permanent musical director."[41]

Periodically, Isadora worked to evolve dances without music. That
it was possible, she never doubted, even if she ultimately regarded it
as a task for "the Dancer of the Future." In 1906 she told a reporter
that the perfect dance should be unaccompanied, "a self-sufficient expression," but that it should also not be shown to a paying audience,
who wanted entertainment and would fail to grasp it.[42] It would be

years before her reliance on concert music for the dance became accepted practice among ballet and modern dance companies, to the point that the dance music of Chopin, for example, thanks to Fokine and *Les Sylphides,* is now widely considered to be "ballet music." In this regard, it wasn't Isadora who convinced the Russian critics — her Beethoven program in St. Petersburg was a unique disaster.

The evening began badly with an atypically poor performance from Isadora's piano accompanist, Hermann Lafont; after the intermission, it was the orchestra, the Petersburg Philharmonic, that failed to perform up to par. The conductor, violinist Leopold Auer, made no attempt to conceal his hostility, refusing even to look at the stage and what he regarded as Isadora's "profanation" of the Seventh Symphony. Auer was criticized by other Russian musicians for agreeing to assist her at all; later he claimed that he had been led into it, without knowing what he was doing. The result was predictable. "Inspiration failed her," Shebuyev wrote, "and her dancing lost its brilliance, faded, wilted."[43]

It would be interesting to have Isadora's own comment on what was plainly an act of sabotage, but she wrote nothing about it. She simply decided not to include the Beethoven program when she got to Moscow. Walking through Red Square on February 17, Craig saw the assassination of Grand Duke Sergei Alexandrovitch, uncle of the tsar and the much-hated governor of the city. "Dook Sergie," said Craig, was blown to pieces by a terrorist's bomb as he left the Kremlin in his carriage: "I only escaped being bombed [myself] because no one had enough courage to throw at such a guy."[44] The rest of Isadora's concerts were canceled owing to public mourning. Altogether, she was glad to leave Russia. A "provincial reaction" had greeted the sight of her "scanty garments" in Moscow; at one of her concerts, booing was heard. She stopped the performance. "This is impolite and unkind," she called from the stage. "This offends me as a woman. Those who do not like it may leave."[45]

Among Russian artists and the avant-garde, Isadora remained a revelation — part dancer, part reformer, "the symbol of the new, young revolutionary Russia," as Andrei Bely wrote. Konstantin Stanislavsky, director of the Moscow Art Theatre, saw her in Moscow and reported that the audience simply hadn't known what to make of her. Stanislavsky described Isadora's first night in his autobiography, *My Life in Art:*

> I appeared at Isadora Duncan's concert by accident, having heard
> nothing about her until that time, and having read none of the adver-

tisements that heralded her coming to Moscow. Therefore I was very much surprised that in the rather small audience that came to see her there was a tremendous percentage of artists and sculptors with [Russian railway magnate and arts patron Savva] Mamontov at their head, many artists of the ballet, and many first-nighters and lovers of the unusual in the theatre. . . . Unaccustomed to see an almost nude body on the stage, I could hardly notice or understand the art of the dancer. The first number was met with tepid applause and timid attempts at whistling. But after a few of the succeeding numbers, one of which was especially persuasive, I could no longer remain indifferent to the protests of the general public and began to applaud demonstratively.

When the intermission came, I, a newly baptized disciple of the great artist, ran to the footlights to applaud. To my joy I found myself side by side with Mamontov, who was doing exactly what I was doing, and near Mamontov were a famous artist, a sculptor, and a writer. When the general run of the audience saw that among those who applauded were well known Moscow artists and actors, there was a great deal of confusion. The hissing stopped, and when the public saw that it could applaud, the applause became general, and was followed by curtain calls, and at the end of the performance by an ovation.

Stanislavsky didn't meet Isadora on her first trip to Moscow. "From then on," however, he "never missed a single one of the Duncan concerts." When she returned to Russia three years later, they became friends. Isadora introduced Stanislavsky to Craig and helped make possible their production of *Hamlet* at the Moscow Art Theatre in 1912. "He belongs not only to his country," she remarked of Craig, "but to the whole world, and he must live where his genius has the best chance to display itself."[46]

Returned from Russia, Isadora immediately embarked on another tour of German cities. At the end of February, she was in Frankfurt. "Pillow soaked with tears," she wrote to Craig — "no sleep. Why aren't you here? Great Big Beds — 2 of them — Hélas! — Poor little me — *alone*." She was traveling with her maid, Anna, and thinking about Craig the whole time.

"Anna is rather awed by my general gloomy mien," Isadora wrote, "& trembles with fear at my frown. She says *es war viel netter wenn Herr Craig war mit* [It was much nicer when Mr. Craig was with us] — *Netter* — My Gods I should think it *war netter*."[47] On the twenty-fifth she could no longer bear their separation: "It just struck me as a Blooming Farce your not being here & I sent a telegram asking you to come. I wonder if you Will?"[48]

Craig answered from Berlin with more than a touch of impatience: "Of course it's a blooming farce. . . . How do I know whether or not I will come? I've sworn to go & work but swears are no use where you are. . . . Come quick back and work with me. How else shall we — can we — be together — and even *then* how is it possible."[49] Already, he relied on Isadora for everything — money, contacts, inspiration — as earlier he had relied on his mother and on every woman with whom he formed any lasting attachment. "I make no vows," Craig warned, in a line Isadora could easily have taken to refer to marriage and not to the love that consumed her. Privately, Craig played a deceptive game, excusable only by the fact that he plainly didn't know his own mind. He wrote in *Book Topsy*:

> In the first days I used to laugh gaily whenever she grew deadly serious about "mein lieber mann" & "Hochzeit" & all the rest of it for I used to say to her, "we are *not serious*" "we cannot be *serious*" — & she would take up the refrain "no, not serious" & then her arms round my neck & mine round her we would kiss lightly or youthfully — never once can I recall her teeth meeting mine — or the tip of her tongue — never once — she kissed as much with the eyes as with the lips.
>
> "no, no" — week after week, "not serious, Topsy," "It can't last Topsy — love never lasts does it Topsy —" & then she would be apt to turn the talk or take a rather offended tone — She could not admit then that love never lasts & could she have really seen into my heart & head she would have seen there the same refusal to believe that our love could die. *Only I had already begun to provide for the future catastrophe so that when it came up I should be able to stand up to it.* This she did not know — how could she.[50]

For Isadora, unaware of Craig's thoughts, their affair led to an unfamiliar confusion about what it meant to be an artist and a woman. She took her copy of Whitman on the road, but "Walt" made her "feel like a tissue-paper fool."[51] Not long after, she was reading Nietzsche on the train: "I feel such extraordinary convolutions going on — one moment I feel I could live on bread & water on the highest mountain top & *think*, and the next as if I'd like to bask all my days in a valley with flowers & *kiss* — & the changes come so quick & unexpected that I feel a bit rattled. Battled — rather say."[52] By the time she got to Göttingen, Isadora had decided that "Nietzsche is [not] the thing for Mother's child to read":

O you you you — I am slipping away from myself and becoming nothing but a longing and reflection, and I tried to tell you the other day my *work* was the principle thing. *Work* — I haven't a thought or feeling left for it — that's the truth — it's this Infernal feminine Coming out at all places.

And yet — how far I am from wishing to be a Man! — but O how happy must the woman be who doesn't know what this tearing to pieces element means.

Her closing was less urgent than usual. "Come if you can," she wrote.[53] Frequently she descended to begging, pleading, baby talk ("I feel dreful," "Topsy me comes if you telegraphs"), and "Hexry" — *Hexerei* — the German word for witchcraft: "Teddy Come along — I'm trying to Hexry you — do you feel it? I Want You to Take The Train & Come — come come come come come . . ."

In Berlin, Craig was working on drawings of Isadora in motion (six of which were published in book form the following year)[54] and on puppets, precursors of the *Übermarionetten* he envisioned in place of actors on the stage. Among his other plans were a theater journal he could edit and publish himself, "so that through that publication I might in time come to change the whole theatre — not plays alone, but playing, sceneries, construction of theatres — the whole thing."[55] Craig's magazine was finally born in Florence, three years later, as *The Mask*, "but in 1905," writes Edward Craig, "he had too much to think about to give all his time to any one project. . . . It was a period of a hundred schemes."[56] At different times Craig planned productions of *The Tempest, Macbeth,* Shaw's *Caesar and Cleopatra* (in collaboration with Max Reinhardt), and Sophocles's *Elektra,* for Eleonora Duse, but none of them came to fruition. There was talk of giving him his own theater, if his letters to Martin Shaw may be taken at their word. Shaw was Craig's only real confidant, whom he repeatedly begged to join him in Germany.

"They've watered me well here & I grow," Craig wrote. "Expect to receive wonderful news within 3 months. I may then have my own theatre & my own company. . . . No women in it boy. Only comrades!"[57] While Duse's production of *Elektra* never materialized (she deemed it unsuitable for touring), Craig's designs were actually completed and sent to her in Italy. The patronage of the greatest names in European theater seemed to him only his due. "Reinhardt, Kessler, Duse, all of them monkeys," said Craig: "I demand my theatre & my rights from the whole pack."[58] In *Index to the Story of My Days,* he admitted his susceptibility to flattery — "indeed I not only like it, I stand in positive need of it"[59] — and it was this weakness, evidently, that led him into his next venture: Direktion Vereinigter Künste (United Arts Management), a booking agency that he hoped would put him on the road to commercial success. More than anything, Craig thought, he needed an agent to promote him.

In Berlin, Craig met Maurice Magnus, a twenty-nine-year-old American expatriate who introduced himself as a journalist and teacher of English.[60] "Little Magnus," as Craig called him, playing on the name, was short, "snappy," and "decidedly shabby in more ways than one." Everything about him was suspect, from his claim to be a morganatic descendant of the Hohenzollerns to his putative list of familiar contacts; nevertheless, Craig chose Magnus as his manager. Together, they established an office in Craig's studio building, hired a secretary, printed contracts and stationery, and obtained a telegraphic address, FOOTLIGHTS (a mocking reference to the one thing Craig hated most about the theater). Magnus would receive £3 a week, rising to £5 when the first bookings came in, no small salary in 1905. The money, of course, would come from Isadora.

Soon Magnus suggested that Direktion Vereinigter Künste represent Isadora on her concert tours. With Craig behind the scheme, she agreed, pledging 10 percent of her receipts to the new agency. That a mess would ensue might have been clear to them all. Magnus was more socialite than businessman, a master gate-crasher, in thrall to the famous and the rich. His motto for success — One needs only to know the right people — appealed to Craig as much as his air of slavish devotion. Most of the time, Magnus could be found at parties and restaurants, "for, bless him," Craig wrote, "little Magnus couldn't think clearly without the help of Martini. Martini was to him as much as the Bible is to a more reverent man."[61] Over the course of the year and beyond, Craig would hire him, fire him, and hire him again, before finally taking over Isadora's management himself, in another quixotic business venture, whose costs were borne by her alone.[62]

The immediate purpose of Craig's foray into business became clear to Isadora in March 1905, when, as evidence suggests, she opened a letter addressed to Craig and discovered that his companion in England, Elena Meo, had given birth to a son in January; not just that, but that Craig was sending her money and had promised to return to her, as soon as he got on his feet. Craig never concealed his affair with

Nelly, as he called Elena, but the existence of the baby, his eighth child and future biographer, Edward Craig, came as a shock to Isadora, who wanted a baby of her own. The depth of Craig's deception was undoubtedly hidden from her even then. As happened periodically, he became nostalgic for England and deluded himself into thinking he was a family man at heart.

"I will win this time, absolutely must," Craig wrote to Martin Shaw, "then I'll return with the spoils of war and lay them at the feet of my son and his mama."[63] The only evidence of Isadora's distress is a letter she sent from Berlin in the middle of March, between stops on her tour: "Dear — I feel awfully ashamed — ashamed is not the word. I feel dust & ashes — it was an awful kind of rage that took possession of me. . . . I'm afraid you will never be able to think of me in the same way again."[64]

In this instance, Isadora would rally quickly, sending Craig a raft of cheerful letters from the road and her blessing on his union with Elena. "Save me from the *Green Demon Jealousy!*" she wrote. "And the *Red Devil Desire for Complete Possessorship* and the ten & twenty thousand friends who accompany them."[65] It remained a struggle, however. She worried that Craig no longer wanted her, that she had overwhelmed him. She begged him to "persue" her, to prove his desire. "I think I is an Amazon," Isadora wrote:

> If you like the persuing idea you'll have to put up with me persuing at the same time & Clash Bang Crash *Collision* in the Middle —
> So long —
> Come along . . .
> I mean
> You must   Come along and *persue me*
> Please Persue Me —
> I'll pretend to fly fine
> If you'll only persue me —
> I'll be more fun than a fox hunt.[66]

For Craig, Isadora's jealous attack was a spur to new heights of misogyny. As always, he kept his deepest thoughts to himself, confronting the problem only on paper, in a notebook he called "Confessions." In light of Isadora's insecurity, the document makes painful reading. It's pure Craig — secretive, self-obsessed, and a disservice to both his lovers. Craig would visit Elena only once in the following year, for two or three days, leaving her with the vague promise of his return and the advice that she drink "oatmeal stout" to strengthen her blood. "He had not the courage to tell her everything about his affair with Isadora," writes Edward Craig, "but merely said that some woman who was infatuated with him was giving him trouble."[67] Elena would wait the rest of her life for Craig to make good his promise of marriage. He wrote to himself:

> I am in love with one woman only [Elena], and though others attract me how could it ever obliterate what exists of her in my heart and soul. . . . But I am keenly attracted to another woman [Isadora], who may be a witch or a pretty child (and it really doesn't matter which) and I find it hard to be away from her. She not only attracts me, she revolts me also. One moment I instinctively smile with her and love to be with her, and the next I want to be away from her and I shrink from her. It is not that she is at all ugly or repulsive — but merely that I am delighted with her or bored.
>
> When she talks about herself incessantly for a quarter of an hour — when she drinks more wine than she needs or wants — when she cuddles up to other people, men or women, relations or not relations — it is not that she does so repulsively but I see they are equally attracted as myself — and I object to be equally anything in such matters.
>
> And my confession is that I have a contempt for her and do not like to feel I have a contempt — because I find her so dear and so delightful.
>
> Still I cannot trust her, and even friendship, much more love[,] demands absolute trust.
>
> Not that I love her — it is not possible to "Love" twice.
>
> And that is where perhaps a clever idiot would get mixed, for though I do not love her, I tell myself and her that I do — Still I also tell her that I am unable to tell what love is. . . .
>
> Love is something a bit less restless and wayward than this. Love regards no other thing or person except through the eyes of the loved one. . . .
>
> Love which torments is not love. Love is all which is dear and beautiful, without fluster or excitement, without excess of laughter or tears, something at ease and gravely sweet — And where love is there is no room for any other thing.[68]

This nonsense must have served the purpose Craig intended — for surely he spared Isadora only the first part of his confession, not the flowery conclusion. She comes back in her letters as a naughty but chastened child, regretting her misdeeds, determined to do better in the future, and possessed of an elastic generosity toward Craig and

Elena. She would be bountiful, she would be large, in keeping with her character.

"Forgive me if I make a mistake but it strikes me you may be worrying about telegraphing money to England," Isadora wrote when Craig prepared to visit Elena in the summer. "Are you? — I meant to go to the Bank today & get some but it was closed — perhaps till then the enclosed will lift the strain?" She signed her letter "in admiration comradeship & love,"[69] and before long was writing Elena herself, pledging her friendship, offering hospitality, and insisting that she was no rival for Craig's affections. What mental and emotional gyrations were required for her to reach this point can only be surmised. Craig caught up with her where and when he could, joining her in Brussels for three days, where "we dug — and played at farmers — danced. Ah! what days. . . . We flitted off. We dug in the fields we were so happy. I always kept saying 'This is not real' — she laughed — if I had not said so I should have died a year or so later. Of this I am certain."[70] In Breslau, where he sketched her from the wings of the stage,

> she danced more perfectly than ever and with more care more freedom more love — there they sat still and stupid. How strange a sight. An ugly little theatre full of ugly and foolish people and on the darkened stage a figure growing at each movement more perfect — lavishing beauty on each side of her as a sower sows rich corn in a brown and ugly field — poems glitter and shimmer all round her, floating in the air with her waiting to be flung out into the air never to return — all there waiting.[71]

"Did I say you had no heart?" Isadora wrote. "But I couldn't have said that — have I not often heard your heart beating — happy me — happy happy me."[72] Her students remembered the day she appeared suddenly at the school, interrupting their lessons to ask, "Tell me, children, what is the greatest thing in life?"

"To dance!" the girls answered.

"No," said Isadora, "dancing is not the greatest thing in life. The greatest thing in life is — LOVE! Is it not true?"

She left the room as suddenly as she had entered it, "delighted with the dramatic effect she had created," according to Irma. "To our astonishment, the prim schoolteacher had turned crimson with confusion." Taking a Bible from her desk drawer, the teacher read aloud from First Corinthians: Though I speak with the tongue of men and of angels, and have not love, I am become as sounding brass, or a tinkling cymbal. . . . And now abideth faith, hope, love, these three; but the greatest of these is love.

"That," said the teacher, "is what Miss Duncan meant when she said the greatest thing in life is love." But the children didn't believe it.[73]

"Love," wrote Isadora, "it's written across the sky."[74]

11

Maternity

Isadora had dreamed about her baby before it was conceived. The figure of Ellen Terry had appeared "in a shimmering gown," she wrote, ". . . leading by the hand a little blonde child, a little girl, who resembled her exactly, and, in her marvellous voice, she called to me — 'Isadora, love. Love . . . Love . . .'

"From that moment I knew what was coming to me out of the shadowy world of Nothingness before Birth. . . . Joy and Sorrow! Birth and Death! Rhythm of the Dance of Life!" She dreamed the same dream twice more and seemed to float on a cloud in performance: "The divine message sang in all my being. I continued to dance before the public; to teach my school, to love my Endymion. But when I told Craig, he looked bewildered: 'What again?' . . . He was restless, impatient, unhappy, bit his nails to the quick, exclaiming often: 'My work. My work. My work.'"[1]

In Brussels, Isadora sat up late one night in her hotel room, listening to the sound of traffic in the street. "The people here are very gay," she reported, "and the students pass singing & crying out — also the noise of the bells and the cars. All this Life — Wonderful and delightful life — Life is splendid — above all things to be *alive*."[2] She had begun work on what she called a "Marvellous Book!" — an essay about women, later published as "The Dancer and Nature."

"Had a wonderful torrent of ideas falling over each other," Isadora wrote to Craig — "Don't know if they are of any worth. . . . It's all a matter of magnetic forces . . . Wonderful. Aren't we wonderful — Love Love Love Love Love." She drew a wave through the words "Waves — love waves — I've been writing about dance waves — sound waves — light waves — all the *same*."[3]

Isadora's first tour of Holland, in the spring of 1905, was one of the untarnished triumphs of her career. The Dutch had never been known as lovers of dance; Isadora may be said to have made them so. Stories about her appeared in Dutch newspapers for weeks before her arrival; her performances in other countries were critiqued, her interviews reprinted, and *The Dance of the Future* was published in translation, as *De Dans de Toekomst*. "Toe Art," said Isadora:

> In Amsterdam by
> Rotterdam
> They dam the Dikes
>   O
> Dam Dam Dam.[4]

But she fell in love with Holland when she got there. "Dutch country so pretty," she wrote, "tulips & hyacinths — fields — and all like someone's back garden . . . and Amsterdam is really too wonderful with all the houses leaning side ways on one another or just falling forward."[5] Her opening night at the Stadsschouwburg on April 12 was sold out — "not a seat remained!" according to Amsterdam's *Nieuwsblad*.[6] As she often did when appearing in a new town, Isadora presented her *Dance Idylls,* with their dreamy minuets, musettes, and tambourins. To these, she added a suite of dances from Gluck's *Orfeo ed Euridice* and closed with "that infernal Blue Danube,"[7] as she now called the most popular dance in her repertory. "The public that didn't understand the earlier dances, and who have been sitting there all evening, should be given something," Isadora told a reporter.[8]

"How does she dance?" asked a critic for the *Algemeen Handelsblad*. "I cannot describe it. I can only give you some idea by saying that she was completely free . . . moving gracefully, in splendor, completely unrestrained, without affectation, scarcely confined by the rhythm of the music, completely free." Among Dutch critics were several who wondered whether Isadora's "mimic interpretation" rose to the level of art — "This reporter would not have been surprised if many in the audience had confused several of the numbers in the program," said one. But with *The Blue Danube* all doubt was forgotten:

> Suddenly the attention heightened, everyone sat up straight, necks craning, binoculars aimed at the stage, when Isadora Duncan appeared, lightly glided on her bare feet and commenced the lilting waltz. The charm of this dance, dancing which is no mere traipsing or skipping but an outpouring of the whole body in melody and rhythm! The hall rose to its feet. The applause was thunderous.[9]

At her second concert in Amsterdam, on April 13, Dutch critics spoke of "the breathtaking succession of movements, the rhythmic gait . . . the highest splendor" of *Iphigenia*. In Isadora's hands, the drama remained what Gluck and his librettist intended it to be: an epic of Euripides, the linear narration of events that led to the sacrifice of Agamemnon's daughter when the Greek fleet sailed for Troy. But Isadora's was the view from the Chorus; in retelling the legend, she danced parts considered secondary or decorative in opera — memorably, the frolics and games of Iphigenia's attendants on the seashore at Chalcis, as they await the arrival of the Greek ships. In the second act, she wore a scarlet tunic for her Scythian and Amazon dances, hurling spears and raising her shield against the imagined onslaught: "She discovers a crown, presents a palm, offers a blow, brandishes a sword, plucks a rose . . . all with motions so simple, yet so subtle, as to seem at once spontaneous and supreme art."[10] Only at the end, when she mounted the steps of the sacrificial altar, her hands raised to strike with the knife, did action and commentary come together in a single moment of dramatic fulfillment. That it was done by suggestion, with no other actors, scenery, or props of any kind, added to the critics' wonder.

Isadora returned to Berlin from Holland in time to be of help to Craig while he wrote *The Art of the Theatre* — amazingly, in just twelve days. He was "more and more restless" — *searching* was the word he used to describe his discontent.[11] Craig's stage designs and woodcuts toured Germany that year, and he followed them, leaving also for England early in the summer while Isadora attended to the children of her school and rehearsed their first performance at Kroll's. August found them relaxing in Tützing, in the Bavarian Alps, where they had gone "to be cool," Craig reported, "as it was a hot summer. There was a well managed hotel there [the Simpson] — and there I sat and cut wood and Isadora read books."[12]

That Isadora was thinking the whole time about the baby she wanted is clear from her appeals to Craig when she returned to the Netherlands in October. For the first time, we learn that she had difficulty with her menstrual periods, what she called her "bad days." She felt that her "feminine insides" could only be helped by a pregnancy. "O — by the way," she wrote from The Hague on October 24, "Topsy were very ill . . . so I guess Vereinig. Kunst can book that tour right along — till next summer. . . . One can not have everything but still it made me pretty glum. . . . Aren't I ever going to have any little Baby of my own but always go on dancing round Strange Foreign Countries & dancing & dancing & dancing. . . ."[13]

She was writing on stationery with the logo Craig had designed for her: the initials ID entwined with daisies and the year, 1905.

On October 10 Craig took "control of all [her] business affairs," momentarily eliminating Magnus from the picture and arranging Isadora's bookings himself. He would receive half her earnings in exchange for carrying her expenses on the road — "theatres, lighting, orchestra and orchestra direction, advertising, railway and carriage expenses."[14] In turn, Isadora would dance "not less than twelve times a month" and get a new program ready by January. She was working on it already: "I do it early mornings — I can't sleep anymore for some reason or other — fall into a sleep about 3 o'clock and wake at 6."[15]

Isadora's second tour of the Netherlands proved as lucky as the first, with the exception that her popularity had roused her detractors in number. "Is it Art or Humbug?" a critic asked in Amsterdam. Writer and playwright Herman Heyermans, who refused to see her, declared that her dancing wasn't fitted to the Dutch frame of mind — not only "because Holland doesn't have the climate for naked legs," or because Isadora was "flagrant in her disregard for shoes and boots," but because "Holland by nature is not a dance-oriented country. . . . We are a reserved population with, generally speaking, introspective, mainly quiet, dignified citizens."[16] To her dismay, the Calvinist intelligence of Heyermans's critique also infected Isadora's musical accompaniment. The finest orchestras in Holland still refused to play for her, angered by her "degradation" of classical music. For the length of her Dutch tour, she was accompanied by the Haarlem Municipal Orchestra, a band she considered third-rate and frequently threatened to dismiss. As it was, she had her hands full trying to cheer up Craig, who in October learned that his "master," Ellen Terry's acting partner, Henry Irving, had died in London.

"The old Angel dead," Craig lamented, "and howling forbidden to us of the masculine gender — and I cannot tell you the state I am in, unrelieved — may my immortal Henry float away and away where ever fancy allows."[17]

By the end of the year, Craig was doubly dispirited. His plans with Max Reinhardt for *Caesar and Cleopatra* had fallen through, as all his plans did, owing to his insistence on total control. In January 1906 his patron, Count Kessler, sent him what sounded like a notice of dismissal: "Reinhardt has written to me, saying he is sorry and amazed at your changing your mind. I much regret it too, as I cannot help thinking this decision of yours a great mistake. However, you must know best, and so I can only wish that you may soon find some other way of realizing your plans." Craig complained in a letter to Shaw: "I am as it were cut off from the Theatre — I who possibly happen to *be* THE THEATRE — Queer."[18] When, also in January, Isadora wrote to say that she was pregnant at last, she understood that Craig's reaction might not be one of unmixed delight. She reminded him that a baby was what she wanted most in the world.

"I have always had that constant longing impossible to control," she wrote, "and I think if it hadn't come I would have gone crazy from the struggle — as it is I can't help feeling happy about it — I *can't help* it — I have the most exquisitely happy feelings at times — but that's no good to you." In the knowledge that there would soon be a sharp decline in their income, she apologized again: "Dr says I can probably dance again next Dec 1 — Listen that isn't so bad."[19] But she must have realized by this time that she would raise her child on her own.

In January 1906 Isadora was in court, answering a charge of contempt against a Berlin bailiff, whom she had "insulted" the year before. A dismissed teacher had brought a complaint against the school; when the bailiff arrived to serve Isadora with papers, she ordered him out of the house.

"If you don't leave right now," she cried, "I'll get a gun and shoot you!" Charges were filed. In court, Isadora defended herself by saying that she had been "nervous and hysterical from overwork." That it was all a comedy, bureaucratic harassment of a famous personality, could be seen from the court's decision to dismiss all charges in light of "the nervous and eccentric character of the accused."[20] But it wasn't the only embarrassment Isadora faced that winter. After three years of glory in Berlin, she found herself mired in petty restrictions and bad publicity.

BAN ON ISADORA DUNCAN read a story in the *New York Times* on January 6. The Berlin wire report, two paragraphs long, ran on the front page: "Miss Duncan dances barefooted, but in a country [Germany] where women, even of the upper classes, sometimes swim in public attired in costumes which would cause their arrest in Atlantic City or Narragansett Pier, it is inconceivable that this circumstance caused the official order."

In fact, it wasn't Isadora's own dancing that roused the prudish forces of Berlin, but the performances of her students. On January 9 the *Kölnischer Zeitung* reported that when the children danced, they were "so scantily clad that [their] sense of modesty was not protected." At the same time, according to Irma, "no one less than the German Kaiserin, Augusta Victoria . . . pronounced herself outrageously shocked at children performing in bare limbs."[21] Since the girls were minors, the police intervened: "The government had just recently extended the laws regarding child protection, forbidding the employment of children of school age and allowing them to appear on stage only with special permission."[22] The ban on their dancing applied only to Berlin and was lifted when Isadora marshaled her forces (Cosima Wagner, Heinrich Thode, Engelbert Humperdinck, and others). But suspicion, once ignited, was hard to put down.

Isadora had ceased to be a novelty in Germany, and the press, as it usually does, turned on a creature it once adored. New personalities in the world of "classic" dance had begun to capture headlines, posing a sometimes direct but always implicit challenge to Isadora's supremacy in the field. Chief among her new competitors were Ruth St. Denis, a twenty-seven-year-old American who had served her apprenticeship as an actress and skirt dancer in David Belasco's company in New York, and Canadian Maud Allan, whose barefoot dances, set to the music of the masters, confirmed the general trend toward imitation of the Duncan style.[23] Both Allan and St. Denis scored their first triumphs in what were called "Oriental" or "Eastern" dances, Allan in her erotic and wildly popular *Vision of Salomé,* and St. Denis, to more lasting effect, in *Radha,* a mystical extravaganza, with exotic sets and scores of extras, in which St. Denis portrayed a Hindu goddess in a series of "sacred dances" that celebrated, then renounced, the power of the five senses.

It never occurred to Isadora, at first, to consider herself the rival of either St. Denis or Allan, whose work she regarded as theatrical entertainment, not the "true" dance of the soul. "And as for some fakir who walks around the stage in an imitation Hindu costume," she told a reporter, "well — you wouldn't write an article about Sir Henry Irving and a knockabout comedian of the music halls?"[24] A few years later, when she heard that American critics had hailed Maud Allan's work as "superior" to her own, she replied, "If that is true, then I can cheerfully retire from the stage."[25] But the press was spoiling for a catfight. "What Duncan has taught, St. Denis can *do,*" said a critic for the *Berliner Tageblatt.*[26] That their dancing wasn't remotely similar — St. Denis choreographed *Radha* using salt and pepper shakers on a kitchen table — did nothing to prevent comparisons.

What was being realized as Isadora moved into her second decade of performing was her own dream of the dance revived, an inexorable forward movement that found its definitive expression in Diaghilev's Ballets Russes. There had been Duncan imitators since at least 1903; now they were all over Europe. In Paris a compelling but oddly listless exotic dancer called Lady MacLeod — later known as Mata Hari — had made a strong impression on the critics, and in Vienna the three Wiesenthal sisters, ballet dancers who crossed over to concert performance, evoked "the soul of the Strauss waltzes" to mounting acclaim. Isadora's high-handedness had won her no friends in the press: "Whether to Brahms, Chopin, Strauss, Beethoven, Wagner, or any other music, Isadora hops gracefully around, arms circling and legs swinging, gazing at the astonished public with the same angel-sweet and naively startled face for the fourth year in a row."[27]

Matters got worse when her pregnancy became generally known. For obvious reasons, at a time when unwed mothers could expect to be abandoned even by their families, Isadora's condition was never announced. But at the beginning of 1906, coincident with the flap over the children's moral condition, she found new trouble among the aristocratic German women whose contributions she relied on to keep the school running.

"When they learned of Craig," Isadora wrote, "they sent me a long letter, couched in majestic terms of reproach, and said that they, members of the good bourgeois society, could no longer be patronesses of a school where the leader had such loose ideas of morals." The letter was hand delivered by Giulietta Mendelssohn, Italian-born wife of the banker Robert Mendelssohn, who "looked at me a bit unsteadily," Isadora recalled, "and, suddenly bursting into tears, threw the letter on the floor, and, taking me in her arms, cried: 'Don't think I ever signed that wretched letter. As for the other ladies, there is nothing to be done with them. They will no longer be patrons of this school. Only they still believe in your sister, Elizabeth.'" If they knew the truth, said Isadora, they wouldn't.[28]

At Grunewald, Elizabeth was newly involved with Max Merz, an Austrian musicologist drawn into the Duncan orbit after seeing Isadora dance in Berlin. Merz had offered his services to the school, and Isadora had accepted them, whereupon Elizabeth, smitten, took him over completely: she became his lover and, sometime in 1908, the mother of a stillborn child. None of this was known outside the Duncan circle. As Isadora toured, Elizabeth and Merz together made decisions at the school, frequently leaving her without word of her students or their progress. When the girls performed in Berlin at the Theater des Westens in October 1905, Isadora, in Holland, asked Elizabeth to send loge tickets to Craig — "Little Beasty she didn't do it. . . . I hear the Audience applauded frantically for the Kiddies. Wish I knew what they did!"[29]

In February 1906, with Isadora's consent, Elizabeth formed the Society for the Support and Maintenance of the Dance School of Isadora Duncan. Nominally a fund-raising committee, the group soon became a receivership, ready to take responsibility for the school as the scandal over Isadora's pregnancy mounted. She would not submit quietly to what she regarded as hypocrisy.

"These women so roused my indignation that I took the Philharmonic Saal and gave a special lecture on the dance as an art of liberation," Isadora wrote.[30] It may have been "The Dancer and Nature,"[31] in which she urged women to discover beauty through the exploration of their own bodies: "Not by the thought or contemplation of beauty only, but by the living of it, will woman learn. And as form and movement are inseparable, I might say she will learn by that movement which is in accordance with the beautiful form." In the stern society of imperial Berlin, where women still lived imprisoned by corsets and foundations, high-laced boots, shifts, brassieres, garters, buttons, and hooks and eyes, Isadora's words were not just mutinous but indecent:

"Any intelligent woman who reads the marriage contract and then goes into it, deserves all the consequences." As for children: "Well, I could give the names of many prominent people who were born out of wedlock." At her lecture, she recalled, "half of the audience sympathised with me, and the other half hissed and threw anything that came to their hands on to the stage."[32]

The issue of marriage, of course, didn't arise in Isadora's relationship with Craig.[33] That spring, his drawings of Isadora were published in Leipzig, Holland, and England. Craig had hoped to display the prints in the lobbies of the theaters where Isadora performed, or as advertising material on posters and kiosks, but the plan proved too expensive and the drawings, in any case, weren't brilliant: "Eventually by scribbling away, he devised some very idealized visions of Isadora gliding through the clouds, prancing in pools of light, and bouncing in the wings of an old-time theatre."[34] Before they met, Craig had never drawn the human figure from life, just as he had plainly come to prefer the thought of Isadora to her actual presence. To Isadora's mind, he seemed "strangely remote."

Kathleen Bruce joined her on the road:

> "Come with me to Brussels," said she, and I went. "Come with me to Berlin," and I went. "Come with me to the Hague." . . . No friends at all had we in these foreign towns. If pressmen came the dancer was self-conscious and austere, and since she talked nothing but American the interviews were brief. We got up early, ran in any park that was near, and did a few gymnastics. Whatever happened later, and terrible things did happen, at that time the dancer was a healthy, simple-living, hard-working artist. . . . She was open-handed, sweet-tempered, pliable, and easy-going. "Oh, what's the difference?" she would say, if I, who hated to see her put upon, wanted to stand out against overcharges. "What's the difference?" . . . She was making enormous sums of money."[35]

In February, Martin Shaw arrived in Berlin, summoned by Craig to assist Isadora on tour as her conductor. At thirty-one, Shaw had just begun his distinguished career as a composer and musicologist; later he compiled *The Oxford Book of Carols* and arranged the music for such familiar Anglican hymns as "All Things Bright and Beautiful" and "Let All the World in Every Corner Sing." His witty reminiscences of Isadora's 1906 tour were published two decades later in his autobiography, *Up to Now*.[36] Shaw recalled the night they met in Berlin:

The theatre was crowded and the audience in a state of ecstatic delight throughout. Isadora provided the whole programme. This in itself is remarkable. I doubt whether any other dancer has ever been able to carry through a whole evening's entertainment unaided. All the time I conducted for her she was the sole performer on the stage. . . .

After the performance I was taken round to see the wonderful creature in her dressing-room. She looked at me with the untroubled gaze of a child and spoke a few words of welcome in an American accent which the extraordinary sweetness of her voice robbed of the least suspicion of harshness. All her movements were deliberate, reposeful, never for an instant hurried or nervous. One simply could not imagine her catching a train.[37]

Emerging from the stage door, we encountered the usual crowd of admirers lining the way to her carriage, to which she walked with a kind of floating sway from the hips. . . . Her serenity made me think of a still, deep lake over which no breeze made the faintest ripple.

For Isadora, the spring tour proved even more arduous than the one before it. She continued dancing during the first months of her pregnancy, ostensibly to support the school, but there can be no doubt that she worked as long and hard as she did in order to keep her lover in pencils, notebooks, and five-course dinners at the best restaurants in Berlin. Craig began to complain about the school — in fact, warning Isadora that it would drain their resources and urging her to be stronger in her resolve when Elizabeth pressed her for funds. In November she had sent money to Raymond, who wrote her "a feverish note" from Paris to say that his pregnant wife, Penelope, "would have to go to 'Pauper Hospital'" if Isadora didn't help them out.[38] From January to May of 1906, she danced all over Germany, Belgium, and Holland, as well as in Copenhagen and Stockholm. How she managed it is anyone's guess, but with Shaw as her conductor, she could at least count on Craig joining her for long stretches of the tour.

Things looked bright enough when they began in Nuremberg, Shaw recalled: "The night came; Isadora Duncan danced in her own divine manner, the music went well, and all was joy. Alas! Never again did I have such an orchestra." In Augsburg the local philharmonic was made up entirely of army officers. "They were most anxious to oblige," said Shaw, "and I liked them, though their playing was, as might be expected, slightly heavy and mechanical. By this time I had learnt to count up to ten in German and so felt a little more confident. . . . I never got to twenty in any part of Europe."

In Amsterdam, Isadora was joined again by the Haarlem Municipal Orchestra, but now she had Shaw to confirm her opinion of the band. "It was a worse orchestra than the one at the theatre in Munich," he remarked: "The players were seated in a room that just held them comfortably — and no more. It was impossible to tell whether [they] were sounding the right notes or not. Added to this, every single one of them had a lighted cigar in his mouth, even the wind players."[39] Isadora had added a *Waltz Evening* to her other programs, dancing to Brahms, Chopin, and *Seven German Dances* of Schubert that "soared to glory," according to the *Nieuws van der Dag.*[40] Her ongoing problems with the orchestra were more frustrating for that — one night she stopped dead in the middle of a dance and declared that she couldn't go on.

"This was naturally jolly for me!" Shaw wrote. "The orchestra sat and listened to her with Dutch phlegm. At the end of her speech she relented and said she would try [the] dance again. But this I refused to do, and we went on to the next item and somehow finished the program."[41] By they time they got to Sweden, they were all exhausted. Craig was "searching" more and more obtrusively, and Isadora, when she wasn't dancing, did nothing but sleep.

The question now arose as to where Isadora would have her baby. That she would need seclusion was never in doubt. At first, she considered Lake Como, in northern Italy. "I believe that Duse is in Milano," she wrote to Craig, "if so I will see her." (Duse and Isadora had met in Vienna in 1903, when they alternated performances at the Karl Theater.) Meantime she stayed at the Villa Albertina in Gautzsch, near Leipzig, the home of friends, a Dr. and Mrs. Zehme, whom she had met through the Mendelssohn banking family. Zehme was a lawyer who specialized in the affairs of artists. "It is very comfy here," Isadora wrote, although her hosts seemed intent on persuading her to give up the baby for the sake of her reputation.

"Perhaps I better curl up and refuse to budge," Isadora wrote nervously: "Every country has its customs and it seems here they hire those amiable old ladies with slaughterous intentions — even Dr. Z. offered to 'adopt' it — I'm really getting scared and *don't* feel like falling over myself to get to Como — if the honest German is such what would the wily Italian be — The future King of Ireland must be protected from these Conspiracies."[42] That their child would be the long-lost king of Ireland was one of Craig's more whimsical suggestions. He left Isadora by herself while she battled the Zehmes in Gautzsch.

On June 12 Ellen Terry celebrated her golden jubilee at the Drury Lane Theatre in London. Craig didn't attend. "Somehow this Jubilee thoroughly upset me," he wrote, "because my father . . . was forgot — like the Hobby Horse!" Since the death of Henry Irving, Craig had felt bereft of a mentor. He blamed the women: "My father, my master and I, all loved the same woman [Terry] — and we all left her for the same reason — a commonplace one: our work called to us, and we went. But we did love her. Strange, it was she who could not follow us."[43] He would employ much the same words the following year, when he parted with Isadora — she, not he, had failed in her devotion.

Isadora must have sensed Craig's desire to leave her, however hard she worked to conceal it. Her letters from Gautzsch reek with insecurity, and when she shortly decided to return to Holland, at Noordwijk, for her delivery, she rushed to assure Craig that she felt "so well & jolly."[44] But she didn't.

"The child asserted itself now, more and more," Isadora wrote later. "It was strange to see my beautiful marble body softened and broken and stretched and deformed. . . . My hard little breasts grew large and soft, and fell. My nimble feet grew slower, my ankles swelled, my hips were painful. Where was my lovely, youthful naiad form? Where my ambition? My fame? Often, in spite of myself, I felt very miserable and defeated. This game with the giant Life was too much."[45]

The town of Noordwijk, now a major Dutch resort, lies on the coast of the North Sea not far from Leiden and the Hook of Holland. For the first weeks, Isadora lived there alone in a cottage on the dunes, Villa Maria, with only a cook for company. Craig appears to have visited briefly after she arrived. "He came and went," Isadora wrote, leaving his dog, Black, to keep her company. Temple Duncan also came to stay from the school. Isadora had wanted several of the girls to join her, but Elizabeth put her foot down — it wasn't long before the press located Isadora's hideout. The story spread that she had married or was about to marry Craig, identified in Dutch press accounts as "her private secretary, well-known stage reformer, and son of Ellen Terry." Reporters caught up with him one day on a visit to Noordwijk, but he would neither confirm nor deny the report: "We keep these matters private in England and are not commenting now."[46]

That summer Craig's *Art of the Theatre* was translated into Dutch. He spent most of his time in Amsterdam, arguing with his publishers and threatening to boil them in oil, but visited Isadora only when the mood struck. "When you comin to see yo poo ole Rabbit?" she wrote at the beginning of July. "Por ole Rabbit is now going for a little tod-dle down to the other end of the beach."⁴⁷ The sea soothed her nerves at an anxious time. She had "thirty times the energy of a normal per-son," said Marie Kist, hired to be the baby's nurse. "The father [Craig] was much more difficult. . . . He was convinced that everyone was stealing from Isadora."⁴⁸ In August she completed a short essay, "A Child Dancing," written after seeing Temple play at the water's edge: "She dances because she is full of the joy of life. She dances because the waves are dancing before her eyes, because the winds are dancing, because she can feel the rhythm of the dance throughout the whole of nature."⁴⁹ With nothing but time on her hands, Isadora also wrote down a series of five hundred exercises for the children, "a regular compendium of the dance," as she proudly described it. Temple scan-dalized their neighbors by dancing naked on the beach.

At the end of August, Isadora summoned Kathleen Bruce to join her for the baby's birth. "I was so inexperienced as to think that hav-ing a baby was a perfectly natural process," she remarked.⁵⁰ She hadn't reckoned on pain, inactivity, loneliness, doubt, or the fear that gripped her, more and more, as her delivery approached. When Craig left her without word for ten days in July, Isadora was frantic. He was in En-gland, visiting Ellen Terry and, of course, Elena. Isadora wrote:

> Dearest — Just rec your letter — you can have no idea how anx-ious I have been — *10* days without a line — I thought you were run over by a London cab — I thought you *ill* — I thought the boat had gone down in the storm Saturday night — I pictured all sorts of fear-ful things that had happened to you — till I got a bad fever and the nurse had to take my temperature every minute. Now I see I was quite *silly,* but you know just at this time one's nerves are not under con-trol. . . . For you dear heart I am so glad you are well, and also glad you see your dear Mother or see any that you love, and I can only re-peat — if there is anyone you care for very much who feels unhappy and wants to come with you she can have half my little house with *all my heart.* It will give me *joy* — and Love is enough for all.⁵¹

Was she serious? Kathleen remembered that during the few days Craig actually stayed with Isadora at Noordwijk, he was "treated as the Messiah; everything was to fall before his slightest wish." Kath-leen's account of these days is both informative and unpleasant. She was the first to concede that Craig, physically, "was not altogether inappropriate. He was tall and well-built, with a mass of long, thick, golden hair . . . good features, high cheekbones, and a healthy color. Only the hands with the low-bitten nails betrayed the brute in him." In his presence Isadora kept a brave face, but when he was gone she "sank back exhausted into the monotony of the long wait."[52] Her own account echoes the tenor of Kathleen's: "I had sudden, sinking moods, when I felt myself some poor animal in a mighty trap, and I struggled with an overwhelming desire to escape, escape. Where? Perhaps even into the midst of the sullen waves."[53] Kathleen recalled a bad night, after a reporter had tried to interview Isadora:

> I woke in the small hours aware that all was not well. I lay still for some time, telling myself that there was nothing unusual afoot. I heard nothing. Nevertheless, after a little anxious listening I got up and peeped very quietly into Isadora's room. The bed was empty. There was no light in the house. The front door was open. I dashed down our usual sandy path to the sea . . . and there, straight ahead in deep water and some way out, I could surely see dimly a head and two hands and wrists extended. The sea was calm. I rushed in. The figure ahead did not move. As I neared it, calling, she turned around with a gentle, rather dazed look, and stretched out her arms to me with a faint, childish smile, saying, "The tide was so low, I couldn't do it, and I'm so cold." . . . With infinite and patient care . . . I undressed and rubbed [her down], filled hot-water bottles, and made hot drinks, murmuring soothing and lullaby-like consolation. "There, there, go to sleep . . . There, there . . . We'll forget all about it."[54]

Thus it continued for another month: the baby, due at the end of August, wasn't born until September 24. Kathleen's diary records that Isadora's contractions began at 5:00 A.M. on Saturday, September 22, and that the baby finally arrived on Monday about noon. Craig turned up for the birth, summoned by a telegram, but neither Isadora nor Kathleen mentioned him in their memories of that day.

"The end of it came at last," Kathleen recalled. "The local doctor, a little, fat, middle-aged Dutchman with a stubbly beard, arrived with a black handbag, containing, he said, anesthetic; this however he left in the hall both then and later. There followed the most terrible hours that I had ever spent. . . . The cries and sights of a slaughterhouse could not be more terrible."[55] Isadora's famous description of her labor, graphic for its time, has entered literature as a feminist cri de coeur:

We were all sitting at tea one afternoon when I felt a thud, as if someone had pounded me in the middle of the back, and then a fearful pain, as if someone had put a gimlet into my spine and was trying to break it open. From that moment the torture began, as if I, poor victim, were in the hands of some mighty and pitiless executioner. No sooner had I recovered from one assault than another began. Talk about the Spanish Inquisition! No woman who has borne a child would have to fear it. It must have been a mild sport in comparison. Relentless, cruel, knowing no release, no pity, this terrible, unseen genie had me in his grip, and was, in continued spasms, tearing my bones and my sinews apart. . . . I suppose that, perhaps with the exception of being pinned underneath a railway train, nothing could possibly resemble what I suffered.

The doctor warned Kathleen that Isadora might "never dance again & certainly not for 8 weeks."[56] But the baby was alive — a girl, and "a perfect miniature of Ellen Terry." Isadora continued:

They say such suffering is soon forgotten. All I have to reply is that I have only to shut my eyes and I hear again my shrieks and groans as they were then, like something encircling me apart from myself. . . .
It is unheard-of, uncivilized barbarism that any woman should still be forced to bear such monstrous torture. It should be remedied. It should be stopped. . . . Don't let me hear of any Woman's Movement or Suffraget Movement until women have put an end to this, I believe, wholly useless agony, and insist that the operation of childbirth, like other operations, shall be made painless and endurable.[57]

Kathleen left Noordwijk on September 30, and Craig, if he stayed any time at all, was gone in a matter of hours. Isadora asked him about a name for the baby, and he answered, "Call her anything you damn please — Sophocles, if you like."[58] For the time, they settled on a nickname: Snowdrop. Not for eighteen months would the child take the name she is remembered by: Deirdre, "Beloved of Ireland." Her mother wrote:

Ah, but the baby! The baby was astonishing; formed like a Cupid, with blue eyes and long, brown hair, that afterwards fell out and gave place to golden curls. And, miracle of miracles, [her] mouth sought my breast and bit with toothless gums, and pulled and drank the milk that gushed forth. What mother has ever told the feeling when the babe's mouth bites at her nipple, and the milk gushes from her breast?

This cruel biting mouth, like the mouth of a lover, and our lover's mouth, in turn, reminding us of the babe.

Oh, women, what is the good of us learning to become lawyers, painters, or sculptors, when this miracle exists? Now I knew this tremendous love, surpassing the love of man. I was stretched and bleeding, torn and helpless, while the little being sucked and howled. Life, life, life! Give me life! Oh, where was my Art? My Art or any Art? What did I care for Art? I felt I was a God, superior to any artist.[59]

Isadora stayed on in Noordwijk until the end of October, "weak on [her] pins."[60] Craig was in Rotterdam, only an hour away, but couldn't bother to help her when she closed the villa and packed his things. An exhibition of his designs was about to open at the Kunstkring: he had his work to do.

12
Breaking Stones

Isadora returned from Holland to Grunewald in November 1906, offering no explanation for the blue-eyed baby she brought with her, except to say that she would soon be "the youngest pupil in the school." When pressed, she remarked only that the child was the granddaughter of Ellen Terry.[1] "During the first weeks," she remembered, "I used to lie long hours with the baby in my arms, watching her asleep; sometimes catching a gaze from her eyes; feeling very near the edge, the mystery, perhaps the knowledge of Life."[2] But the bank account was empty, and Craig, far from sharing Isadora's delight in their child, began agitating that she work on a new dance program and get ready for another tour.

In December, Isadora and Craig went with the baby to Florence, where Craig had agreed to design a new production of *Rosmersholm* for Eleonora Duse — with his 1912 *Hamlet,* one of the only productions of Craig's ever to reach the stage. At forty-eight, Duse was generally acknowledged as the greatest tragic actress of her time, surpassing even Sarah Bernhardt, her only possible rival. Bernhardt was "all over the stage in a play," as Craig told Ellen Terry, "dancing — making pictures — singing — flying — leaping — cooing — crowing — hypnotizing — laughing — in fact enjoying herself."[3] Duse's secret was stillness, tension, controlled emotion; as Isadora said about her own work, "the more reserve the better."[4] Her admiration for Duse dated to 1900, when she saw her in Pinero's *Second Mrs. Tanqueray* in London. It was a revelation:

> At the end of the third act, where Mrs. Tanqueray is driven to the wall by her enemies and, overcome with ennui, resolves to commit suicide, there was a moment when Duse stood quite still, alone on the stage. Suddenly, without any special outward movement, she seemed to grow and grow until her head appeared to touch the roof of the theatre. . . . [It] was one of the greatest artistic achievements I have ever witnessed. I remember that I went home dazed with the wonder of it. I said to myself, when I can come on the stage and stand as still as Eleonora Duse did tonight, and, at the same time, create that tremendous force of dynamic movement, then I shall be the greatest dancer in the world.[5]

Before she mounted *Rosmersholm,* Duse was already widely identified with Ibsen's heroines, having toured Europe for years in *Hedda Gabler* and *The Lady from the Sea.* Her love affair with the Italian playwright, novelist, and future fascist revolutionary Gabriele D'Annunzio became public property in 1900, when D'Annunzio published *Il fuoco,* a barely disguised roman à clef about Duse, from whom he parted four years later. Since then, Duse had wandered the world in moodiness and mystery, alternating between ecstatic bursts of creative energy and protracted fits of seclusion and gloom, to the point that her public image became inseparable from the tragic roles she portrayed on the stage.

In *Index to the Story of My Days,* Craig maintained that he agreed to work with Duse "chiefly for the sake of Isadora," a claim belied by the delighted tone of his letters when the offer arrived. "By this time," writes Edward Craig, "Isadora must have realized that unless Craig got involved in some work soon he would go mad, and it may also have occurred to her that she could not nurse him *and* her baby."[6] Craig and Isadora saw Duse at the Mendelssohns' in Berlin; Isadora remembered "a few meetings of mutual enthusiasm" before Duse asked Craig to work for her. Duse's daughter had also approached him, saying, "Oh, do help Mother, she has no one to help her."[7] The actress was in one of her idles, bereft of D'Annunzio, fearful of the public, and threatening retirement. Isadora acted as interpreter for Craig, who spoke no Italian or French, and Duse, who knew no English.

"I found myself between these two great geniuses," Isadora wrote, "forces which, oddly enough, from the very beginning seemed in opposition to each other. I only hoped to make each happy and to please both. This I accomplished by a certain amount of misrepresentation."[8] It's reasonable to assume that Duse never employed Craig to give her conventional work. Nonetheless, according to Isadora, she was completely taken aback when she saw his sketches for *Rosmersholm*.

"It shall be made into a dream," Craig wrote, "a dream — DREAM." Edward Craig describes his father's finished set as "a dark greeny-blue interior with an opening at the back looking out on to a misty 'beyond'; the mistiness even pervaded the interior and the walls, which seemed more like great curtains merged into the floor like the roots of huge trees."[9] Needless to say, Craig's stage bore no resemblance to the scene described in Ibsen's text: "The living room at Rosmersholm, spacious, old-fashioned, and comfortable." Isadora compared the set to "a great Egyptian temple with [an] enormously high ceiling, extending upward to the skies, with walls receding into the distance. Only, unlike an Egyptian temple, at the far end there was a great, square window." This window led to the first dispute with Duse, as, earlier in Berlin, a door put an end to Craig's association with producer Otto Brahm.

"I see this as a small window. It cannot possibly be a large one," Duse told Isadora, who translated for Craig — whereupon "Craig thundered in English, 'Tell her I won't have any damned woman interfering with my work!'"

"He says he admires your opinions and will do everything to please you," Isadora translated. "Then, turning to Craig, I again diplomatically translated Duse's objections as, 'Eleonora Duse says, as you are a great genius, she will not make any suggestions on your sketches, but will pass them as they are.'" When they got to Florence, Craig instructed Isadora to "keep Duse out of the theatre" while he built the set with the help of two Italian workmen he hired on the street. Thus it fell to Isadora to intercept Duse when she came too near. The actress normally dressed in a brown fur coat, Isadora recalled, with a Russian Cossack's hat on her head. "For, although Duse at times in her life, by the advice of her kind friends, patronised the fashionable dressmakers, she could never wear a modish dress or look in any way *chic*. Her dress was always up one side and down on the other. Her hat was always crooked." Isadora went on:

> I shall never forget the picture of Duse, walking through [the Semplici] gardens. She did not look like a woman of this world, but

rather like some divine image of Petrarch or Dante, who found herself upon the terrestrial sphere by some mischance. All the populace made way for her, and stared at us with respectful but curious eyes. Duse did not like to be stared at by the public. She took all the little by-paths and small alleys, to avoid the popular gaze. Nor had she any love for poor humanity, as I had. She considered most of these people as *canaille* [rabble], and used to speak of them as such.[10]

Rosmersholm was scheduled for only one performance, on December 6, at the Teatro alla Pergola in Florence. Duse intended to take the production on the road after that, although it remained doubtful to the last minute whether she would "pass" Craig's designs or not. On their way to the theater for the unveiling, Isadora reassured her: "In a little while — You will soon see. Have patience."

Inside, Craig was arguing with the stagehands, "now trying to speak in Italian," said Isadora, "now just saying, 'Damn! Damn! Why didn't you put this here? Why don't you do what I tell you?'"[11] Duse was silent when she saw the set — mists, "colossal heights," enormous window, and all: "The scene was a revelation — an extension of Ibsen's imagination: it was not a drawing-room, but 'a place' as unreal as the play."[12] Isadora remembered a collective gasp of astonishment, then saw that Duse was crying: "I do not know what Ibsen would have thought. Probably he would have been as we were — speechless, carried away." After a few minutes, Duse strode to the stage.

"Gordon Craig!" she called. "Come here!" It wasn't yet clear to the company whether she intended to thank him or fire him. But to Isadora's relief, Duse took Craig by the hand. "It is my destiny to have found this great genius, Gordon Craig," she intoned. "I now intend to spend the rest of my career (*sempre, sempre*) devoting myself only to showing the world his great work." According to Isadora, Duse went on "to denounce the whole modern trend of the theatre, all modern scenery, the modern conception of an actor's life and vocation," and declared again that "only through Gordon Craig will we poor actors find release from the monstrosity, this charnel-house, which is the theatre of to-day!"[13]

Apparently, Isadora didn't exaggerate Duse's enthusiasm. "She asks me to work with her in joy and freedom [and] to do three more Ibsen plays at once," Craig wrote to Martin Shaw: "She says 'I will *never* have any other scenes — any more of that other *horrid family*.'"[14] A young actor in Duse's company, Guido Noccioli, confirmed in his diary that "the Signora adores [Craig's] work." She was the only member of her company who did. Noccioli found it "a strange set, all green and illuminated by ten spotlights,"[15] while the actor playing Rosmer, Isadora wrote, appeared to have wandered on stage "by mistake." At the opening performance, when the curtain came up, the audience sat in bewildered silence, then erupted in murmurs "like a disturbed beehive." One voice rose loud enough to be heard: *"Bella, bella."* It was Italy's greatest actor, Duse's Henry Irving, Tomasso Salvini, whose approval allowed the audience to relax. "Let our common sense be left in the cloakroom with our umbrellas and hats," Craig wrote in his program notes. "It is . . . possible now to announce that the birth of the new Theatre, and its new Art, has begun."[16]

The reviews of *Rosmersholm* were sufficiently dazzled to send Craig's spirits soaring. "It was a success, and is," he wrote to Martin Shaw. "Duse was magnificent — threw her details to the winds and went in — She has the courage of 25! She, Ibsen and I played our little trio out, and came home happy." Here Craig added another, decisive tribute: "The pleasure I got from seeing Miss Duncan watching my work with Duse was *infinite*. . . . I care not now whether anyone approves or disapproves of one point in my plan or a hundred — because I have that which *glows* to *accept* it without approval or disapproval."[17] Isadora herself, barely recovered from her difficult delivery and painfully nursing her baby, was tired to the bone by the time they left Italy.

"I can't tell you what I felt when I witnessed your wonderful work in Florence," she wrote to Craig a few weeks later. "Probably you have no idea how truly great & Beautiful it was. It was like something supernatural that a man with a thousand million *geni* at his disposal might create & I felt conscience stricken too that I had perhaps been the cause of you wasting some of your time on me — It would be a *Sin*."[18] Her words came back to haunt her when Craig, in short order, moved to Florence permanently — and alone. "When next I came there it was without her," he noted. "It was then that my hour struck."[19]

Returned from Florence to Berlin, Isadora stayed just long enough to collect her music and costumes and catch a train for Warsaw, sending the baby to the Italian Riviera with Mrs. Duncan and a nurse and leaving Craig to his dreams of glory with Duse. In *My Life* she talks about "a tour to Russia" and mistakenly mentions St. Petersburg, a trip she undertook later in 1907: "Farther and farther north the train sped, until I arrived again in those plains of snow and forest, which now seemed more desolate than ever."[20] Until 1918 Poland was part of Russia, and Warsaw a provincial capital of the Russian empire. A Russian visa was required for travel there, which Isadora had some difficulty obtaining.

"I spent one day going half way to Warsaw & back and the next in rushing around all the Consuls American & Russian trying to get a passport," she wrote to Craig, "completely *Capoot*."[21] Dutch newspapers, calling Isadora "Mrs. Craig," had announced the birth of her daughter before she left Noordwijk in October; a month later, *Javabode* in Amsterdam let the secret out: Miss Duncan had given birth "like an ordinary domestic or seamstress" (in other words, illegitimately).[22] In Catholic Poland, questions were raised about her morals. The director of the Warsaw Philharmonic, hired to accompany Isadora when she began her engagement on December 17, wrote to Craig demanding to know the "name of Miss Duncan's husband." Craig answered tersely: "Not the affair of the public."[23] In her autobiography, Isadora confessed what she had not been able to say to Craig at the time:

> I was not in the least prepared for the ordeal of a tour. . . . The first separation from my baby, and also the separation from Craig and Duse, were very painful. Also my health was in a precarious condition, and, as the baby was only half-weaned, it was necessary to have the milk drawn from my breasts with a little machine. This was a ghastly experience for me, and caused me many tears. . . .
>
> I remember that often, when I danced, the milk overflowed, running down my tunic, and causing me much embarrassment. How difficult it is for a woman to have a career![24]

The first concert in Warsaw was a fine success. Isadora wrote to Craig on December 18:

> I slipped into my old dresses & my old dances last night like a Charm. After rehearsing orchestra all day — & great agony of spirit — suddenly felt myself dancing like a miracle. Art or whatever you may choose to call it — every little finger movement came in its old place. I was hardly conscious of my body at all — I feel I have cause to triumph a bit because I had such a terrible time getting here. It was like one of those heavy dreams where one tries to get places & can't. To cap climax a toothache began on the train Sat. night — my cheek [is] swollen. . . . But last night was a real Joy![25]

Within twenty-four hours, all had changed. "Dear heart — as much as I joy in your presence I am *glad* you are not here," Isadora wrote. "This is all *too much suffering*. . . . I got through the performance some old way tonight but it was awful."[26] Her health continued to get worse. There were ten visits to the dentist before she returned to Berlin in January. Unable to keep food in her stomach, she ate nothing but *"oysters . . . & raw eggs,"*[27] but even this Elysian remedy misfired. "Been dreful ill," Isadora wrote. "Dr. says *poisoned* oysters caviar or something — Am up & better now — [castor] oil every hour all day yesterday — spare you details."[28] There were battles with the orchestra, the agency that booked her in Warsaw, the theater director, the house manager, and the stage technicians. Somehow, two-thirds of Isadora's earnings in Warsaw disappeared into local hands: after the theater took its cut, she made barely enough money to cover her hotel and traveling expenses.

"This *Contracting* and *accounting* is *Death* to any *nobility* of life or thought," Isadora lamented, "you agree — It is Brutalizing & directly hurtful to any true work or inspiration."[29] She drew a sad face on one of her letters: "That's Topsy me — I haven't had anything to eat for 2 days. If any of the German ballet was here I should suspect that it *wasn't* the oysters." Meantime, the bills were piling up. Isadora still owed large sums in Holland after her sojourn at Noordwijk. Recently, she and Craig had borrowed money from the Grunewald school, money that Isadora had earned herself but that Elizabeth badly needed back.

"Don't forget dear to send money to *frl. Kist*," Isadora reminded Craig. "*Grand Hotel de Nice* — San Remo — Italia — or Snowdrop will be complaining."[30] Craig had booked her on another tour of Holland, to commence immediately after Isadora left Warsaw; they owed the baby's nurse four or five months' back salary. "It's rather discouraging trying to work with one's own body as instrument," Isadora confessed at a low moment. "I am too *tired*."

In Warsaw, Isadora began to experiment with orchestral accompaniment for the dances of Chopin, which she had always performed as they were written, for piano. "Musicians will tear their hair," she predicted: "I know it — *Mais que faire?*"[31] Craig was sorry, too, since new orchestration meant new sheet music for the orchestra. "All that will cost something," said Isadora.[32] But she was happy with the result. When she felt Craig receding from her, she talked about their child — "Frl. writes the Baby grows stout & well with *red* cheeks so you must find another name than Snowdrop"[33] — or reveled in the occasional swell of passion that still reached her from Berlin: "Darling — I opened your envelope just now expecting to find a letter but instead found something so sweet so beautiful I didn't know what to do so cried over it. How can you write me such words — anyway they would almost create an angel out of a dustheap, such words as that. Thank you dear I will try to live up to a little part of them at least."[34] Performances in Lodz, seventy miles from Warsaw, were first scheduled, then canceled, owing to riots in town.

"It seems they're marching about Lodz at present amiably killing each other," Isadora reported. She asked the reason for it "& was told indifferently, 'O Socialists!' "[35] Russian revolutionaries, suppressed in 1905, had gone back underground. Two days later Isadora was finished with Warsaw: "I leave night of 10th — no woman in Siberia could be more pleased. . . . Yes I want those kisses I do — I'm coming right along. . . . Get that Brass Band out I'm coming."[36]

For Craig, Italy and *Rosmersholm* were in the nature of an epiphany. Riding on the train to Florence, his son reports, he "felt that at last he had come home. . . . As he progressed farther and farther into Italy, his past life receding from his memory, he was like some insect emerging from its chrysalis; the torpid stage was over — he wanted to fly. He felt that he could."[37] In letters to Ellen Terry and Martin Shaw, Craig quoted Duse on the experience of acting: "Duse said today . . . it is the same with plays as [with] people, one does not love the same person and one cannot always love the same play, but to *renew* love — that is the secret, not to hang on to past & dead things — to sweep all past away & to *continually renew*."[38]

Craig's alliance with Duse came to grief in February 1907, when she summoned him to Nice with a telegram: I HAVE A NEW PLAY THAT IS VERY BEAUTIFUL BUT I MUST DISCUSS IT WITH YOU. CAN YOU COME TO NICE? I SHALL BE PUTTING ON ROSMER FEBRUARY NINTH. DUSE.[39] Craig hoped that Duse would take *Rosmersholm* to Holland, where he had arranged for a theater to produce it. Isadora was dancing in Amsterdam — rather, not dancing there, since at the end of one performance she collapsed on the stage and needed to be carried back to her hotel.

"I think it had something to do with the [baby's] milk," she wrote later, "what they call milk fever."[40] Her doctors spoke of "neuritis" and "neuralgia," essentially meaningless terms applied to "women's complaints" in the absence of serious treatment or social remedy. It isn't known what sort of reception Isadora met with from Craig on her brief return to Berlin — whether she got the "kisses" she wanted or not — but there is little doubt that the creeping physical ailments afflicting her throughout 1907 were to some degree psychosomatic, if also hormonal in nature.[41] Craig sent her a copy of *The Book of Job*, with illustrations by William Blake, a disquieting choice for a woman on the edge of collapse.

"The more I live and experience," Isadora answered, "the more I see of beautiful things like Blake for instance & Bach's music, the more I realize what the right, the *divine* place of Woman is — and it's *not* rushing about doing things — *not* — No — it's like she is in Blake's pictures."[42] According to Craig, Isadora once told him that "all the women must be put back again into the Harems — *all* of them — *all*."[43] That her illness might be traced to the trauma of her daughter's birth, or that she might actually have worked herself into the ground supporting Craig and her other dependents, seems not to have been considered by anyone. Isadora wrote: "Once I danced, yes then I was more like 'tree or wave,' but now I feel just the *beginnings* of being a woman — just the beginnings. The others at my age arrived at it long ago — & I begin to feel it's a d—— pesky thing to be — Yes Infernal. . . . O I tell you I have no caution or care, & if I don't see you soon I will pull myself up by the roots & throw myself in the Sea. . . . Come nice growly Tiger — Eat me up . . . Come Eat me — Put your lips to mine & begin that way."[44]

In Amsterdam, Isadora found the Dutch papers buzzing with gossip about her illegitimate baby — scandalous news to the "proper mamas and still more proper daughters" of Holland, where Isadora had hitherto appeared as "the epitome of purity (a sort of Eve in the pre-fig-leaf period)."[45] A critic for *De Telegraaf* took it upon himself to explode the notion that she was a serious artist: "A high squealing note made her stand on tiptoe, a glissando of the violins caused her to glide over the stage like a lump of butter in a hot pan." The attacks took their toll. The *Nieuws van der Dag* reported on January 28:

> Isadora . . . had begun a Chopin waltz when suddenly she stopped. She advanced toward the orchestra, spoke something to the conductor, and then with considerable emotion . . . explained to the audience that things could not continue this way — the music was much too slow, she had been ill and couldn't get to Haarlem for rehearsals [with her orchestra]. Would everyone please excuse her? "You

are excused, Madame," a clear female voice cried out from the crowd. When, at the end, the forlorn-looking Isadora addressed her audience with *"C'est une soirée manquée"* [The evening is ruined], she was amply reassured to the contrary by the generous and heartfelt applause.[46]

Isadora stayed in Amsterdam for several weeks after her collapse, canceling the rest of her Dutch engagement. Her breakdown had co-incided with her "bad days," which seemed to get worse every month. When she used the words *ill* or *unwell* in her letters to Craig, it was code for cramps and hormonal imbalance. Craig saw her in Amster-dam on January 29 but can't have stayed very long: he returned to Berlin before he went to Nice on February 8 to meet Duse (and not be-fore Duse sent him a thousand dollars).

Since its premiere in Florence, Duse had performed *Rosmersholm* only twice, in Milan and Genoa. Guido Noccioli noted that she had "had the set shifted two or three times. According to her, it has been cut down."[47] Craig arrived in Nice to find the set "cut in half" to fit the stage. "His fury knew no bounds," writes Edward Craig, "and after telling everyone in the theatre what he thought of them in English, with the introduction of various French and German words such as 'cretins,' 'imbeciles,' and 'dummkopf,' he rushed off to find Duse."[48] Isadora described their shattering quarrel on the stage:

> "What have you done?' he stormed at her. "You have ruined my work. You have destroyed my Art! You, from whom I expected so much."
> He went on and on mercilessly, until Eleonora, who certainly was not used to being spoken to in this manner, became furious. As she told me later: "I have never seen such a man. I have never been talked to like this. He towered more than six feet, arms folded in Britannic furor, saying fearful things. No one has ever treated me so. Naturally I could not stand it. I pointed to the door and said, 'Go. I never want to see you again.'"[49]

Craig, of course, told a different story. "Fancy anyone treating the mighty Duse badly," he scoffed, "being cross, banging a table, *I* of all people, too — I who in her presence always dwindled to the age of eighteen or nineteen . . . and never would have dared to say Bo [sic] to her shadow."[50] But Isadora's account is confirmed by Noccioli, who reported "big scenes with the stagehand, the electrician, the business manager, the stage manager, the property man. Great chaos of lan-guages back and forth. . . . Countless insults flew about!" When Duse performed *Rosmersholm* next in Vienna, it was without Craig's sets: "The Signora . . . released her anger on the stagehand, who defended himself violently, and on the business manager, who . . . didn't give a damn." At the end of the day, Duse fired them all. "What they have done to your scene," she purportedly told Craig, "they have been doing for years to my Art."[51]

"I am having hell with Duse," Craig confessed in a letter to Shaw, "but hush, not a word to a soul. . . . I want to fly far beyond that haphazard work."[52] And far from Isadora, who now traveled to Nice, virtually on a stretcher, to set things right. "I hope I.D. comes here to regain her strength," Craig had written earlier. But when she did, it was a different matter. "She is so troubled," he discovered. "She's down, *down*."[53] On February 20 he fled to Florence.

In Italy, Craig settled into a villa loaned to him by American art collector Charles Loeser, the first of several houses he would occupy in Florence over the next seven years. "From now till the middle of 1913 a productive period of my life," he wrote: "All came along this year — 1907: Screens, and SCENE, the 'Übermarionette,' Black Figures, The Mask."[54] *The Mask* was first published in 1908 with the help of a young Englishwoman in Florence, Dorothy Neville Lees, with whom Craig shortly began an affair. (In 1915 Dorothy Lees gave birth to another of Craig's children, David). The "Black Figures" were a series of woodcuts, silhouettes Craig used as models for the *Übermarionetten* that followed.

"So you have a villa," Isadora wrote. "Bedad! It sounds very imposing."[55] From Berlin, maliciously or not, Elizabeth sent her news of Craig's attentions to other women — she was "stage-managing," Isadora decided: "There are lots of [more] clever & prettier people in the world than I — Heaps — if I turn to be jealous of them all I will soon be dead — from the strain."[56] A false indifference was no remedy.

"Visions of Craig in all his beauty in the arms of other women haunted me at night, until I could no longer sleep," Isadora confessed. "Visions of Craig explaining his Art to women who gazed at him with adoring eyes — visions of Craig being pleased with other women — looking at them with that winning smile of his . . . taking an interest in them, caressing them. . . .

"All this drove me to fits of alternate fury and despair."[57] Her letters from Nice, and later from Mont Boron, where she moved to a smaller hotel to escape the "silliness" of the city, are almost unbearably affecting. Craig had proposed that she resume her Dutch tour by March 10:

Joseph Charles Duncan and Mary Dora Gray, Isadora's parents
(DUNCAN COLLECTION).

Joseph Duncan's Pioneer
Land and Loan Bank
of San Francisco
(SAN FRANCISCO PUBLIC
LIBRARY).

Isadora, age three, Oakland, 1880.

Isadora photographed in Fresno, 1892, about age fifteen (KERVEL).

The Duncan traveling show, 1894. Left to right: Elizabeth, Raymond, Isadora, Augustin (DUNCAN COLLECTION).

Double exposure: Isadora dancing, photographed by Raymond Duncan
(DUNCAN COLLECTION).

Raymond, Isadora, and Augustin
Duncan in France, 1903
(DUNCAN COLLECTION).

Loie Fuller in her *Danse du Lys*
(ISAIAH W. TABER, MUSÉE RODIN).

Isadora on the Lido in Venice
(DEUTSCHES TANZARCHIV KÖLN).

Mary Desti with Preston Sturges, circa 1904.

"Romeo," Isadora's first lover, Oszkár Beregi.

Isadora dancing for Rodin at Vélizy (MUSÉE RODIN).

The unfinished walls
of Kopanos, Athens
(DUNCAN COLLECTION).

Isadora and her Greek boy chorus,
Berlin, 1904 (DUNCAN COLLECTION).

Program for Isadora's *Dance Idylls*.

Kissing Beregi at
Philipsruhe, Bayreuth, 1904
(RICHARD-WAGNER ARCHIV,
BAYREUTH).

Edward Gordon Craig
(DANCE COLLECTION,
NEW YORK PUBLIC LIBRARY
FOR THE PERFORMING ARTS).

Isadora and Craig in
Berlin, December 1904.

The Duncan School at Grunewald.

Brochure of the Committee
for the Support and Maintenance
of the Dance School
of Isadora Duncan, Berlin.
The Amazon statue greeted
visitors in the front hall.

Verein zur Unterstützung und Erhaltung
der Tanzschule von Isadora Duncan. E. V.

Isadora as Iphigenia (HOF-ATELIER ELVIRA, MUNICH).

Eleonora Duse.

The Villa Maria at Noordwijk
(DANCE COLLECTION, NEW YORK PUBLIC
LIBRARY FOR THE PERFORMING ARTS).

Eine, die abtanzt.

Schweres Schickſal droht Berlin: Jſadora hüpft für immer davon, begleitet von den
eigenswünſchen des Gerichtsvollziehers und den Abſchiedswinken ihrer Schülerinnen.

"She's dancing out of here," German
satire on Isadora, 1906.

Isadora with Deirdre, 1907
(DANCE COLLECTION,
NEW YORK PUBLIC LIBRARY
FOR THE PERFORMING ARTS).

Maud Allan as Salome.

Isadora and Elizabeth in Baden-Baden, June, 1907 (DEUTSCHES
TANZARCHIV KÖLN).

Isadora photographed
in London, July 1908
(BANCROFT LIBRARY, UNIVERSITY
OF CALIFORNIA AT BERKELEY).

Grunewald girls working with Elizabeth Duncan, Paris, 1909 (PAUL BERGER).

Isadora's pupils outfitted by Paul Poiret, 1909.

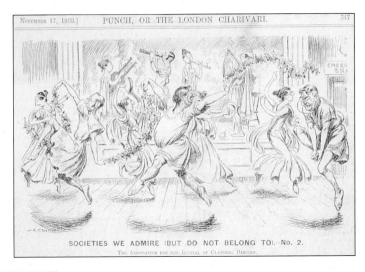

A cartoon in *Punch,* London, 1909.

Program for Isadora and her students, Paris, 1909.

Isadora in Venice (DUNCAN COLLECTION).

The Singer estate at Paignton, England.

Isadora with Deirdre and Patrick, 1912 (PAUL BERGER).

Deirdre and Patrick in Neuilly, photographed
by Anna Duncan two days before they died
(KATHLEEN QUINLAN-DANSMUSEET, STOCKHOLM).

The funeral of Isadora's children and their nurse, Paris, April 1913.

It kills me to say it but I'm afraid March 10th is impossible — O Lord! — I am still lying very flat & pains all over —

I came "unwell" yesterday 22. . . . I will be in bed a week more, the Dr. says, & then it will be at least 2 weeks before I am strong enough to walk — practice dance —

All this is despairing — the constant pain & constant powders. I feel a bit discouraged. Last night I was a bit cracky![58]

The Dr. now says it's a form of nervous prostration. What next? He has just been here — he says no performance possible till the first of April! Otherwise he says I would only fall ill again & hints it would then be a profitable commission for the Undertaker![59]

Getting well is really hard work. My spirits feel equal to anything & then I find my feet dragging & body like lead — Enough to make one Swear Horribly. I am so impatient to be strong — I want to feel the earth spring under me again — I do not wish to die just yet or even by halves — but repeat me those magic words — say you love me & my old husk will fall off. I will bloom up anew for you.[60]

In March, Craig had news that confirmed his decision to sweep away the past. Ellen Terry was married again, this time to an American actor, James Carew, thirty years her junior and three years younger than Craig. "You don't mind much do you?" Terry wrote in a postcard from Niagara Falls. "You are happy that I am happy — aren't you?"[61] In the future, Craig would have nothing to do with powerful women. "How utterly trivial all these 'great' women are," he complained, "how vain they are, and how helpless."[62] Isadora wrote him from Mont Boron:

Dear, you need not worry about me. It is true I am still somewhat ill & [in] a good deal of pain but your power of giving me joy is so great that the dear lines you write me make up for all else. It is perhaps just from having to lie so still & being so much in pain that I have more joy — it sounds a bit Irish but it is really so — life dulls things a good deal & this being in a way half out of life Love shines more clear — So don't worry about me — *I'm not unhappy.*[63]

Gradually, her strength returned. "The neuralgia pains have suddenly left me," she reported. "Queer — Gone as suddenly as they came."

I practice a little each day. The beginning is like breaking stones. One loves to work when once begun, but it is so difficult to reach the right state to begin — sometimes I wish I might dissolve into a mist rather than begin again — The feminine spirit has a special aversion to entering in that land of abstract idea where work is — Indeed only a few in History have succeeded in doing it alone — & then only through suffering, & I object to suffer.

In the margin of this letter, Craig wrote, "Oh dear Topsy!" Isadora continued:

To wrench oneself from Time & place and self & enter where time & place & self do not exist — that is a great pain — but then also a great reward. Is anything comparable to the feeling of having come in contact with that eternal idea of Beauty — a wrench, an awful suffering, a feeling of battering for ages against an impassable barrier, & then suddenly & sharply a glow, a light, a connection with the idea like entering into a God — a happiness indescribable, triumphant.

That's what I feel when I try to work, only many times I get only as far as the suffering & battering & then a blank fall to despair. That there is so much pain connected with so simple an effort I put down to my sex.[64]

As for you — you must follow what your Demon says, I would not dare to say . . . (the Baby is now howling like a veritable Bogie. There — I turned her on her Tummie & she stopped — now she's trying to chew the end of this paper — Well, that's a kiss for Papa —) I can't live without you: that's true. I think my Body & Soul contains parts of you & I long for you, but I'd rather you be a million miles away from me & know you *happy* or at *least* happy you know what I mean.

"Yes. My wonderful Topsy," Craig noted on her letter, "yes! yes! — but don't you protest too much?"[65] By the end of March, she was ready to resume her tour. "Alas — poor me," she wrote, "my heart is torn to pieces — & still I am alive."[66]

The rest was banality — six months of evasion and excuses, mixed with cruelty and reproach. In Amsterdam, Isadora received a letter from Craig saying that Elena Meo had been ill in England and needed his help. It was a way of declaring his prior allegiance.

"I thank you that you wrote to me about N. [Nelly]," Isadora replied. "I have often wanted to speak to you about her. I know it is a good heart & filled with love for you — and I have often thought of her and I thank you because it shows . . . you have forgiven my stupid jealousy of which I have been many times ashamed — but I swear to you there is not a vestige of it left." Her recovery had left her in a state of abounding generosity: "Perhaps it was the pain of the Baby which cleared it all out — only love is left. . . . I mean I can't write what I mean but you know. It's just Love Love Love — the God of Love — & the Kingdom of Love — we will enter it & all who you love with us."[67] So that was no way out. Craig could only find excuses. "I was thinking all the time of *The Mask*," he wrote: "Why should I suppose she might help? Because I supposed she could understand — and she did not understand any deeper than did the others. I was wrong to expect it of anyone. . . . How very idealistic — how absurd."[68]

Isadora returned to Berlin, where she attempted to sort out her finances and "had a good rest — & I feel so well again. I take long walks in the woods with Temple & we both dance for joy of all the opening buds."[69] Her mother brought the baby from Nice; Isadora had closed her apartment and was living at the school. In May she danced again in Stockholm. Craig joined her there, then returned with her to Germany, where they parted in Heidelberg. They pledged to work together in the future; Isadora promised to send money from her summer tour to help with Craig's marionette theater. It was the last time they met as lovers. Craig wrote:

> I went off to Florence — waited, not a word — not a mark arrived . . . I waited & began work — I got 2 men to commence — one a young artist from Bordighera gave up his house there on the strength of my assurance & damme if Madame Duncan didn't let me down & him down & what's worse sent no word of excuse.
>
> From that day I have never forgiven this: I don't mind what anyone does or says to me — but if they in any way show disrespect for my work once I am at work (when warm at it) then click goes the apparatus & it's all over between me & whoever has played me the trick.[70]

So much of Craig's account is purely false that it's a wonder his blushes don't show on the page. Isadora spent the whole summer of 1907 in a fruitless effort to make good on her word, dancing all over Germany in a series of badly managed and poorly attended concerts that left her "tired to tatters" by the time they were finished. In Craig's absence, Augustin acted as her manager. "Gus is good & dear but not very *quick*," Isadora reported. "Dates fix themselves & vanish in the most irritating fashion. . . . We are trying to fall over things too much in a hurry."[71] Far from letting Craig down, she bailed him out by paying off his creditors in Berlin and sent him at least fifteen hundred marks before the summer was over. At the last minute, she began to lose patience. When Craig wrote in July to say that he had broken his foot, she answered tartly, "Take Wings instead."[72]

"I have seldom in my life spent a more disagreeable time since — since you left," Isadora wrote from the road. "I telegraphed you yesterday to know if when things are fixed up here I should meet you somewhere or go to Berlin until performance there. . . . Must do one or other as money is given out. Those small affairs in Heidelberg & Baden only paid hotel bill."[73] On July 12, under a crescent moon, she danced with the children at Mannheim, in a giant outdoor festival celebrating the 300th anniversary of the city, and netted only two thousand marks, half of which she sent to Florence. Isadora and the girls performed on a floating stage in the middle of a fountain in Friedrichsplatz, entering on gondolas lit by paper lanterns. One of the lamps caught fire as they got out of the boat.

"With a single swat of Isadora's hand it was extinguished in the water," wrote the children's drawing master, Konrad Müller-Fürer. "Then, as if nothing had happened, everything proceeded as if it had been rehearsed several times."[74] It hadn't been rehearsed even once — Isadora didn't have the energy. In Baden-Baden she went to the races with Elizabeth and Max Merz. "I placed a bet on a horse for her and she won 80 marks," Merz recalled, "about which she . . . became childishly, infectiously and hilariously overjoyed."[75]

"Making money in summer is like trying to hold water in a sieve," Isadora wrote to Craig. "Things are beginning to go forward but we always need that *Business* man."[76] In Berlin the police ordered a special rehearsal of the children before they danced with Isadora on June 28. "We put all the little girls in long dresses," she reported, "& he looked in vain for a single leg — he asked me to dance also, but I told him that was *quite* impossible." A crowd of five thousand cheered them on that night — "*unheard* of . . . at this time of year."[77] But Craig would not be appeased. He wrote again: "I expected to see you the day after Mannheim — but I suppose you have lost the map — or your head — or some other trifle."[78]

To this impossible statement, Isadora replied: "You will have to tell your people there that they must wait till winter — there is no other way. . . . I wish I could write something to comfort you. . . .

Dearest Dreamer, this is a pretty silly world & I'm afraid you needed someone a bit stronger than your poor Topsy to help you." On her letter, Craig wrote: "All this is Elizabeth's influence."[79] He was so far gone in resentment that he never bothered to see Isadora when she came to Venice in September for a rest.

"I bathe in the sea & am feeling so much better and stronger," she wrote. "If at the end of the week you don't come I will & see you — *if* you want me. Do you?"[80] The word *if* was underlined fourteen times. Craig's feelings weren't softened to know that Isadora was staying at the Danieli, the most expensive hotel in Venice. "Don't expect such wonders of people," she advised him, not long after, "our ancestors were only lately throwing coconuts at each other's heads & swinging by their curly tails."[81]

"And so I expect too much of people . . . ," Craig answered. "Rather do I think we have gone back a stage or two since we hung by the tail and caught fleas as an art."[82] His revenge was quick:

> Later [Isadora] suddenly arrived in Florence: expected to find me willing to go on working with her — but she seemed to me like a sort of stranger & [in] spite of all her dear old attractions nothing could make me look at her as anything more than a wonderful dear thing, across there *on tother side of a river.*
>
> There I put her since there she seemed to be & I never crossed over to her again.[83]

After twenty-four hours Isadora left Florence in tears. "I had found it impossible to kiss her as in the grand days," Craig added, twisting the knife: "Maybe she had heard that the tears of a woman soften the heart of a man who loves her and whom she loves — but I gave no sign that I had seen any tears: from head to foot I suffered, but my cloak hid that."[84] Isadora wrote from Cologne:

> Dear Ted you have a funny effect on your Topsy! You fill me with a Longing & Pain that are terrible. I felt I would rather *die* than leave Florence, & each jog of the train was like torture. It is probably better that I am not there. I have no strength when I am near you — I only want to fly into you & die. It is the music of Tristan [Wagner's *Tristan und Isolde*] that you do not approve of at all, and it is the most horrible suffering — I am *two* people really, & each would be fairly decent if the other wasn't there but the combination is frightful. . . . All my heart's love to you — & what I can't express.[85]

"All's past," Craig wrote, ". . . all's said . . . all's done . . . What now? . . . I loved her — I do so still — but she, the complex she, might have wrecked me. . . . She was a strange, lovely, strong creature, but it seems that I was the stronger."[86] Isadora would depict her break with Craig as a creative necessity, her only recourse if she hoped to save anything of herself at all. "Either Craig's art or mine," she wrote, "and to give up my Art I knew to be impossible: I should pine away — I should die from chagrin."[87] When he read her autobiography in 1928, Craig found it "decidedly libelous," "half bosh, half balderdash," but admitted, in the endless notes, diaries, and treatises he kept about Isadora: "*Tout même* YOU NAUGHTY GIRL."[88] Edward Craig describes their relationship after this: "She would always go on working on his behalf; he would always worship her as a goddess who had appeared to him once, as in a dream."[89]

Part III

PASSION AND THE STORM

(1907–1914)

Now the tune grows frantic,

   Now the torches flare —

Wild and corybantic

   Echoes fill the air.

With a sudden sally,

   All the voices shout;

And the Bacchic rally

   Turns into a rout.

Here is life that surges

   Through each burning vein;

Here is joy that purges

   Every creeping pain.

Even sober sadness

   Casts aside her pall,

Till with buoyant madness

She must swoon and fall.

   — Louis Untermeyer, "Isadora Duncan Dancing"

13

Pim and Pure Pleasure

In May 1907 Isadora turned thirty. She was no marker of birthdays, but she dated her life in graduating epochs and knew a milestone when she saw it. "I was already famous in Europe," she remarked. "I had created an Art, a School, a Baby."[1] In the ruins of her love for Gordon Craig, she would work not just for these but for her own fulfillment as a sexual being. In life as in art, Isadora turned to her body for answers.

"The Baby is having a fine time dancing about & singing '*Das Leben ist so schön,*'" she wrote to Craig the following year. "I hope she will always find it *schön* — she looks like a duck."[2] On tour, she missed them both, "but one cannot have everything," she conceded, "& I have to pay a big price for being so 'truly famous.'"[3] Her reluctance to make a final break with Craig was mixed with a weary tone.

"I love you although you may think my way of showing it is a bit strange," Isadora wrote. "There are times when I can't write — if you ever ask me I'll tell you why some day — if you like the truth — but what is the truth — it's all an illusion. But the Baby isn't an illusion — she's *lovely.*"[4] Later, Isadora confessed that the break with Craig had left her in a "frenzied state." She was fully awakened to the joys of the flesh and suffered intensely from his absence in her bed. "I must find a remedy," she wrote, "and I thought of the wisdom of the Homeopaths. And, as everything that we wish for very much comes, the remedy came." She was dancing in Amsterdam:

> He entered one afternoon: fair, debonair, young, blond, perfectly dressed. He said: "My friends call me Pim."
>
> I said, "Pim! What a charming name. Are you an artist?"
>
> "Oh, no!" he disclaimed, as if I had accused him of some crime.
>
> "Then what have you? A Great Idea?"
>
> "Oh, dear no. I have no ideas at all," he said. . . .
>
> Here was my remedy. I had signed a contract to tour Russia — a long, arduous tournée, not only through North Russia, but South Russia and the Caucasus as well, and I dreaded the long journeys alone.
>
> "Will you come with me to Russia, Pim?"[5]

With that, Isadora took up the gauntlet, staking claim to the timeless privilege of men: the right to choose her lovers as she pleased. She would "live the beauty of woman," as she had argued in her essay "The Dancer and Nature." From 1908 date the first stories of her sexual promiscuity, as well as her much-parodied invitations to "great men" to father children for her. The most famous of these tales, apocryphal, reports a dialogue between Isadora and George Bernard Shaw, who didn't meet before 1918. In the joke, Isadora begs Shaw to sleep with her "on scientific grounds," saying that a baby with her body and Shaw's brains could never fail in life.

"Yes, my dear," Shaw replies. "But suppose it had my body and your brains?" It was such a good line that Shaw sometimes forgot to deny he had ever said it.[6] Isadora offered no apologies for her flight into the physical.

"One cannot make plans for life, or rules for marriage," she told a reporter some years later. "Life comes, and one lives, each day. I am opposed to marriages. I believe in the emancipation of women."[7] The humor that informs her account of her affair with Pim — in particular, the absence of any "Great Idea" — was lost on Craig when he read her autobiography twenty years later. Pim was Willem Noothoven van Goor, from The Hague, and as lovely as Isadora described him. That he was also homosexual, and probably more swain than lover, is plain from her account.

"His whole appearance had the fresh and attractive look of a bed of golden tulips," Isadora wrote. "His golden hair [was] like a bed of golden tulips; his lips like rose tulips; and when he embraced me I felt as though I were floating away on a bed of thousands of tulips in the spring of Holland."[8] Maurice Magnus, who went with her to Russia as her manager, described van Goor's "violent friendship" — that is, his affair — with Anna Pavlova's discarded lover, Joseph Ravicz, whom Isadora eventually took for herself.[9] Pim was only the first on a very long string:

> When we arrived in Petersburg, I was perplexed when the baggage porter demanded eighteen trunks from the train, all marked with Pim's initials.
>
> "But what is this?" I gasped.
>
> "Oh, that is only my luggage," said Pim. "This for my neckties; these two for my lingerie; these for my *complets;* and these for my boots. Then this one contains my extra fur-trimmed waistcoats — so appropriate for Russia." . . . Heretofore love had brought me Romance, Ideal and Suffering. Pim brought me pleasure — just pure delightful pleasure — and at a moment when I most needed it, for without his ministrations I might have sunk into a hopeless neurasthenic.[10]

That Isadora recognized sex as the panacea for her bouts with "neurasthenia" was more to her credit than not, at a time when most doctors would have preferred her to remain neurasthenic for life. She never discussed her love affairs in prurient detail, or even indiscreetly, inasmuch as she took pains to disguise the identities of most of her partners and infused her sexual history with an air of lofty purpose. Isadora didn't live to see Craig's account of his own struggle with sexual imperiousness — "It is not a thing to quarrel with: you must make friends with it" — but she had Whitman's words to guide her: "Give me now libidinous joys only! Give me the drench of my passions. Give me life coarse and rank!" She looked no further than her own family to see the results of repressing her nature. In November 1907 her mother, raging and depressed, went back to San Francisco.

"Wild horses would not hold her," Isadora groaned. "She has cost me a small fortune & now I think dear Brother Gus may take care of her for a time."[11] Later, Isadora would attribute her mother's antagonism to a lack of sexual gratification, but, in fact, San Francisco had just been destroyed in the 1906 earthquake and fire, and Mrs. Duncan's return home carries no weight of mystery. Deirdre's nurse, Marie Kist, remembered Isadora's mother as a "strange woman" who "sometimes disappeared for several days," to be found, after a hunt, in out-of-the-way hotels. "When I'm old, I'll be like that, too," Isadora said.[12] In Oakland Mrs. Duncan turned to her family's old friends the Tread-

wells. She was "very troubled about Isadora's affairs and her not wanting to marry," Florence Treadwell's daughter remembered. "My mother
said to her, 'Well, you raised her that she never should get married.' . . . But she said she never expected that."[13]

Isadora wouldn't see her mother again until 1917. No extraordinary psychology is required to explain the comfort she now found in
erotic adventure and bottles of champagne, even if she realized, at the
beginning, that they were also compensations, buffers against pain.
("Do I contradict myself?" Whitman had asked. "Very well, I contradict myself.") In October, just before she met van Goor, she sent a card
to Craig.

"En route," Isadora wrote. "Rainy — rainy — rainy — dancing
like a Marionette in fits."[14] She stopped in Warsaw with van Goor on
their way to Russia and told Craig in another letter: "I have been en
fête perpetual here — champagne & dancing — it was the only alternative to suicide. The only way to stand [it] was to be continually
drunk!" In the margin of her letter, Craig noted, "Oh — big Fool."[15]

Joining Isadora in Russia were Elizabeth and their pupils, who
danced their rounds and waltzes at the end of her concerts in St. Petersburg. Isadora had summoned the girls in the hope of finding new
funding for the school. "I am devoted to my dancing," she told a reporter later that year, "and I love the little children of my school, but
I am anxious to get someone to take the financial end off my shoulders. A millionaire will do, or a municipality, or an institution. I am
perfectly willing to continue giving my services, but I do wish that
someone would come forward and relieve me of the necessity for finding the money as well."[16] At the end of each performance, she stepped
forward with her plea: *"Aidez-moi! Aidez-moi!"*[17] Soon she turned to
Stanislavsky, hoping to establish the school as part of the Moscow Art
Theatre. Isadora had another goal in Russia: to find work for Craig.
She wanted a rapprochement, if only for Deirdre's sake.

"I've been talking all afternoon to a big manager here about your
work," she wrote to Craig in January. "You see I talk of you, I think of
you always — but when I go to write to you I am overcome." She felt
increasingly crushed by the weight of her responsibilities: "The same
old ratatat of telegrams come in from Mama & from the School —
send 1 thousand send 2 thousand at once — etc. Darn it all, School &
all."[18] Van Goor ran up a bill at their hotel in St. Petersburg that left
even Isadora short of breath. Her impatience was made worse by

Stanislavsky's inability to accommodate her and his failure to respond to her sexual advances.

At forty-three, Stanislavsky had just begun to explore the system of acting known in America as the Method, an irrevocable alteration of the actor's art, in harmony with Isadora's own work in movement and Craig's in design. Stanislavsky later pointed to Isadora as a galvanic inspiration, in a statement as fundamentally Russian as it is generous:

> The necessity to see her often was dictated from within me by an artistic feeling that was closely related to her art. Later, when I became acquainted with her methods as well as with the ideas of her great friend Craig, I came to know that in different corners of the world, due to conditions unknown to us, various people in various spheres sought in Art for the same naturally born creative principles. Upon meeting they were amazed at the common character of their ideas. . . . I did not have the chance to become acquainted with Duncan on her first visit to Moscow [in 1905]. But during her second visit she came to our theatre and I received her as a guest of honor. . . . It became clear to me that we were looking for one and the same thing in different branches of art.

From her conversations with Stanislavsky in 1908 come two of Isadora's most quoted pronouncements. Stanislavsky asked her "who taught her to dance," and she answered, "Terpsichore."

> "I danced from the moment I learned to stand on my feet. I have danced all my life. Man, all humanity, the whole world, must dance. This was, and always will be. It is in vain that people [resist] this and do not want to understand a natural need. . . . *Et voilà tout*," she finished in her inimitable Franco-American dialect. Another time, speaking of a performance of hers that was just over, during which visitors had come to her dressing-room and interfered with her preparations, she explained:
> "I cannot dance that way. Before I go out on the stage, I must place a motor in my soul. When that begins to work my legs and arms and my whole body will move independently of my will. But if I do not get time to put that motor in my soul, I cannot dance."[19]

The motor in her soul was the Method defined, as Stanislavsky revealed it in his well-known books about the actor's art, *An Actor Prepares* (1936) and *Building a Character* (1948). In Method acting, the performer rationalizes the words and actions of the character through his own experience, just as Isadora used music to awaken her own emotions, visions, and dreams. She "met the music," so to speak, as actors would soon meet the texts of the plays they performed and discard centuries of stylized technique. In her letters to Craig, Isadora rhapsodized about Stanislavsky and his troupe. She neglected to say that she had tried to seduce him and failed.

"One night I looked at him," she remembered, "with his fine handsome figure, broad shoulders, black hair, just turning to grey on the temples, and something within me revolted at always playing this rôle of Egeria."[20] (In Greek mythology, Egeria is a water nymph who gives advice to statesmen.) Ilya Ilyich Schneider, who worked as Isadora's secretary in Moscow after the Russian Revolution, remembered the first time he saw her in 1908 as she pulled up in a carriage with Stanislavsky in front of the Art Theatre: "They were holding hands, looking into one another's eyes, and smiling: he with embarrassment, she excitedly and as though surprised. Her smiling face seemed about to burst into laughter."[21] Isadora was nothing but frank in her intentions, drinking late into the night with Stanislavsky and wooing him ruthlessly with talk about art. One night she threw her arms around his neck and kissed him on the mouth. He hadn't known what to think, returning her kiss "with tenderness" but drawing the line after that. Stanislavsky was "too much married," Isadora thought.[22]

As a woman of the theater and "a dancer," working in a profession already assumed to be depraved, Isadora was largely protected from the social consequences a different woman of her time might have met in the same pursuit of pleasure. In society, dancers had no reputation to lose. But Isadora broke the stereotype even among artists, where free love might be taken for granted. "You have to be Isadora Duncan to have the right to come on stage half-naked and not shock anyone," Stanislavsky warned his students.[23] In Russia, home of the ballet, stories of her promiscuity were antedated to coincide with her first visit to St. Petersburg in 1904. Alexandre Benois described a scene at Cubat's restaurant, where Isadora ostensibly danced across the tables and "made a fool of herself" after her debut in the city (at a time, in fact, when she thought of no one but Gordon Craig).

"She was very drunk," Benois reported, "took off her robe and, keeping on a short chemise, improvised a bacchanalian dance ('Je vais vous danser une danse bacchique'), at the end of which she crashed onto the carpet. . . . One of the hosts took her to the Hotel Europe, where she was staying. He told us later that the excited woman would not calm down for some time, but danced, rolled on the floor, and embraced him."[24] Not for nothing did stories of Isadora's profligacy emerge among balletomanes. To the guardians of the academic ballet, she appeared not only as a usurper but as a threat to male domination of the dance. "Ballet is *woman*," George Balanchine would say, but the bodies of ballerinas were, as they still are, shaped by men and a masculine dream of unsexed womanhood.

"Let us applaud Miss Duncan as much as we like," wrote a London critic in 1908; "let us give solemn ear to all the noble lessons she would teach with her toes; but let us not imagine that she, her pupils, or her theories will live one-half as long as the portrait F. A. von Kaulbach painted of her in Munich in 1902."[25] The Kaulbach portrait shows Isadora as a slim and pretty girl, pliable in the ballet tradition. She was now a full-bodied woman, her waist and hips thickened by childbirth, her unbound breasts moving freely with her dance. The horror of balletomanes at the sight of a naturally proportioned female body in motion is conspicuous, inasmuch as almost every critic who saw Isadora dance throughout her career mentioned that her work was devoid of erotic appeal. "Nothing so far removed from the suggestion of the flesh has ever been seen in this city," a critic wrote later that year. "The audience was wild with the ecstasy of art."[26] But purists saw only flesh.

"Everything here is freezing," Isadora wrote from Russia at the end of January, "something unthinkable, the cold . . . long, long stretches of snow & finally the Sea — all frozen. I asked myself when I saw it — Why am I a dancing dervish & why am I up here at the North Pole?"[27] At Stanislavsky's suggestion, she had approached the director of the imperial theaters, Vladimir Telyakovsky, hoping that the Russian state might be persuaded to support the school. Stanislavsky had advised her not to ask for more than fifteen thousand rubles a year, to pledge a return from concert receipts, and "not to abuse the old Ballet too much."[28] But the ballet "was too firmly rooted in Russia to make any change possible," Isadora said, and she gave up the attempt. On February 23 she danced in a gala performance at the Maryinsky, where the children, for the first time, joined her onstage in selected pieces from *Iphigenia*. The evening was an unqualified success.[29]

"There can be no doubt that Isadora Duncan has made a great impression on everybody," Telyakovsky reported in his diary. "Everybody is talking about the classical dances of Greece, Rome, India,

China, and other countries."[30] Around the world, other "art" dancers were making their mark: in Germany, Ruth St. Denis; in Paris, Mata Hari; in the Spanish world, Tórtola Valencia; in London and New York, Maud Allan, Bianca Froelich, Gertrude Hoffman, and "Mlle. Dazié" (Daisy Peterkin, of Detroit, Michigan). The year 1907 saw "a cataclysm of Salomes," in St. Denis's phrase, after the world and national premieres of Richard Strauss's opera of that name, based on the play by Oscar Wilde. Wilde's 1893 retelling of the biblical tale of Salome and John the Baptist proved ripe for portrayal in every art, from Aubrey Beardsley's erotic illustrations in the first published edition to the modernist disharmony of Strauss and the glittering vampires of Gustav Klimt. In 1907 Strauss's *Salome* was banned in England and also withdrawn from the repertory of the Metropolitan Opera: the Met's board of directors had threatened to resign if it was shown again.

What the elite had forbidden, the music halls adored: sex — "exquisitely suggestive, exquisitely evasive, exquisitely graceful" sex, as a London paper wrote about the most successful Salome ever, Maud Allan:

> Her feet, slender and arched, beat a sensual measure. The desire that flames from her lips and bursts in hot flames from her scarlet mouth infects the air with the madness of passion. Swaying like a white witch with yearning arms and hands that plead, Miss Allan is such a delicious embodiment of lust that she might win forgiveness with the sins of her wonderful flesh. . . . Before her rises the head she has danced for, and the lips that would not touch her in life she kisses again and again.[31]

Allan was never alone on the Salome circuit: until 1909, when the craze passed as abruptly as it began, "fatal" dancers in every large city of Europe and the United States worked their variations on Salome and her Dance of the Seven Veils. "Maud Allan parties" became the rage in London, women-only affairs at which "each of the ladies proceeded to outvie her sisters in providing herself with a costume matching in all details the undress effect of Miss Allan's scanty attire." This news was reported at a Berlin dancing conference in "horror-stricken tones," according to the *New York Times;* a debate on the merits of "classic" dancing itself was tabled, "with a view of preserving international peace."[32] In all classes of society, a new dance consciousness was taking hold: a freer, open dance, released from centuries of formality and ancient courtship rituals and turning to ever more elemental and scandalous rhythms. Ballroom dancing was about to be overrun by ragtime and the tango.

In the press, meanwhile, with considerable help from their producers, a "War of the Dancers" was declared.[33] Some critics favored Allan, some Isadora, and some the solo ballerina Adeline Genée, billed by her New York producer, Florenz Ziegfeld, as "the greatest dancer in the world." Having heralded a fad, Isadora now found herself on the far side of it, determined to protect her art from commercialism, sensationalism, and rank imitation. ("But *why?*" she asked a reporter. "Why put us together? One has respect for Mademoiselle Genée. She has trained for many years and won an honorable place in her profession. She is an excellent acrobat. But if you are speaking of an art . . .")[34]

Isadora was back in Russia in April, without the children, for a two-month tour with Magnus that took her into the southern reaches of the empire: Kiev, Tbilisi, Kharkov, Rostov, and the Crimea. "I am trying to make enough money to rest from June to October without dancing & stay quiet some place with the Baby," she explained to Craig.[35] In June, however, having closed the school in Grunewald, she made for London with the children. Her dream of a quiet summer evaporated in the need for funding.

"In my first year in Berlin I made 150,000 marks ($30,000) clear from my dancing," Isadora complained, "and with that money I started my school. . . . Since then I have had to find 50,000 marks ($10,000) every year for its maintenance."[36] The duchess of Manchester, American-born, had suggested to her that she might find money and help in England; not coincidentally, she would also dance on Maud Allan's turf. "Wish me luck!" she wrote to Craig: "We open Duke of York Theatre July 6, under Charles Frohman — it has all been arranged inside of one week & I feel dizzy. . . . If only we have a success . . . I am frightened to death — Pray for us."[37]

In London, Maud Allan's *Vision of Salomé* had played to packed houses at the Palace Theatre for nearly five months. Allan had been hired for a two-week engagement and would stay for two years, praised and excoriated in equal measure: "In naked sensuality, her body calculating, she meets the eyes of Herod; the rhythm of her motion accelerates; she knows what she wants."[38] Allan's Salome came with the unofficial endorsement of King Edward VII, who saw it in 1907, when Allan danced for him privately at Marienbad. The royal performance went ahead even though the king was warned that Allan wore nothing but "two oyster shells and a five-franc piece," a clever but exaggerated depiction of her shimmering veils, headdresses, necklaces, and beads. At the Palace, she broke all box-office records, dancing on a bill that included the comedienne Anita Eddis, "Belle Davis and Her Southern Piccaninnies," "Sam Elton, the Man Who Made the Shah Laugh," and "the Juggling McBans."

Born in Toronto in 1873, Maud Allan was raised, like Isadora, in California and had been dancing in Europe since at least 1903. Her real name was Durrant, not Allan, which she adopted to escape the notoriety that befell her family when her brother, Theodore Durrant, was tried and executed for the murder of two women in San Francisco in 1898. The scandal had made headlines across America, one of the first "crimes of the century." After that, Allan took pains to conceal every detail of her private life. "No one knows my feelings," she said, "and no one shall know them." She was an artist of high ideals, but after five years of performing in Europe with only limited success, she had settled for Salome and "succès de scandale." When they met in Berlin in 1904, Allan and Isadora "disliked each other intensely."[39]

"Four years ago Miss Allan came to me in Berlin and said she was a poor American girl studying dancing, and it would help her so much to see me," Isadora told the New York Times. "So I gave her tickets for every evening when I was dancing. Some weeks afterward she gave imitations of some of my dances and announced herself as my pupil. Now in London she tells an interviewer that she has never heard of me before."[40] Like Isadora, Allan danced barefoot in a Greek tunic. Her Vision of Salomé was set to music by the Belgian composer Marcel Rémy, but normally she danced to Mendelssohn, Strauss, and Chopin. She was "the first to try it & to find that robbery would pay," Craig declared, in a judgment more easily asserted than confirmed: Isadora's admirers were as rude about Allan as any balletomane ever was about "Duncan."

In May 1908, two months before Isadora got to London, The Academy had attacked Maud Allan in an article, "All We Like Sheep," signed pseudonymously by Christopher St. John — in reality, Christabel Marshall, the life companion of Craig's sister, Edith. Marshall reminded readers that not Miss Allan but Miss Duncan, "unheralded, unadvertised, unboomed," had originated the "new art" of classic dancing: "There is very little art in Miss Allan's performance. She herself admits this when she says she has never learned to dance."[41] Ruth St. Denis, in London that same summer, saw Allan at the Palace and described her work as "an adaptation of Isadora's Greek Spring rhythms, the costumes and actions of some of the German actresses in the part of Salome, and a generous sprinkling of my arm movements."[42] In London, St. Denis also saw Isadora for the first time, on a hot afternoon in July. To cash in on the Salome craze, Isadora's producer, Charles Frohman, had billed her as "the Sensation of the Continent" and the children as "Twenty Parisian Dancers." In Edwardian England the word *Parisian* was code for sexual license and "hanky-panky." "And so much for the irony of the world," St. Denis concluded: "Maud Allan might dance before kings and receive a good stipend, but neither she nor any of her successors could be more than a faint echo of [Isadora's] pure spirit of the dance."[43]

In the end, Maud Allan had no successors. "Salomania" didn't survive the arrival of the Ballets Russes and the emergence of Diaghilev's stars, especially Pavlova, who began her own career as a solo dancer in 1910 and obliterated all trace of sirens and severed heads with her *Dying Swan*. Meanwhile, Frohman's attempt to sell Isadora in the Salome mode fell flat. "Her dancing is as finely imagined as it was," wrote the *Times*' Fuller-Maitland, "and she still presents an embodiment of youthful grace and winning innocence. If it is the beauty of early summer rather than of spring, it may be observed that the artist has gained in command of her resources."[44] It wasn't the sort of review to rally audiences from the music hall. As an Englishman, Martin Shaw attributed Isadora's small houses in London to the fact that "there was no sex appeal" in her dancing.

"The extraordinary thing is that [of] all countries in Europe, England has welcomed her least," Shaw discerned. "In St. Petersburg, Berlin, Paris, Vienna, Munich, Copenhagen, Stockholm, Amsterdam, her name was a household word among even the ordinary public. But in London she was almost, judged by her own standard, a failure."[45] At one of her concerts, Ellen Terry, whom Isadora had finally met for the first time, "sprang to her feet" and addressed the crowd: "Do you realize what you are looking at? Do you understand that this is the most incomparably beautiful dancing in the world? Do you appreciate what this woman is doing for you — bringing back the lost beauty of the old world of art?"[46]

"Meeting your mother has been a great thing," Isadora acknowledged to Craig. "She is so marvelous — so Beautiful so kind — She was like a great Lovely Goddess Angel to me — & the two nights she came to the Theatre I danced as in a dream."[47] Craig, of course, was furious to learn about Isadora's friendship with his mother — a "great rapprochement,"[48] as Shaw remarked. He was even angrier when Shaw told him that her stage decor in London had been mistaken for his own work. Craig's bitter recriminations — "It is a direct case of piracy," he wrote, "You have removed from yourself the right to deride the Maud Allans of the variety stage"[49] — filled many pages. He may or may not have sent them to Isadora.

"I have had very nice audiences here," she went on, "as nice as anyplace — & it has cured the terrible fear I had of London engendered by almost starving to death here 8 years ago. I particularly adore to rush in motor cars about this town where I walked & walked & walked so many dreary miles."[50] Her students had seduced the London critics, appearing in a program of German folk songs and dances that supplemented their work with Isadora in *Iphigenia* and must have badly disappointed anyone who came to see Parisian girls. John Galsworthy's description of Isadora's pupils, simply titled "Delight," still moves after ninety years: "There was no tiptoeing and posturing, no hopeless muscular achievement; all was rhythm, music, light, air, and above all things, happiness. Smiles and love had gone to the fashioning of their performance; and smiles and love shone from every one of their faces and from the clever white turnings of their limbs."[51] A report at the end of her London engagement spoke of "Isadora Duncan's Triumph" and remarked that "her season here has been most successful from both the artistic and the financial point of view."[52] The story may have been planted by Frohman, who on July 7 announced that he would bring Isadora to America for a twenty-week engagement.

"A mad idea it is," Isadora told the *New York Times,* "going to America to dance in the middle of August. New York must be a furnace, but Mr. Frohman wants to get me there before the imitations of my dances are done everywhere. Personally, I can't see what difference it makes." In a witty aside, she begged the reporter not to describe her as a "Greek" dancer. "While my dancing owes inspiration to the Greeks," she said, "it is not Greek really, but very modern — my own idea."[53] Her farewell concert in London "aroused the tremendous enthusiasm of a packed house." Fans piled wreaths of flowers on the stage "almost as high as Miss Duncan herself, intertwined with American and English flags."[54] Queen Alexandra had come twice to see her perform, and the children danced privately for the king and queen at the estate of the duchess of Manchester.

"Their majesties graciously shook hands with us," Irma remembered, "and the King wanted to know what everybody else in that over-dressed era was always asking: 'Are you not cold with so little on?' Bored with the same old question, we simply shook our heads and smiled."[55] The duchess of Manchester, Consuelo Yznaga, was a Louisiana "dollar princess," one of many American women whose fortunes rescued British titles in the nineteenth century. In the end, however, she delivered no money for the school — "disillusion once more!"[56]

In London, Isadora saw old friends from her New Gallery days and helped celebrate Kathleen Bruce's engagement to Captain Robert Falcon Scott — "Scott of the Antarctic," whose doomed mission to the South Pole would leave Kathleen a widow in just four years. Neither her students nor Deirdre, nearly two years old, would be with her in America, the former on account of child-labor laws and the latter because it was purely inconvenient to take her. In this, Isadora behaved no differently from any other female star of her era. In an effort to rouse Craig's interest in their daughter, she invited him to see Deirdre in Ostend before she "sailed the briny deep." Craig declined. Soon Elena Meo and their children joined him in Florence, but they hadn't been there long before Craig left for Moscow, where Stanislavsky, thanks to Isadora, invited him to discuss plans for *Hamlet,* a project that wouldn't be realized for another three years. Stanislavsky offered Craig a monthly stipend of five hundred rubles for the duration of his "preparations." In the meantime, Ellen Terry supported his former wife, May Gibson, Elena Meo, and all his children, with the lone exception of Deirdre. "Great success to you," Craig wrote to Isadora — "and keep all the millionaires you find for yourself — you need them."[57]

In New York, Charles Frohman billed Isadora not only as the sensation of the Continent, but "the Rage of London: Miss Isadora Duncan in Her Celebrated Classical Dances." A decade after Augustin Daly's death, Frohman was the most powerful producer on Broadway and the force behind America's "theatrical trust," a national booking syndicate, dominated by Frohman and his brother, Daniel, that held a virtual monopoly on access to commercial theaters in the United States. Among Frohman's legendary stars were Maude Adams, Ethel Barrymore, and Jeanne Eagels, but he overreached himself with Isadora, whom he seems to have signed on only to establish a lock on the suddenly exploding vogue for solo dancing. Newspapers reported that crossing to New York on the *St. Louis,* "Miss Duncan was seen every day . . . with the young men returning from the Marathon races in London. In conversation and whenever they were together, they were talking about feats of strength."[58]

For Isadora to dance alone on Broadway was itself "a feat of endurance," according to Frohman's publicity, "never previously seen outside of Europe. . . . She will be the first example of a single artist devoting a whole evening to dancing, unrelieved by song, skit, or recitation."[59] It didn't work. Frohman had booked Isadora into the Criterion theater on Forty-third Street, where she danced for three weeks, in a heat wave, to small and baffled houses. Nine years had passed since she left the United States — in New York she was hailed again for her role in the Windsor Hotel fire. American audiences as yet had no concept of modern, or "art," dance; the *Times'* first dance critic, John Martin, wouldn't be appointed until 1928. Broadway writers struggled valiantly for words to express what Isadora did: "Terpsichorean interpretations," "dance posturings," "etherealized pantomime." Henry Taylor Parker, writing in the *Boston Evening Transcript* as HTP, spoke for his colleagues when he said: "It is fairest and clearest to name it Miss Duncan's dancing and rest content." Parker went on:

> A dancer could hardly be [more] free from the grosser bonds of flesh and muscles and nerves, from all physical and material conditions that would bind her to the earth. Miss Duncan treads the stage as though it were the air; she moves through the air as though it were the finer ether; the impression, though the eyes do see, is that she is as incorporeal as the sylphs, as fairy-footed as the elves. Her dancing is as intangible, as un-material, as fluid as are sound and light.[60]

Unfortunately for Isadora, sylphs and elves couldn't compete with Ziegfeld's *Follies,* which premiered in 1907, or the wiggling sirens of vaudeville. "There are many in New York who knew her as a clever artist when she lived here some years ago, and of those many were present," the *New York Telegraph* wrote after her opening night.[61] During her curtain calls, she "became confidential: 'This is very sweet of you,' she said. 'Do you really want me to dance again? Haven't you really had enough of it?'" Explaining that she hadn't yet acclimated to the heat, Isadora promised to do better the following week.[62] When it came, however, the hot weather had felled her to such an extent that she cut her performances from seven a week down to four. On August 29 the *New York Times* reported an "enthusiastic reception" for her

Seventh Symphony, to which she had added eight works by Chopin. In the lobby of the Criterion, nevertheless, *Variety* overheard the comments of the producer William Harris and a companion, Abe Thalheimer.

"Miss Duncan is a very neat worker," said Thalheimer.

"Who handed such a lemon to Frohman?"[63] Harris replied. Mary Fanton Roberts, editor of *The Touchstone* and later of *The Craftsman* and *Arts & Decoration,* went backstage to meet Isadora and saw her crying in front of the mirror. "Augustin Duncan, ever gentle and courteous, told me that [she] was too unhappy to talk with anyone, that she wanted to break her contract and go back to Europe," Roberts remembered. "'But,' I said, 'she must not do that. This is not her audience. She should never have danced in this theatre.'"

It was a lucky encounter. With her husband, editor and naturalist W. Carman Roberts, Mary Roberts would lead Isadora to the audience she wanted: "poets, painters, writers"[64] — all of them engaged, in 1908, in an effort to discover and define a specifically American art, a new aesthetic to rival Europe's and replace what was seen as a hopeless and sterile provincialism. The whole history of American art in the first half of the twentieth century must be seen in the light of this common struggle: a new world required a new art form. Among artists, *primitive* was the word of the hour, signifying not savagery or artlessness but directness and purity of expression — "that primitive purity which, every two or three thousand years, reappears from the depth of the abyss of our worn-out conscience to restore to us again a holy animality," as critic Elie Faure wrote about Isadora in Paris.[65]

That same year John Sloan, Robert Henri, William Glackens, and five other painters of the urban-realist Ashcan School, known collectively as The Eight, had mounted a communal exhibition at the Macbeth Gallery on Fifth Avenue and Fortieth Street — less than twenty blocks south of the Fifty-seventh Street showrooms but well ahead of the Beaux-Arts academy in the quest for truth and life in painting. "Don't imitate," Henri directed his students; "be yourself." It was the call to destiny for a generation of artists, the essential cry of self-expression. In 1908 and through two subsequent tours of the United States, in 1909 and 1911, Isadora would appear to American artists as the herald of their collective aspiration, "dancing America" and making forever American the natural dance of the world. Jacob Adler, actor and founder of the Grand Theater, saw her in concert and found himself weeping:

Something happened to me that will change my whole life. There were an exaltation and inspiration in her. All seemed to be inspired with the spirit of Miss Duncan. I had what seemed to me was a peep into a new paradise, and then I felt that everything that I had to this time seen — I had not seen; and everything that I had to this time heard — I had not heard. It was a new world. I saw that she was one of the rare persons of this world, and that her art could, in some strange way, bring completeness to what was, otherwise, so discouragingly incomplete.[66]

According to Isadora, sculptor George Grey Barnard prevailed upon her not to leave New York after she canceled her contract with Frohman. She had gone on the first leg of a national tour, but it was "so badly arranged" that she stopped it in Philadelphia and tore up her contract, "from a feeling of hurt pride, and also out of contempt for [Frohman's] lack of sportsmanship."[67] In September she took the lease on a studio apartment in the Beaux-Arts building overlooking Bryant Park. Here, she lay down her carpet, scattered pillows around, hung her blue curtains, and got to work, "dancing every evening for the poets and artists." Barnard, remembered for his statues of Abraham Lincoln and for the collection of French medieval art he bought and installed at the Cloisters in Washington Heights, was among Isadora's fervid admirers.

"Miss Duncan is the Light of Tomorrow," Barnard declaimed, "a torch that lights the path of progress. . . . She has annihilated whole Louvres of self-consciously built-up art."[68] Outside his studio near Fort Tryon Park, Isadora raised her arms toward the Hudson River and cried, "I see America dancing." She was not unmindful of Barnard's "beautiful frame" and for a time went daily to pose and discuss "new plans for art inspiration in America. . . . I, for one, was willing to give myself body and soul to the task. . . . With every atom of my being I longed to become the mobile clay under his sculptor's hands." But Barnard proved as married as Stanislavsky — "one of those men who carried virtue to fanaticism," Isadora sniffed.[69] In November she met the man who would transform her fortunes: Walter Damrosch, the German-American composer and conductor of the New York Symphony.[70]

In 1908 Damrosch was forty-six, known as a musical innovator, "strongly pro-Wagner" at a time when Wagner was seldom performed in the United States and enjoyed even less. His venturesome tastes didn't prevent Damrosch from becoming one of the leading maestros of the age. He had seen Isadora's *Seventh Symphony* in Philadelphia and, almost alone among musicians, had left the theater in rapture.

"I have never felt the real 'joy of Life' in an almost primitive innocence and glory as in her dance of the *Scherzo*," Damrosch wrote in 1909. "The *Finale* is a 'Bacchanale' of such tremendous intensity that one little dancing figure on a large stage is not sufficient. The stage should be filled with twenty Duncans, but alas, so far our age has produced only one."[71] At her studio in New York, Damrosch saw Isadora's suite of Schubert waltzes and, shortly afterward, invited her to perform under his baton. Her moment had come with the change of seasons.

On November 6, 1908, Isadora made what amounted to a second New York debut at the temple of American music, the Metropolitan Opera. With Damrosch behind her, and New York's music audiences returned from summer retreat, there was no question of a small crowd. "The vast auditorium contained an audience that not only filled every seat," wrote *Musical America*, "but uncomfortably crowded the standing-room, upstairs and down."[72]

Two more concerts with Damrosch followed in November, one at the Met and the other at Carnegie Hall, before Isadora left New York on another tour, a jubilant procession through Boston, Philadelphia, Washington, Chicago, and St. Louis that left her image pressed forever on the American consciousness. On her program for the *Seventh Symphony*, she had quoted Wagner: "This symphony is the *Apotheosis of Dance* herself; it is the Dance in her highest aspect, as it were the loftiest deed of bodily motion incorporated in an ideal mold of tone."[73] Purists still sputtered, but the dancer had won. Socialist Max Eastman, who became editor of *The Masses* in 1912, likened Isadora in her own country to Whitman. "She did indeed fly out like a sunlit bird from that dark mass of prophetic imagery," Eastman wrote. "She rode the wave of the revolt against puritanism; she rode it, and with her fame and Dionysian raptures drove it on. Perhaps it is simplest to say that she *was* the crest of the wave — an event not only in art, but in the history of life."[74]

14

Daughter of Prometheus

In November 1908 a reporter for the *New York Sun* caught up with Isadora at her Beaux-Arts studio. The apartment had been stripped, the walls hung "with soft folds of blue that fall from the cornice and away and swing like summer clouds." A small table held photographs of family and friends — among them, Deirdre, whom Isadora casually identified as "the daughter of Gordon Craig." On the floor and along the walls were pillows and low divans, draped in fabric of blue and white. The *Sun* reported:

> On one of these Miss Duncan is found coiled, like a soft, fussy caterpillar after a 4 o'clock rain. She admits that the rain in her case was a party she gave herself, and the tips of her graceful hands find her temples and press them sympathetically every few minutes. As it is then 5 o'clock in the afternoon and the party has been over only twelve hours there seems abundant reason for the throbbing pulses. . . . Her short, dark hair is coiled and curled in a loose knot at the nape of her neck, parted simply, Madonna-like, about her face, which she describes in a particularly headachy moment as having "an upturned nose and grayish bluey eyes." Many of her press notices speak of her as being tall and statuesque — a triumph of art, for Miss Duncan is in reality but 5 feet 6 and weighs 129 pounds.

She was entertaining a group of poets, according to the *Sun,* guests from the previous night, who had returned "to pay their party call lest they forget it" and uncork the next magnum of champagne. Ridgely Torrence had arrived, "blond and buoyant," with *The Touchstone's* Mary Roberts and her husband, Billy; playwright Percy MacKaye, a leader of the American civic arts movement and son of the actor Steele Mac-Kaye, who introduced Delsarte's "emotional expression" to the United States; Lloyd Osbourne, William Vaughn Moody, Edwin Arlington Robinson, and "a prophet, who is introduced by no other name and seems to vary the species by being treated with honor." The reporter noticed Isadora's feet — "fine, alert, well-shaped. . . . They are feet that have learned not to press unduly on the unpleasant realities of life. They glide over, not down and through. They are feet that are led and do not lead."

That evening, as she did almost every evening, Isadora danced for her guests:

> Amber border lights are turned on, and a yellow disk in the center of the ceiling glows softly, completing the color effects. Miss Duncan apologizes for the incongruity of the piano music.
>
> "There should be no music for such a dance as this," she says, "except such music as Pan might make on a reed cut from the river bank, a flute perhaps, a shepherd's pipe — that is all. . . . It is to revive [the] lost art of dancing that I have devoted my life. . . ."
>
> She has been standing near her parterre of poets when she begins to talk, and when she finishes she is at the other side of the room. You do not know how she got there, but you think of her friend Ellen Terry as she does it, and the latter's nonchalant way of ignoring space.

Isadora's dance isn't described in the *Sun's* report. It is simply said that she became "a pagan spirit" when she began to move, "stepping naturally from a bit of broken marble as if that were the most obvious thing in the world to do. A Galatea, perhaps, for certainly Galatea danced in the first few moments of her release."[1] The shared images of Isadora's contemporaries were all of Greece and its familiar myths; the music she employed for her dances, with few exceptions, was also well known to concert audiences. But what the audience experienced when Isadora danced was startlingly new and cathartic, a window, or a mirror, into the souls of the spectators themselves.

In Chicago, where she gave three concerts at the end of November, local debutantes in lavender tunics sold roses and violets in the lobby of Orchestra Hall, alongside copies of Isadora's *Dance of the Future,* specially translated and printed for her American tour. GIRL'S ART DANCE AIRY AS HER GARB, said the *Chicago Tribune:* "Isadora Duncan's Revival of Greek Steps Brings Calls for Opera Glasses." There followed obligatory comment on Isadora's costume, or lack of it — "There was a gasp of delight from the audience and a general stir of craning necks" — and a Chicago newspaperman's best effort to describe the figure before him: "Her arms were uplifted as though she were gathering ghost flowers in the air. They were bare. Her hair hung in a dark mass around her shoulders. A soft white texture clung carelessly over her bosom and fluttered in the air the dancer made. White feet, like two doves, gleamed on the dark green carpet." At the end of the evening, "the cheers and applause would not stop."

"That was an encore," Isadora cried. "Do you want something more?" The audience roared, and she laughed: "You must go home, you know, for I would stay here dancing all night!"[2] She had recently premiered her rendition of Schubert's *Moment Musicale,* which she later described as a tribute to Pim and the "pure delightful pleasure" she had found after her break with Gordon Craig: "I forgot my chagrin, and lived in the moment and was careless and happy. . . . My performances bubbled over with renewed vitality and joy."[3] Two thousand people were turned away from one of Isadora's concerts in Philadelphia, while the *Harvard Lampoon* paid her tribute in verse:

> We like your dance's swift surprise,
> We hope it doesn't give you pain —
> "La Reine est morte" — *Salome dies!*
> Well, requiescat. "Vive la Reine!"[4]

At her opening night in Chicago, Isadora's audience refused to leave until she had danced both the *Moment Musicale* and the *Blue Danube.* Even then, after "the musicians climbed on the stage and started for the exit," the crowd kept whistling and cheering, until Isadora herself disappeared with a final wave. When she returned to the United States the following year, 1909, Methodist ministers in St. Louis adopted a resolution condemning her as a "Jumping Jezebel." Even at the time, such attacks were lightly dismissed — indeed, they only added to Isadora's appeal.[5] Walter Damrosch's teenaged daughter, Gretchen, saw every Duncan concert her father let her attend and cried at each one, "my first tears shed at the startling quality of beauty," she recalled. "I must have been studying mythology, for it seemed to me that Isadora was Daphne dancing in some ancient glade, and that behind the trees lurked Apollo, but that she, the nymph, did not know or care that he was there. Let him later transform her to a laurel, but now she wanted only to dance alone to the music of Gluck, a wild and happy creature — for she was free."

Like other girls in New York, Gretchen Damrosch repaired to Bloomingdale's after seeing Isadora dance and bought cheesecloth, "enough to outfit a hundred Greeks in kirtles. It was very cheap, eleven cents a yard, and I wanted to be sure I had enough. . . . I made a hole for my head, sewed up the sides, chopped off the bottom, and tied the corded belt of my wrapper around my waist." Gretchen never got further than posing in front of the mirror, however, having discovered immediately that Isadora's dancing was less instant than it looked.[6]

"They thought it was easy to do what they saw her do, because it looked easy," said the actress Margherita Sargent, who later married Augustin Duncan. "Technique, I take it, is the mastery of one's medium of expression to the point at which the means disappears and only the result is seen; they mistook the perfection of Isadora's technique for lack of it, and thought that all they had to do was let themselves go, and the same beauty would come forth." Isadora always discouraged her imitators, whether professional or amateur. Sargent tells the story of a later appearance in New York, when Isadora agreed to take part in Percy MacKaye's "civic masque," *Caliban of the Golden Sands,* and "found herself near a group of 'Greek' dancers" at City College of New York's Lewisohn Stadium.

"If it weren't for you," said one, "we wouldn't be doing this. Don't you feel proud?"

Isadora looked the girl in the eye and answered, "I regard what you do with perfect horror."[7] The forthrightness of her manner and conversation startled even New Yorkers. At a party in her honor in 1909, during her second American tour, she spent the whole evening lying on a sofa, "à la Mme Récamier." Introducing herself, one woman said, "Please, don't get up."

"I have no intention of doing so," Isadora replied.[8] John Butler Yeats, father of the poet, met her at a New York restaurant and "at once understood her to be the oddest and most unexpected person in the world. She forms her own plans and is quite indifferent to what people think or say, for that reason she is never aggressive just as she makes no effort to conciliate any one."[9] In 1908 she caused a sensation when she first walked down Broadway in sandals: "Cars stopped at the delectable vision. Death-dealing automobiles lingered in their course of destruction. Pedestrians stared, turned, laughed or gasped according to their temperaments. . . . But Miss Duncan, undismayed, pursued the even tenor of her way."[10] Yeats told his son in Ireland: "People are much divided about her merits, the rival parties hating each other like the Capulets and the Montagues. The young girls are full of enthusiasm for her. Those a little older puzzled and somewhat shocked, the elder ladies furious. She herself wears a bonnet with a long veil and has a most demure expression."[11] Both onstage and off, she wore lipstick, "but was not in the habit of spending much time over maquillage."[12]

Isadora stayed in New York for a month after her first tour with Damrosch ended, and might have stayed longer, she wrote, "if it had not been for the pulling at my heart-strings to see my baby and my school."[13] She lectured about her school wherever she went that fall, telling the New York Sun: "My children! It is of them I love best to talk. How could I hope to revive the lost art of dancing without their help? If I should die, if I should become disabled, who else would there be to carry on the work on which I have spent all my years and all my resources?"[14] The Sun reported that Isadora's students "are just now enjoying the delights of residence in a château, about forty miles from Paris."[15] In fact, the girls were living, without heat or running water, in one of the outbuildings of the Château Villegenis, at La Verrière, where Elizabeth Duncan had left them, on Isadora's recommendation. If she never knew the circumstances of their confinement, she also never asked — "as an artist Isadora had genius," said Gretchen Damrosch, "as a person she was a goose." With hindsight, Gretchen understood that Isadora's designs on Walter Damrosch had been more than professional:

> She had theories about everything and my father had to listen to all of them. He would watch her across the footlights, enraptured, and then she would come to the house and he and my mother would become rapidly unenraptured, almost frantic. She called my father "Walter" and my mother "Mrs. Damrosch" and still my father remained tied. She urged my father to come to her chilly loft after a performance to really talk about fundamentals but my father said he was hot from conducting and wanted to get home and take a bath. So Isadora had to come to our home to explain to my father in her curiously flat little voice how one should live if one really wanted to live. . . . My mother, who greatly admired her dancing, would praise her latest performance

to the skies. Isadora would thank [her] graciously and then ask if a lamp or two could be turned out because she could express herself better in a dim light.[16]

At her parties in New York, where "champagne flowed like brooks in spring," Isadora surpassed her own record for merrymaking. Her doors were open to anyone with a talent and a friend, preferably male. George Grey Barnard came one night with MacKaye, William Vaughn Moody, and Edwin Arlington Robinson — three American poets whose greatest successes still lay in the future and whom Isadora called her "young revolutionists." She greeted them in the corridor, "like a maenad, with a rout of revelers at her heels," dancing tributes to all three, in sequence. "You know," she said coyly, "dancers were made for poets."[17] In Boston an angry letter to the *Herald* denounced her as a "terpsichorean Trilby," adding that her dancing, "like most odors of the Orient . . . is unmentionable."[18] Isadora called a press conference at the Hotel Touraine to warn that the city had gone "Bacchic." She had seen dancing in the streets.

"Let the women of Boston don their golden sandals and their diaphanous draperies, and go out and dance on Boston Common in the moonlight," she exhorted the reporters. "I look forward to the day when I shall lead the maidens of Boston, clothed in white, with dandelions in their hair, round Boston Common in the spring." When someone asked her if Boston was anything like Athens, she fell over laughing.

"You've got me! You've got me!" Isadora said. "Well, there is some difference. I can't describe it, but if I were in Athens I'd know it at once from Boston. . . . And it's true. A great wave of dancing, of revelry, has swept over your city. All Boston is dancing." She turned to her brother Augustin, who came with her on tour. "What were those people doing, anyway, Gus?"

"The African dodger."

"Truly Bacchic, anyway," said Isadora: "Don't forget to say something about my striking beauty; my features are not classical, but they are — well — oh, yes, and remember that I wore diaphanous draperies. I don't know what I should do if I had an interview where my draperies were not called diaphanous."[19]

Foremost in Isadora's thoughts on her return to Europe was the fate of her school. In April 1908 she had closed the house at

Grunewald and dismissed the staff until further notice. "The petty persecution of the Prussian police made it impossible to continue any longer," she told reporters in New York, only half truthfully: "Not a day passed but some helmeted gendarme put his face in at the door with some impertinent inquiry."[20] In fact, Isadora had grown tired of the continual hunt for support. She "was beginning to allow the unacceptable idea of disbanding what was left of the school to creep in at the edges of her mind," according to Preston Sturges, who, with his mother, Mary Desti, now lived permanently in France. Mary had divorced Solomon Sturges and embarked on a spiritual quest that led her to the cult of Aleister Crowley, the British "black magician," whose reputed orgies and manifestos on the occult had earned him a reputation as "the wickedest man in the world."[21] Mary, for a time his lover and most fervent disciple, was known in Crowley's circle as Soror Virakam — the Server of Light — endorsing Crowley's "satanic" maxim, Do what thou wilt shall be the whole of the law.

It was already Isadora's creed. "For I have never waited to do as I wished," she wrote.[22] In Paris, where she returned in January 1909, she turned to Aurélien Lugné-Poë, the French impresario, director of the avant-garde Théâtre de l'Oeuvre, and Eleonora Duse's manager in France. Isadora invited Lugné-Poë to her hotel suite and greeted him without rising from her divan. "You are Lugni [sic]," she said. "Do what you will with me." She meant to follow her American success at once with a Paris season. "She wanted Paris to know about her school," Lugné-Poë recalled, "and to interest the government or the city in its fate."[23]

At the same time, as she reported in My Life, Isadora turned to telepathy in the hope of attracting money to her cause. "I must find a millionaire!" she said, repeating the phrase "a hundred times a day, first [as] a joke and then, finally, according to the Coué system, in earnest."[24] (The French psychotherapist Emile Coué was the author of the first and most famous dictum of mass-marketed positive thinking: "Every day in every way, I am getting better and better.") One way or another, Isadora persuaded Lugné-Poë to present her with the children at the Théâtre-Lyrique Municipale de la Gaité in Montparnasse (shortened in popular discourse to the Gaité-Lyrique). "Isadora's personality was singular," Lugné-Poë explained, "and there was no other."[25] With her booking secured, she sent for the girls.

Outside Paris, at La Verrière, the Grunewald children were living in a state of uncertainty. Their temporary residence, the Château Villegenis, had once belonged to Jérôme Bonaparte and was now owned by an American, the wife of a steel magnate, Mrs. W. E. Corey.[26] Elizabeth had brought the girls to the château in August 1908 and then disappeared, telling the children that she would be looking after Deirdre in Isadora's absence. (It seems that she retired to give birth to her own child, in fact, born dead.) In the meantime, on the order of Maybelle Corey's mother, a Mrs. Gilman, the girls were banished from the château itself to a small apartment overlooking the stable courtyard — there were four rooms and sixteen girls. Soon their German governess quit, leaving them alone and without money, as Irma reported, "not even a penny's worth to buy an occasional lollipop or a ribbon for our hair."[27] Irma's account of these days reads like a page from *Les Misérables:*

> The winter that year in France proved to be exceptionally severe. It was so cold that the pump froze and the older girls needed to hack the ice away to get water for our cold baths. By then our open sandals had worn thin and had such big holes in them that we were practically walking barefoot in the snow. Our clothing, too, was threadbare and provided little warmth. Fortunately, some coal fires in an open grate provided a little heat in the tiny rooms, otherwise we would surely have frozen to death. . . . Through our tears, hungry as the mice in the wainscotting, we gnawed on raw acorns and chestnuts that we had gathered in the woods for Christmas presents — the only ones we had. We cried ourselves to sleep, lying on the miserable pallets on the floor.[28]

Irma's description of life at Villegenis filled a whole chapter of her autobiography, *Duncan Dancer,* written more than fifty years after the events of that winter and still aching with resentment. Her chronology, among other things, is completely awry, and her account was disputed by some of the other girls. In a letter to her parents, Anna described Villegenis as "very beautiful and interesting." A new governess had been appointed immediately; Max Merz and the drawing master, Konrad Müller-Fürer, were constantly on the scene.[29] And they had Preston Sturges for company — Mary Desti had opened a chicken farm at Fleurines. That winter Preston taught the girls to ride, "which they did with many squeals," in decided contrast to their self-possession in performance.

"They were lovely looking and beautifully built little girls," Preston recalled, "in age slightly above to slightly below me, and all wonderful dancers."[30] It's true that they were stranded in France and that they hated their confinement. In 1908, Anna hadn't seen her family for two years, while Irma wrote to her mother in Hamburg to say that she had "almost forgotten what you look like."[31] Even so, she never faulted Isadora — "our idol, our goddess. . . . Insufficient control and superintendence is the only blame attached to her, since she sincerely believed that by placing us in the trusted care of her sister, she had left us in the best of hands."[32]

In the background, although not behind the scenes, Elizabeth made plans of her own. With Merz, she had turned to Ernst-Ludwig, Grand Duke of Hesse, with a plea for support and funding for the Duncan school. "Ernie" of Hesse was a grandson of Queen Victoria and a brother of Russia's Empress Alexandra, a well-known liberal and patron of the arts in a sea of princely philistines. He warmed instantly to Elizabeth's appeal, finally offering her a plot of land at Marienhöhe, near the Hessian capital of Darmstadt; funding to build a school and dormitory on the property came from different parts of Germany, as surely and smoothly as Isadora's efforts in the same direction proved futile. Neither she nor her students realized, at first, that Elizabeth and Merz's school would be devoted not to dance per se but to "physical culture and racial hygiene." Eugenics was Merz's particular obsession. "A fanatic on the subject," Irma wrote, "ambitious and an opportunist, he managed to exert a kind of Svengali influence over Elizabeth."[33] Other of the girls remembered Merz kindly, as a first-rate musician and needed organizer of the school's curriculum and finances. For now, they were told only that the school would shortly go back to Germany, news they greeted with relief. "Sometimes I sit here and reflect on things," Irma wrote to her mother, "but then I'm gripped with such a terrible longing that I feel like ripping myself to pieces."[34]

When Isadora suddenly reappeared in January, the girls were surprised to learn that she expected them to dance with her immediately: they had had no regular dance instruction for six months. In Paris she rented two apartments in rue Danton, on the Left Bank, one for herself and Deirdre and the other for her students. Isadora had already leased a studio in the Hôtel Biron at 77, rue de Varenne, now the site of the Rodin museum. The eighteenth-century structure, designed by Jacques-Ange Gabriel, enclosed a large, untended garden, kept in a state of chaos in order to remind artist-tenants of their debt to nature. Rodin, Rainer Maria Rilke (who for a time was Rodin's secretary), Henri Matisse, actor Edouard de Max, and the young Jean Cocteau all had studios at Hôtel Biron, which became the site of such raucous entertainments, "Roman" parties, and fêtes champêtres that the French government, which owned the building, shut it down.[35]

From the Hôtel Biron, Isadora captured the Paris beau monde in 1909, a year remembered as a turning point in the history of modern art. At his studio in Montmartre, Picasso had entered his cubist period, in collaboration with Georges Braque. The Italian F. T. Marinetti published the Futurists' Manifesto, with its rejection of art tradition and emphasis on "dynamism," motion, machinery, and speed.[36] Gide, Claudel, Péguy, Mirbeau, Apollinaire, Colette, and Proust were all writing in Paris. That year, Proust completed "Souvenir d'une matinée," the germ of the work that became *A la recherche du temps perdu.* The modern cinema was born in France; Sarah Bernhardt ruled the stage with Madame Réjane and Cécile Sorel, the "brightest jewel" of the Comédie-Française, while in cabarets and music halls, Yvette Guilbert "made the angels swoon" (and was said to be richer than the tsar of Russia). It was the artistic year of wonders, crowned by the opening of the Ballets Russes at the Théâtre du Châtelet in May.

When her students arrived from Villegenis, Isadora dispatched them to the rising star of French couture, Paul Poiret, who outfitted the girls in green silk coats, dresses, and "little green hats" that set them apart in the most fashionable company. Poiret was the first celebrity fashion designer, an event in his own right, who almost single-handedly liberated Parisian women from the prison of tight corsets, jutting busts, shelflike behinds, and muted colors — "lilacs, swooning mauves . . . niles, maizes, straws, all that was soft, washed-out and insipid," as Poiret later wrote: "I threw into this sheepcote a few rough wolves: reds, greens, violets, royal blues, that made all the rest sing aloud . . . the morbid mauves were hunted out of existence."[37]

In 1906 Poiret had offered the first dresses in his high-waisted, loose-cut "Empire line," known in Paris as *le vague,* "the wave." One of these he named for Isadora. Three years later, distilling the era, he adapted Léon Bakst's costumes for the Ballets Russes into eveningwear and launched both a perfume and interior-design business. "Poiret's showmanship was the catalyst that finally changed the way women all over the world walked, held themselves, gestured, ate, spoke," writes Elizabeth Kendall. "Within several years he had caused all dressmakers to raise waists, narrow skirts, and add flowing tunic effects to gowns. It was as if some gigantic hook had let go of women at the base of their backs, releasing them into sinuous plastic poses."[38] When Isadora soon bought her own studio in Neuilly, on the outskirts of

Paris, she turned it over to Poiret for renovation. It would be both home and stage, a cavernous, shrewdly lit shrine to Paris's newfound goddess of dance — *"Fille de Prométhée,"* as poet Fernand Divoire called Isadora at the height of her glory in France: Daughter of Prometheus.[39]

Tickets for Isadora's concerts at the Gaité-Lyrique, where she and her pupils made their debut on January 27, 1909, with the Concerts Lamoureux Orchestra, were sold out within hours of being announced. "A queue of equipages and luxurious motorcars" lined the front of the theater at her first performance. Inside, the audience was "crammed to the rafters."[40] Isadora hadn't danced in Paris since 1904, when she premiered the *Seventh Symphony* at the Trocadéro. Now she presented *Iphigenia,* with her students taking part as her attendants and play-mates, the maidens of Chalcis. "They passed over Paris like a breath of spring," wrote architect Louis Sue — it was "the most stunning, the most original" performance he had ever seen.[41] Edith Wharton came and remembered the event as "a white milestone. . . . It shed a light on every kind of beauty, and showed me for the first time how each flows into the other as the music merged with her dancing. All through the immense, rapt audience one felt the rush of her inspiration."[42]

The Gaité-Lyrique held 2,200 seats, and for the length of Isadora's run none of them was empty. At the end of May the *New York Times* reported that her dancing had created "a furore" in the French capi-tal.[43] In *Le Figaro,* French deputy Joseph Paul-Boncour appealed to the government for "a society to perpetuate the art of this sublime dancer" and a revision of the course of instruction and dance training at the state-run Paris Opéra. Paul-Boncour went further and pro-nounced the ballet dead: "We should go along with [Isadora], along with her as an artist. . . . The state must recognize her usefulness for the public good."[44]

On May 19 Isadora sat in the glittering front row of diplomats, ministers, Russian dignitaries, artists, and Paris beauties at the Théâtre du Châtelet, where Diaghilev presented the first performances of the Ballets Russes: *Le Pavillon d'Armide,* the Polovtsian Dances from Borodin's *Prince Igor,* and an extended pastiche, set to the music of Rus-sian composers, which Diaghilev called *Le Festin.* Later in the season *Les Sylphides* and *Cléopâtre* were added to the repertory. All were cho-reographed by Michel Fokine, with designs by Benois and Bakst.

For his Paris opening, Diaghilev had completely remade the Châtelet, transforming it from a serviceable but unfashionable theater into "a gigantic salon," with seats, carpets, and walls in scarlet red and the foyers and dress circle thick with statuary and potted plants. "The most beautiful actresses in Paris" filled the grand tier at the *répétition générale,* blondes alternating with brunettes at Diaghilev's command: "Not a tail-coat, not a bald head to break through the lustrous semi-circle: only beauty, diamonds and bare shoulders."[45] Among artists, Diaghilev's invited audience included Rodin, Mirbeau, Fauré, Saint-Saëns, Lina Cavalieri, Yvette Guilbert, Fyodor Chaliapin, and the poet Anna de Noailles. "All artists understood that this was more than exotic entertainment," wrote Maurice Brillant. "I do not believe that in the entire history of our theatre there was a more rapid revolution, a more irresistible foreign invasion, or a quicker triumph. The battle, if there was a battle at all, was won on the first night."[46]

The unparalleled impact of the Ballets Russes sprang from Diaghilev's vision of total theater, a ravishing synthesis of music, dance, drama, and design, unlike anything Paris had seen. In the following days, two topics were the talk of the city: the exotic sets and costumes of Bakst and Benois; and Vaslav Nijinsky, whose frank sexuality and fantastic leaps reminded Paris, and Isadora, of something long lost to the art of dance — the male. As Nijinsky replied, when asked if his airborne leaps were difficult to execute, "No, no. Not difficult. You have to just go up and pause a little up there." Fashionable Parisians of both sexes, who pursued him with passion, were dismayed to discover that in life, Nijinsky was awkward, withdrawn, and tongue-tied — an "idiot of genius," said Misia Sert.[47] Isadora was staggered by his grace and prowess. She left no written record of Diaghilev's premiere but never concealed her amazement at Nijinsky and his luminous partners, Pavlova and Tamara Karsavina. All three were "ethereal" artists, in Isadora's view, their "divine genius" transcending the abomination of their form.

"There is this difference between Isadora Duncan and me," Pavlova remarked in 1910. "She lives to dance, and I dance to live."[48] Neither Pavlova nor any ballet dancer would allow that Isadora's technique held a candle to her own. "You see," Pavlova explained, "she never has to get up and dance on her toes, and I do."[49] Isadora applauded Diaghilev's goal of synthesizing the arts but deplored his means on principle. With their painted sets, gushing fountains, and fake greenery, the Ballets Russes seemed to her not an advance but a regression, a step in the wrong direction for a theater that needed simplifying, above all things. A decade later, long after Fokine, Nijinsky, and Pavlova had left the company, Isadora wrote from London: "The

Russian ballet are hopping madly about in Picasso pictures. Very silly — sort of epileptic gymnastic with no strength or center. I often wonder to what domain of Insanity they will hop to next — If that is Art I prefer Aviation."[50]

In the fall of 1909, on a trip to Venice, Isadora encountered Nijinsky on the Lido, where she tried to dance with him,[51] to his embarrassment, and asked him to father her next child. The only source for this story is Romola de Pulszky, Nijinsky's future wife and guardian, but the tale repeats itself so often, with one "divine genius" or another as the object of Isadora's attention, that it can't be dismissed out of hand.[52] For the record, Nijinsky and Diaghilev both praised Isadora's work — "She has dared to give liberty to movement," said Nijinsky, "she has opened the door of the cell to the prisoners"[53] — but as lovers and partners in the dance, they belittled her as an amateur and a rival. In 1912 Diaghilev confessed that the Ballets Russes needed to "search for new trends in movement, but one that will circumvent Isadora Duncan, who doesn't appear to be old-fashioned simply because her talent is so forceful."[54]

At the Gaité-Lyrique, Isadora's concerts continued to pack the house. Her dancing figure was compared to the Nike of Samothrace in the Louvre — better known as *Winged Victory* — to Greuze's head of Athena, to the Pyrrhic dancers described by Plato to illustrate the natural movements of warriors in combat, "be it flinging oneself to the side, drawing back, leaping, or bending."[55] Isadora answered that no matter what was said or written about her, she was bound to be misunderstood. Allan Ross Macdougall, her future friend, secretary, and biographer, reports noisy bands of art students at the Gaité-Lyrique, where Isadora added encores specially for them. Among her most popular works was *Death and the Maiden,* which she had performed without music as early as 1903 and preferred to call *Life and the Maiden,* since it expressed the struggle of existence. Now set to a Chopin mazurka, *Death and the Maiden* never failed to stir the audience.

"I know of nothing more beautiful than the sudden transformation of this young creature, dancing and laughing at life, who suddenly feels herself seized by death," wrote Jeanne Gazeau in *Les entretiens idéalistes.* "It is only a shudder, then an effort to shake off the cold embrace, finally a desperate hardening of her whole being and a supreme convulsion, when she seems to shrink into herself like a flower against the blow, and then falls dead. It is the eternal mystery of death in all its anguished simplicity. . . . I am only reporting the facts: I saw people weeping who were laughing when it started."[56] In her studio Isadora began to explore new movements, "wild and terrifying" motions and gestures that broke completely with her lyrical dances of the past. She was ready to take her art to a deeper and more disturbing level. Fernand Divoire recalled an encore presentation at the Gaité-Lyrique after the orchestra had left and "hundreds of remaining spectators still clamored for more." The piece, untitled, was an allegory of the will:

> "I am going to dance the philosophy of my life," she says. She dances in silence.
>
> She is before a bronze door, is she not? An invisible bronze door, yes, that's it. Invisible and impassable as destiny.
>
> She hurls herself against it. To beat it down with a blow, with a push, with the tremendous dash of youth. And now she lies there, downed.
>
> She returns obstinately, with all the power of one who wills.
>
> And always rejected. . . .
>
> And always conquered by the solid, dumb door. . . .
>
> She finally doubts.
>
> She supplicates.
>
> She gathers all her strength. Oh, it is perhaps her last effort; perhaps the last stone to be thrown; her last pile of faggots to be thrown to the philosophic flames; and then there is nothing more.
>
> But the last twig must be burned.
>
> She gathers all her strength.
>
> AND THE DOOR HAS SHAKEN. Unhinged. IT FALLS TO EARTH.
>
> And that is what is called Victory.

"Oh," Divoire concluded, "may this same will be given to us, to cast down, at the same cost, the door of Destiny."[57]

In February 1909, during the first days of her triumph at the Gaité-Lyrique, Isadora met Paris Singer, the next-to-youngest of the twenty-four children of Isaac Merritt Singer, American founder of the Singer Sewing Machine Company.[58] Named for the city of his birth, Paris Singer was raised in England, where his father had died in 1875, when Paris was only seven, leaving him a sizable portion of the Singer estate and an income from investments estimated at fifteen thousand dollars a week. It is futile to place a current valuation on a nineteenth-century fortune of that size; calculated for inflation, Paris Singer's income from interest alone would now exceed a million dollars a month. His mother, Isabella Boyer, was French, the daughter of a tavern-keeper who had married the aging Isaac Singer in New York when she was just twenty-one. (At Isaac's death, Isabella's six children won precedence over the eighteen others, most of them illegitimate, whom the patriarch had sired with his first wife and a string of litigious mistresses.)

Isaac Singer's reputation for philandering was sufficiently known in New York society to prevent the second Mrs. Singer from breaking into it, and for that reason, shortly before Paris's birth, the family had left Yonkers for Europe. Isaac Singer lived out his days in the mansion he called The Wigwam at Oldway, near Paignton, on the Devonshire coast, which Paris transformed after his father's death into a fanciful replica of the palace of Versailles. Money was no object, and Paris had a penchant for the grand.

He was six feet three inches tall, blond, bearded, "of fine physique, handsome, highly educated, with a Court of St. James['s] air" and the appearance of "a Renaissance king."[59] The tangled negotiations and lawsuits over the disposition of his father's estate convinced the young Singer that his fortune needed sheltering from both lawyers and relatives, and especially from his still youthful widowed mother. At his own request, therefore, "while still in knee pants," Paris Singer was made a ward of the British court, where he became a companion of the children of the future King Edward VII and a favorite of Queen Alexandra. At Cambridge he studied medicine, chemistry, and engineering, at the same time entering the first of many romantic scrapes when he secretly eloped with one of his mother's maids, Henriette Marais. The union was annulled, and in 1887 Singer married an Australian, Lillie Graham, by whom he had five children. Marital ties did nothing to stop his progress as one of the great swains of the Belle Epoque, "a celebrated international Romeo," with a villa at Cap Ferrat; an apartment in the place des Vosges; a town house in Cadogan Square in London (where he also owned a block of Sloane Street); a four-hundred-ton yacht, the *Lady Evelyn;* and his jewel, the Oldway mansion.

Like his elder sister Winaretta, Princess de Polignac, Paris Singer became a generous patron of the arts, which he approached with the same impatient zeal he brought to his quixotic (and usually disastrous) business ventures. Unlike Winaretta, however, whose skill as a painter and musician earned her the respect of the artists who passed through her Paris salon, Singer never honed a talent of his own. Nervous, a hypochondriac, prone to tantrums and sulking, he remained the dilettante par excellence, "the last of the universal men," according to *The New Yorker*'s Alva Johnston, "an artist, athlete, scholar, scientist, art patron, sports patron, philanthropist, and amateur in architecture, medicine, and music." Airplanes, boats, and cars were Singer's enduring passions, along with beautiful women and the march of technology; he installed the wiring system at Edward VII's country estate at Sandringham and later interested Queen Alexandra in a line of electric motor cars, which he hoped would revolutionize private transportation. Although he held no professional degree, Singer nevertheless hung a plaque, P. E. SINGER, ARCHITECT, on the door of his mansion in London.

"Any disappointment in a romantic matter caused him to console himself with architecture," Johnston wrote. "A tiff was enough to start him on a villa or harbor improvement. A broken heart inspired a project for a great medical-research institute, but a reconciliation canceled it." At one point Singer was reportedly engaged in "a search for a compound to abolish all diseases" and "swallowed a new drug called aspirin in such quantities that for a time his life was despaired of."[60] Preston Sturges, who loved him deeply, remembered Singer as "a celebrated collector of antiques, a famous, although invariably seasick, yachtsman, a generous backer of Rudolf Diesel and his inventions, and an encourager and contributing supporter of the great French surgeon, Doyen. . . . He told me to call him Uncle Mum."[61]

By 1909 Singer had separated from his wife. They would not be divorced until 1918, but even before they parted, the list of Singer's sexual conquests had piled up high. "He was very good-looking," said his only daughter, a second Winaretta, "and women threw themselves at him, and he'd had a great many *affaires* — but when he saw Isadora he fell straight in love with her before she fell in love with him, which was quite the other way round, usually."[62] Isadora recalled that Singer had presented himself one morning in her dressing room at the theater: "I remember I had my hair in curling-papers for the afternoon matinée, and it was covered with a little lace cap. My maid came to me with a visiting card on which I read a well-known name, and suddenly there sang in my brain: 'Here is my millionaire!'" She replied to the maid: "Let him enter!"

Thus began the longest and most turbulent romantic attachment of Isadora's life: "He entered, tall and blond, curling hair and beard. My first thought was: Lohengrin. Wer will mein Ritter sein?" [Who will be my champion?].[63] In Arthurian legend, Lohengrin is the son of Parsifal, a knight of the Holy Grail, who sails to Antwerp in a boat drawn by swans and wins the hand of the king's daughter, Elsa de Brabant. Lohengrin marries Elsa on a condition, that she must never speak his name. Isadora never identified Singer in her autobiography, calling him only Lohengrin or "L." She remembered his appearance at the Gaité-Lyrique as a longed-for wind from Olympus. He had brought his daughter with him to show the purity of his intentions. "Don't stay too long because I have business to discuss with her," Singer told the young Winaretta before entering Isadora's dressing room. "You go to her dancing children . . . and you be with them."[64]

With the joining of children, the seduction began. "I admire your art," Singer said, "your courage in the ideal of your school. I have come to help you. What can I do?" During their first conversation, Isadora realized that she had met him before, in 1901, at the funeral of her early patron, Prince Edmond de Polignac, Singer's brother-in-law. "We had met first in a church before a coffin," Isadora wrote. "No prophecy of happiness, that! Nevertheless, from that moment I realised that this was my millionaire, for whom I had sent my brain-waves seeking. . . . For whatever fate, it was *Kismet*."[65] At the end of her engagement, she left for the south of France with Deirdre and all the children of the school, settling into a villa at Beaulieu, while Singer stayed nearby in a hotel at Nice. Before leaving Paris, Isadora had seen Gordon Craig, who "chanced to be passing through." He recalled that they had walked in the Bois du Boulogne as Isadora unburdened her heart.

"She began telling me of the wonderful things Singer might be about to do for her & for her school," Craig wrote. "He had a yacht — something to do with this — at Nice, was it? — She told me & added, 'But I hear he is far too fond of young girls.'" Craig thought it "a nasty mean thing to say about a man she did not quite know but who (evidently) was about to help her with half a million pounds."[66] After they became lovers in Beaulieu, Isadora sailed for Italy with Singer and Deirdre on the *Lady Evelyn*. She wrote:

> I can see it all as if it were yesterday: the broad deck of the yacht; the table set with crystal and silver for lunch, and Deirdre, in her white tunic, dancing about. Certainly I was in love and happy. And yet all the time I was unpleasantly aware of the stokers, stoking in the engine-room; the fifty sailors on the yacht; the Captain and the Mate — all this

immense expenditure for the pleasure of two people. Subconsciously I
was uneasy of mind at the passing of these days, each a loss from the
mark. And sometimes I contrasted unfavourably the ease of this life of
luxury, the continual feasting, the nonchalant giving up of one's being
to pleasure, with the bitter struggle of my early youth. Then quickly I
would react to the impression on my body and mind of the glory of the
dawn as it melted into the heat of a dazzling noon. My Lohengrin, my
Knight of the Grail, should come, too, to share the great idea![67]

In April, leaving Singer and the children, Isadora returned briefly
to Russia, where, as "Kismet" saw fit, Craig had gone to discuss *Hamlet* with Stanislavsky. "For a short moment I was on the verge of believing that nothing [else] mattered," Isadora wrote, "neither the
school, nor Lohengrin, nor anything — but just the joy of seeing him
again."[68] In St. Petersburg she gave a dinner for Craig and Stanislavsky
at her hotel, where they were joined by Isadora's "very pretty secretary," identified, happily for her, only as "Miss S." According to Craig,
Isadora had too much to drink, threw herself at Stanislavsky, "& began to kiss him — he objecting most politely all the time — & she refusing to accept his objections."[69] Seeing this, said Isadora, Craig "flew
into one of his old-time rages," picked up Miss S. in his arms, and carried her into the next room, locking the door behind them.
"Stanislavsky was terribly shocked," Isadora wrote. For half an hour
they knocked and pleaded, until Stanislavsky went home and Isadora
withdrew to her bedroom.[70] The secretary emerged the next morning
just in time to accompany Isadora to her train for Kiev. Craig recalled:

> As I helped to arrange the rugs [in Isadora's carriage] I could not
> help saying with polite smiles that I hoped she had passed a pleasant
> evening anyhow. To this she said neither a yea or a nay but, as was her
> custom when utterly boulversé, she uttered a brief sermon — said she,
> "Try to emulate the virtues of the good *good* man with whom we
> supped last night," & signing to the coachman to jolly well drive on
> she drove away. These sudden bursts of damnèd hypocritical sermo-
> nizing *rarely* seized her — but when they did one stood staggered &
> uncertain whether to weep, laugh, howl, or shoot. . . . Anyhow off she
> went by train to join Paris Singer, her millionaire in whose millions
> she so thoroughly believed & whose millions she came to curse.[71]

At the end of her Russian engagement, Singer met Isadora in Paris
and brought her to his apartment in Place des Vosges, where, "for the

first time," she learned "what the nerves and sensations can be transformed to. *I became a quivering mass of responsive senses in the hands of an expert voluptuary. . . . Like a flock of wild goats cropping the herbage of the soft hillside, so his kisses grazed over my body, and like the earth itself I felt a thousand mouths devouring me.*"* She would reach no ethereal planes with Singer, no heavenly spheres or paths of shining light. All would be played out in carnality, against a backdrop of unimaginable wealth.

"Like Zeus," wrote Isadora, "he transformed himself into many shapes and forms, and I knew him now as a Bull, now as a Swan, and again as a Golden Shower, and I was by this love carried over the waves, caressed with white wings delicately, and strangely seduced and hallowed in a Golden Cloud."[72]

---

* These italicized passages were excised from English editions of *My Life*.

15

To Love in a Certain Way

"All money brings a curse with it," Isadora wrote, "and the people who possess it cannot be happy for twenty-four hours."[1] Thus, in her autobiography, she renounced her affair with Paris Singer. "Even today I simply cannot comprehend how little he understood me and my work," Isadora told Victor Seroff, the Russian pianist who became her lover in 1926. "But, you see, you have never lived with a rich man. . . . That is the trouble, that is the core of it." Seroff reports that Isadora remained "so bewildered about her feelings toward [Singer] that she was incapable of giving a rational account of their union."[2] To another friend she confided, "We loved each other, and I think we hated each other by turns."[3]

They hadn't known each other long before they quarreled, in a clash of American sensibilities that set the tone for all their arguments to come. On the yacht, during their first Mediterranean cruise, Isadora read Whitman's "Song of the Open Road" to her lover, saying that it perfectly expressed her philosophy of life: "Camarado! Give me your hand!" When she finished, she looked up to find Singer's "handsome face congested with rage."

"What rot!" he said. "That man could never have earned his living!"

"Can't you see," said Isadora, "he had the vision of Free America!"

"Vision be damned!"

"And suddenly I realised that *his* vision of America was that of the dozens of factories which made his fortune for him," Isadora wrote. "But such is the perversity of woman that, after this and similar quarrels, I threw myself into his arms, forgetting everything under the brutality of his caresses." Before the end of 1909, they had already broken off and resumed their affair several times, in what became a reflexive pattern of melodramatic scenes and quiet reconciliations. Isadora wrote:

> If I had only realised that the man I was with had the psychology of a spoilt child, that every word and every action of mine should have been carefully prepared to please, all might have been well. But I was too young and too naïve to know this [she was thirty-two], and I prattled on, explaining to him my ideas of life, Plato's *Republic,* Karl Marx, and a general reform of the world, without the least notion of the havoc I was creating. This man, who had declared that he loved me for my courage and generosity, became more and more alarmed when he found what sort of red-hot revolutionary he had taken aboard his yacht. He gradually comprehended that he could not reconcile my ideals with his peace of mind.[4]

Unfortunately for Singer, no evidence exists to contradict Isadora's peevish assessment of his character. In all accounts, he emerges as a gracious but inveterate tyrant, "a capricious egotist"[5] who flitted from one exorbitant project to another without landing for long on any of them. "He was neither creative nor 'interpretive,'" Isadora said, "I mean in his schemes — none of them were ever carried out to the end."[6]

Singer's personality held a deadly combination, a desire to please mixed with a need to be flattered and thanked. Isadora told the story of another Mediterranean cruise, when Singer invited a number of her friends to join them, "prominent men in music, painting, sculpture, poetry and writing," who lay about the deck unshaven — a large sin in Singer's eyes — and refused to see the sights when the yacht anchored at Cairo. Singer erupted in rage, whereupon Isadora said that her friends were "true aristocrats"[7] and that Singer was too thick, or too rich, to know it. She seemed to get pleasure from taunting him.

As to Singer's daily work, over eight years Isadora never discovered what it was. She imagined he must have had an office somewhere to administer his financial holdings — "probably more than one" — but he seemed to spend most of his time on the telephone at home, "making dates for lunches, parties, God knows what." She appreciated the "magnificent libraries" in all of Singer's houses but doubted he had ever opened a book for anything but information.

"He was the busiest man you ever heard of," Isadora told Seroff later. "At one time he was going to build an Italian castle on Cap Ferrat and on Mondays he would be rushing to Paris, and then rushing back to Cap Ferrat on Wednesdays. . . . All those schemes, and always on the grandiose scale, were his diversions, and he thought the same way about my Art. Why should I want to do anything if everything would be served up to me by the magic wand?"[8] At the beginning, Isadora made a point of declining gifts and money from Singer — "not a single jewel," she declared. "He was always talking to me of the way women ran after him for his money and the presents he gave them; and I used to tell him that I was the one exception."[9] She lost her resolve in Paris, however, at least when it came to houses, dressmakers, and the acme of French civilization — food.

"I learned to know all the really good restaurants in the city of Paris," Isadora remembered, "where L. was kowtowed to and treated like a king. All the Maîtres d'Hôtel and all the cooks vied with one another to please him — and no wonder, for he distributed money in a truly royal manner." The girl who once drank goat milk with the rising sun in Athens soon learned "the difference between a *poulet cocotte* and a *poulet simple*[,] the different values of ortolans, truffles, and mushrooms," and the vintage of wines. Having sent her students to be outfitted by Paul Poiret, Isadora went there herself "and fell to the fatal lure of stuffs, colours, for.n — even hats." She excused her indulgence by saying that Poiret was "a genius. . . . Yet this was for me the change from sacred to profane art."[10]

When she returned to the stage of the Gaité-Lyrique in May and June 1909, Poiret put the last touches on Isadora's new studio at 68, rue Chauveau, in the wealthy suburb of Neuilly.[11] She had paid for the place herself, as she liked to remind people, before she met Singer. Set back from the road in a shaded park, a short distance from the Seine, the house had belonged to the painter Henri Gervex, who built it to work on a series of giant murals commissioned by Tsar Nicholas II in honor of his coronation in 1896. Inside, the open studio space measured twenty by thirty meters; a spiral staircase led to Isadora's rooms on the third floor, while Deirdre and her nurse lived in a separate, smaller building on the grounds. Isadora's pupil Irma wrote that walking into the Neuilly house "was like entering a cathedral. The long blue drapes covering the walls and hanging down from the ceiling in heavy folds suggested a Gothic interior. The soft light filtering through alabaster lamps overhead lent a mystic atmosphere."[12] A portrait by Carrière, *Maternité,* hung at one end of the hall. Incense burned; flowers were everywhere. "Filling the veranda were blue hydrangeas."[13]

Upstairs, Poiret transformed Isadora's private chamber into "a veritable domain of Circe. Sable black velvet curtains were reflected on the walls in golden mirrors," she wrote; "a black carpet and a divan with cushions of Oriental textures completed this apartment." The windows were covered, blocking out all sunlight, and the doors appeared to Isadora as "strange, Etruscan tomb-like apertures." She adored the sensualist effect: "The little room was beautiful, fascinating, and, at the same time, dangerous. Might there not be some character in furniture which makes all the difference between virtuous beds and criminal couches, respectable chairs and sinful divans?"[14]

How much of Singer's money went into the renovations at Neuilly is anyone's guess. In Isadora's temple, he was mainly relegated to the background. Visitors remembered Singer as "a strange silent man"[15] who sat stoically through endless evenings of music, art talk, and Duncan-worship. His own theatrical tastes ran notoriously to cabaret and can-can; Singer's idea of a dancing girl was entirely different from Isadora's, and he often left the house when she entertained.

If he failed to appreciate her art, as Isadora believed, Singer was even more put out by her behavior. She insisted that there was a love of the body and a love of the soul and that the two were not the same. "And as my Millionaire was not an artist," said Isadora cruelly, "my soul never belonged to him. It belonged sometimes to other artists, which made him very angry. In me he found a kind of defiance of his will. I suppose that fascinated him."[16] At no point in their liaison did Isadora seriously curtail her attentions to other men. That most of her male friends were homosexual seemed to infuriate Singer rather than console him: he knew that Isadora's pursuits never stopped with her first attempt. "Gone were the days of a glass of hot milk and Kant's *Critique of Pure Reason,*" she admitted. "Now it seemed to me more natural to sip champagne and have some charming person tell me how beautiful I was. The divine pagan body, the passionate lips, the clinging arms, the sweet refreshing sleep on the shoulder of some loved one — these were joys which seemed to me both innocent and delightful." Singer saw it differently, although he, too, found comfort in other beds when Isadora's flirtations and occasional affairs drove him storming from her house. No sooner had he taken another mistress, however, than she would beckon and the game began again. Since breaking with Craig, she had learned that "love might be a pastime as well as a tragedy."[17]

"What mad people the two of us must have seemed to the outside world," Isadora sighed. "Always quarreling, always loving. What a life!"[18] Only a handful of her letters to Singer survive in public archives. They present no surprises, and no high-flown paeans to the power of love. Yet, by her own admission, Isadora did love Singer; in the end, they were bound together by more than a battle of wills. "All these gratifications had their reactions," Isadora wrote, "and there were days when we spoke of that weird sickness — neurasthenia."[19] She left it there, although, by appearances, what she took for neurasthenia might easily have been hangover.

Late in their affair, Isadora asked Singer to tell her what it was about her that had attracted him for so long, and he replied, "You've got a good skin, and you've *never* bored me."[20] According to Isadora, he asked her to marry him many times, an invitation she declined on principle: "Can you imagine me no longer being Isadora Duncan, but Madame Singer? Well, I couldn't."[21] One of her students remembered Isadora saying calmly to Singer, "I can't marry you and sit here playing cards. I have a mission to fulfill."[22]

Isadora and Singer were already locked in combat when Stanislavsky came to Paris in June 1909 and found her "changed beyond recognition." In a letter to his wife, he reported that "Duncan . . . imitates a *Parisienne*," that she had taken him to dinner with Singer at a restaurant "full of courtesans and fops," that Singer was unable to disguise his jealousy, and that Isadora, when they said good night, secretly blew Stanislavsky a kiss.

"All this stupidity makes me despair," Stanislavsky wrote. "Has she really sold herself, or, even worse, is this exactly what she wants?"[23] He was sufficiently upset not to see Isadora backstage after her performance the next night, but she sent Lugné-Poë after him and he was caught. There had been "a big scene," she confided. Singer had left her in a jealous rage. Almost immediately, however, "much to the surprise of Duncan," Singer walked through the door and greeted Stanislavsky in his heartiest baronial manner. Would he come the next afternoon to Isadora's studio "for a lecture and demonstration of the principles of her school?" Stanislavsky accepted and regretted it. He wrote to a colleague at the Moscow Art Theatre:

I don't quite understand what she wants — apparently she expects me to help her with the organization of her school. The point is that a rich man has built a wonderful huge studio for her near Paris. I entered it during a lesson for the children. The mysterious semi-darkness, subdued music, dancing children — all this made a great impression on me. She was genuinely glad to see me and inquired after Muscovites, about Craig, about you, etc. But when the dances ended, she took me upstairs to show her own tiny rooms. I was literally scared. These are rooms not of a Greek goddess, but of a French *demi-mondaine*. When she showed the bedroom, she poked her finger at the lace covering the red wallpaper of a courtesan, saying, "Mister Singer ordered this." She suddenly became quite shy. She then went into a long explanation about how . . . her sister and some German [Max Merz] have signed contracts with all the remaining children and their parents, and there she is with a school but no children, even though she has fed and clothed them for [five] years.[24]

The struggle between Isadora and Elizabeth for control of the school now came to a head. On June 7 Isadora wrote to the children's parents in Germany, announcing that the Duncan school would move permanently to France and asking for legal custody of the girls until they reached the age of eighteen. This was a requirement of the French government, she explained; the children couldn't stay in France without it.[25] Almost simultaneously, however, Elizabeth and Merz announced the opening of their own school in Frankfurt, where they set up temporary headquarters while waiting for their new building in Darmstadt to be completed.

"My own activities have been widely recognized in Germany," Elizabeth reminded the children's parents. "I therefore declare that I am not taking any part in the reestablishing of a new school in Paris, France."[26] Elizabeth understood that German parents would prefer to see their daughters in Germany; Merz, whose ideas on race and eugenics were in no way unusual for the time, insisted on it. In this context, the very words *Paris, France* were sufficient to sound the alarm. Merz later professed "sadness" at what he called "Isadora's antagonism toward our plan. . . . It was so pronounced and unwavering. I had no other intention than to maintain the school for her and Elizabeth. Any desire for personal enhancement in this context was completely foreign to me."[27] Nevertheless, Merz recalled a day at Grunewald in terms that tell the whole story. He and Elizabeth had arrived at the local station from Berlin. As they walked the short distance to the school, "our children" suddenly came running around the corner, "wearing all sorts of colorful clothes."

Elizabeth's face fell. "Oh, God," she said. "Isadora's here."[28] According to Irma, Elizabeth actually "kidnapped" five of the girls in Paris.

"We had not seen her for ages," Irma wrote, "when she appeared one afternoon at our pension all smiles and innocence. Although most of us instinctively scattered like birds, *sauve qui peut,* at her approach, she managed to catch a few of the more trusting ones who had lingered behind." Promising them tea at Rumpelmeyer's, Elizabeth instead took the girls to the Gare de l'Est and hustled them aboard a train to Frankfurt.[29] None of the others remembered anything so drastic, but (as the girls all knew) their correspondence was read and vetted by Elizabeth before it went to their parents: "Unfavorable reports were not allowed out, as these could damage the school's reputation, thereby threatening its existence."[30] In the meantime, Elizabeth kept all of the furnishings of the Grunewald school.

"This is an outrage!" Isadora cried when she realized what had happened. "How is it possible that my own sister should do a thing like that to me?" Irma had "never seen [her] so angry,"[31] but Stanislavsky thought it just as well that Elizabeth won the first round. He had seen Isadora giving lessons to the children. "Alas, nothing will come of this," he wrote. "She is no teacher. . . . No. She'd better dance. Schools should be opened by other people. Craig was right." A few days later Stanislavsky reported:

> You know, I slandered Singer and am sorry now. Yesterday there was a reception at Duncan's. There was a horde of guests including the director of the Comédie Française, celebrated writers, artists, political figures. Singer played the host. . . . He looked after the children as a nurse, spread the carpets out, rushed about, entertained the guests, while she, adroitly posing as a grand celebrity, sat in a white costume among admirers, listening to compliments. This time the barometer of my sympathies suddenly turned and I befriended him and helped him to spread out the carpets and do the children's hair before letting them dance for such a choice society. . . . Singer stopped being jealous of me and entrusted me with taking Duncan in a car, and when we sat there, she started kissing [me], while I was trying to impress upon her that Singer was a charming fellow. In other words, everything got mixed up.

That night Stanislavsky left Isadora a note in her dressing-room:

> You asked my advice. . . . I have understood everything now and
> am able to say: 1) Run away from Paris. 2) Value freedom above all.
> 3) Give up your school, if it has to be paid for at such a price. 4) What-
> ever happens with you — I shall always understand and will sympa-
> thize with you from all my heart.[32]

Before he left Paris, Stanislavsky walked with Isadora and Deirdre
in the park at Neuilly. Deirdre was almost three, "always dancing and
laughing." "A charming child," said Stanislavsky: "Craig's temperament and Duncan's grace. I liked her so much that Duncan promised
to let me have her if she (Isadora) should die. . . . If she leaves me all
her future children, too, I can rest assured that I shall spend my old
age surrounded by a numerous family."[33] He left Paris disgusted with
Isadora's new way of life: "All this makes me ill. I have said goodbye
for good to Duncan."[34]

At the end of their June engagement at the Gaité-Lyrique, while
refusing to concede openly to Elizabeth, Isadora sent her remaining
students back to Germany "for a holiday" with their families. She
would call for them again when her Paris school was ready to receive
pupils. "It was all a muddle," said Theresa, who had just turned fourteen. "Suddenly one day, she sent us all home. Out of the blue, we
were, for no apparent reason, sent away."[35] Isadora must have realized
that most of the girls would find their way eventually to Elizabeth and
Merz. In the meantime, she left Paris with Singer.

"That summer we spent in the yacht off Brittany," she wrote. "Often it was so rough that I got off and followed the yacht along the
coast in an auto." She was restless and upset, worried more than ever
about the future of her work. In September she went with Deirdre to
Venice, without Singer, and learned she was pregnant. Inside the
Cathedral of San Marco, Isadora gazed at the blue-and-gold interior
dome and imagined she could see "the face of a little boy, but it was
also the face of an angel with great blue eyes and an aureole of golden
hair." The thought of another pregnancy left her struggling between
"joy and disquietude." In Milan, where she consulted Duse's physician, she considered an abortion, "filled with revolt that such a deformation should again come to my body . . . [but] tortured by the call,
the hope, the vision of that angel's face, the face of my son." She asked
the doctor to leave her alone to decide:

I remember the bedroom of the hotel — a rather gloomy room — and facing me I suddenly saw a picture, a strange woman in eighteenth-century gown, whose lovely but cruel eyes looked straight into mine. I stared at her eyes and they seemed to mock me. "Whatever you may decide," she seemed to say, "it is the same. Look at my loveliness, that shone so many years ago. Death swallows all — all — why should you suffer to again bring life into the world, only to be swallowed up by death?" . . . Life or Death, poor creature, you are in a relentless trap.

Finally I rose and spoke to the eyes. "No, you shall not trouble me. I believe in Life, in Love, in the sanctity of Nature's Law."

Was it imagination, or did there suddenly shine in those hard eyes a gleam of terrible, mocking laughter?

Isadora returned to Venice and gave Deirdre the news: "You will have a little brother."

"Oh," said Deirdre, clapping her hands. "How sweet, how sweet."

"Yes, yes," said Isadora, "it will be sweet."[36]

The baby would be born on the first of May, 1910, at the same villa in Beaulieu where Isadora fell in love with Singer. The previous October she left Paris for her second American tour — a "most happy, successful, and prosperous" journey, as Isadora recalled it, "for money attracts money."[37] Her program remained essentially the same as the previous year's, with the exception that she had added the *Marche Militaire* and her new suite of Schubert waltzes to the repertory. Carl Van Vechten, writing without a byline in the *New York Times,* still protested what he called Isadora's "perverted use of the Seventh Symphony" but granted she had never been in better form: "Seldom has she been more poetical, more vivid in her expression of joy, more plastic in her poses, more rhythmical in her effects. . . . One of the wildest of her dances she closed with arms outstretched and head thrown back almost out of sight until she resembled the headless Nike of Samothrace."[38]

Isadora's brother Augustin joined her onstage at the Metropolitan Opera, in what were described as "readings from 'Greek Choruses.'" Gus's marriage to Sarah Whiteford had ended by mutual agreement. Their daughter, Temple, would remain in the Duncans' care, a sometime student of Elizabeth's in Germany who "completely rejected being trained as a dancer," according to Merz, "and was just as subtly charming as she was indifferent."[39] Gus had worked as stage manager in Charles Coburn's Shakespeare company and made a hit on Broadway in the cast of Percy MacKaye's *Canterbury Pilgrims*. Coburn, who went on to a long career in Hollywood in avuncular roles, would be Isadora's manager on this and her next U.S. tour, in 1911.

By the time she gave her farewell concert at Carnegie Hall on December 2, 1909, Isadora was unable to conceal her pregnancy. In Pittsburgh "a protesting bevy of Sunday-school teachers" had complained to her sponsors, demanding to know "if Miss Duncan danced in bare feet."[40] Had they learned that she was pregnant, they might have staged an even larger scene in the cause of modesty. Local clergymen in St. Paul, Minnesota, were invited to see her dance for themselves on opening night: "Criticism was disarmed."[41] But in New York a woman came backstage to warn her that she had pushed the limits of license: "But, my dear Miss Duncan, it's plainly visible from the front row."

"Oh, but, my dear Mrs. X.," said Isadora, "that's just what I mean my dancing to express — Love — Woman — Formation — Springtime . . . you know — the fruitful Earth."[42] She returned to Europe not long after on the *Lusitania*, with Temple and Augustin, having told reporters in Boston, "I'm going to Egypt to lay flowers at the feet of the Sphinx — at its paws, I should say. I'm going out on the desert. . . . Remember that I said this mysteriously."[43] The *New York Mirror* reported that Temple, at the age of twelve, "has never worn a pair of shoes."[44]

Shortly before his sister's departure, Raymond Duncan and his wife arrived for their own American tour, in a production of Sophocles's *Elektra* performed in the original Greek. Penelope Duncan played Elektra and Raymond "danced the chorus," also lecturing where he could on the art and music of ancient Athens. "I should like [it] if you will first indicate what you wish me to talk about," Raymond told reporters when they called, "for I must say to you that I know almost everything under the sun."[45] In New York he and Penelope were charged with neglect and fined for allowing their four-year-old son, Menalkas, to walk barefoot in winter.[46] The sight of Raymond and his followers in Greek garb was not easily forgotten.

"In those days," Preston Sturges wrote, "Raymond traveled with a rather large group of his disciples, mostly of the opposite sex, often young, sometimes comely, and nearly always with recently born or about-to-be born babies. This entourage required large quantities of milk, and everybody knows that there is no milk like goat's milk for raising robust babies, so attached to the entourage were a number of goats."[47] At the end of the tour, Raymond and company moved on to the Pacific Northwest, where they spent several months with the

Klamath Indians, "studying their music and teaching them to weave." Even Isadora was at a loss for words. "I am so worried about Ray," she had written a few years before: "Too much Too much." [48]

In January 1910, while she waited for the birth of her child, Isadora and Singer left Paris for Egypt, where they cruised the Nile for two months in a houseboat, chartered from "Cook's Dahabeahs on the Nile." Singer "seemed delighted" at the prospect of becoming a father again. The party started out in Alexandria and sailed to Luxor, Aswan, and finally "into Nubia, where the Nile is so narrow that one can almost touch the banks on either side." When Singer went off to Khartoum, Isadora stayed alone on the boat with Deirdre and enjoyed what she remembered as "the most peaceful time of my life. . . . Our boat seemed to be rocked by the rhythm of the ages." Keeping her company was Hener Skene, a cousin of Kathleen Scott and a pianist, whom she had hired, with Singer's approval, to play "Beethoven and Bach" on a Steinway grand.

"Oh, Mama," Deirdre exclaimed when she saw the Sphinx, "this dolly is not very pretty, but how imposing!" Isadora noted: "She was just learning words of three syllables." Try as she might, she couldn't escape a sense of foreboding or ignore the "beautiful, supple" bodies of the sailors and workers in the fields. "The little life within me seemed to vaguely surmise this journey to the land of darkness and death," Isadora wrote. [49] But her son was born alive and healthy when she returned to Beaulieu, golden-haired as she imagined him. Singer's name was not recorded on the birth certificate, only "Duncan, Isadora, née á San Francisco (États-Unis), profession d'artiste." [50] The delivery had even been easy. "Unlike the stupid peasant doctor" at Noordwijk, Isadora's French physician, Emil Bosson, "knew how to alleviate the suffering with wise doses of morphia, and this second experience was quite different from the first."

"Oh, the sweet little boy, Mother," said Deirdre; "you need not worry about him. I will always hold him in my arms and take care of him." [51] Isadora named the baby Patrick Augustus. "He takes up every minute of my time but when he looks at me with his blue eyes I feel richly compensated," she wrote to Ernst Haeckel in Germany: "This boy will be a monist, and, who knows, there may be some of your great and wonderful spirit in him. We will hope so." [52]

Isadora was due for a showdown with Singer when they got back to Paris. In June they took a suite at the Trianon Palace Hotel at Versailles, where Isadora threw "a great fête" to celebrate her return to the city. The party was Singer's idea; he had given her carte blanche.

"The guests were invited to arrive at four o'clock in the afternoon . . . ," Isadora reported, "and there, in the park, were marquees with every sort of refreshment, from caviar and champagne to tea and cakes. After this, on an open space where tents had been erected, the Colonne orchestra, under the direction of [Gabriel] Pierné, gave us a programme of the works of Richard Wagner."[53] Dinner followed after Isadora had received her guests singly, dressed in a flaming, pleated-silk gown made for the occasion by artist and stage designer Mario Fortuny. As the night wore on, she switched to her tunic and a pair of gold sandals, dancing in and around the tents and lawns to the strains of a Vienna orchestra. Among her guests were Diaghilev and Nijinsky, Yvette Guilbert, Henry Russell, the director of the Boston Opera Company, the Nobel Peace laureate Paul d'Estournelles de Constant, Joseph Paul-Boncour, René Blum, and the writer Georges Maurevert, who remembered "a noisy and joyful dinner, completely devoid of cant or arrogance." Even a steady rain didn't spoil the effect:

> When cigars were served, the cloth of the tent was rolled back and the garden appeared to us magically illuminated, with globes of all shades glimmering through the trees, and the lawns bordered with goblets of light. . . . And what joy . . . to see, circling about, to the sound of gypsy music, on the paths and the lawns, Miss Isadora herself, sometimes leaping under her white veils and fleeing toward distant groves, sometimes triumphant as the Victory of Samothrace, or grave as an antique supplicant.[54]

Only one thing marred Isadora's party: the host made no appearance. About an hour before her guests arrived, Isadora had received a telegram from Singer in London, where he had gone on business, saying "that he had had a stroke and was too ill to come, but that I was to receive the guests without him."[55] She was upset by the news and concerned for Singer's safety, but also impatient. She knew Singer's neurotic obsession with his health. Nevertheless, she joined him in July at his country estate in England, in what she described as an experiment in domesticity. After Patrick's birth, Singer had again asked her to marry him, and again she had refused. Her account of their summer at the Oldway mansion in Devon is an extended comic riff:

> "How stupid for an artist to be married," I said, "and as I must spend my life making tours around the world, how could you spend your life in the stage-box admiring me?"

"You would not have to make tours if we were married," he answered.

"Then what should we do?"

"We should spend our time in my house in London, or at my place in the country."

"And then what should we do?"

"Then there is the yacht."

"But then what should we do?"

L. proposed that we should try the life for three months.

"If you don't like it, I shall be much astonished."

"So that summer we went to Devonshire," said Isadora. She despised Singer's friends among the British aristocracy, mocking their food and dining rituals, endless games of bridge, walks, shooting expeditions, and "the really important business of the day — dressing for dinner." Singer's medical treatment involved an early form of shock therapy, "a sort of cage which had been brought over from Paris," Isadora wrote, "in which he sat while thousands of volts of electricity were turned on him, and he would sit there looking extremely pathetic and saying: 'I hope this will do me good.'" A resident doctor and nurse remained "emphatic," meanwhile, about Isadora's "line of conduct." She was given a room in a separate wing of the house, "and told that on no account was I to disturb L. . . . You can imagine whether this life pleased me or not. In the course of a couple of weeks I was positively desperate. . . . But I had not reckoned on the rain."

"Why don't you dance again — in the ballroom?" Singer suggested when Isadora's patience reached its limit. Since his father's death, he had expanded and remade the Singer Wigwam in the image of a royal palace, replete with a marble staircase, cut by Lebrun for Louis XIV and originally intended for Versailles. In the ballroom, Singer hung Gobelins tapestries and a giant painting by David of Napoleon's coronation. "It seems that David made two such pictures," Isadora wrote dryly, "one of which is in the Louvre, and the other in the ballroom of L.'s house in Devonshire." The imperial temper of the decor left her seething.

"How can I make my simple gestures before these," she complained, "on the oily, waxed floor?"

"If that is all that troubles you," Singer said, "send for your curtains and your carpet."

"But I must have a pianist."

"Send for a pianist."

Isadora telegraphed Edouard Colonne, director of the Colonne Orchestra in Paris: SPENDING SUMMER IN ENGLAND, MUST WORK, SEND PIANIST. Colonne sent André Caplet, his assistant director and first violinist, "a strange-looking man with a very large head," as Isadora recalled him, "which oscillated on a badly made body. . . . This person was so unsympathetic to me that he gave me a sense of absolute physical revulsion whenever I looked at him or touched his hand." Caplet, remembered as the composer of *Miroir de Jésus,* was a musical prodigy, a friend and collaborator of Debussy who died during a gas attack in World War I. Isadora never used his name in her autobiography.

"How is it possible that Colonne has sent you?" she asked when Caplet arrived at Oldway. "He knows I hate and detest you."

"Je vous demande pardon, Madame," Caplet replied, *"le cher Maître m'a envoyé . . ."* Singer was both gleeful and relieved. "At least I have no cause for jealousy," he said.

Isadora blamed the ensuing fiasco on the rain. Bored and annoyed, she set to work with Caplet at the piano, practicing behind a screen so she wouldn't have to look at him. When a guest of Singer's upbraided her for her bad manners, she agreed to invite Caplet on the drive she took each afternoon in one of Singer's fourteen automobiles. Even then "a feeling of such disgust" came over her that she cut the drive short, "rapped on the glass and told the chauffeur to turn and go home." She wrote:

> The country road was full of ruts and, as the car turned, I was thrown into the arms of X. [Caplet]. He closed his arms around me. I sat back and looked at him, and suddenly felt my whole being going up in flames like a pile of lighted straw. I have never felt anything so violent. And, all of a sudden, as I looked at him, I was aghast. How had I not seen it before? His face was perfectly beautiful, and in his eyes there was a smothered flame of genius. From that moment I knew that he was a great man. . . . How was it possible that from such violent antipathy could be born such violent love?

On their return to Oldway, Isadora and Caplet went to the ballroom, where they made love on the floor, underneath the piano. So Isadora told Victor Seroff, at least. She had left Deirdre and Patrick in Paris and was free to indulge herself: "From that day in the auto we had one obsession, to be alone — in the conservatory, in the garden, even taking long walks in the muddy country lanes; but these violent passions have violent ends, and there came a day when X. had to leave the château, never to return. We made this sacrifice to save the life of a man who was supposed to be dying."[56]

Singer found out about Isadora's affair with Caplet by listening in on their phone conversations. She made no attempt to hide it, in any case. "I have never made a secret of love," she declared. "My maid, who was devoted to me, warned me that my Millionaire was suspicious, that the staff were carrying tales to him. But I didn't mind. When one is in love, one does not mind." Afterward, Isadora agreed that she had treated Singer badly — that her affair with Caplet, conducted under Singer's nose, was one of the few things in her life she truly regretted: "I should have waited till he had recovered." Her remark betrays her own appreciation of her sexual nature. She knew how faithless she could be, how "impossible" for a man like Singer. She told a friend:

> [Caplet] and I parted, after ten days of love. And on the tenth day I loved him less than on the first. That is life. . . . For ten days our love was a very perfect thing. After that . . . It is not a pretty fairy story, but it is true. In it is a piece of the real me, that I cannot help. I was made to love in a certain way, just as I was made to suffer in a certain way. I've always loved, and I've always suffered. I shall go on loving and suffering until the end, I expect.[57]

Isadora returned to Paris under a cloud in the fall of 1910, "somewhat wiser and sadder" but determined "for the hundredth time . . . that hereafter I would give my entire life to Art."[58] In England she had begun work on her full-length performance of *Orpheus,* with music from Gluck's *Orfeo ed Euridice,* which premiered at the Théâtre du Châtelet on January 18, 1911. Isadora had studied Gluck's score since 1898, at least, and had already presented several versions of the work. But this *Orpheus* was different — a violent and unsettling dance that showed the world a new Isadora. She had begun to explore themes of darkness, hopelessness, and resistance already at the Gaité-Lyrique. In "The Dance of the Furies" from *Orpheus,* she portrayed both the demons and the tormented souls of the underworld, in a "terrifying, horrible, repulsive" depiction of corruption and despair. It is said that even Elizabeth, when she saw her sister's Furies, "was startled by the facial contortions and grimacing she witnessed."[59] Charles H. Caffin, who saw "The Dance of the Furies" at Carnegie Hall when Isadora returned to New York in February 1911, surmised that it had "less of the abstract, impersonal quality" of her previous work:

> Here the expression of concentrated venom and malice is carried out with an intensity and detail more dramatic, savage, earthly than in the earlier dances. The muscles harden in the face and limbs, the movements are abrupt, fierce, now bowed and now angular. The carriage of the body is stiff and inflexible, and then quivers and vibrates like a bow-string, loosed from the hand. . . . It goes without saying, after all, that a spirit so sensitive as Miss Duncan's to the diverse moods of joyousness and gaiety cannot fail to respond to the deeper emotions.[60]

Duncan scholar Kay Bardsley identifies Isadora's *Orpheus* as "the earliest representation of ugliness" in the dance: "No longer was Duncan evoking the endearing qualities of a woodland nymph, a wild bacchante, or a beauteous maiden facing the menace of death. Now her intent was to personify the menace itself."[61] In *Orpheus*, Isadora's doomed souls are fated to lift boulders on their backs, while their torturers lunge and claw in a frenzy at the damned. When Orpheus finally appears in the underworld, the demons fall madly to the floor, sweeping the ground with their hair in repetitive circular motions, as if ready to smash their skulls on a rock. Following Gluck's libretto, the central theme of the piece is the triumph of love over death. To balance the horror of the underworld, Isadora also portrayed the radiant souls in the Elysian Fields in "The Dance of the Blessed Spirits," but there were many who thought she brought more conviction to her Furies than to her saints. As Caffin observed when she opened in New York, "This dance is something of a tour de force. It fascinates one by the virtuosity displayed in wedding a borrowed convention to the free expression of the dancer's own nature."[62]

Isadora's third and last tour with Walter Damrosch and the New York Symphony was neither the happiest nor the most successful. She arrived in New York on the *Provence* on February 10, 1911, and announced that she would reopen her school within the year, in either Paris or the United States. "Other artists spend more than this school will cost on their jewels," Isadora told reporters on the dock. "Well, this is my jewel."[63] She had left America two years before, complaining about its lack of culture, "saddened, or perhaps angry, over the failure of the leaders of taste in her own country to extend to her any such appreciation as her work has commanded in the capitals of Europe."[64] Now, the *New York Tribune* noted that she had "put behind her all her old ideas about sackcloth and ashes for art's sake" and dressed stylishly, in gowns by Poiret, Fortuny, and Lucile of Paris: "The simplicity of the Greek gave way to the frills of the Frank . . . as far as Miss Duncan was concerned." But she was tired of Europe's "hothouse atmosphere, and [had] come over for a moral tonic."[65]

On her 1911 tour of American cities, Isadora danced Bach's Suite no. 3 in D (including the "Air on the G string"), along with *Orpheus* and selected pieces from Wagner: the dance of the flower maidens from *Parsifal* (described as "a subtle waltz of seduction"),[66] the Bacchanal from *Tannhäuser,* the dance of the apprentices from *Die Meistersinger von Nürnberg,* and the romantic *Liebestod* from *Tristan und Isolde.* She had gone to "the master" for inspiration, still searching for the pure blend of music, drama, and form that Wagner had set as his own creative task. But critics were doubtful: an impatient tone could not be missed in their reviews. "She tries to do more with the new music than she has ever done before, the result is less," wrote Henry Taylor Parker ("HTP") in the *Boston Evening Transcript;* "moreover, the conquering Russians have come, and there were times last night when somehow the spectators saw Miss Duncan through and beside the beautiful phantom, as it were, of Anna Pavlova."[67]

In 1910 Pavlova had quit Diaghilev's company and set out on a solo career, touring the United States with her Russian partner, Mikhail Mordkin, and ravishing audiences from coast to coast with her signature *Dying Swan.* Ruth St. Denis and Loie Fuller were also dancing in America, the latter still encircled by her "bevy of brightly colored butterflies." In the *New York Times,* Carl Van Vechten welcomed back Isadora with the remark that she was "directly responsible for a train of barefoot dancers who have spread themselves, like a craze, over two continents in the last five years." A recent and ardent convert to the ballet, Van Vechten had long objected to Isadora's use of concert music for the dance. Now he faulted her conception, too, dismissing her Bacchanal as "very pretty but hardly as bacchanalian as might have been expected." Van Vechten surrendered to the *Suite in D* only because "several numbers of this suite bear the names of dances, so Miss Duncan cannot be taken too much to task for using them for her purposes."[68]

On February 15, when she unveiled the *Liebestod* from *Tristan,* Walter Damrosch took the precaution of warning the audience at Carnegie Hall that what they were about to see was not just "controversial" but "largely experimental." Wagner's own notes on the *Liebestod* describe a soaring arc of desire, from "the tenderest shudder" to "the most terrible outpouring of an avowal of hopeless love." The music itself was deemed unfit for children, unmarried women, and virtuous wives.

"As there are probably a great many people here to whom the idea of giving pantomimic expression to the *Liebestod* would be horrifying," Damrosch continued, "I am putting it last on the program so that those who do not wish to see it may leave." No one did, Van Vechten reported, "except possibly the usual few who are obliged to catch trains."[69] The critic for the *New York Sun* was completely bewildered: "Mr. Damrosch played the prelude, and then the figure of Miss Duncan was dimly visible against the draperies at the back of the stage. When the finale began and the lights went up it was seen that she was lying on her stomach. She arose in a few minutes to her knees. But it was some time before she got to her feet." When she did, she stood transfixed, moving slowly and softly to an internalized rhythm "too impalpable" for Carnegie Hall. Her motions seemed obscure, her gentle swaying less erotic than expected or hoped for: "There were no long leaps upward and forward about this dance, if it could possibly be described as a dance, since it bore no more relation to that act than an occasional run backward and forward."[70] Caffin reported "flashes of exquisite beauty, so ethereal that they could not be held for more than a moment. . . . In some of her ideas, no doubt, Miss Duncan has run so far ahead of her age that the latter is left in doubt as to the direction of her path."[71] By the time she reached Boston, she faced half-empty houses.

"The boxes yawned in emptiness," wrote Henry Taylor Parker, "above stairs and below, the audience was scanty; the social and aesthetic contingents that used to profess the utmost joy in Miss Duncan were lacking; the throng of the merely curious had declined into scattered hundreds of spectators, many of whom were elderly women." Parker was not alone in observing that Isadora had "grown somewhat too stout of leg and body. Her comeliness suffers thereby, and the suggestion of middle age which her detractors have found in her is emphasized."[72] Poet Witter Bynner met her in Buffalo, where she "petted [him] a little" and regaled him "with exclamations of self-pity, lamenting over the lodging of a cinder in her eye."

"To think that I should have been seeking my poet all over America," Isadora cried, "and should at last be able to set on him only one good eye!" Bynner wrote to a friend on March 28, 1911:

She draped a shapely arm over the other — which was in fact swollen and unsightly — and murmured against time and fate. "I was beautiful in Atlantic City," she pouted, a baby in face and affectations, "and, since I had written you that I was there and waited for you [i.e., a poet], you should have come. Each morning and evening I looked through my window to see if there were not a troubadour on a white horse speeding up the boardwalk. And there was nothing but vulgarity."

Isadora invited Bynner to supper at her hotel, arriving late

in deep brown furs and a rosy scarf caught diagonally across the unfit eye. . . . First greeting us, then looking in gentle dissatisfaction upon her chair at the table, [she] said to the waiter: "Take this away and bring a sofa": a request that induced in him only amazement of visage and imperfection of service in that he brought instead, to her disgust and to the table, a capacious armchair. Of which she inquired in a still small penetrating voice: "Is that what you call a sofa? . . . What? — not a sofa on this floor?" and dismissing the misfortune by accepting the armchair for a less picturesque pose than she had intended on the sofa [wrote] for me . . . on the cloth of the table where the champagne stood coolly bubbling, her prospective itinerary, places and dates, among which with delightful misspelled allurement was "Cinsinatto."[73]

Returned to New York, Isadora took comfort in the arms of another "artist-genius," the baritone David Bispham. "He came to all my representations," she remembered, "and I went to all his recitals and afterwards, in my suite at the Plaza, we would have supper and he would sing to me, 'On the Road to Mandalay,' or 'Danny Deever,' and we laughed and embraced and were delighted with each other."[74] The magic was by no means gone. Parker praised Isadora's *Suite in D* — "In all her dancing and miming here, she has never been so truly of the Greek marbles" — and, unlike Van Vechten, succumbed completely to her Bacchanal: "Here she compassed a clear, soft beauty of sensuous rapture, a still ecstasy, a languor that was like a slow and lovely relaxation into sleep and dream. There are verses in 'The Faerie Queen[e]' of the enchantress reposing in the forest alone, that are not more beautiful."[75] Still, Isadora was happy to leave New York in April.

"One comes back to one's own country and one hopes for a little sympathy and recognition," she complained to journalist Arthur Ruhl, "and one either isn't noticed at all, or you write nothing but twaddle. . . . They send people to me who know nothing of dancing, nothing of art — nothing. . . . Why don't they send a sculptor?"[76] A New York paper wrote: "It was evident from her conversation . . . that she is hoping the public has learned to appreciate her art, but successful or not, she is prepared, she asserted, to leave her skeleton with the critics."[77] She wouldn't dance again until November, after another round of wooing and another angry parting with Singer.

"I shall never forget my return to Paris," Isadora wrote in *My Life*. "I had left my children at Versailles with a governess. When I opened the door, my little boy came running towards me. . . . I had left him a little baby in the cradle."[78] In a letter to Mary Fanton Roberts, Isadora remarked that Patrick was "perfectly Beautiful & seems to have the sweetest character. I am unhappy at being away from him. . . . He looks like Paris, only his nose is turned up like mine."[79] She resolved to spend more time with her children; Patrick was "delicate" and needed her attention. "I think it would be difficult for women who are not mothers, and even for some who are, to understand fully Isadora's love for her children," Roberts wrote later. "They were something splendid to her, and she guarded them and watched over them and taught them the beautiful things of life in a way that was supremely touching and inspiring."[80] She also played Santa Claus on Christmas Eve, dressing up as Père Noël with gifts for the children in a performance few were privileged to see.[81] "Dear Baby — Be good," she wrote to Deirdre before her last American trip. "Be careful of the stairs and the elevator. Mama will come back soon."[82] Victor Seroff remembered that "whenever Isadora mentioned her children in conversation, she invariably left me with an impression of her almost uncanny physical, animal love for them."[83]

At the end of April 1911, Kathleen Scott came to Paris and, predictably, disapproved of Isadora's approach to motherhood. Kathleen had just returned from New Zealand, where she said good-bye to her husband, Captain Scott, as he sailed on his fatal mission to the South Pole. She brought her own baby with her, Peter, about a year older than Patrick. In her diary, Kathleen described her visit to Isadora's studio in Neuilly:

> She has it absolutely empty, with just a dull bluish carpet, two or three exquisite bas-reliefs, and a great mirror. A grand-piano and an immense divan looked mere specks in the great place. I found her in bed with her two babies. Patrick is just a year, so pretty, but oh! so fragile — such a contrast to mine. They are rearing him all wrong. He

wears too many clothes, has hot baths, and is half-starved. We went to the Opéra Comique and got home very late, but Isadora got into her dancing dress and danced for me, and I lay on a divan, and there were colored lights. Oh, dear me! — very wonderful indeed.[84]

In July, Kathleen and her baby joined Isadora at Boulogne, where Singer's yacht was due to meet them. Isadora and Deirdre "came in a big motorcar to meet us, both dressed in Poiret gowns looking perfectly beautiful," Kathleen recalled.[85] Not long after, Augustin and Elizabeth arrived. Isadora and her sister had reached a tentative agreement about the students of the school. Elizabeth and Merz would continue to house and instruct them, while the best of the class — Irma, Anna, Theresa, Erika, Gretel, Lisa, and Isabelle — would join Isadora onstage in Paris when she wanted them. It was news the girls had received with delight.

"I had not heard from Isadora for two years when, quite unexpectedly, she came to see us," Irma recalled. The students hardly recognized her in her Paris finery, nor she them in their "uncomfortable, unbecoming" school uniforms. In Elizabeth's hands, the girls were bound over to Merz and his theories of maidenhood and *Körperkultur,* their dancing now "resembling in every respect the stiff drill of soldiers on parade," Irma thought. "Month after month, year in and year out, we still kept the spark alive and continued to dance the way Isadora had taught us,"[86] but her absence from the school made impossible any progress in that direction, and the girls found no encouragement from Elizabeth and Merz. "I only wanted to protect the school from one danger," Merz would write, "from the artistic ambitions of the semi-talented, from the thought that one or the other of the girls should ever try to become a 'little Isadora.'"[87]

Life with Elizabeth became increasingly regimented. Her school at Darmstadt wouldn't be finished until the end of 1911; in the meantime, the girls toured Germany "to make propaganda and drum up trade in the form of paying pupils," dancing in "gray woolen underwear" while Merz lectured on hygiene, race, and the supremacy of Swedish gymnastics. "A clever man," said Irma ruefully, "obsessed with a theory to propound, he developed a natural bent for lecturing. He would get up and lecture at the drop of a hat anywhere, any time."[88] A note from Anna to her parents confirms the tone of Merz's regime. "I'm already fifteen years old," Anna wrote. "Yesterday I went to a marvelous lecture on termites."[89]

At the First International Hygienic Exhibition in Dresden in 1911, where Isadora caught up with her students, Merz and Elizabeth won the gold medal. The exhibition "was the most important demonstration of the modern way of life before the First World War," according to a German history of the Duncan school. "The pupils lived in Dresden for several months, studying all aspects of the many sections of the exhibition. They were, in effect, a part of the Exhibition."[90] The girls gave demonstrations of their physical prowess, while plaster casts of their torsos, arms, and legs sat on display in the central hall, next to a transparent replica of the human heart pumping blood. "But this is a morgue!" Isadora remarked sourly.[91] On leaving, she asked Elizabeth to bring Irma with her when they met on the yacht in July. Irma joined the party at Ostend, where Isadora put her in a room with Deirdre and Patrick.

"The last time I saw [Deirdre] she had been a mere infant," Irma wrote. "Now five years old, she looked me over carefully before asking timidly, 'Who are you?'"

"I am your new playmate," Irma answered. "I hope we shall be friends."

"Have you seen my little brother?" Deirdre asked. "His name is Patrick and he is twelve months old." Later, the memory of Deirdre came close to breaking Irma's heart: "She was such a beautiful child, so exquisitely made." Isadora had asked Irma to teach Deirdre some dancing steps. "I had never taught anyone," Irma wrote, "and so Deirdre, Isadora's little daughter, became my first pupil. She also suggested I teach her some simple piece of poetry like William Blake's 'Little Lamb, who made thee? / Dost thou know who made thee? / Gave thee life, and bid thee feed / By the stream and o'er the mead.'" For Irma, the question had only one answer — Isadora: "Getting into bed beside her sleeping children, I had the sweet sensation of actually being one of her children, too." When Irma met Singer the next morning, Isadora urged her to call him "Uncle Paris."[92]

That summer the yacht sailed to Mont-Saint-Michel and the Channel Islands — Singer hoped to get as far as Norway or St. Petersburg by the end of August. Kathleen remembered a chaotic week at Boulogne, where Isadora and Singer first fought, then made up, and then parted, several times. "Everybody felt the idiocy of the thing, but nobody said a word," wrote Kathleen. Isadora behaved outrageously, flirting with the sailors, the officers, her guests, and an old friend of Kathleen's, a Captain Sykes, who had come to Boulogne "for a spree."

Sykes was "very intelligent and very nice and beautifully a gentle-man," Kathleen reported. "The charming way he warded off Isadora's advances was delightful." But Singer was appalled. There was another quarrel; "both were too proud to open the door between their rooms," and Isadora soon left for Paris. When she came back, it was Singer's turn. "Isadora and Paris are more married than the most married people I ever knew," Kathleen concluded. "How easily and how stu-pidly these things happen."[93] Soon Isadora decided that the yacht would take Kathleen and Peter across the Channel to England. Kath-leen wrote on August 10:

> Isadora arrived and we moved the whole party from the hotel to the yacht, Isadora's two children, my one, and the nurses and maids. . . . Out we set gallantly to sea, full of good intentions. No sooner out of the harbor than the babe Patrick began to yell. It was quite rough. My babe was on my knee. "No like it! — Sick, feel sick"; and then he was, very, and then so was I and so was the nurse, and so was everybody else. Still we went on, Patrick yelling and howling all the while and Isadora grey with terror. She implored me to go and say we must turn and go back, but I couldn't get up or speak. . . . My babe and the nurse were in the same condition and now the water was com-ing overboard in great waves. It was a gay party! At last, and it seemed after infinity, the order was given to return.[94]

Isadora cut the party short in the middle of August. Patrick had developed a fever and she was anxious to get him to Dr. Bosson in Nice. She was "finished" with Singer, she said, and he with her: "This human life seemed so heavy beside my dreams of Art."[95] After the Paris premiere of *Orpheus,* music critic Pierre Lalo had attacked her in *Le Temps,* deploring her "useless, obscure motions," her "false sim-plicity and affected naiveté," and her complete lack of training — "not even a shadow of technical competence," Lalo wrote. "Merely fluttering about and trying to express her soul, this presumptuous American . . . thinks she is creating a revolution." Lalo had even de-nounced Isadora's students, "heavy little girls from beyond the Rhine, whose ankles were as thick as their thighs." Always it was the natural female body that roused critics of this type, but it was a "stupid" pub-lic, Lalo insisted, who bore the blame for Isadora's success: "They are the dupes of a Parisian pro-Duncan coalition composed of snobs: ring-leaders, agitators preying on the bovine throng, who blindly follow the caprice of fashion." (Anticipating cries of xenophobia, Lalo added that he would welcome any foreign artist into France "who is a Wagner, Tolstoy, or Ibsen — not a Puccini, Caruso, or Isadora Duncan." At that, she was in fine company.)[96]

From Nice, Isadora went to Venice, the city she invariably chose to adjust her thinking — *"pour changer les idées,"* as she said. Rumors spread that she had decided to give up the stage. Leo Stein heard that Singer, eager to be rid of her, had agreed to buy Isadora a château at Saint-Cloud "for 2,000,000 francs, I believe."[97] She was back with Singer in October, however, or at least at his town house in London, where she went with Augustin to confer with classics scholar Gilbert Murray about performing his translations of the works of Euripides. "Generally speaking, I came to the conclusion that the dance in itself, the pure dance for dance's sake, can no longer offer a full artistic satisfaction either to the connoisseur or to the true artist," said Isadora. What sounded like a retreat was, to her mind, the only possible advance. She would go back to the tradition of the Greeks, where dances did not exist separately in the theater, but as the integrative expression of music and the spoken word.[98]

On October 1 Isadora and Augustin signed a preliminary contract in which she pledged "to devote her genius for a period of three years" toward the establishment of a permanent theater company, with Augustin at the helm. Isadora would direct "the plastic movements, dances and stage deportment of the principals and chorus" and would dance herself "in such of these productions as it shall be mutually agreed upon lend themselves to her purpose."[99] Augustin tried to interest Gordon Craig in the project, but Craig hadn't softened toward Isadora. He had seen her again earlier in the year, when he came to Paris, hoping to start a French edition of *The Mask,* and stayed for two months, following Mary Desti from salon to salon while Mary tried to convince him that "she could find all the money and support he needed."[100]

Mary, too, was riding high, having broken with Aleister Crowley and married a Turk, Vely Bey, whose father was supposedly a vice admiral of the Turkish fleet and "personal physician to the Sultan" of Constantinople. When her new mother-in-law gave her a family recipe for skin cream, with Singer's backing, Mary opened a perfume and cosmetics emporium on rue de la Paix, the Maison Desti, marketing her lotion "to the vampire trade" as "Le Secret du Harem."[101] It wasn't long before Craig's letters and notebooks flooded over with complaints about "American women," Isadora, and Paris, France, the city that had "cooked her & dressed her up — absolute murder of the girl."[102]

"The men are asses, the women are foul," Craig wrote to a friend in America. "Champagne, the arts of Greece & millionaires are all reconciled under the table. . . . The nicest people seem to become fakes when they get [to] drinking champagne in Paris."[103] Isadora, in particular, was drinking buckets of champagne: "After a performance which would always excite her tremendously she was so *strung up* that she needed something that would slowly release the tension. She would insist on a supper — & these suppers were very often bacchic sorts of affairs — not exactly Greek in theory — but Parisian." If her career had suffered, Craig thought, it was her own fault; she would not "give up frivolling for her art." Worse, she had become a gossip:

> Of certain men who were childishly devoted to her she would say things calculated to do them great harm. . . . It was always of people's sexual affairs she spoke — as though hers were so very perfect. That is queer. . . . She was an artist & to be critical of the relationship of men & women — even of men & men, & women & women, is not exactly the happiest theme for an artist to pounce on. . . . I was very fond of Topsy Duncan. . . . But slowly & surely Topsy grew very vague [and] "Madame Duncan" grew more & more horrific. I'm not sure that this third party wasn't a performance, but anyhow it was a most unpleasant one & a role she really had little sense to assume.[104]

In November, putting rumors of her retirement to rest, Isadora danced with her star pupils at the Châtelet in an expanded version of *Iphigenia,* in which the girls were given larger parts and the actor Jean Mounet-Sully "spoke verse interludes." It was the first endeavor in Isadora's plan to mix dancers and actors on the stage. "I am pampering a big dream . . . ," she told journalist Michel Georges-Michel. "I want not 50, not 500, but 5,000 pupils. . . . I would wish for the whole world to dance with me!"[105] But the Châtelet season was plagued by controversy. First, the Paris Opéra refused permission for Isadora and her students to perform the *Tannhäuser* Bacchanal, whose rights it had held since the Paris premiere in 1861. Next, complaints were lodged with the Paris police concerning "the commercial exploitation in Parisian theatres of young children, parading around in skimpy outfits and baring their naked legs." For Isadora, it was a throwback to Berlin, which she had left precisely in order to avoid this kind of "petty persecution." Someone was foolish enough to tell her that "all child dancers in Europe end up as prostitutes."

"Look at these children," Isadora exhorted the crowd at the

Châtelet, when the girls came out on stage. "They are healthy and robust; eyes are clear and no one is tired or weakened. To the contrary, listen as they breathe freely. Do you think it is wrong for them to dance?"[106] Theresa recalled how Isadora put "the motor in her soul" while waiting to go on stage: "She prepared herself for it like a ritual. Standing in the curtains and listening to the music, she would go into herself, growing from minute to minute in power, so that she appeared terrifying to her pupils and the stage hands."[107] At one of her Châtelet performances, a shoulder strap on her tunic broke loose, exposing her breasts. The following night, police were posted at the theater to make sure she stayed fully clothed. Isadora was enraged, even more when she learned that the police had decided to investigate her for "indecency." This time, she did threaten to retire.

"If they annoy me about this," she told Georges-Michel, "I will dance in a forest naked, naked, naked . . . with the song of birds and elemental noises for an orchestra."[108] Singer was moved to action. Not long after, he purchased a plot of land on rue de Berri, just off the Champs-Elysées, and announced that he would build Isadora a theater of her own. It was the gift she was waiting for. Here, at what Singer would call Le Théâtre du Beau, she could house and train her students, work with Augustin, and, as she hoped, provide "a meeting place and haven for all the great Artists of the world."[109]

In January 1912 Isadora and Singer returned to Egypt on the yacht, this time with a large and boisterous party that included the painter Jules Grandjouan, a French count and countess with the names Tristan and Isolde (de Bérault), and Hener Skene, the young musician who had played for Isadora on her first trip up the Nile in 1910. Skene had become her favored accompanist and "my best friend and comforter in those days," as she wrote. "He adored my Art, and was only happy when playing for me. He had the most extraordinary admiration for me of anyone I have ever met."[110] Different sources suggest that Skene was something of a wild man, a sexual predator and batterer who, with Mary Desti, formed part of Aleister Crowley's mystical cult in London.[111]

In her autobiography, Isadora never mentions this second trip to Egypt. Singer had bought a villa in Alexandria, where they both insisted they wanted to live permanently. In Isadora's case, "Isis" had come home. Both of her children were with her in Egypt in 1912, along with Elizabeth and Irma, once again brought as a companion for

Deirdre.[112] "To a young girl of my age," Irma wrote, "it was something straight out of the Arabian Nights. . . . During the day we watched mud huts and ruined temples glide by. At night, when the stars shone so brightly they looked like small moons, the air was filled with the curious native chanting of the crew." At Abydos, the temple of Osiris was still half buried in sand. Irma ventured out on what she thought was a boulder and found herself caught on the roof of the temple itself, "with a drop of fifty feet on either side." Panicking, she heard Isadora's "quiet voice" coaxing her down: "Don't turn! Keep steady; look straight ahead and walk to the end. You can get off there."

At Kom Ombo, between Luxor and Aswan, Irma learned a harder lesson. The party had docked at the temple of Horus, where Skene played for the guests after dinner. On deck, Irma dreamed of "forgotten centuries" and vanished gods; "Beethoven's *Moonlight Sonata* came floating through the air," followed quickly by Elizabeth, who announced that Isadora wanted Irma to dance for the company. Alone, without the other girls, Irma was terrified. "I dreaded the outcome," she wrote; "and, hoping I would be let off, I said quite truthfully that I had not brought my tunic."

"Well, that doesn't matter," Elizabeth answered, handing Irma a silk nightgown. "Here, wear that."

"Oh, no! Tante Miss, I really cannot go!"

"Nonsense! . . . Just do as I tell you and let's have no more fuss."

"With these words," Irma wrote, "she led me by the hand to the temple, like a lamb to the sacrifice. . . . I was forced to dance here against my will by the twin personalities who so far had shaped my life."

"Ah, here she is," said Isadora as Irma entered the temple court. "Are you going to dance for us, my dear?" Her guests were sitting on broken columns and slabs of stone. To Irma's dismay, the pianist, Skene, had disappeared. "I don't know what to dance," she stammered, "without music and everything. . . ."

"On such a wonderful moonlit night," Isadora countered, "in this beautiful temple, surely inspiration should not be lacking. Dance anything you fancy, whatever comes to mind." Irma never knew how she got through it: "Only one thing came to my mind and that was to run away as fast as I could. . . . I turned and swayed and leaped around . . . until my sense of utter inadequacy struck me dead in my tracks."

After a silence, Isadora rose and addressed her guests. "Have you noticed how entirely unrelated her dance movements were to these extraordinary surroundings?" she began. "She seemed to be completely unaware of them. What she did just consisted of some pretty little dance gestures she has learned — very nice, very lighthearted, but not in the slightest degree in harmony with the almost awesome sense of mystery that pervades this place and of which you are all, I am sure, deeply aware." Irma was horrified. She had never before seen her goddess with such monstrous clarity, and after Isadora herself had danced in and out of the massive temple columns, she heard the delighted cries of her teacher's friends: *"C'était magnifique, magnifique!"* In Paris, Lugné-Poë had complained that Isadora, for all her sensitivity in performance, seemed curiously "indifferent to suffering." He had reproached her for it, but she only laughed.

"Lugni, drink," she said. "We'll talk tomorrow."[113]

16

One Great Cry

In 1912, apart from brief appearances in London and Rome, Isadora's energies went into establishing her theater in Paris, where dance would fuse music with poetry and retrieve its place at the summit of the arts. "Miss Duncan intends to stage Greek tragedies in a vivid and artistic manner," wrote the London *Daily Mail*. "The pupils of her school will form the chorus for the pieces, and the venture will be supported by well-known poets, musicians, actors, and actresses. No effort will be spared to make the theatre a real temple of art."[1] That summer, Singer hired architect Louis Sue to design the building in rue de Berri, in the heart of Paris's wealthy eighth *arrondissement,* off the Champs-Elysées. Next, Singer turned to a crash course in Western theater, taking command of the project with an enthusiasm that amazed Isadora.

She had come back from Egypt bearing "Allah's best points," according to American news reports: "[Her] theatre is not to be like other theatres, just like the fair Isadora is not like other girls. It is to be just an amphitheater . . . more like a cockpit or the scene of a billiard match, only that the center space is to hold Isadora and her twinkling bare toes."[2] In fact, Isadora wanted "a democratic theatre," with special prices for artists and students and nothing that catered to "the over-fed rich," as Singer quoted her in a letter to Louis Sue.[3] Isadora never stopped digging at "L. and his millions"; to her surprise, he agreed with her plans.

"I have been living in the theatre for some weeks and I know my way about it with my eyes shut," Singer wrote proudly to Louis Sue. "The more I think of it the less I care for the idea of having boxes since they would be right at the back of the theatre in the very heart of your enthusiasm and . . . would be occupied by the people least likely to be enthusiastic."[4] Isadora's correspondence with Singer reveals a still touching devotion between them, a weary familiarity, reflecting all too plainly the turmoil they endured as lovers.

"Dearest," Isadora wrote when Singer complained about their mounting bills, "I wonder if you know that when I receive a kind letter from you I feel strong and happy and can *work,* and when you write me unkindly I am so depressed I feel heavy & can not think of work — you probably do not know that you have this power — or you would not use it so ruthlessly." Her health had not been good, for neurasthenic or other reasons. "I am working trying to get in Condition," she wrote, "but as I am very tired it will probably work better when I have a rest. . . . I will leave next Wednesday for Plombières but if there is any chance of your coming to see me I would go any place you suggest." As always, there were quarrels and separations, when Isadora's careless approach to money or men became more than Singer could stand. A note from Isadora in the summer of 1912 put the onus on him: "If I am no longer any pleasure to you, tell me now. . . . You know I never accepted anything from anyone before I met you — and I cannot *bear* the idea of taking things from you unless you love me. Answer me the *truth.*"[5]

While waiting for her theater, Isadora practiced day and night with Hener Skene, not caring about time or performance pressures but only the joy of her work and the "preoccupation" of art. Daylight never penetrated her studio in rue Chauveau, hung with her heavy curtains and lit only by soft lamps. Michel Georges-Michel saw her there in September 1912 and left a chilling depiction of the Neuilly house: "Dante before the seventh portal of Hell suffered a distress less dismal, no doubt, than did your servant at the dancer's walls. A dark park, large trees hiding a tall building — strange and without windows." Inside, all was dimness. The cascading folds of Isadora's blue curtains seemed "heavy as with tears." Georges-Michel peered through the gloom to the upper balcony, where Isadora suddenly emerged through "clouds of incense, like a glittering deity out of this nightmare heaven. . . . A point of gold, then azure, she grows taller as she descends the eleven turns of the stairway to the unhappy marbles below."[6] Her trips to Egypt left their mark on her style: Singer now called her "Isis."

"L. delighted to give dinner-parties and fêtes," Isadora wrote, "and often the vast studio was turned into a tropical garden or a Spanish Palace, and there came all the artists and celebrated people of Paris."[7] The 1912 social season was the most extravagant in memory, the dying starburst of the Belle Epoque. Only two years separated Europe from World War I and the end of a way of life. In 1913 French couture set the world on its head when women's day dresses, "so tight from hip to ankle that they showed the outline of the thighs," also began to sport necklines "as low as evening gowns." The "peek-a-boo" blouse made its appearance; skirts were slit up the side. In the *New York Tribune,* Paris correspondent Kate Carew gave the tone of these last, careless years: "We are garbing ourselves like Solomon in all his glory; India, the Orient, all the corners of the world have been scoured for fabrics and ideas. We are to unite every color of the rainbow on our persons. If we have a yellow skirt we are to balance it with a green coat and purple hat. . . . We are to walk abroad looking like Post-Impressionist pictures, or Futuristic efforts, or Cubist atrocities."[8] Both opium and cocaine could be found at parties.

In June 1912 Paul Poiret hosted his Olympian Ball at Versailles, where the guests appeared as characters from Greek myth, as depicted in the age of Louis XIV. Poiret came as Jupiter, "with curled golden hair, curled golden beard, draped in an ivory veil and shod with buskins." Under the trellises, "pyramids of watermelons, pomegranates, and pineapples" sat on a sumptuous buffet. "Bacchic serving-women crowned with vine leaves poured out new wine. . . . In front were tubs filled with scarlet shrimps, baskets full of grapes, cherries, and gooseberries."

That night Poiret's guests consumed more than eight hundred quarts of champagne. Isadora arrived as a woodland nymph. "Drunken with wine and with the splendor of the scene," she called for music and danced "a delirious improvisation" with Poiret on the terrace of the Pavillon du Butard. "Certain of the guests were moved to tears at so much beauty come together," Poiret wrote modestly.[9] Rumors of orgies spread quickly through Paris. It was a season of sexual scandal.

In May, Diaghilev had presented Nijinsky in his own choreography of Debussy's *Afternoon of a Faun,* igniting a moralistic furor that made Isadora's recent adventure with a broken dress strap seem nothing by comparison. Nijinsky's "onanistic gesture" at the end of the ballet — having failed in his pursuit of a bathing nymph, the faun takes her discarded scarf and apparently ejaculates into it — raised an outcry in the press and led to diplomatic consultation between Russia and France.[10] Newspapers reported "a new reign of prudery" in the French capital: "A crusade against these daring innovations was started at once, public opinion strongly denouncing the degenerating influence of . . . Russian ballet, and more especially of some so-called aesthetic soloist dancers"[11] — namely, Isadora Duncan. At a party given by the actress Cécile Sorel, Isadora broke through the crowd in pursuit of some handsome guest, knelt, and handed him flowers, saying, "Tonight, you are my god. I will dance for you."[12]

"She seemed not to care what impression she made in private, or even in public," wrote Lugné-Poë: "She wore an air of smiling shamelessness that suited her."[13] Dancers at the Paris Opéra, meanwhile, were banned from wearing "flimsy dresses" in performance: Nijinsky's costume in *Afternoon of a Faun* had made him look *"plus nu que nu"* — more naked than naked — and "the too obvious pantomime" of his choreography "deliberately contrived to be bestial," as Gaston Calmette, editor of the conservative daily *Le Figaro,* complained in a front-page editorial. Jean Cocteau left a picture of Nijinsky after a performance of *The Specter of the Rose,* "bowing and smiling to thunderous cheers as he took his fifty curtain calls, and the poor athlete backstage between bows, gasping and leaning against any support he could find, half fainting, clutching his side," his valet spitting cold water into his face to keep him from falling over. It seemed to many a description of Europe itself in the last days before the war.[14] Michel Georges-Michel described Isadora, dancing along the avenue de l'Opéra one night in the company of Jean Mounet-Sully and looking exactly like Carpeaux's statue *La Danse* (which was also condemned as indecent at its unveiling in 1868). An American friend of Gertrude Stein reported to her family in Oakland that Isadora was "so very lovely" to look at — "from a distance." They had met briefly at the theater: "Between numbers, when everyone promenaded, she was standing just at the door of her loge, talking French to seven men. I sat with my glasses glued to her the whole time."[15]

In September, Isadora and Singer motored through Germany with Deirdre and Patrick on their way to the Bayreuth Festival, where

Singer sat through four hours of *Parsifal*, evidently without complaint. He seemed impatient to please Isadora, going so far as to invite Craig to collaborate with them on their plans for her theater in Paris. It had been a good year for Craig. In January, after four years of preparation, his *Hamlet* had finally opened at the Moscow Art Theatre to unparalleled acclaim, granting him a degree of celebrity and recognition he had only dreamed of up till then. In Paris, where he spent most of 1912 with Elena and their children, Craig worked on an illustrated edition of *Hamlet* and enjoyed the high patronage of Countess Greffulhe, who hoped he might eventually do for the French stage what he had done for the Russian and who reluctantly loaned him to Singer when Isadora pleaded for his assistance.

Singer offered Craig fifty thousand francs to work with Louis Sue on the stage construction and lighting of the Théâtre du Beau. At first, Craig accepted, purportedly with the understanding that Isadora would have no part in the proceedings. "There are too few ideals in the theatrical world for one to be lost," Craig wrote to Singer in July. "In the planning and execution of your scheme I would earnestly urge you to exclude from your counsels all and every *performer*."[16] When he withdrew from the project in October, it was because Singer had refused to deny press reports that the theater was being built expressly for Isadora: "Now although anyone might be honored to build a theatre for Miss Duncan I have made it one of my rules lately to work for no performer however highly gifted or eminent, & I cannot break it. . . . I am very sorry — & I had hoped things would have been different."[17]

In the interim, Craig was unable to avoid a reunion with Deirdre, whom he met as a virtual stranger in Neuilly. Years later he professed to be shocked that she had not run joyfully into his arms: "With all my children, especially the dear little girls, *all understanding* has ever been between us — always — and somehow little Deirdre seemed frozen . . . no tender leap towards me — no eager smile. . . . Can you imagine what that meant to me? No eager smile no run to me — and to her it must have been strange."[18] Craig went back to Florence, where tirades followed in his notebooks about "Isadora and her millionaire." In February 1913, with money Elena had raised in England, he would open his own school of stagecraft and design at the Arena Goldoni. It died in eighteen months, with the outbreak of war.

The loss of Craig to her theater plans left Isadora regretful and depressed. She seems to have turned on Singer in response. In November she threw a "Persian" party, offending Singer so badly by her flirting that he left her studio, with the remark that there was no room for him in it. "On this particular evening the champagne flowed as freely as it always did when L. gave a fête," Isadora observed coolly. "By this time I was somewhat initiated into the different intrigues of Paris, so I was able to put together couples who I knew wished it, thus causing tears on the part of some of the wives"[19] — Paul Poiret's, for example: Poiret recalled that Isadora had plied him with kisses in front of his wife and that she said good night to Singer "with considerable affectation. Then everyone danced, and above all, She danced, magnificently, marvelously, divinely, as only She knew how."[20]

At three in the morning, Singer returned "like a thunderclap." He found Isadora in her bedroom with the playwright Henri Bataille. Gossip specified that Bataille was "kissing Isadora's foot" when Singer entered,[21] raging and swearing. Leaving the house a second time, he paused long enough to shout that he was through with Isadora and her theater, too. "This had a somewhat damping effect upon the guests," she wrote, "but in a moment turned my mood from comedy to tragedy." Bataille was an old friend, "like a brother," she protested, but Singer wouldn't be talked down. "His curses fell upon my ears with the empty clanging of demon bells," said Isadora: "The world seemed suddenly transformed to an obscene Hell." Two days later Singer left for Egypt, with another woman.[22]

With Singer gone, apparently for good, Isadora accepted a six-week engagement to dance in Russia. It was there that her apprehensions of tragedy began. "Probably the past, the present, and the future are like a long road," she reflected later. "Beyond each turn the road exists, only we cannot see it, and we think this is the future, but the future is there already waiting for us."[23] Isadora had long been susceptible to psychic visions, "troubled by hallucinations" and "strangely influenced by evil omens and curses," according to Mary Desti; it was "the Irish" in her, Mary thought.[24] In January 1913 she arrived in Kiev with Hener Skene and took a sleigh from the station to their hotel. It was daybreak and the city was covered in snow:

> Hardly awakened from sleep, suddenly I saw on either side of the road, quite clearly, two rows of coffins, but they were not ordinary coffins, they were the coffins of children. I clutched Skene's arm.
> "Look," I said, "all the children — all the children are dead!"
> He reassured me.

"But there is nothing."

"What? Can't you see?"

"No; there is nothing but the snow — the snow heaped up on either side of the road. What a strange hallucination! It is fatigue."[25]

Isadora wasn't convinced. "I thought it was my Death approaching," she wrote to her friend Georges Maurevert later in the year. "And then one night in the train I heard Chopin's *Funeral March* all through the night and I had a sort of vision that so impressed me that I danced it the following evening, just as I had seen it, without a rehearsal, for the first time." In St. Petersburg she came down with a fever and made out her will. "And during all my tournée in Russia," she told Maurevert, "I was haunted by this presentiment of Death and I ask myself now if it is possible that the word *accident* exists. This thing coming towards me, I sensed its approach."[26]

On February 22 Isadora saw one of the last performances of Craig's *Hamlet* at the Moscow Art Theatre, and afterward joined the company for "a grand supper à la Russe" with the Stanislavskys.[27] She may have known that Stanislavsky had once suggested her for the part of Ophelia, saying that she was the only performer living who could capture Ophelia's "stillness." Craig had vetoed the idea, although he thought of Isadora in designing the role, marking her initials in the text of Act III, scene i, when Hamlet spurns Ophelia: "I loved you not." Craig noted further: "The scene is love, love, love — over & over again — no fury — no anger — nothing but love in agony."[28] From the Hotel Astoria, Isadora wrote to Louis Sue, the architect for her Paris theater, saying that she was "desolate . . . disconsolate. . . . Lots of 'success' but that doesn't mean happiness!" She had written to Singer in Egypt, but he didn't reply: "I'm living here like a *monk,* and apart from moments of exaltation and ecstasy [on the stage] it's very *depressing.* . . . What a joy it will be to see my Patrick and Deirdre again. I am Homesick. . . . My soul is drying up."[29]

At the end of her Russian engagement, Isadora left for Berlin, where Elizabeth met her with the children and her pupils. The "sinister foreboding" would not lift. With her students, Isadora gave three concerts in Berlin and again found herself dancing the *Marche Funèbre,* haunted by the image of "one going forward in the world suddenly crushed by a terrible blow. . . . I danced a creature who carries in her arms her dead, with slow, hesitating steps, towards the last resting-place."[30] By the time she returned to Paris, she was seriously alarmed.

In her studio she saw "great black birds flying about" and jumped from her chair at a dinner she gave for Lord Alfred Douglas, with the words, "Did you see anything pass just then before the curtain? . . . Three black cats ran across there. This is most extraordinary. I believe I am losing my mind." Douglas, a Catholic convert, was so unnerved that he went next door and "baptized" Deirdre and Patrick while they slept.[31] Isadora never knew it — it was her own death she expected.

In the last week of March, Isadora was joined by her leading pupils and Temple Duncan for concerts at the Trocadéro. The girls arrived from Germany over the protests of Merz, who feared that once in Paris, they might never return. Elizabeth, who came along as chaperone, insisted that they be billed on Isadora's program as the "Students of the School of Dance at Darmstadt."[32]

At the Trocadéro, Isadora presented *Orpheus* in concert with the Colonne Orchestra and chorus, with readings by Jean Mounet-Sully and arias from Gluck sung by tenor Rodolphe Plamondon. The mystic poet and playwright Joséphin Sar Péladan introduced the evening with a lecture on Greek tragedy.[33] Singer might have abandoned the Théâtre du Beau, but Isadora remained steadfast to its vision, devoting fully half of the Trocadéro concerts to poetry, chorales, and the work of her students — "slender young girls in rose-colored scarves and crowned with flowers," as Fernand Divoire described them. "They are grown up now. . . . Isadora dances with them and is part of them. And the delighted audience applauds and applauds, freed of all everyday worries and care, left with no other thoughts but those of grace and youth eternal."[34] It was Divoire who gave the girls their unforgettable name: Les Isadorables.

On April 9 Isadora moved her company to the Châtelet, where she presented *Iphigenia* to sold-out houses. That same week, the new Théâtre des Champs-Elysées opened on avenue Montaigne, with Bourdelle's bas-reliefs of Isadora embedded in its walls. Her image was everywhere apparent in the finished building, from Bourdelle's sculpted fresco above the entrance, depicting her in an imagined dance with Nijinsky, to Maurice Denis's painted figures of the nine Muses in the auditorium. In France, Isadora Duncan had become monumental. It seemed to critics in Paris that she had reached her apotheosis.

"Is she not tragic?" Bourdelle exclaimed when he saw Isadora dancing at the Châtelet. Turning to his companions, he said, "She seems to be dancing in the face of Death. Truly, she has Death before her."[35] He never knew what it was that had made him think so. The *New York Sun* reported that Isadora was "called back repeatedly" at one of her concerts, "until the asbestos curtain was lowered to show that she would not come back [again]. Mounet-Sully, who was present, urged her to go back and dance Chopin's Funeral March. Miss Duncan said she would not do this, although the audience was demanding the dance, because it might bring her misfortune."[36]

Alone in her studio, Isadora woke to the vision of "a moving figure, draped in black," which stood at the end of her bed and gazed at her "with pitiful eyes." The "double black cross" Poiret had designed on the gold doors of her bedroom, which she once thought merely bizarre, now seemed to her an incontestable augury of doom. In desperation, she consulted Dr. Bosson, who told her that her nerves were "overstrained" and ordered a rest.[37]

Accordingly, Isadora and her children left Paris for Versailles. On April 18 she awoke to brilliant sunshine and the warbling of birds. Mary Desti joined her at the Trianon Palace and remembered that she had "never seen Isadora so happy or tender." Rodin came to tea with his secretary, classicist Mario Meunier, who was working on a new translation of *The Bacchae* at Isadora's request. That night, dancing at the Châtelet, she felt new energy surging through her:

> I remember that evening so well, for I danced as never before. I was no longer a woman, but a flame of joy — a fire — the sparks that rose, the smoke whirling from the hearts of the public — And, as a farewell, after a dozen encores, I danced last of all the "Moment Musicale," and as I danced, it seemed to me that something sang within my heart, "Life and Love — the Highest Ecstasy — and all are mine to give — are mine to give to those who need them." And suddenly it seemed as if Deirdre were sitting on one of my shoulders and Patrick on the other, perfectly balanced, in perfect joy, and as I looked from one side to another in my dance, I met their laughing, bright baby faces — baby smiles — and my feet were never tired.[38]

After her performance that night, Isadora came back onstage ten times to acknowledge the cheers of an audience that refused to leave. She was smiling, "her arms raised as if to touch the crowd, offering her hands, and standing for a long time afterward in the wings, propped-up, immobile, as if looking for the last time at her frenzied admirers."[39] As she prepared to leave the theater, Singer walked into her dressing room. Isadora had heard nothing from him since their quarrel in November. "He seemed deeply affected by my dancing that evening and by our meeting," she wrote, "and proposed to join us at supper at Augustin's apartment in the Champs Elysées Hotel." She hadn't known what to think, but when Singer failed to appear later that night she was "bitterly disappointed." "I had been deeply glad to see him, for I loved him always and longed to show him his own son, who had grown strong and beautiful in his father's absence." Discouraged, Isadora returned to Versailles with Mary.

The following morning, April 19, the children were in high spirits, "dancing and singing all over the place," as Mary recalled.[40] They woke Isadora by jumping on her bed: "Patrick was more than usually boisterous, and amused himself by turning over the chairs and as each chair fell he shouted with joy." Their Scottish governess, Annie Sim, tried to quiet him: "Please, Patrick, don't make such a noise; you annoy Mama."

"Oh, let him be," said Isadora. "Think what life would be, nurse, without their noise." She was still in her dressing gown when the telephone rang. It was Singer. Would she come to lunch in Paris and bring the children?

That morning Isadora, Deirdre, Patrick, Mary, and Annie Sim rode into town in a rented Renault, driven by an agency chauffeur, Paul Morverand.[41] The car was considered old-fashioned even in 1913, tall and narrow, with a crank engine, and closed against the elements at a time when luxury convertibles were the rage. It was raining hard by the time they got to Paris. Isadora stopped first in Neuilly, where her students had arrived for a rehearsal in the studio. Irma remembered that Patrick, while waiting for his mother to get ready, gave "a cunning imitation" of her curtain calls, bowing deeply and waving to an imaginary crowd.[42] Mary went to the Maison Desti, while the girls joined Isadora, Augustin, and the children for lunch at an Italian restaurant with Singer. It seemed to Isadora that all quarrels were forgotten. Singer hoped to revive the Théâtre du Beau.

"It will be Isadora's Theatre," he said.

"No," said Isadora, "it will be Patrick's Theatre, for Patrick is the Great Composer, who will create the Dance to the Music of the Future." Singer was in a splendid mood and suggested that the party spend the afternoon at the Salon des Humoristes, but Isadora and the girls had scheduled a rehearsal with Hener Skene. About three o'clock, they arrived back at Neuilly.

"Will you come in with the children and wait?" Isadora asked the governess, Annie Sim. She would practice only for an hour or two.

"No, madame, I think we had better return [to Versailles]. The little ones need rest."

Isadora bundled the children in the car, covering their legs with lap rugs: "Then I kissed them and said, 'I will also return soon.' And then, in leaving, little Deirdre put her lips against the glass window. I leaned forward and kissed the glass on the spot where her lips were at that moment. The cold glass gave me an uncanny impression." Waving good-bye, she turned and went into the house:

> I threw myself down on the couch. There were flowers and a box of bonbons that someone had sent me. I took one in my hand and ate it lazily, thinking, "Surely, after all, I am very happy — perhaps the happiest woman in the world. My Art, success, fortune, love, but, above all, my beautiful children."
>
> I was thus lazily eating sweets and smiling to myself, thinking, "L. has returned; all will be well," when there came to my ears a strange, unearthly cry.
>
> I turned my head. L. was there, staggering like a drunken man. His knees gave way — he fell before me — and from his lips came these words:
>
> "The children — the children — are dead!"

The Renault had driven only a few hundred yards along rue Chauveau to the intersection of boulevard Bourdon, which runs parallel to the Seine embankment.[43] Stopping short to avoid a collision, the car stalled facing the Seine. Morverand, the chauffeur, got out to crank the engine. Later he insisted that he had left the gear in neutral and secured the parking brake. When the engine turned, however, the car shot forward across boulevard Bourdon, jumped the pavement at the other side, and careened down the grassy slope of the embankment into the river. Morverand ran to stop it, getting as far as the running board before he was knocked to the ground. "Shrieks from the two children and the nurse" were heard as the car plunged into the water.[44] Morverand remained screaming on the pavement, "beating his head madly." Then he tried to run but was blocked by the crowd already gathered at the river's edge. *The Times* of London reported on April 20:

> A number of workmen, who were drinking on the terrace of a neighboring café, had witnessed the accident, and they behaved with great promptness and courage. One of them dived several times into the water, but was unable to locate the submerged car. Others of them

ran to the nearest fire station and alarmed the fire brigades of Neuilly and Levallois, who were quickly on the scene, followed at short intervals by men of the Paris brigade, and by M. Hennion, the new Prefect of Police. M. Hennion telephoned for divers from the station of the Island of Saint Louis. A large motor boat was also soon requisitioned and its crew were the first to succeed in locating the submerged car in the bed of the river. Strenuous and indeed desperate efforts were made to get it to the bank, but an hour and a half elapsed before the crew of the motor boat by means of ropes and anchors finally managed to haul it ashore.

There was a heart-rending scene when the door of the car was opened and the children were found clinging to their dead nurse.

According to press reports, it wasn't Singer but Augustin who broke the news of the accident to Isadora — her true relationship with Singer could not be acknowledged in the press. Gus was drawn to the river by the wail of sirens. He arrived to witness the car being raised and thus also saw the bodies removed — first Annie Sim, then Deirdre, then Patrick. The nurse had wrapped lap rugs around the children. The faces of all three were "stricken with indescribable terror." When Gus realized what had happened, he attacked the weeping chauffeur "with his fists, beating him about the face and screaming," until police pulled him away.[45] Morverand kept crying, *"Ah! quel malheur! Quel malheur!" Excelsior* wrote: "The witnesses and even the firemen, well accustomed to scenes of tragedy, couldn't restrain their tears."[46]

The bodies were carried across boulevard Bourdon to a tobacco shop, and from there to the American Hospital in Neuilly, only a few blocks from Isadora's studio. Undoubtedly, Augustin telephoned Singer. The children's bodies were already at the morgue before Isadora learned what had happened. She wrote:

> I remember a strange stillness came upon me, only in my throat I felt a burning, as if I had swallowed some live coals. But I could not understand. I spoke to [Singer] very softly; I tried to calm him; I told him it could not be true.
>
> Then other people came, but I could not conceive what had happened. Then entered a man with a dark beard. I was told he was a doctor. "It is not true," he said, "I will save them."
>
> I believed him. I wanted to go with him, but people held me back. I know now that this was because they did not wish me to know that there was indeed no hope. They feared the shock would make me insane, but I was, at that time, lifted to a state of exaltation. I saw

everyone about me weeping, but I did not weep. On the contrary, I felt an immense desire to console everyone.

Mary Desti returned to her apartment late that afternoon, to be greeted at the door by her secretary: "Quick, quick, you must go to Isadora's immediately. They have been telephoning like mad for the last half hour."[47] Mary was tired and answered that Isadora could wait. Within seconds, Elizabeth was on the line: "Tell Mme. Desti to come immediately, immediately. It is most urgent."

On her way to Neuilly, Mary paused to buy flowers for Isadora: "I knew she intended having the Queen of Naples[48] there for tea and I supposed she just wanted me to come." At the studio she saw "an immense crowd, policemen, and terrible excitement. I thought, 'Oh, she's having a great party.'" Upstairs, Isadora stood "in the middle of the room with [Singer's] arms around her." She reached out her hands: "Mary, tell me it isn't true, it isn't true. My children are not dead."

"Of course, they're not."

"Don't lie to her," said Singer. "It is not the time for that."

"Oh, Mary doesn't know," Isadora cried, "doesn't know what happened." Elizabeth entered and swept Mary into the hall: "Mary, for God's sake, don't lose your head. . . . The babies are drowned, Mary; in the Seine."

Mary had run from the house and quickly down the street to the American Hospital, where she saw the children's bodies on a marble slab, along with "a sight that has filled all the rest of my life with a nightmare. There was the poor little English nurse and imprinted on her face and staring open eyes and wide open mouth, the horror of the whole tragedy." When she realized that there was nothing to be done, Mary went back to the studio and "found Isadora sitting like one in a trance, giving orders unconsciously about everything. . . . She asked me had I seen the babies and was there any hope and I told her, 'No, none.'"

"We must notify Ted at once," said Isadora. "It will break his heart." Her telegram to Craig in Florence gives the measure of her calm: OUR LITTLE GIRL DEIRDRE WAS TAKEN FROM US TODAY WITHOUT SUFFERING MY BOY PATRICK IS TAKEN WITH HER THIS SORROW IS BEYOND ANY WORDS I SEND YOU MY ETERNAL UNDYING LOVE = ISADORA.[49]

Mary asked whether Isadora wanted the bodies brought home. She did. In cases of accidental death, with investigation pending, Paris police normally refused permission to remove corpses from the morgue. "After tremendous difficulties," the matter was arranged by Gaston

Calmette, editor of *Le Figaro,* who, along with dozens of Isadora's friends, had rushed to the studio upon hearing the news.

"Isadora," said Calmette, "command me in any way, in any way. Let me be of some help to you." She answered: "No, there is nothing, nothing, nothing to do."[50]

The bodies were released about eleven o'clock that night. Mary had prepared a sofa in the downstairs library, "where I arranged and dressed them, combing and curling their golden locks. There they lay, hand in hand like two smiling angels." In death, Deirdre's arm was placed protectively around Patrick, and their heads were turned inward, touching.

"Going upstairs I asked Isadora if she would like to see them," Mary wrote. "Like a stone image, with Augustin on one side and me on the other, she came down the long stairs to her immense studio, and as we entered the library, oh, so gently, so gently, she knelt beside them, taking their little hands in hers, and with a cry that has pierced my heart ever since, whispered, 'My children, my poor little children.'"[51] Isadora later described that moment:

> Only twice comes that cry of the mother which one hears as without one's self — at Birth and at Death — for when I felt in mine those little cold hands that would never again press mine in return I heard my cries — the same cries as I had heard at their births. Why the same — since one is the cry of extreme joy and the other of sorrow? I do not know why, but I know they are the same. Is it that in all the Universe there is but one Great Cry containing Sorrow, Joy, Ecstasy, Agony, the Mother Cry of Creation?[52]

For the next three days, Isadora never slept or changed her clothes. Two doctors stayed at the studio, urging her to rest and offering her sedatives, which she refused. Singer was so distraught that he checked into a clinic. In London, Mrs. Patrick Campbell wrote to George Bernard Shaw: "Such a day one would have loved only to have thought of life and happiness. I open the paper to read of Isadora Duncan's heart rending sorrow — poor Singer — poor Ellen Terry, poor Gordon Craig — poor all of us that have hearts to ache."[53]

Before dawn on Sunday, April 20, students from the Ecole des Beaux-Arts arrived in Neuilly and covered Isadora's garden and trees with white blossoms — "all the white flowers they could find in Paris," Mary wrote.[54] "Owing to the peculiarly distressing nature of the accident," said the *New York Times,* "nothing that has happened in a long time has so touched the hearts of Parisians. . . . All Paris is in mourning."⁵⁵ Hundreds of Isadora's friends and acquaintances streamed through the studio on Sunday and Monday to offer their condolences. Patrick's toy wagon, a gift from Jean Cocteau, still sat in the courtyard, along with his pet goat, which wandered the grounds "looking for its master," according to reports. Maurice Ravel approached "that unfortunate house" trembling and afraid: "It is too frightful and so unfair!"⁵⁶ Outside, Bourdelle was seen pacing back and forth, holding his head in his hands, "muttering wildly." Mary persuaded him to come in, where he fell on his knees and, weeping, lay his head in Isadora's lap.

"She looked at him as the Mother of God might have looked," Mary wrote. "I can't explain just what it was. She was in the most exalted state, as though some great spirit of pity had taken possession of her and she was sorry for the whole world."⁵⁷ Word reached her that the chauffeur, Morverand, had been arrested on charges of "culpable homicide." She immediately sent a letter to the Paris public prosecutor, asking for his release. "I wish to assure you that I do not bear him ill will," Isadora wrote. "He is a father, and I need to know that he has been released to his family before I can regain some measure of calm. . . . It is for the peace of my soul that I make this appeal for pity." Morverand was let go without penalty.⁵⁸

In the meantime, rumors flew. Newspapers reported on April 21 that Isadora would leave the stage and "devote the rest of her life to the care of the poor and sick as a hospital nurse. As soon as she has recovered from the shock . . . it is said she will leave for the field of operations in the Balkans and join the Bulgarian Red Cross." The story originated when Raymond arrived in Paris from Albania, where he and his followers had set up a relief operation for refugees of the Balkan War. The colorful configuration of the Duncan clan posed a challenge to reporters. Raymond "caused a sensation on alighting from the train in his customary costume of ancient Greece,"⁵⁹ while Augustin, whose divorce from Sarah Whiteford wouldn't be final until August,⁶⁰ lived openly in Paris with the actress Margherita Sargent; they, too, had a child, Angus, born in 1911.

In the wake of the tragedy, the press never disclosed that Isadora's children had been illegitimate. The *New York Times* stepped cautiously around the issue: "Isadora Duncan held unconventional ideas in regard to marriage and motherhood, and never lacked the courage to uphold her views whenever the subject was discussed among her friends."[61] Many papers reported that she was prostrate with grief, sobbing, crying her children's names, and "refusing to be consoled." In fact, she was still in shock: "The unhappiness was too great for tears. I could not weep. Crowds of friends came to me weeping. Crowds of people stood in the garden and the street weeping, but I would not weep."[62] She didn't break down until her students came to see her on Sunday.

The girls had learned about the accident only a few hours after it happened, when Augustin, "in a frantic state, his clothes dripping wet," came to their pension in search of his daughter, Temple. Mary Desti arrived the next morning with the whole story. "She told us to pack our things," Irma recollected, "since we would leave for Darmstadt immediately." They learned that Isadora's doctors had requested their presence, in the hope that seeing them might shake her out of her trancelike state. Irma wrote that they were barely able to distinguish Isadora's figure in the darkness of the studio, sitting in a tall chair, "immobile, like a statue, her head thrown back and eyes closed, tears streaming down her face. Standing close beside her, I could not control my wild sobbing when she looked at me and, taking me in her arms, held my head close to her breast. Through my sobs I heard her say in a gentle, pitiful voice, 'You must be my children now.'"[63] The girls couldn't speak a word, Anna reported, "but only cried and felt for her. . . . For us, personally, as well as for the future of the school, this is a decisive moment. May all be well. I only hope that Isadora will be able to bear it."[64]

In Florence, Gordon Craig had received Isadora's telegram announcing the children's deaths. He wrote in his daybook: "The wind drops and the sun comes out and all is calm — April 20th, 1913."[65] Nothing in Craig's experience or temperament could prepare him for a calamity of such proportion. "No, I can't say anything not one word," he wrote to Isadora. "I've said a million written and written — thought & thought — & all useless — all of no use. Only I can repeat my dear my dear many million times. Hear that continually."[66] A longer letter followed:

> Isadora, my dear — not I alone but all of us, feel we claim some share of your sorrow — and take it.
> Dear — dear ———
> You are bearing all the grief which would have been theirs — then dry your eyes for them

Be sure the Gods are looking at you now
& I am sure you are bearing yourself nobly.
And as all their little griefs fall to your share now, so also does all
their pride & splendor become yours again by right.
Dear and great Isadora now is your time.
To say I love you would not cover the whole.
I take your fingers your hands in mine & I pray a great prayer.[67]

From Neuilly, Isadora answered with another telegram: YOUR
WORDS AS THEY HAVE ALWAYS DONE BRING ME COMFORT AND IF THERE IS
COURAGE FOR A GRIEF LIKE THIS I WILL TRY AND FIND IT LOVE TO YOU AND
YOURS TED = ISADORA.[68] She wasn't equipped to oversee the details of the
funeral, insisting only that the children be cremated, not put "in the
earth to be devoured by worms." Again, Gaston Calmette intervened
with the authorities: under French law, cremation was forbidden to
anyone who hadn't requested it.

"I had one desire," Isadora said, "that this horrible accident
should be transformed into beauty. . . . Augustin, Elizabeth, and Raymond sensed my wish, and they built in the studio a huge mound of
flowers, and when I was conscious the first thing I heard was the
Colonne orchestra playing the beautiful lament of Gluck's 'Orphée.'"[69]
A Catholic priest who came to the studio offering spiritual comfort
was sent packing. "I am a pagan," Isadora answered. "It is not in your
heaven that I shall see my children again. . . . I don't want a church; a
mother's heart is deeper than all temples."[70]

The funeral service took place in the studio on the morning of
April 22. The bodies were taken from the library and placed on a
catafalque at the center of the Duncans' floral tribute. Deirdre and
Patrick lay in open coffins. Annie Sim did not — no amount of cos-
metic labor had been able to remove the look of agony from her face,
which remained covered with a sheet.

"Very early more wreaths began to arrive to swell the mass of flowers already covering the coffins," wrote the *New York Times*. "A little
before 10 o'clock men and women famous in the artistic and literary
life of Paris began to assemble, and by 10 A.M., when the funeral ceremony began, the studio was thronged with about seven hundred
people."[71] Cécile Sorel watched as Isadora, flanked by her brothers
and sister, "passed before us like a shadow on the way to the room that
held the coffins. Then she seemed suddenly stricken by the reality of
what had happened. Her knees gave way, she reeled, collapsing into

the folds of a gray curtain. Then, slowly, as if the slightest sudden movement would cause her to fall again, she raised herself." She said a short good-bye in private, then retired to the third-floor gallery, where she collapsed again at the rail, surrounded by her family, Mary, and Sorel.[72]

Craig had asked Count Kessler to represent him at the funeral. "Take on my behalf two tiny bunches of some flower one buys in a great city on a quay & put them there for me — will you," he wrote. "I can be of no use or I would have left last night for Paris. . . . I don't know yet how to think or feel — Now one becomes [a] complete fool — *useless*."[73] Kessler reported on April 23:

> Yesterday, the poor little creatures were laid to rest. There was a most beautiful, moving ceremony in the studio, *the most moving ceremony I have ever been to*. Nothing but exquisite music, Grieg's "Death of Aase," then a piece of Mozart, that seemed to embody the tripping of light, childish feet on soft grass and flowers, and a wailing, infinitely moving melody of Bach. I thought my heart would break. Poor Isadora behaved splendidly. She knelt behind her sister and two brothers on the balcony. Then the coffins were carried out, through the garden all strewn with white daisies and jessamin [sic], to the white hearses drawn by white horses; everything most admirable in taste and *restraint*. I haven't spoken to Isadora since the tragedy; but her brother Augustin tells me, that she bears up wonderfully; and others, who have seen her, tell me she is really *heroic, encouraging* the others, saying *there is no death*, really great in her terrible grief. . . . Everyone in Paris is moved to the depths of their heart.[74]

The coffins were taken in procession across Paris to the cemetery of Père-Lachaise, where the remains of Chopin, Balzac, Talleyrand, Champollion, Oscar Wilde, and Héloïse and Abélard are interred. Isadora rode with Elizabeth and Mary in a closed carriage. "We all went out too," said Preston Sturges. "The men, on foot, followed the enormous hearse to the crematory. . . . As we walked by on the streets, all the men we passed stopped and took their hats off, the police saluted, and the women crossed themselves."[75] During the service Singer had broken down and thrown himself on the catafalque, crying that he loved both children as his own: he didn't make the trip to Père-Lachaise.

On the ride to the cemetery, Isadora held tight to Mary's hand. "No tears, Mary — no tears," she said. "They never had a sorrow and we must not be sorrowful today. I want to be brave enough to make death beautiful, to help all the other mothers of the world who have lost their babies."

In the event, it proved too much for her. At Père-Lachaise another funeral was in progress and the final services were performed in the crematorium itself. "Some one decided the ceremony of burning the three dear bodies must take place at once," Mary recalled. Isadora hadn't planned or expected to witness the cremation and "looked like gray marble" as the caskets went into the flames.

"I turned to her and begged her to leave," Mary wrote. "I think she would have died had we stayed another instant."[76] Isadora, wearing "a motor cloak and veil," was "so weak and pathetic" on leaving the crematorium that she had to be assisted to a waiting car: "In the furnace room, masses of white roses and lilies were thrown."[77] Annie Sim's ashes were sent to her family in England. The children's were placed side by side in two niches at the Père-Lachaise columbarium, numbers 6793 and 6805, where simple plaques were later installed, giving no information apart from their names, Deirdre and Patrick.

The most difficult task lay ahead — to separate Isadora from the tragedy that had engulfed her. After the funeral Mary suggested that she come to her apartment for a rest, but Isadora declined.

"I have a great mission to do," she said.[78] She returned to the studio and "sat for hours just looking into space." Mary never left her side: "Later the others returned and noticing a terrible restlessness about Isadora, and fearing what she might do . . . I asked Raymond not to leave her, but not to let her know; that he was to follow us if she insisted on going out." About midnight Isadora rose, put on her cloak, and strode into the night. "I told her I would die if she would leave me," Mary wrote. "I could not possibly stay alone. I must go with her."

"Very well, then, Mary," said Isadora, "come, but you must let me decide for myself."

They walked to the embankment where her children had died, "and she sat gazing for a long time into the waters of the Seine. . . . Then up and down, in one street and out another, for two hours she tore along at a terrific pace," Raymond following unnoticed in the shadows. Finally, she stopped: "Mary, I've decided to see it through. Nothing matters to me now but maybe I can help others." Mary took her home, and together they lay down on Isadora's bed. She was "sobbing very quietly," Mary wrote. "I put my arm under her head, and in a short time she slept."

Mary, too, was exhausted. About five in the morning, she "heard the outer gate open and footsteps crunch on the gravel." Careful not to wake Isadora, she rose and passed Singer on the stairs, "his face alight with such beauty that he looked like a god." Relieved, knowing the bond that held them, Mary left the house without a word, "returning to my own home, knowing he was the only person who could console her."[79]

17

The Rock of Niobe

Within days of her children's deaths, Isadora left Paris for Corfu, the northernmost of the Greek islands in the Ionian Sea, where Raymond had established a base of operations in the Balkan War of 1912 and 1913. Raymond's relief efforts blossomed into the dream of a self-supporting community in the nearby province of Epirus, where thousands of refugees, on the verge of starvation, had collected in the Albanian port of Agii Saranta. Raymond taught "the homeless souls" to weave on antique looms and was soon selling their work in London at a profit, which he returned to Albania in the form of food, tools, and wool.[1] "The whole country is in need," he told Isadora. "The villages devastated; the children starving. . . . Come and help to feed the children — comfort the women."[2]

Isadora arrived on Corfu with Augustin and Elizabeth. On May 14, while waiting to cross to Agii Saranta, she wrote to architect Louis Sue:

> We are here in a villa overlooking the sea — completely isolated —
> one can walk miles among the olive trees without meeting *anybody.*
> I have spent two very difficult weeks — it is so difficult some-
> times. Horror itself conquers me and in spite of all my efforts I fall into
> emptiness — in a sort of hell — it is terrible. . . . I try to wear myself
> out with long walks — but night comes always when I cannot read

any more or think and I fall a prey to tortures. What is surprising is that the body still lives. . . .

I am awaiting Raymond's return. . . . It is so beautiful here — I would like so much if, instead of sending you these stupid words in my bad French, I could send you the view from my window — on the wide space of the sea — I can see right to the mountains on the opposite side which seem to float in the azure between earth and heaven — like a vision of a promised land. . . . Sometimes looking out on it I think that maybe I'm dead with my children and have entered Paradise — and I feel them close to me — and then comes again the cruel physical suffering — my eyes will never see them, my hands never touch them again, and I see once more the poor little things waving their little hands — in the automobile driving off — and I want to scream.[3]

Isadora had left Paris in a daze, fearing either to go or to stay, but confident that whatever she did would bring no relief for her suffering. "When real sorrow is encountered," she wrote, "there is, for the stricken, no gesture, no expression. Like Niobe turned to stone . . ." In Greek mythology, Niobe was a mother, queen of Thebes, whose pride in her children led to their slaughter by the gods. After wandering the earth in desolation, Niobe was transformed into a rock, from which a river of tears was said to flow. For Isadora, the metaphor was real. "Those who were with me say that for days and weeks I sat only staring before me," she reported. "I took no account of time — I had entered a dreary land of greyness where no will to live or move existed."[4] As for dancing, she couldn't think about it.

"I know that my real self died with my children," Isadora wrote from Corfu. "I do not recognize what remains. . . . If I continue to exist it will be as another creature, kinder perhaps. But I'll never dance again."[5] When Raymond brought her to Agii Saranta, she cut off her hair and threw it in the sea, in a dramatic gesture of mourning. "Mme. Duncan [has] turned her face in the direction of the old world from which she received her life's inspiration," said the *Paris Herald*.[6] The plight of refugees helped distract her from her sorrow. On May 31 Isadora wrote to Craig:

We have bought tents and provisions and are going back to erect shelters for the children. It is terrible to see the results of war — no one trying to help these poor people — If we can save some hundreds of little children I will say Deirdre & Patrick are doing it for me — We live while there on a little boat as there are no houses — and I lie all night looking up at the stars — Sometimes towards morning I see a marvelous liquid shining one — I think myself is there — what is left of me here — only a poor shadow.[7]

She returned to this theme repeatedly in the months ahead. There was "nothing left," she wrote; her children were "the best part" of her, "all the joy, the strength and the inspiration of my art." Inevitably, no kind of mental effort could free her from a burning sense of guilt. To Elena Meo, who sent a generous note of sympathy, Isadora answered in distress: "What shall I do with it — all my life gone — and my work too — for how shall I ever *dance* again — how stretch out my arms except in desolation. If I had only been with them, but the nurse had my place."[8]

In Paris the rumor circulated that Isadora had danced at her children's funeral.[9] It shocked her to the core, at the same time driving the myth of Niobe even more deeply in her mind. Preston Sturges recalled that sympathy quickly turned to blame among "professional pulpit-pounders" in France, who detected in the death of Isadora's children "the hand of God the Avenger. . . . Others spoke more gently but with no less evident satisfaction. The events, they said, spoke for themselves."[10] Before leaving Paris, Isadora had issued a statement of thanks to the city, gallant indeed in its sentiments. "My friends have helped me to realize what alone could comfort me," she wrote. "That all men are my brothers, all women my sisters, and all little children on earth are my children."[11] Count Robert de Montesquiou, generally regarded as the nastiest man in Paris, decried her for her egotism. "Evidently, all men are her brothers," he hissed; "for not one is her *husband*. But all women wouldn't want to be the sister of a courtesan, nor all children, her bastards."[12]

Isadora never knew how widely she was faulted for the tragedy that tore her life in half. Craig's ruminations on this subject were especially cruel, coming as they did from a man who paid no more attention to his children than he did to their discarded mothers. "Never need she have lost her loved children had she realized that to have children entails having obligations," Craig wrote. "*Someone* must care for them — & that someone is always MOTHER. This truth she never seems to have faced up to. . . . Never could they have died as they did die with their MOTHER watching."[13] It's tempting to forgive this unimaginable outburst in the knowledge that Craig himself was racked with a guilt he couldn't express. "Only I, in all the world, seem to have no heart," he wrote to Martin Shaw. "It could at least break, if I had one. . . . All suffering, or what I fancied to be such, is wiped out; all misunderstandings too."[14] To Isadora, Craig wrote that he was "mad about something outside myself" and lacked the strength to look within: "A glimpse of myself — if I dared to lift the veil — might kill me."[15]

With Raymond, Isadora walked "fifty miles a day" through the mountains of Epirus, carrying bread, blankets, and what she hoped was comfort to the children of the war. "To help those poor starving mites over there does something to keep me from dying in my desolation and despair," she wrote to Craig in July, "and then I think Patrick and Deirdre would like to see those little ones eating & singing — and who knows perhaps among them we are saving some great Spirit for Future times — anyway what else can I do." It was better "to weep with the stars looking down," she wrote, than alone in a room, or a madhouse, where she feared she would be before long: "All my life seems like a fine ship on the rocks and no hope of ever going [on] another voyage. Also my poor head won't work right anymore." In her first months of grief, it helped to reminisce: "Do you remember I sent you a little picture of Deirdre sitting on the Great Temple at Karnak — looking up so calmly & sweetly — That is how she was — more & more bright & sweet & gay — She would never have agonized through life as I have — when I looked at her I always thought — mine is all broken pieces & disaster — hers will be beautiful & Complete." In her letters, Isadora began to express her conviction, a desperate prayer, that life itself was "only a bad dream, a mirage . . . this abominable bad dream of matter . . . these infernal appearances that are *Shams*."[16]

Sometime that summer Singer arrived on Corfu from London. It isn't known under what circumstances he had parted with Isadora in Paris after the children's funeral. "If this sorrow had come to me much earlier in life," Isadora wrote, "I might have overcome it. . . . If a great love had then enveloped me and carried me away — but L. did not respond to my call."[17] In *My Life,* she attributed Singer's sudden appearance on Corfu to their "telepathic bond. . . . I had the hope also that by a spontaneous love gesture the unhappiness of the past might be redeemed to feel again that stirring in my bosom; that my children might return to comfort me on earth."[18] She hoped to conceive another child. Louis Sue reported that Singer was shocked at her suggestion, finding it "frivolous and inappropriate."[19] Isadora wrote only that "my intense yearning — my sorrow — were too strong for L. to stand. One morning he left abruptly, without warning. . . . I saw the steamer receding over the blue waters, and I was left once more alone."[20]

Late in July, with Raymond's wife, Penelope, Isadora left Corfu for Constantinople. "I feel I can no longer look at all this misery," she confessed. "I have a longing to sit in a mosque with one quiet lamp — I long for the feeling of Persian carpets beneath my feet." Her narrative of the Turkish excursion in *My Life* took on a more than usually phantasmal tone. In Constantinople she saw a fortune-teller, who promised that "after many wanderings," at the end of her life, she would "build temples all over the world. . . . All these temples will be dedicated to Beauty and Joy because you are the daughter of the Sun." On the same trip, Isadora rescued a young actor from suicide over a broken love affair, only to find that the object of his affection was "a lovely youth of about eighteen" named Sylvio. There followed a spirited defense of homosexuality, with reference to the love of Zeus and Ganymede. "As I have always been a student of Plato," Isadora wrote, "and, indeed, consider his 'Phaedrus' the most exquisite love-song ever written, I was not as shocked as some people might have been. I believe the highest love is a purely spiritual flame which is not necessarily dependent on sex."

What seemed like a strange digression in fact reflected Isadora's rebounding defiance of her critics, public and private. She had seen as much suffering as she cared to in Albania. "No doubt there is a great difference between the life of the artist and that of the saint," she remarked.[21] "I can already hear the voices of all the so-called good women of the world saying: 'A most disgraceful history.' 'All her misfortunes are only a just requital of her sins.'"[22] Delivering Penelope to Raymond, she boarded a steamer for Trieste and made her way back to Paris.

In August 1913, from Neuilly, Isadora issued a statement denying reports that she had accepted an engagement to dance in South America. She found the suggestion "infinitely shocking. . . . It seems to me that if I could think of dancing at this moment it would be a crime against life itself and against the great lesson of death which I am trying to learn in silence. It will be a long time before I can even dream of my work again."[23] Nevertheless, she did dream of it. "Sorrow came so suddenly into my life," she told the *Paris Herald,* "taking from me without warning all that made life beautiful. . . . I cannot understand the meaning of the past, or grasp the portent of the future. . . . Time alone can help me to know what I must do. Life after all is war, and the future uncertain."[24] In a note to Hener Skene, Isadora asked him to find "a chorale or hymn by Bach or Palestrina" on which she could work. "I completely despair of life," she wrote, "but perhaps I could make some thing beautiful in movement in the midst of a *requiem* — which might comfort some people on Earth such as myself — Please search for me."[25] The empty house in Neuilly proved more than she could bear. She was thrown into fits of weeping and thought she could hear her children's voices in the garden. In September she went to England, where she stayed in Kent with Deirdre's grandmother, Ellen Terry. "I am half mad with grief and pain," Isadora wrote to Craig, who was then with Elena in London, "and I wanted to feel your Mother's arms about me — as I used to dream they were before Deirdre was born."[26]

Of her own mother, long estranged, Isadora mentions nothing. Max Merz's diaries confirm that Mrs. Duncan stayed at the Darmstadt school for several months in 1913, but there is no record of any contact or correspondence between her and Isadora. That fall Augustin took the girls on tour in Gluck's *Echo and Narcissus,* describing it to Isadora as "a great success and a great advance and a *tiny step* forwards towards your great idea."[27] Her friends all began to urge her to get back to work, but even Gus, she reported, "had no power to break the spell which bound me."[28] In London, at Craig's suggestion, Isadora met Elena — Elena Craig, as she signed herself — and departed in bitter contempt. "Your *own* Nellie has no place in her heart except her all-absorbing ferocious & jealous love for you," she protested in a note to Craig. "I am sorry if you don't understand. . . . Think of the morning Deirdre was born & perhaps you will — and if you can't understand at least pity me."[29] Craig stopped in Paris on his way back to Florence. "I thought I would go & see the river where the little girl went over," he wrote to Elena, "so I drove down there & got out & dropped grain of the white heather Teddy gave me. I didn't want to call at the house up the road — but the place still has tragic signs — Very tragic — can't explain but there are marks, clear & speaking."[30]

By November, Isadora was in Italy, having driven alone from Paris over the Alps. "Only when I was in the car and going at seventy or eighty kilometres an hour could I get any relief from the indescribable anguish of the days and nights," she wrote.[31] She went from Milan to Venice, Rimini, Florence, and finally Viareggio, on the Tuscan coast. Here she was reunited with Eleonora Duse, whom she later credited with saving her life.

Since 1909 Duse had been in retirement, partly from ill health, but more "shamefully," Isadora thought, because she lacked "the capital necessary to carry out her ideas of Art as she wished."[32] In Viareggio they saw or wrote each other daily — "The Tragic Dance promenades with the Tragic Muse," Duse remarked as they walked on the beach. "She never said, 'Cease to grieve,'" wrote Isadora, "but grieved with me, and, for the first time since [the children's] death, I felt I was not alone. . . . Often, when I walked with her by the sea, it seemed to me that her head was among the stars, her hands reached to the mountain-tops." In New York, Isadora had once told reporters, "I do not dance every day, for the same reason that [Duse] does not play every day. She told me that her physical strength was equal to it . . . but that her emotions were not."[33] Recently diagnosed with emphysema and battling what she considered to be vulgar legends about her life and personality, Duse wished Isadora would stop talking to the press altogether. "*If you see* journalists," she warned in a note, "I pray you not to tell them that I am unwell. You don't know how to *hide yourself* from the crowd, and I don't want the crowd to find me."[34]

Indeed, at the Grand Hotel, Isadora was "pestered by strangers" and soon took a villa nearer to Duse, "a large, red brick house set far back in a forest of melancholy pine-trees, and enclosed within a great wall." In a burst of short notes and telegrams, which she sometimes sent to Isadora two or three times a day, Duse advised her not to seek happiness, not to "tempt Fate," and to guard her grief against the encroachment of time: "*Ne perdez pas la bonne douleur! Ne perdez pas la bonne douleur.*" [Do not lose this good sorrow.][35] But hope was "a hard plant to kill," Isadora thought, "and, no matter how many branches are knocked off and destroyed, it will always put forward new shoots." In *My Life,* she reported that she had tried to drown herself in Viareggio: "I thought I would swim so far that I should be unable to return, but always my body of itself turned landward." One afternoon, she imagined that she saw Deirdre and Patrick walking arm in arm on the strand. She ran after them, "followed — called — and suddenly they disappeared in the mist of the sea-spray." Isadora began to fear that she would break completely:

> I had for some moments the distinct feeling that I was then with one foot over the line which divides madness from sanity. I saw before me the asylum — the life of dreary monotony—and in bitter despair I fell upon my face and cried aloud.

I don't know how long I had lain there when I felt a pitying hand on my head. I looked up and saw what I thought to be one of the beautiful contemplation figures of the Sistine Chapel. He stood there, just come from the sea, and said:

"Why are you always weeping? Is there nothing I can do for you — to help you?"

I looked up.

"Yes," I replied. "Save me — save more than my life — my reason. Give me a child."[36]

The man was Romano Romanelli, a young sculptor from a prominent Florentine family. Isadora hadn't met him for the first time on the beach. They knew each other from Paris, where Romanelli was part of Rodin's circle; he also sculpted a bust of Isadora after he became her lover.[37] "When I felt his strong youthful arms about me and his lips on mine," she wrote, "when all his Italian passion descended on me, I felt that I was rescued from grief and death, brought back to light — to love again." By December, eight months after her children's deaths, she was pregnant and "entered into a phase of intense mysticism. I felt that my children's spirits hovered near me — that they would return to console me on earth." Before long, Isadora convinced herself that Romanelli was "a second Michelangelo" and that their child, depending on its sex, would be the reincarnation of either Deirdre or Patrick. "I was so tired," Isadora wrote, "of the constant horrible pain."[38]

Duse was appalled. "Nothing of that which is irreparable is understood by this magnificent and dangerous creature!" she wrote to Lugné-Poë in Paris. "Her generosity is quite as great as her error of imagination."[39] Evidently, the matter caused a breach between them. "I never could have imagined that such a supreme artist as Duse could be so narrow-minded," Isadora remarked.[40] She was so exalted by the turn of events that she didn't mind when Romanelli, already engaged to another woman, broke off their affair: "I felt he had saved my reason, and then I knew I was no longer alone."[41] Summoning Hener Skene from Paris, she left for Rome. "What courage," wrote Duse, "what strength, what folly. . . ."[42]

Isadora remembered her first Christmas without the children as a time of ritual mourning. "Rome is a wonderful city for a sorrowful soul," she observed. "I was as a ghost who had wandered on the Appian Way for a thousand years, with the great spaces of the Campagna and the great arch of Raphael's sky above. Sometimes I lifted my arms to the sky and danced along — a tragic figure between the rows of tombs."[43] A note from Rome to Fernand Divoire declared, "I am dead — and walk among the Saints and Martyrs — *Saluez mes amis.*"[44] Before leaving Viareggio, with "faithful Skene" at the piano, Isadora had danced the adagio movement from Beethoven's *Sonata Pathétique* in a private performance for Duse. "It was the first gesture I had made since the 19th of April," she declared.[45] Duse's response belied her doubts. "If a dream of art takes you far, far away from here," she urged Isadora — "*chère,* what joy to see you take flight again toward the light. Without work, without risk, life is nothing — a dream empty of dreams."[46]

In Rome, Isadora began to compose new dances. "It was sad enough," she wrote, "but I said to myself: 'Nevertheless I am not in the tomb or the mad-house — I am here.'" After Christmas a telegram came from Singer, imploring her to return to Paris. Hoping for the best, she went.

Singer had prepared a suite at the Hôtel Crillon, where Isadora told him about her pregnancy and her "mystic dream of the children's reincarnation." She recorded only that "he hid his face in his hands" before offering her complete funding for her school. In 1912 Singer had bought the Hôtel Paillard in Bellevue, an eighteenth-century mansion on the heights of Paris, overlooking the Seine, which at first he intended to endow as a hospital. Instead, it would be the first home of Dionysion, Isadora's new temple of dance. Singer gave her Bellevue outright and promised as much capital as she might need, if she would "leave all personal feeling aside and, for the time being . . . exist only for an idea." The offer was apparently made in complete sincerity, with no other motive than to rescue Isadora from grief. "Seeing what a tangled mesh of sorrow and catastrophe this life had brought me," she wrote, "in which only my Idea always shone bright and untarnished above it all, I consented."[47] For the time, she refrained from captious remarks about the rich.

The house at Bellevue was built in 1837 by Louis XV, as a gift for Madame de Pompadour. Pillaged during the French Revolution, the estate then passed through many hands before becoming a hotel and restaurant at the end of the nineteenth century. Isadora found the interior "rather banal" and set Poiret and Louis Sue to work on new designs. The dining rooms were transformed into two dance studios, the *salon bleu* and the *salon blanc*. In the first, starkly decorated in Isadora's trademark style, performances, lectures, and receptions would be held; in the smaller *salon blanc,* her students would practice dance under reproductions of the Parthenon frieze.[48] Bellevue had more than sixty rooms, and Isadora appealed for fifty children, girls and boys, to be raised "in the spirit of the art" she had created. Her inclusion of boys in the hunt for new students must be seen as a tribute to Patrick. At the same time, she insisted that none of the children be younger than six: she wanted no one in the new group of pupils to remind her too strongly of the two who were missing.[49]

Looking out from the terrace over the Seine valley, with Paris in the distance, Isadora could see the curve of the river where her children had died. On her programs and publicity for the school, she inscribed words from the Thirtieth Psalm: "Thou hast turned for me my mourning into dancing." The name *Dionysion* was chosen not for its evocation of satyrs and nymphs but as a symbol of the birth of art.

The school at Bellevue was structured on the exact lines of Isadora's first school in Grunewald, with the difference that her senior pupils — the six Isadorables: Anna, Theresa, Irma, Lisa, Gretel, and Erika[50] — now took the role Elizabeth had occupied as dance instructors. Isadora was tired of their coming and going, Anna said: "She wants a decision to be made, either we stay with her all the time or she stops teaching us completely."[51] Augustin extended Isadora's invitation to the girls at Darmstadt just after Christmas. "And that was the end of our association with Tante Miss," Irma wrote firmly.[52] Max Merz, "hysterical," threatened to throw himself from a window, according to Anna — "Yes. At least, he was trying desperately to make Elizabeth change her mind."

"You don't know what you're doing!" Merz cried, when Elizabeth gave her consent to the girls. "This is ruin for us!"[53] The Isadorables arrived at Bellevue in January 1914 and moved there permanently in March. "I intend to continue working with Isadora," Anna wrote her father, "to 'be true' to the idea, as Isadora expresses it and as she has lived her whole life." Anna wouldn't forget Darmstadt and all it had done for her: "I just see it as a step forward. If fate is ever to allow me to make something of myself, then I have to choose Isadora as my *Meister*: after much thought and conviction, that is the conclusion I have finally come to."[54]

For the seven months of its existence at Bellevue, Dionysion came near to fulfilling Isadora's dream of a "school of life," where dance, music, poetry, and drama combined with academic instruction in an atmosphere of harmonious dedication to art. "I believed that this school at Bellevue would be permanent," she wrote, "and that I should spend there all the years of my life, and leave there all the results of my work."[55] As at Grunewald, Isadora charged no tuition or maintenance fees, taking full financial responsibility for the children in exchange for the "loan of their souls and expanding minds."[56] She confined her own teaching to private sessions with the Isadorables, however; pregnant, she made few appearances anywhere. The girls themselves took charge of the new students, who came and went according to their skill. Only one boy survived the cut: Jean, an eight-year-old from Paris. Mary Roberts came to Bellevue for a visit and found Isadora in "a charming room which Poiret fitted up" and where she hung Carrière's painting "of a mother gathering to her breast the spirits of her lost children. Isadora cherished this picture more than any other possession she had."[57]

In April 1914 Irma, Anna, Lisa, and Theresa went to Russia with Augustin; his new wife, Margherita; and Hener Skene to find students for the school. By June there were about twenty in residence. The girls were charged with auditions as well as instruction, Isadora finding it too painful to take more than a collective interest in the children's lives. "Often," she wrote, "I went to my room to weep alone." The actress Elsa Lanchester, who spent several months at Bellevue as a child, reported that Isadora was "usually covered from head to foot, even her face, with the finest veiling of the palest color." Her interaction with her new students consisted of little more than motivational speeches.

"Sometimes Isadora would rise from her divan and herd us over to one of the great long windows overlooking the Seine," Lanchester remembered. "She would point to some climbing pink roses growing wildly over an old trellis pergola, and, as a few of the petals fell, she would say, 'They dance, now *you* dance!' Then, with a Christlike gesture — both hands outturned — she would bid us scatter. And we did."[58] After three months Isadora felt confident in proclaiming "the hope of some new movement in humanity. . . . These were the future dancers of the Ninth Symphony of Beethoven."

With her flock around her and Singer's funds again at her disposal, Isadora returned to the dream of her own theater, which she hoped to construct on the grounds at Bellevue. Louis Sue's original model for the project stood in the *salon blanc* next to a statue of Isadora dancing, one of three made in Berlin in 1903 by sculptor Walter Schott. Friday af-

ternoons were given over to performances by the students, followed by
an open house, at which Isadora's guests might include Rodin, Maeterlinck, Henri Bergson, Jean Cocteau, "a Russian prince, members of the
Royal Family of England ... ministers, ambassadors, all the *haut
monde* of Paris," as Mary Roberts wrote.[59] Ellen Terry came, and Duse
arrived from Italy in the spirit of rapprochement. One day Isadora
hoped to present Duse as Antigone in the Great Festival Theater she
envisioned, "to which the people of Paris would come on great fête
days" to see Greek tragedies performed by the leading actors of the age,
with her own students dancing the Chorus to the music of a symphony
orchestra that Singer had promised to endow. Lanchester remembered
"superb food, good clothes, trips in Rolls-Royces to the Louvre and
Versailles. We were all beautifully dressed, and each of us had a warm
coat of a different color. We must have looked like a living rainbow."[60]

On Saturdays dance classes at Bellevue were conducted for the
benefit of artists, who sketched and modeled the children at work.
The girls — and little Jean — moved outdoors in good weather, running and dancing on the lawns and through the trees to such striking
effect that Rodin was heard to say, "If I had only had such models
when I was young!" Rodin's property at Meudon was only a short
walk from Bellevue. André Arnyvelde, writing for *Le Temps,* visited
the school one weekend when the master arrived.

"There's a great joy," Isadora said, "a great blessing in my house. A
god has come down to us." Settling a cushion at Rodin's feet, she knelt
and practically sang, "As Brunhilde at the feet of Wotan." Arnyvelde
saw that she sat before Rodin "like the believer at the eucharist." With
the help of her colleagues and friends, she would give France another
Bayreuth.[61] Rodin repaid the compliment by telling Mary Roberts,
"Isadora Duncan is the greatest woman I have ever known. . . . Sometimes I think she is the greatest woman the world has ever known. *Elle
est suprême!*"[62]

A regular visitor at Bellevue was Gabriele D'Annunzio, the Italian
poet and soldier of fortune and Duse's former lover, whom Isadora
had first met in 1912. In her autobiography, she reports that D'Annunzio arrived at her studio one day with the express intent of seduc-
ing her. "This was no compliment," wrote Isadora, "as D'Annunzio
wanted to make love to every well-known woman in the world and
string them round his waist as the Indian strings his scalps." To her
own surprise, she resisted: "It was a heroic impulse."[63] Notes from
D'Annunzio to Isadora during her recent trip to Rome would suggest

he did not give up the attempt: "*Douce amie,* would you like me to come pay you a little visit? I am only a spirit. D'Annunzio."[64] When he compared Isadora to "the trees, the sky, the landscape," she felt like Eve with the serpent. "That was the genius of D'Annunzio," she said. "He made each woman feel she was a goddess in a different domain."[65]

At Bellevue, D'Annunzio bravely told Isadora that the death of her children was "the most fortunate thing that could have happened to her as an artist." She disagreed. Grief, she said, "clogs the spirit, numbs the soul; there is no impulse to self-expression in sorrow — only a desire to keep still and be let alone."[66] Isadora referred to her sorrow constantly in discussing the birth and mission of Dionysion, going so far as to seek a legal injunction against a cabaret in Paris that had parodied the school in a musical revue. "My own career has collapsed," Isadora wrote in her complaint: "I am trying to give my art to others. . . . In the name of my grief, in the name of mothers who are now entrusting their children to me, out of respect for the dead, I ask that this theatre caricature be stopped." Her request was denied, but the cabaret was ordered not to speak or otherwise indicate Isadora's name on its stage.[67]

On June 26, 1914, Isadora's new students made their public debut at the Trocadéro, in a three-hour program led by the Isadorables. Anna took the central role in Schubert's *Marche Héroïque,* a dance of grieving women, described as Isadora's tribute to her children. Eight months pregnant, Isadora herself sat hidden from view, in a private box. "At certain parts of the programme the audience rose and shouted with enthusiasm and joy," she recalled,[68] a memory borne out by the elated tone of the girls' reviews: "Long ago Isadora had trained them, had taken their soft, childish arms in her divine hands, curved their tender necks, straightened their shoulders and aligned their heads, and finally, by the caressing touch of her grace through their yielding bodies, initiated these virgins into the mysteries of rhythm."[69] Not knowing about Isadora's pregnancy, the audience was "visibly stunned" when she failed to appear onstage. Prudence aside, it was part of her design, the proof that her art would survive, despite her loss. At the Trocadéro, she was heard to say, "In two years, it will be quite good."[70]

In just two days, the Austrian Archduke Franz Ferdinand was assassinated at Sarajevo. Bellevue would perish in the stampede to war.

In the summer of 1914, while Isadora waited for the birth of her third child, "a strange oppression came over the earth. I felt it," she wrote, "and the children felt it too. . . . An uncanny pause seemed to hang over the land."[71] In France the coming of World War I coincided with the national scandal over the murder of Gaston Calmette, editor of *Le Figaro,* shot to death in his office by the wife of Joseph Caillaux, French minister of finance; Caillaux's efforts to preserve peace between France and Germany in 1914 had led Calmette, a staunch nationalist, to denounce him repeatedly as "Germany's man" and a "Socialist dupe." At home, Caillaux promised to "smash [Calmette's] face in," whereupon his wife, Henriette, "a woman of character and considerable stupidity,"[72] bought a Browning revolver, arrived at the *Le Figaro's* offices in the Champs-Elysées, and pumped four bullets into Calmette's body, killing him on the spot. Calmette was an old friend of Isadora's and had proved especially helpful to her at the time of her children's deaths.

"It was a tragic event," she wrote about Calmette's murder, "the forerunner of the greater tragedy. . . . I was much shocked and saddened by this news." Talk of war held no meaning for her: she was not a political thinker. "While I had been planning the renaissance of the Art of the theatre . . . ," she wrote with perfect candor, "other forces had been planning war, death, and disaster, and, alas! what was my small force against the onrush of all this?"[73] When the war came, Isadora threw herself body and soul behind the Allies, especially in the cause of France, her spiritual home and the nation that had hailed her as a goddess. "That marvellous message of defiance," she wrote, "the wonderful enthusiasm that was to lead to miles of devastated country and graveyards, who can say if it was right or wrong?"[74]

Not long after their Trocadéro concert, wanting solitude for her delivery, Isadora sent her students to England for a vacation at Singer's estate in Paignton. For several weeks she was alone at Bellevue, where she fell prey to "a deep depression." She was worried about the child: "It seemed to me that the movements of the babe I bore were weaker, not so decided as those of the others had been. . . . I suppose I was also very tired from the effort I had made to change grief and mourning into new life."[75] Most of Isadora's staff had left for the summer, among them many who vanished with the first rumor of war. A fire in the house on July 15 sent her in panic back to the Hôtel Crillon in Paris.[76] Mary Desti found her there, nervous and afraid. Mary brought a cradle with her, "all hung with white muslin," and Isadora now focused her whole attention on it: "I kept my eyes on the cradle. I was convinced that Deirdre or Patrick was coming again to me."

On August 3 Germany declared war on France, turning Paris into a chaos of mobilization and euphoria. Mary Desti observed it from the Maison Desti on rue de la Paix: "Our bookkeepers, doormen, and other men employed around the place ran out shouting, stuffing razors in their pockets, and five minutes afterwards, down the street, they were handed bundles of military uniform, fitting them in any haphazard way. Such joyous shouting, shrieking, and hurrahs." Within two days the city was transformed, its art packed away in crates, its cinemas, theaters, and nightclubs shut down, with an early curfew and a night-time blackout, imposed in anticipation of German zeppelin raids. One by one, the roads leading in and out of Paris were blockaded to the en-emy. "Hundreds of soldiers were already tearing up the pavements of Paris and barricading these entrances," Mary remembered, "as there were rumors that the Germans were already at the gates."[77] With light-ning speed, the kaiser's army had advanced as far as the Marne valley.

At the Crillon, Isadora booked a second room for her doctor, Emil Bosson, who received his notice of military service just as she went into labor: "It was a hot day, and the windows were open. My cries, my sufferings, my agony were accompanied by the rolling of the drums and the voice of the crier." Singer had left her a car, the only means of transportation as French soldiers were herded to the front. In labor, Isadora went from clinic to clinic in search of a competent doctor, but at each one, Mary wrote, she cried "with a shriek, 'Take me out, take me out of this place!'" Finally, they headed for Bellevue, passing through the military blockade on the strength of Isadora's name. A doctor was found at the last minute, "a very well known Parisian specialist," who arrived with a nurse to help with the delivery. Isadora wrote:

> The doctor kept on saying, "Courage, madame." Why say "Courage" to a poor creature torn with horrible pain? It would have been much better if he had said to me, "Forget that you are a woman; that you should bear pain nobly, and all that sort of rot; forget every-thing, scream, howl, yell —" or, better still, if he had been humane enough to give me some champagne. But this doctor had his system, which was to say "Courage, madame." The nurse was upset, and kept on saying, "Madame, c'est la guerre — c'est la guerre." . . .
>
> Finally I heard the baby's cry — he cried — he lived. Great as had been my fear and horror in that terrible year, it was now all gone in one great shock of joy. . . . Outside my window and door was a running to and fro and voices — the weeping of women — calls — discussions as to the mobilisation, but I held my child and dared, in the face of this

general disaster, to feel gloriously happy, borne up to the Heavens with the transcendental joy of again holding my own child in my arms.

Her happiness lasted only a few hours. "We understood very quickly that this exquisite little child who looked like a Donatello statue hadn't a chance of living," Mary wrote sadly. "His lungs refused to expand despite everything science could do."[78] Isadora later believed that the baby was frightened from the world by the war. "I whispered, 'Who are you, Deirdre or Patrick? You have returned to me.'[79] Suddenly the little creature stared at me and then gasped, as if choking for breath, and a long whistling sigh came from his icy lips." She called for the nurse, who took the boy away and left her in agony for more than an hour. Oxygen arrived from Paris, but the baby died by nightfall. "I believe in that moment," Isadora wrote, "I reached the height of any suffering that can come to me on earth."

Isadora's third child never had a name. At Bellevue she "heard hammer-taps closing the little box that was [her] poor baby's only cradle" and surrendered to her role as a shattered madonna: "As I lay there, torn and helpless, a triple fountain of tears, milk and blood flowed from me." Her overtly Christian image spoke to the horror of mass slaughter and destruction, "for in that death," Isadora wrote, "it was as if the others [had] died again — it was like a repetition of the first agony — with something added." When she returned to dancing in 1915, she would fuse her private suffering with the grief and rage of the world at war. Her dance, never equaled for lightness, became colossal and stark. Her gestures were larger, slower, stronger, "rooted in universal sorrow."[80] With grief came defiance, not of her own fate alone but of all forces that sought to deny the freedom of the spirit: tyranny, oppression, terror, and death. After 1914 all of Isadora's dances would be hymns of deliverance — the personal became political by virtue of the world catastrophe.

"She still dances and poses with a beauty that she only among the dancers of our time may compass," Henry Taylor Parker observed the following year. "It is a larger and more opulent beauty as of broad, full and expanding line. It is a more plastic beauty, that, were marble a fluid medium, might easily be transfused into it."[81] In the greater portion of her *Rédemption*, composed in 1916 to the music of César Franck, Isadora never left her knees, "leaving expressive movement to the neck, throat, shoulders, head, and arms."[82] Critics remarked that both age and passion had exacted a toll on her body, but "it would have been impossible for her, in those years, to go on giving her old programs as if nothing had happened to her or to the world," according to her sister-in-law Margherita Duncan: "The change in Isadora's work was not substitution, but evolution."[83] The *New York Sun* saw her *Rédemption* in 1917:

> Miss Duncan was discovered upon the deep shadowed stage, utterly prostrate, her white robes draped down upon her huddled figure as upon a thing grotesquely useless and inert. Then slowly, laboriously, the stir of life came; one could see it only in the trembling fingers at first, then along the uplifting arms. Then to knees, then to full height — and the figure could stride and assert itself in broad, deliberate motion. It was all a cycle of slow gestures, unalterably slow and stern, every inward impulse of it seeming to find fight and oppression from the unseen force without. And when, in the end, self-mastery came, with head high and face gladdened with the pride of peace, it was as if a great battle of humanity unlimited had been enacted through one strong, transparent soul.[84]

Only a few days after her infant's death, Isadora gave Bellevue to the Dames de France for use as a military hospital. It seemed "only natural" under the circumstances. "Even the artists said, 'What is Art?'" she wrote. "'The boys are giving their lives, the soldiers are giving their lives — what is Art?' And if I had had any intelligent sense at that time, I should have said, 'Art is greater than life.' . . . But I went with the rest of the world and said, 'Take all these beds, take this house that was made for Art, and make a hospital to nurse the wounded.'"

When the first casualties arrived, Isadora greeted them in the *salon bleu* and saw that her curtains and bas-reliefs had been removed and replaced with "cheap effigies of a black Christ on a golden cross." Her heart fell: "I felt that Dionysus had been completely defeated. . . . My Temple of Art was turned into a Calvary of Martyrdom and, in the end, into a charnel-house of bloody wounds and death." When she was well enough to travel, she left Bellevue with Mary for Deauville. "Bellevue!" she wrote. "My Acropolis, that was to have been a fountain of inspiration."[85]

At Deauville, Isadora stayed for several weeks at the Hôtel Normandie, a refuge for "many distinguished Parisians" who, for one reason or another, had not yet joined the fight. Isadora remembered Robert de Montesquiou's "light falsetto voice" and Sacha Guitry's "irrepressible fund of stories and anecdotes," but the effort to be amusing fell flat as the trainloads of wounded rolled in.[86] "Everything in Deauville . . . stopped like a clock whose pendulum someone has reached in and grabbed," said Preston Sturges, whom Mary had dispatched to the coast to supervise Maison Desti's fashionable Deauville branch.[87]

At the casino, the most famous in France, "where but two weeks before all the beauty and grace of Europe had gathered to gamble, dance, or dine," camp beds replaced the gaming tables, "each containing a broken piece of humanity, with terrible, sorrowful eyes wondering what it was all about."[88] Unlike Mary, Isadora was never trained or certified as a nurse, so she performed errands for the wounded, "writing letters home, reading and doing the countless little things that bring cheer,"[89] but the ceaseless reminder of death and dying worked havoc in her mind. She began a violent love affair with the chief physician at the casino hospital, "a short man with a black beard," whom she later recognized as the same doctor who had tried to rescue her children on the Seine embankment: "I looked. The mist cleared away. I gave a cry. I remembered. That terrible day. The doctor who came to me to bid me hope." The attachment grew morbid and Isadora soon cut it off. "I could find no relief either in Art, in the rebirth of a child, or in love," she wrote. "In every effort to escape, I found only destruction, agony, death."[90]

At the start of the war, fearing for their future as German nationals in England, Singer sent the Isadorables to New York, along with the rest of the new students from Bellevue. With Kathleen Scott's help, Elizabeth and Merz soon followed, with the pupils of the Darmstadt school. In November Isadora decided to join them. Sending to Bellevue for her winter clothes, she received, by mistake, a trunk filled with Deirdre and Patrick's discarded effects. She fainted: "When I saw them there . . . the little dresses they had last worn — the coats and shoes and little caps — I heard again that cry which I had heard when I saw them lying dead — a strange, long, wailing cry, which I did not recognise as my own voice — but as if some cruelly hurt animal called its death-cry from my throat."[91] In the eighteen months since her children died, her hair had turned white. With henna, she dyed it red and embarked on her phantom voyage, a solitary, accusing figure in mourning for the world.

Part IV

DECRESCENDO

(1914–1921)

And they keep a wounded distance

    With following bare feet,

A distance Isadoran —

    And the dark moons beat

Their drums. . . .

More desolate than they are Isadora stands,

    The blaze of the sun on her grief;

The stars of a willow are in both of her hands,

    And her heart is the shape of a leaf.

With the dark she wrestles, daring alone,

    Though their young arms would aid;

Her body wreathes and brightens, never thrown,

    Unvanquished, unafraid.

Till light comes leaping

    On little children's feet,

Comes leaping Isadoran —

    And the white stars beat

Their drums.

    — Witter Bynner, "Opus 1" (1916)

18
Dionysion 1915

Isadora arrived in New York on the Cunard liner *Franconia* on November 24, 1914. Within a week, she took a studio at 311 Fourth Avenue, on the corner of Twenty-third Street, and announced that Dionysion would continue its work in America for the duration of the war. Wherever she traveled now, her tall blue curtains followed in steamer trunks, ready to be hung on a moment's notice, blocking out noise, views, and natural light to create an instant stage and salon. Rose-colored scarves of Liberty silk, draped over mirrors, lamps, and Isadora's intimate, low divans, completed the hermetic effect. Home now lay in her decor, "a great space, silent and high, separated from the world."[1] Isadora called it "the Ark," with reference both to the deluge in Europe and her intention to start her work fresh in the United States.

Isadora found her students living at the Simeon Ford estate in Rye, on Long Island Sound, where they were photographed together on the rocks to celebrate her arrival, "a happy band of war refugees."[2] Singer stayed in England, where his Oldway mansion, like Bellevue, became a military hospital. For reasons never explained, his support for the school also dried up. There is no record of a quarrel, but Isadora would see Singer only once, briefly, before the fall of 1916.[3]

With the Isadorables in New York were the remaining pupils from Bellevue, a mixture of French, Russian, Italian, and Polish children, remembered now by their first names: Colette, Yvette, Annette, Suzanne, Vala, Ala, Mila, and Jean, the lone male. For four days after their arrival in September, in the absence of guardianship papers, the younger children had been detained on Ellis Island.[4] It was the first of what Isadora took to be successive insults in her home country, whose indifference to the war in Europe left her indignant and aroused. "Coming from bleeding, heroic France," as she put it, the American life of complacency, moneymaking, and self-satisfaction seemed to her not only shortsighted but complicit in the destruction of Europe.[5] From the moment she stepped ashore, perversely, she denounced the United States for its "sterility," its "pointless amusements," its "unjust laws," and its failure to recognize the value of her work. Unfortunately, her effort to revive Dionysion collided with a skeptical press and a public that already regarded "classic" dancing as a relic of the past.

"Miss Duncan is usually thought of by Americans (New Yorkers in particular) as a queer-looking woman who wears very few clothes, and those of weird and sketchy cut," wrote the *New York Evening Mail*. "They know she dances, but just how they are not sure, or why." It was left to the *Mail* to pronounce MISS DUNCAN NOT "QUEER" in a headline[6] — in regard to American dancing, she was only out of step. In 1912 James Reese Europe's Clef Club Orchestra had appeared at Carnegie Hall for the first time, introducing fashionable New York to syncopated rhythm. A year later the phenomenal success of Irving Berlin's "Alexander's Ragtime Band" set the seal on a new era in popular music. Dozens of new dances emerged: fox-trot, turkey trot, grizzly bear, bunny hug, chicken scratch, etc. "Dinner" and "tea" dances were the rage; in a swoop, social dancing was liberated from the ballroom, spilling out into restaurants, hotels, nightclubs, and dance halls: "Men clutched their partners, bent them backwards, flung them about in the most suggestive ways. Gone were modesty, reticence, restraint, femininity!"

A backlash was only to be expected. In 1913 the mayor of New York denounced "the lascivious orgies going on in the so-called respectable dance-halls in this city," enacting a series of ordinances designed to thwart pickups in public places. Anti-vice societies linked jazz to white slavery and opium dens, while the editor of the *Ladies' Home Journal* fired fifteen of his female employees who had confessed to dancing the turkey trot on their lunch hour.[7] A new beat ruled — loud, wild, and permanent.

To Isadora, the lightning spread of "animal dances" seemed like a raid on the gods. Nowhere does her character emerge more unattractively than in her remarks about "the tottering, ape-like convulsions [of] the South African Negro . . . wriggling from the waist downwards" in ignoble expression of sexual desire. Her racism was endemic and her modesty not feigned. Sex itself was "a fine thing," she wrote, urging that "bans on the realization of sex" be placed instead on "the frivolous caricatures and symbols of sex" in jazz and ragtime dancing. On Broadway, Vernon and Irene Castle transformed the fox trot into a glamour act, dancing cleaned-up versions of the original, but the substitution of the wholesome for the base did nothing to appease Isadora. "Very little is known in our day of the magic that resides in movement," she would warn, "and the potency of certain gestures." It would be better for American girls to indulge in "a real orgy, which, after all, might not be so hurtful to them — since a real orgy might, like a real storm, clear the atmosphere for purer things. . . . For we are no longer in the state of the primitive savage, but the whole expression of our life must be created through culture and the transformation of intuition and instinct into art."[8]

New York in 1915 was a Mecca for any radical, the front line in the battle for freedom of speech and self-expression in America. Among artists and intellectuals — a word only recently coined — two events had fused into one mission in 1913, when the bloody silk workers' strike in Paterson, New Jersey, organized by the Industrial Workers of the World under "Big Bill" Haywood, Carlo Tresca, and Elizabeth Gurley Flynn, coincided almost to the hour with the International Exhibition of Modern Art at the Sixty-ninth Regiment Armory in Manhattan. More than twelve hundred works of mainly European painters and sculptors, from Ingres and Delacroix to the futurists and cubists, completed the break with academic tradition that the urban-realist Ashcan School had begun. Duchamp's *Nude Descending a Staircase* was the most talked-about work on display, condemned by critics as "disgusting" and "deranged" and satirized everywhere ("an explosion in a shingle factory," "an orderly heap of broken violins"). The *New York Times* warned in an editorial: "It should be borne in mind that this movement is surely a part of the general movement, discernible to all the world, to disrupt, degrade, if not destroy, not only art but literature and society too."[9] For artists and reformers, however, the Armory Show and the Paterson strike expressed the same quenchless impulse — "that every individual should be made free to live and grow in his own chosen way," as Max Eastman, editor of *The Masses,* expressed it in his autobiography.[10]

At the age of thirty, Eastman was the acknowledged leader of New York's Young Intellectuals, that storied group of artists and romantic revolutionaries in Greenwich Village that included Eastman's fellow *Masses* editor Floyd Dell; journalists Hutchins Hapgood and John Reed; painters John Sloan, John Marin, and Marsden Hartley; stage designer Robert Edmond Jones; Lincoln Steffens; Emma Goldman; Walter Lippmann; and Edna St. Vincent Millay, whose much-kissed lips could no longer tell "what loves have come and gone." From the Village came the image of the New Woman, embodying every horror known to the American heartland. By 1914 the New Woman had asserted her right to vote, love freely, marry and divorce at will, practice birth control, and keep custody of her children, with or without their fathers' consent. At a time when the Gibson Girl had barely faded from memory, Village women wore loose-fitting sweaters and smocks, smoked in the street, and washed their hair every day — hair they had begun to cut into progressively shorter bobs. "Having studied Freud," said Louis Untermeyer, "[they] began to exhibit their inhibitions and learned to misquote Havelock Ellis on a moment's notice."[11]

In a general sense, every Village radical was a socialist. Even Lippmann, who broke with the intellectuals' left wing in 1914 as a founding editor of *The New Republic,* began his career in American letters as the organizer of the Socialist Club at Harvard. What Lippmann's generation sought in socialism, however, wasn't the workers' paradise as much as the artists'; few among the intellectuals ever joined the Socialist Party. Whitman and Freud were the gods of Greenwich Village, and the *The Masses* was its testament, a journal of leftist reporting, fiction, poetry, and illustration, calling for universal liberty through personal emancipation. Art, in this view, was no other than politics: if a woman was free to cut off her hair, she could also write poems without rhymes — and she did.

Indeed, Village radicalism's most durable legacy lay in its embrace of women's liberation, even if the practice of free love in the Village drove most of its participants into marriage (and not a few into institutions). Village feminism was a politics of the body, not the voting booth, "a product of the evolutionary science of the nineteenth century," as Eastman's colleague Floyd Dell affirmed in his first book, *Women as World Builders:* "When the true history of this movement is written it will contain more about Herbert Spencer and Walt Whitman, perhaps, than about Victoria Woodhull and Tennessee Claflin. In any case, it is to the body that one looks for the Magna Carta of feminism."[12] And it was to Isadora that radicals looked for the Magna Carta of the body. "She was the extreme outpost of the movement for woman's emancipation," Eastman concluded. Dell took a Byronic view: "When I think that if I had lived and died in the darkness of [the nineteenth] century I should never have seen with these eyes the beauty and terror of the human body, I am glad of the daylight of my own time. It is not enough to throw God from his pedestal, and dream of superman and the cooperative commonwealth. One must have *seen* Isadora Duncan to die happy."[13]

Isadora's solidarity with the Village rebels remained an attachment of the spirit. Soon enough she would call herself a Bolshevik and a "red," but, if anything, she was anarchist, not socialist, referring always to a higher authority than the state — in her case, the religion of beauty and the dance. To Isadora's mind, the only good law was an abolished law; Eastman wrote later of "the admirable force of character with which Isadora insisted on being half-baked." Village rebels would claim her for the cause not as a thinker but as "a mind and a moral force," in Eastman's words: "America fighting the battle against Americanism, that was Isadora."[14]

In May 1915 *The Masses* put Isadora on its cover, in a candid sketch by John Sloan of her *Marche Militaire*. "What do you think of my drawing of Isadora?" Sloan wondered. "Her friends like it, and her enemies are crazy about it."[15] She had aged — in 1915 she turned thirty-eight. She had put on weight and was drinking heavily, her favored Pommery champagne never far from reach. With her hair cut short and dyed, she wore heavy cloaks and robes, felt hats, turbans, tocques, and scarves. "She seemed a curious combination of old washerwoman and Great Mother of the Gods," said Dell.[16] Meeting Isadora at her studio, Percy MacKaye's daughter Arvia remembered her as "an unusually beautiful woman, in soft, flowing garments, with large dark eyes of an almost tragic depth and beauty. It is the mystery and depth of those large wonderful eyes which stays with me especially"[17] — a depth captured on camera, as Isadora's dancing never would be, in a series of portrait photographs made in New York by Arnold Genthe.

To later generations, Isadora's refusal to allow her dancing to be filmed remains the most dismaying revelation of her career. After her death, she was quoted as saying that she preferred to be remembered "as a legend."[18] No doubt she did, but her experiences of early photography had greatly predisposed her against the form. She could make no natural motion while posing for the camera. In the cinema, just born when her career began, Isadora saw nothing but "flickers." Film couldn't reproduce her dancing, in any case, without the music that inspired it. Had she lived into the sound era, she might have reasoned differently, but when Genthe met her in 1915 he found her "shy of the camera," offering excuses whenever he suggested that she sit for him.[19]

Born in Berlin, Genthe began his career in San Francisco, where his pictures of Chinatown and the 1906 earthquake made photographic history. Four years later his studio moved to New York, and with it his brand of "natural photography." Genthe's subjects were never posed — often they never knew when their pictures had been taken. With its glamorous lighting and chiaroscuro effect, Genthe's technique owed more to painting than to Kodak. "It is true he pointed his camera at people and took their photographs," Isadora would remark, "but the pictures were never photographs of his sitters but his hypnotic imagination of them. He has taken many pictures of me which are not representations of my physical being, but representations of conditions of my soul, and one of them is my very soul indeed."[20] She didn't say which, but told Genthe: "When I am alone and look at it, after a while my face fades out and the faces of my children take its place." Genthe reported that she had finally consented to sit for passport photographs: "I made some pictures that might answer that purpose, and when she discovered that photographs could be taken so rapidly, and without her having to be conscious of it, she was quite eager to have me make others."[21]

Twenty-four of Genthe's portraits of Isadora were later published in a portfolio edition,[22] including several made at Dionysion headquarters on Fourth Avenue. Of these, the most famous shows Isadora, seated, looking into a crystal ball, with the Isadorables grouped around her. The girls made their American debut on December 3, 1914, at Carnegie Hall, with the New York Symphony. Isadora didn't appear with them. After their detention on Ellis Island, there had been rumors of "German spies," and she wanted to show them on their own. "We had quite a big success for America," Anna wrote to her father, "and Isadora, who sat in the loge, was very pleased with us, that's the main thing."[23] The image of a mystical, free-loving priestess and her nubile acolytes registered in the press.

"I want them to know about my girls," Isadora told a reporter for the *New York World.* "My girls are like the Knights of the Grail! and come to earth when there are wrongs to be redressed."

"So they, and you, do come to earth occasionally?" The question exactly reflected the smart, modern tone of the time: the following year Dorothy Parker began writing ad copy for *Vogue.*

"You are too young to talk of such things," Isadora replied, "much too young. You are a mere child. You don't know anything." She added: "Don't call me Miss Duncan. It sounds like a cook. Call me Isadora. Everybody calls me Isadora."[24] Two policemen arrived at her studio one night, demanding to know "what kind of a place this is." She handed them a wad of bills. "There," she said, "go and get a nice supper somewhere and some good German beer. I know how you must hate what you're doing."[25] The *Sun* left a picture of the Isadorables as they reached maturity:

> The little girls of the early blue-and-white stage have grown up into miniature Isadora Duncans. . . . They are known only by their Christian names. Anna, the eldest, is actively concerned with the affairs of the world around her. Theresa and Irma come next, an impulsive and spirited pair. Liesel [Lisa] is long-haired and long-legged, physically the best dancer of any of them.
>
> Gretel is a thoughtful child, filled with a sense of her dignity and somewhat mystified with the American manner of doing things. Erica, being the youngest, is also the most serious. She has recently had her hair bobbed, but not quite so short as Isadora Duncan's. One must be conservative in such matters.[26]

When Isadora herself returned to the stage in January 1915, in her first public performances since her children had died, her program was weighted with religious themes, her dances accompanied by conductor Edward Falck, soprano Marguerite Namara, and Augustin Duncan's readings from the Bible: "Blessed are they that mourn: for they shall be comforted. They that sow in tears shall reap in joy." The hope alone was sufficient for Isadora's purpose — she would never soften in her hostility to churches. At the center of her new work was Schubert's "Ave Maria," which she composed in two versions, one for herself alone and another with the Isadorables as angels. Lisa remembered Isadora dancing among them "so divinely . . . we praying around her . . . each with two children at our side, whirling around her like a celestial vision."[27] The *Ave Maria* would remain in her repertory for the rest of her life, a permanent tribute to Deirdre and Patrick.

At the close of her concerts, Isadora again stepped forward to plead for funding and students for the school. Having asked for fifty children at Bellevue, she called for a thousand in New York, and one of the city's empty armories to house them. "In our school we have no costumes," Isadora said, "no ornaments — just the beauty that flows from the inspired human soul, and the body that is its symbol, and if my Art has taught you anything here, I hope it has taught you that. . . . If I were only a dancer I would not speak, but I am a teacher with a mission."[28]

Unfortunately, Isadora's new program generated some of the worst reviews of her career. "Miss Duncan seems to have experienced a change of faith as to the purely artistic purpose of her performances," Henry Taylor Parker remarked in the Boston Evening Transcript. "They are sicklied over now with the pale cast of some very immature and hasty thought of some kind. It is a most disheartening and amateurish mixture of music and recited literature, from the Bible and other sources entirely unsuited to any such purpose."[29] Schubert, the Beatitudes, and a host of angels seemed like a throwback to Queen Victoria in a nation alive to new music and art. "As a conscientious artist," furthermore, wrote Sonya Levien, "[Isadora] should have refused the inartistic assistance of her brother, Augustin Duncan, who in a voice of dole insisted on depressing the audiences. . . . Her failure was due not to lack of talent, but rather to an unconscious over-indulgence of egotism."[30] Village feminist Henrietta Rodman, in a feature for the New York Tribune, as much as stated that the most revolutionary of dancers had lost touch with the times. Rodman met the Isadorables at one of Isadora's frequent open houses and was struck by their unthinking devotion to their teacher's ideals. Young Jean had opened the door.

"You come to see us?" said Jean. "Let me lead you in. See I speak ze English? We all speak ze English, but not vera much." The Isadorables spoke English fluently, along with German and French, but "the one weakness of their education," Rodman thought, was "their lack of contact with the harsh and ugly realities of our present-day life. It is Isadora Duncan's theory that children should move always in a world of 'sweetness and light!'"

"I am preparing them to be priestesses of beauty," Isadora answered frostily, "not factory-girls."[31] As if to prove a point, she brought her students to the Lower East Side and gave a free concert at Jacob Adler's Grand Theater. "Some people said to me, 'If you play a symphony of Schubert on the East Side the people will not care for it,'" Isadora reported at her next Met concert. "Well, we gave a free performance — in a theatre without a box office — so refreshing! — and the people sat there transfixed, with tears rolling down their cheeks; that is how they cared for it." Her contempt for American values never extended to "the masses," a trait she shared with Village intellectuals. "My work is appreciated by those people in the gallery," she declared, "because only the poor people of this country are intelligent." She added, to thundering applause, "I expect to be arrested in the morning."[32]

Early in 1915 Mary Roberts, George Grey Barnard, and other of her friends in New York established the Committee for the Furtherance of Isadora Duncan's Work in America. Ultimately, the group had more than fifty members, ranging from Robert Henri and Ellen Terry, lecturing in New York that season about Shakespeare's heroines, to sculptors Paul Manship and Gutzon Borglum, Theodore Dreiser, Eastman, Lippmann, and John Collier, the pioneering social worker and cultural anthropologist of New York's People's Institute. Linking them all was Mabel Dodge, whose salon at 23 Fifth Avenue, just north of Washington Square, was the point of rendezvous for the whole of New York's avant-garde — "Socialists," as Dodge wrote, "Trade-Unionists, Anarchists, Suffragists, Poets, Relations, Lawyers, Murderers, 'Old Friends,' Psychoanalysts, I.W.W.'s, Single Taxers, Birth Controlists, Newspapermen, Artists, Modern-Artists, Club-women, Women's-Place-is-in-the-Home Women, Clergymen, and just plain men."[33] In 1915 Dodge had just returned from a decade in Europe and a tempestuous affair with journalist John Reed. "Many famous salons have been founded by women of wit or beauty," Eastman observed; "Mabel's was the only one ever established by pure will power."[34]

In 1914, just before Isadora arrived in New York, Dodge had helped Elizabeth Duncan settle the Darmstadt school in its wartime headquarters at Croton-on-Hudson. "The Duncans were a clan who were indivisible in the spirit, but who, upon the stage of the world, strove to wangle the prizes from each other," Dodge wrote later. Elizabeth was "shrewd . . . sagacious like a nanny goat," while Isadora "set curious forces loose about her, flowing up and out from her flesh. . . . She lay on the French *chaise longue* and the room grew different. There was something frightening about her actual presence in a place; the vibrations became loosened up, broader, more incalculable. She made one nervous. Anything might happen."[35] Dodge spoke from experience. In January 1915 she wrote to their mutual friend in Paris, Gertrude Stein:

I am up to my neck in Duncans this winter. John Collier & I got a school started for one of them [Elizabeth], & for Isadora we are engaged in the maddest project of getting her the Armory, where she can teach a thousand unemployed people's poor children to *dance* & feed & clothe them & charge rich people sums to come in & see her teach 'em. And we're going to get up some great out of door festivals for her in the Stadium at Cambridge & in New Haven's *Bowl!* We're perfectly insane in our plans but sometimes insanity works![36]

Dodge soon arranged a meeting at Isadora's studio with John Purroy Mitchel, the "boy mayor" of New York, a thirty-five-year-old Irish Catholic liberal, the youngest man ever elected to the office.[37] Isadora was to "charm the mayor" out of his Armory while her students danced, Dodge recalled: "How carefully we planned it! I got Walter [Lippmann] interested in it because I knew he would give 'cachet' to the event and we invited several 'eminent' men to come and make it appear more significant to the Mayor. [John] Collier was to bring him at four o'clock, and Isadora was to do the rest." Dodge reported in her *Intimate Memories:*

> The place was large and dim and romantic-looking, with a few shaded lamps burning. It was a contrast to the hard, bright city streets we had left, and Isadora in a flowing Greek dress, ample and at ease, made us look and feel dingy and utilitarian. Particularly the men, as they stood beside her, appeared stupid, inexpressive and as though cut out of wood, there was such a radiance about her compared with other mortals. I could see Isadora appraising them as she glanced them over. Others came forward: Augustin Duncan, with his round, candid forehead and tip-tilted Irish nose, [Margherita] Duncan, his wife, a tall, adequately Grecian type with pale gold hair and flowing draperies, and some of her young girls: Anna, Lisa, Theresa, Irma. . . . They were lovely, with bodies like cream and roses, and faces unreal with beauty whose eyes were like blind statues, as though they had never looked upon anything in any way sordid or ordinary. . . . I felt myself to be shorter and more square than I had ever been in my life, and my gloves suddenly ceased to fit my hands.[38]

When the mayor arrived with Collier, Isadora cried out in surprise: "Why, I thought you would be an old, old man with a long, white beard! . . . You, the mayor of New York? You certainly don't look like the mayor of this big city. You look like a very intelligent and handsome young man."[39] Taking Mitchel by the arm, she led him to her largest divan, low to the ground and scattered with pale orange cushions. Mitchel "saved himself just in time," Dodge noticed, "and, looking somewhat wildly about him, made a dash for the piano stool. [It] gave a swift turn as he struck it, nearly upsetting him, but he laid hold of the piano and steadied himself, still holding his derby hat protectively against his solar plexus."

Isadora sank to her cushions "with movements like falling water." Her students had gathered around her, the smaller children with "their flower faces turned up toward her as to the sun." Propping up on an elbow, she gazed at Mitchel: "'Mayor!' she cried in a ringing voice, 'why don't you release that poor woman you have in prison for murdering her children?'"[40]

The woman was Ida Sniffen, an unmarried mother jilted by her married lover and indicted for poisoning their two children. Isadora had written twice to the *New York Sun,* arguing that Sniffen suffered "not from 'wickedness' but from the blunders of the present-day laws, conventions and prejudices. . . . There is no such thing as murder. There is no death. There is only transformation and transformation and transformation."[41] To Dodge's dismay — "Oh, Medes and Persians!" — Isadora harangued the mayor on this theme: "How do you suppose she feels shut up in there? How can *anyone* be certain that she did it? How can anyone believe a mother would or could kill her children?"

Mitchel coughed and looked around for help. "That matter is not within the province of Mayor Mitchel," Collier interjected. "Now, I have told the Mayor something of your methods of teaching. He would be interested, I think, if you could show him some of them."

"Oh," said Isadora, "my methods of teaching are probably very different from anything *he* has ever known!" She gestured to her students: "*These* children have always had a *beautiful* life. Look at them! *They* don't have to get up in the morning and go down to breakfast with their cross fathers and mothers! *They* don't have to go to school with horrid dirty school books in satchels! *They* don't have to go to church on Sunday and listen to stuffy old men in ugly buildings!" As she spoke, Dodge observed, her dress slipped from her shoulder and exposed her breast. Soon she was talking about her lovers: "The last time I was here I had three poets. I went away and now when I come back they are all gone. . . . Gone! One is dead, one has gone crazy, and one is married. . . . But others appear." She looked defiantly at the mayor: "*That* is education. Living education."[42]

Across the room, Isadora's other guests were conversing eagerly, desperate for the moment to be over. Her voice rose louder and louder: "Who are these people? What do they know about art or what can they understand of my work? Who are these women? Wives with feathers!"[43] When Mitchel asked if the children would dance or not, she answered shortly, "Oh, I do not think the children feel like dancing this afternoon." Then she settled back into her cushions, "perfectly happy . . . stretching herself with a lazy long reach and laughing softly."

Lippmann sent an angry note to Dodge the following day. "I'm utterly disgusted," he wrote. "If this is Greece and Joy and the Aegean Isles and the Influence of Music, I don't want anything to do with it. It's a nasty, absurd mess, and she is obviously the last person who ought to be running a school. I want you to let me off the committee; you can tell the others I'm too busy." All the same, Lippmann's closing lines betrayed a lingering ambivalence. "Please don't show this letter to anyone," he added: "Just let me slip out as quickly as I can. And some day soon take me again to see the children dance."[44]

Needless to say, nothing came of Isadora's meeting with the mayor. Dodge didn't try another time.

In February, Isadora returned to dance at the Met, where she reprised her Schubert program and denounced both the U.S. government and "the rich" as "crude, vulgar, cold, heartless, barren and inartistic." Said *Musical America*: "Our ambitions lie in electric signs and dollars, our art in office buildings, and Miss Duncan is sickened of us."[45] Similar speeches rang out wherever she appeared that winter — it wouldn't be possible for her to remain in such a country. "I am going to an island in the Greek Archipelago to live on bread and onions and worship beauty," Isadora declared. "What is there left [for artists] in America, but the ships to take them to lands where their efforts are appreciated?"[46] If she was looking for sympathy, she found it. At the first of two "farewell" concerts on February 25, her dancing earned twenty-seven curtain calls and her speech brought the house to its feet.

"What a pity that Miss Duncan delayed it so long!" Sylvester Rawling wrote archly in the *New York World*. "None of her points missed fire, and almost every sentence evoked applause." Rawling went on:

> Miss Duncan excused her berating of Americans for their ignorance of Art on the score that she was born in America and that, like the man who poured invectives upon the woman who had rejected

him, she loved us. She was taking herself and her school away to a foreign land, she said, to give it the proper atmosphere.

"Stay with us!" yelled an enthusiast.

"Build me an opera house on the east side and I will," she replied.
"Give me an auditorium that will seat 2000 people free, 2000 people
for ten cents a chair and 2000 people for twenty-five cents a chair. It is
a crime to force art-loving people to sit suffocating up under the eaves
of a great house like this!"

"Right you are, Ma'am!" yelled a man who was one of the suffocating victims.[47]

That same night, with what seemed like gratitude, Isadora announced that Otto Kahn, the international banker, had offered her the
use of the Century Theater on Central Park West. Kahn, a director of
the Century, was New York's most liberal arts patron, a German-Jewish
expatriate, broker, deal-maker, bon vivant, and chairman of the board
of the Metropolitan Opera. Known for his embrace of democratic
causes and the avant-garde, he was the kind of capitalist Isadora could
reckon with. She had received him in her studio in a conciliatory frame
of mind, according to Mary Roberts: "He was very restrained and distraught and evidently wished Mrs. Kahn were with him."[48] But Kahn's
offer gave Isadora the chance to put theory to the test and realize her
vision of a unified theater. "As the Greek dances were the forerunners
of the Greek drama," she proclaimed, "so we believe we are laying the
foundation for the development of a great universal art."[49]

Isadora's new season at the Century commenced on March 25,
1915, and ran through the month of April, an ambitious mixture of
her regular dance programs, solo concerts, "religious offerings" for
Easter, and three Greek tragedies, staged in collaboration with Augustin. A sixty-five-piece orchestra and choir of 180 voices materialized under the direction of Edward Falck. In the spirit of democracy,
Isadora removed the first fifteen rows of the Century's seats to make
room for the stage, which jutted out from the proscenium arch and
covered the floor. Other marks of privilege disappeared on her instruction — the private boxes, founder's loge, and walls of the theater
being draped with the same blue fabric that hung at the back and sides
of the stage. Isadora would charge two dollars for the remaining orchestra seats, but only a dime for the upper balcony, where "the
people" sat. Genthe never forgot the look on Otto Kahn's face when he
saw what she had done. It was the most quixotic theatrical venture of

her career, remembered by poet Witter Bynner as "an exciting laboratory unique in American history."[50]

The most talked-about of Isadora's three Greek plays was *Oedipus
Rex*, for which she directed the crowd scenes and the movement of the
Chorus. Augustin, who also played Oedipus, took charge of the actors
and text. Two large flights of stairs composed the set, backed by mov-
able blocks and lit by a board of lights behind Isadora's curtains: "The
effect from the auditorium was as though one was looking into miles
of azure air; as though one could easily walk until one were tired back
through the amazing blue."[51] Isadora insisted that the stairs be "realistic," of the same height and width as the steps of a Greek temple. Margaret Wycherly, who played Jocasta, promptly fell on her face in
rehearsal and was bandaging her knees when Isadora appeared to find
the source of the commotion.

"Her looks said that the fault lay in me," Wycherly remembered,
"not in the Greek tradition. Sure in her perfect training and control,
she mounted as I had to the platform from the wings, took one step
down, and then with a child's surprise at grown-up deceit [said], 'Why,
these are impossible! Cut little half-steps on the upstage side . . . we'll
use them.'"[52]

Both critically and financially, Isadora's Century programs failed:
there seemed to be no connection between her dancing and the hasty,
pedantic tenor of her productions. Liturgical readings, choruses, and
"prosy" translations of Sophocles seemed less organic than imposed.
"While genius has privileges the public has rights," Rawling advised.
"It was all high art, full of moral uplifting . . . but to one in the audience, at least, it was boresome." With most of the seats selling for ten
cents, Isadora swiftly emptied her bank account. At a matinee performance, when she danced Chopin waltzes and mazurkas, a woman
cried out: "That's what we want! We don't go to the theatre to be made
sorrowful, but to be made happy!"[53] On April 9 Isadora announced
that her mind was made up — she would leave the United States for
more sensitive shores. That night she told the crowd:

> There are people here tonight that have paid as much as $100,000
> for a painting by some old master of Europe. The cost of one of those
> paintings would support my school for a long time. I suppose that
> twenty-five years after I am dead they will come along and build an
> immense theatre, just about as ugly as this one, and try to start the
> work that I am doing now. . . . I could build up a school for about one-

quarter of what this hideous theatre cost. But only the rich people here can make it possible for me. But the rich people of America are so criminally unintelligent that it seems there is nothing left for me but to take the ship and emigrate.[54]

As the season went on, Isadora's behavior became more erratic. Irma remembered the scene that erupted when Augustin gave her a speaking part in the chorus of *Iphigenia*. "Take her away! Take her away!" Isadora cried. "What is this, Gus? She can't do that; take her away!" Augustin prevailed, but Isadora's resentment at seeing her authority challenged almost caused a breach between them.[55] She ruled by fiat, ordering "masses of roses" to deck the stage during one of her concerts, despite the fact that she had run out of money to pay for them.

"Do you call that 'masses of roses'?" Isadora asked her new manager, Frederick Toye, when she inspected the stage.

"We can't afford 'masses,'" Toye answered.

"How wonderful!" said Isadora. "You always know what everything costs! I just know what I want."[56] Pianist George Copeland, who accompanied her in her Chopin concerts, remembered that she declined to rehearse with him even once.

"You don't understand," Isadora said. "It's the *music* which is important. Play as if I were not there, as if you were simply playing a recital alone, and it will be all right." The same condescension allowed her to state, when Copeland complained that she was late for a performance, "We must teach the American public the art of repose."[57] Preston Sturges, now living in New York with his mother, worked on *Oedipus* "as assistant stage manager, call boy, and backstage elevator operator to bring down whole elevator-loads of additional mourners and wailers" for the Chorus. It was also Preston's job to cue the thunder and lightning for Augustin's big scene, when he "staggered out of the Theban palace with his eyes gouged out and hanging down on his cheeks." Inevitably, things got mixed up: "All the audience saw was a man waving his arms and all they heard was the thunder. . . . Thus ended my first job in the theatre," Preston wrote. "I was sixteen and a half and didn't come back . . . for a long time."[58]

On April 23 the Century season ended abruptly after four weeks, when Isadora's students were evicted from the building by the order of the New York fire department. "The trouble was that the girls had been sleeping in the opera house, and this was against the law," the *Times* explained.[59] That night, escorted by the Isadorables, the smaller children moved to the Empire Hotel on Broadway and Sixty-third Street, "wearing their blue and red hoods and cloaks and hugging their dolls and toys tightly." Isadora withdrew to the Majestic and "gave way to her emotions." The following day she failed to appear for either of her two scheduled performances. She would leave New York to "philistine darkness" just as fast as she could pack.[60]

A last humiliation was in store. Having lost more than $12,000 on her Century experiment, Isadora appealed for "some millionaire" to absorb the rest of her debts: U.S. Customs threatened to confiscate her theater trunks, with all her carpets and curtains. Help came from the Dionysion committee, banker Frank Vanderlip, and Paris Singer, who settled Isadora's most pressing accounts, and from New York merchants, who ultimately forgave more than 80 percent of her debt.[61] The *New York Telegraph* reported that "up to within two hours of [her] sailing it was a question whether the exponent of Greek dancing would be permitted to leave the country. . . . So close to the hour of departure were the arrangements completed that the final papers were signed by Miss Duncan on the pier, under the direction of her attorney."[62] And still she railed against "America" and the stingy rich.

"Of tact or self-control she had very little," Genthe noted sadly, "nor did she wish to have. She was the complete and willing tool of her impulses."[63] Mabel Dodge was harder: "Calling it Dionysian to quaff great goblets of wine did not lessen its evil influence upon her. . . . No one could stop her or control her, ever. . . . Lovers — lovers — and wine — with nothing allaying that hunger and thirst in her, and no way of understanding it, no realization. . . . Like all tragedies, Isadora's came from not knowing."[64] Before leaving the country, she called on stage designer Robert Edmond Jones at a New York hospital, where Jones was recuperating from an operation. With George Cram Cook, Susan Glaspell, Hutchins Hapgood, and Eugene O'Neill, Jones was a founder of the Provincetown Players and had designed the set for the 1913 *Pageant of the Paterson Strike* at Madison Square Garden; earlier, in Florence, he had tried to study with Gordon Craig but was firmly rebuffed. He greeted Isadora on a spring afternoon through a haze of medication:

> She is wrapped from head to foot in a great mantle of violet velvet and her hair — coarsely cropped as if by the shears of some shepherd on the hills of Hymettus — is crudely died with pure henna. On her arms

she wears long gloves of violet suede reaching to the shoulder, of a style that was once called *mousquetaire*. A figure of mourning and flame . . .

My first impression is one of violence. There is a suggestion of fierce movement about her, an atmosphere of storm. She is like the corposant on a mast head. All other images fade away before the sheer intensity of the grief that is in her eyes. I am face to face with ruin, with unending bitterness, with woe beyond description. . . . Then I hear her voice. It is unexpectedly light in quality, allusive, not sharp, and oddly *absent*. It is an American voice, an Irish voice, and in some curious way a humorous voice.

"You have been very ill, very ill . . . you are getting better . . . you will soon be well, I know it. . . ." Then suddenly, querulously: "Don't you know what's wrong with you? It's those hideous brick buildings across the street! They would make anyone sick! That's what's the matter with you Americans! Why do you live in such ugliness? You are all going to die of it some day. It's going to kill you all, every last one of you. . . . Where have you been, all of you, all your lives? Haven't you ever gone anywhere? Haven't you ever seen anything? Haven't you ever loved anybody? Hasn't anybody ever been kind to you? What *is* it that makes you willing to live with such hideous things around you?"

As she left, Isadora paused in the doorway. "Just you wait!" she told Jones. "I'll give you something to take your mind away from those buildings! In a little while you'll forget there *are* any buildings!"[65] She sailed to Europe with her students on May 9, 1915, on the *Dante Alighieri*. At the last minute, "crying into her handkerchief" as the ship prepared to sail, Isadora called out to Mary Desti, who had come to the pier to say good-bye with Preston: "Mary! If you don't come with me, I don't know what I'll do!"

Isadora "leaned against the stanchion," Preston remembered, "the better to sob. Mother, sobbing, too," ran up the gangplank, crying to Preston as she went: "Do the best you can, darling. Keep things going. I'll send you some money as soon as I can!" Mary left New York without even an overcoat — with no luggage and no money.

"At the rail," Preston wrote, "Mother and Isadora started laughing, and it turned out that what they were laughing at was the face of the purser when he discovered that not only *Mother* didn't have any money for her ticket, but that Isadora didn't have a dime either."[66] As they pulled out into the Hudson, with the girls alongside, they were waving French flags and singing "La Marseillaise."

19

South America

On May 7, 1915, two days before Isadora left New York, a German U-boat torpedoed the British liner *Lusitania* off the south coast of Ireland, killing nearly twelve hundred passengers and crew in an attack that came without warning. Among the dead were 128 Americans, including Isadora's former manager Charles Frohman. A wave of anti-German feeling erupted in the press; coming on the heels of atrocities in Belgium and France, the sinking of the *Lusitania* did more than anything else in the war to sway American opinion against the kaiser. Increasingly, the European conflict was seen not as the death struggle of rival empires but as a "war to end wars," the last battle between freedom and tyranny, democracy and despotism. Isadora's pleas for American intervention would find a more receptive audience when she next returned to dance in New York.

Having sailed to Italy by the southern, safer route, Isadora intended to go straight to Athens, "with the idea of camping on Kopanos" in Raymond's still unfinished reproduction of Agamemnon's palace. An angry scene erupted on the voyage from New York, when she learned that her manager, Frederick Toye, whom she had asked to arrange a tour for her in South America, arranged one instead for the Isadorables, without their teacher. That Toye apparently acted without the girls' knowledge didn't soften Isadora's response. DISCOVERED

TOYE'S COMPLETE DISHONESTY, she cabled Mary Roberts in New York: GIRLS TRAITORS.[1]

By the time they reached Naples, Isadora had stopped speaking to her students — they had already told her that they wouldn't go with her to Greece. Italy had just entered the war on the side of the Allies, and the older girls, traveling on German passports, refused to risk safety for art: there was no telling which way Greece might go. Raymond Duncan had returned to Athens from Albania, moreover, and taken possession of Kopanos with his full entourage. "Wanting no part of that," wrote Irma, "we put our collective foot down. . . . But it took a real mutiny on her pupils' part before [Isadora] would change her mind."[2]

Ultimately, "after numerous tragedies,"[3] Isadora deposited her nineteen charges at a *pensionnat* in Geneva, Les Hirondelles, a combination boarding and finishing school for girls. On a trip to Paris to raise funds, she borrowed heavily from "money-lenders" and mortgaged her house in Neuilly, then returned to Switzerland, settling till October in a hotel on Lake Geneva. Mary Desti disappeared that fall, having persuaded Edith Rockefeller McCormick to invest in her new line of cosmetics and "Desti's Ambre Cigarettes."[4] Soon Isadora fell in with an "amusing" crowd of Polish draft dodgers, "a group of beautiful boys in shining silk kimonos" and their wealthy patron, "an older man — large, blond, with a form resembling Oscar Wilde." Isadora never spoke about homosexuality without euphemism, or concealed her irritation at its tenacity. Playwright George Middleton remembered her stricken face one night at her studio in New York when she greeted "an approaching male vision" with the words "*Who* is this beautiful creature coming toward me? But who *is* this man?" and the answer came back in a sibilant falsetto: "I am ———— ————!"[5] Gay men, more and more, would form her entourage.

"Their evident indifference to feminine charms rather piqued my pride," Isadora confessed. In Switzerland she put her powers to the test and persuaded one of the Polish party to drive her to Athens, where, far from "camping on Kopanos," she installed herself at the Hotel Grand Bretagne and began to agitate for Greece's entry into the war.[6]

"The modern town was in a tumult," Isadora reported. "The fall of Venizelos [sic] was proclaimed on the day after our arrival, and it was thought probable that the Royal Family would be on the side of the Kaiser."[7] Eleuthérios Venizélos, the Greek prime minister and founder of the Balkan League, had been dismissed by King Constantine I despite a solid parliamentary majority. The queen of Greece was the kaiser's sister, and the king himself a field marshal of the Prussian army; wartime Athens was a nest of spies, divided between royalists and Venizélos's populist, pro-Allied supporters. At a dinner for old friends in her hotel, Isadora heard a group of German officers toasting victory. Her guests that night were all royalists (among them Constantine Mélos, the king's private secretary), but she rose defiantly and cried, *"Vive la France!"* Later, she gathered a crowd in Syntagma Square, led them in singing "La Marseillaise," and "endeavored to dance the Athenians into a sense of their responsibilities," marching at the head of a column to Venizélos's house. The prime minister declined to show himself but sent Isadora a dozen roses for her trouble.[8]

Thus another adventure foundered. By December, Isadora was back in Paris, where she recuperated from a bout with typhoid fever at the Hôtel Meurice. "Yes, I went to Athens but things are in a deplorable state there," she wrote to Mary Roberts. "Oh where are the Heroes of Greece?"[9] When she recovered from her illness, she rented a house at 23, avenue de Messine, a dark mansion with a winding staircase, studio, and palatial reception hall. Isadora's own property in Neuilly had been occupied by French refugees since the start of the war. She wouldn't have lived there even if she could: Paris was filled with memories.

"The sight of any little child who entered the room suddenly, calling 'Mother,' stabbed my heart," said Isadora, "twisted my whole being with such anguish that the brain could only cry out for Lethe, for Oblivion, in one form or another."[10] Fernand Divoire, now editor of *L'Intransigeant,* remembered Isadora's reaction when she heard that the child of a mutual friend had fallen ill: "At the sound of the word *child,* she buried her face in her arms and sobbed for more than an hour."[11] New York papers reported that she was "keen to go to the front and dance to the soldiers in the firing line. Her ambition, she says, would be for a shell to fall on her at the climax of one of her dances, so that she and the creation of her art might die gloriously at the same delirious moment. Too ridiculous!"[12] Isadora wrote:

> The most terrible part of a great sorrow is not the beginning, when the shock of grief throws one into a state of exaltation which is almost anaesthetic in its effects, but afterwards, long afterwards, when people say, "Oh, she has got over it" — or "She is all right now, she outlived it"; when one is, perhaps, at what might be considered a merry dinner-party to feel Grief with one icy hand oppressing the

heart, or clutching at one's throat with the other burning claw — Ice and Fire, Hell and Despair, overcoming all — and, lifting the glass of champagne, one endeavours to stifle this misery in whatever forget-fulness — possible or impossible.[13]

From January to April 1916, Isadora gave what amounted to a con-tinuous party at avenue de Messine, a nightly open house for French government ministers, deputies, senators, journalists, and hundreds of soldiers "ranging from private to general." It was her patriotic duty, she maintained, a way to repay her adopted country "without any regard for expense, simply that those soldiers [could] have their part of the great illusion and forget."[14] As time went on, she became a hero-ine to soldiers in the trenches and the most prodigal hostess in wartime Paris. Maurice Dumesnil, a young pianist on leave from the front, recalled the night when "some twenty-five poor devils, dressed almost in rags," arrived at her house uninvited. Isadora dispatched a taxi to buy food and wine for the new arrivals, an enormous extrava-gance in wartime. "Everybody was shocked."

"Oh, poor things, they are artists," said Isadora, "and they were so hungry! It was the least I could do. Who can tell? Perhaps among them is a future Carrière, or a Rodin." The cost of her bounty never fazed her. "Money, money, what does it matter after all?" she asked Dumesnil. "You see, I've had a long career already, and there was never a moment when I wasn't worried financially. . . . We must be confi-dent that things can be arranged. They always arrange themselves."[15] Unavoidably, Isadora fell deeper into debt — she had borrowed money "at fifty per cent" and spent most of it on parties and champagne. By April both her landlord and the *directrice* of the Isadorables' school in Switzerland had threatened her with eviction. She would need to dance again to pay the bills.

Isadora began by inviting Dumesnil to play for her every morning at eleven o'clock.[16] She planned "a great program" at the Trocadéro, a benefit for the Armoire Lorraine produced by the French ministry of fine arts. She would premiere the monumental works of her maturity — the *Marseillaise,* the *Rédemption,* and *Pathétique* (Tchai-kovsky's Sixth Symphony), a dance of careless charm transformed into "a battle charge . . . totally unbridled, a plunging, tearing at the enemy, a fury not to be stopped."[17] Isadora had first heard the sym-phony in 1906 and had recently performed the second, scherzo move-ment in New York. Her finished version included the final *adagio lamentoso,* an expression of "supreme sorrow and complete hopelessness" in mourning for the fallen. Presented as "the story of the present world struggle," the *Pathétique* would drive audiences to patriotic frenzy.[18]

Inspired by her looming debts, Isadora now booked her tour of South America, under the management of the Argentine impresario Walter Mocchi. She would make no money at the Trocadéro — all the proceeds went to war relief — but insisted on paying Dumesnil while she rehearsed. "My time was supposedly two hours [a day]," he remembered, "but I don't know of one instance when I remained less than four, and I was sorry when I had to go." Tickets for the Paris concert sold out in a matter of hours.

Isadora hadn't danced in Paris since the death of her children. She arrived in her dressing room "beaming," having paused to acknowledge the cheers of the crowd. "A case of champagne stood in a corner," Dumesnil noted, "but she did not touch it until the intermission, when it was necessary to whip up her energy for the second part of the program." When she appeared onstage, the audience stormed in applause. Among the spectators were the French minister of war, thousands of soldiers on leave from the trenches, and Rodin, who became "wild with excitement" when Isadora ended her *Pathétique* lying still on the ground, the dying chords of the music suggesting the rhythm of a beating heart: "His arms went through the air like the wings of a windmill, and he seemed to shriek, although his voice was lost among the general shouting." The unbilled addition of the *Marseillaise* brought the audience roaring to its feet.

According to Isadora, she first danced to the music of "La Marseillaise," the rousing national anthem of France, at the Metropolitan Opera in 1915. "It was a call to the boys of America to rise and protect the highest civilisation of our epoch," she wrote later — "that culture which has come to the world through France."[19] With its call to arms and cries for vengeance against tyrants, the anthem is by nature incendiary, symbolic not only of France's struggle but of the cause of world revolution. Isadora's ultimate version, the tour de force of her career, used the first four stanzas of Rouget de Lisle's text and the music adopted as official by the French government in 1887, slightly different from today's. In it, she combined the full range of her dramatic power with poses copied directly from Rude's sculpted *Marseillaise* on the Arc de Triomphe — the "Genius of War" summoning the nation to arms. In her final pose, she "stood filled with patriotic fury," her left breast bared in evocation of Delacroix's *Liberty Leading the People*. Well aware of its value as wartime propaganda, Isadora still insisted that her *Marseillaise* portrayed a deeper, human theme. It wasn't just France that filled her thoughts.

"In a robe the color of blood," wrote Carl Van Vechten, who saw the *Marseillaise* in New York the following year, "she stands enfolded; she sees the enemy advance; she feels the enemy as it grasps her by the throat; she kisses her flag; she tastes blood; she is all but crushed under the weight of the attack; and then she rises triumphant with the terrible cry, *Aux armes citoyens*." Not a word was spoken, "but the hideous din of a hundred raucous voices seems to ring in our ears."[20] At the Trocadéro, the audience "wept unashamedly" and joined in singing the anthem as Isadora, "imperiously, with proud, wide gestures, beckoned to a great unseen army that seemed to fill the stage at her magnetic command."[21] For another hour she danced Chopin waltzes, mazurkas, and preludes, until the lights finally went down and "she actually fell on the couch" in her dressing room. "I did my very best," she said as her maid wiped the sweat from her body with a sponge. "I think I've given the best performance of my life."[22]

A second concert at the Trocadéro was quickly scheduled for April 29. In the interim, Isadora traveled to Geneva, where she gave two concerts at the Grand Theatre with the Isadorables and earned just enough money to pay their school fees. It was not a happy trip. For reasons both politic and temperamental, the Swiss received Isadora's wartime program less passionately than had the French. Her pupils had been left to knit and needle for months under the watchful eye of a Madame Dourouze — their reception, too, was cool.[23] After her first performance, "to chase the blues away," Isadora got drunk at a lakeshore restaurant, refused to get in the car after dinner, "and wanted to go to the garden, dance in the moonlight and descend to bathe her feet in the clear waters of the lake." Later, brought home by Dumesnil and poet-playwright René Fauchois, she fell in the lobby of her hotel, waving away assistance with the words "You are drunk! And besides, *vous êtes des mouches* [you are flies]!" The next morning there was no sign of her distress, nor did she apologize for her behavior. It was a scene Dumesnil would witness repeatedly when he accompanied Isadora to South America as her conductor — in Paris he never saw her drunk. She left Switzerland promising the Isadorables that their martyrdom would not continue much longer.[24]

The second Trocadéro concert proved as rousing as the first. "I will

not attempt to describe, in detail, an event which surpassed anything that I have seen in my career," wrote Dumesnil. At the end of her performance, Isadora pledged to dance the *Marseillaise* "all over South America." She had returned to Paris to discover that her landlord had impounded her possessions for nonpayment of rent. Before the house was padlocked, Dumesnil managed to rescue five of Isadora's cherished Carrières, lowering the paintings down the side of the building into the arms of Fauchois and Fernand Divoire. "I must not lose my Carrières," Isadora insisted. "I must not." Never had she been so firmly rebuffed. Dumesnil called it "a turning point."

Isadora's theater trunks had been stored at the Trocadéro; there was nothing to impede her immediate departure. On May 13, just ahead of her creditors, she left Paris from the Gare d'Orsay, wearing "an entirely green outfit: a long gown, a soft felt hat, and a scarf," twisted several times around her neck. "No jewelry," wrote Dumesnil, "except a magnificent large emerald worn on the front of her dress." If she had sold it, she could have settled her debts on the spot.

"Erin," said Isadora. "I am partly Irish, you know."[25]

Until February 1916 Maurice Dumesnil was an officer of the "automobile service" of the Thirteenth Artillery Regiment in Paris. Complications from pneumonia had earned him an honorable discharge, a point he emphasizes in the book he later wrote about Isadora, *An Amazing Journey: Isadora Duncan in South America*.[26] A student and disciple of Claude Debussy, Dumesnil would go on to a respectable career as a recording artist and champion of his master's music (in 1932, the same year he wrote about Isadora, he published a manual for musicians, *How to Play and Teach Debussy*). In her autobiography, Isadora says little about the South American tour and almost nothing about Dumesnil, calling him only "the pianist" or "my pianist," with no other comment on his work.[27] Since she normally withheld nothing in praising her accompanists, her omissions can only have grated on Dumesnil's nerves: *An Amazing Journey* has the unmistakable feel of payback.

"I will admit frankly that Isadora was just spoiled . . . ," Dumesnil observed. "She had been made a goddess everywhere, and treated as such. She was used to having everybody worship at her shrine, and took it as an insult if anyone ever attempted to act differently."[28] Outside of newspaper gossip, there was never a suggestion of romance between them. This may have been the problem, particularly as Dumesnil,

throughout the South American tour, saw Isadora take lover after lover along the route. Dumesnil was a man of more than physical delicacy, fussy, fretful, and easily shocked. He had entered Isadora's orbit at a moment of unique vulnerability, footloose in wartime, when "piano playing was regarded as frivolous" and "anyone 'in mufti' was looked upon as a slacker . . . Yellow."[29] Mabel Dodge reported on the virile temper of Paris at the time: "The cafes surged with officers in brand-new uniforms and shining eyes. The male population of Paris was as lustful as the Roman mob."[30] At every point in his *Amazing Journey,* Dumesnil is at pains both to prove his masculinity and to divorce himself from Isadora's rampaging indiscretions.

They sailed from Bordeaux to New York on the *Lafayette,* leaving after midnight in accordance with wartime regulations to minimize the risk of enemy attack.[31] Isadora almost missed the boat, having encountered the violinist Jacques Thibaud on the train from Paris and disappearing with him for several hours in Bordeaux. Thibaud was the first of the men she called "divine . . . ravishing" to her pianist's startled ears. On landing in New York, she made a short speech to the press and left Dumesnil to handle the pack of reporters: "Is it true that Isadora had to get out of Paris quick, because of her big debts? . . . Did she have a special bathtub in which she bathed in nothing but champagne? . . . Is it true that at one of her receptions she danced entirely naked?" Dumesnil answered that Isadora liked champagne too much to waste it in a bath: he was already doubtful and put out.

At the Plaza, Isadora waited for the second leg of her trip.[32] A year after her failure at the Century Theater, her contempt for America had only amplified. "Everything here is commercial," she advised Dumesnil. "The public is stupid. They're like a flock of sheep." Almost immediately she discovered the Manhattan cocktail, "which she liked very dry" and added to the list of her daily potations: "At the luncheon, she ordered Sauternes first, then a bottle of red Burgundy, and champagne with the ice cream. By that time, she had become quite excited." Invitations poured in from old friends "and she went out a great deal," usually not returning until well after dawn. It occurred to Dumesnil only slowly that she was never without a lover; he had met one of Isadora's swains "in the elevator, early morning and in full [evening] dress!"

"Oh! . . . he is divine . . . ravishing," said Isadora.

"As much as Jacques [Thibaud]?"

"Oh, yes. But . . . so different!" After a few days she stopped rehearsing for the tour: "She said that it didn't matter, as all she needed was to keep fit by going through a few minutes of gymnastics and exercises. . . . She had indulged in every luxury of food and drink."

On May 21, before an audience of twenty thousand people, Isadora took part in the inaugural pageant of Percy MacKaye's *Caliban of the Golden Sands*, an epic, open-air festival at City College's Lewisohn Stadium, commemorating the 300th anniversary of the death of Shakespeare. More than fifteen hundred actors, singers, and dancers joined a Broadway cast "with songs, hobbyhorses, and maypoles," in "the biggest dramatic entertainment ever presented within the limits of this city," according to the *New York Times*.[33] "Let's do it anonymously," Isadora had suggested. "It'll be fun to see how they react, and if they recognize me."[34] Midway through the program she appeared, unannounced, in "a great beam of white light," arms lifted, moving slowly across the giant field to the music of Arthur Farwell and MacKaye's translation of Sophocles: "Many are the wonders of time, but the mightiest wonder is man."[35]

"Your idea of a pageant is fine," Isadora told MacKaye, "but it won't put you anywhere. It'll be above their heads."[36] She sailed for Buenos Aires on the *Byron* in the second week of June, having persuaded Augustin to come along as her manager. "I'm tired of taking care of my own affairs," Isadora complained. "An artist cannot be a businesswoman at the same time." As they pulled out of harbor, she waved to the Statue of Liberty. Dumesnil was traveling without a contract, on the promise of payment "out of the first receipts" in Buenos Aires.[37]

The *Byron* was a British liner, "old and decrepit." It would take three weeks to reach Argentina. On board, suddenly alarmed about her laziness, Isadora found no place to exercise. "I'm afraid I'm getting fat," she confessed. "I musn't do that! When we get to Buenos Aires I'll take a few Turkish baths and it'll vanish like magic." Meantime, she walked around the deck each day, escorted by Spanish painter Ernesto Valls. As always with Isadora, it was love at first sight — *coup de foudre*. "He is an extraordinary genius," she declared.

"She is my inspiration, my leading star," said Valls. "She is a Greek goddess!"

Also on board the *Byron*, to Valls's dismay, were a group of New York prizefighters, headed to Brazil for a boxing competition. "How beautiful these men are," Isadora remarked as she watched them spar on deck. "In ancient Greece, they could have been an inspiration to the artists." Two of them, at least, were seen "leaving her cabin."

Dumesnil's narrative continues in this vein. Isadora's supply of champagne had disappeared within a few short days. Before long, she consumed the entire stock of the ship on credit: "Although she was careful of what she ate, she observed no restrictions as regards the drinks." When the champagne ran out, she scolded the headwaiter for a "lack of service. He answered by telling her that she was an 'unusual customer.'" Augustin tried to reason with her from time to time, but to no avail.

"Why worry?" said Isadora. "The ocean is beautiful. We have peace. No wires, no letters, no lawyers, no creditors. No trouble of any kind. We are alone with the water and the sky." As they passed the equator, the heat became ferocious: "The flying fish had appeared. . . . The Southern Cross! . . . At night, the water was phosphorescent, and the boat seemed to cut through liquid fire." Inevitably, Dumesnil encountered a stoker from the engine room scuttling down the hallway one morning outside Isadora's cabin, "only half dressed." Later that day he couldn't restrain himself.

"How did you sleep, Isadora, on such a stifling night?"

"Oh, I had a perfectly glorious night."

"You don't mean . . . Why . . . he was only a stoker!"

Isadora broke into a lecture. "Life is made of contrasts, of changes," she said. "And at times, as a contrast, it is refreshing to pass from an artistic to a plain, unsophisticated, merely human expression of nature." Ernesto Valls had been moping around the ship for several days.

"Think of the life of those poor men down by the furnace, and the hours of toil and labor they have to put in," Isadora went on. "Here we are on deck and lying comfortably on soft cushions. . . . No one ever thinks of the inferno below. It seems to me that at least one of these poor fellows should be given a little happiness. I had one last bottle of champagne and I shared it with him." She paused. "And you know . . . he had the legs of an Apollo!"

The *Byron* reached Buenos Aires in the first days of July, having stopped at Salvador (Bahia), Rio de Janeiro, and Montevideo. Neither Isadora nor Dumesnil had any experience of a nation of freely mixed races — "Colored people!" as Dumesnil exclaimed.[38] Isadora used the French word *nègres*, — either "Negroes" or "niggers," but in either case pejorative. The tour would expose her native prejudice in the harshest possible light. "In every garden bloomed the red hibiscus," she reported later on, "and the whole town of Bahia teemed with the promiscuous love of black and white races."[39] She was captivated by the atmosphere of open sexuality. In the bay of Santa Catarina, when a fistfight broke out on the *Byron* between Valls and another suitor, she dismissed them both without a care: "She was quite intoxicated, sat with one hand on her hip, and held a cigarette with the other. A red and green scarf, picked up from somewhere around, flew in a war-like manner around her neck. . . . 'You're nothing but a couple of flies! Flies . . . nothing but a couple of flies.'"[40]

Calamity struck immediately on arrival in Buenos Aires.[41] Isadora had shipped her carpets, curtains, and musical scores separately by freighter. There was no sign of them at the dock or the customs house. Nor could the ship be tracked, owing to wartime security. *"Nous sommes perdus!"* Isadora whispered (We are lost!). At her hotel, an-other Plaza, she met Renato Salvati, an assistant to her impresario, Walter Mocchi. Salvati reassured her as to the scores: they could be obtained from the opera library. For curtains of any kind, she could purchase new ones "at one of the London furniture houses." She would find Buenos Aires the most sophisticated of cities. Mocchi would have come himself to receive her, but he was "too busy with the operatic season . . . to occupy his time with minor details of management."

Isadora's opening, already sold out, was a week away. Whether through Mocchi's discourtesy or some demon of her own, she made up her mind against Argentina. "What's the idea?" she cried to Dumesnil when Mocchi's office asked for a full list of her programs and the dates on which she would dance them. An orchestra had been hired to accompany her three times a week — she could choose the dates herself.

"I'm not in the habit of preparing my programs like an opera sea-son," Isadora replied. Who could say what she would feel like dancing after the premiere? Who could say that she would feel like dancing at all? "I'm an artist, not a machine." Mocchi's secretary replied that the firm couldn't work with "temperamental women." Augustin was al-ready white in the face, having gone with Isadora to Maples and pur-chased two thousand dollars' worth of "inferior" blue curtains on credit, to be paid for, of course, "from the first receipts." More worried than ever, Dumesnil returned from a walk in the city to find Isadora surrounded by a new crowd of male admirers: "Where they came from and how they had been introduced to her I didn't know."

She "made a sensation" as she strode into the Plaza ballroom for an afternoon tea before "many distinguished families of Argentina," dancing the tango for the first time. "From my first timid steps I felt

my pulses respond to the enticing, languorous rhythm of this voluptuous dance," Isadora wrote, "sweet as a long caress, intoxicating as
love under southern skies, cruel and dangerous as the allurement of a
tropical forest."[42] A number of men had "swarmed around her," to the
evident displeasure of their mothers and sisters.

That same night, despite warnings from her new friends, Isadora
insisted on being taken to La Boca, the international slum and red-
light district of Buenos Aires. There she sat "motionless" in a pornographic movie house, "her eyes literally pinned on the screen," while
prostitutes plied their trade in and out of the rows of seats. Suddenly,
before Dumesnil could stop her, she ran from the theater, crying, "Oh,
my God!" The next day she was "exceedingly depressed," talking
about white slavery, pornographers, and "those simple-minded girls."

"Poor creatures," Isadora said. "I think it's the most miserable
kind of degradation. . . . When the low-down criminals who carry on
that abject trade are caught, they should be shot, hanged or guil-
lotined." Dumesnil was "puzzled. . . . Perhaps Isadora's reaction was
aimed at the mental, rather than the physical attitude" of prostitution.
On the night before her opening, she went to Pigall, "the best known
nightclub in Buenos Aires," where she danced the tango with a line of
gigolos until three in the morning. Surrounded by men, drinking from
each of their glasses in turn, she called out: "I will now interpret for
you the national anthem of this great country. Long live Argentina!"

"The audience did not know what to think," wrote Dumesnil.
"The more distinguished portion, seated in the boxes, seemed to be
shocked beyond words." Having finished her dance, Isadora tossed
her sandal to an admirer in the crowd. "The second sandal soon followed, but it was thrown in anger, at some people . . . who had obviously laughed at her."

Dumesnil woke the next day to the sound of frantic pounding on
his door. Three of Mocchi's assistants "bounded in," talking so heatedly that Dumesnil could catch only a few words: "Broken the contract! . . . Lawsuit! . . . Responsible! . . . Hold the money!" A clause in
Isadora's contract forbade her to dance in any public place without the
consent of her manager — her tango performance at Pigall was the
scandal of the city. Dumesnil managed to avert an immediate disaster,
but the ship had already sunk. At her Buenos Aires opening, Isadora
detected "a lack of magnetism" in a self-consciously cultured audience,
to whom stage dance hitherto had meant only ballet. (Indeed, Isadora
was billed as a *bailerina,* as female dancers normally are in Spanish.)

Dumesnil remembered "a magnificent exhibition of dresses and jewelry" and a crowd that "seemed cold and indifferent . . . surprised, deceived, and to tell the truth, bored by Isadora's conception of art."

The following morning a savage critique in *La Nación,* one of Buenos Aires's leading dailies, declared flat out that Isadora Duncan was "not a dancer. . . . All she did was stand, taking at times a few steps from one side to the other, or stoop, while she looked up and raised her arms above her head." There were further "discourteous remarks" about her weight and the size of her legs. Dumesnil received glowing reviews. A cartoon appeared in *Ultima Hora,* showing two men in opera dress.

"Did you understand Isadora Duncan's art?" said one.

"No, but I admired the cut of Dumesnil's tuxedo," said the other.

Isadora professed indifference. *"Ce sont des nègres,"* she declared. *"Ils n'ont rien compris."* (They're niggers. They understood nothing.) The second concert fared no better than the first, and the third was performed without Dumesnil, who refused to play for Isadora's "all-Wagner" program. "We were here on a semi-official tour of propaganda," he protested. "The first two nights she had interpreted the *Marseillaise,* thus siding openly with the Allies. . . . I felt it was impossible for me to take the baton that night, and I told her so frankly."

"Wagner is a great international genius," Isadora countered, "a world figure who belongs to all nations alike." She was adamant: "A genius like Wagner is not a Boche." Dumesnil enlisted a substitute conductor, but the ill-timed program failed miserably. Ticket sales had already dropped substantially since opening night. When latecomers arrived, chattering in their seats, Isadora stopped the orchestra and addressed the half-empty hall.

"I had been told, before coming here, that I would find the Argentinians very primitive, and uneducated," she began. "I had been warned that they would never be able to understand my art. . . . The people who warned me were right. You are nothing but a bunch of niggers!"

Backstage, Dumesnil listened in mounting horror: "I was astounded. This time, it was the collapse, the end of everything."

"I am afraid you do not understand me when I speak in English, so I'm going to tell you in French," Isadora continued: *"Vous êtes des nègres!"*[43]

For the record, apart from Dumesnil's account, there is no confirmation of this dismaying scene. New York papers reported in September that Isadora had "met with the same disastrous financial results" in Buenos Aires as she had at the Century Theater the year before, "and it is said that she vented her opinion of the Argentineans and their capability to appreciate the True, the Good and the Beautiful . . . in no uncertain terms."[44] Mocchi soon canceled the rest of her engagement. He would pay her nothing and confiscated her curtains as collateral. In a letter to Fernand Divoire after the Wagner concert, Isadora described Argentina as *"un pays de Barbares"* (a country of Barbarians). The women were "beautiful animals" and the men "handsome brutes," but there were "no artists" among them; she had only one desire, "to return to Paris — with all the trouble I have there, I still have compensations — but here — nothing — and no one."[45] She had transformed her hotel suite into "a Hindoo temple," strewn with flowers, veils, and cushions for her seemingly endless string of suitors. Dumesnil talked to the hotel maids and "heard of visit after visit, at all hours of the day and night."[46] Isadora wrote Divoire: "If you knew how tired and unhappy I am . . . Oh! I want to come home."[47]

Augustin left Argentina immediately after the Wagner fiasco, sent by Isadora to Switzerland to "arrange something" for her students, who once again faced expulsion from their *pensionnat*. Within a month Dionysion would cease to exist. The smaller children went home to their parents (including Jean, who later became a dancer with the Paris Opéra), while the Isadorables embarked on a dancing tour of Switzerland at the suggestion of the composer Ernst Bloch.[48] Augustin arrived in time to act as their manager. "It was [our] success as a group," Theresa wrote later, "without Isadora for the first time . . . that gave us the opportunity to find our own strength as soloists and individual artists."[49] The Isadorables had mutinied.

Isadora was already in Montevideo when the news reached her that her school had been dispersed.[50] Unable to pay her hotel bill in Buenos Aires — she had run up $4,000 in charges — she left her emerald pendant and ermine coat to cover her costs. A new impresario had entered the fray, Cesare Giulietti, "a perfect Rossini type," who booked Isadora for performances in Montevideo, Rio de Janeiro, and São Paulo in Brazil. At the last minute Walter Mocchi released her curtains as a favor to Dumesnil, who had yet to be paid for his services.

Isadora was so glad to leave Buenos Aires that when her curtains failed to arrive in Montevideo, she laughed it off: "I feel that I could even dance without any decoration at all. I could dance right there in the public square." Her faith was rewarded on opening night by the most admiring audience she had seen since leaving France:

> After many encores, shouts of *"La Marsellesa, la Marsellesa!"* were heard all over. Again, they wanted the *Marseillaise.* Isadora was very tired, and hesitated about yielding to the request, but fifty young enthusiasts climbed upon the stage, dragged her out and began to sing the anthem, while two of them sat at the piano and began playing it, without giving me time to come back to my chair! Others stood around singing in chorus and waving their arms as they sang. It seemed as if the spirit of the great Revolution inspired them, and the whole thing was almost a duplicate of the scenes which had taken place at the Trocadéro three months before. . . . After the performance, a parade was organized and accompanied us to our hotel, while many people sat around and commented upon the unforgettable evening.[51]

Dumesnil attributed Isadora's success in Montevideo, in part, to Uruguay's traditional rivalry with Argentina, but it was no different in Brazil, where her audiences in Rio de Janeiro erupted in cheers and "tremendous manifestations. . . . One, two, three, five encores didn't quench the outpour of enthusiasm which seemed to run through the spectators like wildfire."[52] As a precaution, Isadora had given names to her program of Chopin preludes, nocturnes, and polonaises: "Ecstasy," "Destiny," "Elegy," "The Poet's Harp," "Belgium in the War," "Poland Enchained," and so on. Local critics hailed her as "a cosmic expression . . . original, unexpected, more sensed than understood."[53] "Like Venus born of the waves, so does Isadora rise out of the waves of Harmony . . . to charm the universe."[54] When it became apparent that Giulietti was pocketing most of her profits, Dumesnil stationed a paid agent at the box office. By the time she left Rio, Isadora had earned enough to settle her debts in Buenos Aires and hire an expensive car to take her around town — her emerald and ermine were promptly returned. At her last concert she was "recalled more than thirty times" and wept openly onstage as poets and students read tributes to her work.

And still Dumesnil "puzzled" over the character of a woman who ultimately left him "panic-stricken." Isadora's escapades in Rio and Uruguay were less rowdy than before, although one discarded lover cornered Dumesnil to rant about her faithlessness: "After me, there had been six other men there. Yes! It makes seven altogether in six hours! She's a . . . ! She's a . . . !"

Dumesnil cut him off. "Oh! that gossip," he wrote. "What treasures of imagination are wasted in inventing stories, rumors, and scandals of all kinds!" Ultimately, he received payment for four months' work. "I'm going to tell you what you are," said Isadora as she handed Dumesnil the check. "You're a fly, nothing but a fly. Get out of here. . . . You're worse than Mocchi!!"[55] Her tour concluded, broke but out of debt, she returned to New York on the *Vestris* — as it happened, with the same group of prizefighters whose bodies she had so admired on the voyage out.

20

"I Tell You She Drives 'Em Mad"

"When we reached New York, no one came to meet me," Isadora wrote, "as my cable had not been delivered owing to war difficulties." The voyage from Brazil was "sad and lonely," despite the presence of the boxing team and the attentions of "an American named Wilkins, who was always drunk." Not knowing where to turn, she telephoned Arnold Genthe: "What was my surprise at being answered by a familiar voice, but not the voice of Arnold. It was Lohengrin, who, by a strange coincidence, had just gone in to see Genthe that morning." Broke in Buenos Aires, Isadora had thought of cabling Singer for help but confessed that she had no idea where he was: "When he heard that I was alone at the docks, without funds and without friends, he at once said he would come to my aid. . . . I had a curious feeling of confidence and safety, and I was as delighted to see him as he was to see me." Singer had taken an apartment on West Fifty-seventh Street, where Genthe captured the reunited lovers on film in a moment of genuine tenderness — "L. was in one of his kindest and most generous moods," Isadora wrote. Her debts were paid, champagne flowed, and "life became wonderful" once again, "through the magic power of money."[1]

On the day of their reunion, at his own expense, Singer booked the Metropolitan Opera House for Isadora, where she appeared on

November 21, 1916, in a benefit concert for the families of French artists impoverished by the war. Seating was by invitation only, with Oscar Spirescu conducting the same program Isadora had danced at the Trocadéro in April (in New York, she added her solo *Ave Maria*).[2] In the audience were Mayor John Mitchel, Anna Pavlova, Otto Kahn, Gertrude Vanderbilt Whitney, "the diplomatic representatives of the Allied nations," and "as many of the dancing students in New York" as Singer's messenger boys managed to hunt down.

"It was a tremendous undertaking," Mary Roberts recalled, "and when we neared the day of the performance we were offered as high as $100 a ticket, but none were sold." When Isadora began the *Marseillaise*, the doors to the hall were thrown open, "and as she came to the stage a strong wind came in off the street and her draperies were blown back against her body. . . . She was really a ravishing sight and the audience rose to its feet and cheered her."[3] For Isadora, it was a perfect triumph.

All too disastrous was her performance after the concert, when she joined Singer and a number of their friends for dinner at Sherry's. "About a hundred guests were to come in afterwards to dance," Arnold Genthe reported. Singer took Genthe aside before Isadora arrived:

> "I have placed you next to her," he said. "You know she never eats before a performance — she's had nothing all day but a cup of coffee at breakfast. I want you to see that she doesn't drink anything until she has had some solid food."
>
> Isadora had scarcely sat down when she said, "I'm dying of thirst. I just have to have a sip of champagne."
>
> I have never seen her in better form than she was during the dinner. As a rule, she paid very little attention to clothes. And she cared nothing at all for jewelry. But that evening, to please Singer, she wore an exquisite white chiffon frock and a diamond necklace which he had just given her. All went well until the dancing began. I was talking to Isadora when all of a sudden her face lit up. "Do you see," she said, "that dark, handsome young man over there? . . . I want you to go over and bring him here."
>
> I did as she asked and they proceeded to dance a tango that astonished the guests by something more than mere grace and rhythm.[4]

The identity of Isadora's tango partner has never been established. Genthe describes him as "a typical lounge lizard"; others as "Maurice [Mouvet], the well-known ballroom dancer of the period."[5] Not in dispute is the way Isadora danced — "in a fashion one doesn't exhibit in public"[6] — or the fate of Singer's diamond necklace. Max Eastman told the story of Singer's mounting fury:

> They danced with so little restraint that Lohengrin finally got up . . . lifted the slender swain by the pants and collar, and carried him through the door. When Lohengrin returned, Isadora was standing in flames of ice, if for her sake there can be such things, in the center of the floor.
>
> "If you don't like my friends," she cried, "I don't want your jewelry!"
>
> She ripped off the fabulous necklace and, with a gesture between Mars God of War and Zeus the Rain-bringer, scattered the flashing gems in every corner of the room, and marched out in the wake of the beautiful tango dancer. Arnold Genthe was standing near the door, and as she passed him she murmured, without turning her head: "Pick them up."[7]

By all accounts, this contretemps was soon resolved — Singer remained in a gift-giving mood. Witter Bynner recalled a conversation between Singer and Isadora as their romance moved unavoidably to its conclusion. "If you could only . . . cease making these public scandals, there's nothing I wouldn't give you!" Singer said.

"What would you give me?" Isadora asked.

"Madison Square Garden."

"What are your conditions?"

"That you always behave yourself with dignity in public."

"I'm not sure that I can meet your conditions," Isadora answered.[8] At the end of December, "restless still and weary with the social round," she left New York, at Singer's suggestion, for a vacation in Havana.[9] Allan Ross Macdougall, then working as Singer's secretary, accompanied her to Cuba as a sort of chaperon. "With Dougie [Singer] did not have to be jealous," Isadora explained. In his early twenties, handsome, red-haired, "with the most engaging smile and a contagious laugh," Macdougall was happily homosexual, enjoying a thousand dollars a week in pocket money as Singer's amanuensis. Isadora described him as "a Scotchman and a poet," calmly confiding that she had hoped to "convert" him on their trip: "I got as far as getting his head close to my breast, but when I thought he might go to sleep . . . I gave it up."[10] Macdougall would be her first biographer.

"This evening we had a grand dinner with wines and many bad speeches and silly toasts," Macdougall wrote to Bynner from the ship to Havana. It was Christmas Eve 1916. Isadora had brought a portable gramophone and danced the hula on deck, "with a very boisterous drunk man, while the onlookers shouted and howled and laughed so that even the wash of the waters was not heard any more." Later she asked for silence, donned a green velvet cloak, and danced an allegory of the birth of Christ to Bach's "Air on the G String." "What a moment to have lived!" Macdougall exclaimed. "Not all the sermons preached in every church in Christendom could equal in spiritual eloquence that dance."[11]

Directly opposed to the joy of Christmas was Isadora's theme at New Year's, when she danced "the dance of Christ crucified" at a bar in Havana, before "the usual assortment of morphimaniacs, cocainists, opium smokers, alcoholists, and other derelicts of life."[12] In January she went to Florida, where Singer shortly joined her at The Breakers in Palm Beach. The town did not yet enjoy its reputation as the rich man's paradise, a status imposed on it in large part by Singer, who returned in 1918 and bought up hundreds of acres of land, at the same time funding construction of the Spanish-style Everglades Club, the sanctum sanctorum of Palm Beach's restricted social cabal. Local legend insists that Palm Beach was the scene of Singer's final break with Isadora, when he found her in the arms of the boxer "Kid" McCoy, onetime inventor of the corkscrew punch. She is supposed to have left Palm Beach "throwing a curse in her wake."[13] If so, she stayed with Singer until March 1917, after he paid to bring the Isadorables from Switzerland to New York. True to his word, Singer took a $100,000 option on Madison Square Garden and offered the arena to Isadora as the new home for her school.

"What do you think I am, a circus?" she cried. "I suppose you want me to advertise prizefights with my dancing!" Singer broke the news over dinner at the Plaza, where a party of Isadora's family and friends had gathered: Augustin and Margherita, Elizabeth, Genthe, Mary Desti, and George Grey Barnard. On hearing Isadora's sarcastic response, "Singer turned absolutely livid. His lips were quivering and his hands were shaking. He got up from the table without saying a word and left the room."

"He'll come back," said Isadora. "He always does."

But he didn't. "She sent her brother, her sister-in-law, Mary Desti, and finally her pupils to plead with him. He was adamant. Her letters to him went unanswered. All funds were stopped."[14] Macdougall, too, lost his post as Singer's secretary, and with it his lavish allowance. He was among the first to enlist when the United States declared war on Germany in April. ("Do you wonder that Dougie went to pieces . . . ?" Isadora asked.)[15]

The following year, sinking deeply into hypochondria, Paris Singer finally obtained a divorce from his wife and married Joan Balsh, the nurse who supervised the soldiers' hospital at his Paignton estate. Palm Beach became their second home, where Singer worked with architect Addison Mizner to transform the Florida swamp into what now contains the largest concentration of private wealth in the United States.[16]

Isadora's fatal breach with Singer coincided with her opening, on March 6, in an encore of her program at the Metropolitan Opera, this time before a paying audience that overflowed the house and included half a thousand standees. Only a month remained before President Woodrow Wilson, provoked by Germany's resumption of unrestricted submarine warfare, asked Congress to declare war on the Central Powers.

"At that time," Isadora wrote, "I believed, as did many others, that the whole world's hope of liberty, regeneration, and civilisation depended on the Allies winning the war."[17] She had not misjudged her target. On a tide of nationalism, her program played to packed houses at intervals through the end of April, billed as *The Spirit of a Nation Drawn into War* and ending each night with the *Marseillaise,* now transformed into a showstopping display of American patriotism.

"Those who like to see pretty dancing, pretty girls, pretty things in general will not find much pleasure in contemplating the art of Isadora," wrote Carl Van Vechten. "She is not pretty; her dancing is not pretty. She has been cast in a nobler mold and it is her pleasure to climb higher mountains." Critics vied in their effort to describe the deluge of emotion Isadora inspired in a public now roaring to beat the Hun, "as vehement and excited an expression of enthusiasm as it would be possible for an artist to awaken in our theatre today," according to Van Vechten.[18] The *New York Sun* reported in its opening-night review:

> The performer, unaided this time by her troupe of young girls, held the thousands of eyes riveted upon her every beautiful gesture, and incited a clapping of thousands of hands, which during every dance had had to clinch in a stemming of emotion. And at the end of all, when came the "Marseillaise," there came an uproar such as sub-

scription nights rarely have accorded Metropolitan stars . . . made by an audience which had leaped to its feet and which remained there to join in the final strains of the "Star Spangled Banner." The heavy golden curtains had to swing back many times in order that Miss Duncan could acknowledge the cheers which sometimes reached the height of pandemonium. . . . And when at the end, it was encored, and the American anthem trumpeted in behind it, [she] had only to tear off her outer skirtlet and discover herself in the Stars and Stripes. It was daring — but the audience, not entirely unacquainted with that sort of thing in other sorts of entertainments, seemed to like it.[19]

That night, Isadora's closing speech contained nothing of antagonism or resentment. "This is no time for art and artists," she began. "Men should want to serve in the trenches and women should nurse the soldiers." Shouts from the audience of "No! No!" led her to add that she would stay in the United States for the duration of hostilities: "I feel that America is on the brink of a great awakening and that now it is going to be a really interesting country to live in."[20] Draped in the American flag, she kissed it as she said good night, igniting another torrent of applause.

On March 15 Nicholas II abdicated the throne of Russia, ending three hundred years of Romanov rule and heralding the fall of tyrants across Europe. No doubt remained that the United States would join the Allies — the country was war-mad even before a despairing President Wilson gave in to the inevitable. The collapse of Russian autocracy had removed an embarrassing weight from Allied shoulders. Now the war really could be seen as a fight "for democracy and against absolutism," as Wilson's secretary of state, Robert Lansing, affirmed at a cabinet meeting: "By entering the war now, the United States would be battling for the democratic ideal."

Still reluctant, Wilson finally conceded. In his speech to Congress he echoed what was briefly the national sentiment: "The great, generous Russian people have been added in all their naïve majesty and might to the forces that are fighting for freedom in the world, for justice, and for peace."[21] The promise of liberal democracy, in both the actual and the jingoistic sense, had never shone so brightly.

"On the night of the Russian Revolution I danced with a terrible fierce joy," Isadora wrote.[22] Assisted by her students, she dedicated her program of March 28 to Russia's fledgling utopia, soon to be strangled by a Bolshevik coup that seemed to her equally prophetic: "Here at last is a frame mighty enough to work in. . . . Here one feels that perhaps for the second time in the world's history a great force has arisen to give capitalism, which stands for monstrous greed and villainy, one great blow."[23] Only fifteen blocks north, as Isadora expected, a three-ring circus played at Madison Square Garden, the forum that might have been hers had she not finally insulted her millionaire.

On April 6 Isadora drove to Washington to hear the proclamation of war and, "at white heat," composed a dance to Tchaikovsky's *Marche Slave*.[24] Five days later she added it to her repertory, standing alone on the stage, "head bowed, knees bent," her hands apparently tied behind her back. Van Vechten wrote:

> Groping, stumbling . . . she struggles forward, clad only in a short red garment that barely covers her thighs. With furtive glances of extreme despair she peers above and ahead. When the strains of "God Save the Tsar" are first heard in the orchestra she falls to her knees and you see the peasant shuddering under the blows of the knout. The picture is a tragic one, cumulative in its horrific details. Finally comes the moment of release and here Isadora makes one of her great effects. She does not spread her arms apart with a wide gesture. She brings them forward slowly and we observe with horror that they have practically forgotten how to move at all. They are crushed, these hands, crushed and bleeding after their long serfdom; they are not hands at all but claws, broken, twisted, piteous claws! The expression of frightened, almost uncomprehending, joy with which Isadora concludes the march is another stroke of her vivid imaginative genius.[25]

Almost immediately, Isadora's critics attacked her new dance on political grounds. Tchaikovsky's *Marche Slave* is a brassy, crashing celebration of imperial might, not noticeably in tune with the groans of the masses — Isadora's shackled, weighted movements turned the music on its head. "This antithesis or dissonance of gesture against music roused some storm in the audience," she confirmed.[26] In the modernist *Little Review*, editor Margaret Anderson lambasted her for "turning music into stories of war and religion," adding an "adolescent brain" and "a body that was never meant to move in rhythmic line" to the list of her imperfections: "Isadora Duncan ran, jumped and skipped and stamped and swooned about the stage. . . . [She] felt a great deal. She shook her head and arms in such a fury of feeling that she appeared to be strangling; and when there was no way of reaching a further intensification she shook her whole body in a kind of spasm of human inability to bear the grief of the world."[27] Van Vechten confessed that he warmed only slowly to Isadora's now gargantuan technique; at the end of the night, he was cheering with the rest. Her gifts as a tragic actress had found their ultimate expression in the cause of war.

"People — this includes me — get on their chairs and yell," Van Vechten reported in a letter to Gertrude Stein. "It is very exciting to see American patriotism thoroughly awakened — I tell you she drives 'em mad; the recruiting stations are full of her converts. . . ."[28] Isadora's impassioned speeches and apparently shameless manipulation of "an American flag of filmy silk" brought shouts from the audience of "every variety . . . from bravo to the rebel yell."[29] With the Isadorables dancing "defiantly" alongside her in the *Marche Lorraine,* trailing scarves of billowing Liberty silk in red, white, and blue, Isadora "really achieved for the first time the whole of her aesthetic dream," according to Max Eastman: "My vice of admiration never carried me more dangerously near to worship."[30]

In general, Isadora's friends on the American left were annoyed and dismayed by her new incarnation as a militant patriot. Almost all Village radicals opposed the war, as did *The Masses,* whose editors, including Eastman, went on trial the following year for "conspiring to obstruct enlistment." The case concluded in a hung jury and was finally dropped by the federal government, but *The Masses* itself was shut down by the Espionage Act in August 1917. Eastman struggled for years to reconcile his passion for Isadora's art with the "difficulties" of her personality and what he saw as her lack of any coherent intellectual or political position. Despite her best efforts, he remained unseduced.

"She looked, in the first place, like one of El Greco's Irish Mick-like angels with a turned-up nose," Eastman wrote, "a very difficult kind of nose, in my opinion, for an angel to wear, and still more for a Grecian dancer. . . . It was something in Isadora as a person that I did not like . . . a sort of didactic, blue-stocking assertiveness. You will find it in the great free-lovers as often as the old-maid saints." Eastman went on:

> She had made a cult of impulse and impracticality, rapture and abandon. She had dimmed her own native good sense, drugged her cerebrum consistently, all her life long, with romantic notions of what her classic art, and art in general, demanded and consisted of. . . . Not only was she a smatterer and a mental dilettante; that, as a dancer, she had every right to be. But she was, in her sparkling way, an obscuran-

tist. . . . She cultivated an attitude of irrelevance to fact and rationality as though it were an intellectual virtue — as though it were a part of being "radical." That was the thing that made her impossible to me as a companion. We shared so many views and attitudes, and I admired not only her art, but her courage, kindness, wit, and true-heartedness, so fervently that this single repelling element stood very clear in my mind. . . . I wanted her to be great and real, a classic in the mode of Walt Whitman, all the way through.[31]

When Isadora herself was investigated by the U.S. government later in 1917, it was less for her radical views and pronouncements than her attachments to Germans and foreigners in general. Since 1914 German and Russian diplomats and visiting dignitaries had mingled freely at Isadora's parties in New York. Elizabeth Duncan's transplanted school at Croton was composed almost entirely of Germans, from the students, teachers, and staff to the presiding *Geist*, Max Merz, now lecturing a handful of American children about racial purity. When one of Elizabeth's students complained about "propaganda," the school was placed under federal surveillance. Another girl was found to be seven months pregnant, fueling rumors of free love on the Hudson.[32] To make matters worse, Isadora told reporters that "the only man in America" who understood her work was "a Russian Jew who writes for a paper on the East Side of New York." America's first Red scare had barely begun, but the European war had redefined espionage: in October 1917 Dutch dancer Margarete Zelle — Mata Hari — would be shot as a spy in Paris.

That spring and summer, Isadora went from party to party and bed to bed, as if in mad reaction to her rupture with Singer. "It became fashionable to boast of having had a week with Isadora," said Agnes de Mille, "whether true or false, the chance of contradiction being slight."[33] Carl Van Vechten recalled the night he danced with Isadora at a party in the Village — "I even carried her in my arms! . . . And Isadora related how she had rolled around in the damp gutter with a sailor the night before, which she remembered in the morning when she discovered her white lace dress was all blue."[34] In May she turned forty, indignant at the notion that time could wither her style. Even so, she began to take years off her age (five years later, she would claim to be thirty-eight). Only her students knew how seriously her diet of parties and alcohol imperiled her work.

"Sometimes we would have to tie her with silk reins and lead her on stage as if we were a team of horses leading a chariot," Anna remembered. "There were other times we needed to surround her as if it were part of the routine, so her falling down would not be obvious. I always thought that Isadora had a strange death urge. But she would become revived and rigid. She was a proud woman."[35] As she grew older, she gave full rein to her mystical, "Irish" streak: "She believed in everything so long as it was irrational: fortune telling, astrology, Couéism, visitation in dreams, palmistry, premonitory visions."[36] Max Eastman was nearly seduced over a Ouija board.

"Do you really believe in this?" Eastman asked Isadora.

"Of course I believe in it, don't you?"

"I believe you might get up something out of your unconscious."

"Unconscious, bosh! We're communing with Destiny."[37] At the Met, her students watched from the wings and feared that when the time came for them to dance by themselves they would never escape her shadow. "The gods carried her," Anna said: "The gods cared for Isadora."[38]

At twenty-two, Anna Denzler was the eldest of the Isadorables, the self-described "Kommandant of our little troupe"[39] and Isadora's frankest critic among the girls. In Switzerland, at Isadora's request, all six had signed contracts, pledging to remain as her students through the age of twenty-one, whereupon they could stay or leave, as they chose. The price of allegiance was steep.

"If one of us should go out on our own," Anna explained in a letter to her parents, "which after all she can't prevent, we're not permitted to bill ourselves as her students."[40] Slowly, the girls realized that Isadora meant to keep them with her permanently, "subject to her every whim," as Irma complained.[41] Isadora had said all along that she wasn't training dancers for the stage but as "priestesses" and future teachers of her art. They would all go back to Bellevue when the war was over. They would rebuild the school.

Early in 1917, with anti-German feeling at a peak in the United States, Isadora authorized all six of her students to take the surname Duncan for professional purposes. "This was done legally through the New York courts," Irma wrote. "Her intention was to adopt me and her other five original pupils as her daughters."[42] Irma insisted on this even though no adoption ever took place: in light of the death of Isadora's own children, her gesture assumed the character of a benediction. All the girls remained in awe of their teacher and grateful for "the grand adventure" she had given them. "There was never a dull moment," Anna conceded. "She saw to that."[43] They only wished Isadora would allow them to expand, "to be independent," in Irma's words. "Not merely financially, but artistically independent. . . . A God-given right, so to speak."[44]

In 1917 Irma turned twenty, Theresa, twenty-two, Lisa, nineteen, Gretel, seventeen, and Erika, sixteen. The girls' discontent turned quickly to anger. When they pleaded for the right to perform on their own, Isadora answered that they needed to work harder on their dances — in fact, her dances — and that she would not allow her work to be shown on the stage until it was perfect, "or as near to perfection as possible." She placed no such restriction on herself, as the Isadorables knew. Her intransigence "became a constant source of friction and contention between us," Irma recalled, and "threatened to come inevitably to a head-on collision of wills." No evidence suggests that Isadora directly manipulated the girls' loyalty by reference to Deirdre and Patrick; even so, Theresa detected "a maternal feeling of such monstrous proportions that it had to vent itself continually like a volcanic eruption."[45] Anna was more blunt, attributing Isadora's opposition to an aging woman's jealousy and regret: "She had become an extraordinary psychological study. . . . I am fully convinced that Isadora's second great tragedy in life was that she could not cope with advancing age."[46]

In fairness to Isadora, she had more on her mind than suppressing her students' ambitions. Her school was her legacy, however precarious, all she had to preserve and continue her work. "Rodin surrounds himself in his studio with slabs of marble," Isadora said. "I want to surround myself also; my block of marble — my pupils."[47] She hadn't raised them from the ground to become "Broadway attractions" — by 1917 America had begun to laugh at "classic," barefoot dancers. Arnold Genthe recalled the day Isadora saw "a photograph of young women in chaste draperies" in a Sunday newspaper supplement, their arms spread wide and heads thrown back in apparent simulation of ecstasy. The caption read: "Modern Maids in an ancient Greek dance."

"This is the kind of thing that the general public blames me for," Isadora grumbled.[48] Later she described her visit to an unidentified dancing school in New York where the teacher stood before rows of budding Terpsichores crying, "Undulate, girls, undulate! Isadora says: 'Undulate!'"[49] The 1910s had seen a mass proliferation of dance and dancers' images in the United States, gorgeously and fantastically presented by such pioneers of glamorous art photography as Genthe, Alfred Stieglitz, Edward Steichen, and Adolf de Meyer and epitomized in the pages of *Vanity Fair:* in 1918 Genthe's portrait of Isadorable Lisa Duncan, holding a torch of liberty as "the Angel of the Battlefield," graced a poster for the American Red Cross.

In 1915 Ruth St. Denis and her husband, Ted Shawn, had opened the Denishawn School of Dancing and Related Arts in Los Angeles, teaching every kind of dance, from ballet and "plastique" to Dalcroze's eurythmics,[50] in a program famously advertised to improve body, mind, and soul. Dance was "too great to be encompassed by any one system," Shawn believed: "The individual and personal thing in Dancing is the finest thing anyone can offer."[51] The result was the great grab bag of styles and influences, overwhelmingly theatrical, that gave substance to the first generation of American modern dancers: Martha Graham, Doris Humphrey, and Charles Weidman all trained at Denishawn. In Hollywood, St. Denis choreographed the "Babylonian" dance sequences in D. W. Griffith's *Intolerance* and instructed silent-film stars in the art of Delsartean gesture and emotional expression; Denishawn students routinely found jobs in the movies. "Either we work in a pure spirit of charity or we make money," St. Denis said. Among her better-known clients were the Gish sisters, Mabel Normand, Blanche Sweet, and Louise Brooks, the unforgettable Lulu of G. W. Pabst's *Pandora's Box.*

In technical virtuosity and splendor of presentation, Denishawn was frequently compared to the Ballets Russes — proof to Isadora of "the error that is born of imitation unsupported by original thought."[52] She and the girls spent the summer of 1917 on Long Island, at Long Beach, where Isadora rented an oceanfront cottage after exhausting her resources in New York. She had pawned Singer's necklace and later sold her ermine and emerald: "As I was now practically penniless, it would, no doubt, have been wiser to have invested the proceeds . . . in solid stocks and bonds, but of course this never occurred to me, and we spent a pleasant enough summer. . . . We had no studio, but danced on the beach."[53] Irma recalled an unbroken flow of guests, from the composer Edgard Varèse to violinists Fritz Kreisler and Eugène Ysaÿe; the German painter Winold Reiss, later famous for his portraits of Native American life; Hans von Kaltenborn of the *Brooklyn Eagle;* Stuart Benson, poet and editor of *Collier's;* and the leaders of the New York wing of Dada, Marcel Duchamp and Francis

Picabia, with whom Isadora conducted an especially rambunctious affair. Mary Desti stayed at Long Beach for most of the summer, along with Elsa Maxwell, professional partygoer, future columnist, and author of the splendid advice "Never complain. Never explain. Never apologize."

On Long Island, Isadora enjoyed her first and only encounter with Sarah Bernhardt, the reigning legend of the Paris stage, then recovering from an operation in New York. Arnold Genthe offered to introduce them.

"How do I know she wants to meet me?" Isadora asked — according to Genthe, she had "a certain kind of humility" among the great: "What have I to give to one of her divine genius?" The day came when they encountered Madame Sarah on the boardwalk, "being wheeled towards us in her chair." Bernhardt said to Isadora, "Sit down here beside me."

"Ah, that would be too great an honor," Isadora replied. "I ought to be at your feet." Only then did she remember that Bernhardt, at seventy-three, had just had her left leg amputated.[54] "She did not generally take life too seriously," Irma suggested, "only her art."[55] Mercedes de Acosta, the Prince Valiant of American literary lesbians, met Isadora for the first time on the beach at Amagansett and "felt that the dunes, the reeds, the beach, the sea — all of these — in some strange way mingled with her and she was part of them." They would meet again later in Europe with resounding consequences.

"Always go barefooted whenever you can," Isadora advised Mercedes. "With your feet free your whole body assumes a natural grace. Contacting the earth barefooted revitalizes brain and body. It is a wonderful health cure. . . . Let me see how you move your body. Come, let's run." When they stopped, panting, Isadora seemed pleased: "Not bad — not bad. I wish I could have trained you when you were four years old. I could have made a dancer of you." Suddenly she began to talk about her children. "There is a fallacy in the saying that time heals any grief," she declared. "I do not believe this. I think in time we learn to hide grief so as not to become tiresome and boring to others. When my children were killed, I died too. . . . I, too, am dead." Mercedes recalled:

> I approached Isadora altogether differently from any other person in my life. I not only approached her differently but I also evaluated her differently and, in a manner of speaking, I saw her differently. I am quite sure of this. . . . In after years when many people were critical of her, I was always tolerant — tolerant of her violence, her recklessness,

of all her wild and uncontrolled love affairs. I understood all these passions in her as I could say I understand thunder, or a hurricane, or, in the case of her love affairs, as I understood a great cosmic maternal urge. Isadora was always the great mother in all her expressions of love — she could never truly be a mistress or a wife. She wanted ceaselessly to give of herself to all her loves as a mother gives to her child. And she gave herself indiscriminately because mothers, of which she was the supreme one, do not discriminate among their children.[56]

The wildest of Isadora's lovers in America was Francis Picabia, the short, hypersexed, drug-crazed Cuban-French artist and Dadaist, whose private fortune funded a great part of the Dada enterprise in New York. Manic, alcoholic, and addicted to opium, Picabia defined himself thus: "There is nothing modern about making love; however, it's what I like to do best." After his death, his widow reported that he had owned seven yachts and 123 automobiles, and "that was little compared to his women." In Isadora, briefly, he found the perfect playmate.

"Picabia could not live without being surrounded morning and night by a troupe of uprooted, floating, bizarre people whom he supported more or less," wrote Juliet Gleizes, who lived with her husband, French artist Albert Gleizes, upstairs from the apartment Picabia shared with Edgard Varèse in New York. At any hour a knock might come on the Gleizes' door, followed by Picabia's voice: "We are having a party. Come down."[57] One day Isadora presented him naked to their friends — she "thought nothing of nudity either," according to Louise Norton,[58] who summed up the spirit of the group: "Beauty for the eye, satire for the mind, depravity for the senses! Of such is the new kingdom of art. Amen." By this time Picabia's "steady diet of opium and sex alternated with delirium tremens, tachycardia, and preoccupation with death,"[59] which seemed only to strengthen his appeal to Isadora. "If you ever get tired of being Mme. Picabia, send me a telegram!" she told Picabia's next mistress of record, Germaine Everling. "Because I'd like to be, and this time — legitimately!"[60] (In the meantime, she consoled herself with violinist Eugène Ysaÿe and, according to report, with Elsa Schiaparelli's husband, William de Wendt.)

In September, Isadora returned to the city, taking a studio in the just completed Hôtel des Artistes on West Sixty-seventh Street. There followed "two distracted months"[61] with no money, no concert bookings, and increasingly heated arguments with the Isadorables. The girls, too, had found love on Long Island; the days were gone "when we lived like ensorcelled virgins in the depths of the woods," Theresa remarked, "hidden away from the world that might claim our hearts."[62]

"New York is no place for young girls," Isadora warned her disciples, urging them to "continue [their] studies" and "teach little children"[63] when she left for California in November, on what she hoped would become a national tour. But it was too late to stop the Isadorables' progress. Theresa fell in love with New York gallery owner Stephan Bourgeois, Irma with Edna Millay's future husband, Eugene Boissevain, Lisa with Max Eastman, and Erika with Winold Reiss, who helped cultivate her talent for painting and for whom she would soon leave Isadora and the troupe. Of all the girls, only Gretel seems not to have had a regular beau in New York; when she took the name Duncan, nevertheless, Gretel began to call herself Margot. More than ever the Isadorables wanted to dance — and live — on their own terms. Instinctively, they turned to Uncle Gus, Augustin, the gentlest and best loved member of the Duncan clan.

After twenty-five years on the New York stage, where he was known as a "modest violet" among actors, Augustin Duncan had finally come into his own. Gus was "an actor of the old school, robustious, full of voice and gesticulation," according to a press review in 1919, the year of his monumental success on Broadway in St. John Irvine's Irish tragedy, *John Ferguson*.[64] That same year, Augustin became one of the founding directors of the Theatre Guild in New York; with his contacts and advice, he helped launch the career of America's first heroic black actor, Paul Robeson.

Since the death of her children, Gus had given unstintingly to Isadora. He had helped her at each opportunity, had neglected his own family for her sake, and watched sadly now as she tried to stifle the Isadorables' hopes. "Why?" Anna wrote in later years. "Because he more than any person on this earth was devoted to her art, and believed in it so deeply and sincerely, that it should be saved for future generations and posterity to see, that he was willing to sacrifice his own career . . . for her cause."[65] Witnessing the girls' distress, Gus risked even more: in defiance of his sister, he arranged for the Isadorables to perform as a group at the Liberty Theater under the sponsorship of his friend and mentor, Isadora's onetime road manager, Charles Coburn.

"[I] am sure it will be a success if you believe in it," Anna wrote to Gus in gratitude. "*Alors en avant vers la victoire et de courage. . . .* It is a great life if we do not weaken."[66] The girls had already appeared for several nights at the Liberty when Isadora, to whom Gus broke the

news, cabled from California: I FORBID IT. THE GIRLS ARE NOT YET READY
FOR PERFORMANCES OF THEIR OWN. . . . [67] She was dancing in Los Angeles, where a hostile critic remarked that she "followed the music as a
bear might pursue a mouse" and where, in Pasadena, a young Julia
Child and her siblings, hiding behind bushes past their bedtime,
watched her dance at a garden party their parents gave in her honor.
Agnes de Mille, the future choreographer of *Rodeo* and *Oklahoma!* and
niece of Cecil B. De Mille, saw Isadora at a matinee at the Mason
Opera House.

"Children were taken as to a shrine," de Mille reported. "What they
saw, alas, was a prematurely aged and bloated woman, coarsened by
terrible trials, laboring through gossamer steps and classical evocation."
De Mille was eight years old at the time. The program ended with the
Marseillaise "and we had to stand," she remembered:

> Everyone wept for various reasons. I became aware that this audi-
> ence was reacting quite differently from any other theater or moving-
> picture audience I had ever before experienced. Nothing was happening
> onstage that seemed to me worthy of tears, yet they wept. Isadora wore
> a blood-red robe which she threw over her shoulder as she stamped
> to the footlights and raised her arms in the great Duncan salute. . . .
> This was heroic and I never forgot it. No one who saw Isadora ever for-
> got her.[68]

Bound by legal contract, using Isadora's name and Isadora's
dances, her students had no choice but to cancel the rest of their engagement at the Liberty. Augustin found himself "in an awkward position for having negotiated the whole thing with Coburn," Irma wrote.
"I believe it left a wound that never quite healed. . . . And there was
our displeasure. If she did not consider us ready now at the age of
twenty, she probably never would, we told ourselves."[69] They were right.

21

Sunk in Sorrow, Tossed in Joy

On November 19, 1917, Isadora arrived in San Francisco on the ferry from Oakland that her grandfather, Colonel Thomas Gray, first ran for profit in the 1850s. OAKLAND GIRL IS BACK HOME WITH WREATH OF FAME read a morning headline. To waiting reporters, she looked "slender and languid and very beautiful. She wore a Colonial costume, with a billowing cloak and gown"[1] and a black veil that covered her face. Redfern Mason, music critic for the *San Francisco Examiner,* met Isadora later that day at the St. Francis Hotel and pronounced her "a tired woman, deprecating any attempt to discuss her art and life in a few moments." She had just read the news of the death of Rodin. The "Great God Pan" had died two days earlier in Paris, at the age of seventy-seven.

"It is difficult to think of Paris without Rodin," Isadora told Mason that night at the St. Francis. "But Paris will never be without Rodin — his spirit is there." Her own art would die with her, she feared. Mason sensed that her return to the city "must have been an ordeal."[2] After ten years Isadora saw her mother again, writing nothing about their meeting except that Mrs. Duncan looked "very old and careworn. . . . I could not help contrasting my sad face and the haggard looks of my mother with the two adventurous spirits who had set out nearly twenty-two years ago with such high hopes to seek fame and fortune. Both had been found — why was the result so tragic?"[3] Mason called her "a pessimist" — "she talks like a Buddha spoiled by anarchism."[4] He would become her lover before she left California.

The 1906 earthquake had destroyed all eight of San Francisco's downtown theaters. Isadora performed at their most durable replacement, the Victorian-style Columbia (now the Geary), which opened in 1910, not far from the site of her birth at the corner of Geary and Taylor Streets. Nothing remained of the Duncan homestead now but "an empty place of rubble and sand, some weeds and nothing more."[5] At the Columbia she pulled out all the stops, dancing the leading works in her repertory over the course of four matinees: *Iphigenia*, the *Seventh Symphony*, Schubert, Tchaikovsky, Chopin, Brahms's waltzes, and always, in closing, the *Marseillaise*. In a second patriotic dance, Elgar's *Old Glory*, Isadora appeared as "Columbia incarnate, her eyes aflame, the intoxication of liberty in her cheeks." War fever gripped San Francisco — in the audience, women were knitting for the doughboys.

"That'll get recruits!" said a man next to Mason. "And he was right. The house went wild." A few blocks away, the Ruth St. Denis Dancers were performing at the Tait, but the day, and the critics, belonged to Isadora: "After all, this is the Hellas of the western world. . . . It was dateless art, the free play of a spirit that was old when the pyramids were young and is new now that they are crumbling."[6] The *San Francisco Bulletin* compared Isadora to Michelangelo and preferred her to any ballerina: "She has all of Pavlova's art, which she has made but a foundation alone for the spirit of a poet."[7] No homecoming welcome could have been more complete.

At the St. Francis, Isadora greeted Florence Treadwell Boynton, her earliest friend from Oakland, now married to a San Francisco attorney but still wearing Greek robes and sandals and raising her eight children in Berkeley on a diet of peanuts and honey. Florence was a Christian Scientist, a vegetarian, an advocate of outdoor schools, and the mistress of Berkeley's Temple of the Wings, built to her specification in 1914 in imitation of a Greek temple, without walls and open to the sky. Here, Florence lived out her free ideas, gave birth to her children under a grape arbor, and opened a successful school of dancing in the spirit of Isadora. "She was the only woman my mother wanted to keep up with," Florence's daughter recalled[8] — the Boynton family taught dance in the Berkeley hills for more than sixty years. Florence described Isadora's return to San Francisco in a memoir:

At her hotel, I received instructions to come right up to her apartment. I shall never forget the arms of love when Isadora opened her door and took me in. It was as if those arms of love could enfold all humanity in compassionate pity. Isadora with the lovely face, the deep thoughtful eyes — a great soul washed of much of the human element through sorrow and afflictions! . . . I had taken with me a young musician and my youngest child, three years of age. But Isadora could not endure the presence of a little child, so the musician and the baby waited in the reception room. . . . I said to Isadora, "I did not know you would feel this way or I would not have brought the child." She then apologized as for a weakness, but later referring to the incident said, "Of course no one could understand," in a way entirely foreign to Isadora, as if grief had an aristocracy of its own. . . .

Abruptly she said, "Look at me, I am a wreck." All one was conscious of was her beautiful face as she was heavily draped like the prophets of the Sargent [murals] in the Boston Library. . . . [She] seemed to cling to me and want me not to go; she insisted that I return the following evening and told me that I might bring my two little daughters.

When Florence arrived again at the St. Francis she found Isadora flirting with Redfern Mason:

She was gowned in black lace. She was brilliant, exquisite in thought and facial expression. . . . When [Mason] departed, early in the evening, Isadora jokingly and in play asked him when she should go to the priest to be "shrived and wived" and he replied in the same playful mood. She also said she never slept at night and to phone her after midnight.[9]

Mason was only one of Isadora's lovers in California. In Los Angeles, through their mutual friend Eugène Ysaÿe, she met pianist Harold Bauer, who had seen her dance in London years before and won her heart by saying that the event had changed his life. "To my amazement and delight, he told me that I was more of a musician than a dancer," Isadora wrote, "and that my Art had taught him the meaning of otherwise inscrutable phrases of Bach, Chopin, and Beethoven."[10] Bauer was a virtuoso, "prince among pianists,"[11] one of the first musicians to champion the work of Ravel and Debussy and a man of modest pretension. "I'm just a piano-player," he said, "with artistic principles and opinions like wax — *hot* wax, at that."[12] Isadora called him "my musical twin-soul." Bauer told of her reaction to his execution of a Chopin étude, "in the course of which the music appears to indicate a tremendous crescendo followed by a diminuendo, reaching the end of the phrase."

"You are playing this wrong," said Isadora. "This phrase must continue to crescendo until the end, and when it is finished after that you can fall down to a softer level."

"But . . . I must make this diminuendo," Bauer answered, indicating the sheet music.

"It cannot be done that way because if it were I would have nothing to do with my arms," Isadora replied. Later Bauer saw Chopin's original manuscript and was able to confirm her hunch: the composer's directions had been altered in subsequent printings.[13] He marveled at Isadora's musical intuition — in an interview with Mason, Bauer called her "that glorious woman."[14] Mason, in turn, let Isadora write the review of one of Bauer's concerts, which he published in the *Examiner* under his own byline: "Great Art is the highest and most dependable religion we have today and the message of a Beethoven through the Soul of a Harold Bauer a thousand times more [conducive to faith] than the dogma of any religion."[15] Not since Hener Skene had Isadora found a pianist so in tune with her ideas; but Skene had died on the western front in the early days of the war.

On January 3, 1918, Isadora and Bauer gave a joint recital at the Columbia Theater in San Francisco, an all-Chopin program they rehearsed for several weeks "in a wonderful collaboration of art." Mason felt the bond between them: "So intimately and perfectly did their art merge that it was difficult for the audience at the Columbia to tell which — if either — was the inspiration and which the inspired. . . . She danced with sheer joyousness, not in a crude realism . . . but in surges of psychic ecstasy and despair, upliftings of the spirit, the fantasy of dreaming, a divine drunkenness in which the mystery that veils music was momentarily lifted."[16] At their curtain call, Isadora took a chaplet of roses someone had thrown from the audience and laid it on Bauer's piano, at the same time bowing deeply from the waist. Bauer's wife arrived in San Francisco soon after and put an end to the affair.

Isadora went back to Mason, whose jealousy amused her. "Do you want me to be walking on my bare knees on broken glass?" she asked. "Aren't you glad I can still dance a Bacchanal & that sometimes in a quiet landscape I wish for a Faun to part the bushes and leap forth and seize a not unwilling nymph?"[17] Her California tour manager purportedly had absconded with her box-office earnings; Isadora's concert with Bauer was held as a benefit to rescue her finances. "Everything I get is taken away from me," she told Florence Boynton. "I have always gotten everything I have set my heart upon, but I have no sooner acquired my wish than it has been snatched away." Florence wanted to scream when she saw Isadora's *Ave Maria:* "She portrayed the parting [of her children] and lifted them upward, releasing them to the heavenly sphere. This was repeated so incessantly that it was almost insanity. . . . It was unendurably pathetic." Later, leaving her hotel for dinner with Mason, Isadora said, "'Florence, go home to your children,' almost like a warning, as if she realized she was taking me from them; and also as if in all the world it was that which she most desired to do, to go home to her own."[18]

"Can you know what it is to have had 3 Babies — & now have simply — arms?" Isadora wrote in a letter to Mason. "Can you understand to suffer so that one rushes to the Delirium of perhaps a false joy?" The Boyntons had hoped she might bring her school to the Temple of the Wings, but when local officials unaccountably denied her permission to dance at the Greek Theater in Berkeley, where Ruth St. Denis had performed just a few months before, Isadora turned her back on San Francisco. "I have shrieked aloud with agony," she wrote to Mason, "& I have screamed with joy but I won't no I will never admit" — and then she broke off. "I will tell you the rest when I see you — soon — *n'est-ce pas?*"[19]

By April 1918 Isadora was in Paris, having quarreled bitterly with her brother Augustin and the Isadorables as she passed through New York. The girls resented and refused her suggestion that they go back to Elizabeth's school, now under Mabel Dodge's patronage in Tarrytown, while Isadora tried to raise money abroad. "I am going back to France," she had said, "because I find conditions here more than I can bear. . . . I feel utterly disheartened and much too discouraged to continue."[20]

With Augustin's backing, and despite their teacher's opposition, the Isadorables would soon embark on a tour of American army camps with pianist George Copeland, billing themselves as the Isadora Duncan Dancers. Angry and defeated, Isadora ran up an enormous hotel bill in New York before Mary Desti persuaded Gordon Selfridge, the department-store king, to buy her a one-way steamship ticket to London. The Maison Desti had done well in the war: apart from

Mary's "ambre" cigarettes, Preston Sturges, before enlisting in the Army Air Corps, invented a "kiss-proof" lipstick, Red Red Rouge, that made his mother a lot of money.

"Many years ago I promised Isadora I would stand by her to the end," Mary wrote, "and on many occasions I gave up everything, flew to her whenever her school was on the rocks — but never was it so badly on the rocks."[21] The majority of Isadora's friends regarded Mary as a destructive influence, determined to indulge Isadora in any wildness or extravagance. According to Mercedes de Acosta, Mary "worshiped her to such an extent that she had taken on some essence of Isadora. Often Mary seemed to run things while Isadora behaved like a soft, purring kitten. But things were just the contrary. Isadora completely dominated Mary and, although it was true that she purred, it was the purring of a spoiled child. . . . Isadora always got her way. She could make anyone who opposed her wish seem like an absolute brute."[22]

Sailing to London, on her first night out, Isadora tripped and "fell down an opening in the deck, a drop of about fifteen feet." The fall sprained her hip and put her in bed for the rest of the trip. "Gordon Selfridge very gallantly put his cabin at my disposal," she wrote — she had reminded him of their first encounter in Chicago at Marshall Field's in 1895, "when a hungry little girl asked him for credit for a frock to dance in."[23] All the same, Selfridge disappeared when they got to London.

"I'm afraid it needed you," Isadora wrote to Mary — "& London needs you. . . . I find it a bit dark & *triste*. . . . I feel rather lost."[24] Kathleen Scott found her in rented rooms in Duke Street, St. James's, near Piccadilly Circus, "very fat, but still Isadora," and consorting with a "fat old freak called Angelo." To Kathleen, it seemed "sad oh so very sad." Alone, Isadora "wept at her lonely and sorrowful condition" and declared her life to be a failure — *"Ratée!"*[25] Later she wrote:

> I spent some terrible and gloomy weeks in that melancholy lodging, completely stranded. Alone and ill, without a cent, my school destroyed and the war appearing to go on interminably, I used to sit at the dark window at night and watch the air raids, and wish that a bomb might fall on me to end my troubles. Suicide is so tempting. I have often thought of it, but something always holds me back. Certainly if suicide pellets were sold in drug stores as plainly as some preventives, I think the intelligentsia of all countries would doubtless disappear overnight in conquered agony.[26]

One encounter brightened the London gloom. Through Kathleen, Isadora finally met George Bernard Shaw, Britain's greatest living man of letters (and an Irishman by birth). Kathleen had sculpted a bust of Shaw and they "got on together to perfection," although Shaw, in most company, "rather sat on the other guests." There was no chance of that with Isadora, who "made impassioned love" to him, according to Kathleen.[27] "Are you Shaw?" she asked.

"I am," said Shaw.

Isadora's arms rose in delight. "Come to me," she said, "I have loved you all my life!" Shaw remembered that she was "clothed in draperies" and that her "face looked as if it had been made of sugar and someone had licked it . . . rather like a piece of battered confectionery." As she aged, Isadora wore heavy makeup, eye shadow, and thick red lipstick: "She looked, in wine-red draperies, like a full-blown peony."[28]

"Though I may not be much to look at I'm very good to feel," Isadora joked,[29] leading Shaw by the hand to a sofa, where "for an hour," he wrote, "we performed the last act of *Tristan and Isolde*. . . . I can't remember all we said to one another, but I know the audience, which listened to every word, was very much amused. I think at first my hostess was a little nervous of how I would take the situation!"

On leaving, Isadora invited Shaw to her flat, "where, she declared, she would dance for me undraped. . . . She said just what she liked. Yet there was more in her than that. Somehow one didn't feel like telling her to go to the devil."[30] Kathleen did, before Isadora left for France. There were other drunken escapades and sloppy scenes, one in particular among the Bloomsbury group, when Isadora tossed herself at Virginia Woolf's brother-in-law, Clive Bell, crying, *"Je ne suis pas une femme! Je suis une génie!"* [I'm not a woman! I'm a genius!][31] She was "laid up for two months in London," as she later complained to Mary Fanton Roberts, "very broke in every sense of the word. . . . Augustin hasn't written me a line neither has Elizabeth."

At length, after "an agonizing time" and by "selling all the last trinkets,"[32] Isadora reached Paris, where she took another high-interest mortgage on the Neuilly house and moved to the Hôtel Palais d'Orsay. Here she saw old friends, such as remained from before the war: the poet Divoire, Mario Meunier and his sister-in-law, painter Christine Dalliès, and actress Cécile Sorel, whose bounty and patience saw Isadora over the worst humps of that spring. None of her friends or family in America answered her letters or appeals for money. "New York seems like some awful nightmare," she confessed to Mary Desti:

"If you could persuade Paris [Singer] to cable 1000 it would be salvation."[33] Even Mary didn't reply.

"Have sent you 6 letters and 4 cables," Isadora wrote on April 16. And ten days later: "Still not a word from anyone. . . . *Please* write me news. . . . What is Augustin doing — and the girls? . . . I am living here on Hope."[34] An affair with the flying ace Roland Garros helped take her mind off her troubles. Garros had just escaped from a German prison camp and had the distinction of being the first pilot in World War I to shoot down an enemy plane by firing through his propeller. On their way home from a party, Isadora watched a zeppelin raid with Garros in the place de la Concorde and danced to the crashing of bombs in the empty square, her companion applauding, his "eyes lit up by the fire that fell and exploded quite near us. He told me that night that he only saw and wished for death." So did she, or so she thought when the mood was on her. "I suffer from Neu-ras-then-ia," she wrote, "which malady translated means Incurable Sorrow & Heartbreak. I rush about the world trying to find a remedy — There is none."[35]

"Ace" Garros was killed in action in October 1918, only a month before the Armistice. By then Isadora had met the "Archangel" of her memoirs, pianist and composer Walter Morse Rummel. Christine Dalliès, now working as Isadora's secretary, introduced them in July. "What a pendulum is life," Isadora reflected, "the deeper the agony, the higher the ecstasy — each time the lower sinking in sorrow, the higher tossed in joy."[36] She described her first sight of Rummel in terms that recalled her meeting with Gordon Craig:

> When he entered I thought he was the picture of the youthful Liszt . . . so tall, slight, with a burnished lock over the high forehead, and eyes like clear wells of shining light. He played for me. I called him my Archangel. . . . And during the booms of the Big Bertha, and amidst the echoes of the war news, he played for me Liszt's "Thoughts of God in the Wilderness," St. Francis speaking to the birds, and I composed new dances to the inspiration of his playing, dances all comprised of prayer and sweetness and light, and once more my spirit came to life, drawn back by the heavenly melodies which sang beneath the touch of his fingers. This was the beginning of the most hallowed and ethereal love of my life.[37]

At thirty-one, Walter Rummel was one of Europe's best-known concert pianists, a former student of Leopold Godowsky and grandson of Samuel F. B. Morse, the American painter, inventor, and pioneer of telegraphy. Raised in Berlin but an American citizen, Rummel had lived in Paris since 1908, devoting himself to the study of early French music. His interest in plainsong from the age of the troubadours led to friendship and collaboration with Claude Debussy, the most modern of composers, whose music nevertheless issued straight from the French academic tradition. Before he was thirty, Rummel had edited two anthologies of early music, arranged choral works by Bach and Vivaldi for the piano, and was known as a performer of intense originality both in Europe and the United States, where he premiered a collection of Debussy's *Préludes* in 1910. Indeed, Rummel was one of the few pianists Debussy could tolerate playing his work — a "prince of virtuosos," in the composer's words.[38]

"One does not congratulate a sunset," Debussy wrote to Rummel in 1917, "nor does one congratulate the sea for being more beautiful than a cathedral! You are a force of nature."[39] Shaw heard Rummel in London and told him afterward: "You make Chopin stand out ten times bigger than he is." As a pianist, Rummel was gifted with a strong rubato, "a lyrical approach, and an effortless technique." A Paris critic noted that he was more artist than technician, aiming "to identify with the composers he plays and to put us directly in contact with them." Like Isadora, Rummel was given to prophetic dreams: through his mother, Leila Morse, he became a disciple of the German mystic Rudolf Steiner and a fervent anthroposophist. "His hair was long and hung upon his cheeks," wrote Frances Gregg, who knew Rummel in Paris when they were both in thrall to the modernist circle of Ezra Pound and Hilda Doolittle ("H.D."): "Those cheeks were pallid, a dewy robust pallor; his eyes were blue and like the Ice King's, so that to look into them was to think of Norse icebound wastes of water and scudding clouds."[40]

In her collaboration with Walter Rummel, Isadora's art reached new dimensions and what was probably its highest refinement — during their three years together, she won some of the best reviews of her career. Rummel was more than her accompanist and lover of record; he became her "musical advisor," helping her to mine "the primordial and impersonal emotion that rises from the innermost depths," as he described it in an essay printed for Isadora's theater programs.[41] This is what she had wanted from Harold Bauer: a happy cooperation of art and ardor, "an entire new domain of musical expression." That Rummel was ten years younger, married, and almost impossibly good-looking didn't disturb her. At forty-one, she had no fear of other women. "What nonsense to sing always of love and spring alone," she scoffed. "The colours of autumn are more glorious, more varied, and the joys of autumn are a thousandfold more powerful, terrible, beautiful. . . . I was the timid prey, then the aggressive Bacchante, but now I close over my lover as the sea over a bold swimmer, enclosing, swirling, encircling him in waves of cloud and fire."[42]

At first, Isadora and Rummel worked together without any thought of performing, for the joy of it, in a studio on avenue de Montesparn loaned to them by the actress Madame Réjane. Later in the summer of 1918, they moved south to Cap Ferrat, where they stayed for long stretches, through 1920. Isadora loved the Riviera. Her "first-born child" with Rummel was a Schubert impromptu. "It was like the dream of Catholics dead and gone to Heaven," she wrote. "Now and then we issued from our retreat to give a benefit for the unfortunate or a concert for the wounded, but mostly we were alone, and through music and love, through love and music, my soul dwelt in the heights of bliss."[43] For a time, evidently, Isadora drank nothing but milk; she was "reading The Lives of the Saints in forty volumes," as she wrote to Mary Roberts, and confessed to being "finally out of breath from this unequal battle with Destiny. . . . Dionysos has been a too Strenuous God to follow — *Je me repose*."[44] When she finally caught up with the Isadorables and learned that they were touring America, she responded generously, with advice. The girls would cherish her letter for the rest of their lives:

> Please don't let anyone persuade you to try to dance to Debussy. It is only the music of the *Senses* and has no message to the Spirit. And then the gesture of Debussy is all *inward* — and has no outward or upward. I want you to dance only that music which goes from the soul [upward] in mounting circles. . . .[45]
>
> Plunge your soul in divine unconscious *Giving* deep within it, until it gives to your soul its *Secret*. That is how I have always tried to express music. My soul should become one with it, and the dance born from that embrace. Music has been in all my life the great Inspiration and will be perhaps someday the Consolation, for I have gone through such terrible years. No one has understood since I lost Deirdre and Patrick how pain has caused me at times to live in almost a delirium. In fact my poor brain has been more often crazed than anyone can know. Sometimes quite recently I feel as if I were awakening from a long fever. When you think of these years, think of the Funeral March of Schubert, the *Ave Maria,* the *Redemption,* and forget the times when

my poor distracted soul trying to escape from suffering may well have given you all the appearance of madness.

I have reached such high peaks flooded with light, but my soul had no strength to live there — and no one has realized the horrible torture from which I have tried to escape. Some day if you understand sorrow you will understand too all I have lived through, and then you will only think of the light towards which I have pointed and you will know the *real* Isadora is there. In the meantime work and create Beauty and Harmony. The poor world has need of it, and with your six spirits going with one will, you can create Beauty and Inspiration for a new Life. . . .

Dear children, I take you in my arms. And here is a kiss for Anna, and here one for Therese, and one for Irma, and here is a kiss for Gretel and one for little Erika — and a kiss for you, dearest Lisel. Let us pray that this separation will only bring us nearer and closer in a higher communion — and soon we will all dance together *Reigen*. All my love. Isadora.[46]

Two years followed in relative peace, the calmest and most confident time Isadora had known since the death of her children. In her memoirs, she gave credit to Rummel: "Each time a new love came to me, in the form of demon or angel or simple man, I believed that this was the only one for whom I had waited so long, that this love would be the final resurrection of my life."[47] Two works of Liszt soon entered her repertory, each on the theme of sorrow and renewal: *Les Funérailles* and *La Bénédiction de Dieu dans la Solitude,* Liszt's "personal" expression of the human soul rising into heaven. Both were showpieces for Rummel's virtuosity.

Throughout their association, Isadora gave Rummel equal billing in what were advertised as joint recitals. With Rummel, she tackled Wagner again, working from Liszt's and other piano transcriptions of *Tristan, Tannhäuser,* and *Parsifal.* She revised and edited her extensive Chopin repertory into a single program of hope and rebirth, an allegory of the coming peace called *Poland Tragic, Poland Heroic, Poland Languorous and Gay.* When she took the Chopin package to Belgium after the war, Isadora changed the title to *Belgium Tragic, Belgium Heroic,* etc. It never failed to receive an ovation. In Rummel, she had found her perfect musical partner:

My Archangel had a very sweet sense of compassion. He seemed to feel all the sorrow which made my heart so heavy and which often caused me sleepless and tearful nights. . . . Often as I danced and he played, as I lifted my arms and my soul went up from my body in the long flight of the silver strains of the Grail, it seemed as if we had created a spiritual entity quite apart from ourselves, and, as sound and gesture flowed up to the Infinite, another answer echoed from above.

I believe that from the psychic force of this musical moment, when our two spirits were so attuned in the holy energy of love, we were on the verge of another world. Our audience felt the force of this combined power, and often a curious psychosis existed in the theatre such as I had not known before. If my Archangel and I had pursued these studies further, I have no doubt that we might have arrived at the spontaneous creation of movements of such spiritual force as to bring a new revelation to mankind.[48]

As to love, Rummel was divorced shortly after meeting Isadora. His first wife was Thérèse Chaigneau, a fellow musician, highly regarded, who "went insane" when Rummel left her; she spent the rest of her life in a Swiss asylum. Women in Rummel's life always seemed to come to grief: Margaret Cravens, a young American in search of art and beauty in Paris, shot herself in 1912, after Rummel announced his engagement to Chaigneau. To Isadora, "the miracle of love [was] the varied themes and keys in which it can be played."[49] In her autobiography, she wrote discreetly about Rummel's sexuality — rather, the lack of it — telling Victor Seroff later that he "preferred to make love to himself behind the closed doors of his room" and that she had spent most of her nights with Rummel alone and frustrated.[50] "He did not give way to passion with the spontaneous ardour of youth," Isadora wrote, "but, on the contrary, his loathing was as evident as the irresistible feeling which possessed him. He was like a dancing saint on a brazier of live coals." She had her hands full not scaring him away: "To love such a man is as dangerous as difficult. Loathing of love can easily turn to hatred against the aggressor."[51]

In October 1918 Isadora and Rummel left Cap Ferrat for a tour of the French provinces, getting as far as Marseilles, Bordeaux, Nantes, and Geneva before the global flu epidemic cut short their itinerary. Up to 40 million people died in the 1918 plague, nearly five times the number that had perished in World War I up till then. Just as suddenly, in November, the war ended. With a stroke of the pen, the Germans were defeated, to be replaced by a new and, ostensibly, more lethal enemy — socialism, Bolsheviks, "Reds." What was the Great War about? John Dos Passos wondered in *Nineteen Nineteen*, contemplating "the vast new No Man's Land of Europe reeking with murder and the lust of rapine, aflame with the fires of revolution."[52] Among Woodrow Wilson's Fourteen Points for peace was the call for "intelligent and unselfish sympathy" and cooperation with Russia's newborn Soviet state, but Wilson's idealism went the way of all nobility at the Paris Peace Conference in 1919. A generation of men had been wiped out in the European slaughter; Germany lost, only to rearm and rise more hideously in the years ahead. The war stopped, but it never ended.

After the Armistice, Isadora and Rummel returned to Paris, with the hope of reopening Bellevue, both as a school and the "new Bayreuth," Isadora's ultimate legacy to the French nation. She had served France well in the war and gave no thought to abandoning her role as a national heroine. "We watched the victory march through the Arc de Triomphe," she wrote, "and we shouted, 'The world is saved.' For the moment we were all poets. . . ."[53] Allan Ross Macdougall, still in American uniform, caught up with Isadora in her suite at the Palais d'Orsay early in 1919. She introduced him to Rummel, and they took a walk through the Tuileries gardens before lunch. Macdougall wrote:

> I can still remember her sprightly step, her high good humor and her jokes about the classical statues that sprout all over the gardens. I still recall, too, the excitement of the lunch served in Isadora's salon. There was the dancer's favorite Pommery Sec to celebrate our reunion and a special sole dish. After the first taste of the sole she asked the waiter if he were sure the fish were fresh. Turning to me, she said: "How does it taste to you, Dougie?" I could only say that for me, after months of slumgullion and cheerless chow, it was ambrosia. But Isadora, with a grand wave of her hand and a backward toss of her short auburn hair told the hovering waiter to remove it. "The poor boy," she said to him in French. "The poor boy is an American *poilu* whose taste has been dulled by his terrible war experience!"
>
> During the rest of the regal meal I remember . . . Isadora telling me that the American Army had taken over her big Bellevue house outside Paris for its art school, under Lorado Taft [the Chicago sculptor]. There was a laughing promise that when they were all cleared out and I, too, was demobilized, we would all — including the six "Isadorables" — be installed there in an idyllic, arcadian existence, where nothing else would matter but the Dance, Music and Art.[54]

But nothing would be the same in Paris after the war. To the survivors, France's golden *avant-guerre* seemed as distant and unreal as the days of Marie Antoinette. In 1919, when the U.S. Army finally decamped, Isadora found Bellevue in ruins. The house had served as a hospital for five years; it had been shelled in the war and was partly burned. Paul Poiret's "weird" decorations in the hallways and rooms were lost forever. "Still, we thought, why not rebuild it?" Isadora wrote. "And we spent some deluded months endeavouring to find the funds for this impossible task."[55] More than ever, she feared that her dance would not survive her. It became her essential lament.

On July 24, 1919, Isadora and Rummel gave a concert in what had once been the *salon bleu* at Bellevue, charging a hundred francs a ticket for a select group of friends, colleagues, and national dignitaries. The sum raised was only a fraction of what Isadora needed to restore the house. *"Il ne faut pas que Bellevue meure!"* she cried to her guests. (Bellevue must not die!) That day Isadora danced her Chopin tribute to Poland. In the *Marche Funèbre,* said Fernand Divoire, "she was not just the chief mourner but the tombstone, too, and death, and the deceased, and resurrection, and immortality."[56] Sisley Huddleston, Paris correspondent for *The Times* of London, remembered how anxious Isadora had been before the performance: "She had lost that lightness, that suppleness. . . . I shall not forget the accents of her voice, when she said to me: 'I have learned so much in the school of sorrow.'" During the dance itself, she sprained her ankle. "It is not money that is needed," she concluded, "it is a miracle."[57]

With Rummel and Christine Dalliès, Isadora soon left Paris for a tour of Switzerland, arranged by her former manager Maurice Magnus — "little Magnus," as Craig had called him in Berlin. Later in 1919 the trio found its way to North Africa, on a tour of Arab countries about which little is known. The journey lasted a month. Christine Dalliès snapped pictures of Isadora and Rummel in their desert garb — it is reported to have been "a happy time."[58] Rummel wrote Divoire from Algeria: "In the sun at last — a marvelous chance to open the School here, many Negro pupils, government backing with big subsidy and a splendid site. . . . Isadora enthusiastic. Sees the future of the dance in Africa."[59] What went wrong with the venture no one knows. The woman who supposedly shouted, "Niggers!" to an audience in Buenos Aires left no record of her African tour.

Passing through Rome with Rummel on her way back to Paris, Isadora sent a note to Gordon Craig. They had met only once since her children died: "I should love to see you if you are free — telephone tomorrow — or send me a word — Isadora."[60] On her personal stationery she still used the crest Craig had designed for her in Berlin in 1905. Craig, too, felt nostalgic: "If ever I have wept those tears were all joy . . . if ever I have hurt you I have hurt myself far more — you have never hurt me. . . . I have nothing to forgive, and everything to remember."[61] He wrote after Isadora's visit:

> We came together again for a brief moment in Rome . . . the night of December 12 [1919], Friday . . . This to a day was 15 years after we had first met. . . . We walked & walked arms linked in the darkest Rome (it was as we passed an occasional shaded lamp, for the lights were dimmed in Rome, that I turned my head to see her dear face.) — we talked of nothings as we walked & again our hearts SANG — we were weeping as we walked but we walked all that away & ended smiling. Just to stand together was to us supreme intoxication.[62]

According to Craig, Isadora hoped to revive their romance. "For so long I have only turned my head looking back & weeping for the past," she wrote the next day. "Now when I see you Life seems again full of Hope & Joy & Enthusiasm, & everything seems possible, Even a Future!"[63] Craig was touched but "knew it would be wrong — an error in every way."[64] His life had settled down comfortably in a villa near Rapallo, sometimes with Elena, but more often not. A number of women came and went, with or without a baby. Craig's son Ted, now working as his assistant, described Isadora as "sad and disillusioned" during their one and only encounter.[65] Craig did his best to cheer her up when she left:

> Don't forget — you are a great being — Act as you have always done — greatly — my beloved — & when in doubt — go one better. . . . "The past" — "the present" . . . "future" . . . all these are words which have some meaning when used in speaking of most people — *they have nothing whatever to do with you* — They have not touched you, nor can they. . . . Dear dear dear Isadora . . . All the days & years with their sorrows of regret dance with me at this moment with LOVE. . . . You are one of the greatest of beings comparable only with — no one.[66]

Isadora's concert engagements in 1920 were prodigious, comprising a *Festival of Music and Dance* that brought her to the Trocadéro in March and April, Holland and Brussels in May, and back to Paris in June for the close of the season at the Champs-Elysées. She wrote to the press about the new aim of her work, offering her art to the nation as "spiritual concerts," a healing force, "consolation to the sorrowing and to the afflicted." Where was the joy of the Allied victory? Isadora demanded: "Who among you can proclaim joy today?" Paris was filled with "profane music" and shiny amusements. "Distraction can be destruction," Isadora warned.[67] Her reviews were mainly reverential — "A priestess . . . a goddess . . . She is a whole temple, this woman!" — and her name alone still filled the Trocadéro. But "like most of us," a critic wrote, "she is not as young as she was."[68] Sisley Huddleston thought Isadora had "gained as well as lost" with the years but doubted she could take her work much further:

> She was slower, heavier, more deliberate in her movements, and indeed had reduced her movements to a minimum. She employed fewer and fewer gestures, stood stationary in the center of the stage. She was at times a mere point which held the eye while one listened to the music. . . . With all her great gifts, it is necessary to remind her that the Greek dance had its roots in popular feeling and popular understanding, and it is putting too great a strain upon her admirers to ask them to be satisfied with witnessing the faint stirring of an arm from time to time.[69]

"To think that it was once at my feet . . . all Paris," Isadora told a reporter, "and now . . . I guess there's nothing left to me but Greece." In the end, defeated, she sold Bellevue to the French government for a million francs, consistently reported as being "a fraction of its true value." The mansion would be used thereafter, as it still is, for scientific and military research.

"Don't think that I'm feeling sorry for myself," Isadora said as she looked at Paris a final time from the rooftop: "I don't in the least feel like crying over spilt milk . . . but I would like to come up here at night, alone, and just bay at the stars like some lost dog. I think I'd feel better!"[70] At least she was out of that "awful muddle," as she wrote to Craig. "How wonderful it would be to walk with you in the Temple of Karnak. . . . Perhaps if we went to Karnak or Abydos we would find our former ghosts — who were probably les très chic types & knew better how to adjust themselves to this Earth than me." Craig left a note on Isadora's letter: "My dear — my dear."[71]

At Easter, Isadora added Berlioz's *Enfance du Christ* to her *Chopin Festival* and her regular offerings of Beethoven, Schubert, Tchaikovsky, and Wagner, whom she continued to perform despite a general ban on Wagner's music in France. A sour and grudging spirit infested Paris after the peace of Versailles: for the first time, Isadora heard her *Marseillaise* attacked as "impious" and disrespectful, "an affront to the public!" With the war now won, "tampering" with the national anthem "to indulge choreographic whims" seemed to many a desecration of the great sacrifice. "Botch the works of foreign composers!" a critic warned Isadora.[72] Beyond that, she paid the price of any middle-aged woman in the performing arts. "If you didn't see her when she was twenty, you never saw her at all," said Russian ballet critic André Levinson.[73] Levinson was the ultimate ballet purist, and Isadora's body, as it aged, proved more than his vision could compass. By 1920 it was plain that her art, once revolutionary, had grown apart and aside from the dominant trend of dancing in the theater.

"Who, then, said this woman was a dancer?" asked Paris journalist Pierre Scize. "The most agreeable of mimes, a tragedian, perhaps, a sculptor, as well. A dancer? Truly no!"[74] That same year, the Ballets Russes and the avant-garde Ballets Suédois both performed in Paris, leading a wit to remark that, with Isadora, "the Cause, the Effect, and the After-Effect" had appeared in a single season.[75] Isadora responded manfully: "I have but opened a door. This door must never be allowed to close."[76]

Through everything, from stages still heaped with flowers at the final curtain, Isadora talked about her school. "Give to me," she cried, "ask your president to give to me, one hundred war-orphans and in five years I will give you — this I promise — beauty and riches beyond imagining." If France declined to help her, she warned, she would "go to Russia with the Bolshevists."[77] The announcement brought gasps from her audience. After the revolutions of 1917, Russia was still at war — White versus Red. So feared and despised were the Bolsheviks in Europe, and so scarce any reliable information about them, that a Russian friend of Isadora's had told her they were "slaughtering four-year-old children and hanging them up by their limbs in butcher shops." Isadora answered, "Well, if this is all true, then I *must* go."[78] She would open her school "on Mars" if she had to and leave "with pleasure . . . by the next scientific rocket!"[79]

"I know nothing about [Soviet] politics," Isadora insisted. "I am not a politician. But I will say to the leaders 'Give me your children, and I will teach them to dance like Gods or . . . assassinate me.' They will give me my school or they will assassinate me. For if I do not have

my school I would like better to be killed. It would be much better."
To her audience at the Théâtre des Champs-Elysées, where her dancing figure ringed the auditorium in the murals and bas-reliefs of Bourdelle and Maurice Denis, she continued:

> When I was twenty-two [sic] I offered my school to Germany. The
> Kaiserin responded that it was "Immoral!" and the Kaiser said it was
> "Revolutionary!" Then I proposed my school to America but they said
> there that it stood for "the vine . . . and Dionysos." Dionysos is Life, is
> the Earth, and America is where they drink lemonade. And how can
> one dance on lemonade? I then proposed my school to Greece, but the
> Greeks were too busy fighting the Turks. To-day I propose my school
> to France, but France in the person of the amiable Minister of Fine
> Arts gives me a smile. But I cannot nourish the children in my school
> on a smile. They must live on fruits and the milk and honey of Hymet-
> tus . . . As for me I await.[80]

With the money she earned from the sale of Bellevue, Isadora
leased a house at 103, rue de la Pompe, in the fashionable Passy district. The building contained a small theater, called the Salle Beethoven,
and here, with Rummel, she continued to work. "How pitiful that
earthly passion should have put an end to this holy pursuit of highest
beauty," she wrote. "For, just as in the legend, one is never content but
opens the door for the bad fairy, who introduces all sorts of trouble."

In April, Isadora had cabled her students to join her in Paris. In
August they arrived, "young and pretty and successful. My Archangel
looked upon them — and fell — fell to one."[81] It was Anna.

22

The Bad Fairy

For two years the Isadorables had enjoyed an independent success in America, dancing from coast to coast, and often in towns where Isadora herself had never appeared. Between 1918 and 1920 Augustin arranged two long tours for the girls, the second under the management of Sol Hurok, the Russian-born impresario, then just starting his career. Hurok began as a small-time concert-booker for left-wing and labor organizations and went on to become the American manager of Anna Pavlova, Marian Anderson, Isaac Stern, the Ballets Russes, and Isadora — a mighty list, dense in temperament. "If they're not temperamental, I don't want them," Hurok famously said. "It's in the nature of a great artist to be that way."[1] In time, "S. Hurok Presents" would be synonymous with foreign dance performance in America.

Hurok booked the Isadorables on a recommendation, having discovered that they "sold out six performances at Carnegie Hall in June — an unheard-of achievement."[2] With George Copeland and, later, Beryl Rubinstein at the piano, the girls' success was impressive around the country; genius being mortal, their ensemble work probably left a more lasting impression on American modern dance than Isadora's solo concerts did. "Dancing as pure abstraction (without drama)," writes Elizabeth Kendall, "dancing as ensemble patterns — these were Isadora's advanced concepts that lodged themselves here in the twenties through Denishawn's cruder efforts."[3] Sigmund Spaeth reported in the *New York Mail*:

> There can be no doubt of the fitness of the Duncan Dancers to carry on the unique art created by Isadora Duncan. It makes little difference whether they appear singly or in groups, always they impart the same involuntary thrill that comes only when art is based on something very real. . . . Whether it is Anna's interpretive art, or the rhythmic certainty of Theresa, or Lisa's airy leaps, or the dramatic eloquence of Irma . . . there is always the effect of a youthful spontaneity, a direct challenge to everything that is artificial and insincere.[4]

In San Francisco, Redfern Mason met Mrs. Duncan at the Isadorables' concerts, "happy to see her daughter's art pulsating and young in another generation." For Mason, like many, "Lisa of the golden curls" was the most compelling of the six, "kin to Undine of romantic legend." They all stood out in different ways: "Erika, the dreamy-eyed . . . Margot, the sylph . . . Theresa, the loveliest of all . . . the most like Isadora . . . waltzing, whirling through an immense quiet."[5] Anna reported "warm and enthusiastic houses" wherever they went, but these were not words to describe Isadora, and the girls knew it. Her dance revolution was already accomplished; in America the mood was cynical, satirical, and "sophisticated." A critic in New York objected to "so much stress put on emotion for emotion's sake" in the Isadorables' dancing, adding that their technique "needs a lot of watching, especially in the feet where all but the little, yellow-haired Lisa seem to be stiff."[6]

In October 1919, still hoping to rescue Bellevue, Isadora first approached the girls about returning to France. "If you knew how happy it makes me to receive letters from you, you would all write oftener," she scolded Irma that fall. "Perhaps you would all like to come in the spring? But tell me frankly your ideas and wishes. . . . If you were here we would study the 9th Symphony [of Beethoven] to celebrate the Peace." She had stopped writing to Augustin and Elizabeth, she said, "as they never answered even *once*."[7]

In Paris, Isadora had Raymond to contend with. Penelope Duncan had died of tuberculosis in Switzerland in 1917. Raymond came back to Paris with thirty of his followers; a new companion, Aia Bertrand; and his mature philosophy of actionalism, which held that the industrial machine, not love of money, was "the root of all evil" and from which Raymond derived a new technique of dance and stage movement, based on "all actions of normal human labor."[8] At his shop on the Right Bank, Raymond sold his colony's handwoven goods and became a magnet for American tourists. Isadora called him "the chamber of commerce in Greek disguise," according to Irma, who added: "A sack of beans and goat's cheese go a long way, [and] he had cleverly invested in real estate."[9]

In May 1920 Raymond took Isadora to court to keep her from giving the name Duncan to her students. His suit was overturned, but not his determination. The Isadorables were *"vampires, vipères et cochonnes,"* in Raymond's opinion — vampires, vipers, and swine[10] — who never did and never would understand the gift Isadora gave them, a gift he, Raymond, with the rest of the Duncan family, had helped give to her. The girls heartily returned his dislike. "With his long hair," Irma wrote, "rolled up into a ribbon stretched across his forehead, dressed in long-fringed, graying, woolen, homespun garb, he looked more like an Indian squaw . . . than a neo-Greek."[11] Isadora's friends avoided Raymond as a matter of course (he lectured them against drinking, smoking, and meat-eating, among other things), but Isadora, even with a lawsuit on her hands, refused to hear a bad word about "little brother." They were drawn more tightly together when they learned that their mother, Mary Dora, was dying in California. Raymond would bring Mrs. Duncan to Paris the following year, after Isadora left for Russia.

On May 16, 1920, the *New York Times* reported that the Isadorables had failed in their petition to become Duncans by law — evidently Isadora neglected to send her written consent. What became of the case after that is difficult to track, but certainly the girls were never "adopted" by Isadora, as is commonly supposed. Three of them — Irma, Anna, and Lisa — would use the Duncan name for the rest of their lives. Erika, the youngest, now chose painting and Winold Reiss, her teacher, over a doubtful career on the stage. Erika had already decided to leave the group when Isadora's second summons came, in April 1920. She proposed to teach her students new dances from the *Pathétique,* Beethoven's Seventh, and the last two movements of Schubert's Seventh Symphony, "her hymn to the goddess Diana." The girls were badly divided in their response.[12]

"She says we can meet anywhere," Anna told her parents, "what she means by that I don't know. . . . My place is now here [in America], and I really can't — none of us can wait around Isadora any longer without working until she actually feels like teaching us something. If we dance with her in Paris it will be in only one or two numbers. I'm sorry to have to say this, but it is true."[13] Theresa wanted to leave for France on the next boat — "We needed [Isadora] and felt under obligation for all she had done and meant to us"[14] — while Lisa and Margot wanted the older girls to decide. Irma refused to go without a contract, finally. Hurok had already booked the six into Carnegie Hall in October; Irma demanded Isadora's written guarantee of release at the end of the summer.

To everyone's surprise, Isadora agreed. "But once I held it in my hands," Irma wrote, "I instantly realized the complete futility of this gesture. It was just a piece of paper."[15] The *Times* reported laconically on the Isadorables' last performance in New York: "As usual, they did it very well, and the two known as Anna and Lisa did it a little better than the others. A few of the things that Lisa did with Chopin . . . were just a little bit better than anything else — but there, perhaps, nature contributed even more than art."[16] Irma noted on May 27: "So all is well. This is Isadora's birthday."[17]

The girls arrived in Paris at the end of June, only to learn that they were headed for Greece, to Kopanos, which Isadora meant to reclaim after Raymond's departure. "Let us all go to Athens and look upon the Acropolis," she declared, "for we may yet found a School in Greece." She had written to Greece's newly restored strongman and premier, Venizélos, asking his help in founding a national gymnasium of Duncan dance in Athens. Upon returning to power, Venizélos had exiled King Constantine and the Greek royal family and erected a puppet monarchy under Constantine's second son, Alexander, who was married to a commoner and obediently became one with the people. Thus, Isadora could think of modern Greece, like Soviet Russia, as "a new world" in the making. Venizélos's warm response to her ideas settled the matter: he offered Isadora the use of the Zappeion for rehearsals. There she would train "a thousand children for great Dionysian festivals in the Stadium."[18]

Isadora, Rummel, and the girls were packed and ready to leave Paris in July, when Anna came down with appendicitis. "This necessitated a change of plans," Irma wrote.[19] Having booked passage to Greece from Venice, Isadora sent the other girls ahead to the Lido with Christine Dalliès, keeping Rummel at her side while she waited for Anna to recover. The normally quiet and brooding Rummel had responded warmly to the girls.

"My Archangel," Isadora wrote, "among this bevy of flower-crowned maidens, resembled Parsifal in Kundry's garden, only I began to notice a new expression in his eyes, which spoke more of earth than of Heaven. I had imagined our love so strong in its intellectual and spiritual fastness that it was some time before the truth dawned on me."[20] Her effort to keep Rummel to herself had misfired: alone with Anna, Rummel fell in love.

"We expected Isadora [in Venice] today," Irma wrote in her diary on August 7, "but no sign of her yet." Then:

> *August 8* (Sunday): They came today. . . . Isadora invited me for a gondola ride. . . . She appeared to be in a state of shock. Very taciturn and morose. It seems she and the Archangel had a serious quarrel.
>
> *August 13* (Friday): Seems that Anna and the Archangel have fallen in love. Isadora is awfully jealous. She made us all move to the Danieli, forsaking the Excelsior and the Lido. I said to Christine: *"Cette histoire avec Anna et l'Archange est vraiment embêtante. Il parait qu'elle est amoureuse de lui, mais lui [il] aime beaucoup Isadora."* [This business with Anna and the Archangel is really a pain. It seems she's in love with him, but he loves Isadora.][21]

Anna later maintained that her affair with Walter Rummel was nothing but an innocent flirtation until they returned to Paris from Greece, in the fall of 1920. On Irma's evidence, this seems inexact, but no record tells how far the romance had progressed before Anna and Rummel, separately, left Isadora or how the three managed to live together for as long as they did, out of respect for their higher selves, that is, as artists. "One can't argue about this kind of thing," Isadora decreed. "Either one is [in love] or one isn't."[22] Anna remembered "four months where I had to grind my teeth and be terribly sensible to be able to stay on."[23] At first, Isadora hoped only to wait out the crisis. Rummel's love was music, not women, as she well knew, and she was Isadora: she believed in free love and the emancipation of her sex. For reasons of policy as well as pride, she could regard no other woman as her rival, much less Anna, one of her "little pupils." But Anna was "so lovely looking, so small and delicate and white," seven years younger than Rummel, with dark, almond eyes "and then that husky voice. . . ."[24] When Isadora intercepted "a meeting of their eyes, flaming with equal ardour in the scarlet sundown," she fell to jealousy like any other mortal:

> All my experience availed me nothing, and this was a terrible shock to me. From then on, an uneasy, terrible pain possessed me, and

in spite of myself I began to watch the indications of their growing love with feelings which, to my horror, sometimes awakened a demon akin to murder. . . . Never to such a degree had I been possessed by such a terrible passion as I now felt. I loved, and, at the same time, hated them both. . . . I cannot understand such a possession now, but, at the time, it enmeshed me and was as impossible to escape as scarlet-fever or small-pox.[25]

By coincidence, Isadora met up with Edward Steichen before she left Venice, where the photographer had gone in search of a rest after separating from his wife, Clara. Isadora and Steichen had known each other for years, both in Paris and New York. Clara Steichen, always jealous of Steichen's women friends, routinely accused them of adultery and dragged Isadora's name into a New York divorce court the following year. "How on earth a person can execute — can daily *live* such beautiful things as her dances & still have such a common *low* view of life . . . is beyond me," Clara Steichen said. Isadora told Steichen that there was nothing so "terrible or immoral as a virtuous *woman*."[26] Now she lured him to Athens with the pledge that, when they got there, she would let him film her dancing on the Acropolis. If only to pique Rummel's interest, she needed a more attentive male companion — Rummel had retreated into his music, overcome with guilt about his feelings for Anna. Apart from the Isadorables, the only other woman on the trip was Christine Dalliès, a painter and "an old maid," as she has gone down on record, "or rather an old bachelor in skirts."[27] They all left for Athens on August 17.

At the last minute Anna balked: surely it would be better for all if she went back to Paris. "Be sensible," Isadora commanded her in an urgent note. She would stick to her own principles, at least: "In any case I will not start out for Greece with Walter unless you come — He would simply be sad & miserable all the way and no possibility of work or pleasure either. . . . All these things are too important to let personal feelings interfere — I beseech you be reasonable and you will not regret it."[28] The party arrived in Athens on August 22, in the hottest days of summer.

"We found Kopanos a ruin," Isadora wrote, "inhabited by shepherds and their flocks of mountain goats." Immediately, she put the girls to work with wheelbarrows and brooms; installed her carpet, curtains, and piano; and hired an architect to construct a new roof for the building. There was still no water on the property. For weeks the girls did little but cart and carry, reliving Isadora's bare-knuckle experience of Kopanos in 1903. "Every day we went to the Acropolis," she wrote; "it was for me an intensely touching sight to see the youthful forms of my pupils . . . realising a part, at least, of the dream that I had had there sixteen years before." If the girls arrived from New York with "certain affectations and mannerisms," they lost them quickly under Isadora's watch: "I taught my pupils each day, and continued plans for the school in Athens, upon which everything seemed to smile."[29]

At the Parthenon, predictably, Isadora withdrew her pledge to be filmed by Steichen. "She always said she was so completely overwhelmed by what she felt there that she could not pose," Steichen recalled. He finally captured her portrait one morning with a borrowed Brownie camera as she stood in the west portal of the Parthenon:

> She did promise to pose for me for some still photographs. . . .
> The camera was set up far enough away to include the whole portal
> wall. The idea was that she was to do her most beautiful single gesture,
> the slow raising of her arms until they seemed to encompass the whole
> sky. She stood there for perhaps fifteen minutes, saying, "Edward, I
> can't. I can't do it. I can't do it here." But finally, after several tries, I saw
> the arms going up. I waited to catch a particular instant near the apex
> of the movement. Then we went around to the portico with its line of
> columns. She removed her cloak and stood there in her Greek tunic.
> And here she contributed what only an artist like Isadora could con-
> tribute. She made a gesture completely related to the columns. . . . She
> was a part of Greece, and she took Greece as a part of herself.

Steichen's portraits of Isadora at the Acropolis are among the most famous pictures ever taken, published later that year in *Vanity Fair* and reproduced in dozens, if not hundreds, of volumes of American art photography. Another shows Isadora with Anna and Theresa at the Erechtheum, their arms raised and flattened on their heads in line with the capitals that support the caryatid columns above them, Isadora standing just higher than the girls, half in and half out of immortality. *Wind Fire*, Steichen's stunning portrait of Theresa alone on a high rock outside the temple, the wind blowing through the silk of her tunic so hard that it looks like flame, betrays the impermanence and evanescence of dance: "The wind pressed the garments tight to her body, and the ends were left flapping and fluttering. They actually crackled." Like Rummel and Anna, Theresa and Steichen had coupled off. "Unlike Isadora," Steichen said, "Theresa had no feelings of conflict."[30] Again Isadora's aim misfired: she encouraged the girls to find beaux in Athens, hoping it would take their minds off their careers. It didn't help that Rummel was still racked with guilt and broodier than ever, leaving Anna and Isadora both in doubt of his intentions.

"My feelings have not changed in either sense, and I am eaten by a terrible struggle and whirlwind," Rummel wrote to Isadora later — he addressed her as "Great One" in their correspondence: "I love the child [Anna], but not enough to separate her in my feeling from you, nor to want her to separate from her work, nor through her to lose you."[31] One woman had already killed herself in frustration over Rummel — it fell to Isadora to strive for "spiritual heights above all this." She couldn't banish Anna from the only home she had known, nor did she want to lose her Archangel, "who was," however, "more and more rapidly taking on the resemblance of a human being." At a demonstration for Venizélos in the Athens Olympic stadium, Isadora pledged to create "a thousand magnificent dancers" for Greece and was crowned with a wreath of laurel before fifty thousand people — in these times, she could forget about Rummel and Anna altogether: "What do petty passions matter in face of my Great Vision, I thought, and beamed at them with love and forgiveness." One ardent glance between the lovers, however, "silhouetted against the moon," sufficed to throw her completely off track. "The only resource I had was to assume an armour of exaggerated gaiety and try to drown my sufferings in the heady wines of Greece," she wrote. "There might certainly have been a nobler way, but I was not then capable of finding it. . . . But probably everyone seeks to avoid their own disaster and torment in the only way they can."[32]

By the end of September, all the girls were sick. Margot's health was always fragile. Theresa had sunstroke, Lisa a cold, Anna a blood infection, and Irma strep throat: "Isadora suffered mostly from bad humor."[33] She reacted snootily when Steichen read Carl Sandburg's venomous attack on Reverend Billy Sunday, the American "baseball preacher," from a spot on the Acropolis where Pericles had once addressed the city of Athens. Sandburg was Steichen's brother-in-law, "the new Whitman," critics said: "You come along squirting words at us, shaking your fist and calling us all dam fools so fierce the froth slobbers over your lips. . . ."

"That's wonderful," said Isadora, whom Sunday had frequently attacked at his revival meetings, "but is it poetry?"[34] Tensions mounted until Irma, early in October, reminded her of their contractual agreement.

"She told us quite frankly that she opposed our return to the States," Irma recalled. "A huge argument resulted. . . . I suggested quite logically, so it seemed to me . . . that we fulfill our contract and then return to her. But she would have none of this."

"I did not bring you up to teach you my art, only to have you exploited by theatrical managers!" Isadora cried. Irma could take her "ugly Broadway spirit" back to New York — by herself. There would be a boat leaving that day, no doubt, from Piraeus.

In shock, Irma packed her things. The other girls were silent — they had "meekly given in."[35] Later that day, Irma appealed to Isadora from the Hotel Angleterre:

> What a waste and what a crime. . . . I can't thank you for what you have done for me, because it has been all in vain. On the contrary, I should rather curse the day you took my hand and led me to the school — your hand that always pointed upwards, that made us feel that there is something beyond, something greater than Life. . . . Willingly I wanted to be led and now you turn around with a frown on your face and point your finger at me and say that you see into my soul and what you see is . . . Isadora, do you really think you have the eyes of God? Maybe only small, very small, earthly, petty things are obscuring your vision. Perhaps if you had tried to look with a little more love and understanding you would have been able to see.

Isadora preferred to forget the quarrel — on her own terms. "Do not believe the words which were wrung from me in anger by your extraordinary exasperating attitude," she told Irma in reply. "You must confess that the things you say sometimes would make a saint angry." In a second note she softened and repeated what Irma already knew: that her art, their dancing, was "not for *you* or *me* but *for the generations to come*. . . . I only have a few more years to do it. Won't you help me? Before I die, at least one hundred beings must *understand* the work and give it to others. . . . I don't ask any of you to sacrifice all your Life for the School. I only want you to give a part of each year to helping me. . . . Come this morning & work — Forgive any thing I have said that has wounded you. I did not mean it."

Irma stayed. "I think if we don't speak to each other we understand each other better," she told Isadora. Isadora thought so, too.

"Your letter has made me *happy*," she wrote. "Now, hand in hand, we will go forward and conquer the world in *harmony* and *love*."[36]

Neither her own jealousy nor her students' rebelliousness ended Isadora's plans for the school in Greece, but a monkey bite to the leg of the shadow king, Alexander, who died of blood poisoning from his wound in October 1920.[37] With Alexander's death, Venizélos fell, the legitimists were back, and Isadora returned to France, her hopes crushed another time.

In Paris the Isadorables took a furnished flat not far from Isadora's house in rue de la Pompe. "Here we were left to struggle along financially as best we could," Irma reported. "The famous contract we signed with Isadora, being of no further value, we tore up and threw away. Dissention was in the air."[38] It was too late for the girls to rescue their season in New York; to the dismay of their manager, Hurok, they now canceled their spring tour as well.

"Everyone knows we have been with Isadora and would expect something new from us," Anna explained in a letter to Augustin Duncan. "Do you remember when I once told you that I thought there was *a curse* over us girls? Well, I am convinced now."[39] Not till later did they discover that Isadora had also been in touch with Hurok, angling for her own American tour through a new agent and manager, Norman Harle, a friend of Mary Desti. From New York, Augustin wrote to Harle that no American producer would risk money on Isadora, "as confidence in her likelihood of fulfilling a contract, once made, is down to zero."[40]

Isadora refused to believe it. The girls had "cheapened her art and finished her in America."[41] Soon her most worshipful friend, Ruth Mitchell, arrived in Paris from New York with tales of the girls' disloyalty, "working up Isadora against us," as Anna complained.[42] In May 1915, after her failure at the Century Theater, Mitchell, a stranger, had paid for Isadora and her students to return to Europe; she asked no reward but Isadora's friendship. "Her name was Ruth," Isadora wrote — "Ruth who said: 'Thy people shall be my people; thy ways as my ways.' And such a Ruth she has been to me ever since."[43] The girls despised her.

"Me for another world," Anna sighed: "We are doing the most beautiful thing in art, and yet it takes so long to be born, and I fear . . . the storm will destroy it before its time."[44] Anna recalled her last rehearsal with Isadora before she left the troupe: "We were working on Wagner's *Parsifal*. She had shown us girls . . . just once, a great upsweeping gesture with which we had to cross over to the other side of the studio, passing by Isadora, who was down on the floor kneeling. After we had repeated these movements, she got up, went over to a couch and broke into a loud, sobbing cry." Calling Anna to her side, Isadora threw her arms around her and said "that what I had just done was all that counted. If I could convey the exalted mood of these few gestures, as I had done, then it was worth all her efforts with us."[45]

When her *Parsifal* premiered at the Trocadéro in November 1920, for the first time Isadora gave her students champagne before the concert. "It won't hurt you and may put you in the right mood for the seduction scene," she said. Irma thought Isadora looked like "the Goddess of Seduction" herself, "in a long cream-colored satin gown, a flowing red velvet cape, and a crown of red and white roses in her auburn hair."[46] Her Wagner program played to sold-out houses through November and December, along with a resurrected *Orpheus* and the always prudent "lighter" evenings of Chopin, Schubert, and Brahms. A two-page tribute, signed "W.M.R." — Walter Rummel — appeared in Isadora's printed programs; in an essay on *La Bacchanale,* she wrote about "terrible desires coming to climax." Many critics were ecstatic. Here was "heavenly nourishment" for a jaded world: "Standing erect, her hand signals the canopy of heaven and the revelation of divinity. It is simple and it is great."[47]

At night, often till morning, Isadora danced the tango in clubs and cabarets around Paris. She returned with a will to designer fashions, appearing in evening gowns and cocktail dresses by Poiret, Lucile of Paris, and the new star of French couture, Coco Chanel, assisted by Russian Grand Duchess Maria Pavlovna, narrowly escaped from the Bolsheviks and exiled to Paris "in her nightgown." Isadora's favorite club was El Garron in Montmartre, where she danced to "Latin tunes," played by hulking Argentinians with accordions. It was a wild time in Paris, "both blinding and new," said modernist painter and "tubist" Fernand Léger, the victim of a gas attack in World War I, whose 1919 oil on canvas, *The City,* saw cylinders, rectangles, planes, and color as "a mechanical ballet," "an unleashing of forces [that] filled the world."[48]

In the Salle Beethoven on rue de la Pompe, Isadora revived her late-night suppers, where "guests strolled in, strolled out, and from low divans supped principally on champagne and strawberry tart. . . . Week after week came people whose names she never knew. They were like moths."[49] The Russian Revolution had brought tens of thousands of exiles to Paris. The Ukrainian Chorus played at the Théâtre des Champs-Elysées, Jacques Copeau at the Vieux-Colombier, and Suzanne Desprès, under Lugné-Poë, at the Théâtre de l'Oeuvre. Deprived of intimate relations with Rummel, after years of professional friendship, Isadora added "Lugni" to the list of her lovers, along with the sculptor and archaeologist Theodore Reinach, who "sent her ravishing letters about the language of flowers along with cheap bouquets of forget-me-nots that cost 20 sous." Isadora declared that Reinach was right to save his money — he would need it later "for the funeral wreath" he would doubtless send when she was dead.[50] Michel Georges-Michel attended a private dress rehearsal in the Salle Beethoven and, peering through the smoke of burning incense and flickering candles, remarked that it was "enough to make mystics swoon and the godless weep. . . . In the studio of Mme. Duncan, as in a temple, you proceed slowly and speak in a soft voice."[51] At her parties, women were seen dancing together, kissing, and sniffing cocaine.[52]

Margot's health hadn't recovered from the trip to Greece — only four of the Isadorables joined Isadora at the Champs-Elysées in January 1921, when she closed her season with a Wagner reprise that included the *Dance of the Flower Maidens,* the *Dance of the Apprentices,* the *Liebestod,* the *Tannhäuser* Bacchanal, and "a beautiful, etherealized choreography for the Holy Grail music" from *Parsifal.*

"To dance to Wagner with this corpulence," a critic sputtered, "this Isadora! . . . She's a national glory!"[53] Others were less kind. "You know in advance just at what moment she will employ those famous attitudes of hers," wrote *Le Figaro's* Antoine Banès: "Expressed by simple facial poses and automatic gestures, the 'Death of Isolde' becomes almost incomprehensible, and as for the 'Ride of the Valkyries' — reduced to a single *cavalier seul* — it is lamentable." The Paris critic for the *Dancing Times* took up the cry: "Madame Duncan, like *la vie chère,* is still with us, [but] the spell cast by her past achievements and undoubted talents would appear to be on the point of dissipating."[54] Many regretted that she had not given the Isadorables more to do. Thus provoked, Isadora took out her anger on the girls. She had once been Psyche in her own drama; now, in theirs, she was Aphrodite, the jealous mother of love.

"I realized that none of my best intentions and efforts . . . was of any use," Anna wrote later. "I knew she used the situation between Walter Rummel and myself as an excuse to cover the real reasons of her resentment towards us. Her exaggerated assertions, that we were absolutely incapable of performing her art and work to her artistic satisfaction, [were] too hurtful."⁵⁵ In February, Rummel bolted — he, too, wanted the best for all concerned. "Oh, I know I gave the initial blow," Rummel wrote to Isadora from Monte Carlo. "I now give up all hope. I was ready to do everything, all, not with a spirit of sacrifice, no but from my heart — But I see that is all over. . . . Everything is breaking down. . . . Well, let it break, break and crash."⁵⁶

This time, Isadora had no difficulty in persuading Rummel to come back — "Rummel's temples are narrow and it's obvious he'll never go mad," Debussy had said⁵⁷ — whereupon Anna, in desperation, quit the scene. "I came to the conclusion, after thoughtful deliberation, to eliminate myself from this emotional upheaval. . . . I gave up the man I loved more than anyone else in the world for the sake of the future of her school." Anna remembered:

> I went to tell [Isadora] of my decision. It was to be the last talk we had together. During the two hours discussion she destroyed a large bouquet of red roses, by breaking off the petals in a very nervous way and throwing them all over the floor and on her bed, on which she was reclining. I could not help but think of the times I had watched her strewing white petals so exquisitely in her lovely 'Musette' from *Iphigenia*, or when she danced an improvised encore how graciously she would throw some flowers to the orchestra for their beautiful playing. But this treatment of the roses was evidently consonant of her inner struggle of the last months. . . . I left Isadora and did not follow her to Russia.⁵⁸

In her last note to Isadora, Anna never flinched. "Keep to the heights where the gods have put you," she warned, "and don't sink to the human depths. Anna tells you this, your grateful and heartbroken pupil, who for sixteen years stood by you in sorrow and joy."⁵⁹

Isadora's invitation to Russia came from Leonid Krassin, the high Bolshevik diplomat, commissar, and deputy to the Soviet Trade Commission in London in 1921. For two weeks in April, Isadora appeared with Rummel and the London Symphony Orchestra at the Prince of Wales Theatre, where Krassin, "one of the most cultured and charming of all the Bolshevist leaders," saw her dance the *Marche Slave*. After the concert, according to Allan Ross Macdougall, "they discussed briefly and somewhat banteringly the idea of the dancer's going to Russia to found a great school of the dance. Krassin promised to do all in his power to facilitate the scheme."⁶⁰ A few days later Isadora stated her conditions in a letter to Anatoly Vassilievitch Lunacharsky, the Soviet commissar for education and the arts. She wrote:

> I shall never hear of money in exchange for my work. I want a studio-workshop, a house for myself and pupils, simple food, simple tunics, and the opportunity to give our best work. I am sick of bourgeois, commercial art. . . . I am sick of the modern theatre, which resembles a house of prostitution more than a temple of art, where artists who should occupy the place of high priests are reduced to the maneuvers of shop-keepers selling their tears and their very souls for so much a night. I want to dance for the masses, for the working people who need my art and have never had the money to come and see me. And I want to dance for them for nothing, knowing that they have not been brought to me by clever publicity, but because they really want to have what I can give them. If you accept me on these terms, I will come and work for the future of the Russian Republic and its children. Isadora Duncan.

Not long after, a telegram arrived for Isadora from Lunacharsky: COME TO MOSCOW. WE WILL GIVE YOU SCHOOL AND THOUSAND CHILDREN. YOU MAY CARRY OUT YOUR IDEA ON A BIG SCALE. Isadora answered at once: ACCEPT YOUR INVITATION. WILL BE READY TO SAIL FROM LONDON JULY 1.[61] She was "very surprised" to discover that Rummel would not go with her.

"I am tired, tired, and want to rest with you," Rummel wrote to Anna. His letter was sent through Christine Dalliès: Anna still lived in Paris but, for the moment, out of self-protection, refused to let Rummel know where.

"Dear Baby, I am very sad and quite at the end of my strength," Rummel went on: "There is no use in speaking of it all, and talking will only complicate matters and bring more misunderstanding. . . . Isadora wants to go to Russia. . . . Maybe it's for the best; perhaps there they will better understand her wild, disorganized nature."[62] Anna had only one comment: "Lord help her." She wrote to Augustin Duncan on May 10: "Alas, not even my flying out of town made her come to her senses. But at least she did go to London with Rummel and had wonderful artistic success. Financially, of course, a failure, since the impresarios were friends of Mary [Desti] Sturges. But artistically she conquered London of all places and I am really glad for her."[63]

Indeed, just when critics in Paris seemed to forsake her, the English suddenly discovered a great artist in Isadora Duncan. She had worried that her defense of Bolshevism would kill her at the box office, but she played to good houses for most of the run; few believed she would really desert her "life of luxury" for the hardships of Soviet Russia. Her plans for the new school were considered, at first, to be just another dream out of reach.

"Let us rejoice that Isadora Duncan has returned to us with a crown of Titian hair on a Junoesque figure," wrote J. T. Grein in the *Illustrated London News*. There were "two Isadoras," Grein proposed: "The one is the artist who knows what is 'great and good and beautiful'; the other is a kinswoman of the late P. T. Barnum, he who knew so well that a blare goes further than a whisper. . . . To Isadora Duncan's better half, my salaams!"[64] Ernest Newman raved in *The Times* of London: "She has overcome criticism, and in these days her genius is realized. She found dancing an art: she will leave it a language." Newman's tribute stands as the ultimate accolade of Isadora's late career:

> It is not as a dancer that she stands out among her contemporaries. . . . What she gives us is a sort of sculpture in transition. Imagine a dozen statues expressive, say, of the cardinal phases of despair — the poses and gestures and facial expressions of the moment in which each of these phases reaches its maximum of intensity. Then imagine some hundreds of statues that represent, in faultless beauty, every one of the moments of slow transition between these cardinal phases, and you get the art of Isadora Duncan. The soul becomes drunk with this endless succession of beautiful lines and groupings.
>
> The muscular control they imply is itself wonderful enough, but more wonderful still must be the brain that can conceive and realize all these faultless harmonies of form. She seems to transfer her magic even to the fabrics she works with; no one who has ever seen it can forget the beauty of the slow sinking of her cloak to earth in one of her dances; the ripples in it move the spirit like a series of soft, mysterious modulations in music.
>
> Her secret, so far as we can penetrate to it, is apparently in the marvelous cooperation of every cell of her brain and every movement of her face and limbs. . . . The most wonderful illustration we had of this was at a certain moment in her miming of the "Ride of the Valkyries," when, in dead immobility, she gave us an incredible suggestion of the very ecstasy of movement, something in the rapt face, I imagine, carried on the previous joy of the wild flight through the air. The sudden cessation of physical motion had the overwhelming effect that Beethoven and Wagner now and then make, not with their music, but by a pause in it.[65]

One who never forgot Isadora's last appearances in England was Sir Frederick Ashton, still a schoolboy at the time but later the director of Britain's Royal Ballet. "I didn't think I'd like it," Ashton remembered, "but I was completely captivated. . . . The way she used her hands and arms, the way she ran across a stage — these I have adapted in my own ballets." Fifty years later, at Covent Garden, Lynn Seymour would dance Ashton's *Five Brahms Waltzes in the Manner of Isadora Duncan,* the nearest thing to homage of the Duncan style yet created for the classical ballet. "I got an impression of enormous grace, and enormous power in her dancing," said Ashton: "She had a wonderful way of running, in which she what I call 'left herself behind,' and you felt the breeze running through her hair and everything else. And she had the most beautiful square feet, I remember, and the most impressive hands, and she wasn't really the old camp that everyone makes her out now, she was very serious, and held the audience and held them completely."[66]

In Paris, Irma, Theresa, Lisa, and Margot were left sitting on their hands. "The only way we knew how to earn a living was by giving public performances," Irma pointed out, "though every time we did, we ran counter to our teacher's wishes." When a concert manager approached them about a French tour, they wrote to Isadora for permission to accept. She gave it, on the condition that she receive a third of the Isadorables' fees after expenses and that they restrict their dances to pieces they had already known and performed for years.

IPHIGENIA . . . , Isadora wired from London, SCHUBERT WALTZES MARCHE MILITAIRE . . . NO CHOPIN OR ANY MODERN MUSIC. Her restrictions were absurd — the Isadorables had danced Chopin successfully all over the United States. In their anger and frustration, they "foolishly let off steam" to Mary Desti and another of Isadora's friends in Paris, Dolly Votichenko, wife of a Russian timpani player. "We had no one else to help or advise us," Irma wrote.[67] Dolly and Mary, of course, went at once to Isadora with the news of her pupils' discontent.

"If you could only learn a bit of discretion," Isadora wrote the girls from London, words that normally never crossed her lips. "I assure you that this can do you no good and my patience is almost at an end. . . . Please work & live simply — read & study — and either be true to me or leave me on your own names & your own responsibility." A second letter, sent from Brussels when Isadora and Rummel arrived there at the end of April, was even sterner:

Dolly Votichenko . . . says that the way you all speak of me made her think that I was possibly some sort of Monster. And in fact she re-peated to me word for word what Mary had already told me. This is really too much and my patience is at an end. That you should speak of me this way is simply disgusting. . . . And to crown this you tell Dolly that I am *jealous* of you as an Artist — really my poor children I think you have all taken leave of your senses. . . . In the meantime I beg you not to tell every little stupid idea in your heads to strangers. . . . Your present attitude toward me seems to me to make further relations very difficult. I am, as Harle says, "fed up."[68]

Isadora returned to Paris in May, alone, having said good-bye to Rummel in Brussels. There is no record of their final parting — Rummel would return briefly to Anna before abandoning both. "When at length I found myself alone in that house in the Rue de la Pompe, with its Beethoven Salle all prepared for the music of my Archangel, then my despair had no words," Isadora wrote. "I could no longer bear the sight of this house in which I had been so happy; indeed, I had a long-ing to fly from it and from the world."[69]

Irma remembered Isadora's homecoming differently. "Who wants to go to Russia with me?" she asked the girls. Only three of them could even consider it: Anna and Erika were gone, and Margot already showed signs of the "galloping" tuberculosis that would take her life in 1925.

"I'll go wherever you want to go," Irma answered. Theresa and Lisa were less sure of themselves, and not a little surprised at Irma's willingness to sacrifice for the cause. "I knew I could count on you," Isadora said, gazing coldly at Lisa and Theresa. She would give them time to think it over.[70] In the meantime, the Paris papers "fairly brimmed over with the news" of her decision to leave for Russia: "Re-porters swarmed all over her house."[71] On May 29 Isadora took their questions, insisting again that she knew "nothing of politics."

"Perhaps I am becoming a Bolshevist," Isadora said, "but all my life I have wanted to teach children, to have free schools and a free theatre. . . . The Soviet is the only Government that cares about art nowadays and about children." Asked if she wasn't afraid of food shortages and other inconveniences of war and revolution, she shook her head. "I fear spiritual hunger. . . . Privations do not count in ad-vancing toward my ideal. It is the dream of my whole life that is being realized." In France the press condemned her outright. "Her confi-dence in Bolshevik generosity is touching," wrote *Le Figaro*. "We know the Soviet is always ready to help artists — sometimes even to reach a better world."[72] Isadora answered briskly, "Every artist worth anything has always been vilified. It is the price the world demands for the beauty we evoke."[73]

At a farewell party in the Salle Beethoven, Russian friends of Isadora's begged her to reconsider. Famine was spreading in Russia, and fresh tales of cannibalism had reached the Paris émigrés. The journalist Cécile Sartoris, present that evening and writing as Séverine, remarked that Isadora's face seemed "like the surface of a lake where the ripples pass, like a mirror reflecting the rapid race of clouds."

"Don't worry, Irma," Isadora said, noticing the look in her disciple's eyes. "They'll eat me first. . . . There is a whole lot more of me than there is of you."

"And if you are hungry?" Sartoris asked.

"We will dance so as not to think of it," said Isadora.[74] Before leaving, she opened her leather-bound guest-book, a gift from Gordon Craig, and wrote "boldly, in red ink, that henceforth it would be kept in Moscow."[75]

Part V

RUSSIA

(1921–1924)

And then he grew up,

And a poet what's more,

Of limited power

Yet ready and smart,

And he called some woman

Aged forty or more

A despicable strumpet

And the joy of his heart.

— Sergei Esenin, "The Black Man"
(translated by Gordon McVay)

23

Comrade Duncan

On her way to Russia, Isadora went first to London, where she danced at Queen's Hall and saw a fortune-teller with Irma and Mary Desti. "She was told she was going on a long journey," Mary wrote, much amazed, and after "many worries and vicissitudes," she would be married for the first time: "You will be married. You will be married. And within a year."[1] Isadora laughed "ungraciously" and "refused to listen to any more nonsense."[2] In the last lines of her autobiography, she put all of her aspiration for Russia: "Adieu, Old World! I would hail a New World."[3]

Among her students, finally only Irma went to Moscow. Isadora had waited as long as she could before leaving Paris, hoping to see her mother, whom Raymond would take care of until Mrs. Duncan died the following April. But the boat from San Francisco was delayed: Mrs. Duncan arrived in Paris on June 4, 1921, a day after Isadora left the city. "Leaving on the 4 o'clock train for Brussels," Irma wrote in her diary. "Poor little Gretel [Margot] has to stay behind all by herself. I don't believe we girls shall ever live together again."[4]

They didn't. Isadora danced with Theresa, Irma, and Lisa for the last time in London on June 27. "There was no 'final break,'" according to Theresa,[5] who soon returned to New York and married art dealer Stephan Bourgeois. Lisa declared that she was "simply plain scared of the Bolshies" — she hoped to tour the United States with Anna and Margot, when Margot's health improved. Both asked Irma for help in explaining their plans to Isadora.

"It turned out exactly as we had feared," Irma wrote; "grand hysterics on [Isadora's] part and a flood of tears on theirs. 'Ingrates,' she called them." She had counted on more than one assistant to help her in Russia. When Irma took Lisa and Theresa to the train for Paris, Isadora called after her: "And you, Irma, are you also leaving me?"

Irma assured her that she was not: "I had given her my solemn word and I meant to keep it."

"Thanks," said Isadora. "You are all I now have left in this world." Just a few hours later, however, when she returned to their hotel, Irma found Isadora in the midst of "a gay party," dressed in a white tea gown of French lace and surrounded by friends, drinking champagne. Seeing Irma walk in, someone said, "Here comes the *school!*" Isadora took up the cry: "I propose a toast to Irma. Here is to the school! God bless her!"[6]

In London, Isadora said good-bye to Ellen Terry, who watched her dance the *Marche Slave* at Queen's Hall and afterward remarked, "I never saw true tragedy before." According to her daughter, Edith Craig, Terry kept "a great affection as well as admiration" for Isadora — "this wayward genius, not her daughter-in-law, but her daughter-in-love, the mother of her fairest grandchild. . . . Little Deirdre's untimely death . . . was one of the tragedies of which Ellen Terry could not speak."[7] In her curtain speech, Isadora paused to acknowledge Terry's presence. There was one in the audience "far greater" than she: " 'Let us applaud her, let us rejoice in Ellen Terry!' she cried, holding out her arms with one of those primal gestures that seemed to some almost indecent."[8] They said their farewells in Isadora's dressing room, two icons of perseverance and regret. "Oh, Lord — it is a queer world," Terry wrote to Isadora that night. "Well well! — or rather ill, ill — We must cheer up. We'll soon be dead."[9]

Isadora had told the press that she expected to spend ten years in Russia. "I will give my art to the Russians," she declared, "whom I adore and who will support me with splendid musicians and disinterested enthusiasm."[10] Leonid Krassin had promised her not just a thousand Russian children but Nicholas II's palace at Livadia for her school, high on a rock in the Crimea, overlooking the Black Sea, near Yalta. Isadora's students would live and dance in rooms built for the tsar's own daughters. She either didn't know or preferred to say nothing about the Bolshevik slaughter of the Romanov family in 1918, the gruesome details of which had just begun to appear in Western books and newspapers.

"Life in Europe is passé," Isadora went on. "It is too hopelessly bourgeois ever to understand what I am really after. Of course, I realize that present conditions in the Soviet Union are difficult for a regime in the throes of stabilizing itself. But it can't be as bad as the papers make out, or the Bolsheviks would not have sent this friendly invitation."[11] At no time, then or later, did she address the reality of Bolshevik terror, murder, and oppression; in the early years of Soviet communism, crimes of war and revolution could be considered as unavoidable. "I see only the Ideal," Isadora declared. "But no ideals have ever been fully successful on this earth."[12] According to Mary, she left for Moscow in full belief that "she was on her way to Paradise, where all was perfect love, harmony, and comradeship — where there were no stupid rules or convention of any kind — and where the children would all belong to her great school. There was no limit to her ambition." Gordon Selfridge gave her "all the supplies she needed" for the trip, along with an enormous food basket containing "every sort of canned goods that one could possibly use."[13] At a dinner in London, nevertheless, Krassin's wife had a word with Irma: "She has no conception of what she has to face. I don't want to discourage her, but I am warning you. You will all have a very difficult time."[14]

"Mary, you should come with me," Isadora pleaded as she boarded the *Baltanic* with Irma on July 13. "You should come with me. Why stay in this place of sorrow and trouble?"[15] Her friend Ruth Mitchell had arrived from America and would sail with them as far as Tallinn, in Estonia; after that, they were alone, with only Isadora's maid, Jeanne, for company. Jeanne was Isadora's personal dresser and factotum, described as "a gorgeous, full-breasted woman"[16] "livid with fear" at the thought of going to Russia. The compulsory equality of Soviet society led her to cry on her first night in Moscow: *"Non! Non! Qu'on me laisse tranquille! Je ne veux pas être la camarade de Madame!"* [No! No! Leave me alone! I don't want to be Madame's comrade!][17]

"We were told all sorts of terrible stories," Isadora reported in Moscow. "Irma and I would be raped at the frontier, and even if we succeeded in getting as far as Petrograd we would have to drink soup with chopped-off human fingers floating about in it."[18] The boat stopped overnight at Gdańsk, where Irma saw her mother for the first time in seven years. "We just sat and held hands and looked at each other for a long time," Irma wrote. "What really was there to say?" Her life with Isadora had made them strangers.[19]

At Tallinn the *Baltanic* was met by Ivy Litvinov, the English-born wife of Soviet Russia's assistant secretary for foreign affairs. (Litvinov would go on to be Soviet foreign minister and later ambassador to the United States.) Isadora was disappointed: she had expected to be greeted by a "Bolshevik with red flannel shirt, black beard, and a knife between his teeth." It was the same on the way to Moscow: Isadora and Irma rode second class with "a very timid young man" in spectacles, a Soviet courier who spoke English and proved invaluable along the route.[20]

When the train stopped for Customs at the Russian border, Isadora walked to buy fruit and flowers at the local market, returning an hour later like the Pied Piper, with a throng of children in tow, to whom she gave an impromptu dancing lesson on the station platform and "all the candy and sweetstuffs she could find in her baggage." She was "thrilled beyond telling" to enter Russia and wanted "to join the Communist party on the spot. . . . She felt like some great hero arriving in Valhalla."[21] It didn't occur to her until she got to Petrograd — St. Petersburg — that anything in Russia might have changed for the worse. She had seen the city last in 1913, just before her children died. Walking along the Neva, she looked sadly at the palaces that lined the river, battered and dark after the flight of their owners: "This one was a present from the Grand Duke [Sergei] to the ballerina Kschessinska . . . ; that palace over there, with the gaping shell-holes, once belonged to [Grand] Duchess [Vladimir] who came to all my performances."[22] The town looked "dead and infinitely sad."[23] Isadora was glad to leave it.

The express train to Moscow, boarded at midnight, took twenty-eight hours to reach the capital, twice as long as it should have: "Peasants and whole families with their samovars and their bedding crowded each station. Some of them, it was said, had waited a week to get a train."[24] Isadora and Irma finally arrived in Moscow at four in the morning on Sunday, July 24. The journey from London had taken eleven days. Draped in scarves and a bright red cape, her lipstick and eyeliner freshly applied, Isadora prepared to meet her compatriots:

> She waited a few minutes to give the reception committee a chance to be sure she had arrived. Then, her feet scarcely touching the earth, she stepped from the train, expecting to be engulfed in the embraces of countless comrades and children. She had visions of them all in red shirts, waving red flags, and welcoming her to their midst, but

no one paid the slightest attention to them but the guard, who looked at them most suspiciously. How different it all seemed from what Isadora had imagined! Soldiers everywhere. She seemed to be thrown back into the midst of war. Everyone looked at the other with suspicion. Courtesy and politeness had dropped from the world.[25]

Isadora stood shocked and embarrassed on the station platform. Had the Kremlin not received her telegram? "No friendly welcoming voices, no wreaths or festive garlands" — she was "mystified by this strange lack of elementary consideration." The young courier who shared their compartment now offered his services, taking Isadora and Irma as far as the Soviet foreign office, headquartered since the revolution in Moscow's Metropol Hotel. There they waited outside in a taxi, "cold, and feeling deserted by God and man," until a friendly face appeared at the car window — Count Florinsky, formerly attached to the imperial Russian legation in New York. In the war Florinsky had often joined Isadora's late-night parties at Long Beach.[26]

No one could find Lunacharsky, the commissar for arts and education, whom Isadora had expected to meet first, at the head of a long line of Soviet dignitaries. Florinsky took the travelers to his hotel, cooked them an omelette, and found them the last room in the house, "sheetless and without pillows," where they tried to sleep, despite a horde of flies and *"grands rats"* that left Jeanne, the maid, "weeping hysterically." Isadora went down to the hotel restaurant in "a Callot Soeurs creation" and felt badly out of place: "I found, after meeting others, that a real communist is indifferent to heat or cold or hunger or any material sufferings." She, "a poor pagan sybarite,"[27] was not. After a walk through Moscow with Irma and "a little Bolshevist" they met at dinner, she went back to the train. "He talked," Isadora wrote, "more and more inspired, until by dawn we were also ready to die for Lenin and the cause."[28]

On Monday, Lunacharsky was at his desk, brought back from the country in July to deal with Russia's newest crisis. Lunacharsky was a journalist, historian, critic, and playwright as well as a devout Old Bolshevik, a favorite of Lenin, who, despite Lunacharsky's known homosexuality, admitted to "a weakness for him. . . . He's an excellent comrade!"[29] In that respect, Isadora couldn't have found higher protection in Russia. Lunacharsky confessed that he had never expected her to come — "When Duncan announced her intention of coming to Russia, shrieks of astonishment and indignation were heard"[30] — and that no preparations whatever had been made for her reception. "Duncan" was not what he expected:

> Dressed in a strange attire that was a mixture of a rich Cook's tourist and some kind of Grecian tunic, she had scarves waving about her almost as in a dance. She had extraordinarily sweet, sort of China-blue eyes, very naïve and kind. . . . In her Anglo-French dialect she insisted that she was prepared to live on black bread and salt, but requested a thousand girls and boys from the poorest families, whom she promised to turn into the most graceful people. . . . Duncan has been called the queen of Movement, but of all her movements, this last one — her coming to Red Russia in spite of being scared off — is the most beautiful and calls for the greatest applause.[31]

With the appearance of Ilya Ilyich Schneider, Lunacharsky's appointed deputy, Isadora and Irma were soon installed in the apartment of Ekaterina Geltser, a leading dancer of the Bolshoi Ballet, now on tour in southern Russia. Schneider was a friend of Geltser, a slim young man of thirty, with a background in journalism, theater, "aesthetics," and ballet history. His first service would be as an interpreter — Isadora spoke no Russian at all.

And who was Geltser? she asked. A great ballerina? Schneider "looked at her as though she had asked: who is Stanislavsky, or who is Chaliapin? To be so great a dancer and not to know one's contemporaries!"[32] Later, aroused, Isadora thumped her chest and cried, "I am red, red!"[33] Schneider began to wonder what she was made of when he went to collect her luggage at the station and found it "piled two yards high with trunks, hampers and suitcases." His experience with dancers was not entirely useless.[34] "I did all the work with Isadora when she was in our country," Schneider wrote later. "I managed her school . . . I wrote all of her articles and letters in Russian."[35] During their first conversation, Isadora began covering the lampshades in Geltser's apartment with pink silk shawls.

"I can't bear white light," she said. Then, with an alarmed look at Geltser's decor: "The difference between the pretty and the beautiful is too great." Irma walked in suddenly, "a very slim girl in a long, silk peignoir."

"This is Irma," Isadora said casually, "the only one of my pupils who decided to come with me to Russia." Jeanne appeared next with "jam and marmalade, chocolate bars, biscuits, and some kind of small packets in greaseproof paper. . . . Isadora said [they] were starch-reduced rolls, for she was afraid of putting on weight."[36] But Schneider had eyes only for Irma. They were engaged by the end of the year.[37] Isadora had no idea how eagerly Irma would take to living in Moscow and running the school.

Isadora's first visitor at Geltser's was Konstantin Stanislavsky, much aged since she last saw him and "not happy" with the Soviet regime — Stanislavsky had had "terrible times" in the revolution. Now he was staging Tchaikovsky's *Eugene Onegin,* his first experiment with opera and a waste of effort, in Isadora's opinion. *Onegin* was "too sentimentally romantic" for such stirring times, she declared. With a look of swagger that must have left him speechless, she gave Stanislavsky her best advice: "*Cher, grand artiste:* you are faced with this dilemma; either you must consider your career at an end and commit suicide, or you must begin a new life by becoming a communist!"[38]

Isadora had no difficulty becoming a communist herself, untroubled as she was by any consideration of politics, theory, economics, Russian history, or the working of government. After only a week in Moscow, she caused a scene at a party held in the former palace of Russia's "sugar king," Pavel Kharitonenko, still "decorated, and over-decorated, in Louis XV style," with gilt furniture, Gobelins tapestries, and painted ceilings. Isadora arrived in a red dress and turban, only to find her comrades listening to a young soprano, dressed as a shepherdess, singing French country songs at the piano. She was outraged: "What do you mean by throwing out the bourgeoisie only to take their places? . . . *Plus ça change, plus c'est la même chose!* . . . You are not revolutionists. You are bourgeois in disguise. Usurpers!" She ran out.[39] The incident was talked about all over Moscow.

"In those years there were only about eighteen Moscow actors and artists who were members of the Communist Party," Schneider pointed out. "The rest, all three thousand of them, were neither interested nor involved in politics."[40] Even Lunacharsky, writing a tribute to Isadora in *Izvestia,* mentioned that "Comrade Duncan is going through a phase of rather militant communism that sometimes, involuntarily, makes us smile."[41] Most of the first days she spent walking through Moscow, where "everything could be had for free," if she found the right freebooter, swindler, or black marketer.[42] At night she went to the theater: "In those days admission was free and she was always a welcome guest."[43] She was perpetually hungry in Moscow and, when autumn came, perpetually cold.

"We found the streets littered with every conceivable object *but* gold," Irma wrote. "Money in any kind of currency was out of circulation. . . . Wherever one looked, one saw endless lines of people queuing up for food. We, too, were put on rations, or *paiok* as they called it for artists."[44] Outside Moscow, famine broke out — more than 5 million Russians would die of starvation over the next two years. Had it not been for the American Relief Association (ARA), which shipped millions of tons of food to Soviet Russia under the direction of future U.S. president Herbert Hoover, the death toll might have doubled or tripled (as it did a decade later in the Soviet famine of 1931–32).

In August, Lunacharsky took Isadora to an orphanage outside Moscow, where she asked the children to dance their "peasant dances" and declared that they desperately needed new ones. "These are the dances of slaves you have danced!" Isadora cried. "All the movements go down to earth. You must learn to dance the dance of Free People. You must hold your heads high and throw out your arms, wide, as though you would embrace the whole universe in a great fraternal gesture!"[45] On Sparrow Hills, the wooded rise above the Moskva River, she met Nikolai Podvoysky, the Bolshevik commissar who had led the attack on the Winter Palace in November 1917. With Trotsky, Podvoysky had organized the victorious Red Army and was now occupied with "a small army of athletes," designing the Soviet system of physical education. Isadora was smitten with Podvoysky, whom she called "a God-like man,"[46] and equally with his young helpers, "who were wearing only shorts and . . . busying themselves round the samovar, throwing fir cones, blowing up the fire."

"I don't suppose you've ever seen such a huge samovar," Schneider remarked innocently.

"Aber so ein schöner Samovar," Isadora answered in German: *"So ein schöner Samovar hab' ich nie gesehen!"* (But such a beautiful samovar. Such a beautiful samovar I've never seen!)[47] When she got home that night, "still vibrant from contact" with Podvoysky and his crew, she wrote a tribute to the commissar that she later sold to the *Daily Herald* in London: "Like Prometheus, this man would give to humanity the flame for its regeneration." It was the first time Isadora had earned money from writing, and "she was more thrilled by the receipt of that check," said Irma, "than ever she had been by the enormous sums received for her dancing, or by the applause of her admirers."[48]

The Russian summer of 1921 was rainy and cold, but Isadora accepted Podvoysky's invitation to spend the rest of it in a log cabin on

Sparrow Hills, away from the bourgeois atmosphere of Geltser's apartment. "In your life you have known great theaters with applauding publics," Podvoysky said. "That is all false. You have known trains de luxe and expensive hotels. That is all false. Ovations — false. All false." If Isadora hoped to serve Russia, she must go among the people: "Dance your dances in little barns in the winter, in open fields in the summer. Teach the people the meaning of your dances. Teach the children. Don't ask for thanks!"[49]

Podvoysky was the sort of communist Isadora hoped to know better, but there would be "no entangling alliances," as she quickly discovered, "in the manner of the former Grand Dukes and the dancers of the Imperial Ballet." The commissar proved as straight as a stick. Isadora stood a whole week of "the simple life . . . sleeping on the floor, enduring the most primitive hygienic arrangements,"[50] until frustration and boredom got the better of her and she stormed back to Moscow, demanding children, demanding work, demanding the school she was promised.

"She must not lose courage," Podvoysky told Schneider, "she must not complain, and she must not be surprised. . . . We need her."[51] Podvoysky later disclosed that Lenin himself had "given instructions" about Isadora: "Duncan did not appear with us accidentally. . . . 'If she does something in excess [Lenin had said], let us correct her by advice, but the more attention we pay to what she is doing the better the results will be.'" Lunacharsky sat her down and talked about the suffering of the Russian people, the revolution, and the civil war: "Isadora opened her small mouth, and at some point in my tale, very large tears streamed from her blue eyes in a torrent. The strangest thing was that in those hungry, striving years, we did find a building for her school . . . and that, in the end, we did dance."[52]

At the end of August, Isadora, Irma, Schneider, and Jeanne moved to Prechistenka 20, a rococo mansion of palatial ambition in one of Moscow's formerly most fashionable districts. Prechistenka runs directly away from the belfry of Ivan the Great at the Kremlin, a broad avenue in neoclassical style that was long associated with artists, poets, Decembrists, and other liberal Russian minds. Number 20 belonged to another ballerina, Alexandra Balashova, now exiled to France. Isadora saw the move as a favorable omen: "She wondered how long it would be before the whole ballet would finally cede to the dynamic freedom of her Art and her School."[53] (Curiously, Balashova had tried but failed to sublet Isadora's house in rue de la Pompe before she left Paris. "It was some sort of progress," Isadora said.⁵⁴)

Prechistenka 20 was built in the eighteenth century for the Smirnov vodka family. Its last occupant before Isadora was Béla Kun, the Hungarian communist, who "filched everything, including the bric-a-brac," according to Irma. "He had even stripped the silk damask off the walls."⁵⁵ But the house was in good condition for the times, with tall, intact plate-glass windows, a large entry hall, a marble staircase surrounded by a rosewood balustrade, and two ballrooms on either side of the entry. Upstairs the rooms bore names — Blue Room, Oriental Room, Turkish Room, Empire Room — but each was carved uniformly with bas-reliefs of Napoleon and Josephine, "eagles, ciphers and medallions" on all the ceilings, columns, doors, and cornices.⁵⁶

"A quadrille!" Isadora cried as she viewed Prechistenka for the first time. "*Changez vos places!*"⁵⁷ It took several weeks to clear out the peasant families and government dependents squatting in the building; the school did not open for general auditions until October. "Beds, mattresses, and bedding for the first forty '[D]unclings,' crockery, pots, and pans, etc., were all brought into the school," Schneider wrote, "which already had a service staff of sixty people." "They came in pairs: two porters, two maids, two typists, two chefs."⁵⁸ Academic instruction would be undertaken by the state. Every two weeks Jeanne went to the Kremlin to collect the extra rations for "brain-workers" — white flour, sugar, tea, and caviar — which Isadora invariably disposed of the same day at one of her parties. As everywhere, she threw her door open to guests, "mostly half-starved poets and artists." Normally, the only food in the house were potatoes, cooked in various ways — "*sauté, pont-neuf, soufflé, lyonnaise . . .* [and] as *pommes en robe de chambre* — potatoes with their jackets on."⁵⁹

At her first official dinner in Prechistenka, Isadora entertained Leonid Krassin with the *Ave Maria*: "This was the rhythmic dedication of the Isadora Duncan School."⁶⁰ It annoyed her to discover that conductors and musicians in Moscow still refused to play for her, on the grounds that her dancing profaned great music. Schneider had trouble finding even a rehearsal pianist. A young musician, Pierre Lyuboschitz, finally took the job, "and with his arrival the house was filled with music: the majestic chords of Liszt's *Funeral March,* the victorious chariots of a Chopin polonaise, the desperate *Etude in D sharp Minor* of Scriabin."⁶¹ Into this and a second Scriabin étude, her first compositions in Russia, Isadora poured "all the horror and the ghastly relentlessness" of her imagination of the Volga famine.[62] The actor Vladimir Sokoloff, a rising star at the Kamerny Theatre, was so far undone when he saw the Scriabin works at Prechistenka that he asked Isadora not to dance them for anyone else.

"And half smiling, half seriously," Sokoloff remembered, "she answered me after short consideration: 'Very well, then . . . They are yours; I give them to you.'" Sokoloff, one of Russia's greatest actors, may have been Isadora's first lover in Moscow:

> She had a tremendous influence on me. She was a revelation to me. A great person in life. Not only a dancer but a tragic actress. . . . She was the only person I had ever met who was not a conformist . . . and her eccentricity was nothing but the immense and tragic solitude in which always and wherever she happened to be, she lived . . . a solitude which was her fate from the first to the very last day of her phenomenal career. . . . All I consider as being really important in my art, I have learned from her.

"Do you know that you are a Tragedian?" Isadora asked — up till then, Sokoloff had played only comedy at the Kamerny. It was "news that all but made [him] faint." Isadora's advice to actors was specific: "A great thing you cannot express with a hundred gestures, but with ONE. Just remember how persuasive a little scarce gesture can be." As to persuasion: "Whenever you work, go into the forest. Act for the trees, the sky, the grass at your feet. You will be happy then, and happy people are always convincing."[63]

Isadora herself grew "gloomier and gloomier" as summer turned to fall and there were still no children at the school. Bracing her for worse news, Lunacharsky had already told her that she would have only forty or fifty students to start. Lenin's New Economic Policy, by which Soviet Russia converted temporarily to a free-market system, would be promulgated in November. The state could not afford to fund a thousand children anywhere.

At last, late in September, Schneider received permission to place a notice in The Workers' Moscow, advertising the opening of "Isadora Duncan's school for children of either sex between the ages of four and ten." Preference would be given to "children of workers." Isadora took a hammer and nails to the Napoleon ballroom, laying her carpet and hanging her curtains. A "hideous" chandelier she covered in pink and yellow silk, draping the room's only other furnishing, a portable heater, with "a piece of blue stuff." When she was done, the light in the room looked "like a blue sea or a southern sky." This would be the children's rehearsal studio.

"If it's going to be a revolution, then let it be a revolution!" Isadora cried. An emissary from Lunacharsky's office had arrived with a plan of instruction for her students, "reduced almost to the rules and regulations of a ballet school." Isadora had only one comment, scrawled in red ink at the top of the document: *"Idiot!"*[64]

On the first day of auditions, the children flocked in hundreds to Prechistenka, "little girls of the Moscow working class: intimidated bambinos with pigtails or close-cut hair, with freckled faces, with fearful astonishment in their eyes, with worn-out dresses."[65] Over several days Isadora and Irma chose 100 of them for further trials. They would train them all through October and November, "determining their musicality, sense of rhythm, and line" and imparting the bare essentials of Duncan dance: "They were first of all taught to walk naturally, but beautifully, to a slow march; then to stand, swaying their bodies rhythmically, 'as if blown by the breeze,' said Isadora."[66] She restricted her teaching to two hours in the evening, from five to seven, leaving Irma with the harder task of routine instruction, "the strenuous, physical effort and exertions required to whip a solid mass of untrained humanity into a semblance of agility and grace," as Irma put it.[67] For the moment, the children continued to live at home. All 100 would appear with Isadora at the Bolshoi Theatre on November 7, the fourth anniversary of the Bolshevik Revolution, in a command performance for the Soviet hierarchy. After that, Isadora would pick the best two score as her pupils. As the performance grew near, she became more and more nervous. Russian theatrical life differed greatly from before the war.

"There are two or three Art theatres with such futuristic ideas that Stanislavsky seems quite old-fashioned," Isadora wrote to Augustin in New York. Nothing like Soviet ideology had yet descended on Moscow artists.[68] In the early 1920s the Russian theater was alive and innovative — to many of those in it, Isadora seemed "quite old-fashioned," too. V. E. Meyerhold, formerly Stanislavsky's colleague at the Moscow Art Theatre who now directed the State Higher Theater Workshop in his system of "biomechanics," pronounced her "absolutely out-of-date and totally obsolete."[69] As sterner political times approached in Russia, her work would find official disfavor for its "mysticism."

"I teach the children to look above them," Isadora protested, "to look around, to be conscious of the whole universe: is that mysticism?"[70] She never suspected that an awakened consciousness might be subversive to the Soviet state. On November 7 her Tchaikovsky program packed the Bolshoi with three thousand people and left "ten times that number" standing in the street. Isadora was assured that tickets would be given by priority to soldiers and workers, most of whom remained outside in the snow, "a mob of disappointed, stamping, pushing men and women. They were only kept from rushing the doors of the theatre by a vigilant cordon of police." Inside were the Bolshevik leaders, including Lenin, "various commissars, government officials, the heads and officials of the trade unions, representatives of the Red Army, and all the foreign correspondents. . . . A colossal number of theatrical youth broke through the controls and flooded the Bolshoi from first tier to last."[71]

When Isadora appeared — heavy, middle-aged, her hair the color of fire — gasps were heard in the audience: "The transparent chiton on a no-longer-young woman and the absence of a brassiere" shocked the typically prudish Russian sensibility.[72] That she would dance the *Marche Slave,* with its echoing strains of the tsarist anthem, had been discussed for days in the press. Lunacharsky himself had vetted Isadora's performance "to see if [her] interpretation of the music had anything treasonable about it." It remained for Isadora to convince *Izvestia* "what an inspired artiste can make of such an old-fashioned thing."[73]

After the *Pathétique,* all eyes were on the former imperial box, where Lenin sat with his colleagues. "I saw quite clearly his face, full of feeling and so expressive," said a witness who sat only a few yards away. "Like a sensitive mirror, it reflected the minutest movement of gesture of the artist." During the *Marche Slave,* as Isadora depicted "a bent, oppressed, heavy-laden" slave suddenly liberated from bondage, Lenin leaned forward in his seat, gripped the balustrade, and finally "stood up and, joining the general expression of admiration, shouted loudly at the top of his voice, 'Brava, brava, Miss Duncan!'"[74] *Izvestia* felt safe in declaring: "Against the background of the hated tsarist hymn triumphed the revolution. . . . The allegory was understood by everyone."[75]

At the end of her Bolshoi program, Isadora danced not the *Marseillaise* but Russia's new anthem, *L'Internationale.* From the official standpoint, all was triumphant:

But the thrill of the evening for the enraptured audience came when . . . the orchestra began to play the *Internationale,* and Isadora moved to the center of the stage. There she stood firm-footed, statuesque, draped in red, and began to mime the overthrow of the old order and the coming of the new: the brotherhood of man. And as the people all stood up, singing fervently the words of their hymn, they seemed like a revival of the antique chorus commenting on the heroic gestures of the central figure on the stage.

When the dancer had mimed the first stanza, the singing audience saw Irma come from a corner of the stage leading by the hand a little child, who was followed by another and another — a hundred little children in red tunics, each with the right hand held high clasping fraternally the left hand of the one before, moving against the blue curtains, forming a vivid, living frieze, and then circling the vast stage, and surrounding, with childish arms outstretched towards the light, the noble, undaunted, and radiant figure of their great teacher.[76]

On the day Isadora chose resident students for her school, Schneider and Irma handed out red tickets to the lucky forty and green ones to the others, many of whom fell apart in sobs at not being chosen. For several days their irate and desperate parents kept Schneider's office busy; Isadora wrote to Augustin that she still hoped to find "a great *salle*" in Moscow, "where I will teach five hundred children each day. . . . It looks as if all the children in Russia wanted to come to this school, and it is very touching to see the eagerness of these children, and their desire to learn something beautiful."[77]

The Dunclings were given tunics and had just begun to work with Irma when they were suddenly sent home: winter had come, and there was no wood to heat the school. Soon Lunacharsky came to explain the New Economic Policy to Isadora. Shops were now open; all theaters would begin charging admission, "and it would also be possible for Comrade Duncan to give performances before paying audiences."[78] She could keep the house on Prechistenka for as long as she liked. According to Irma, "Isadora's idealism was blown sky high."[79]

"I have left Europe and Art that was too tightly bound with commercialism," she complained in *Izvestia* on November 23, "and it will be against all my convictions and desires if I shall have to give again paid performances for the bourgeois public."[80] Nevertheless, by December she was dancing for money at the Zimin Theatre, and to larger crowds than had seen her at the Bolshoi.[81] With her own "*dingy,*" she said, using the Moscow slang for cash, she would pay for the school:

"For the realization of my Ideas . . . I need only a big and warm hall. About feeding and clothing the children I have already received a promise from the A.R.A."* With fuel in the fire, and food on the table, the children came back and at five o'clock sharp were led, two by two, into the Blue Room, Isadora's private studio and workspace.

"Isadora stood facing us and showed us how trees sway and swing in the wind, while the leaves (our wrists and fingers) keep slightly fluttering," said Yulia Vashentseva, one of the first girls to occupy the dormitory at the Duncan school. "The movements of her arms and hands were incredibly beautiful. Even we, such small children, could understand this."[82] In their recollections of Isadora, not recorded before the 1960s, the Russian children would echo the words of the first girls at Grunewald, suddenly "transported to another world. . . . The walls were hung with blue curtains, the huge chandelier, camouflaged by a large pink scarf, sent diffused light over Isadora. Wearing a red mantle, she sat in an armchair, more beautiful, more majestic than anything I had ever seen or dreamed of in my life."[83]

At Christmas 1921, on the invitation of Ivy Litvinov, Isadora gave the free concert she wanted, a repeat of her Tchaikovsky program for workers and peasants at the Zimin. "No government has yet understood that through music it can inspire the masses with the might and power of its ideas and convictions," she wrote in *Izvestia,* calling for the Bolshoi to stay open one night a week for free performances under the NEP.[84] She paid small attention to the critical assessment of her work in Moscow, much of it savage. Innovators panned her outright, Meyerhold joining the legion of male critics who insisted that Isadora was "not a dancer because her movements [lack] the basic variety found in classical ballet." But ballet, too, was out of favor in the early Soviet days. Moscow was crazy for American jazz, anything new, anything forbidden or exciting. Isadora divided her notices into "very good" and "very bad." The worst were provoked by "the decay of her body," her "massive" bare legs and "wobbling breasts," one or both of which routinely fell out of her tunic when she danced — "not a pretty sight."[85]

"With a gesture full of chastity and grace she would replace it to the murmur of the orchestra seats and considerable din from the gallery," said the actor and choreographer Alexander Rumnev, who served briefly as gymnastics instructor at the school. "She treated this

---

*Records of ARA correspondence with the Duncan school in Moscow are at the Hoover Institution on War, Revolution, and Peace, Stanford University.

as an absolutely natural thing and was not confused in the least by the reaction in the auditorium."[86] Rumnev begged her to consider convention and wear a brassiere but at forty-four, such a thing could hardly faze her. She was bothered only when she heard herself attacked and ridiculed as an opportunist who had come to Moscow to profit from the Russian disaster.

"It is important that I am surrounded only by friends and people who understand me," Isadora told Schneider. "I can foresee great difficulties. The Tsarist ballet is still supreme here. . . . It will be like that until a fresh wind starts blowing."[87] She could have left Russia at any time without embarrassment, Schneider pointed out: with the withdrawal of state funding, her Idea had been made impossible. Pressed to explain why she stayed in Moscow, Isadora answered, "If you must know, it was a choice for me between seeing all those depraved, sugary sweet women crying around me, 'Oh, Miss Duncan, you are so wonderful . . . you remind me of . . . my mother used to tell me . . .' and the images of men such as Podvoysky — and he was not the only one."[88] With the money she made from her first concert at the Zimin, she bought a Christmas tree for the children.

In the fall of 1921, Isadora met Sergei Esenin, the twenty-six-year-old "poet of the revolution."[89] With Anatoly Mariengof, his best friend and collaborator in Moscow, Esenin led what was called the circle of imaginist poets (sometimes imagists, but unrelated to any such circle in the West). The group had a reputation in Moscow for "hooliganism" and drunken high jinks. Blond, blue-eyed, with a face at once "cherubic" and "depraved," Esenin, at twenty-six, was already well embarked on a cycle of alcoholic destruction that amazed even Russians and his bibulous confreres. Isadora knew what lay in store for her when she took him home from a party on the night they met.

"I couldn't bear to have a hair on his golden head hurt," she told Mary Desti later. "Can't you see the resemblance? He's the image of little Patrick. Patrick would look like that one day, and could I allow him to be hurt?"[90] All accounts agree that, at their first encounter, Isadora took the lead. She had accepted an invitation from the painter and designer George Yakulov and dressed for the occasion as if she were still in Paris, all in red, made-up, perfumed — Isadora told Mary that she had "wanted to look devilish."[91] Mariengof wrote in his memoir of Esenin, *Novel Without Lies:*

She advanced slowly, with grace. She looked round the room with eyes that seemed like saucers in blue delft, and her gaze was stopped by the sight of Esenin. Her mouth, small and delicate, smiled at him. Isadora then reclined on the couch, and Esenin came and sat at her feet. She ran her fingers through his curly hair and said: *"Solotaia golova!"* (Golden head!)

We were surprised to hear her say these two words, she who knew only about a dozen Russian words all told. Then she kissed him on the lips, and again from her mouth, small and red like a bullet-wound, came with [a] pleasant caressing accent, a Russian word: *"Anguel!"* (Angel!)

She kissed him again and said: *"Tschort!"* (Devil!)

At four o'clock in the morning, Isadora Duncan and Esenin left.[92]

As they rode home with Schneider, Isadora and Esenin were so engrossed with each other that the driver circled Prechistenka three times before they noticed where they were. He had driven around a church.

" 'He's married us!' Esenin cried, shaking with laughter."

"Marriage!" said Isadora, when Schneider translated. She was smiling. "Marriage!" Then they talked "all through the night," Schneider wrote, in gestures, because Esenin spoke no English and Isadora no Russian. Thanks to her carefully hung curtains and scarves, "the night was long in Duncan's room."[93]

24

Wayward Child

$\int$ergei Alexandrovitch Esenin was "a hard and naughty cherub," Max Eastman wrote, "a sweet melodic singer of the drunken sloppy perfumed sappiness of whores and sophomoric hooligans."[1] In 1921 he was also the most famous poet in Russia — "famous enough [even] before the revolution to be invited to read his poems to the tsarina," as Eastman pointed out. "She said that they were beautiful, but very sad. 'So is all Russia,' he answered."[2] In Moscow the riotous imaginist circle of which Esenin was the showman and star provided a welcome antidote to seven years of war, revolution, and hardship. Having once pledged "to overthrow everything, to change the structure of the universe,"[3] Esenin presented himself now as a dandy, in top hat and patent-leather shoes, "playing the part of leader of a kind of 'golden youth' in impoverished, hungry, cold Moscow . . . charming the public, showering them with pretty images and then suddenly shocking them with some obscenity."[4] When Isadora met Esenin, she was forty-four, eighteen years his senior. The imaginists were recently famous for urinating on convent walls.

"His eyes were light-blue and beautiful," a childhood friend of Esenin's recalled. "He always looked you straight in the eyes. His mouth was very mobile and expressive. His hair was soft and perfectly fair."[5]

A herald of both Russian revolutions in 1917, Esenin, four years later, felt betrayed by the new regime. "I am ceasing to understand what revolution I belonged to," he wrote in 1923. "I can see only one thing — that it was neither the February nor the October. Evidently there was and is concealed in us a kind of November."[6] For decades Soviet biographers downplayed this truth, sanctifying Esenin's largely fictitious image as poet laureate of the revolution over the dangerous and violent exhibitionist he undoubtedly became. In Russia, Esenin remains a figure out of legend, a martyred knight of the peasant class, always youthful, adored for his simple, sorrowful verses, and sentimentalized beyond recalling. No Russian youth visits Moscow without a stop at Vagankovskoe cemetery, where Esenin lies buried beneath a bust of his head and torso, and the faithful pray, eat, sleep, sell drugs, read poetry, and speechify in perpetuity. At the millennium, Esenin is the Jim Morrison of Russia.

"His poetry had a sincerity, an extraordinary musical quality that enthralled even those who disapproved of him," said Ilya Ehrenburg.[7] By the time he met Isadora, Esenin was already alcoholic, reputedly epileptic, and alternately depressed and elated. "His life, although few can have expected it then, was increasingly to be a fight against boredom and a deepening melancholy," writes his English-language biographer, Gordon McVay: "Underlying this was a more serious dissatisfaction with the consistent behavior required by the conventions of everyday life . . . a reality which alcohol, and, ultimately, only death could negate."[8]

Against all evidence, most Russians still believe that Isadora "ruined" Esenin — according to Mariengof, it began the night they met at Yakulov's party in Moscow. The next day Mariengof found Isadora with Esenin in the Blue Room at Prechistenka, where "chairs, armchairs, and tables were hung with light French fabrics, Venetian shawls, and brightly colored Russian scarves." Isadora apologized for the decor. Mariengof, who spoke some French, acted as interpreter:

> "It is Balashova's fault. It's a terrible room. Isadora has bought far too many scarves in Russia." . . .
> On a little table by the bed stood a big picture of Gordon Craig. Esenin took the photograph, looked at it attentively, and then asked, "Your *mouge?*"
> "What is *mouge?*"
> "Husband: spouse."

"Yes, he is my husband; but bad husband. He work and write all the time. Craig is a genius."

Esenin pointed his finger to his chest, saying: "I also genius. Esenin genius — Craig nothing."

He then slipped Craig's photograph under a pile of old newspapers, saying, "*Adieu!*" to it.

Isadora was enchanted, and repeated, "*Adieu!*" making a gesture of farewell toward the picture.

"Now, Isadora," said Esenin, "dance! Dance for us." He felt like Herod calling for the dance of Salome.[9]

From that moment, in Mary Desti's words, "Isadora was never to know an hour of peace, and it was not very long before she discovered her young poet was not only a great genius but also a mad one."[10] As Isadora is blamed in Russia for Esenin's demise, so Esenin in the West has been faulted for hers. Irma told of the night, just three days after she met Esenin, when the tranquil mood of Isadora's evening salon "was shattered by a dozen feet pounding on the stairs and half-a-dozen drunken voices lifted in raucous laughter and vinous wit." Into the room came Esenin with his friends.

"I'm going to dance for all of you!" Isadora said quickly. She had just performed a Chopin mazurka and moved on to a waltz, which she danced with "rapturous joy and seductive grace." Finished, "her eyes radiant," she reached out her arms to Esenin and asked him how he liked it: "The interpreter translated. Esenin said something coarse and brutal that brought howls of . . . laughter from his drunken friends."

"He says it was — awful," Schneider stammered, "and that he can do better than that himself." Then he began to dance around the room, jumping, kicking, and waving his arms at "the crestfallen and humiliated Isadora."[11] From the beginning Esenin treated her with open contempt.

"At times he seemed to love her as much as he could, never leaving her side for a moment," poet Ivan Startsev remembered. "At other times he would stay by himself, turning to her from time to time, cruelly, coarsely, even striking her and cursing her with the most vile street language. At such moments, Isadora would be especially patient and tender, attempting to calm Esenin by any means."[12] Irma stated the case: "He was a wayward, willful, little child, and she was a mother passionately enough in love with him to overlook and forgive all the vulgar curses and the peasant blows."[13] Indeed, on Mariengof's evidence, she seemed to enjoy them: "Later Esenin became her master. Like a dog she kissed the hand that he raised to strike her. . . . And yet he was only the partner . . . a partner tragic and without a will. . . . It was she who led the dance."[14]

Anatoly Mariengof was Esenin's closest friend, probably also his lover, and until 1921 his inseparable companion and roommate in Moscow. His descriptions of Isadora, while credible enough, reflect the jealousy and anxiety all the imaginists felt when she appeared in Esenin's life, but especially "Tolya," who earlier that year had married the actress Anna Nikritina. Some believe that Esenin took up with Isadora only to make Mariengof jealous. When Esenin was sober, there was no one more charming; but when he drank, said another poet-friend, Valentin Volpin, "he changed sharply, there appeared about him a kind of evil, unquenchable fervor, and in such a state he spoke sharply, was completely intolerant, rather inappropriately praised only his own talent, and would not stand for any objections. Sometimes this mood . . . gave way to a melancholy sentimentalism accompanied by laments over fate and failure which he felt to be persecuting him."[15]

In 1917 Esenin had married actress Zinaida Raikh, who bore him a son and daughter in short order. The marriage was dead in two years, Esenin giving the reason that Raikh had lied to him by telling him she was a virgin when they met. (Raikh went on to marry Meyerhold; both were murdered by Stalin in the 1930s.) In Moscow he had also enjoyed a liaison with a local girl, Anna Izryadnova, but questions about his sexual experience are not, as many Western and all Russian historians insist, the invention of a later, theory-driven age. Maxim Gorky recalled in a letter to Romain Rolland: "I saw Esenin right at the beginning of his arrival in St. Petersburg [in 1915]. He was short and delicately built, with golden curls, dressed like Vanya in *A Life for the Tsar,* blue-eyed and shining like Lohengrin. He was welcomed by his confreres as a gluttonous person might seize a strawberry in January."[16] In Mariengof, he found what intimacy there was. "There are only passions," Esenin declared. "Love does not exist. . . . I like sucking a woman dry, drinking her right up, then I don't need her anymore."[17]

When Mariengof unexpectedly married Anna Nikritina in 1921, Esenin left the room and the building they had shared for two years. "I cannot and will not sit on the edge of someone else's nest," he said.[18]

His poem "To Mariengof" speaks to the heart of their friendship: "Ah, Tolya, Tolya, it is you, it is you, / For one more moment, one more time. . . ."* Mariengof wrote later:

> Esenin did not fall in love with Isadora Duncan, but with her fame, her world-wide fame. And he married her fame, not her — not an [aging], somewhat heavy, but still beautiful woman with dyed hair. He derived pleasure from walking hand in hand with this world-wide celebrity along the streets of Moscow, appearing with her at the Poet's Café, at concerts, at theatrical premieres, and hearing behind his back the whisper of many voices in which the two names were interwoven: "Duncan-Esenin . . . Esenin-Duncan."[19]

On Isadora's part, explanations were unnecessary. "You know, I'm a mystic," she told a reporter. "While I slept my soul left my body and ascended into the world where souls meet — and there I met the soul of Sergei. We fell in love immediately."[20] On more earthly terms, she had no illusions. "She understood perfectly well that for Seryozha [a Russian diminutive for Sergei] she represented a passionate infatuation and nothing more, and that his real life lay elsewhere," said Nikritina, who stayed married to Mariengof for more than forty years. "Whenever they visited us and sat down on our broken bed, she would say: Here there is something genuine, here there is love." Isadora bought Nikritina a bridal veil as a gift, remarking, with a sadness that seemed like insight, in regard to men: "It is important to be the last, and not the first."[21] She called Esenin "my last love," in any case, and "used to write 'Esenin is an angel' most assiduously in lipstick on walls, tables and mirrors," according to Mariengof.[22] Esenin taught her Russian obscenities and invited her to "Drink with me, you scabby bitch!" when he went to the Stable of Pegasus, the nightclub he owned jointly with the imaginists.

"He's not at his best tonight, poor Sergei," Isadora told Walter Duranty, the New York Times' Moscow correspondent, one night at the café, "but there's one thing I'd have you know, and it's this; the boy's a genius. All my lovers have been geniuses; it's the one thing upon which I insist." That night Esenin read his poetry and Duranty understood better that Esenin's art, like Isadora's, was a language of its own: "The poem was raw and brutal but alive and true. . . . Line after shattering line banged the consciousness of that motley crowd. . . . When

---

*"Poem to Mariengof," translated by Vitaly Chernetsky, in Kevin Moss, ed., Out of the Blue: Russia's Hidden Gay Literature, an Anthology (San Francisco: Gay Sunshine Press, 1997), 156.

he stopped there was not a sound. Everyone — cab men, speculators, prostitutes, poets, drunkards — all sat frozen with pale faces, opened mouths, and anguished eyes."

Isadora looked coolly at Duranty. "Do you still think my little peasant boy has no genius?" she said.[23] She would take Esenin to Europe and the United States, expose him to culture and great minds. "She was fleeing from her art," Max Eastman thought,[24] but as Russia turned from "wood" to "iron," in Esenin's central image, the poet needed Isadora as much as she needed him.

From November 1921 until they left Russia six months later, Esenin spent almost every day with Isadora at Prechistenka. He was writing his epic drama about the eponymous eighteenth-century rebel Pugachev, a chronicle of the peasants' revolt against Catherine the Great. A drinking friend asked him when he found time to write.

"All the time, always," Esenin answered. "I do not write with a pen. I merely put the final touches on it with a pen."[25] Eventually Isadora decided that she ought to learn Russian if she wanted to understand what her poet was saying. "I do not recognize any language except Russian," Esenin made plain, "and if anyone wants to talk to me, he'd better learn Russian."[26] Thus the English tutor at Prechistenka began to teach Isadora, beginning with the simplest Russian phrases: "What is this?" "It is a pencil." "What kind of pencil?" "It is a red pencil."

"Yes, that's very amusing," said Isadora. "But I think you'd better teach me what I ought to say to a beautiful young man when I want to kiss him . . . and things like that." Irma kept the notebook with her Russian exercises, in which she entered sentences she wanted translated: "I worship the ground you walk on!! I won't forget you. . . . You may come into this house as if it were your own."[27] Once, Schneider saw Isadora alone in her room, "shaking a fist at the three angels with lutes eyeing her from a picture on the wall" — she insisted that "one of the angels was the spitting image of Esenin."[28] When the imaginists lured him briefly out of Moscow, however, on an aborted trip to Persia, she took to her bed and refused to eat. Esenin came back but left again, in the pattern that continued as long as they were together.

"Esenin always seemed to be hurrying off somewhere to some mysterious rendezvous for which he feared he might be late," Irma observed. "Because of this mad habit, Isadora made him a present of a beautiful, thin, gold watch."[29] Inside she put her passport photograph, the only retrievable item when Esenin, erupting in rage, later smashed the watch against a wall. Neither Esenin nor Isadora could remember what started the quarrel. Isadora once called Schneider urgently to the Blue Room, where he found Esenin clutching a friend roughly by the beard.

"Why didn't you come?" Isadora whispered. "He's been holding him like that for twenty minutes." Normally Schneider had a calming influence on the poet: "He somehow quieted down at my appearance. Isadora made use of that. It was impossible to be angry with Esenin: his face suddenly beamed with an angelic, childlike smile and there was an embarrassed look in his blue eyes."[30] During one of his fits of fury, Schneider carried Esenin, speechless, his body stiff with rage, into the bathroom and ran his head under the taps, leading Isadora to worry only that he might catch cold.[31] Stories of her drinking with Esenin may or may not be exaggerated. Nikolai Klyuev, Esenin's first — and openly gay — patron, visited Prechistenka and left a picture of Isadora gulping brandy at dawn out of the house samovar. Schneider protested that she had no samovar, although she did ask him one morning to drink vodka and go with her for a walk.

"Into the fresh air! Into the fresh air!" Isadora cried. "It isn't such a bad idea to go for a walk now, is it?"[32] She became frantic when Esenin disappeared for any length of time. She pictured him "lying with his throat cut in some haunt of 'apaches'" and begged for help from his imaginist friends. "Don't imagine that I am speaking like some enamored school-girl," she wrote; "no — this is devotion and maternal solicitude."[33] Frequently Esenin turned up at Mariengof's with a bundle of clothes under his arm, looking "serious and determined."

"This time it's definite," he would say: "I've said good-bye to Isadora." Mariengof wrote:

> Two hours later the porter from Prechistenka would arrive with a letter. Esenin would write a laconic, definite reply. In another hour Mr. Schneider . . . would come. Finally she herself would appear, her lips swollen and her blue eyes shining with tears. She would fall down at his feet and throw her arms around his legs, and he would tell her to go away. Then, smiling tenderly, she would say, "Sergei Alexandrovitch, I love you."
>
> It always ended in the same way: Esenin picked up his little package and departed. . . . Of course, if Isadora had not been so insistent he would have returned to her voluntarily. He did so on other occa-

Isadora relaxing on Singer's yacht, Egypt, 1912 (MUSEUM OF THE CITY OF NEW YORK).

Paris Singer (left) and Isadora (right) in Egypt
(MUSEUM OF THE CITY OF NEW YORK).

Inside Bellevue:
the *salon bleu*
(DUNCAN COLLECTION).

Isadora's second
school, at Bellevue.

Isadora (at right,
in hood) in the
Red Cross Hospital
at Bellevue,
August 1914.

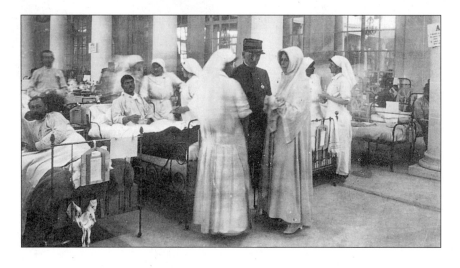

Duncan students dancing on the lawn at Rye, New York, November 1914
(MUSEUM OF THE CITY OF NEW YORK).

Isadora with
her students on
the rocks at Rye.

Ellen Terry with Anna Duncan,
New York, 1914
(KATHLEEN QUINLAN-DANSMUSEET,
STOCKHOLM).

Isadora with Paris Singer
in New York on the deck
of the S.S. *Lafayette*,
May 1916, on her way to
South America (MUSEUM OF
THE CITY OF NEW YORK).

A program for Isadora's
"Century Season," 1915.
It was the first time one of
Isadora's students (Irma)
used the name Duncan.

Isadora with Ernesto Valls
and Maurice Dumesnil
(right), Salvador, 1916.

Isadora in *La Marseillaise*, 1917 (Arnold Genthe).

Isadora and Dougie (Allan Ross Macdougall), Palm Beach, January 1917.

The Isadorables in a scarf dance. Left to right: Theresa, Irma, Lisa, Anna (ARNOLD GENTHE).

Isadora in the ruins of Bellevue with a canvas by Eugène Carrière, 1919 (DUNCAN COLLECTION).

Walter Rummel
(KATHLEEN QUINLAN-
DANSMUSEET,
STOCKHOLM).

Isadora at Cap Ferrat, 1920.

At Kopanos with Rummel and the girls, Athens, 1920. Standing, left to right: Anna, Margot, Rummel, Lisa, Theresa; seated: Isadora and Irma (Duncan Collection).

One of the few photographs of Isadora dancing, Athens, 1920, from a photograph by Edward Steichen (Joanna T. Steichen).

Isadora in the Parthenon, photographed by Steichen (JOANNA T. STEICHEN).

Isadora with admirers,
Paris, 1920.

Prechistenka 20, home of the
Duncan School in Moscow.

Isadora and Irma with
the Russian "Dunclings,"
Moscow, 1921.

Isadora and Esenin on their wedding day, with Irma, May 1922.

Isadora and Esenin, held up by Immigration on the docks in New York, October 1922.

Isadora in Paris after leaving Russia.

Victor Seroff, 1926
(DUNCAN COLLECTION).

Isadora with Seroff in Nice
(DANCE COLLECTION,
NEW YORK PUBLIC LIBRARY
FOR THE PERFORMING ARTS).

Program for Isadora's concert with Jean Cocteau and Marcel Herrand, designed by Cocteau, Nice, 1926.

Isadora and Mary Desti on the beach at Juan-les-Pins, September 1927.

Isadora inspired many artists.

Walter Schott.

Friedrich August von Kaulbach.

Edward Gordon Craig
(DANCE COLLECTION, NEW YORK PUBLIC
LIBRARY FOR THE PERFORMING ARTS).

Léon Bakst.

Auguste Rodin
(DANCE COLLECTION, NEW YORK PUBLIC
LIBRARY FOR THE PERFORMING ARTS).

Romano Romanelli, father
of Isadora's third child.

José Clará.

Jean Cocteau.

Emile-Antoine Bourdelle,
from a 1915 program.

Francis Rose (DANCE COLLECTION,
NEW YORK PUBLIC LIBRARY
FOR THE PERFORMING ARTS).

David Levine, 1964.

(San Francisco Performing Arts Library and Museum)

sions later on, when Isadora's strength failed to support the violence of her attachment.[34]

By March 1922 Esenin was a wreck. "I live roughly . . . without a place I can call my own," he complained to a friend. "I am constantly disturbed by all sorts of good-for-nothing loafers. . . . I simply don't know how to get rid of these stupid fools and I'm getting thoroughly ashamed of burning the candle at both ends."[35] Isadora threw herself into work, dancing "every evening," alone, in what Schneider called her "red" studio: "One could hear Scriabin, Liszt, Beethoven (the *Fifth Symphony*). . . . Isadora could not bear monotony in anything; she invariably got excited by some new idea that came into her head, the next inevitable *grossartige Idee*." The children went regularly to performances of the Moscow Symphony, the Maly, and Stanislavsky's Art Theatre but never, to Schneider's astonishment, to the Bolshoi Ballet. "They will be enticed by those fairy-tale spectacles," Isadora warned: "They are not yet able to distinguish between spectacular and natural, beautiful movement."[36] At the school, private lessons in English and French supplemented the state curriculum. Pupil Yulia Vashentseva recalled:

> Isadora was concerned with the spiritual side of dancing, and her demonstrations were incomparably beautiful and hard to imitate. Isadora always wanted us to have a technique stronger than hers or even Irma's, and it was Irma who saw to this. She developed our elevation by making us jump over a string, lifted higher and higher by two girls. We could do nearly full splits in the air. We also danced on high pointe. . . .
>
> But the really important thing was the absolute fusion of dance with music. Isadora had the ability to convey the minutest light and shade of the music in her dancing and gradually she developed this skill in us. We really danced *music,* not merely *to* music. Isadora's lessons expanded our horizons and lifted us to a higher plane.[37]

In February, Esenin went with Isadora to Petrograd, where they stayed at the Hotel d'Angleterre, near St. Isaac's Cathedral. "The wine cellars of the Hotel d'Angleterre were famous, and stocked with all the best pre-war vintages in uncountable pints, quarts, and magnums. Esenin soon discovered this fact; and soon discovered also that traveling with Isadora gave him a sort of *cachet*." At least once, the poet of the revolution was seen running naked through the halls of the hotel and had to be carried to his room.[38] Isadora had larger things on her mind. She asked Schneider to introduce her at the Maryinsky Theatre with a lecture and an explanation of her intentions for the school. Schneider balked.

"These people want to know and have a right to know. . . ." Isadora answered. "I came to Russia for the sake of these spectators. Do you mean to say they won't want to know why I am here?" Schneider relented but admitted to stage fright on their opening night. She poured him a glass of champagne.

"Drink it," she said. "I understand the state you're in."

"Why, if I drank it, I wouldn't be able to say anything at all," Schneider countered.

"I shouldn't have offered it to you if I didn't realize how nervous you are," Isadora said. "Drink it. I know from experience: it will give you the necessary courage." At her first concert, she was greeted with "thunderous applause" and "rapturous shouts."[39] So good were her reviews that at least one critic slammed her on that account, disgusted that Petrograd newspapers refused to "print anything but dithyrambs and rapturous reviews about Comrade Duncan."[40] In subsequent concerts there were reports of faint applause and catcalls, while on February 13 the orchestra rebelled, "mix[ing] up the major and minor keys, sometimes entering incorrectly, sometimes slowing down too much or, on the contrary, 'running away' from the conductor. Realizing that it was a case of sabotage, [he] kept turning from right to left to make both sides of the orchestra play in unison, but without success."[41]

At a special performance for Russian sailors — among them the crew of the battleship *Aurora,* heroes of the revolution — the electricity went off in the Maryinsky. Undaunted, Isadora asked for a lantern, which she held over her head for more than an hour while the audience sang revolutionary songs. Schneider remarked that "even the most talented producer" could never have imagined such a climax.[42] "When masses sing it is always beautiful," Isadora said: "I shall never forget what I have heard tonight."[43] Neither did Esenin. He appeared in her dressing room after the concert. "He looked as if he were in a trance, or still seeing some kind of vision," Isadora recalled. "I have never seen him look as beautiful. When he put his arms around me and repeated several times 'Sidora . . . Sidora . . .' I felt for the first time that he really loved me."[44]

On April 12, 1922, Isadora's mother died in Paris. Isadora had had the usual forebodings, turning pale as she sat with Irma one night at the Ouija board and saw the stylus spell out the name DORA. That night she couldn't sleep. "She saw visions," Irma wrote, "and relived again all the hours she had spent in the company of the wonderful human being who was her mother."[45] A guilt-loading letter from Elizabeth did nothing to cheer her spirits. Elizabeth had gone back to Berlin from New York in 1920 and reopened her school at Wild Park near Potsdam, in one of the kaiser's former palaces. She wrote to Isadora:

> Called to Paris by three telegrams from Raymond, I arrived within forty-eight hours to find our mother waiting with a shining face and a great beauty of expression for the final parting with her children. That she made this long journey from California for this purpose I know — otherwise she would never have had the strength. . . . I am surprised to find us, her children, so small. We are so small beside her simply heroic lines. . . . We should all be here with her together — It is my great regret that we are not big enough — She passes on as ever The Leader. All Love Elizabeth Duncan.[46]

"From that moment, Isadora became more and more restless in Moscow," Irma wrote. "She felt that she must leave Russia for a while."[47] Irma and Schneider's engagement had already been announced in the New York papers; in Moscow they needed only to sign a register to be considered husband and wife. In March, Isadora had transferred artistic direction of the school to Irma in case of her absence. Schneider became headmaster and Isadora's de facto representative in Moscow. Soon she announced plans for a party at Prechistenka to be held in the style of a Gypsy cabaret, where the children would show what they had learned, Gypsies would sing, she would dance, and everyone would go home stuffed with blinis. Even Esenin tried to dissuade her — her audience would come only to drink, he warned; the word *gypsy* carried "associations" in Russia.

Isadora ignored him, printing posters to advertise the event. A note arrived from Lunacharsky: "The notices you issued have met with an unfavorable reception by our Party leaders. I must warn you that everything you do should be kept within the limits of the strictest decorum."

"Dear Comrade," Isadora answered, "the words 'within the limits of the strictest decorum' do not exist in my vocabulary. Will you, please, explain what you mean?"[48] Her decision to leave Moscow for Germany in May would be put down to reasons of health. She took Esenin with her "first, because he was a very sick man, in need of the examination and care of a specialist; second, because he was a poet who required, so she thought, new horizons."[49] Esenin's friends all believed the trip was fatal to him.

"After all, I'm not going abroad in order to loaf about London and Paris, but to conquer," Esenin told Mariengof.

"Conquer whom, Seryozha?"

"Europe! . . . Do you understand? . . . At first, of course, I'll conquer Europe. . . . And then. . . ." Later he put it exactly: "I'm going . . . in order to show the West what a Russian poet is like."[50]

Only a week after her mother's death, Isadora cabled Sol Hurok in New York: PROPOSE TOURNEE TWELVE WEEKS OR MORE MYSELF IRMA GREAT RUSSIAN POET ESENIN AND TWENTY PUPILS. . . .[51] Hurok replied that October would suit — he sought Pavlova's advice about bringing Isadora to New York. "With the children, too!" Pavlova exclaimed. "Good. Very good."[52] Hurok agreed to pay the expenses of the tour and guaranteed Isadora forty thousand dollars net. But October was too long for her to wait — she and Esenin would leave Moscow by plane.

"It did not put her off to be told that since the air service had been started between Moscow and Germany, there had never been any private passengers, or that the price would be staggering — at least a thousand gold rubles!" Irma wrote. "She was going, she said, if it was the last act of her life."[53] Permission from Lunacharsky had to be obtained for Esenin's departure. He gave it, with the advice that Isadora and Esenin marry before they left Russia. According to Victor Seroff, Lunacharsky even made it a condition of their departure. "He'll be exposed to all sorts of dangers," Lunacharsky said. "Your name would be his protection — that is, if he were Isadora Duncan's husband."[54]

Different accounts offer a puzzle of motivations for Isadora's decision to break the rule of her life by marrying Esenin. Irma wrote: "She remembered quite well the barbaric hounding of another great Russian, Maxim Gorky," whose harassment by the press and police when he toured the United States with his common-law wife in 1906 was a lesson to freelovers everywhere. "So for the sake of a peaceful and fruitful tour in the Land of Liberty . . . Isadora Duncan went through the formality of a Soviet marriage."[55] She was roused to new fervor on May Day 1922, when, as she remarked, the streets of Moscow "were like crimson roses. Thousands of men, women, and children, with red handkerchiefs about their heads and red flags in their hands, swept by singing the *Internationale*. . . .

> 'The Earth shall rise from its foundation
> We have been naught, we shall be all!'

"As I looked and listened I wished with all my heart that this song could be radioed around the whole earth," Isadora wrote.[56] No legal contract bound a married couple in the new Soviet Union, or any financial obligation. Either party could end the union at will, without penalty or loss. Isadora was undoubtedly sincere when she told a reporter on her upcoming tour:

> I am absolutely, unutterably and vehemently opposed to all legalized marriage. I think the wedding ceremony is a most pernicious foe to the poor little victims of marriage — the children. If it were not for this dreary, monotonous, miserable, wretched, inane life-mating of humdrum Mrs. Brown with crabbed, cranky, shifty Mr. Brown, the poor little Browns might have had some chance in life. . . . I was forced into marriage by the silly laws of the lands I had to travel through as an artist. I married my husband to get him past the customs officers. . . . That's why I married, and that's only why.[57]

She was thrilled on the day of her wedding, nonetheless, May 2, 1922. "A wedding! A wedding!" Isadora cried: "Write us your congratulations! We will accept presents! . . . Plates, saucepans and frying pans! . . . For the first time in her life Isadora has a lawful husband!" Mariengof mentioned Gordon Craig.

"No! . . . No! . . . No!" Isadora answered. "Seryozha is Isadora's first husband. Now Isadora is a fat Russian wife!"

What about Paris Singer?

"Singer? No!"

"D'Annunzio?"

"No! No! No! No! Seryozha is Isadora's first lawful husband."[58] Esenin himself told the writer George Ustinov: "You don't understand anything! She's had more than a thousand men, and I'm the last."[59] At the Registry of Civil Statistics, she signed her name, "Isadora Duncan, *en alliance,* Esenin-Duncan." She was an *"artiste"* by trade, Esenin a *"littérateur."* Their wedding photo shows Irma turned away in a dramatic gesture, as if repudiating the union.

"I advised her not to take her husband to either Western Europe or America, foreseeing nothing but disaster," Irma wrote. "She would not listen to me, and I certainly wanted no part of the mad ménage. . . . And so I stayed [in Moscow], come what might, for better or worse; resolved to do my utmost to make this thing I helped to start a success."[60] Mariengof went to the wedding party at Prechistenka and saw Esenin "looking with violent hatred" at Isadora, "who was crimson with vodka and chewing painstakingly, perhaps with teeth that were not her own. . . . He found it somewhat easier to kiss this fifty-year-old woman when he was drunk. . . . And he went to their broad marital bed . . . in a state of intoxication."[61] Before leaving Moscow, Isadora asked Schneider shyly to alter the birth date on her Russian *laissez-passer,* the only legal document she would have in the future.

"It's for Esenin," she said. "We don't feel this difference of fifteen years in our ages, but when it's written down here and we hand our passports to strangers, it may make him feel uncomfortable."[62] On May 5, 1922, Esenin wrote to Klyuev: "I'm very tired and my last illness from a drinking bout made me so run down that I am even afraid to write to you in case I hurt you unnecessarily."[63] He never mentioned his marriage, or Isadora. Leaving Moscow's airport four days later, at the purported age of thirty-eight, she gave Esenin a mixture of "lemon and champagne" and scribbled a will in pencil: "In case of my death, I leave my entire property and effects to my husband. In case of our *simultaneous* deaths, then such property is to go to my brother [Augustin]. Written in clear conscience. ISADORA DUNCAN."[64]

25

"How Russian! How Russian!"

Isadora's "honeymoon tour" with Esenin, fifteen months of alcoholic bedlam and disaster, began in Berlin on May 11, 1922, when they checked into the Hotel Adlon as husband and wife. Standing east of the Brandenburg Gate, the Adlon was Berlin's finest and most expensive hotel and the day-and-night haunt of American foreign correspondents, who ran a poker game at one of its bars. No special introductions were needed before Isadora made a speech. The flight from Moscow had been rough, she said, "with violent winds"; it was good to be back in civilization:

> I love the Russian people and intend to go back next year. Nevertheless it is very comforting to return to a place where one can have warm water, napkins, heat, etc. One has other things in Russia, but poor weak humans that we are, we become so accustomed to luxuries that it is very difficult to give them up. Not that the Russians believe in giving up luxuries. On the contrary, but they believe in luxuries for all, and if there is not enough to go around, then every one should have a little less.[1]

Isadora's tipsy picture of the Soviet paradise seemed confirmed by her own and Esenin's appearance. "They arrived at Berlin . . . full of joy and happiness," Mary Desti wrote. "Isadora was radiant. All who knew her . . . still contend that she looked scarcely a day older than Sergei." Esenin looked marvelous anytime, Mary added — "it really didn't matter what he wore. He always looked beautiful except when he was in one of his terrible epileptic spells and then he looked like nothing so much . . . as the reincarnation of the devil. His whole personality changed, including the color of his eyes and his hair. One could never believe he was the same man."[2]

Esenin's epilepsy, never medically confirmed, would go only so far to cloak his manic personality as Isadora's tour progressed. According to Mary, she left Russia with "only one idea in mind, and that was to show the beauties of the world to her young poet. . . . Isadora often declared that she was his Virgil and would lead him through the world, opening his eyes to all the precious beauties in art."[3] Esenin, on the other hand, "in his mad little brain," cared for nothing but drinking, money, and clothes — rings, watches, "costumes, boots, caps, overcoats, silk shirts, pajamas," handkerchiefs, shoes, scarves — he took to the capitalist world "like a child . . . pushed into a monstrous toy shop and told he could do what he liked."[4] Rarely could Isadora drag him to a museum or a concert without stopping off first and last at the tailor's.

"He bought everything that attracted his eye in the way of lotions," Victor Seroff reported, "and he bathed, shampooed his hair, and perfumed himself so much that Isadora . . . remarked: 'He is such a child. He had never had these things in his life. I couldn't bear to chide him for it.'"[5] At the Adlon, "feeling they were very smart," Esenin appeared in a neat blue suit, a crimson tie, white canvas shoes, a top hat, cane, and spats. He began to powder his hair in the manner of an eighteenth-century aristocrat and wore Isadora's pancake and rouge when they went out in public.

"This blond angel is my husband," Isadora told Joe Milward, an American freelance reporter in Berlin.[6] They were sitting in the Adlon bar and she was feeding Esenin from her plate.

"I keep him eating steak tartare to keep him interested," Isadora said. "Do you think he may get bored?" She seemed to know that she was living in a comedy, offering Milward a madcap explanation for her predicament: "The only difference between a Russian marriage and a Russian divorce is that the marriage office is open only in the afternoons. The divorce office is open only in the mornings. . . . Isn't that excellent psychology! I'll never divorce Esenin. Even if I should want to, I'd never manage to get up in time."[7]

"She looked lovely that noon," Milward wrote, "with her gleaming red bobbed hair, her clear, deep blue eyes alive with mischief and wisdom." Traveling with Esenin, Isadora was grateful for anyone who spoke English. "I don't know any Russian," she explained helplessly, and Esenin refused to speak anything else. Milward continued:

> He had vehement reasons for this decision. He said that Russia was alive, that he was a genius of Russia and that he could not permit his genius to be contaminated by the use of languages of dead cultures. He stuck to his guns with the exception of two words: *genius* and *kaputt*. When he talked about himself he used the word *genius*. When he talked about the people, the arts, or the culture outside Russia he used the word *kaputt* and defined it first by slashing his throat with his finger followed by a gleeful pop of his tongue. . . .
>
> It was not true that Isadora and Esenin talked only in pantomime. She had learned about 400 Russian words. Pronouns were tagged to verb infinitives. Nouns were used without articles or declensions. . . . Supplemented by signs and gestures it was possible to discuss any subject. . . .
>
> One of the first things Esenin told me was Isadora's age. Each time he hurled himself into a rage he would point his finger at Isadora and shout, *"Zhenshchina ochen staraya!"* ("Woman very old!") He illustrated this by shaking four fingers in my face, followed by eight fingers. After these exhibitions, Isadora explained that Esenin suffered from *névrite*. "*Névrite* is a disease of genius," she told him. "Almost every genius has suffered from it."

Milward soon discovered that Esenin's *névrite* came and went with the drinks, being nothing but Isadora's own "neurasthenia," resurrected in French:

> I never saw him sit with either a book or a pencil in his hand, and seldom without a glass of cognac or a bottle of vodka. Day after day he was surrounded by hours of talk in languages he refused to understand. . . . One day after lunch, in the middle of a violent show of rage, he grabbed a carving knife from the table, turned, winked at me, and drove the other luncheon guests out of the house. Years of training as a roughneck enabled him to act out very exhausting performances. If this expenditure of energy were not sufficient he would rush down to the street and disappear into a bar. . . . The first time Esenin stormed out of the Adlon and disappeared into Berlin, Isadora almost had *névrite* herself.[8]

Esenin's "first recorded scandal abroad" took place on May 12, 1922, in the Russian House of Arts (Dom Iskusstva) at the Café Leon in Nollendorfplatz. Like Paris, but closer to Russia, Berlin was a center of the Russian emigration — literary, intellectual, conspiratorial, and fraught with rivalry, old and new. The House of Arts was a mainly liberal club where, until the Soviets cracked down on travel abroad, émigrés and Soviet writers could still meet one another — the house organ, *On the Eve,* published two of Esenin's poems within days of his arrival in Berlin.

"It was large, ill-lit, with a pervasive smell of German cigarettes and cigars mixed with sauerkraut, fried onions, and stale coffee," wrote composer Nicolas Nabokov, who rarely missed a Friday-night reading at the House of Arts.[9] Esenin had just finished reciting his poetry when Isadora appeared in a blaze of red silk and "proposed that they should sing the *Internationale.* . . . She and Esenin began to sing and they were joined by many people in the café. But some White guardsmen who were also there began shouting, 'Down with them!' and interrupted the singing by whistling."

"It's no use — you won't outwhistle me!" Esenin cried, jumping up on a table: "We are the best scandal-makers in the world."[10] He took delight in antagonizing Russian monarchists and former tsarist officers, who now found themselves working in Germany as waiters and taxi drivers. "Did I raise hell there because I was drunk?" Esenin asked later. "Was it so bad? I raised hell for our revolution!"[11] It suited Isadora to think so, too, in forgiving moods. "Like all geniuses, he's cracked," she said: "Mad as a hatter, strong, full of vitality. Poetic!"[12] She ordered a car, "a Buick five-seater," to take them around town. They were filmed for the newsreels and waved at the cameras with cigarettes in their hands.

"You're a bitch," said Esenin, grinning for the reporters.

"And you're a dog," said Isadora.[13] Later she told a friend on the Riviera: "He was a great poet, even if he did knock me about."[14] Photographs show her alternately bright-faced and exhausted in Berlin; unlike Mary Desti, Nicolas Nabokov thought that Isadora looked her full age and more. Russian men generally did.

"I had heard that she had aged," Nabokov wrote in his memoir, "but I was stunned by what I saw. . . . Her baggy face was glistening and red. One eye was covered with a black patch [where Esenin reputedly had hit her]. Mascara and lipstick were swimming inordinately on her lips and her brow. She wore a rumpled-looking Greekish tunic with a deep décolleté and an equally rumpled mauve shawl that covered her hair and neck."[15] Maxim Gorky joined the Esenins for dinner one night at the home of writer Alexei Tolstoy, who, like Gorky, soon returned to the Soviet Union. Gorky considered Esenin to be "the greatest poet of the new generation" and blamed Isadora unequivocally for his destruction.

"He gave a magnificent reading," Gorky reported, ". . . then he kicked Duncan in her international posterior and said to her: 'You shit.' I am a sentimental man, and I cried quite shamelessly at the sight of such a lethal combination of genuine Russian poetry and illustrious European vulgarity."[16] After dinner Isadora danced: "Aging, grown heavy, with a red, ugly face, shrouded in a brick-colored dress, she wheeled and writhed in the cramped room, clutching a bouquet of crumpled, faded flowers to her breast, and with a meaningless smile frozen on her fat face."[17] Gorky had never liked what he called "intellectual dancing" — he saw Esenin turn away sharply when Isadora finished and knelt at his feet.

"Let's go somewhere, where there is noise," Esenin said.[18] Nabokov remembered the night he took Isadora — "my mare," "the bitch" — to a gay nightclub.

"Men get undressed there and bugger each other on the stage," Esenin remarked hopefully. "I want to see it." At the next table was Count Harry Kessler, Gordon Craig's former patron, to whom Esenin took a transparent and violent dislike: "I never saw so many *Tyotki* [aunties] in one place! . . . Oh, shit. Tell him to stop ogling or I'll smash his . . ."

"Will you stop, Sergei!" said Isadora. "Stop being obscene!" Nabokov, too, was drunk, and the last thing he remembered was "Isadora's purple, irate face as she tried to hit Esenin with a vodka bottle."[19] When she found him on the ledge of their hotel window, "threatening to cast himself into the street," she put it down to "Russian melancholia. . . . This only convinced her that he really possessed the true artistic temperament."[20] And "when she simply could not stop him from breaking everything in their room at the hotel," Isadora joined in the game and gleefully smashed crockery against the walls.

"Seeing this," wrote Victor Seroff, "Esenin became perfectly petrified, fell on his knees before her and begged her to stop. 'Sidora, Sidora,' he murmured. He wanted to call a doctor. 'For a while the trick worked,' Isadora said with apparent satisfaction."[21]

To reporters, Isadora talked constantly about Russia, giving inter-

views in Berlin to plead for her school and praising the work of the
American Relief Association, in the now severely escalated Russian
famine. However, according to a report in the émigré press, "No matter what you ask her — about life in Moscow, the revolutionary masses,
art, famine — the conversation involuntarily turns to S. Esenin. 'I
love Russia so' . . . and then the invariable conclusion: 'I am in love
with Esenin.'"[22] Disregarding politics, Esenin took an uncompromis-
ing view of the Russian exiles, whom he held in contempt for their desertion of the motherland. "Though we be Asiatics," he wrote to
Schneider in Moscow, "though we smell and aren't ashamed to scratch
our backsides in public, our souls haven't the corpse-like stench theirs
have. There can be no revolution here."[23] From the moment he landed
in Berlin, he affected to despise the West.

"I was so bored," Esenin explained. "When we were still flying in
the airplane I asked them to show me Berlin from on high. They
showed me — there, they said, down below, where you can see the
lights. I couldn't refrain from spitting right down onto the Germans'
heads."[24] He spat at Isadora, too; on the night they dined with Gorky,
he read "a poem about a dog: the dog's puppies are drowned, she sees
this happen, and then she runs about, howling as she goes, for it
seems to her that the moon in the sky is her puppy."[25] Esenin wrote his
"Song About a Dog" in 1919, well in advance of meeting Isadora; still,
he seemed oblivious to the pain she must have felt on hearing the
poem explained to her. "I wept," she reported later, "and when he finished I asked him, 'Now Sergei, tell me what would you say if such a
thing had happened to a woman?'"

"To a woman? A woman?" said Esenin. He spat on the floor: "A
woman is a piece of shit! But a *dog!* Ah! a dog!"[26] Mary Desti, for one,
felt obliged to defend Isadora. "She might support Esenin and forgive
terrific battles with him," Mary wrote, but "she was never the slave
type, and . . . in all their quarrels she was more than his match."[27]
Having once endured a two-year affair with Aleister Crowley, Mary
might not have seen anything askew in Isadora's capacity for abuse.
Victor Seroff compared her partnership with Esenin to George Sand's
with Chopin: "Maternal feeling played no small part in their attitude."[28] Elsewhere in Berlin, it was the era of the flapper, of Tiller
Girls, cabaret, and the "new woman," for whose unfolding Isadora
had appeared to dedicate her life. In Esenin's case, unfortunately, liberation from Russia only reinforced what can be seen as an extreme,
but not atypical, Russian attitude toward women.

"How Russian! How Russian!" Isadora cried when Esenin fell into his rages. *"Esenin krepkii . . . oschegne krepkii!"* [Esenin is strong . . . very strong!].[29] She had the same idea about Esenin that she did about Russia itself, Gorky complained: "This lady praises the Revolution in the same way a theatre lover praises the successful premiere of a play. She should not do it."[30] With Esenin, no one who knew her understood why she did, apart from the obvious, if inadequate, explanation — that she loved him.

"I do not think there was ever a woman [who] understood more maternally her role of *inspiritrice* than did Isadora when she took Esenin to Europe," wrote Belgian poet Franz Hellens, who later that year translated Esenin's *Confessions d'un voyou* (*Confessions of a Hooligan*) into French. "This was a sublime act, for it meant for her a sacrifice and the assurance of sorrow. She had no illusions about this, knowing that the period of tormented happiness would be short; that she would live in a dramatic disequilibrium. . . . For Isadora passionately loved the poet. I saw that this love, even at its beginning, was already a sort of despair."[31] Walking one day on Kurfürstendamm, Isadora and Esenin met the Tolstoys, with their four-year-old son, Nikita. Isadora "knelt before the child in the street and then strode away unseeing" — like a figure out of Sophocles, Natalya Tolstoy thought. "The divine Isadora! Why had Time been so cruel to this absurd genius of a woman?"[32] Years later Nikita recalled Esenin, "a young man with hair lighter than straw, not white like an old man, but light gold. And a woman with hair that was lilac. And the lilac lady came over and embraced me and then sobbed."[33] According to Allan Ross Macdougall, Esenin's contempt for Isadora knew no restraint:

> What a rare lyric confession this roughneck could have made of that day in Berlin when, coming into the hotel room and finding his wife weeping over an album containing portraits of her unforgettable Deirdre and Patrick, he ruthlessly tore it from her and, throwing it into the fire, cried in a drunken rage, as he held her back from saving her precious memorial: "You spend too much time thinking of these ——— children!"[34]

In June, Alexander Kusikov came to Berlin and vanished with Esenin for several days on an imaginist debauch. Berlin in 1922 was already "the babylon of the world," according to Stefan Zweig — "bars, amusement parks, honky-tonks sprang up like mushrooms. . . .

Along the entire Kurfürstendamm powdered and rouged young men sauntered . . . and in the dimly-lit bars one might see government officials and men of the world of finance tenderly courting drunken sailors without any shame. Even the Rome of Suetonius had never known such orgies as the balls of Berlin."[35] Indeed, Isadora's command of Esenin and the situation never seem to have failed her when she perceived that his sexual interests had strayed. By the time she caught up with Esenin and Kusikov, she was "like a demon of destruction."

"Leave this brothel immediately and follow me," Isadora commanded. Meekly, Esenin did as he was told — the scandal was duly reported in émigré newspapers.[36] While looking for her husband, Isadora had stopped at the American consulate, in quest of a new passport. Her own had been confiscated by Russian authorities when she entered the Soviet Union and was subsequently lost. Now, she learned that under U.S. immigration law, an American woman who married a foreign national automatically lost her U.S. citizenship. Therefore, outside of Russia and those few countries that had already recognized the Soviet Union, Isadora was stateless. She had hoped to be in Paris by the end of June. Joe Milward wrote:

> In desperation she and Esenin called on the French consul, who refused to grant a visa for them because Esenin was a citizen of a government which had not yet been recognized by France. Into the middle of this muddle a letter arrived from Isadora's bank in Paris returning a check she had cashed on her arrival in Berlin, on which payment had been refused, explaining that a number of creditors had attached her bank account and that none of her funds in the bank could be used until said creditors had been satisfied.

It appears that Isadora owed nearly fifty thousand francs to Parisian banks, moneylenders, and shopkeepers. Sending Milward to Paris with her power of attorney, she instructed him to settle her accounts from what remained in the bank and to call on Cécile Sorel as soon as he arrived. Sorel was the "favorite" of former French President Raymond Poincaré. "Tell her Esenin and I must have a special visa and it's as good as done," said Isadora. From her trunk she took a large bolt of red velvet, "about ten feet long and three feet wide. It was heavily brocaded with pearls, precious and semiprecious jewels — rubies, emeralds, and amethysts," which she might have sold herself in order to raise money.

"This is the train of a court dress that belonged to the tsarina of

Russia," Isadora said quietly. "It was looted from the palace during the revolution. . . . Take it to Sorel."[37]

With Esenin, Isadora spent a quiet week at Elizabeth Duncan's re-opened school in Potsdam, then piled in the Buick for a tour of the Rhineland. Esenin needed a cure, she decreed. "Berlin is very quiet and dull — was delighted to leave it," she wrote to Irma in Moscow. "The house in Grunewald was lost thru the war — etc. The lawyer handed me the absurd sum of 90,000 marks for it. All my moneys properties etc. in Paris were attached so we have had nothing but difficulties. . . . Hope everything can be cleared up soon." The postwar German inflation had just begun. In January 1922 the Reichsbank issued the first ten-thousand-mark note: by the end of the year, a billion marks might buy a sausage and a roll.

"I am enclosing a check as [an] experiment," Isadora went on; "if you succeed in cashing it I can send other — to send money thru bank is impossible."[38] After that, Irma heard nothing more from her. From Wiesbaden, Esenin wrote to Schneider:

> The atmosphere in Berlin made me go to pieces. My nerves are so on edge I can hardly walk. . . . I don't drink anymore and am starting to work. If only Isadora were not so crazy and would allow me to settle down somewhere, I could make a lot of money. . . . [Her] affairs are in a terrible mess. . . . As if nothing were the matter she rushes by car now to Lübeck, now to Leipzig, now to Frankfurt, now to Weimar. I follow her in silent obedience for she becomes hysterical whenever I disagree with her.

To this, Esenin added a postscript: "My warmest greetings to Irma. Isadora married me a second time and is now no longer Duncan-Esenin, but just Esenin."[39] There is no record of another civil service, however, and neither of them would have set foot in a church. "What can I say about this most terrible realm of philistinism," Esenin wrote from Düsseldorf, "which borders on idiocy? Apart from the foxtrot there is almost nothing here. I've not met one human being so far, and see no trace of one. Mister dollar is terribly fashionable, but no one gives a damn for art."[40] A letter to Mariengof was even gloomier: "How I would like to leave this nightmarish Europe. . . . It is an endless graveyard. These people who move faster than lizards are not people, but worms who eat their dead; their houses are coffins and the Continent is the grave. Those who did live here died long ago. . . . In Berlin I made, of course, many scandals and a lot of noise."[41]

"Isn't he adorable?" said Isadora. *"Isn't he a darling?"*[42] Before leaving Berlin, Milward secured her the services of a Russian interpreter. This was Lola Kinel, a twenty-three-year-old Polish writer who published her memoirs of the job in a lively autobiography, *This Is My Affair.*[43] Kinel's extended duties embraced anything that Jeanne, the maid, refused to do. Thus, she found herself sorting Isadora's trunk of personal and theatrical mementos — "a sort of *résumé,* a printed *résumé,* [of] her life as an artist and her life as a woman — or shall I say courtesan? For, I think, she was the greatest courtesan of our times, in the rich grand old sense of this word." The large wicker hamper was one of a dozen trunks Isadora transported with her on tour:

> There were programs innumerable in all the languages of the world; there were thousands of press clippings — bunches of them in rubber bands and stray ones which fluttered about the trunk and the room. There were packets with letters and many single ones, letters beginning with "Dearest" or "Darling" and "My very own" which I sorted according to their handwriting and which I didn't read. And then there were the photographs — of many men: clever men, old men, middle-aged men, and young men. Beautiful young men. . . . I placed them face downwards, for once during that long afternoon Esenin came in and, seeing all the photos of the handsome young men, he grew pale and his eyelids grew pink, which was a sign that he was vexed.[44]

Over time, Kinel came to know all of Esenin's "signs" — for the moment, he had sworn off alcohol: "I understood then . . . why Esenin's face was so grey and his lips blue, and why he was often so terribly tense. He had been drinking for several years, drinking heavily, as most Russians do, and this sudden complete stop must have been a bad strain on his nerves."[45] Esenin's sexual obsessions expressed themselves constantly in lewd and lurid remarks. "I am not going to beat around the bush — or cheat," Esenin told Kinel. "I want absolute freedom — other women if I like. If [Isadora] wants my company, I shall stay in her house, but I don't want any interference."

"I can't tell her that, Sergei Alexandrovitch," Kinel protested. "Please!"

"You have to! It's your job!"

"I won't!"[46] The poet made a display of pointing out "aunties" when he saw them. "One bed. See?" he said when Isadora hired

British pianist Ralph Lawton to help her rehearse for her upcoming tour. Lawton arrived with an American friend, and the two of them shared a hotel room.

"Perhaps the fellows are poor," Kinel suggested.

"Poor like hell. They always take a room with one bed. Jeanne told me."[47] Kinel described the summer as "an education." When Esenin asked her to translate his poems into English, she was "a bit frightened and a bit shocked. . . . I knew that it was a sacrilege and an impossibility both. Esenin's poetry is almost purely lyrical: it is music expressed in terms of Russian words, of Russian phonetics, and so could never be rendered into any other language."[48] But Esenin insisted: he intended to become as famous as his wife.

"How many millions of people will know me if my poems appear in English?" he asked Kinel.

"We began to count on our fingers: England, 40,000,000; the United States, 125,000,000; Canada, 10,000,000 perhaps — I wasn't sure. . . . Australia! New Zealand! India!"

Esenin clapped his hands and turned to Isadora. "A dancer can never become very great because her fame doesn't last," he declared. "It is gone the moment she dies."

"No," said Isadora, "for a dancer, if she is great, can give to the people something that they will carry with them forever. They can never forget it, and it has changed them, though they may not know it."

"But when they are gone, Isadora? . . . People may come and admire you — even cry. But after you are dead no one will remember. Within a few years all your great fame will be gone. . . . No Isadora!" Kinel wrote:

> All this he said in Russian, for me to translate, but the last two words he said in the English intonation, straight into Isadora's face, with a very expressive, mocking motion of his hands, as if he had waved the remnants of the mortal Isadora to the four winds. . . . "But poets live," he continued, still smiling. "I, Esenin, shall leave my poems behind me. And poems live. Poems like mine live forever."
>
> Beneath the obvious mockery and teasing tone there was something extraordinarily cruel. A shadow passed over Isadora's face as I translated what he said. Suddenly she turned to me, her voice very serious: —
>
> "Tell him he is wrong, tell him he is wrong. I have given people beauty. I have given them my very soul when I danced. And this beauty did not die. It exists somewhere. . . ." Suddenly she had tears in

her eyes and she added in her pitiful, childish Russian: *"Krasota nie umiray."* (Beauty not dies.) . . . With a characteristic gesture, [Esenin] pulled Isadora's curly head towards him and patted her on the back, saying mockingly, *"Ekh,* Duncan." . . . Isadora smiled. All was forgiven.

Soon they were arguing about God — the Bolsheviks had banned the word from Russian books and newspapers.

"But Bolsheviki right," Isadora insisted. "No God. Old. Silly."

"Ekh, Isadora!" said Esenin. "Why everything comes from God. All poetry and even your dances."

"No, no. Tell him that my gods are Beauty and Love. There are no others. . . . All the hell is right here on earth. And all paradise." Kinel observed that she stood very tall, "like a caryatid, beautiful, magnificent, and fearful," as she gestured toward the bed she shared with Esenin and cried in Russian, "with tremendous force: — *'Vot Bog!'* (This is God!)."

"Esenin sat in his chair, pale, silent, and completely annihilated." Kinel slipped from the room.[49]

When Milward got back from Paris, he brought Isadora the balance of her French bank account, about forty thousand francs. Milward had paid off bankers, lawyers, the Swiss sanatorium where Raymond Duncan's wife had died, and the painter Sylvestre Bonnard, who had briefly rented Isadora's studio in Neuilly until a water pipe burst and caused a wall and ceiling to collapse. Bonnard sued Isadora for the inconvenience and won the value of "one unpainted work" — ten thousand francs, by judgment of the court. "Isadora took such 'stupidities' in her accustomed cheerful, smiling stride," said Milward, who joined the Esenins and Kinel on their tour of the Rhine.

"Incidentally, we saw very little of the Rhine," Milward wrote. "Isadora was a night person. It was usually about 3:00 P.M. before the car started for the next stop." The goal of each afternoon was to find a place to stay for the night, with a good restaurant and a supply of 1911 champagne. During her years with Paris Singer, Isadora had learned "that the most delicious champagne had been made from grapes grown in the summer of 1911, due to that year having had a perfect climatic combination of sun and rain"; and Milward was sent to inquire, at every hotel and inn along the route, if Miss Duncan might be accommodated in this regard. "If the answer [was] yes, we stopped there for the night."[50]

Isadora called Singer "the Grand Duke," Milward discerned: "This or that 'happened during the time of the Grand Duke,' she would say. 'The Grand Duke married his nurse in order to get away from me.'"[51] To Milward, she also confided her resentment of Walter Rummel: "I went [to Russia] because I discovered that my Archangel was making love to my pupil in the afternoon." It wasn't Rummel and Anna's affair per se that disturbed Isadora, but his deception, "the manner in which this liaison had been kept from her. In her references to it the words *deceit* and *disloyalty* occurred again and again."[52] Esenin had only to suggest going back to Russia to throw her into a panic: "He could get anything if he threatened to leave. . . . He was highly intuitive. It was almost as if he could smell what he couldn't understand."[53]

In July the Esenins left for Brussels on the advice of Cécile Sorel, whose influence with "certain people" stopped at the German border: it would be easier to obtain French visas in Belgium. Esenin had already written to Maxim Litvinov: "Dear Comrade Litvinov, would you be so kind as to help us get out of Germany to proceed to the Hague? I promise not to sing the *Internationale* in public."[54] Isadora entered Belgium on a transit visa, as a touring performer, having hastily arranged concerts at the Théâtre Galéries with the help of Eugène Ysaÿe. Esenin came along as her "manager," by sworn affidavit. True to Sorel's word, their French visas were delivered on arrival in Brussels.

"You would probably not believe your eyes," Esenin wrote to Schneider on July 13: "Almost a month now since I've taken a drink." Isadora still counted on Irma to join her with the Russian children. "We await your arrival impatiently," Esenin concluded. "I await you, in particular, because Isadora has no notion of practical matters, and I find it very painful to watch the pack of bandits that surrounds her."[55]

One of the "bandits" was American writer Herman Mankiewicz — "Mank" — who found himself broke in Berlin at the height of the inflation and went to work as Isadora's publicity agent, hoping to make enough money to get back to New York. "This German is ruining my Yiddish," Mank complained.[56] A natural comedian and a heavy drinker, he kept the Esenins company through many a jarring night.

"They were loving," Mank's wife, Sara, remembered, "but both sort of out of control. Lots of laughter. And that madman — nobody could understand him. She would tell him things in English, and he would pretend to understand — laugh boisterously and start quoting Russian poetry — and she would stamp her feet and get up and do a revolutionary dance. It was terribly exciting and funny."[57] If Mank eventually fell out of favor, it was only because he insisted on a salary — he remained indifferent to Isadora's dancing. "The diva has danced twice and she ain't so good," he wrote to Sara from Brussels. "On the whole there's a fleshiness and lack of fire that makes it impossible to keep up any illusion."

When Mankiewicz quit in Paris, still unpaid, Isadora threw "a random handful of cash at his feet" and "railed at him for his disloyalty."[58] She had had a "remarkable" advance sale of $12,000 in Brussels, and the Trocadéro guaranteed her ten concerts with the Russian children, if she could get them into France. Isadora was warned about making "Red propaganda," however, and was kept under surveillance: she and Esenin were reputedly the first Soviet citizens to enter France. When Schneider cabled that the Kremlin had refused to let her students leave Russia — "she entirely overlooked the fact that such a tour would have entailed enormous expense"[59] — Isadora threw up her hands in disgust. Irma wrote calmly in *Duncan Dancer:* "That summer and the following winter, I lived on the simple fare the school provided . . . while my foster mother toured the States. All my efforts were concentrated on my forthcoming debut as a solo dancer in Moscow."[60]

Two months remained before Isadora's tour began in New York. "But there had never been two months without problems in the life of Isadora Duncan," Milward wrote, "and there never would be. . . . Instead of showing Paris to Esenin, she decided to spend a month showing him Venice."[61] According to Franz Hellens, her house on rue de la Pompe really was full of bandits: "She had leased it to an American, who went home without paying the rent, taking her best carpets with him. . . . Her servants were all stealing from her; a crowd gathered every night in her kitchen to eat off her bounty. Esenin didn't mind, but Isadora didn't dare put a stop to these orgies."[62]

In Venice, the Esenins lived for two weeks at the Hotel Excelsior on the Lido, where Lola Kinel was finally dismissed for insubordination: she had refused to send two telegrams to Moscow that Esenin, drinking again, wrote in a stupor.

"I'm terribly sorry," Isadora said as Kinel packed her bags. "It's Esenin. He hates you now." The women formed a bond in Venice as they tried to keep the poet from harming himself. One day, Esenin disappeared "for a walk."

"He mustn't be left alone when he is in this state," Isadora warned. "He might kill himself or someone else." With Kinel, she scoured the length of the Lido looking for her husband — she suspected that he had fallen asleep beneath a tree: "It was noon of a day in August — the hottest month in Italy. . . . We drove very slowly, stopping at every bush, clump of brush, or bit of hedge that looked as if it might conceal a man." Isadora drank champagne in the car as they searched:

> The wine had made her dreamy and she rambled on in a half-reminiscent way. She talked with a humor and irony peculiar to her, which were delicious. She spoke of her lovers, of the strange fate which seemed to give her only eccentric men for lovers; she discussed the nicest way to commit suicide — for that is what she intended to do if we found Esenin dead. She ate salted almonds, which she liked so much, having purchased a whole bagful of them from a little street vendor. She offered me some and then said, half seriously: —
> "But I oughtn't to die without writing my biography. It's amazing, you know. You could help me write it — you like to write."
> "No one could do it better than yourself, Isadora."
> "Oh, but I am too lazy . . . I hate to hold the pen."
> The afternoon ebbed away; we had looked at all the bushes on the island and we returned to the hotel. I was very tired, and even Isadora looked drooping. . . . The last thing I heard her say, as she stretched luxuriously on the sand, was: "No, I don't think I shall commit suicide yet; my legs are still very beautiful."[63]

Her poet found, Isadora returned to Paris with less than fifty francs in her pocket; she spent the last money she had on a bottle of Coty perfume. Esenin caused a scene at the Comédie-Française, leaping from his seat when Cécile Sorel appeared onstage. "If this is the French national theatre and that woman the greatest actress in France, give me a drink!"[64] Esenin cried (thankfully, in Russian). Somehow Isadora found the money to pay Franz Hellens and his Russian wife, Maria Miloslavskaya, for their translation of Esenin's "Hooligan" poems.

"I saw them almost every day," Hellens wrote, "sometimes in Isadora's little house in the Rue de la Pompe or sometimes at the Hotel Crillon, where they had taken refuge from domestic difficulties."[65] Unable to settle her bill at the Crillon, Isadora decamped to the Majestic, where the management demanded payment in advance. Insulted, she took a taxi she couldn't pay for to the Trianon Palace in Versailles, where she had spent the last night with her children before they died. Here the staff was more sympathetic, bowing discreetly when Isadora asked that the bill be sent to her later. Another friend of Esenin's, Vladimir Vetlugin, had turned up in Paris. Isadora made him her secretary — Esenin would need someone to talk to in America, she explained. All three were set to sail from Le Havre in the last week of September. Hellens saw the Esenins at rue de la Pompe just before they left:

> I arrived when they were still at table and found them in a strange and somber humor. They hardly spoke to me. They were clasped together like two young lovers. . . . As his wife showed herself to be more nervous than usual, seeming to lose the admirable coolness, the sense of measure, the rhythm which was the foundation of her art and also her nature, Esenin took it into his head to get her drunk. There was no bad intention on his part; quite the contrary. It was his own way of calming shaken nerves. He forced her wheedlingly, softly, lifting the glass himself to his wife's lips. As the effects began to show themselves I read more clearly in the dancer's features the despair that she usually knew how to hide under a calm and smiling air. . . . That evening I understood that these two beings, notwithstanding their differences, could never separate without tragedy.[66]

At the sight of the Atlantic Ocean, Esenin "began to roar with laughter." The restaurant on the S.S. *Paris* was "somewhat bigger than our Bolshoi Theatre," he reported. It took him five minutes to walk from his stateroom to dinner, passing by libraries, movie theaters, swimming pools, bars, and dance halls. Esenin was astounded: "The world I had previously inhabited struck me as terribly comic and absurd. . . . From this moment I stopped loving beggarly Russia."[67] Broke or not, Isadora sailed in a *suite de luxe*. Her manager, "Mr. Hurok," would pick up the bill, she told the Cunard Line, showing the bursar her signed contract. Milward spoke of her "American resourcefulness — she called it her 'Irish.'"[68]

"As a dancer," Isadora was heard to say, "I am a really good orator."[69] As an orator, she would find nothing but trouble in the United States. She arrived without a passport, with only her Russian travel documents and visas for herself and Esenin: it never occurred to her that Isadora Duncan might be mistaken for anyone else. On the voyage to New York, she drafted a statement, "Greetings to the American People,"[70] and gave it to reporters when the *Paris* docked a week later, on October 1, 1922.

"We are the representatives of young Russia," Isadora began. "We are not mixing in political questions. We believe the soul of Russia and the soul of America are about to understand each other." She knew how bad the situation might be for her husband. At the height of the first Red scare, in 1919, anarchist Emma Goldman and her companion, Alexander Berkman, were deported from New York to Russia on the order of the U.S. attorney general, along with hundreds of other real or suspected socialists, aliens, and "undesirables." J. Edgar Hoover had just taken charge of what became the Federal Bureau of Investigation, born under Prohibition in a paranoid hunt for bootleg liquor and Red propaganda. Race riots broke out in the South and Southwest; thousands of immigrants were arrested and deported without trial. Isadora seriously misjudged the intensity of American Russophobia.

"It was not suspicion but sheer, unreasoning terror," Sol Hurok wrote; "it was not mistrust but the bitterest hatred." Isadora's new manager was himself Russian, although a naturalized American, and could ill afford the kind of trouble she and Esenin brought to his firm: "As the first slap was dealt her, a lesser soul would have quailed and fled; a wise one would have sealed her lips and danced. But Isadora was neither weak nor wise."[71] Women in America had just been given the vote. Her greetings continued:

> We have come to America with only one idea in mind — to tell of the Russian conscience and to work for the *rapprochement* of the two great countries. It is only the field of art that we are working. No politics, no propaganda. . . . In Russia there is an avid thirst to study America and her sweet people. May it not be that art will be the medium for a new Russian-American friendship? May the American woman with her keen intelligence help us in our task! . . . America — our last but greatest hope! Greetings and thanks to the American people!

When the *Paris* docked in New York Harbor, Isadora and Esenin were met on deck by Customs officials and forbidden to leave the ship. They received no explanation for their detention. Hurok found Isadora in the first-class lounge, "in her long cape and white felt hat, holding court for a vast gathering of reporters and photographers."[72]

"Can you tell me why I am being detained?" Isadora asked sweetly. "This man here" — she pointed to an immigration official — "is impossible." Someone suggested that she might be in "hot water" as an emissary of Lenin. She laughed. "Why, I never saw Lenin or Trotsky in all the time I have been [in Russia]," she said, her eyes wide with innocence (in fact, she saw Lenin at the Bolshoi in November, but they were not introduced). "And my husband is just a young Russian poet. He's no politician, but a genius. [We] are viséd properly and we aren't coming here to spread propaganda."[73]

While she talked, Isadora kept her arm protectively around Esenin, "who, in honor of the occasion, had powdered his hair like a Louis XIV marquis."

"What's the idea with the powder?" someone asked. The newsmen broke apart, laughing.

Isadora patted Esenin on the cheek: "It was explained that poets and artists in general were privileged to practice their own conception of style."[74] Despite the difference in their ages, "both appeared to be genuinely in love and took no pains to conceal their mutual adoration." Esenin was "an imaginative poet" — "his press notices call him melancholy, but he seems the most cheerful Bolshevik that ever crossed the Atlantic." Several times Isadora paused to reassure him in French: "*Sois tranquille.*"[75]

That night the captain of the *Paris* invited the Esenins to remain on board as his guests: "In this way they were saved the humiliation of passing the night in the immigrant quarters of Ellis Island." Isadora had been firm about that: "I am an American girl, and am proud of it, but I will never go to Ellis Island. I will return to Paris on this ship before I will suffer the indignity of being sent to Ellis Island."[76] When Hurok left the boat, he was strip-searched, news that ran high in the columns and headlines. Hoover's men were looking for "invisible writing."

"There is just one thing that astonishes me," Isadora remarked before retiring. "That is to hear that the American government has no sympathy with revolutions. I had always been taught that our great country was started by a revolution. . . ."[77] Hurok wrote:

> The next morning the papers had denials from the Bureau of Immigration that any orders had been issued to detain her. [Columnist] Heywood Broun wrote caustically of the "blundering boorishness" of America's welcome to Isadora. . . . A statement was issued later, explaining that she had been held by the Department of Justice because of her long residence in Moscow, and because there was some suspicion that she and her husband might be acting as "friendly couriers" for the Soviet Government, carrying secret documents.[78]

At eleven A.M. on October 2, Isadora and Esenin were brought to the Customs office at the Cunard Line pier:

> There all their baggage was opened and thoroughly inspected. . . .
> Every article was examined; all wearing apparel being turned inside
> out and all pockets felt; even the soiled linen did not escape poking
> and shaking. All written matter was microscopically peered at; all
> printed matter in what seemed to be the Russian language — mostly
> Russian poems and classics — was confiscated. And sheet by sheet all
> the orchestral and piano music was turned over, explanations being
> demanded from the dancer as to the meaning of her marginal notes on
> several of the scores.[79]

On the assurance that she would not be held there overnight,
Isadora finally relented and agreed to go to Ellis Island for an interview. She emerged two hours later with a grin. "Pronounced innocent," she said — "not guilty!" The New York Tribune reported that
"the three inspectors composing the review decided that there was no
ground for [suspicion], and that the only thing revolutionary about
Isadora was her bizarre costume." She looked "like a Wild West cow-
girl," in a blue tailored suit, striped in yellow and red, with an orange
blouse, "a red caracul hat," and boots of soft red leather.[80] Esenin
bowed to the Statue of Liberty as a Coast Guard cutter took them back
to shore — Isadora only waved. She gave a speech at the dock:

> I feel as if I were acquitted of murder. They seemed to think that
> a year's residence in Moscow had made me a blood-thirsty criminal
> ready to throw bombs at the slightest provocation. Then they asked
> me silly questions, such as, "Are you a classic dancer?" I told them I
> didn't know, because my dancing is quite personal. They wanted to
> know what I looked like when I danced! How do I know? I never saw
> myself dance. . . . Among other absurd things they wanted to know
> what Sergei and I thought of the French Revolution!
>
> Before I set foot on Ellis Island I had absolutely no idea that the
> human mind could worry itself into figuring out all the questions that
> were rapidly fired at me today. I have never had anything to do with
> politics. All my time in Russia has been spent taking care of little or-
> phans and teaching them my art. To say or even hint that I am a Bol-
> shevik is Rot! Rot! Rot![81]

That day Isadora walked forty blocks from Battery Park to the
Waldorf-Astoria, "a triumphal parade of one," Hurok wrote, carrying
a wilted bouquet of roses left over from the day before.[82] "Ellis Island
inspectors who detained the dancer and her husband did not wish to

talk about it," the *Tribune* disclosed. "They insinuated that they were acting under the instructions of the State Department . . . and that there was nothing unusual in the proceedings."[83] Esenin seemed overwhelmed, and when photographers asked Isadora to pose for pictures, she refused. "Too many wrinkles," she said, laughing and pointing at the sun.[84] Her first three concerts at Carnegie Hall sold out in a single day.

Isadora danced her Tchaikovsky program on Saturday, October 7, before an audience of three thousand people: "Outside stood hundreds of others waiting in the vain hope of obtaining even a foot of standing room. . . . When the program was ended, the audience stood cheering the dancer and seemed loath to leave the hall. Isadora came forward to speak."[85] The *Times* remarked that Russia had been kind to her: "So slender she looked that it seemed the Isadora of former days."

"I come to you from Moscow," Isadora began. "But why must I go to Moscow after illusions that don't exist, when you in America also need the dance for your children?"[86] She had gone to Russia only because America refused to help. "I give you invitations," she cried, quoting Whitman, and won another ovation from the sophisticated crowd:

> I know the American nervous child, because I was one myself. Soon I hope to show you fifty Russian children dancing Beethoven's *Ninth Symphony*. I can bring that to life in New York — make it more real than Broadway. . . . Why does not America give me a school? . . . America has all that Russia has not, Russia has things that America has not. Why will America not reach out a hand to Russia, as I have given my hand? . . . Why am I alone? I composed [the *Pathétique*] for sixty children, but I am always alone. My pupils are seduced by either the Rheingold or something else. I am always alone![87]

"Thus began the Duncan progress through America," Hurok wrote. "From that day never a phone rang but I trembled to answer it."[88] Isadora reached Boston on October 22 and found nothing but rudeness and incomprehension. Henry Taylor Parker of the *Boston Evening Transcript* alone praised her work, but even the gallant HTP remarked that "the merciless years" had "stiffened" her: "Even the vivid life of that outflung pose and motion of joy — now part of the working capital of every dancer the world around — no longer vibrates upon ear and eye."[89]

Esenin caused an uproar before Isadora's concert in Boston by hanging a red flag from a window at Symphony Hall. "Long live Bol-shevism!" he cried to the street. It was the first salvo in the noisiest ex-plosion of Isadora's career.

"He's a darling, but what can I do?" Isadora asked Hurok, who telephoned nervously from New York. "He had a drink or two. Mr. Hurok, don't be disturbed. He won't do it again."[90] But he did, at her Saturday matinee. The Boston critics had been merciless that morn-ing, mocking Isadora's age, her weight, her legs, her dyed hair, and her "tedious" interpretations of Wagner. Parker captured the local mood in his next review, headlined ISADORA INCONTINENT. . . . Silence on the part of the aggrieved artist is normally counted the wiser way."[91]

"Thank God the Boston critics don't like me," Isadora cried at her second concert. "If they did, I should feel I was hopeless. . . . I give you something from the heart. I bring you something real."[92] The au-dience was filled with "young boys and girls," according to press ac-counts, "students from Harvard and the young men and women from the Boston Art and Music schools." At the end of the *Pathétique*, hold-ing her red Liberty scarf high over her head, Isadora waved it from side to side and shouted: "This is red! So am I! . . . You were once wild here! Don't let them tame you!"[93]

What happened next isn't certain. Isadora insisted that she never "mismanaged [her] garments," but the Boston audience, one way or another, caught sight of her naked breasts. According to Hurok, who wasn't there, she made sure that they did, ripping her tunic down de-liberately while crying out, "You don't know what beauty is! This — this is beauty!"[94] One reporter insisted that the offending breast fell out of Isadora's tunic while she was dancing.[95] Parker remembered it happening when she "answered recalls or stretched a congratulatory hand to the conductor." As always, the critic was polite: "The out-come . . . was a degree of bodily revelation unbecoming to a middle-aged woman, too obviously high in the flesh. It was the negation of the sculptural beauty that she professes to seek."[96] *Musical America* added archly: "What the good people of Boston must have suffered from a flimsy garment which slipped repeatedly can only be realized by those who know the Bostonians."[97] As it happened, the *Boston Transcript* had run a series of Bolshevik scare stories that week, "The Red Movement in the United States." Boston was already "apprehen-sive. Isadora's words blew it up."[98]

"I'M RED!" CRIES ISADORE DUNCAN. STAGE REMARKS FOLLOW REPULSIVE

DANCE. AUDIENCE IS DISGUSTED! — such were the headlines as far away as Oregon.[99] "She looked pink, talked red, and acted scarlet!" in another account.[100] The *Chicago Tribune* reported on October 23:

> In concluding one of the most amazing performances ever witnessed in Boston, Isadora Duncan, modern originator of the classical dance, waved a flaming red scarf which a moment before had been the major part of her costume . . . and shouted: "This is red! That is what I am!"
>
> She shook the symbol of revolt in the faces of the spectators, most of whom were standing, and cried: "Don't let them tame you!"
>
> The remarks from the stage followed a dance program that shocked and disgusted the vast audience . . . to such an extent that three-quarters of them left the hall, mid the taunts of the daring performer. . . .
>
> Mme. Duncan came on the stage to dance Tchaikovsky's "Symphony No. 66 [sic]." Her costume was exceedingly scant . . . and the upper part persisted in slipping down.
>
> Later as the contortions and writhings of the dancer became even wilder, it slipped down only to stay down. The crowd held their breath for it seemed the dancer would leave behind what little she had left on her body.

Before long, Isadora found herself banned on the order of James M. Curley, Boston's vastly popular (and vastly corrupt) Irish mayor. "No further licenses to perform" would be issued to Miss Duncan, Curley proclaimed, "in view of the duty the city owes to the decent element. I beg to say that this suspension, after the recent disgraceful performance by the dancer, will continue as long as I am mayor."[101] Three departments of federal government — Labor, State, and Justice — all announced that they would investigate the Esenins and, if cause were found, deport them. "I'd like to be Secretary of Labor for fifteen minutes," Reverend Billy Sunday exclaimed: "I'd send her back to Russia and Gorky, that —" The best Sunday could come up with was "Bolshevik hussy."[102]

Before leaving Boston, Isadora called a press conference at the Copley Plaza Hotel. She hadn't meant "red" in the Bolshevik sense, she said (no one believed her), but as Gorky meant it when he divided the world into three kinds of people, black, red, and gray. The black were purely destructive; the red, creative: "And if I am a 'Red,' as they say, then those who go about so busily taking the alcohol out of wine,

the beauty out of the theatre, and the joy out of living, are grays."[103]
Hurok had already begged her to stop making speeches. She continued to lecture the press:

> Why should I care what part of my body I reveal? Why is one part
> more evil than another? . . . If my Art is symbolic of any one thing, it
> is symbolic of the freedom of woman and her emancipation from the
> hidebound conventions that are the warp and woof of New England
> Puritanism. To expose one's body is art; concealment is vulgar. . . . I do
> not appeal to the lower instincts of mankind as your half-clad chorus
> girls do. . . . My body is the temple of my art. I expose it as a shrine for
> the worship of beauty.[104]

It was too late for explanations. "My manager tells me that if I
make more speeches the tour is dead," Isadora told her audience in
Chicago. "Very well. The tour is dead. I will go back to Moscow where
there is vodka, music, poetry, and dancing. . . . Oh, yes, and Freedom!"[105] Hurok gave her a nickname: "Woman from Mars."[106]

26

Just a Wee Bit Eccentric

"Boston? — *pouf!*"[1] said Isadora. "I did not tear off my dress. . . .
I could not possibly have torn my dress off. It was fastened over the
shoulders and around my hips and waist by elastic bands."[2] From city
to city, she demonstrated as she talked — the Boston incident pursued
her like no other in her career.

"And this is the little red dress which frightened Boston!" Isadora
cried at Public Hall in Cleveland. "I've worn this dress for twenty
years. Is it so shocking? Is Cleveland more hardboiled than Boston?"
She "whirled around on one bare foot," lifting the edges of her tunic.
A policeman appeared at the front of the stage.

"I am not going to say anything against the United States government," Isadora added quickly. "I love America! Who wouldn't? Who
couldn't?" To a local critic, her dancing looked "easily imitated, and
one may expect comedians impersonating her to be the life of more
than one party in Cleveland."[3] Half the audience had already walked
out: "She was hissed, she was hooted, she was booted, they threw
things at her, and left the hall."[4] One who stayed was poet Hart Crane,
a Cleveland native, not yet fully embarked on his own flamboyant
journey to the brink. Crane would use Isadora's image and words —
"No ideals have ever been fully successful on this earth" — as em-
blems of American heroism in his narrative masterwork, *The Bridge*.

From Cleveland he wrote to share his "excitement at seeing Isadora Duncan dance." She gave her Tchaikovsky program:

> It was glorious beyond words, and sad beyond words too, from the rude and careless reception she got here. It was like a wave of life, a flaming gale that passed over the heads of the nine thousand in the audience without evoking response other than silence and some maddening cat-calls. After the first movement of the *Pathétique* she came to the fore of the stage, her hands extended. Silence — the most awful silence! I started clapping furiously until she disappeared behind the draperies. At least one tiny sound should follow her from that vast audience. She continued through the performance with utter indifference for the audience and with such intensity of gesture and such plastique grace as I have never seen, although the music was sometimes drowned out by the noises in the hall. I felt like rushing to the stage, but I was stimulated almost beyond the power to walk straight.[5]

In Chicago, Isadora's first stop after Boston, she told her audience that she felt "much younger now" than when she had last been there — she owed her good health to her love of music and the attentions of "a young husband."[6] Cancellations poured into Hurok's office from around the Midwest, "punctuated by the indignations of mayors and leading citizens."[7] The Hearst newspaper chain, known the world over for its yellow reporting, stopped just short of calling for Isadora's execution on charges of treason. (Mata Hari set the precedent: dancers had been shot before.) "No artist was ever more foolishly and cheaply presented by the cheaper journalism of our time," *The New Republic* confirmed. "The report of her in some of our newspapers was beneath all contempt, an outrageous level of poor jokes and dirty implications."[8]

By November 1922 Isadora was back in New York, greeting reporters at the Waldorf in a hat "not unlike the popular flapper's model" and insisting that her tour would not be killed by negative publicity.

"I am here to rest and recover from the persecution I have suffered from the American press throughout my trip," she complained. "Every time I come to America they howl around me like a pack of wolves. . . . Why is it that my dances are copied in girls' schools all over the country, yet when I appear in person I am subjected to calumny on all sides?"[9] On November 14 she gave the first of two farewell recitals at Carnegie Hall and insisted again that she was not a Bolshevik. "People had said to her that she ought not to make speeches," the *New York Times* reported dryly, "but she wanted to make this little one."[10]

"I preach only love," Isadora said. "The love of mother for her child; of lover for wife — and of my own for the top gallery!"[11] When she talked about Soviet Russia in New York, the audience rose and cheered: "She stated that her idea of communism was everybody singing and dancing together."[12] Julia Levien, later one of America's premiere Duncan dancers and teachers, recalled the wonder she had felt as a child watching "this grand, statuesque woman" in Carnegie Hall: "After the performance, Isadora came to the front of the stage and asked for money for her school in Russia. And from the top of the balcony, from all the boxes, money floated down. . . . A rain of dollar bills. And Esenin picked it up."[13] John Sloan arrived late, as he reported in a note to Robert Henri:

> Bad luck! . . . I couldn't get away until 10:30 & saw but one number . . . wonderful. She is as ever she was and will be always — strong bodied, not fat, beautiful human being — and the reserve of her art — and her loneliness, as a goddess is lonely — A full house but none of the swells. She deals such incautious apparently ingenuous slaps to them they have I suppose gradually found it best to stay away. Or then maybe never came. Last evening she said speaking of millionaires "You see I know about them I lived with one for eight years" — that has a twist for the Puritan tail in it hasn't it. I hear it said that "she lacks tact" — well, so does God Almighty and many another artist is like His Reverence in that way.[14]

In Indianapolis, where she danced at the end of November, four policemen stood in the auditorium to make sure Isadora remained fully clothed, while another waited in the wings to arrest her if necessary. She made no speech that night, content to let the city's Babbitt-like mayor, Lew Shank, defend his position. "Isadora ain't fooling me any," Shank told reporters. "She talks about art. Huh! I've seen a lot of these twisters and I know as much about art as any man in America, but I never went to see these dances for art's sake. . . . If she goes to pulling off her clothes and throwing them up in the air . . . there's going to be somebody getting a ride in the wagon."[15]

Isadora dismissed Shank's nationally published remarks as "Disgusting! Disgustingly vulgar! . . . Two nude women can dance at a banquet of business men — but I'm not allowed to give an interpretive dance wrapped in a blanket!"[16] Perhaps in reaction to her restraint

in Indiana, she let herself go in Kentucky. ISADORA SMIRCHES ART! said
the *Louisville Courier:*

> The climax came when a fastening of her dress at the shoulder
> broke, affording portions of her anatomy here — and portions of her
> anatomy there — full exposure, an exposure the audience might have
> forgiven as accidental if the dancer had not neglected, when the dance
> was ended, to cover herself. . . . Perhaps her reputation for the unex-
> pected and the unconventional in art persuaded some few to attend
> her performance. Perhaps there were reasons for the police being sta-
> tioned on the stage in other cities. Louisville thought better of her and
> was mistaken.[17]

From Louisville, Isadora moved to Kansas City, St. Louis, Memphis, Milwaukee, Detroit, Toronto, Toledo, Cleveland, Baltimore, and
Philadelphia: "Her tour was to end in Brooklyn, where a performance
had been arranged in the Academy of Music for Christmas Night."[18]
On December 4, from Memphis, she also announced that she would
give a Christmas Eve sermon at St. Mark's-in-the-Bouwerie Episcopal
Church in Lower Manhattan, an invited lecture called "The Moraliz-
ing Effect of Dancing on the Human Soul." A reporter noted that she
seemed "oddly inconsistent in her public pronouncements. . . . Sometimes she exulted in her revolutionary ideals and other times she denied them. It is doubtful whether she ever went beneath the surface of
communism to understand it."[19] In every town, Isadora raised eye-
brows by sending Hurok or his representative immediately to find a
bootlegger. Hurok added: "Never was a woman more generous in sup-
plying her enemies the ammunition with which to destroy her."[20]

It is assumed, but not documented, that Esenin went with Isadora
on each leg of her American tour. "It was Isadora, Isadora, only
Isadora," Hurok wrote.[21] After an initial burst of enthusiasm, followed
by an epoch of pure bewilderment, Esenin had soured on the United
States. "It would be enough to make one hang oneself," he wrote to
Mariengof on November 12:

> Isadora is a most splendid woman but a bigger liar than Vanka. All
> her banks and big houses she boasted to us about in Russia are all non-
> sense. We're stranded here without a kopeck waiting till we have col-
> lected enough for the fare back to Moscow. . . . About myself I'll
> say . . . that I just don't know how to behave and what to live by now.
> Before, there was always the consolation [of] "abroad" . . . but now

that I've seen it I pray God not to die spiritually and lose my love for my art. . . . Goodness me, I'd sooner get smoke in my eyes . . . only not be here, not here.[22]

In Memphis, where Esenin became drunker than usual, Isadora left him sitting alone in a speakeasy at four in the morning. It was the only time Hurok saw her "attempt to discipline" the poet — he found his way home that night by himself.[23] "He was conscious of being regarded as 'the young husband of the famous Duncan,'" Mariengof insisted: "He saw this 'young husband' almost in every glance and heard it in every word. . . . And his trip became for him one long torment, torture, insult: He broke. This explains much."[24] Two years later Esenin recalled:

> Once I saw a newspaper-seller on the corner, and my face was in every newspaper. My heart gave a leap. There's real fame for you! . . . I bought a good dozen papers from him, and rushed home, thinking — I must send this to so-and-so and to what's-his-name. And I asked someone to translate the words beneath my picture. And they did so: "Sergei Esenin, the Russian peasant, husband of the famous, incomparable, enchanting dancer — Isadora Duncan — whose immortal talent . . ." etc. etc. I was so furious that I tore the paper to shreds. . . . So that's fame for you! That evening I went down to the restaurant and, as I recall, I got really drunk. I drank and wept.[25]

In New York, Esenin spent long hours in bars, reputedly in the company of Claude McKay, the Jamaican poet, socialist, and leading figure of the Harlem Renaissance. "Perhaps he considered this a protest against race discrimination," one of Esenin's biographers writes, "or perhaps he was simply attracted to this man who, because of his color, belonged to the oppressed for whom Esenin always felt great sympathy." Others have read a different significance into Esenin's attachment to "The Black Man," whoever he was: "He lived his life / In a land, you see, / Of the most repulsive / Deceptions and vices." Invariably, when Esenin met strangers in America and said that he was a poet, the answer came back: "But that's not a job! What else do you do?"[26] Sometimes he became "as angry as a demon" and clutched Isadora by the throat. "I am thinking of making the Woolworth Building my tombstone," Esenin declared, "by jumping down from its tower . . . carrying the last poem I am going to write."[27]

At their hotel in Cleveland, reporter Archie Bell heard Isadora and Esenin exchange exactly one word in English.

"Automobile?" Isadora asked.

"Automobile," said Esenin, whereupon he left the hotel with the chauffeur, "for air." How did they manage to communicate? Bell wondered: "Is love the universal language?"

"Love between nations is much more important than love between individuals," Isadora said.

"You read Russian?"

"No."

"Yet you know [Esenin's] poetry is wonderful?"

"Yes." When she added that communism was "the greatest thing since Christ," Bell looked doubtful. "What is right or wrong cannot be measured by its success," Isadora replied.[28] Her interviews were filled with epigrams and womanly advice: "Art is greater than governments. . . . Age is only self-hypnotism. . . . Women, if they will, can prove the power of mind over matter."[29] Demanding the right of reply, she gave an interview to Hearst's *American Weekly:* even in San Francisco she had been called a "Soviet dancer," her hair "a Bolshevik shade of red."[30] (It didn't help her reputation that Hurok advertised her as "Isadora Duncan, the Famous Russian Dancer.") She began by saying that "America makes me sick — positively nauseates me" — and that this was no figure of speech:

> America produces in me a definite malady — I know the symptoms; I have felt them here on other visits. Stupid, penurious, ignorant America. . . . You feed your children here canned peas and canned art, and wonder why they are not beautiful. You will not let them grow up in freedom. You persecute your real artists. You put them under the heels of fat policemen, like the ones who sat on the platform of my concert in Indianapolis. You drug your souls with matrimony. You import what art you have, which isn't much. And when anyone tells you the truth you say, "They are crazy!" . . .
>
> It's the smugness, the sanctimonious righteousness, the "God bless me and my wife, my son John and his wife, us four and no more, Amen" quality to America that crushes my soul. . . . Bah! Bah again! I have had about as much chance this winter in America as Christ had before Pilate. We both were doomed before we even spoke. When I think of some of the experiences I have lived through on my American tour it makes me want to be a Christian. It makes me feel even that mean.[31]

Back in New York at the end of December, Isadora learned that her sermon at St. Mark's-in-the-Bouwerie had been canceled on the order of Episcopal archbishop William T. Manning. The bishop had "received letters of earnest protest from many parts of the country" and promised "that the dancer referred to will not speak at St. Mark's Church nor appear professionally in any connection with the church or its services." Apparently, Isadora's name was too hot to mention. At the Brooklyn Academy of Music on Christmas night, she was drunk during her performance. Word had come from Paris that Sarah Bernhardt was dying.

"Isadora now suddenly took it into her head that the appropriate thing to do was to dance a prophetic funeral march for the French actress," wrote Joseph Kaye in *The Dance Magazine*. Different accounts of her embarrassment agree that her pianist, Max Rabinovitch, at some point "angrily stalked off the stage" and refused to go back for an encore. Isadora began to hum Brahms's Waltz in A-flat: "To this accompaniment she began dancing and continued for a short time. But the effect was so grotesque and eerie that she realized it would be better not to go through with it." One report states that she made a wrong turn and crashed into the piano: "She waltzed away from the center of the stage to the exit and disappeared."[32] Later she explained "that 'doctorized' or 'etherized' champagne was responsible for the fiasco." The Prohibition liquor she drank in America "would kill an elephant."

"We had some champagne," Isadora calmly told the morning papers: "My husband and I are both accustomed to wine. We drank some and it made us both very ill." In a plea for sympathy, she mentioned that it was Christmas, "a season that means much to those who have children and is very trying to those who have lost theirs. . . . Don't be hard on me. I wanted to dance at my best."[33] At her last two concerts in Carnegie Hall in January, Kaye wrote, "it was clear to everyone who felt for her that Isadora Duncan was now steadily walking towards her end. That tumultuous and glorious achievement for art was closing. The sun was setting."[34] Margherita Duncan saw one of Isadora's last performances and remembered the enduring beauty of her *Ave Maria*:

> I was so moved that I felt I must speak with her, and went to her dressing-room immediately, a thing I seldom did during the intermission. We wept together, both shaken by the experience we had just lived through. And she said: "Now I have finished. I have said all I have to say tonight. But because the manager insists upon variety, I must go on and do the *Seventh Symphony*, and I have no heart for it. I should stop now."

She was right. The rest of the program was only an indication of what she used to do, and it was a violation of her artistic conscience to reproduce an outgrown conception. It was the only time I ever saw her give less than a fresh creation of living emotion in a dance.[35]

Isadora left New York as she arrived, to blaring headlines. According to Hurok, her tour made money, but she found herself broke at the end of it, lacking the funds even to buy steamship tickets for Europe. ("As for me," she told the *American Weekly,* "I would rather be free than out of debt.") She didn't know yet that Esenin had stuffed his trunks with "seven or eight thousand dollars" in cash, along with "half of Isadora's clothes" and his own extravagant new wardrobe. "My God," Isadora said when she discovered her husband's treachery in Paris — "can it be possible that I have been harboring a viper in my bosom?"[36] Esenin guarded his privacy and possessions practically at the point of a knife; Vetlugin, moreover, his hired companion, proved "nothing short of a tragedy," according to Isadora's friend Ruth Mitchell: "He is absolutely incapable and has been a tremendous financial drain."

"I am writing to you with a very heavy heart," Mitchell went on in a letter to Joe Milward. "Isadora is now surrounded by so many threatening troubles that I really don't see how she is going to pull through. The fact that she has only herself to blame does not help matters or especially inspire her few remaining friends to struggle on her behalf."[37] Hurok remembered a frantic phone call from Isadora one morning at about three A.M. Esenin had attacked her: "'Come quickly! He's killing me!' There was stark terror in her voice panting over the wire."

When he arrived at the Waldorf-Astoria, Hurok found Isadora and Esenin both asleep, passed out on their bed. "It was shortly afterward, as I recall, that the Duncan-Esenin menage departed the Waldorf, at the Waldorf's request, and found refuge at the Brevoort on lower Fifth Avenue."[38] Max Merz, in New York on business for Elizabeth's school, saw Isadora at a friend's apartment, where she had fled from Esenin's blows. "She was mortally sad like a hunted animal. I expostulated with her, and said she should no longer submit to this unworthy treatment, but she replied with her characteristic gentle smile: 'You know, Esenin is just a peasant, and the Russian peasant has a habit of getting drunk on Saturdays and beating his wife!'"[39] At the Bronx apartment of Yiddish poet Mani Leib, Esenin punched her in the face after she danced for the guests: "He started to yell about her showing off for the dirty Jews. . . . He attacked her, tore her clothes and they pulled him off."[40]

"What do you think of my darling?" Isadora asked Hurok the next morning, without regard for his reply. According to Mary Desti, she borrowed money from Paris Singer to get back to Europe. How she managed it isn't clear: she had approached Singer earlier in Paris, "in memory of our love for our child," and was sharply turned away. "He won't help me because I am with Esenin," Isadora told Milward.[41] Her departure from New York on February 2, 1923, was reported on the front page of every newspaper in the city.

"No interview!" Isadora cried as she strode onto the deck of the *George Washington,* a "dry" ocean liner, where she hoped Esenin might at least find a respite from drinking. The temptation was too much for her. "I lost four months of my life on my American visit," she said. "It was martyrdom." Her parting shots at the country of her birth were taken as proof of her disloyalty: "I really ought not to say a word to you newspapermen. . . . You newspapermen wrecked my career. . . . I'm going back to Russia. I'd rather live on black bread and vodka there than on the best you've got in the United States. . . . If I didn't get out of this country soon, I'd be killed by the liquor anyhow."[42]

A month later, on March 10, the U.S. Department of Labor confirmed that Isadora had forfeited her American citizenship by marrying Esenin and that if she wanted it back, like "any other alien," she "must prove herself to be a person of good moral character, attached to the principles of the Constitution of the United States."[43] As her ship prepared to sail, she unwound her red scarf a final time and waved it at the crowd on the dock. Of course, she said, she and Esenin were "revolutionists. All geniuses worthy of the name are. . . . So good-bye, America! I shall never see you again." As she walked away she beckoned to her husband: "Come, Sergei, someone is probably watching us even here. We shall go to our stateroom. It is ours, even though we borrowed money to get it."[44]

If anything, Esenin's condition grew worse when he returned to Paris with Isadora. "You ask me what I did abroad?" he told a friend. "What I saw there and what amused me? I saw nothing there, apart from pubs and streets." His unflattering portrait of the United States would appear as *The Iron Mirgorod,* the title taken from Gogol's parable of the ultimate Russian provincial town. "The power of ferro-concrete, the grandeur of the buildings, have cramped the American's brain and narrowed his vision," Esenin wrote. "It was dark, confining. I could hardly see the sky. People were rushing about, but no one cared about you — that really hurt me."[45] Simultaneously, the prospect of returning to Russia filled him with dread.

From the ship, Isadora cabled Mary Desti: IF YOU WOULD SAVE MY LIFE AND REASON MEET ME IN PARIS.[46] The supposedly dry *George Washington* held as much synthetic liquor as any American backwater — Esenin was carried off the train from Cherbourg, wrapped in a bundle of furs, when he arrived with Isadora at the Gare du Nord on February 11.

"Mary, Mary, oh, Mary," Isadora kept saying, "at last you have come to save me. . . . Promise, Mary, never to leave me again." Two nights later Esenin wrecked their suite at the Crillon. "Mary, I might as well tell you the truth," Isadora confessed. "Sergei is just a wee bit eccentric."[47] She had left the hotel before the melee began, fearing for her life. "The beds were broken," Mary reported, "the springs on the floor, the sheets torn into shreds, every bit of mirror or glass broken in bits — in fact, it really looked like a house after a bomb had hit it."[48] It took "six policemen" to subdue Esenin that night and haul him to the nearest jail. Isadora went with Mary to Versailles, where reporters tracked her down: "The bloom is off the rose," said the *Paris Tribune*.

"I never believed in marriage," Isadora remarked sadly, "and I now believe in it less than ever. . . . Some Russians can't be transplanted, you know. That was the tragedy of Nijinsky." Artists shouldn't marry in the first place, she said before launching into a tirade against the United States: "America was founded by a bunch of bandits, adventurers, puritans, and pioneers. Now the bandits have the upper hand."

In Paris the police agreed to release Esenin only on the condition that he leave France. Using the last of Singer's money, Isadora sent him to Kusikov in Berlin, where the Soviet consul could arrange for his transport to Moscow. "I go to Russia to see my two children by a former wife," Esenin told reporters as he left Paris with Jeanne, Isadora's maid: "I am devoured with paternal yearnings. . . . *Zut!* I am a father." When asked if Isadora would join him later, he answered that she would, eventually: "I know her. Now she is angry, but — that will pass."[49]

In fact, Isadora was ill at Versailles, running a fever and more upset than Mary had ever seen her. "Everybody knows he's crazy," she told *Paris Tribune* reporter Lorimer Hammond: "He can smash things up in Moscow and no one will care because he is a poet."[50] In open letters to the press, she begged for privacy and respect: "If this sort of journalism continues, we will have your reporters coming into no matter what house of misfortune or grief and making a joke at the tears of the mourners. . . . No one will be safe from their malice, and the poor public will be the continual dupes of their gross and uncomprehending vulgarity."[51]

In Berlin, Esenin had his own harsh words for Isadora. On February 19 the 8-Uhr Abendblatt reported in its headline, LIEBER IN SIBIRIEN — ALS GATTE DER DUNCAN ZU SEIN (BETTER TO BE IN SIBERIA THAN DUNCAN'S HUSBAND). The report that followed couldn't have been more insulting. "Russia is vast," Esenin said, "and I will always find a place where this terrible woman cannot reach me. . . . She was never willing to recognize my individuality and she always wanted to dominate me. She wanted me as a slave." His remarks wounded her deeply, hard as she tried to excuse them. "It was hell which I bore for six months," Esenin said. "But then I couldn't stand it any longer. I fled, and now I feel well again for the first time since my wedding day, as a free man, dependent on no one."[52]

From Paris, Isadora dispatched a telegram to Kusikov: ESSENTIAL THAT ESENIN WRITE TO THE 'CHICAGO TRIBUNE' TO REFUTE INTERVIEW SAYING HE NEVER LOVED ME AND STAYED WITH ME FOR STATUS. ARTICLE SHOWS HIM IN A BAD LIGHT. WIRE NEWS. ISADORA DUNCAN.[53] Kusikov answered shortly that Esenin "would certainly commit suicide" unless Isadora joined him. He showed no sign of leaving for Moscow and continued to attack her in provocative one-liners: "I love Isadora madly but she drank so much I could not stand it. . . . Duncan has worn me out so much that I've begun to look as if I'd been raped." Before long, however, Esenin began to miss her. Soon he himself was sending telegrams to Isadora — "five or six telegrams a day," Mary remembered, "all of which kept Isadora's temperature soaring. The doctor could do nothing to make her sleep." She was convinced that Esenin would shoot himself without her.

"Mary, dear," Isadora finally said, "if you are really my friend, find a way to take me to Sergei or I will die. I can't live without him. I don't care what he has done. . . . Find out where we can get a car to take us to Berlin."[54] There followed six weeks of aimless adventure, traveling, scenes, and reconciliations, which Mary recorded in detail: "Heavens! here we were without a penny, yet she wanted to go by auto to Berlin. Nothing ever seemed impossible to her. . . . The utter disregard for everything conventional and for all life that had so brutally destroyed her seemed to give her some respite from sorrow." A hired car got them as far as Strasbourg, where the driver refused to enter Germany. Isadora found another, which promptly "banged into a bridge, break-

ing down." Despite Mary's remonstrations, she spent the night drinking in Strasbourg.

"Why does no one ever let me enjoy myself as I like?" Isadora
wailed. "I am doing no harm: I who pass my life giving happiness to
others." Mary remarked that she was "like the sun; she smiled and you
would go to your death foolishly, feeling you were doing some great
brave deed." Three more cars broke down on the way to Berlin. Anxious
though she was about Esenin, Isadora insisted on a detour to Bayreuth,
where she left a hundred roses for Cosima Wagner and met "a very
charming young man" at a restaurant, who took them as far as Leipzig.
"Swift movement was as necessary to her as breathing," Mary wrote.
"She only lived when going like mad, resting now and then for food and
drink. . . . I cannot understand how we were not killed twenty times
over." In Berlin, Esenin and Kusikov were waiting to meet them:

> As we drove up in front of the Hotel Adlon . . . a flying leap
> landed Sergei in our car, he having bounded straight on to the engine,
> over the chauffeur's head into Isadora's arms. . . . There he was in flesh
> and bone, his golden hair waving in the electric lights. He had thrown
> his cap away as he sprang — an expensive but beautiful gesture. For
> what did he now need a hat? His love, his darling, his Isadora was
> here, so away with the hat. He would just as quickly have thrown his
> coat and boots after it.
>
> This was not posing; these two *exaltés* were beyond the con-
> sciousness of their surroundings. The police finally disbanded the on-
> lookers, and by a little urging we persuaded the lovers to descend; but
> as to what hotel they wished to go, or whether the poets had engaged
> rooms for us, we could get no answer of any kind.[55]

"When in doubt," Isadora said, "always go to the best hotel." That
night she and Esenin checked into the Palace, along with Mary and
about half a dozen of Esenin's Russian friends. "Rooms for all,"
Isadora commanded. "They are my party." It would be "a Russian
evening,"[56] she declared, also inviting the Soviet consul and his staff
and not caring about stragglers who came along for the ride. Buckets
of vodka and champagne disappeared in a matter of hours. "I am prepared to [say] that there was never a more Russian evening since the
world began," Mary wrote:

> Things began to fly. Sergei always threw the first thing he got his
> hands on, irrespective of what or at whom. Unfortunately for the dig-

nity of the State, the [Soviet] Minister's head . . . caught the first plate of fish. . . . Before we knew quite what had happened, there wasn't a thing left in the whole apartment. Sergei meanwhile hurled abuse at Isadora and myself, which mattered not to me, as I understood not a word of it. Three or four of his friends tried to hold him down. They might as well have tried to stop the waves of the ocean, such strength as this boy had in these paroxysms. . . . The morning after, we got a very polite note from the management, saying the suite was engaged for that afternoon, and would we please be out of there by twelve noon?[57]

The scene repeated itself wherever the Esenins appeared. From Berlin they went to Weimar, and from Weimar back to Strasbourg. "I begged Isadora to return with me to Paris," Mary protested, "and again begin seriously to work. Or, if not, she should go at once to Russia to her . . . school. But she must leave Sergei. She replied that it would be like deserting a sick child, and that she could never, never do it." Her own fast talking got Esenin back into France. The party retreated immediately, however, when the only car Mary could find turned out to be a "closed" vehicle, not a convertible. "With the greatest difficulty we got Isadora to agree to ride in this car," Mary wrote. "She loathed them. . . . It had something to do with the death of her children who were drowned in just such a one. She began to beat the windows frantically, and in desperation we returned to the hotel."[58]

When they finally reached Paris in the middle of May, Isadora and Esenin were evicted from three hotels in as many days. At last, they moved back to her house on rue de la Pompe:

As there was no money, there began the daily sale of furniture, books, pictures, mirrors, anything and everything. Each day Isadora would smilingly say, "Well, what shall we eat today — the sofa, the bookcase, or perhaps that old chair?" . . . Things got very bad indeed. Sergei had continued his wild scenes every three or four days until Isadora no longer dared to stay in the house alone with him. . . . One night he made a spring and dashed head-first through the window, smashing the glass as he passed through, but not even scratching himself. . . . I went home and was awakened in the middle of the night by Isadora's coming in and saying she could stand no more — that we must find some way to rent or sell the house, as she intended to send Sergei to Russia at once.[59]

The spur to Isadora's determination may well have been Esenin's most recent escapade, when he turned up at a Russian restaurant, insulted the ex-aristocrat waiters, and landed in the street, beaten and denuded of his watch, top hat, coat, socks, and shoes. He was no longer safe in the West, Isadora decided — Lunacharsky was right. Lisa Duncan saw Isadora for tea at rue de la Pompe and wrote to Irma in Moscow: "It seems there isn't a cent in the house and the [cook] is paying for the food."[60] Lisa, herself desperate for money, was dancing at a Paris music hall for fifty francs a night with a male partner, thus breaking two of Isadora's cardinal rules. Isadora made no criticism to her face: she would need to dance her own way back to Russia, scheduling two concerts at the Trocadéro, on May 27 and June 3, 1923.

Isadora's first recital was apparently a success, despite a second-act mishap, when she sank to the floor in a sitting position during a Scriabin étude "and continued to sit there . . . unable to get up. She sat there for about forty seconds," Joe Milward wrote, "which is a long time for nothing to be happening on a huge stage." Milward added: "Nobody laughed. One could have heard a pin drop."[61] Critic André Levinson, commenting "reluctantly" on "the physical decay of an artist and the inevitable ravages of time," needed to say nothing more: "I see again the dancer, arms crossed as on an imaginary crucifix, torso slumped, knees bent, limbs . . . brutally apart. Then the head falls, the torso following it, and the short hair brushes the floor."[62]

After the concert Isadora was joined onstage by artist Kees van Dongen, Raymond Duncan, and Charles Rappoport, the Russian-born French deputy and socialist leader. "My friends of twenty years," she began: "Come nearer, look at me. I have two things to say to you. First, they write that I am a Bolshevik. . . . Do I have the look of a Bolshevik?"

"No! No!" came shouts from the house. Again Isadora asked for money for the school, and again "the bills rained down on the stage, as a little before rose petals had done."

"Thank you, thank you," said Isadora. "Now I will tell you the second thing: I don't know how to dance at all; not at all. That is, I don't know if I know. When I was a very little child I dreamed of smashing the bourgeois mold and remaking the world. Do you understand? . . . I was the first communist. At present —" but Rappoport burst out laughing. "If she continues to talk about sociology," he said, "I'm going to dance."[63] The audience, with Isadora, broke into cheers. Only Esenin was annoyed. During a reception after the performance, at about three in the morning, he came down the stairs at rue de la Pompe, "golden hair rumpled," crying in Russian: "Band of bloated fish, mangy sleigh rugs, bellies of carrion, grub for soldiers, you awoke me!" Grabbing a candelabrum, "he swung it towards a mirror, which crashed to the floor."

Someone called the police: "Soon four *agents cyclistes* arrived, and Esenin was carried off, softly saying, *'Bon politzie. Aller avec vous!'*"[64] The next morning Isadora sent him to a sanatorium at Saint-Mandé — Esenin complained later that she had put him in "an asylum." He was home in several days, dried out, contrite, and "very quiet and good" during Isadora's second Trocadéro concert, a Wagner program. The *Tannhäuser* Bacchanal "was wilder than ever," Lisa thought: "She danced as though hell itself had entered on scene — the public was just a trifle astonished."[65] Also in the audience was American dramaturge Harold Clurman, later a founding member of the Group Theatre in New York. Clurman remained baffled by Isadora's art ("I was in the same plight as my friend the composer Hans Eisler . . . when, after seeing Martha Graham dance, he admitted that he had 'not understood one leg'") but never forgot the power of her presence: "Watching her, I experienced something close to fear and exaltation. Her dancing . . . commanded something like worship." Clurman went on:

> Her voice as she addressed the audience after the recital had a certain melancholy, a quiet, plaintive flow from out of a lost sphere. Apart from its spirit, her speech was not altogether coherent. She spoke of her first struggles in Paris. She reminded us of how poor she was and how she had spent her last sous to sit in the gallery to see the fabulous Mounet-Sully in *Oedipus* at the Théâtre Français.
>
> Then she paused to defend herself against her critics. One of them, André Levinson . . . "There's a certain critic in Paris, André Levinson . . ." she began, upon which a gentleman in evening dress in a first-tier box cried out, "He's a dirty Jew!" "I like Jews," Isadora countered in a subdued, tender tone, and the audience applauded. But she was unable to go on. The touching mood of her farewell to Paris had been broken, and she wandered off stage in a kind of daze.[66]

"I need not tell you of many things Lisa told you already in her letters," Anna Duncan wrote to Irma that same week. "It is a great Tragedy that is now passing with Isadora, and I think the final curtain will come soon."[67] Anna's romance with Walter Rummel had already ended, Rummel having told her so in a letter as cold as ice: "I do not miss you and have quite decided to live alone and to be alone. You must make your own life, do not count on me."[68] Not long after, Rummel remarried, this time an Englishwoman, Sarah Harrington, who stuck it out for several years. Anna's bitterness would be hers for life.

"I am still after six months of separation trying to forget an unhappiness which has taken from me all I believe and hope for Love," Anna wrote. "You will perhaps understand me Irma dear. . . . I am only trying to do what I can to go on with our work, as long as it is still good and strong enough, but otherwise *tout m'est égal*. I do not believe in Love and feel like laughing at Love."[69] The same disillusion had infected Lisa, who, despite several affairs, carried a lifelong torch for free lover Max Eastman: "I have lost much, perhaps all faith in humanity and the world — one thing I know [is] that we all live for ourselves and that *au fond* we are always alone. . . . But we girls have something to fight for and live for — our work is the most beautiful recompense for our little sorrows and tears."[70]

On this point, Anna advised her colleagues: Isadora's lawyer had written to her in February, while she was dancing in Nice, warning her to take Isadora's name off her posters and programs.[71] Anna refused, but when she, Lisa, and Margot toured America later that year, on the advice of their manager, they issued a joint statement "disavowing Isadora Duncan's political beliefs and making clear to the general public that they have no connection whatever with this woman."[72] Lisa told Irma in Moscow: "I think you are a little wonder, I admire you immensely. . . . I hope dear that you will be strong enough and have reliable friends . . . because I am afraid your peace will be short." Esenin had seen an article in *Izvestia* praising Irma's work at the Duncan school in Moscow. "So he screamed with all the *Schadenfreude* and malice" he could muster, Lisa reported: " 'Oh! Irma *bolshe* success!' — 'Bravo Irma!' and Isadora didn't say anything."[73] Milward described one of Esenin's last attacks of *"névrite"* in Paris. After his release from the sanatorium at Saint-Mandé, Isadora had hired "two strong male nurses" to keep him from drinking. The effort failed:

> Suddenly . . . Esenin ran down the stairs into the salon. He was stark naked. In his right hand he held a five-foot length of two-by-four studded with protruding nails. He had disabled one of his attendants by a well-placed kick in the groin. The other followed him at a respectful distance.
>
> "Where is Isadora?" he yelled. "Where is Isadora? I am going to kill her!" He used the word *kaputt*. . . . He meant it.[74]

On June 16 the Russian émigré writer Dmitri Merezhkovsky, author of respected studies of Tolstoy and Dostoyevsky and a religious trilogy dear to Russian hearts, *Christ and Anti-Christ,* denounced Isadora and Esenin in a letter to the *Journal d'Eclair.* Esenin's Bolshevism was nothing but "drunkenness and scandal," Merezhkovsky declared, while Isadora, "with [her] tired legs . . . still endeavors to amuse the Trocadéro public by means of dancing embellished with propaganda."[75] Two days later she was reported to be reading Victor Margueritte's scandalous novel of sexual love, *La garçonne,* and said that it seemed "an exact picture" to her[76] — Pierre de Louÿs, author of the lesbian love song, *Chansons de Bilitis,* was "among the many distinguished patients" Esenin had met during his incarceration at Saint-Mandé.[77]

"Honesty is no longer in style," Isadora told a reporter. "It seems you can no longer expect a man to be honest; if he is agreeable that is all you can ask."[78] For Merezhkovsky, in a published reply, she wished "a very peaceful old age in his bourgeois retreat, and a respectable funeral with black plumes and black-mittened hired mourners." She quite understood that he "could never live in the proximity of such beings" as Esenin and herself, "talent always being shocked by genius."

"As for me," Isadora went on, "I prefer being burned alive at the stake in Moscow, while thousands of children in red tunics dance about me singing the *Internationale.* . . . And even were I legless I might still create my Art."[79] Another altercation with the police shortly put Esenin back in jail: on July 11 French authorities gave him an exit pass and twenty-four hours to leave the country. He got as far as the Belgian border, where he discovered that he had no visa. Back in Paris he "[threw] himself on his knees before Isadora [and] said he could not live without his adorable wife. . . . He would never be separated from her again."

Finally, on the next attempt, Isadora left Paris with her husband. They went again by way of Berlin, where Mary saw them off. "As the train pulled out they stood," Mary wrote, "with their pale faces, like two little lost souls. . . . I returned to Paris, and a week later entered a hospital, a complete wreck."[80] Isadora would spend another year in Soviet Russia, but less than a week of it with Esenin. The honeymoon was over.

27

Genius and Kaputt

During the fifteen months of Isadora's absence from Moscow, Irma and Schneider had remade the school, partly on their own initiative and partly as a result of hostility toward Isadora among Soviet bureaucrats and ideologists. Schneider remembered "bitter fights" at the commissariat of education, "heatedly debating the question of which one of its departments should be put in charge of the school. Was it an institution for social education or a school for professional training?" Isadora would insist that it was neither, but the Kremlin still "poked about for 'systems' and 'methods.'"[1] In the new Soviet Union, strength and utility unavoidably took precedence over beauty and the soul. Even the state ballet school briefly saw its funding dry up in the first years of communism.

Schneider began by reducing the staff at Prechistenka and opening the school to paying students, whose tuition provided for the upkeep of the advanced classes, from whom "a paying 'parallel' group was formed to provide for the upkeep of the main contingency."[2] In the summer the senior class helped Irma teach hundreds of children the essentials of Duncan dance at open-air stadiums in Moscow. A Free Spirit in a Healthy Body became the motto of the school.

With Isadora gone, Irma stepped into the limelight as a performer and celebrity in Moscow, "a venture that would have been impossible," she knew, "while [Isadora] remained in charge of artistic matters. I slowly came to the realization that, if I wanted to make a name for myself in Russia, it was now or never."[3] In her dispatches from *The New Russia*, American journalist Dorothy Thompson left a picture of Irma at work at Prechistenka, teaching the children "to throw their arms earthward whence all good comes and revel in the free, untrammeled expression of their revolutionary souls."[4] Inevitably, Irma was accused of usurping Isadora's place.

On April 14, 1923, Irma and twelve of the Dunclings danced at the Comedia Theatre in Moscow, where *Izvestia* noted that the children had "made great progress" under Irma's tutelage — "a big step forward from what we saw last year."[5] This was the press report Esenin had seen in Paris that he used to taunt Isadora: "Bravo, Irma!" Irma's success in Russia was never so great that she was mistaken for her teacher, however: with Isadora gone, nothing impeded the imposition of Soviet ideology on the school. "There could be no question of defraying the expenses of the school by the few performances we could give," Schneider confessed. "I therefore sent a telegram to Isadora in Paris, insisting on her immediate return to Moscow."[6] She arrived at Nikolaev Station with Esenin on August 5:

> As she descended from the train she looked harassed and worried. She was in reality very glad that she had finally arrived at the end of an extremely tiring task; she had brought back her poet, as she had promised herself she would, to the place where he belonged.
>
> The object of her solicitous care [Esenin] stumbled down the steps of the coach. He was inebriated . . . as much, perhaps, from the overpowering emotional excitement of being back again in Russia as from the effects of the continual stream of vodka that had flown down his patriotic throat. . . . And in his riotous joy he had smashed all the windows of the coach.[7]

"*Hier bringe ich dieses Kind in sein Vaterland,*" Isadora told Schneider through gritted teeth, in German, "*aber ich habe nichts mehr mit ihm zu tun.*" (I'm bringing this child back to his homeland, but I have nothing more to do with him.) Esenin understood more than she supposed. "Ilya Ilyich," he remarked to Schneider over lunch, "when we were abroad [Isadora] said that you and Irma were 'swine,' but now she's all over you."

"*Das ist eine Lüge!*" cried Isadora. (That's a lie!)

"No, it isn't! You did say that! . . . She said that you and Irma were exploiting her art."

"*Er lügt* [He lies]!" Pressed to account for herself, Isadora stammered that Esenin had misunderstood her, "but I was quite sure that what Esenin had told us was true," Schneider wrote. Irma, "looking pale, hung her head" and said nothing.[8]

That August, thanks to Schneider's connections, the Duncan school found itself vacationing in the country at Litvinovo, a "former estate" outside Moscow, where the children "swam, played, studied French and English," and worked a garden to provide food for the winter. Isadora drove out to see them on her first night back, walking the last three miles to the farmhouse after dark, when yet another rented car broke down. "The children," Irma wrote, "who had been on the *qui vive* all day . . . sent out scouts with lanterns to signal the arrival of their teacher." When they saw Isadora, they shouted with joy and "danced her up to the house."[9] Her students' words belie Irma's judgment of Isadora's minimal impact on their dance training.[10] "Something seemed to 'switch on' [when she saw us]," said one of the girls: "She became another person altogether."[11] Schneider wrote:

> Her art of the dance, the beautiful naturalness of movements, their inconceivable lightness and expressiveness — Duncan knew how to transmit it all to her pupils as though her own blood ran in [their] veins. . . . She came to life in the movements of her pupils, in the turns of their heads, in the forceful movements of their outstretched arms, in the characteristic way in which they threw out their knees to create a single supple line from the leg to the torso and from the forearm to the hand. Again and again we saw a resurgent Isadora before us.[12]

At Litvinovo it rained. Esenin was quickly bored and insisted that they return to Moscow. His friend Lev Povitsky saw him at Prechistenka a day or two later, surrounded by "travel requisites, trunks, silk underwear and clothing." Isadora had left the room.

"You've done well for yourself, Sergei Alexandrovitch," Povitsky said.

"I'm leaving here tomorrow," Esenin whispered quickly: "His eyes grew dark and he knitted his brow."[13] At the Stable of Pegasus he got drunk on the first glass of wine and wept to Mariengof about his trip abroad: "I translated your poetry and published my book in French but it was all a waste of time. Nobody wants poetry there . . . and it's adieu to Isadora!" That night he "started a scandal, hit someone, swore, broke crockery, overturned tables and tore up ten-ruble notes." Finally, when they left the club in a taxi, Esenin's head fell on Marien-gof's shoulder "like some strange, useless, cold, ivory ball."[14] He refused to go back to Isadora.

"Something must have happened to him," Isadora concluded. "He's been hurt. He's had an accident. He's ill somewhere."[15] Irma took her in hand. "You've had enough disgraceful scenes all over Europe and America," she said. "You're seriously ill and must have medical treatment at a spa." To her surprise, Isadora offered no resistance, but submitted "meekly" — she had run out of ideas.

Irma bought tickets for the Caucasian mountain resort of Kis-lovodsk, "a sort of expropriated Saratoga Springs,"[16] whose curative Narzan water was the most famous in Russia. "[She] told me that if Esenin turned up Isadora was not to see him," Schneider wrote. On the third day, he did.

"Isadora is going away," Schneider said.

"When?"

"Altogether — from you."

"I want to see her," Esenin demanded. When he found her in the Blue Room, he bent down and caressed her face. "I love you very much, Isadora," he whispered. "I love you very much."[17] For once, she was slow to forgive:

> Looking at him more sternly than she had ever done before, she told him in her broken Russian that if he went off again without telling her where he was going and how long he was going to stay it was the end. She would not spend another three days worrying about him. And in any case she was leaving Moscow that night.
>
> He left the room laughing incredulously. Later that same day, however, in the evening, just before the Southern Express pulled out of Kazan Station, he appeared on the platform. He was quite sober and smiling. By some method best known to himself he had found out from which of the many Moscow stations his wife was leaving, and had come to say good-bye. Touched by his appearance, she tried to persuade him to come on the train. He needed the rest. It would do him good after all the emotions of the return.

Esenin declined to leave Moscow that night but promised to join Isadora in the Caucasus when Schneider went down later in the week.

Within hours of her departure, of course, he was gone, this time permanently. Isadora wouldn't know the truth for several weeks: "Before the last bell rang they bade each other farewell most tenderly, almost as though it were their first parting. And Isadora continued waving her scarf until he was well out of sight."[18]

By sheer coincidence, the first person Isadora met when she stepped from the train at Kislovodsk was Max Eastman, in town to work on a biography of Leon Trotsky "who was resting there." Eastman was buying milk at the station "when here came Isadora and her daughter-in-the-dance, Irma, walking right into my arms like long-lost friends from home." Isadora was in splendid form, "full of 'greatness' as she always was," predicting the ultimate triumph of communism everywhere and calling Esenin the finest poet since Pushkin, Whitman, and Poe. Her "mad passion" for Esenin was "not purely masochistic," Eastman conceded. "It was still a gesture toward her childish notion of the sublime." He did not enjoy their talk: "All the reasons we had for intimate and cozy conversations . . . became, since such conversations were ruled out by my embarrassment, reasons for staying away."[19]

Eastman brought Isadora and Irma to their hotel and disappeared, to be "seen no more," Irma wrote, "either closely or at a distance." Still, the encounter was fortuitous. After two weeks' rest Isadora concluded that "she ought to be up and doing something" and decided on a tour of the Caucasus, beginning with performances in Kislovodsk. Her first concert was nearly canceled by the Cheka (the Russian secret police) when the strains of "God Save the Tsar" rang out during an outdoor rehearsal of the *Marche Slave*.

"The few early promenaders who were not taking their [mineral] bath that day could scarcely believe their ears," Irma wrote. "Before the unwitting [conductor] had put his musicians through a third repetition of the march, he was faced by an angry Cheka official who demanded to know what the brazen recitation of the Tsarist hymn meant." That night the police warned Isadora "that she could not go on unless the *Marche Slave* was taken from the program." She went on anyway, appealing to the audience with help from a translator in the front row:

> Isadora began: "There are members of the Police back stage."
> (The audience stirred uneasily.) "They have come to arrest me!" (The

audience settled back to enjoy the fun.) "They have come to arrest me if I attempt to dance for you this evening the *Marche Slave* of Tchaikovsky. But I'm going to dance it even if they arrest me afterwards. After all, the prison cannot be much worse than my room at the Grand Hotel." (Here the audience laughed uproariously at the dancer's thrust. The majority of them were fellow guests and sufferers at the vermin-infested caravanserai.)

At that moment the volunteer interpreter, who had remained silent, said in a loud voice: "You need not worry, Tovarisch Duncan. You can begin your performance. As President of the Soviet Ispolkom I give you permission to dance the Tchaikovsky march."

The excited public applauded wildly, and Isadora, with a word and a smile of thanks to the President, withdrew back stage.

The Cheka would not be cheated so easily. The following night three officers arrived at the Grand Hotel to arrest not Isadora, but Schneider, on grounds of "counterrevolutionary activity." Schneider had fallen from a horse and sprained his leg. He was lying in bed when Isadora, alerted to his plight over dinner at the *Kursaal,* "hurried back to the hotel."

"*Svoloch!*" she cried — Bastard! — when she saw the guard in Schneider's room. "Yes, *Svoloch! Svoloch!*" It was "the lowest Russian word she knew." Suddenly she remembered Eastman and Trotsky, Soviet minister of war and effectively Lenin's second-in-command. Grabbing a hotel porter, her way "lit by a flickering lantern," Isadora ran to the great man's villa with a note of appeal. Two more Cheka men barred her way into the house:

> They refused to let the strange and excited woman past and called the officer of the guard. Having demanded her business, he said it was impossible for anyone to see Tovarisch Trotsky. In the end she handed him her pencilled note to take into the villa, and after a wait he came back to tell her that she could return to the hotel. Everything would be all right.
>
> When she descended the hilly road and finally reached the hotel, she found [Schneider's] room in disorder, for every drawer and trunk and bag had been searched and examined. The armed soldiers left . . . but not before they had told Isadora . . . that they would have their revenge for all the insults they had received from her that evening. Isadora's reply was to repeat with more intense vigor and expressive disdain the one word: "*Svoloch!*"[20]

Having roused the Cheka, "Isadora felt that it might be safer for her and her friends to move farther afield."[21] They went next to Baku, on the Caspian Sea, and thence to Tbilisi, the capital of Georgia. In the Caspian oil fields, Isadora danced for the workers free of charge and won a terrific reception. "It can be stated without fear of contradiction that it was a triumph for symphonic music, a triumph for Duncan."[22] Her performances in Tbilisi were extended by demand; against her better judgment, she also agreed to watch the students of a local dancing school demonstrate their *"plastique."* She arrived with dread at the event.

"The 'plastic' schools and studios had greatly multiplied in Russia long before the revolution," Schneider observed. "They adopted from Duncan only the 'bare feet,' chitons and tunics, 'serious' music, carpets and curtains, but forgot the main thing — naturalness of movement, simplicity, and expressiveness." Clutching a wreath of white roses, Isadora watched silently while "the very tall and almost naked pupils came out on the platform and arranged themselves in chessboard-order. The show began with Sibelius's *Valse Triste*." After a few minutes, Isadora nudged Schneider with her elbow.

"Warum?" she said — Why? Soon "she nudged me again," Schneider wrote, "more strongly this time, and repeated the question more loudly: *'Warum?'* I began to say something quietly to her in an attempt to avoid a scene, for by now I knew Isadora very well."[23] It was too late. She jumped from her seat.

"What you are doing is dreadful, dreadful!" Isadora cried. "Oh, it's terrible! No! No! don't show me any more!" Walking to the stage, she dropped her roses in front of the girls and said, "I place these flowers on the grave of my hopes!"[24] Schneider thought she was lucky to escape unharmed: "Isadora and Irma went out into the vestibule. They were followed by loud booing. I could hardly stop the crowd from rushing out after them."

"I knew it would end like that," Irma said.

"Then why didn't you tell me earlier?"

"But you all insisted so much," Irma answered, smiling.[25] The tour concluded at Batum, "blistering under the scorching heat of the last days of August."[26] Here Isadora stayed at a villa on the Black Sea, put at her disposal by the regional Soviet: "Palms, cypresses, and magnolias drooped in the unbearably hot sunshine."

"The tropics!" Isadora exclaimed. "How wonderful it is here!" After that, it rained incessantly: "Isadora gazed wistfully at the wet, bleak cypresses. . . . 'I hate them,' she said. 'They are the trees of the dead.'" With an air of mystery, she whispered to Schneider: "Don't tell anyone that, but nature — nature is terrible!"²⁷

That night Isadora disappeared into town; Irma found her two days later, "installed, quite gay and smiling, in the apartment of a young man," a Georgian poet who in turn introduced her to other poets and "black-eyed Ganymedes. . . . Soon they had elected her their Muse."²⁸ It was just the tonic she needed to overcome her obsession with Esenin. He had sent her a letter at Kislovodsk: "Dear Isadora! I am very busy with literary matters and cannot come to you. . . . Things are going splendidly for me . . . and I am now being offered a lot of money for a publishing venture. I wish you success and health and that you should drink less. . . . Love, S. Esenin."

Isadora ignored the gist of Esenin's message. She wired him back on August 22: DARLING VERY SAD WITHOUT YOU HOPE YOU COME HERE SOON I LOVE YOU FOREVER ISADORA. She heard nothing more until September 10, when a cable arrived at Tbilisi: DON'T SEND ANY MORE LETTERS TELEGRAMS [TO] ESENIN HE IS WITH ME. . . . YOU MUST COUNT ON HIS NOT RETURNING TO YOU. GALINA BENISLAVSKAYA.²⁹

According to Schneider, "Isadora was crushed by that telegram, but she pretended only to be hurt."³⁰ Benislavskaya, called Galya, was an old friend of Esenin's, a decorated heroine of the revolution, who until recently had believed that she stood no chance of winning the poet's romantic affections. Neither would she enjoy them very long. "Compared to Isadora we are all pigmies," Galya wrote grimly.³¹ She would shoot herself later on Esenin's grave in Moscow, on the first anniversary of his death.

Isadora still refused to comprehend. I'VE RECEIVED TELEGRAM EVIDENTLY FROM YOUR SERVANT BENISLAVSKAYA, she cabled back: HAVE YOU CHANGED ADDRESS I ASK YOU EXPLAIN. No matter how blunt Esenin became — I LOVE ANOTHER AM MARRIED AND HAPPY — she took her time releasing him. "These telegrams harassed him and got on his nerves dreadfully," Galya wrote. "This was a period when Sergei Alexandrovitch stood on the brink of doom, when he himself sometimes said that nothing now could help him."³²

From Batum, Isadora went to Yalta, hoping that the luxurious Crimean climate would prove too tempting for Esenin to resist. ("That's where my school should be!" she lamented when she saw the Romanov palace at Livadia, which Krassin had rashly promised her in London;³³ the same building would house the Yalta Conference in

World War II.) As late as January 1924, after all communication between them had ceased, she still expected Esenin to come back to her.
"Everyone knows he is my husband," she told his next mistress, an actress, to whom Esenin began dedicating his verse: "For the first time I
sing of love . . ."[34] Isadora expected to see him when she returned to
Moscow at the end of September, but he was nowhere to be found —
he had fled to Petrograd upon hearing that she was back. He "was
in a panic," Galya wrote, "he wanted to hide somewhere, vanish."[35]
When Isadora and Esenin finally met at Prechistenka (the date is unknown), a scene of some kind ensued. "Don't you think it's in bad
taste to scream in Isadora's room in front of people about your love for
another woman?" Schneider wrote to Esenin. "I see only shame and
lies coming from you, and after the scandal of last night, I can only tell
you that I do not want to see you again."

After that, as far as is known, Isadora met Esenin only once more,
when he arrived drunk at Prechistenka to collect a wooden bust of
himself made by sculptor Sergei Konenkov. He left at once, dropping
the sculpture several times and cursing as he went: "Sullenly and
shakily he rose to his feet; and then reeled out of the room to wander
later about the byways of Moscow."[36] On November 22 he was arrested at a bar with three imaginist friends for making "anti-Semitic
remarks" about Bolshevik leaders. "The police examination records
say the [poets] were only slightly intoxicated," Walter Duranty reported in the *New York Times,* "which all who know Esenin may, however, doubt."[37]

Four nights later Isadora danced at the Bolshoi, where the first
Oktabrina christening took place at the Fifth Congress of the Women's
Section of the Communist Party. Duranty called it "a weird substitute"
for the Christian rite of baptism: "On a stage decked with red banners
and slogans, a young father and mother brought a baby girl out to the
footlights, before the red-draped tables of the Executive Committee,
and dedicated her to communism. The offering was accepted by the
aged priestess of the Red International, Klara Zetkin, and by [Nikolai]
Bukharin, himself aflame with devotion to Russia's new religion." At
that time, Bukharin was leader of the Comintern and editor of *Pravda:*
he would be shot by Stalin in 1938. Duranty continued:

> With sublime incongruity, of which the spectators seemed uncon-
> scious, the proceedings closed with a ceremonial christening dance by
> Isadora Duncan and her pupils, to the sacred strains of Schubert's "Ave

Maria," an astounding epilogue to the thunderous roll of the "International," sung before. . . . Every woman in the audience watched . . . as though it were a living child that lay under Isadora's outstretched arms. Then the music swelled and the dancers raised their hands to Heaven as if in prayer. . . . Anywhere but Russia the scene would have been banal, even ridiculous, but here it is not. Atmosphere, innate dramatic sense — call it what you will — it was simple, natural, and terribly impressive.[38]

Isadora spent most of the night of the christening ceremony chatting in her dressing room with Russia's eminent woman Bolshevik, Alexandra Kollontai. Kollontai had recently been named Soviet ambassador to Norway, the first stage in her removal from the center of Soviet power. She was Russia's leading champion of women's rights and a well-known advocate of free love, convinced that "erotic friendships" were the key to party solidarity and revolutionary ardor. Kollontai's influence with the Bolsheviks had once been so great that her recommendations about Russian women and children were virtually decreed as law when Lenin came to power. Now she was blamed for "instability between the sexes" and 100,000 Russian divorces in 1922 alone. While they waited to appear onstage, Isadora and Kollontai split a bottle of vodka and talked about love, sex, and men. When Duranty saw Isadora later that week at Prechistenka, she had plainly reached the end of what he called her "Esenin period." The poet was out of jail long enough to tell reporters that he was "finished with Duncan." If she wanted a divorce, she could get it herself.[39]

"He really is too impossible," Isadora told Duranty. "If it were only women I wouldn't mind so much, but Sergei's trouble comes out of the bottle. . . . It was bad enough in America, but here his crazy goings on interfere with the work of my school, which I won't have. So that ends my first experience of matrimony, which I always thought a highly overrated performance."[40] A friend saw Esenin at the Stable of Pegasus and noticed that he kept running in and out of the lavatory, from where he emerged "enlivened, brisk and extremely stimulated. At first I did not understand what it was, but then I grasped it: he was taking cocaine."[41] In a Moscow park he agonized about Russia's future: "Can't you hear the skyscrapers growing? It's the same as America, just as accursed and murderous."[42]

In January 1924 Esenin entered a sanatorium. By September Isadora could write to Allan Ross Macdougall: "You will be pleased to hear that I have not seen the turbulent Esenin since a year."[43]

✳   ✳   ✳

After Esenin's departure, Schneider saw an unexpected change in Isadora: "She shut herself up in her shell, never mentioned Esenin's name, did not attempt to arrange any meeting with him, and outwardly seemed absolutely calm. She devoted herself entirely to her work with the children and seemed to be interested only in the problems of the future of her school." The hunt for money was a constant distraction. Having arranged one day to meet Lunacharsky in his office, Isadora saw "a very stately and rather plump woman [walking] proudly and importantly through the reception to the exit."

"Who's that?" she asked. Schneider answered that it was Lunacharsky's deputy, Yakovleva, that she was a "left communist," and that she was "in charge of all the financial affairs of the People's Commissariat for Education."

Isadora was silent for a moment. Then she said: "Come on. We are wasting our time here. That woman wears a corset."[44] She wrote to Augustin:

> The children in the School are simply a Miracle. The first school [Grunewald] nothing in comparison, but — Hélas — How shall we feed them — The Government gives nothing, the A.R.A. also is no more. We do not know from day to day when the School will cease & it will be a crime, for such Beauty of movement and Expression I have never imagined could come true. . . . It is a wonder that it still exists. Our only hope is that they may send us help from America.[45]

By "they" Isadora meant American communists and their sympathizers. "If you can find some money to help . . . I would be most grateful," she wrote to Louis Schaffer, editor of Chicago's *Daily Forward,* in December 1923: "We are forced to pay very dear for electric light fuel and even water food & clothes. . . . From one performance . . . I have bought wood for the winter — with a second performance flour, potatoes, etc." That month Isadora danced twice at the Bolshoi — "one alone Wagner," as she told Gus, "and one Schubert with children — Great Enthusiasm and enough *dingy* to live on for two weeks." It was "discouraging" to write to America, she added, "as nobody answers." She told Schaffer:

> The children are at present in splendid health & working with enthusiasm & they are most of them so talented that it will be a thousand pities if this two years work sacrifice & effort is to be lost. . . . If

the school is helped for the next few years I am confident that it will then be self supporting — & we will be able to enlarge it to the number of two or three hundred children.[46]

Her students in Moscow were the last Isadora would have — and the best, in her estimation. "How she loved dancing with us on the stage!" said Maria Mysovskaya ("Moussy"), one of the first girls to enter the school. "She managed to kiss us in the course of the dance and whisper, '*Moye detie, moye detie*' [My children, my children], and we emerged into the wings with blots of lipstick on our cheeks, but didn't we adore her!"[47] At the start, Isadora also accepted boys at the school: the girls were forbidden to tease them. Two sexes required separate dormitories, however, and the education of males was shortly dropped. The dances Isadora composed at Prechistenka were based on Russian workers' songs and appropriate to either sex: *With Courage Comrades March in Step; One, Two, Three, Pioneers Are We; The Young Guard,* etc. Under the pressure of state ideology, her choreography foresaw the imminent direction of modern dance: "In contrast to the lyrical, free-flowing style usually associated with Duncan, most of these dances have a blunt, bound, rooted look to them. . . . The body image emphasizes tension, especially through lunging thighs, laboring arms, and clenched fists. . . . The group formations are decidedly architectural."[48]

The best known of Isadora's Russian pieces is *Warshavianka,* set to a revolutionary working song of 1905 and depicting the heroic endurance of the proletariat: "The action is based on the motif of a leap to victory with red banner held high. As the first group rushes forward leading the attack, *Boom!* They all fall down and die. The next group picks up the banner to mount the next leap to victory, and so on."[49] *Dubinushka,* too, is a dance of solidarity and cooperation, "two parallel lines working together rhythmically to pull a rope," while in *The Blacksmith* the dancers "raise themselves up and unchain themselves, fists held forth, hair swinging to the refrain."[50] Always, the emphasis is on victory and sacrifice. Rehearsing *Warshavianka,* a student recalled, Isadora didn't like "the way we fell on the floor from the 'merciless volleys.'"

"Don't you know how people die?" Isadora asked. "She then collapsed in perfect unison with the music, only to rise slowly and resolutely when coming back to life in order to join her comrades and pick up the banner from their hands."[51]

In February 1924 Isadora left Moscow for a tour of Ukraine, dancing in Kharkov, Rostov, Krasnodar, Ekaterinoslav, Kiev, Vinitza, and Odessa. The tour was delayed for several weeks owing to the death of Lenin in January. "Deeply moved," Isadora stood in line in subzero temperatures "with millions of other people" to pay her respects to the fallen leader at the House of Soviets in Moscow: "Her feelings found expression in two revolutionary funeral songs which she danced in memory of Lenin at all her performances." She lost thirty pounds on her Ukrainian tour "and looked perfectly beautiful, slender and taller with her flaming red head poised high on her graceful neck."[52] Filled with energy, she went to Leningrad (as Petrograd was now renamed), took a suite at the Hotel Europe, and spent more money in a month than she had in a year at Prechistenka. Schneider, now acting as headmaster, confessed to "a dull feeling of irritation. . . . She had done nothing to help the school with the money she received for her [Ukrainian] performances."[53] To him, at least, it became clear that the Duncan school wouldn't survive if its founder and namesake had access to the bank account.

In May Isadora accepted an invitation to dance at Vitsyebsk, four hundred miles from Leningrad, and was nearly killed on the way back at Pskov when her chauffeured convertible "broke in two. The front part with the driver turned somersault. The back half with [Isadora] was hurled over into a ditch."[54] She was thrown from the car "and hit her head, but luckily she had fallen into a puddle and the water had softened the blow."[55] It was the first round in a volley of bad luck that would drive her from Russia in September. "I have always believed that my end would come in a motor accident," Isadora said. Broke, bruised, but "full of animal spirits," she returned to Moscow and immediately arranged another Ukrainian tour, this time with the children. She had left an unpaid bill at the Europe in Leningrad "that seemed to her intimates like the war debt of one of the lesser powers."

In Kiev a heat wave hit. Audiences stayed away, and after two weeks "the financial condition of the School was no better than it had been. Most of the money earned went to pay the expenses of the orchestra and the hotel bills."[56] Sending Irma and the children back to Moscow, therefore, Isadora struck out alone toward the Volga, the cities of central Asia, and the Ural Mountains, dismissing the orchestra to save on expenses and taking only her pianist, Mark Meichik. With them was her Russian concert manager, Zinoviev, nicknamed Zino and sometimes Darling. On July 28 they reached Ekaterinburg, capital of the Red Urals and the city where Nicholas II and his family were murdered in 1918. "Perhaps the killing here of a *certain* family in a cellar has cast a sort of Edgar Allan Poe gloom over the place," Isadora wrote, "or perhaps it was always like that. . . . You can't imagine anything more fearful." She went on:

> We arrived here more dead than alive after 5 nights on the r.r., twice changing trains & waiting all day in villages without hotels. . . . This tournée is one calamity after another, for although I dance to large publics of communists & workmen no one has money to buy tickets except the new bourgeoisie & they cordially detest me. When we have a little money Meichik takes it all on the pretext that he will not play unless he receives all the money at once & after that he calmly sits by & watches us starve. He is a wonderful Tovarisch and ought to be sent to *Rimsky Kreim.**
>
> I have no books or papers — I had hoped you would send some here. Why do you not send us news. We read in the newspapers that the S[oviet] Gov. is now handsomely supporting the School. Is that true?
>
> Well we hope Siberia may turn out better — Volga & Turkeystan [sic] are countries to be avoided. With love to all
>
> In haste — Isadora.[57]

In fact, the Soviet government wasn't supporting the school. That summer Irma and the students again taught dance to workers' children in Moscow, this time at the newly completed Red Stadium on Sparrow Hills: "They romped about in the sun singing their revolutionary songs, and from pale sallow children of the city streets they grew during the summer months to happy, sunburned, and healthy dancing humans."[58] According to Schneider, Irma's hard work "brought to an end the unceasing attacks" on the school,[59] but it could no longer be called Isadora's.

"We were twelve days in that awful Ekaterinburg," Isadora wrote from Vyatka on August 12: "You have no idea what is a living nightmare until you see [that] town . . . no restaurant . . . no coiffeur. The only remaining fossil of that name, while burning my hair off with trembling fingers, assured me there was not one 'Dame' left . . . they shot 'em all." Bookings for the major towns of Siberia had fallen through, and she was trying to get back to Moscow:

> In Perm we did not make expenses — and arrive here without a kopeck. This is a village with awful hotel — bed bugs mice & other

*Properly, *Narimsky Kraim,* that part of Siberia "where all speculators and crooks were sent."

agreements. . . . It is too awful. I haven't had a bottle of eau de cologne no soap no tooth paste since a month. The beds are made of boards & populated. The halls are splashed with the filth of ages & blood stains & pistol shots in the mirrors. . . . My hair is quite white for lack of a Henna champoo [sic] — & I feel extremely *kaputt*.

   . . . With love to Ilysha [Schneider] & the children & love to you —
     Sterbende [Dying]
      Isadora[60]

By the end of August, Isadora finally reached Moscow, where five hundred children in red tunics greeted her from the street on her arrival at Prechistenka: "They cheered her and she smiled back and waved her red scarf to them. . . . She said to those who stood by her: 'What do all my hardships matter after this: these half a thousand children dancing and singing in the open air with fine, free movements?'"[61] For the rest of the summer, she assisted Irma at Red Stadium, writing Macdougall on September 2: "Everyone can say what they please, in spite of the catastrophe and suffering and all, the *idea* of the New World is born here, and nothing can kill it."[62]

Thus confident, Isadora gratefully signed a contract for a tour of Germany, which "Irma and her friends had arranged for her in her absence."[63] Whether the friends were Irma's or her own isn't clear. At one of her last appearances in Moscow, the fourth in a series of farewell concerts at the Kamerny Theatre, she thanked the Russian people for the welcome they had given her and commenced to tell the audience the story of her life.

"You must all forgive me," she said, "if I seem somewhat egotistical . . . but my Life is so tightly bound up with my Art, it is so much one and the same, that I must always refer to it." She spoke about her father, Joseph Duncan; about her mother; and about her family's poverty and hardships in California, saying that she had been "forced" to become a dancer "out of necessity. . . . That is why I don't like children to dance before the public for money, as I experienced what it meant to dance for a piece of bread. . . . I say to the child: 'Put your hands here on your breast, then lift them up higher and higher to the stars. . . . Embrace the whole world with your arms. Reach out. . . . There is a place for you in the Universe.'" Ideologically speaking, she left Russia in the nick of time.

"I went to Russia hoping to create something big," Isadora concluded, "something grandiose. The word *Bolshevik* — meaning Big, I thought. . . . All I needed for that was a big place to work in. And now three years have passed and I have waited in vain."[64] On her first night in Berlin, she told a friend: "The effigy of Lenin in Red Square symbolizes the New Russia. They have embalmed the Revolution."[65] Her final performance at the Bolshoi, on September 29, was arranged by the wife of Politburo president Mikhail Kalinin and attended by "the leaders of the Communist Party and 4,000 young Pioneers and Communist youths." At the end of the night, "with one of her impetuous movements of generosity," Isadora opened her handbag, took out all the money she had earned at the Kamerny Theatre, and scattered it among the children and the crowd.[66]

Part VI

"SANS LIMITES"

(1924-1927)

Then give me a mood of the mountain tops,

And the sacred presence of song;

And I shall resume where the last star stops;

And my chant shall be clear and strong.

My words shall be writ in the world-heart's blood,

And sung to a cosmic lyre;

Whose sighs are a wind, and whose tears are a flood,

And whose love is the central fire.

    — Louis K. Anspacher, "Invocation"

     ("To Isadora, April 8, 1917")

28
Love and Ideals

Isadora left Moscow, telling Irma and Schneider that her absence would be brief: she wanted to collect some things she had left in storage in Berlin and would return with better weather in the spring. On the way out of Russia, her plane crash-landed twice, first on takeoff outside Moscow and later in Königsberg (Kaliningrad). She described the mishaps as "marvelous experiences" to reporter George Seldes, who caught up with her at the Hotel Eden — after her adventures with Esenin, Isadora bypassed the Adlon. "Years in Moscow have not weakened Miss Duncan's vitality and joy of living," Seldes wrote tactfully. But where was her husband?

"There's no real marriage in Soviet Russia," Isadora answered; "consequently I am not divorced now."[1] That was all. She was late for her first performance at the Blüthner Saal on October 3 and apologized to the audience after the *Pathétique*. "I find it difficult to dance," she said, "my heart aches."[2] Dorothy Thompson wrote in the *New York Evening Post:* "Critics who have followed her were willing to agree with her confession . . . that her days of solo performances are over."[3] Seldes saw Isadora later at a party given in her honor by "a rich German or American with a magnificent apartment." Among the guests were the chorus of an imported musical comedy, *Little Jesse James* — six American showgirls, blond, "beautiful in the magazine cover sense, and all but one available." Seldes recalled in a letter to his niece, actress Marian Seldes:

> By the time I arrived Isadora had had too much, as usual, and was stretched on a couch, fat and bloated. We, however, tried to cheer her up, and then followed the cruel scene I refer to. The six American chorus girls, who knew nothing of classic dancing to say nothing of ballet, improvised their own dance, an American musical comedy dance, around and around the couch where the half-drunken Isadora lay with glazed eyes — each chorus girl kicking up her legs and all singing some chorus from one of their latest American shows. It is a scene I'll never forget although it is one of the few things I have witnessed I have never before cared to write or even tell anyone.[4]

At the Blüthner Saal, Isadora ended her program with the *Internationale* and a last defense of communism. "All her dancing was a form of political expression," wrote American correspondent Sam Spewack, "and she hoped by stalking about the stage in a red veil . . . to convert the world."[5] Soon she found herself in a press war with Russian dancer Mikhail Mordkin, Pavlova's former partner, on tour in Berlin by permission of the Soviet government.

"She can't dance and uses politics as an excuse to appear on the stage!" Mordkin scoffed. "We who can dance are hampered at every turn by politics. Isadora Duncan has done more to kill Russian dancing than any living person." It was noted in published reports that Isadora and Mordkin had once been friends.[6] Her final ostracism from the world of dance coincided with the degeneration of the Ballets Russes and a rudderless period in ballet. George Balanchine, the next savior of the form, would banish Diaghilev's innovations in favor of a strict neoclassicism and heaped abuse on Isadora, whom he saw in Russia, in the decisive expression of anti-Duncanism.

"I thought she was awful," Balanchine declared. "I don't understand it when people say she was a great dancer. To me it was absolutely unbelievable — a drunken, fat woman who for hours was rolling around like a pig. It was the most awful thing. . . . She was probably a nice juicy girl when she was young."[7] In Paris, Lisa Duncan was still dancing in nightclubs, adding to Isadora's fears for her legacy. "If she wishes to go to such filth she ought at least to take her own name," Isadora complained. "When she knows what I have suffered and gone through to keep my name from the music hall, and then she drags it there."[8] Seldes asked her what she meant to do next. "It is uncertain," she said. "The only thing I think is that I will continue to devote my life to training children."[9]

It is impossible to discover the reason for the collapse of Isadora's German tour. "I have signed three contracts and been swindled three times," she reported. "The last for Hannover. When the time came, the agent didn't have the money for the R.R. ticket. They are all swindlers." Anxiously, she telegraphed her new tenant at rue de la Pompe. She had given him the house for "a ridiculous sum." No answer came. Isadora concluded: "This Europe is quite impossible. I am homesick for the soldiers singing and the children singing. . . . The children here look like Muffins compared to the Russians. I am not, perhaps, competent to explain what has happened *there,* but here *nothing* has happened, and the people are just simply stopped." Her letters to Irma in Moscow became more urgent:

> ["*Beginning of October*"] It seems my fate in 1924 is to be tragically stranded. I am still waiting here for something — God knows what — Berlin is simply fearful. Better to sell matches on the streets of Moscow. Here is no spirit; everything congested with *Patriotismus* and fatherland. It is awful. . . . I danced two evenings *without receiving a penny*. . . . Altogether it is Hell!!! And I spend my time wondering which sort of poison doesn't hurt the most. I don't want to take any of the fearful kind. . . . Write me what is happening. If you can fix the contract for Siberia I will come. Love to you and to all the dear children. Love — Isadora. *Poor thing.* Love to you all. Maybe I die tonight.

At the end of October, Isadora moved from the Eden to the Central, a "second-rate" hotel near the Friedrichstrasse station. "Everything seems to be standing still," she wrote — "why? I feel like an aeroplane '*en panne.*'"[10] In Berlin the Russian daily *Dni* compared her dancing to "autumn leaves, beautiful in their decay, fading colors, wonderful as the twilight that precedes night."[11] But gallantry from critics was rare. "What a lamentable Odyssey has been the life of Isadora Duncan during the last years!" crowed *The Dancing Times* in London.[12] Isadora wrote to Irma on November 27:

> I cannot move from here! Since four weeks the hotel will serve no more food. An American friend brings me a slice of roast beef a day, but he has no money either. . . . *Elizabeth has deserted me* and gone to visit a rich friend in Vienna. *Her school in Potsdam won't even let me in.* I was ill for two weeks with a bronchitis, and now, to cap the climax,

an ulcerated tooth. I have telegraphed to Raymond, but he is in Nice and apparently *can't* or *won't* do anything. Germany is the limit, simply fearful. I don't know what's going to happen next. . . . Yours in a dying stage, Isadora.

Isadora's "American friend" was Allan Coe, a student pianist living on an allowance in Berlin with his friend and lover, a singer named Martin. According to Mary Desti, Isadora had presented herself at Elizabeth's school after leaving the Eden and was told by Max Merz that her sister was in Austria. When she protested that she had no money and no place to stay, Merz answered that it was her own fault and shut the door. Coe's allowance, too, was soon cut off when his American sponsors learned that he was leading "a wild, debauched life" in Berlin.[13] "Frightfully anxious," Isadora wrote to Irma:

> [16 December 1924]: Why don't you answer my telegrams and letters? Since six weeks I am without any word from you, although I repeatedly sent *Luftpost* letters and telegrams. . . . Are you ill? Does the School still exist? I can obtain no passport here from the Russian Embassy. Please do whatever is necessary to obtain this passport for me and also a divorce from Sergei Alexandrovitch — God bless him, but he's no good for a husband.
>
> I may have to return to Moscow, as here my allowance to stay expires in a week. *Every country has refused me a visa* on account of my *"political connections."* What are my *political connections?* Where are my political connections, I would like to know? I am utterly stranded and lost here in a very hostile city. I haven't a single friend. . . . They have even refused me a visa on a contract for Vienna. Perhaps I. [Schneider] had better get on an aeroplane and come here and save me, otherwise you will soon be sending a wreath to my funeral. But why haven't you answered a single letter or telegram for six weeks?
>
> Love to the children, if they still exist, and to you and to all friends. YOUR DYING ISADORA.

In Russia, Irma had left with the children on a tour of the Volga — she claimed not to have seen Isadora's letters until it was "too late" to help.[14] Urgently, Allan Coe wrote to Macdougall in Paris: "We boys have given our last cent, and we all three are broke — stranded! Honest to God!" On the back of the letter, Isadora scrawled: "Where is Raymond? . . . Perhaps if you asked Walter [Rummel] he would do something — or his dear brother, who really is my friend — Frank —

Pour l'Amour de Dieu sauvez-moi."[15] Seldes called on Isadora at the Central and found her "fat, frowsy, all puffed out," and in a belligerent mood. "God, I wish I were back in America," she said, the surest sign of her distress.

"I think the poor woman was starving," Seldes recalled. "She hopped around from subject to subject like a cricket."[16] His report to the *Chicago Tribune* on December 14 caused a sensation:

> Isadora Duncan is at the end of her rope and does not know how to pay her rent or where her meals are to come from next week, she told the correspondent today. Two courses are open to her, she said. The first is to sell her houses in Paris, which is difficult, because France will not give her a visa to visit Paris, and the second, to publish 1,000 love letters received in her prime.
>
> When asked about the love letters, Miss Duncan said:
>
> "I have no hesitancy about them. Ever since I got into trouble because of my work in Russia and my last tour in America I found that I had no friends. Nobody sticks to you when you are in difficulties, so why should I hesitate about publishing these letters? They are going to ruin a lot of families, but why should I worry?"[17]

She opened a trunk and showed Seldes her treasures. "Please note that this is genuine Isadora," Seldes wrote later. "I think most of the biographies are bunkum. *De mortuis nil nisi bunkem.* It is not a pretty picture."[18] He went on:

> "These are from D'Annunzio," she said, handing me some blue papers written in a large florid way some twenty words to the page. "And these from Gordon Craig." Pages not written but drawn. Every letter a work of art. . . .
>
> "And these are [Paris Singer's] — very plain — a business man's hard handwriting. Here are some from — well, I won't tell you the name now. He was my lover once, young and beautiful — now he's married and has three children and writes no more great poetry."
>
> She held her finger clumsily over the name, hiding only half of it. . . . "Esenin's are in Russian," she said. "You won't understand them. But they are beautiful."[19]

In a letter to Irma six weeks later, Isadora denied Seldes's story flat-out. "I was offered by the *Chicago Tribune* a sum for my 'memoirs,'" she complained, "but afterward it all turned to *blackmail*, and they wrote fearful articles by way of revenge."[20] One of these had quoted her further:

> "The ethics of publishing love letters?" I put in.
> "Let us drop talk about ethics in this matter."
> "But are not love letters in a sense sacred — meant for their recipients, or at most for a remote posterity?"
> "Fuddle," said Miss Duncan firmly. "Why! I propose to publish them just to prove that love is not the sacred thing poets talk about. Love is an illusion. I propose publishing my love letters to prove it is an illusion; to show up their writers; to convince foolish youth that there is no such thing as love."
> "Have you really 1,000 love letters?"
> "Heaps more than 1,000. . . . Yes; love is the world's great make-believe. I ought to know. . . . I shall show them up; I shall name them all!"[21]

Seldes's reputation for integrity in reporting was unmatched in American journalism. He kept the telegram the *Tribune* sent authorizing him to buy Isadora's autobiography — "containing love letters" — for $5,000. "And the truth was that at her ultimatum I brought her a quart of gin," Seldes added, "when I came to fix the memoirs, because she cried for it, cried real tears as if heartbroken, and also threatened: No gin, no deal." On December 20 Seldes hired an English stenographer to take Isadora's dictation; he added "only two commas" to her first chapter, "Love and Ideals."[22]

> I want this book to be something worth leaving behind. It will be worth doing only if it is a book which will help people to live. I want to tell the truth about my loves and my art because the whole world is absolutely brought up on lies. We are fed on nothing but lies. We begin with lies and half our lives at least we live with lies. Most human beings today waste some twenty-five to thirty years of their lives before they break through the actual and conventional lies which surround them.

She went on to discuss Lenin, Christ, Buddha, children, artists, and dancing — "I am not a dancer. I have never *danced* a step in my life" — in what Seldes called "a strange and not too sober jumble of opinions, anecdotes, childhood reminiscences, mentions of her notable lovers, family life in San Francisco, art, love, and passion." He asked Isadora again what had happened to Esenin.

"Oh," she said, "Sergei has gone into the Caucasus . . . to become a bandit. He writes he is going to be a robber to get thrills."[23] She didn't consider herself married any longer but had been denied a French visa on the grounds that she was Esenin's wife. ("You see before you a poor exile," Isadora sighed to another reporter on December 30. "It seems the Revolution is only awaiting my arrival in Paris.")[24]

"But you are a Bolshevik?" Seldes asked.

"No, I am not a Bolshevik. All I did was work for the starving children. . . . Men have loved me, but my only love has been children." Here she spoke as an expert:

> What mankind calls love is only hatred in another form. In the flesh there is no love. I have had as much as anyone of that sort of thing . . . men foaming at the mouth — men crying they would kill themselves if I didn't return their love. Love — rot! I had just barely come on the stage when it began. . . . From all sides I was besieged by all sorts of men. What did they want? Their feelings, I know now, were the feelings they have for a bottle of whiskey. They say to the bottle, "I'm thirsty. I want you. I want to drink you up. I want to possess all of you!" To me they said the same things. "I am hungry. I want you. I want to possess you body and soul." Oh, they actually add the soul, when they plead for the body.
>
> Was that love? No. It was hysteria. . . .
>
> When I was in Moscow I saw little children lying huddled asleep in doorways and on rubbish heaps. Would this be possible if there was love in the world? . . . Was that love? . . . If there is such a thing as love in the world, would people allow this sort of thing? Could they go to their comfortable houses knowing that there are children in such distress? So long as little children are allowed to suffer, there is no true love in the world.

At the end of the day, Seldes's stenographer quit, unwilling to hear any more of Isadora's tale. "I don't like her ideas," the secretary said, "and I can't permit myself to work for a woman who drinks gin." A replacement was hard to find on short notice; meanwhile, Seldes's story of Isadora's plight had moved her friends to action. When he returned to the Central a few days later, he met "an entirely sober and considerably different Isadora." She was packing her trunks, on her way to Spa "for the cure."

"She said she had got a sum of money," Seldes wrote. "It was rumored that one of her former lovers had supplied it to keep the memoirs from being written." Isadora hoped to spend the coming winter in

Nice. "I'm going to have a theatre again," she said. "You must come and see my first performance."

"And your biography," Seldes asked, "and the letters?"

"Oh, that's all finished. Publish my memoirs now? What do you think I am? An old woman? Am I dead? Only the dead publish memoirs. I'll have time enough when I am dead to write them. . . . Life is changed . . . life begins again."[25]

Not one of her former lovers but an American friend, Russian-born newspaperman Isaac Don Levine, settled Isadora's accounts in Berlin and helped her reach Paris in January 1925. Selling love letters was beneath her, Levine had said. He, too, hoped to pry her memoirs out of her and for months worked valiantly to that end.[26] "At last I arrived here," Isadora told Irma on February 2. "I am hardly alive, just gasping."[27] That same day her former pupil Margot died of tuberculosis at a Paris hospital. She was twenty-six. Isadora had delayed going to see her and fell into a depression on the news of her death: "I simply almost gave up entirely . . . I confess — I can't understand — the whole scheme of things is *too* unbearable."[28]

In March Isadora left for Nice by car with Raymond, who had opened another studio on the Riviera, amid considerable controversy. In 1923 a painting of Raymond's called *Maternity* was banned from exhibition in Paris, "on grounds of indecency." He followed it with another called *The Flesh,* which was promptly cut to pieces by an outraged vandal.[29] "Paris is weary of men who disguise themselves as carnival-time Athenians," a critic wrote, "and walk the streets with bare legs and dirty feet so that they can sell rugs of doubtful quality at high prices."[30] Raymond denounced the city as philistine, bourgeois, and loose in its morals. Gertrude Stein had a joke at his expense: "Oh, Raymond, Raymond . . . I remember when you used to drink sherry! . . . Why . . . before you became a Greek . . . you used to wear carnations in your buttonhole and smoke long cigars."

"You have an excellent memory, Gertrude," Raymond answered, "probably due to the fact that you keep repeating things over and over." This swipe at her writing wasn't lost on Miss Stein. Raymond described the silence that followed as "agonizing."[31]

"It really wasn't funny," Isadora said. On their drive to Nice, "when little brother Raymond got out to crank the Ford, the peasants would watch him with great interest. Oh, no! they never laughed. They were very grave and polite!"[32] Raymond offered to install her in an apartment over his shop near the Nice promenade, but after several weeks of sleeping on wooden benches, Isadora looked elsewhere for shelter. The Riviera sunshine and the closeness of the sea lifted her spirits. "My motto," she wrote: "*'Sans Limites.'*"[33] Soon Georges Maurevert, one of her oldest friends in France, persuaded the Hôtel Negresco, Nice's most expensive, to give Isadora "a small room with bath at a greatly reduced rate,"[34] the so-called *tarif d'artiste.*

At the end of March, Isadora located a new studio, a converted garage at 343, promenade des Anglais, in the "California" district on the western edge of Nice. "A friend" had agreed to rent it for her — apparently, the money came first from Augustin and later from Ruth Mitchell in New York.

"It is a perfect gem," Isadora wrote to Irma. "A little theatre twice as big as the Rue de la Pompe with a stage, footlights, etc."[35] In a letter to Mary Desti, she added that she was "stranded as usual and have no money to fix it up — on receiving this if you can telegraph me $200 I could get my carpet from Paris & a Piano — & work again."[36] Through Macdougall, she tried to sell her unpublished essays on the dance, but no one wanted them. "I spent a fearful year in Russia half dead from cold and starvation & seeing everyone else starve too," Isadora wrote to Mary. "Couldn't you hint delicately to Theresa & Anna that they might at least pay me the usual 10% *Author's* rights — in using my work — as they are doing!!!"[37] Then, in April, she was stung by a hornet while indulging in the new craze of sunbathing: "Her right arm began to swell dangerously and she became quite ill."[38] Isadora wrote again to Mary:

> All the Calamities of the Universe seem to fall on my poor head. I was poisoned by a demon in [the] shape of a fly and had to be rushed to Hospital for [an] operation to save my arm. I am getting well now but very shaky. I was about to sign a contract for a tournée of France. I have a wonderful little Theatre by the Sea. . . . If you and Augustin could see your way to send me $50 a week until I can work again I will be able to refund it all in October when I have a prospect of a great deal of money for a contract — France and Spain.[39]

So it continued — "a contract" was just on the horizon. In New York, Mary talked to publisher Horace Liveright about Isadora's still unwritten memoirs, but it would be another year before Liveright agreed to a deal, and then only through Isadora's new Paris agent,

William Aspinwall Bradley. Isadora met Bradley and his French wife, Jenny, on the Riviera about this time. A cable to Mary requested on April 18: BRING CONTRACT BOOK ISADORA. (Another had already arrived from Raymond's companion, Aia Bertrand: ISADORA HERE ALONE ILL CABLE DOLLARS.)[40] Frank Harris, the Irish-born author of *My Life and Loves*, stepped in to give Isadora writing advice, along with Maurevert and Spanish laureate Blasco Ibañez. "Get a stenographer," Blasco insisted: "If you can't write them, speak them! . . . It's not difficult. . . . And you will gain millions and millions of francs! A name like yours represents a hundred editions!"[41] On April 21 the *New York World* reported: ISADORA DUNCAN PLANS MEMOIRS BUT WON'T INCLUDE LOVE LETTERS. She received the *World's* correspondent while recuperating from her "fly" bite at the Negresco.

"Why am I hounded and tortured?" Isadora cried. "I want to write about my art, and everyone insists on talking about my body." In writing, she hoped to find "the same freedom of expression" she had found in dancing; what the result would be, she couldn't say: "My memoirs will not, however, be the chronicle of a female Casanova, as so many seem to expect. There are other and better things to write about in life, though this crazed century thinks otherwise."[42]

For two years Isadora moved back and forth between Nice and Paris, "in the clatter of scandalized tongues, among the kidding faces of reporters, the threatening of bailiffs, the expostulations of hotel-managers bringing overdue bills." John Dos Passos's moving portrait of Isadora in *The Big Money* — "She couldn't stop drinking or putting her arms round the neck of the nearest young man; if she got any cash she threw a party or gave it away" — is a modernist reduction of fact. "She was afraid of nothing," Dos Passos wrote. "She was a great dancer."[43] Zelda Fitzgerald, who met her under trying circumstances at a restaurant in Saint-Paul-de-Vence, remained cynical about Isadora to the end: "She had got too old and fat to care whether people accepted her theories of life and art, and she gallantly toasted the world's obliviousness in lukewarm champagne."[44]

On the night they met, Zelda threw herself down a flight of stone stairs when Scott Fitzgerald began to flirt with Isadora. The Riviera was "vivid with dresses just down from Paris," Fitzgerald wrote, "and giving off a sweet pungent odor of flowers and chartreuse and fresh black coffee and cigarettes, and mingled with another scent, the mysterious thrilling scent of love. Hands touched jewelled hands over the white tables; the vivid gowns and shirtfronts swayed together and matches were held, trembling a little, for slow-lighting cigarettes."[45] In the summer of 1925 Zelda was fresh from an affair with French aviator Edouard Jozan and a suicide attempt with sleeping pills. Perhaps more pertinent, she was already obsessed with becoming a ballet dancer, the kind Isadora loathed. According to Zelda biographer Nancy Milford:

> It was perhaps ten o'clock and they had just finished their meal. . . . At a nearby table sat Isadora Duncan surrounded by three admirers. Gerald Murphy said: "Scott didn't know who she was, so I told him. He immediately went to her table and sat at her feet. She ran her fingers through his hair and called him her centurion. . . ."
> Zelda was quietly watching Scott and Duncan together and then suddenly, with no word of warning or explanation, she stood up on her chair and leaped across both Gerald and the table into the darkness of the stairwell behind him. "I was sure she was dead. We were all stunned and motionless." Zelda reappeared within moments, standing perfectly still at the top of the stone stairs. Sara [Murphy] ran to her and wiped the blood from her knees and dress. Gerald said, "I don't remember what Scott did. The first thing I remember thinking was that it had not been ugly. I said that to myself over and over again. I've never been able to forget it."[46]

A decade later Scott Fitzgerald recounted the conversation he and Isadora began before Zelda's leap cut short their acquaintance. Fitzgerald had complimented Isadora as "a revolutionary American woman and artist."

"My granny's Irish blood . . . ," she answered.

"I'm Gaelic too," said Fitzgerald.

"I could tell from your writing. You're our dancing writer, just as Nietzsche is our dancing philosopher." She gave him her room number at the Negresco: "Fitzgerald had heard that Isadora sometimes chose a lover for the night in this fashion, but he felt her interest in him was due to her needing help with her book."[47] Her presence on the Riviera, with the Fitzgeralds and others, helped turn it from a winter resort into a year-round haunt of the "lost generation" — Gertrude Stein's original description of the American expatriate writers and artists who settled in France after World War I. "Nobody was in Antibes that summer," Fitzgerald wrote, ". . . except me, Zelda, the Valentinos, the Murphys, Mistinguet [sic], Rex Ingram, Dos Passos,

Alice Terry, the MacLeishes, Charlie Brackett . . . Marguerite Namara, E. Oppenheimer, Mannes the violinist, Floyd Dell, Max and Crystal Eastman . . . just a real place to rough it and escape from all the world."[48] Journalist Pierre Loving counted among Isadora's friends in Nice Richard Le Gallienne and his daughter Gwen, artist Adolph Dehn, the English poet Anna Wickman, and celebrity painter Lillian Fiske, who "piqued" the Riviera with her saucy remarks.

"All civilized people have *la nostalgie de la boue*," Fiske proclaimed — "a longing for the gutter. Why not admit it?"[49] At the Hôtel Welcome in Villefranche, Jean Cocteau failed his first detoxification for opium addiction, broken over the early death of his lover, Raymond Radiguet, and working on the script of *Orphée*. Stravinsky and Picasso both lived nearby. In Nice, American Monroe Wheeler, newly arrived with his companion, Glenway Wescott, saw Isadora frequently at Vogade, a café in the center of town near the marketplace.

"She would go to Vogade for a morning apéritif before shopping, crème de cacao laced with vodka or gin, to fortify herself," Wheeler remembered. "She would sit there. The shops would close. No shopping. So there was nothing to do but have another drink."[50] Loving described Isadora's two "pigeons," pianist Walter Shaw, a friend of Cocteau's, and his American lover, both from Boston, "who became features in Isadora's circle. . . . It was fortunate that their liberal allowances were sufficient to cover the liberal education that Isadora was willing to provide them."[51] Wescott remembered her "half-naked, moist, damp & whiskey-breathed & sweet, loveable . . . fluttering her hands, almost a benediction, over her fallen mouth, her fallen breasts, her brewer's belly, her skin like mother-of pearl."[52]

At the Victorine film studios, director Rex Ingram welcomed Isadora to the set of Blasco Ibañez's *Mare Nostrum,* where she also met a parade of celebrities visiting the fashionably sinful Côte d'Azur: Rudolph Valentino, Mary Pickford and Douglas Fairbanks, Charlie Chaplin, Anita Loos, Harpo Marx, Carl Laemmle, Maxine Elliott, and future Hollywood director Jean Negulesco, working at the time "as a *danseur mondain*, twirling American ladies around the dance floor" of Isadora's hotel. Negulesco remembered Isadora ungallantly as "a fat slob. She was fat. She was foolish. Often she was embarrassing, sometimes diabolical, devilish, but never stupid." Negulesco recalled a dance recital at Isadora's studio, after she had finally secured her carpet and curtains:

The people invited that night were Jean Cocteau, Richard Le Gallienne, Marie Laurencin, Picasso, Marguerite Jamois, Rex Ingram, Walter Shaw . . . my fiancée Winifred, and I. On a platform a few steps higher than the floor, all of us were seated on enormous, comfortable cushions of the same color as the draperies.

Some twenty tall church candlesticks with heavy unlighted candles were spaced around the walls and front (furnished by Rex Ingram, courtesy of Metro-Goldwyn-Mayer).

The décor was majestic in its simplicity. It was in complete darkness. A Bach sonata on a record player weighed heavily on us. It was Isadora's way to embarrass us into silence with heavy, almost funereal music. By the last note we were emotionally moved — quiet, relaxed.

Then on the waves of a new record Isadora appeared suddenly between two curtains holding a single lighted candle, dressed in a simple white classical toga, barefooted, hair free, not moving, still. It looked as if she listened only to the music. . . . She was there but not with us. She was there not to dance but to listen, to be still. She was like a stopped frame in a film, stopped in motion, not moving, just projecting. She moved. Or did she move? How long before she was in front of the first candlestick giving light? Her bare feet did not move; there was no moving of her toga; she was ahead of the music. You felt that in her motionless attitude — completely oblivious of her surroundings — she was trying to convey the very essence of music, and dance.

Isadora followed what Negulesco called "this miracle" with a Chopin mazurka, for which she had grown too old and stout: "We were quiet — not shocked, not embarrassed. Her grotesque nudity was unnoticed. We looked at and followed every leap and languorous swaying not as a dance but as a plastic tragedy." When she left the stage, "a long, sinful silence" ensued, until Cocteau finally spoke: *"Elle nous a donné la réponse. Isadora a tué la laideur"* — She has given us the answer. Isadora has killed ugliness. It was what she had promised Diaghilev, Pavlova, Benois, and Bakst in St. Petersburg in 1904. Negulesco went on:

Later that night some of us — Isadora, Cocteau, Rex Ingram, Walter Shaw, Winifred, and I — piled in the big sedan of Rex and drove to Marseilles to Chez Basso for a midnight bouillabaisse. The port was full of sailors, and so was the restaurant — young sailors. Cocteau and Walter were in heaven. We didn't finish ordering before Walter brought to the table a handsome blushing young sailor. An animated quarrel started between Isadora and Jean Cocteau as to who would get the tempting morsel.

Jean was ahead in the argument when Isadora started to moan like a child: "Sweetest Cocteau, you had the one last night. Let me have this one." And turning to us: "Make him realize how unfair he is."

In happy chorus we gave our pacifying verdict: "She is right. It's her turn." To which, sulkily, he agreed. "She can have him. But this is the last time."

Strange that two giants became two envious animals contending in bad temper over an embarrassing intimate problem.[53]

Isadora's life in Paris in these years was much the same as her life on the Riviera, with the exception that she had come to loathe the city, its weather, and its high prices. For more than a year she tried to persuade the French Communist Party to support her Moscow school — better yet, to bring the Russian children to Paris, where they could serve as the "nucleus of a great proletarian dancing institution." Her efforts in this direction were the last thing she hoped for "in a grandiose way," according to Macdougall,[54] now writing columns from Paris for American magazines under a range of pseudonyms and alter egos.

"If they will give me a thousand children, I will bring here my best students from Moscow," Isadora wrote to novelist André Arnyvelde, who interceded on her behalf with French communist officials. "But you must impress on the leaders of the Party that for all this capital is necessary."[55] It became her refrain: "All we really need is a little capital. . . . You must keep after them; the way to get things done in this world is to keep after them."[56] Russian pianist Victor Seroff met Isadora that year when she appeared amid a buzz of voices at the salon of a Mrs. Marvin in Montmartre. Seroff was playing when Isadora entered the room:

> She came up to the piano after I had finished. . . . One noticed at once her lovely arms, with their fine small hands, and the line of her neck and shoulders was magnificent. Her whole body moved beautifully as she walked calmly and gently across the room. She wore a simple, loose suit, and on her head was a shapeless felt hat, with a rather large brim, which seemed to express her personality. Her voice was low and gentle, and it had a tone which gave her whole character a quality of naivete. Her face was tired and looked as if she had rouged it without looking in the mirror, and around her eyes . . . she had streaks of black and blue make-up, which did not quite hide the small wrinkles under the eyelids.

"Please play that piece over again, do you mind, I came in only at the end of it." . . . She sat with her hand drooped on the piano and her head down while I played, looking up once in a while and breathing, and she seemed to resemble a harmonium . . . the emotions of her face expressed the music which was flowing through her. When afterwards I saw Isadora listening to music, she always had that same attitude. One felt that no worries and, in fact, nothing else in the world, existed for her at those moments.

"He's a genius," said Isadora when Seroff finished playing. "Doesn't anybody know he's a genius? I have a nose for genius." She turned to her hostess. "Is he your lover?" she asked.

"Why, no, Miss Duncan, he is my guest."

"He must be somebody's lover?" Isadora said, looking around the room. "Well, he is nobody's lover, then I will take him for myself. I always take genius for myself. Genius needs me." She gave Seroff her phone number at the Hôtel Palais d'Orsay. "Walter," she called to Walter Shaw, "give me some paper, Walter always has paper with him, Walter is my secretary, we are writing my Memoirs now." She chatted with Seroff a while longer, promised to meet him at a later time, then left the party, saying, "Come, Walter, we must write Memoirs. We have a taxi waiting. We are very busy, writing Memoirs."[57]

Isadora soon moved from the Palais d'Orsay to a furnished flat in rue des Sablons, and thence to rue Frankoville in the Muette district, her rent paid at each one by a dwindling array of benefactors. From Italy, when he heard of Isadora's distress from friends in Paris, Gordon Craig wrote to Paris Singer, asking if he couldn't help her to solvency. Singer answered that he had already: "Although I did not hear of the trouble in Berlin I did hear when little Margot died in Paris and I immediately telegraphed my Agent to supply our friend with all necessary funds without letting her know the source. . . . I hope that the danger we both anticipated to her is over and done with."[58] It wasn't. Lotte Yorska found Isadora in her Paris flat reading the Song of Solomon. "She looked so perfectly happy that I thought reports must be exaggerated," Yorska recalled.

"Just how much money have you left, Isadora?"

Isadora laughed, and looked in her purse. "Let's count together," she said: "Five francs, thirty centimes."

Yorska began to cry. Why did Isadora refuse to dance in "commercial" theaters? She had been offered fifty thousand francs to appear for two weeks at the Champs-Elysées, where her own image danced with Nijinsky over the entrance.

"Never, never!" Isadora answered. "I've never criticized any artiste who sold her body to save her art, though I don't believe art can be saved that way." She had tried it and knew: "Art is sacred. It is the most sacred thing in the world, after children. . . . When I posed for Bourdelle for the bas-reliefs, I thought that theatre was going to be a Temple."[59] The English writer Richard Wallace saw Isadora in Paris with Walter Rummel's brother Frank, a painter. Wallace described the scene in a letter to Craig:

> Late one Sunday afternoon we were in Frank Rummel's studio . . . and in the very dim light, there appeared from the direction of the door a figure in a grey squirrel coat. A very pale face with huge dark eyes and a very scarlet mouth — Frank jumped up from the divan where he was reclining with three or four ladies and presented her — Miss Isadora Duncan — There was that little awed silence that follows the entry of a newcomer and Miss Duncan settled into an arm chair and asked for brandy instead of tea. She took a huge one saying that she was cold and then in rather a charming voice told how she had had nothing to eat that day — and that while hunting around her kitchen she had discovered a can of sweet corn. Her description of trying to open it with curling tongs and nail scissors and finally making a hole in the lid through which dripped one grain of corn at a time was told in a rather amusing way though in reality it was rather pitiful. . . . She seemed singularly without bitterness and quite free from any pride or shame about it all — and showed a sense of humor too.[60]

"Don't worry dear, something will happen," Isadora told Lotte Yorska. "You've brought me lilies and fruit. I shall dance in front of the lilies, and I shall eat the fruit after deserving it." She confided to Yorska that in Paris she thought constantly about her children: "Do you know that I see them every night? That is why I'm afraid of the night. . . . Read me the Song of Solomon." When Yorska finished, Isadora, too, was weeping: "Set me as a seal upon thine heart, as a seal upon thine arm: for love is strong as death."[61]

At the end of November 1925, Isadora went back to Nice. "Nothing was happening in Paris," she wrote. "My lease up, *et pas de gîte pour ma tête*. . . . What to do? Suicide, or wait, or what?"[62] On December 28, while getting ready for a party, she heard that Esenin had killed himself in Leningrad.

"No, no, no, no!" Isadora cried when James Thurber, writing for the *Chicago Tribune,* reached her on the phone at the Negresco.[63] "She was asked several other questions, including one as to whether she had ever thought Esenin would end his life violently," Thurber reported, "but she held the phone without response. After nearly a minute, she silently hung up the receiver."[64] In the end, alcoholism, insomnia, delirium tremens, and paranoia had proved too much for Esenin: after leaving a psychiatric clinic, at the age of thirty, he hanged himself from a heating pipe at the Hotel d'Angleterre, having first slit his wrist and left a poem in his blood:

> *Goodbye, my friend, goodbye*
> *My love, you are in my heart.*
> *It was preordained we should part*
> *And be reunited by and by.*
> *Goodbye: no handshake to endure.*
> *Let's have no sadness — furrowed brow.*
> *There's nothing new in dying now*
> *Though living is no newer.**

Esenin's death coincided with a tightening of the Soviet grip on Russian writers and artists. A rash of romantic suicides followed in his wake. For two days his body lay in an open coffin, first at the Leningrad Section of the All-Russian Union of Writers and then in Moscow's Press House, where a banner hung outside the building: "The body of the great Russian national poet Sergei Esenin lies here." During the burial at Vagankovskoe cemetery on December 31, "people crowded everywhere — on the trees, on the fences round the graves, and on the high snowdrifts." A woman's voice cried out before the coffin was lowered in the ground, "Good-bye, my fairy tale!"[65] From Nice, Isadora issued a statement to the press:

> The news of the tragic death of Esenin has caused me the deepest pain. He had youth, beauty, genius. Not content with all these gifts, his audacious spirit sought the unattainable, and he wished to lay low the Philistines.
>
> He has destroyed his young and splendid body, but his soul will

*"Goodbye, My Friend," translated by Geoffrey Hurley.

live eternally in the soul of the Russian people and in the souls of those who love the poets. I protest strongly against the frivolous and inaccurate statements printed in the American press of Paris. There was never between Esenin or myself any quarrel or divorce. I weep his death with anguish and despair. ISADORA DUNCAN.[66]

After Isadora left Russia in 1924, Esenin had married again — illicitly, since he and Isadora weren't divorced — this time, Sofia Tolstoy, granddaughter of Russia's greatest writer. Esenin and Sofia were already separated at the time of his death. Various court cases in Russia to decide the disposition of his estate concluded eventually in Isadora's favor, although she brought no claim to it and took no part in the proceedings. Esenin's fortune, greatly amplified by the sale of his poetry after he died, was estimated at around 300,000 francs, which Isadora refused to take for herself.[67]

"I have made one vulgar gesture by marrying," she wired the Soviet authorities. "I would not make another by divorcing. Since according to your laws I am the sole heir to Sergei Esenin's estate, I wish to state my wish that his entire estate be given to his mother and sisters."[68] To Irma, she confessed that she had "wept and sobbed so many hours about [Esenin] that it seems he had already exhausted any human capacity for suffering. Myself, I am having an epoch of such continual calamity that I am often tempted to follow his example, only I will walk into the *Sea*. Now in case I *don't* do that, here is a plan for the future."[69]

29

Seraphita

"There are only two things left," Isadora said, "a drink and a boy."[1] No evidence suggests that despite her insistence on "genius" in her lovers, she meant it as anything but a witticism. To a Paris reporter, she remarked cleverly, "Sometimes I thought my heart was broken, but it was only bent." In July 1926 the headline appeared: "ISADORA FINDS GLUE FOR BROKEN HEART. Dancer Falls in Love With 'Beautiful Italian.'" The story told:

> It was fête day [July 14] in a certain little apartment way over somewhere beyond the Étoile. A woman in a glorious sea-green robe — she's the only woman in Paris who wears frocks to her ankles — was busy hanging up garlands, stringing Chinese lanterns, seeing to it that the spaghetti had been cooked to the last degree of the delicious. In her fine dark eyes was a happy light. And she said that, metaphorically speaking, there were vine leaves in her hair. She sings lines from a jazz hit: "I'm in love again! I'm in love again, and I'm darn glad of it!"
>
> "I'm in love again. Which is all that counts at the moment. The name of my adored? Does it matter? Ah, well, say that it's 'Seraphita' or anything beautiful. He is an Italian, the most beautiful Italian that ever was born: the offspring of Apollo and the sun. . . . There's nothing in life but love."

"Well, aren't there bankruptcy and broken hearts, also, dejected spirits?"

"Look at me. Am I broken-hearted? Do I seem dejected? Am I a forlorn creature pacing the streets, mourning over the ashes of the past? There is no past for any woman, unless she elects to dwell in it." . . .

She turned briskly, though that is too ungraceful a word, to find the tack hammer and to nail up another garland to the child of Apollo and the sun, whose name is S. Franchetti, though really this is unimportant.[2]

More important than the forgotten Franchetti is the name *Seraphita,* which Isadora would give to any young sailor, waiter, shop clerk, or "tempting morsel" that took her fancy in the future, as well as to Victor Seroff, the Russian pianist she had met in Montmartre and who became her next lover of record. In literature, Seraphita is a sexually ambiguous youth, male at first glance but constantly changing gender, and thus the decisive object of desire. Whether Isadora thought of Balzac's *Séraphita* or the original title of Melville's *Billy Budd* makes little difference. Harlem poet Claude McKay, now living on the Riviera, wrote that, apart from Edna St. Vincent Millay, Isadora was "the only other white woman I knew who was so unreservedly esteemed by all kinds of men. . . . [She] was like a great flowing river through which the traffic of the world could pass." In Marseilles, McKay took her for a tour of the old port, with "a slav adventurer" — not Victor Seroff — whom she found especially attractive: "And as we three went wandering through the garbage-strewn alleys, the old girls in the shifts and tights in their holes in the walls were so startled by the picture of Isadora Duncan and her long Grecian scarf floating over the muck and misery of Marseilles, that they forgot their business of snatching hats."[3]

"Her skin possessed a remarkable whiteness quite natural to it," wrote Pierre Loving. "It was soft and well-kept. It brought memories of her glorious past . . . at least to those who remembered that ancient Greek sculpture was painted."[4] Sometime in 1926 Isadora went with Seroff and Walter Shaw to a party at the Russian embassy in Paris, where she seemed to have a lot of friends. "Though at the time [she] did not have enough money to leave the house without police attendance," Seroff wrote, "she was talking in a grand manner of bringing her entire school of dancers from Moscow to Paris." Normally, she went anywhere she was invited, no matter where or for what, "for she felt in a temporary state of mind, and she had not money to buy a sandwich." Indeed, at the Soviet embassy she looked around for one.

"Walter," Isadora cried, "nobody brings us sandwiches! Where are the caviar sandwiches? Walter, we must have sandwiches!"[5] When they left that night, she told Seroff: "Now you're done for; now you're as red as I am; you might as well come and stick by me now." She had become "very shy of her appearance," knowing how easily she was recognized; walking with Seroff, she imitated the indignation of crowds: "That Bolshevik! She's always carrying young men with her! She says he's her secretary! Have you heard of her last scandal? Such a vile woman!"[6] At a dinner in Paris, twenty-five people heard American socialite Manya Barnwell, on seeing Isadora, chastise their host, Count Etienne de Beaumont: "My dear man, if I had known that you would have that red whore here, I would never have set foot in your home."

Isadora looked shocked for "a split second," Seroff remembered. Then she turned to the butler, smiling. "Do you have something sweet in the house?" she asked. "I feel the need of it just now."[7] Painter Sir Francis Rose described the effort of her friends on the Riviera to persuade an unidentified American millionairess to lend Isadora money, "under certain conditions. It was, however, a complete failure." Isadora disappeared when the woman came for tea, turning up the next morning "very scantily dressed, wandering along the jetty of the Villefranche harbor." When she saw her prospective benefactress on the promenade, she tore a strand of "huge pearls" from the woman's neck and tossed it in the water.

"The pearls were recovered by Italian sponge divers in helmeted suits," Rose remembered, "after all the local fishermen had tried in vain to recover them. No scolding could make Isadora repent or apologize; she felt that she had done right. . . . She was above charity, especially with conditions."[8] Rose himself was later the object of Gertrude Stein's dictum: "Rose is a rose is a rose." Stein would collect his paintings with the same fervor she brought to Picasso's and Pavel Tchelitchew's. Jean Cocteau attended Rose's seventeenth-birthday party at the Hôtel Welcome in Villefranche:

> Lady Rose [Rose's mother] had invited only English officers and their wives. Around eight o'clock, a strange procession appeared on the road that leads down to the harbor. Crowned with roses, Francis Rose supported on his arm Madame Isadora Duncan in a Greek tunic. She was very fat, slightly drunk, and escorted by an American girl, a pianist, and some people picked up along the way. The astonishment of Lady Rose's guests, her anger, the entrance of the procession, the fishermen pressing their faces against the windows, Isadora kissing

me, Francis very proud of his crown — that was how the birthday party began. A deathly silence turned the guests to statuary. Isadora laughed, draped herself over Francis. She even stood up and dragged him into the window recess. It was then that Captain Williams, a friend of the family, played his part. . . . He strode across the dining room, approached the window, and shouting in a tremendous voice, "All right, old lady, let go of that child!" he brought his cane down on the dancer's head. She fainted.[9]

Nothing in Victor Seroff's memoirs of Isadora indicates where or when they became lovers. Seroff was the most prickly of her biographers, an essential witness to her final days who loathed her other friends en masse, while claiming privileged status as her closest confidant. No one else seems to have thought of him that way. "He was no great genius at all but a great sponge," according to Max Eastman, "more shrewd and more steely cruel than Esenin."[10] Mary Desti found him "just the antithesis of Sergei in every detail. Small, black eyes and a shock of black curly hair, a decidedly Oriental and Semitic type of countenance, but [with] the merriest little smile in the world . . . gentleness itself."[11] Most remembered "Vitya," when not as a boy toy, then as Isadora's "young accompanist," an impression he was anxious to dispel.

"Isadora realized that our [professional] collaboration could not be harmonious," Seroff wrote tersely. In Paris he kept his own studio in the Bois de Boulogne, shaded "in a private estate surrounded by high walls," where Isadora came to listen to music and avoid her creditors, the dreaded *huissiers*. She called it "the home of Alice in Wonderland. She enjoyed its quiet. She felt secure," telling Seroff that his playing was essential to their "'*solitude à deux*.' . . . She wisely preferred that I remain a musician, a pianist who was always there to discuss music with her, or play it for her enjoyment."[12] Seroff was twenty-five, roughly half her age. "She seemed to find him a bad accompanist, but a good lover," Jenny Bradley concluded. When they dined in public, Isadora refused to let Seroff drink wine.

"You have to be very unhappy to drink," she said. "You haven't suffered yet. So wait."[13] Seroff waited forty-five years before publishing *The Real Isadora*, much of which he cribbed from other memoirs, without attribution. While undoubtedly her intimate, Seroff was not her closest friend. No man could assume that role any longer.

*   *   *

After Esenin's death, Isadora stayed in Nice until Easter 1926. "It's so terrible to think that God has given me the secret of beauty," she told a journalist on the Riviera, "which He gives to so few of us, and yet I've no longer the power to give it to the world. It's all there, inside me; there, there, waiting to come out."[14] Francis Rose described her studio at the far end of the promenade des Anglais, facing the water at Henri Plage, "a kind of large shed or garage, stuccoed a faded pink salmon; the windows were boarded up, and on the peeling blue paint on the small door were a lot of graffiti; in the center a heart, with the signature Jean deeply engraved. This was Cocteau's symbol. . . . The building looked abandoned and unoccupied, as a lot of rubbish was piled around it . . . It was here that Isadora worked and danced."[15]

"Now I have carpet, stove, piano," she told Irma, "thanks to dear *Augustin,* who gradually sent me the funds to get these things and to keep the studio." In New York, Augustin was going blind, although Isadora didn't know yet how serious his condition was. She had become a vegetarian by necessity, "like Raymond, and have gone back to my simple dresses of Grunewald, and *sandals,* and bare feet. The little time I stayed in Paris, I realized that life there was finished with silk stockings at 75 francs a pair."[16] Prices in Paris had more than quadrupled since the war. "If we are to die, better arrange a meeting and die together. At the last extremity come here. You can sleep in the studio, bathe in the sea, and we will always find a meal."[17]

A Good Friday program of sacred music and dance was arranged to pay Isadora's quarterly rent, due on April 15. She described it to Irma as "a great success. A hundred tickets were sold at [a] hundred francs a ticket and great *Stimmung* and enthusiasm. The studio was lovely with alabaster lamps, candles, incense, heaps of white lilies, and lilacs. Quite like the Archangel's times."[18] Had she known that the Duncan school in Moscow would live on, at least in name, until after World War II, Isadora might have understood better when Irma, without alerting her, left for a tour of Siberia and China with the children. Isadora heard nothing more about it until the end of 1926. Calling Irma "a bandit," she drafted a letter of protest to the Soviet government:

> This is the first word I have heard from the school for six months, and the first knowledge I have had that they are in China. I wish to protest that this School which I formed at the sacrifice of my fortune and person, and for which I [am] naturally boycotted by all former friends and audiences in Europe, should be allowed to pass from my

control and into the hands of private speculation. These sacrifices that I made, I made gladly for the cause of the people; but when it comes to the exploitation of my work . . . without so much as asking my advice — I must protest! . . . Comrade Lunacharsky wrote of my school: "Isadora Duncan wanted to give a natural and beautiful education to every child. The Bourgeois society, however, did not understand this and put her pupils on the stage to exploit them for money. We will know how to act differently."

I ask *when?*[19]

By June 1926 Isadora was in Paris at the Hôtel Lutétia on boulevard Raspail, on the Left Bank near the park at Sèvres-Babylone. All the money she had earned from her Easter concert went to pay for the pianist, the florist, the rent, and a Mathis touring car, which she hired and drove north in order to meet Christian Rakovsky, the Soviet envoy to France. Rakovsky was "very enthusiastic" about bringing the Moscow school to Paris, Isadora reported, "but always the same cry: 'No Money.'"[20] Journalist Joseph Kaye observed: "This was the last interview Isadora had with the comrades on the Paris school idea. The glamorous dream of a great proletarian dancing institute which would serve as a model for the entire world sagged like a punctured gas bag, wrinkled and collapsed."[21] Kaye placed Victor Seroff's transition from friend to lover exactly here. Seroff was too discreet, or too Russian, to confirm or deny it.

"Look at me," Isadora cried, "I haven't even enough money to get my hair washed. I am a sight, like an old witch. You people do nothing for me!"[22] Occasionally Charles Rappoport, on behalf of the Socialist International, took a bill from his wallet and gave it to Isadora, "who would weep, touched at his kindness, and refuse the money. He would try to persuade her to accept it, and only once she did reluctantly consent to do so." To lift her spirits, she played tango music on her gramophone, dancing around her room at the Lutétia with Seroff's umbrella as a partner: "Then, throwing away her properties, she would say, 'Look, that's all I can do here! I have no piano. Think of it, I have no piano! It is just as if *you* had no piano. That's all I can do here. Ugh! If I see these pink walls much longer I will go out of my head!'"[23] James Joyce told Robert McAlmon that his daughter, Lucia, would study dance with Elizabeth Duncan in Germany, "as the more famous sister, Isadora, was not holding classes now."

"She's not even holding her liquor," McAlmon quipped, where-

upon Nora Joyce broke in: "Ah, the poor soul . . ."[24] Pierre Loving
wrote: "People in general had fallen into the habit of saying, 'Poor
Isadora!' . . . Small wonder that she presently tried to surround herself with youth and brightness. She loathed the idea of getting old, of
decay, of the slow dying of a penniless ex-dancer, once famous all over
the world."[25] In 1926 Josephine Baker appeared at the Paris Revue
Nègre in her *Danse du Sauvage,* "doing dances that she never would
have dared to do even in Harlem, and in such a state of chocolate nudity!" as Macdougall exclaimed.[26] Macdougall would become the particular object of Seroff's contempt, owing to his "lapses into what
Isadora preferred to call 'Lesbian' rather than feminine ways . . . gossip, lies, and — especially futile and trivial in themselves — treach-
eries. In her latter days, after spending an evening with her so-called
friends . . . Isadora would simply shake her head as if trying to get rid
of everything she had heard."[27] Seroff wrote:

> They were almost invariably homosexual, both the men and the
> women. . . . Not being an expert in psychiatry, I would not assert as
> axiomatic that lying, intrigue, and treachery are necessarily character-
> istic of that third sex, but at the time when Isadora was most in need
> of firm ground under her feet, her friends did seem to be singularly af-
> flicted with such habits. . . . And yet I could understand her tolerating
> this band of ne'er-do-wells. . . . For Isadora truly needed a counterbal-
> ance to my sober and pessimistic appraisal of her position.[28]

In fact, Seroff had a rival, Isadora's new "archangel," Mercedes de
Acosta. Since they last met on Long Island in 1917, Isadora and Mer-
cedes had seen each other only briefly, during the Paris run of Mercedes's play, *Jehanne d'Arc.* Involved at the time with Eva Le Gallienne,
her Joan of Arc, Mercedes arrived in France the following year with
Alla Nazimova, then at the tail end of her silent-film career. Nazimova
and Isadora knew each other already from the Hotel des Artistes in
New York; Isadora's acquaintance with other American lesbians in
Paris had occurred as a matter of course: Natalie Barney and Romaine
Brooks, Djuna Barnes, Janet Flanner and Solita Solano, Sylvia Beach,
and Gertrude Stein. In 1926 Flanner, *The New Yorker's* correspondent
in Paris, was working on Isadora's profile for the magazine.

"On the Continent she is more widely known today than any
other American of our decade," Flanner wrote, "including Woodrow
Wilson and excepting only Chaplin and Fairbanks, both of whom, via

a strip of celluloid, can penetrate to remote hamlets without ever leaving Hollywood. But Isadora has gone everywhere in the flesh."[29] Flanner's lover, Solita Solano, described Isadora's habit of inviting "people, any people, for drinks at cafés, then someone solid, a non-drinker, would have to be found who would be good for the final bill; J[anet] was caught once, but not twice. One night she held us both by force at the Lutétia, but she soon fell asleep and when she began to snore, we carried our shoes out of the door and fled down the stairs and out into the rainy midnight."[30] Of all America's expatriate "odd girls," so far as is known, only Mercedes took the prize.

"Say what you want about Mercedes," Alice B. Toklas declared, "she's had the three greatest women of the 20th century."[31] Two of these were Greta Garbo and Marlene Dietrich — the third Toklas left to the world's imagination. Dietrich's daughter, Maria Riva, remembered Mercedes as "a Spanish Dracula with the body of a young boy, jet-black hair cut like a toreador's close to the head, chalk-white face, deep-set black eyes permanently shadowed." Tallulah Bankhead compared her to "a mouse in a topcoat."[32] Born to wealth, the daughter of Cuban aristocrats and sister of fabled society beauty Rita de Acosta Lydig, Mercedes was married to the artist Abram Poole, a technicality that in no way inhibited her pursuit of women. Strictly speaking, she was bisexual — as she put it herself, one of "the half-toned people."

"To the outward form of sex which the body has assumed, I have remained indifferent," Mercedes wrote. "I cannot understand these so-called 'normal' people who believe that a man should love only a woman, and a woman love only a man. If this were so, then it disregards completely the spirit, the personality, and the mind, and stresses all the importance of love to the physical body."[33] Flanner, a former lover, left a tribute to Mercedes, handwritten in the shape of a flower and leaves: "Her shoulders were slight miracles of tailoring and God: her waist was thinned like a finger long embraced by a ring. . . . She had a small white body, like a small marble park, in which her eyes lived as brown nightingales. Her shoes were those of ladies who used to be heeded."[34]

In the middle of June 1926, Mercedes de Acosta landed in Paris and "ran into a man who said, 'I know you are a friend of Isadora Duncan's. I hear she has behaved so badly that everyone has abandoned her. I am told that she is in a hotel on the Left Bank, practically starving.'" Mercedes's autobiography, Here Lies the Heart — "and lies and lies," a critic growled — is a classic of allusion and innuendo:

"Room sixty-seven," the porter said. "Shall I announce you?" But I was already halfway up the stairs. I knocked timidly and hearing *"Entrez!"* I opened the door. Facing me and sitting up in bed was Isadora. A small lamp was lighted on the table beside her, but a scarf (the eternal scarf) was thrown over it, and the room was in semi-darkness. "Archangel!!" exclaimed Isadora.

(I was dressed in a white cape without a hat and she afterwards told me she had been lying there praying for help at that moment. As I stood in the doorway the light from the ceiling in the hallway fell on my head in rays, and for a moment she really thought I was a celestial being.)

"I thought you were an archangel from another world come to help me in answer to my prayers," she said. "I think you are an archangel. I shall always call you that from now on. How did you find me?"

Mercedes learned that Isadora already owed a large bill at the Lutétia, and that the management had refused to extend her any further credit. "I asked her why her friends hadn't helped her," Mercedes recalled.

"I have spent their money and not repaid them," said Isadora blankly.

"Did they ever think you would repay them?"

"That's just it. I spent their money which is just what they should have expected me to do. What else is money for but spending?" Mercedes laughed. "Please don't scold me," said Isadora. "I am hungry." After a dinner of strawberries, roast chicken, and wine, she called for her Mathis from the Lutétia garage. "The sun had just risen," Mercedes wrote.

"Au soleil!" cried Isadora. *"Allons au soleil!"* They drove to the racetrack at Longchamps, ate breakfast at Le Coq-Hardi, then went to the Guaranty Trust Company, where Mercedes withdrew enough money to settle Isadora's Lutétia account and leave her something for the future. Isadora seemed "very pleased."

"All that first day she begged me not to leave her," Mercedes wrote. "She came back to my hotel and I talked to her about her life, and said that she absolutely must stop squandering it and pull herself together and begin to dance again." There was the lingering question of her memoirs. "I am not a writer, and I would not have the energy to write," Isadora insisted. As to dancing, those days were done:

"Nonsense," I said. "You will be helped to do both."

"Who will help but you, my Archangel?"

"You will be given Divine Energy, if you will only call upon it," I said.

She took my hands and said, "Your hands are so strong. You are strong. Do you know that you are giving me new life? . . . Deep down in the inmost part of my soul, I believe every word you say. . . ."[35]

It can't be determined how far Isadora's friendship with Mercedes had advanced before Mercedes left Europe later in 1926. On a photograph dated June 28, just after they met, Isadora inscribed the words: "Mercedes, Lead me with your little strong hands & I will follow you — / To the top of a Mountain / To the end of the world / Wherever you wish — Isadora."[36] But only fragments of her letters to Mercedes survive in her hand, and only one bears an identifying salutation.

"Dear," reads a card, "Will you ride with me in the Bois from 3–4 —? At 4 I go to Lawyer — but then am free." A scribble follows: "All night the crystal clearness of your eyes . . ." That the notes are written to a woman is plain, and that the woman is called "Archangel" identifies Isadora's correspondent: "Angel — I await your coming as the soul in Hell the *Last day* of Ten Thousand years of Tortures — In your absence of five centuries I have been feeding from the hand of that Super Demon *misnamed* Seraphita, a diet of Live Coals and *Vitriol*." Seroff's hostility to "homosexuals" and "ne'er-do-wells" in Isadora's entourage needs no other explanation. A poem was found among Mercedes's papers:

Arch Angel
from Another Sphere
God sent to
light my pathway
here.
I kneel in Adoration
dear.

My kisses like a swarm of Bees
Would find Their way
between thy knees
& suck the honey
of thy lips
Embracing thy
Two slender hips.

— Isadora to Mercedes, 1927

Another note from Isadora sits calmly in the de Acosta archive, addressed to *"Adorée"* and torn at the top:

> I have played with your flames and been horribly burned. I thought I knew already every mortal suffering, but now I see the worst was still in store for me — I suffer *fearfully* — but I accept it because the source is so *beautiful*. . . . But how to live with this passion in my veins . . . I beg you not to make fun of me. I may die from it. I'm horrified to realize that only now have I known love for *the first time*. Don't laugh . . . a little word . . . if there is any pity in your heart for me. Respect my secret — I am tortured and ready to cry Mercy. Isadora.[37]

After Mercedes left Paris, Ruth Mitchell materialized to carry the pieces of Isadora's life. "Aunty Ruthy" was the only one of her friends whom Seroff credited with "utter selflessness,"[38] as did everyone on the scene, except Isadora. She told Joe Milward, "The only people who try to help me are those who get something out of it for themselves" — in Mitchell's case, "the privilege to visit her wherever she happened to be," Milward wrote, and thus exchange her "drab life . . . for a part in the excitement and glamour which surrounded her. . . . It was evident that Isadora felt that Miss Mitchell's expenditure [was] modest payment for the values she continued to receive."[39]

Finding both the Lutétia and Isadora's rented car a waste of money, Mitchell bought a used Renault and drove her back to Nice, after long detours to restaurants, vineyards, and country inns that cost more than a month in Paris would have. On the Riviera, at Juan-les-Pins, she insisted on stopping, swimming, and sunbathing for several days, at Mitchell's expense: "The sea acted on Isadora as an elixir. She became quite another person, so gentle, tender. . . . She began seriously to want to dance."[40] In Nice she took a small apartment, again with Mitchell's money, where Francis Rose came to sketch her and gossip about their friends. "I was a precious, spoilt youth," Rose confessed: "She was a goddess of madness — of mad freedom — and of liberty without a torch."[41] He wrote:

> She lived next door to her studio in a tall 1900 apartment building that was so thin and high that it seemed to be only a façade of shutters and balconies for a film set. Her flat was on the first floor, furnished with fake Louis XV furniture from the Galeries Lafayette, aspidistras in pots from oriental bazaars, and dyed bullrushes in fake Sèvres vases. There were crochet-work antimacassars, curtains, and

tablecloths in all the rooms. The walls of her untidy bedroom were covered with photographs of her innumerable lovers: famous writers, negro boxers, millionaires, sailors in uniform, and a few royal princes. Her bed was festooned with grubby mosquito-nets, and the old-fashioned bath-tub in her dressing-room was filled with oddments which had to be moved constantly by the "pigeons." . . . They were men of a type who can look after a beautiful, aging woman, and they fought hard to prevent her from drinking anything she could lay her hands on. I remember her mixing a cocktail . . . out of eau-de-Cologne, Pernod, brandy, and the dregs from nearly empty wine bottles, which she had kept hidden in her bidet.[42]

In the shuffle of many memoirs, Isadora's "pigeons" become interchangeable — any gay men in her company bore the label, "a chorus of male magpies paced by the resonant bells of Isadora's voice."[43] By now, Walter Shaw was involved with French actor Marcel Herrand, who participated with Isadora and Cocteau in a recital at her studio on September 14, 1926. "Marcel Herrand was a pretty, doll-like boy, who dreamed of becoming an actor," Seroff wrote snidely, "but whom meanwhile I sometimes found sobbing in Isadora's arms about the infidelities of Walter Shaw. Except for malicious gossip about Isadora, which they exchanged with their Lesbian colleagues, they were harmless and caused Isadora no particular anxiety."[44] In fact, Herrand did become one of France's foremost actors — nothing Seroff says about him, Shaw, or any of Isadora's friends can escape his paranoia.

Isadora's concert with Cocteau was one of two she gave in Nice that fall (the other being a Liszt program on September 10): "For the program cover Cocteau made a neoclassic drawing called 'Mysteria-Nice'; the studio was decked with flowers; Isadora danced by candlelight . . . while Cocteau read from *Orphée* and from his latest poems" with Herrand.[45] Sometime during the concert, inevitably, Isadora "bared her breasts." Glenway Wescott praised her dancing, and she answered, "Well, I don't know, can't tell. . . . When I was a lovely young woman I danced like a lovely young woman; when I was a mother, I danced like a mother, and now I dance I suppose like heaven knows what."[46] British journalist and playwright Sewell Stokes, "hanging about Isadora" in Nice with painter Gabriel Atkin, met her first at her apartment with the pigeons and Raymond, who had arrived on some errand.

"Raymond — and four beautiful young men," said Isadora as she came in the room; "all looking like a frieze by Titian." Ruth Mitchell was with her: they had just come back from a drive.

"She had not been inside the flat for two minutes before the atmosphere was charged with an indescribable mysticism," Stokes wrote. "From the moment of her entrance, the room became as much a part of her as her own body, and all of us were moving round her like planets round the sun." Isadora held out her hands to the newcomers and asked them to stay to dinner. "There's nothing in the house to eat," she admitted, "and I'm too poor to buy anything, so we'll have to go round to the restaurant next door for a meal. And Ruthie will pay the bill. . . . We'll have a *wonderful* dinner. . . . *Such* a dinner."

"We'll have a little cold meat, and some potatoes — for the *others*," Mitchell interjected. Isadora had been trying to lose weight for her concerts.

"Poor Ruthie," she told Stokes, "it's really a shame. She's so good to me, and I behave so badly. . . . But I love potatoes — and young men. That's my trouble!" At dinner she found the light too bright and covered the table lamp with a straw hat she wore. "She looked in the crude light like the kind of figure Aubrey Beardsley might have designed to scare away birds from his window-box," Stokes wrote. "Soon after this there was a crackling sound, and the unpleasant smell of burning straw."

"There goes my poor hat," Isadora sighed. "It cost fifteen francs and I've only got one other. Never mind, in *[L'] Eclaireur [de Nice]* this morning my name was mentioned among the bathers on Juan-les-Pins beach. 'Isadora Duncan' — it was printed quite clearly. So I'm famous at last."[47] In November she grew restless and drove back to Paris with Mitchell, Shaw, and Herrand. Mitchell returned to New York and left Isadora the Renault. "The fact that I seemed unable to get her one step forward during three years of effort, was a greater disappointment than anyone can know," she wrote to Mary Desti in 1927. "She had had a dread these past years of dying alone and unloved."[48] Stokes describes Isadora as she left for Paris in her squirrel coat, "badly split down the back. . . . She looked really sorry for herself. . . . And from that time, until my last glimpse of her . . . I never saw that expression leave her dear face."[49]

In Paris new trouble loomed in the shape of Isadora's overmortgaged property in Neuilly. She had thought of selling the house the year before, offering Lotte Yorska 20 percent of the deal if she could find a buyer. Nothing came of it. Now a Paris court ordered that the house be sold at public auction to settle Isadora's debts. A loan of 300 francs in 1922 had mushroomed to more than 10,000 four years later; the Neuilly studio was already mortgaged at 150,000 francs and would bring double that at open sale.[50]

"The Paris newspapers came out with long columns describing Isadora's plight," Seroff wrote, "and to everyone's surprise painters and sculptors donated their works to be sold for Isadora's benefit, actors and actresses, music hall performers, and scores of art students generously contributed according to their means."[51] Bourdelle offered Isadora the cast of a sculpted bacchante, at the same time advising her not to sell it for less than 30,000 francs. A committee formed,[52] with Yorska as treasurer and three writers at the helm, Cécile Sartoris, André Arnyvelde, and Alfredo Sides, a friend of Mercedes's, who once shocked a rally of New York suffragists by offering to carry a banner that read: *"I am for killing all men and letting women run the world."*

"Needless to say," Mercedes wrote, "the average male did not like Alfredo. . . . He took it as a compliment."[53] Seroff's report was in character: "He was favored by homosexuals of both sexes. . . . The committee provided an excellent excuse for constant meetings, at which the female members and the 'boys' exchanged the latest gossip about their respective clans in preference to discussing the practical aspects of their project."[54] From the Lutétia — a hotel she now called the "Lusitania" — Isadora complained: "My old friends are getting a lot of publicity saving my house but they are letting me starve here." Yorska answered that it might be "deceiving the public" for her to bargain over Neuilly when she had no intention of living or working there again: "She said she would never set her feet in [the] Neuilly house on account of tragic memories."[55] Isadora was only annoyed.

"Why is everybody so *practical?*" she asked Sewell Stokes: "The men and women I meet think life is just Monday, Tuesday, Wednesday, Thursday, Friday, Saturday, Sunday — and then the funeral! That's all they think. I can't understand it."[56] When she tried to raise money by herself, things invariably went awry. American heiress Peggy Guggenheim, just married to painter Lawrence Vail, saw Isadora at the Lutétia "in great straits, but, nevertheless, she gave us champagne. I'm sure she hoped I would help her out of her difficulties, but I am afraid I didn't." Isadora called her "Guggie Peggleheim" and advised her not to let marriage get the better of her: "Never use the word *wife!*"[57] Before leaving Paris again, she remembered that Joe Milward still held her French power of attorney. She arranged to go to a lawyer to have it revoked, but when Milward turned up to collect her, she suggested a cocktail party instead: "It's being given for Marie Dressler. It'll be fun. . . . Let's forget about that old power of attorney." Milward held it till he died but never exercised his rights.[58]

By December, Yorska's committee had raised enough money to forestall the Neuilly sale. Isadora returned to the Riviera with Seroff. "I begged [her] to give up Nice and to come and live with me," Yorska wrote, "so she could concentrate on her memoirs without having to think about money. She said she would come if I would allow Vitya to come and stay also. This I could not accept."[59] After a few false starts, they ended up again at the Negresco. "It's no use people trying to make me economize," said Isadora. "You can't make an elephant ride a bicycle."[60] On December 11 she sent a note to Dolly Votichenko: "For Heaven's sake come around or telephone and let's go to the Cinema. Otherwise I am likely to jump into the *Sea* & it will be the only thing like Sappho that I ever did for you know I never wrote poetry — for one." If she was thinking about Mercedes, she gave no other clue of it: "Don't you want to go to the Cinema? O — dear what a World."[61]

A month later Isadora made headlines again when she did, indeed, walk into the sea in an apparent suicide attempt. She had been dining with Seroff and their guests, among them Alice Spicer, an American friend of Seroff's, whom he hadn't seen in several years. Spicer had too much to drink at dinner and withdrew to the bedroom to lie down. Seroff followed her.

"He locked himself in the bedroom . . . and refused to answer Isadora's knocking," Max Eastman wrote. "She pounded the door and cried out that she would die by her own hand if he did not let her in. And she did go and put on the long purple cloak in which she was accustomed to dance the *Marche Funèbre* of Chopin, and walk solemnly out into the night . . . straight on into the blue Mediterranean up to her neck."[62] Reading an account of the incident in the *Italian Mail*, Gordon Craig remarked skeptically: "Knees perhaps."[63] Seroff called it "an utterly insignificant incident. . . . Her actions were motivated by her general depression, and the details of the incident were inaccurately reported."[64] Since it embarrassed him badly, Seroff's gruffness can be appreciated. Isadora told Stokes:

> What really happened was this. I was sitting quite alone, feeling very miserable, when suddenly I knew that I didn't want to go on sitting there any more. I said to myself that I just didn't want to go on living any more; that nobody wanted me to. Only it seemed as if

somebody else, and not myself, was telling me that. Really a most curious feeling. And when I got up and went out to walk into the sea, I
was quite sure that somebody was leading me very gently by the arm.
I distinctly remember thinking how wonderful it was going to be, not
to have any more worry, and also that none of the responsibility of
ending my life would be mine, because somebody else, the somebody
who had hold of my arm, was responsible.[65]

In Paris, the news of Isadora's distress horrified the Neuilly committee. She sent Seroff north "to give them a true account of her condition"[66] — in another report, Seroff quit Nice on his own and left
Isadora "inconsolable." Stokes was with her when a reporter at the
Negresco toasted the new year, 1927: "To your health, Miss Duncan!"

"My health is all right," Isadora snapped back. "It's money that I
want."[67] Once and for all, it seemed that her memoirs were the only
solution. Isadora told Stokes that what she had written so far made
her want to weep: "I did the other night. . . . Full of cliches, not literature at all. . . . I don't want to write them . . . unless I can have heaps
of time, and write them properly, all myself."

"And you don't want the scandals mentioned?" said Stokes.

"Of course I do, but properly mentioned. . . . Nothing about my
life is private any longer. I belong to the public so much that whatever
I said would be better for them to hear than what they've already
heard."[68] She gestured toward the mountains above Nice: "To think
that those are the same hills that inspired Nietzsche." Isadora had already told Stokes, "If I had been a man I might have done for dancing
what Wagner did for music."[69] Two days after Seroff left for Paris, Will
Bradley arrived with a contract for her book.

If more confusion about the authorship of *My Life* were possible,
Victor Seroff provided it by accusing Mercedes de Acosta of doctoring
the text. In her own memoir, *Here Lies the Heart,* Mercedes describes
how Isadora "struggled and suffered" over the first chapters, which
she drafted herself in Nice and at the Lutétia. "Many days I locked her
in her room and only let her out when she slid a number of finished
pages under the door," Mercedes wrote.[70] Seroff had "never read a
sillier lie." But it was "unfortunate indeed that she did eventually get
hold of Isadora's manuscript, for her free editing of it supplied Isadora's
life story with de Acosta's own interpretation, especially obvious in
her characterization of the men who were close to Isadora."[71] Gordon

Craig took the same way out when he read Isadora's autobiography in 1928.

"You are quite wrong about it because she did write it and every word of it," Mercedes later protested to Craig. Craig noted on her letter: "Really." Mercedes went on: "I was with her myself when she wrote many chapters before my eyes" — Craig's note: *"Really!"* — "and she read me month to month what she had written until it was finished."[72] Mercedes's typed copy of the book's first chapters bears a note in her hand: "These chapters were given to me by Isadora as she wrote them — These chapters I took to publishers in an effort to get an advance for Isadora." Mercedes brought the manuscript to Boni & Liveright, where her friend T. R. ("Tommy") Smith was editor in chief.

In the meantime, Isadora also gave her chapters to Bradley, who at the end of 1926 clinched the deal with Liveright. Isadora's contract promised her a total of $1,500, to be paid through Bradley in monthly installments, until a manuscript "of not less than 70,000 words" was completed. Bigger money would no doubt come from serialization. "Isadora Duncan will not mind my saying, I am sure, that her temperamental reputation is rather well known," Smith concluded. "Please impress upon her the serious responsibility, if she makes the contract, of carrying it out as quickly as possible."[73] Bradley brought the papers for Isadora's signature to Nice in January 1927.

"It's not very good, is it?" she asked Macdougall when she showed him the contract. "But it's signed. And now I must go on and finish it. . . . But how can I write? You must help me."[74] She asked the same of Glenway Wescott, whose first novel, *The Grandmothers,* had just been published to wide acclaim. Isadora considered Wescott "a very great writer," according to their friend Bernardine Szold: "Not just a writer but a man of letters, a great man of letters. She was working on her memoirs and she asked him to correct them and he said 'Darling Isadora, it would be blasphemy for any mortal to change one word of your book.'"[75] She would need to dictate the rest of the story if she hoped to write it at all. Pierre Loving described her method of composition:

> Realizing that it was going to be uphill work for her, [Bradley] proposed a regular monthly stipend, which was thought sufficient to cover her own personal expenses and a secretary's salary. . . . Her secretaries — there was quite a procession of them — had to be patient and flexible, willing to drink with her, willing to begin at midnight and work till

dawn, if necessary. Isadora rarely got into a talkative frame of mind before evening, and alcohol played its part in untangling the knots in her
memory and making the story flow smoothly. She was often irritable
and temperamental with her secretaries, but most of them didn't mind:
They all felt that they were humble instruments in her service, and the
one thing that mattered, after all, was the book.[76]

Isadora's first secretary in Nice was Ruth Nickson, an Englishwoman, whose company she found "worse than having a governess.
She keeps interrupting . . . 'Miss Duncan, you don't mean to say
this . . . you simply cannot.' Can you imagine it? What am I to do?"[77]
She wanted her book to be "like Whitman's *Leaves of Grass,* only
franker. A book that will be explosive and awaken the whole world."
Macdougall confessed later that he had helped her "editorially" but
insisted that Isadora wrote *My Life* — or spoke it — by herself: "Undoubtedly Mr. Bradley . . . had a hand in the further revision of the
manuscript before it was delivered to the publisher. In the Liveright
office the book was cut and edited; not everything Isadora, aided by
her numerous collaborators, had written was kept in. The book was
made safe, in other words, for American audiences."[78] According to
Seroff, Mary Desti helped Isadora with the passages about Paris
Singer. There is no reason to suspect Mercedes's influence on the finished product more than any other.

Early in February 1927 the management of the Negresco presented Isadora with a bill for nine thousand francs. "There was also a
printed note from the office saying that if [it] were not paid that night,
Madame Duncan would have to vacate her room," Macdougall wrote:

> Isadora was furious with indignation. . . . Miss Nickson was dis-
> patched to see if it were possible to talk the manager out of the
> idea. . . . In a few minutes he was in the room, bowing deferentially to
> Isadora reclining on the bed. Looking up sweetly at him she said: "I do
> not understand why you bother me with this absurd matter of a bill for
> a paltry nine thousand francs. After all you know who I am. You know
> that I have been one of your most famous and regular clients. There
> have been nights when I spent in your halls double and triple the sum
> of this bill. I have no money at the moment. . . . My money is all in
> Paris, tied up in this fight about the house. If I am to get it, I must go
> there. I am planning to go there tomorrow. . . . If you feel you must
> have security for this absurd bill, I will leave you my Renault car
> which is at present in the garage."[79]

Thus Isadora got rid of Miss Nickson; the Negresco even bought her a first-class ticket to Paris, while keeping her car and all her trunks. "I received a telegram asking me to meet her at the station," Seroff remembered. "There were many trains from Nice, but I inquired which was the most expensive, and I calmly waited for her to get off the train *de luxe*. She stepped down and asked me to give the porter ten francs, as he had paid for her dinner."[80] *My Life* would be finished in September.

30

The Ride to Glory

In Paris, Isadora refused to go back to the Lutétia, whose manager had offended her during her last stay by mentioning how much money she cost the establishment. Bradley recommended the new Studio-Apartment Hôtel in Montparnasse, across from the Dingo Bar at 9, rue Delambre. The modernist complex, just completed, contained forty split-level suites, each with a studio and bath and, upstairs, a bedroom and balcony, "rather luxuriously appointed. Its simplicity and spaciousness provided just the right atmosphere for Isadora."[1] On Bradley's allowance, she lived in suite 29.

From February to August 1927, Isadora worked on *My Life,* sticking to "the dictation method," according to Macdougall, apart from the opening chapters already written: "In silence and tears she also wrote out the parts telling of the tragic deaths of Patrick and Deirdre."[2] When asked how the book was coming, she liked to reply, "Well, I've written twenty-thousand words, and I'm still a virgin." Soon, it became 50,000 and a problem for Boni & Liveright. Seroff remembered a telegram from New York: ENOUGH OF YOUR HIGHFALUTIN IDEAS SEND LOVE CHAPTERS MAKE IT SPICY.[3] "All the publisher wants is my love affairs," Isadora complained to Minna Besser, one of her Paris stenographers: "'More about your love affairs,' they cable." She was pleased to meet anyone young: "She smiled and said, 'You should see the women Bradley has sent. Do you think I could work with such faces around me?'"[4]

At the Bradley apartment on Ile Saint-Louis, when Isadora came to fret about her manuscript, Jenny Bradley served "American cocktails" from recipes provided by Harry's New York Bar: "If cocktails were needed to keep Isadora's confidence and flow unshaken then cocktails would be served."[5] She began each day by looking through her address book, Seroff wrote: "And almost every day she would introduce me to some man or woman saying: 'This is my most faithful friend. What would I ever do without him! Now, he is going to help me. We all must keep on the job.'"[6] Despite her protests, she enjoyed making her manuscript "spicy," telling Seroff that what it needed were "pornographic pictures" and lessons in love-making to shock "all those females," who told her, "Oh, Miss Duncan, your memoirs must be thrilling! We're so anxious to read them!"[7]

Janet Flanner's profile of Isadora appeared in *The New Yorker* on January 1, 1927, a year of triumph for Americans in Europe. Not yet using her pen name, Genêt, Flanner signed her piece "Hippolyta," after the Amazon queen, and painted Isadora in the same, mythic hue: "She is the last of the trilogy of great female personalities our century produced. Two of them, Duse and Bernhardt, have gone to their elaborate national tombs. Only Isadora Duncan, the youngest, the American, remains wandering the European earth."[8] Almost simultaneously, in February Lotte Yorska appealed in *Comoedia* for money to buy back the Neuilly house, announcing that Isadora's "Temple of Art" would be endowed as a school and permanent memorial and that her cause was "the cause of France."[9] Isadora began to worry that her friends all wrote about her as if she were dead. "Oh the hell with them anyway!" she cried to Seroff. "People say I drink, but how can one face them without it?"[10] Flanner continued:

> No one has replaced Isadora in her own country and she is not missed. Of that fervor for the classic dance which she was the first to bring to a land bred on "Turkey in the Straw," beneficial signs remain from which she alone has not benefited. Eurhythmic movements now appear in curricula of girls' schools. Vestal virgins frieze about the altar of fire at St. Mark's-in-the-Bouwerie on Sabbath afternoons. As a cross between gymnasia and God, Greek dance camps flourish in the Catskills, where under the summer spruce, metaphysics and muscles are welded in an Ilissan hocus-pocus for the female young. . . . Only

Isadora, animator of all these forces, has become obscure. Only she with her heroic sculptural movements has dropped by the wayside, where she lies inert like one of those beautiful battered pagan tombs that still line the Sacred Road between Eleusis and the city of the Parthenon.[11]

Isadora read Flanner's profile in time to complain about it in *My Life*: "How one's motives are misinterpreted!"[12] She resented her agent's "insufficient advances," writing to Mercedes on February 25 that they came "too late to pay for the barest necessities of each day."[13] So far, Bradley had given her only $600 of her $1,500 advance. It wasn't enough for "peace of mind," Isadora said — she would need at least a thousand for that, "at once."

"In order to give an adequate idea of my life I see that the entire book will take at least three hundred thousand words," she wrote to Boni & Liveright in a letter that must have caused some panic in the editorial office, "and would suggest having it published in two volumes. First: Memoirs of Youth. Second: Maturity. Kindly pardon me as I again repeat that the quality of my writing depends entirely on whether I have capital to write the book in peace of mind."[14] Whatever answer she received is lost to history and the Liveright archives — probably Bradley talked her down from the ledge. But the lopsided narrative of *My Life* confirms that, as time ran out, Isadora began to hurry. "With a kind of Yankee astuteness," she refused to write about Esenin and her years in Russia, telling Bradley that the book would be banned in the United States if she did. As it was, she feared her manuscript would be seized by U.S. Customs as "immoral."[15] Max Eastman, returning to New York on his first visit home since 1922, saw Isadora at Gare Saint-Lazare as his train left the station:

> Much had happened both to me and the world in those five years, and the moment of leaving Paris was one of high emotion. I was standing at the car window, laughing and yet inwardly sobbing at the sadly funny excitement of seeing people part from their friends, the old inexorable mystery of transition, when suddenly I heard Isadora Duncan's rich voice making music of my short name: "Max, Max — good-by, good-by!" She raised her hand when I caught sight of her, and stood still with it in the air, moving slowly in a serene and strong benediction. A great beam of that energetic and celestial, and yet also mischievously Irish, light she had in her eyes shone to me. She looked very great. She looked like a statue of real liberty.[16]

On May 21 Isadora joined a crowd of 100,000 people at Le Bourget airfield to greet the arrival of Charles A. Lindbergh in *The Spirit of St. Louis,* which Lindbergh had piloted from New York to Paris in 33 hours and 30 minutes on the first nonstop solo flight across the Atlantic. "Isadora looked wan but she was as excited as all the rest of us," wrote *Chicago Tribune* correspondent William L. Shirer: "There was an unholy jam of people in the little terminal but we managed to edge toward the bar, where Isadora, as usual, ordered a glass of champagne." When Lindbergh landed, she joined the general pandemonium and "tossed her felt hat into the air. . . . [She] was suddenly overcome by patriotism."[17] Her conflicted feelings about the United States were never resolved: that year she also took up the cause of Sacco and Vanzetti, Italian anarchists convicted of murdering a paymaster and guard at a shoe factory outside Boston. Shirer began to think of her "in a new way that spring. To me, she had become something of a saint."[18]

"The Sacco-Vanzetti case is a blot on American justice," Isadora told an Illinois superior court judge visiting Paris in August 1927. "It will bring down a lasting curse on the United States, a curse deserved by American hypocrisy."[19] She had just returned from a demonstration at the American embassy, where a Paris gendarme, recognizing her, said indulgently, "Isadora, go home. This is no place for artists." Minna Besser recalled how she looked on the night of Sacco and Vanzetti's scheduled execution in Massachusetts — "statuesque, in dramatic supplication; arms wide spread, head held upward . . . in a crimson robe draped from neck to floor. Two tall candles glowed on the fireplace mantel, the only strong lights in a room made somber by dark scarves covering lamps."[20]

Mary Desti returned to Paris and Isadora in May 1927, nearly four years after they had last seen each other in Berlin. In the quest for money, Lotte Yorska had made a list of potential donors from among Isadora's friends: "We thought of all the people I could send cables to. . . . I said, 'What about Mary Desti?' and she answered, 'I don't have to cable to Mary for whenever she has money she sends some to me. She is the only real woman friend I've ever had.'"[21]

The trouble was that Mary had no more money. Sometime during World War I, she had lost track of her Turkish husband, Vely Bey, and concluded, without knowing it, that he must be dead. "The thought having tiptoed into her mind," wrote her son, Preston Sturges, "she was nearly persuaded of the matter a few days later and absolutely certain of it by the end of the month, at which time, bearing up courageously under her widowhood, she married a young Englishman called Howard Perch, also known as Punch." It was Mary's last stab at matrimony; by 1927 Perch hád gone the way of the others: "Inevitably, one day while walking down the Champs-Élysées on the arm of her new husband, my mother saw her old one walking up. . . . It all ended pleasantly, of course, since my mother, motivated only by the highest sentiments, never loused people's lives up on purpose."[22]

After Isadora left Berlin with Esenin in 1923, Mary went back to New York, where, in time, she wrecked the Maison Desti, along with Preston's immediate finances. In the spring of 1927 Solomon Sturges came to the rescue, pledging $1,000 a month to Mary's cosmetics business, on the condition that she give it outright to Preston. She did, after Preston also promised her a monthly income. "Presently Father's first check for a thousand dollars came," Preston wrote, "and Mother packed her things. Just before locking her trunk, she threw in a beautiful bright red batik shawl for Isadora. . . . Mother sailed on April 23, and joined Isadora in Paris on the thirtieth."[23]

This is not how Mary remembered events in her book, *The Untold Story.*[24] According to her, Isadora's mother had appeared to her in a dream, beseeching her, "Mary, Mary, go quickly to Isadora. She needs you." Since this is how they explained the world to themselves and to each other, Mary's report can be taken as her authentic recollection: "May Day in Paris — I had arrived late the night before from America to find Isadora." That she did. "But when I glanced about the room and saw glasses, lemons, bottles untidily everywhere, my heart sank into my boots. . . . She seemed to feel my thoughts, although I tried to smile, and with an expression like the martyred Christ, she said, 'This is the first of May, Mary dear.' That was all. I remembered then that the first of May was Patrick's birthday."[25]

Mary took a small apartment on boulevard des Capucines, next door to the Olympia music hall. Isadora hated the place — Lisa Duncan had made a hit at the Olympia — and visited only to take Mary out on the town. "She won't try to economize, refuses to eat except at the best restaurants, and wants to drink the most expensive wines," Mary reported to Preston — "she feels the world owes it to her — well I guess it does."[26] Together they went to the Marchesa Casati's *bal des roses* at Saint-Germain, where Isadora refreshed her acquaintance with Grand Duke Alexander Mikhailovitch, the late tsar's cousin and the most rakish of the Romanovs, who thrilled to her tales of the Soviet Union and promised to share them with his surviving family. "You see how popular I am with royalty," Isadora told Mary later. "They don't seem to fear my Russian Bolshevik reputation." The marchesa herself was a great eccentric, who once appeared at a party dressed as Saint Sebastian, the arrows piercing her costume rigged with electric lights: "Unfortunately when the contraption was plugged in it short-circuited, giving her a severe electric shock." Mary wrote:

> I knew very well that if Isadora had a few glasses of champagne, nothing would stop her from thoroughly enjoying herself and from everybody else doing the same, and seeing that all these people more or less expected her to act in a wild manner befitting her recent reputation, I induced her to leave in the very midst of the festivities so that afterwards these people might say, "What false stories one hears of Isadora!"
>
> She felt the same as I did the next day but also that she had paid a terrible price for their good opinion and had wasted a great opportunity.[27]

In *The Untold Story,* Mary wrote kindly about "Vida," her stenographer's transcription of "Vitya" Seroff. Isadora introduced him as her pianist: "He is the sweetest boy in the world, and incapable of scandal of any kind."[28] Seroff returned the favor by writing about Mary with venomous condescension, calling her "an illiterate megalomaniac"[29] and depicting her essentially as a scheming nincompoop (while excusing her from the taint of lesbianism). Mary was more concerned about Isadora's reckless expenses. "I believe creating these daily difficulties were what made life possible," she wrote; "it kept her shattered thoughts from the one great sorrow eating at her heart. . . . I went home many a night and cried till morning, with vexation that I could in no way stop this sheer slide to destruction."[30] One night Eva Le Gallienne burst into the Studio-Apartment Hôtel with a pack of friends and many bottles of wine. Isadora called her "my beautiful spiritual daughter."

"What a party! What a night!" Mary remembered: "Isadora screaming with laughter, said, 'Mary, dear, you have only to sit still and concentrate, and behold the Gods answer.'"[31] When Edward Steichen came through Paris with his new wife, they sat up late with Isadora singing popular songs — "all the American songs we know," Isadora commanded: "They sang for hours — 'Swanee,' 'Old Black Joe,' 'The Sidewalks of New York,' 'Molly and I and the Baby,' singing until they cried." Steichen remarked later: "She was one honest-to-God American."[32]

In June, Irma came to Paris from Hamburg, where her mother had just died, and effected some kind of reconciliation with Isadora. Almost everyone who knew her claimed to have had presentiments of her death, not surprising in the circumstances, especially since Isadora spoke constantly about dying. "We had taken leave of each other many times without shedding any tears," Irma remembered. "But this time it was different. We both must have sensed this, for we clung together as fond pupil and teacher, daughter and foster mother, and dearest of friends."

"When will we see each other again?" Isadora asked.

"Soon, I hope," said Irma.

"I'll come to Russia when I receive the money from my memoirs," Isadora promised.[33] Irma had hoped to stay in Paris long enough to see her dance at the Théâtre Mogador at the end of June: "When I told her I had come expressly to see her performance, she informed me that it had been postponed till July [8]. She begged me to stay on, but this was quite impossible: I had too many engagements booked for the summer."[34] Isadora remained "suspicious" of Irma to the end.

She needed to lose weight before she danced at the Mogador. Her performance would be staged and underwritten by the Neuilly committee and writer Cécile Sartoris. For a month Isadora drank nothing but a glass of wine with dinner and went each day to Orcier's Baths. "I talked dancing, and art, and getting thin, until she would have liked to throw me from the window," Mary remembered, "but she always finished by doing what I wanted."[35] Orcier featured a system of "bathing and steaming reduction" that had brought Isadora "to condition more than once. . . . Every concert was an ordeal."[36]

"I don't dance anymore," Isadora told Jenny Bradley. "I only move my weight around."[37] Sitting with Sartoris at a café on the Champs-Elysées, she complained that advertising for her forthcoming concert was insufficient: "Isadora pointed across the street to an enormous, two-story sign on a building. . . . 'That is what we ought to have,' [she] said. 'Why don't you get a sign like that?'"[38] But of all her friends, only Seroff remembered the Mogador concert as anything but a triumph; Seroff's attitude toward the Neuilly committee excluded his participation. With Albert Wolff conducting the Pasdeloup Orchestra,

Isadora danced the *Rédemption,* the second movement of Schubert's Unfinished Symphony, the *Liebestod* from *Tristan,* and the *Ave Maria,* which, as usual, brought the audience to tears. "Who will ever forget the ineffable gesture of the maternal arms cradling nothing?" Macdougall wrote.[39] Among the varied audience were Yvette Guilbert, Eva Le Gallienne, Cécile Sorel, Ford Madox Ford, Charles Rappoport, Lisa Duncan, Anita Loos, silent-film star Mary Miles Minter, sculptor Jo Davidson, reporter Floyd Gibbons, Marilyn Miller, and the Dolly Sisters.

"They gave her an ovation," wrote playwright George Middleton. "After a dozen recalls she moved to the front of the stage and stood there, silent. Then, as the house suddenly hushed, with a single outward flowing motion of arms and hands she expressed what no words could have conveyed."[40] Macdougall noted that Isadora gave no speech that afternoon: "No word to her cheering audience. To many of her old friends there was something a little sad in this omission."[41] Her dressing room after the performance was crowded with well-wishers.

"Oh, God," wrote Mary, "how beautiful. . . . I rushed back immediately and found her bathed in tears of joy."[42] Cécile Sorel asked Seroff to bring Isadora to dinner at her apartment when she had rested, "without those noisy women." But "it would have taken several policemen," Seroff wrote, "to rescue Isadora from the adoring clutches of her passionate female admirers."[43] Mercedes de Acosta had arrived from America especially for the event.

After the Mogador concert came "a period of waiting," according to Macdougall, "for results from the sale of the serial rights of [*My Life*]."[44] Bernardine Szold saw Isadora at a lunch given by Elsie Arden on rue de l'Université, "talking disconnected talk about Russia, and smoking one cigarette after another, or rather, lighting one and after a puff or two tossing it over her shoulder out the window and immediately starting on another. The next day Elsie had to pay for burnt awnings all the way down the side of the building to the ground floor."[45] At this time, too, on the evidence, Isadora wrote her erotic poems to Mercedes. "I am going to see whether you love me or not," she told Mercedes as she peeled the leaves from an artichoke. *"Aimez-moi, un peu, beaucoup, passionément, rien du tout. Aimez-moi, un peu, beaucoup** — ah, *beaucoup,* that's something, but it is not enough."[46] Seroff's hostility to "noisy women" increased:

*Loosely translatable as "She loves me, she loves me not," etc.

Beneath a forehead Broad and Bright,
Shine Eyes, Clear wells of light.
A Slender Body, soft, [Hard], White,
To be the Source of my delight.[47]

"Incorrigible Isadora!" Mercedes exclaimed in *Here Lies the Heart:* "Did she ever have a worse enemy than herself?" Seroff and Isadora were effectively at odds by the time she returned to Nice at the end of August. She had dragged him on a train to Le Havre to say good-bye to Mercedes when the latter sailed for New York. "The train went so fast we thought it would rock off the track," Mercedes wrote. "Isadora said she hoped it would and that we would all be killed together." In Mercedes's cabin, she begged to be taken to America, although she had no money, no ticket, and no passport.

"I am homesick," said Isadora. "I want to go home. Please take me with you. Hide me here in your room until the boat sails and then we will go to see the Captain. He is French, and civilized. He will understand." Mercedes wondered later if she ought to have done it, "risk or no risk."[48] On her way out, Isadora ran into George Middleton, who was sailing on the same ship.

"Isn't one American going to give another American a goodbye kiss?" she asked. Middleton gave her "as good an American sample as I could muster," while Seroff looked on.

"How you kiss!" Isadora said.

"Old stuff, Isadora." She laughed, and the whistle blew: "She stepped carefully down the gangplank. She paused. Then she slowly turned. Another pause, and her long scarf blew frantically in the wind trying to escape from her neck. . . . I heard her call: '*Au revoir.*'"[49] Mercedes found two roses on her pillow, one white, one red, along with a card: "The white reaching toward the sky is YOU, darling; and the red is the earth — ME. I adore you — ISADORA."[50]

"At last I have learned, and am beginning to realize that money is the most important thing in the world," Isadora said. "If I had my life to live over again, instead of giving it away, I would gather it in, keep it and hide it."[51] In August, Bradley sold the British serial rights to *My Life* for 400 pounds, a hundred of it to be paid immediately and the rest six weeks later. It was enough to cover Isadora's bill at the Studio-Apartment Hôtel and take her to Deauville, where what remained of the advance disappeared in four days.

"Now is the time to reap a little of the rest and beauty we are enti-
tled to," Isadora declared. "Now I refuse absolutely to be poor. I will
die first. I hate shoddy, shabby poverty."[52] Seroff declined to go with
her when she went back to Nice with Mary, promising instead to join
them there several days later. His friend Alice Spicer, with her companion, Ivan Nikolenko, a filmmaker, agreed to drive them down —
the same Alice Spicer whose intimacy with Seroff drove Isadora into
the sea the year before. Nikolenko hoped to persuade her to record
her dancing on film; Spicer had only three days to spare for the trip
and warned her there could be no "loitering." Seroff wrote: "Knowing
the four members of the party, I was convinced that the journey was
not going to be pleasant."[53] In fact, he got to Nice before they did,
Spicer having abandoned Isadora and Mary in Lyons. They had loi-
tered a great deal. Mary wrote:

> Isadora replied she had never heard such brutality, that she had
> been driven at break-neck speed against her will. Alice explained it
> was the only way she could get there in time. Isadora said the really
> important thing was getting her to Nice, and if Alice reached there,
> getting back really ought not to matter. Alice then suggested if Isadora
> didn't like the car and the way it was driven, she could very easily get
> out and take another, and that if she preferred the train, she would
> loan her enough money for two second-class tickets from Lyons to
> Nice, as that was all the money she had with her. Had it not been for
> the mention of second-class, all might still have been well.

Isadora refused to go to Nice by train, second-class or otherwise,
asking Mary to rent a car and chauffeur for the rest of the trip with a
postdated check. "Raymond would certainly advance her this sum as
soon as we got to Nice," wrote Mary. "I let myself be persuaded to do
this rather dangerous thing, but truly she looked like death, and the
heat was something unbearable."[54] Before they parted, Nikolenko
caught Isadora for a few minutes on film — "smoking a cigarette, riding in a car, that sort of thing," as Spicer wrote later. "Then a very
serious Isadora, the wind blowing against her hair — only her profile. . . . She was absolutely lovely — 'photogenic' as they say — Her
dance pictures would have been beautiful."[55] That Isadora finally
agreed to have her dancing filmed is not in dispute; again, she wanted
to lose weight first. As soon as she left Lyons with Mary, her mood
lifted:

Before we had gone a mile all the joy of heaven seemed to descend on her. . . . We were gay and joyous and happy. She threw her hat in the air. "Mary you're the only person in the world I can bear. I don't know why, but everything others do irritates me. They don't understand." We sang and laughed like children on a holiday, and it didn't matter in the least to her if we rode until midnight. She was splendid. . . . For the rest of the journey there was nothing but happiness until we struck the [seasonal] forest fires raging all along the Côte d'Azur. This affected Isadora as though it were a personal matter. She couldn't bear to see the lovely landscape and forests spoiled by the fires.[56]

In Nice, Raymond refused to contribute anything more to Isadora's extravagance. For a week she and Mary stayed at the Grand Hôtel at Juan-les-Pins, until the mist of Isadora's fame evaporated and the hotel management realized she was broke. Seroff lasted for only a few days: "Debts began to accumulate, with no prospect of paying them, and after the first day I felt like returning to Paris, for there was no hope of my being of any aid or of being able to work." Isadora called him "a coward for leaving," but they parted on fond terms; Seroff promised to come back when he had found some money.[57] Isadora wrote to him on September 11, "I miss you dreadfully — We are in a H—— of a fix here. . . . Think of me & play Scriabin — perhaps you will be nearer to my spirit when the body with all its material nuisance is not there — There are a few inspired moments in life & the rest is *Chipuka* [rubbish, in Russian]."[58]

According to Mary, Isadora "keenly felt" Seroff's defection and resented it: "We didn't discuss it, but I knew what was happening in her mind." Soon they left Juan-les-Pins for a small hotel near Isadora's studio in Nice, where they were obliged to pay a week's rent in advance. "I told you never to go to a cheap hotel," Isadora grumbled. "It's maddening." That night they walked, in Mary's recollection, from Nice back to Juan, a distance of about fifteen miles, where they found a small restaurant near the water, "a little hut with a kitchen at one end." It was called Tétu, after the owners. Over dinner, Mary remarked that "the wine looked like rubies." Isadora answered: "No, like blood." Mary went on:

She held her glass up to the light, and as she did her eye caught that of a young man seated behind me who was dining with three others. I saw her smile and bow as though drinking to someone.

I turned and said, "Good Heavens, that's a chauffeur you're drinking to."

"Oh, Mary, how bourgeois you are! He's nothing of the kind. Have you no eyes? He's a Greek god in disguise, and that's his chariot out there." She pointed to a lovely little Bugatti racing car, with red, white and blue circles around the tail. Sure enough, it was his car. A few minutes [later] they left, and as he drove off she waved to him, and he bowed. She said to me smiling, "You see I'm still desirable" — then I knew how badly Vida's desertion had hurt her.

While she was in Paris, Isadora's landlords in Nice had padlocked her studio — she got inside by promising to vacate the premises permanently on October 1. Ugly as it was on the outside, Mary found the interior "almost too beautiful, like an old church, and yet one felt some peculiar, malevolent influence there." On another empty check, they hired another car, riding aimlessly along the Riviera coast and corniche roads. "Never for a second did she want to rest," Mary remembered, "and had it not been that the chauffeur had an unfortunate habit of wanting to sleep now and then, she would never have stopped. . . . All the way we sang 'Bye, Bye, Blackbird,' and I'm sure the people passing thought we were daft."

> Pack up all my care and woe
> Here I go, singing low
> Bye bye blackbird.
> Where somebody waits for me
> Sugar's sweet, so is she
> Bye bye blackbird . . .[†]

Fortune changed again when Mary convinced the Hôtel Negresco to buy Isadora's impounded Renault: "Also my money had arrived from America. We were again in the favor of the gods. Then there followed such feasting, visiting, restauranting, night-clubbing, as only millionaires might have supported!" Most afternoons Isadora spent on the beach at Juan, followed by drinks at the Carlton in Cannes, where on September 10 she saw her former lover, Dadaist Francis Picabia, and his patient wife, Germaine.

"Francis, do you still love me?" Isadora asked.

"'Of course I do,'" said Picabia, "looking roguishly about at his wife." That night he invited Isadora and Mary to dinner at a bistro they had found, "the quaintest little restaurant, where they make marvelous bouillabaisse." Of course, it was Tétu, where Isadora had seen

[†]Words by Mort Dixon (1926).

her "Greek god" and his car. "It's just fate, that's all," she concluded, asking the proprietors to give the young man her address if he came in again, "as she was most anxious to buy a car like his." Plainly, this was a ruse — it wasn't the car she wanted: "The old lady smiled her same wise smile, saying he was sure to be there the next day." Isadora began to call him "Bugatti," ignoring Mary's protests that she behave herself.[59] "Mother tried as gently as possible to say that any young man who coveted a woman not only twice his age, but approximately twice his weight, was hardly worth having," Preston wrote later. "This just made Isadora angry."[60] She had turned fifty in May.

At her studio, Isadora began work on a dance to Liszt's *Symphonie zu Dantes Divina Commedia:* "She had never heard this music and when it came to her attention she was swept away by enthusiasm."[61] Bernardine Szold saw her at a lunch in Antibes given by artist Robert Chanler for Glenway Wescott. Wescott's first novel had just won the Harper Prize:

> There must have been twenty of us there. . . . We'd already had too many courses and were feeling a little drowsy from the warmth of the sun and the good rich food inside us, when someone asked Isadora about her brother Augustin in New York, who had been having dreadful trouble with his eyes.
>
> Isadora had just heard that he was practically blind. She burst out in such a bitter tirade that we were all appalled. There was no justice on earth, no mercy in heaven! She knew one man who was a saint, and that was Augustin. "And do you see, do you see how justice works?" she cried. "A beautiful soul, a saintly person — find one who can say a harsh word against my brother Augustin. And this is his fate, to be blind. Why couldn't it have been one of us, Bob?" she exclaimed across the table to [Chanler]. "We've been selfish, we've been greedy all our lives. . . . What would it matter to us or the world if either of us, or both of us, were blind?"[62]

Later that day, as a joke, Chanler and Isadora announced their engagement. Chanler was an heir to the Astor fortune, "a Rabelaisian realist in his use of language, and a generous-hearted Bohemian in spirit."[63] Once married to Italian opera star Lina Cavalieri, "the most beautiful woman in the world," Chanler had signed a paper giving Cavalieri "everything he possessed including his money," and she had abandoned him on their wedding night (this from Mercedes de Acosta, whose sister Maria was married to Chanler's nephew). Chanler's brother John, locked in an asylum when Bob and Cavalieri married, sent his best wishes by telegram, at the same time coining a new word: WHO'S LOONY NOW?[64] "I believe I had better marry you to save you from trouble," Isadora told Chanler. Szold went on:

> It WAS a funny idea. Those who knew Bob and those who knew Isadora will understand how very incongruous just the thought of it was, but we all went on making nonsensical jokes about it until finally someone said, "Let's make it a hoax and wire the New York papers." It took a bit to send a straight cable to New York, and none of us had many francs with him, but we each dug up something and two of the party, scarcely able to walk at the thought of the commotion it would arouse, dashed off to the telegraph office.[65]

In Nice, Isadora looked over the manuscript of *My Life* a final time and regretted what she saw. "She told me that it was the only thing she had ever done just for money," Wescott recalled, "and she was ashamed, and having spent the money she could not give it up."[66] As they expected, her mock engagement to Chanler brought reporters on the run. On September 13 Isadora told the Associated Press: "For the first time I am writing for money; now I am frightened that some quick accident might happen."[67] Wescott did his best to reassure her, without success: "It was worse than I knew, she said. Not only was the style poor and stilted, there was bad grammar in it. There had been many objections to her dancing, but there had been no bad grammar in that; and she wept. So I promised to come on the next Wednesday or Thursday and have a look."[68]

At the last minute, Isadora reconciled with Paris Singer, "Lohengrin," whose fortunes had also declined since they parted in 1918. In 1926 the Florida land boom burst, leaving Singer not just poorer but exposed to criminal charges of fraud over land, loan, and construction deals, which also involved an enormous, never-occupied hotel on what is now Singer Island, off Palm Beach. Singer was eventually acquitted on all charges[69] but spent most of the rest of his life in Europe; when the New York stock market crashed in 1929, he was badly hit. According to Jenny Bradley, Isadora had put "an Irish curse" on him,[70] but she was willing to lift it when Singer came to see her in Nice at Mary's urgent persuasion.

"I have seen your mother and she says she is getting ready to give you 'what for'!!!!" Singer had written to Preston Sturges from Paris. "I told her you had everything well in hand and she said she knew it, especially the cash and that she could not live on broken promises and your neglect."[71] Preston would soon marry heiress Eleanor Hutton, daughter of Marjorie Merriweather Post; all his life he remained close to Singer and his circle, who provided him with the raw material, if more were needed, for *The Palm Beach Story.* That Mary was spending most of her money on Isadora, Preston must have known. On September 11 she approached Singer again, at his villa in Cap Ferrat — Les Rochers — only fifteen miles from Nice.

"Isadora begged me to go to Lohengrin," Mary insisted, "who was now in his magnificent château. . . . She felt sure he would do something to relieve her financial distress." At first Singer refused: "He replied that under the circumstances he could do nothing. It would only be wasted if he did; he believed nothing could check Isadora's downward rush." Mary went back to Nice to give her the bad news.

"I always knew you were grand, Mary," Isadora said. But two days later, on September 13, Singer appeared unannounced at her studio. She had decided to sell the furniture.

"I thought I'd drop in to see if you have had lunch," Singer began.

"Oh, please don't speak of lunch," said Isadora, at the same time deftly kicking a champagne bottle under a couch. Mary left them alone together.

"But, my dear, why did you go away?" Isadora asked her later. "I should have loved you to hear all the things he said. He is a lovely, lovely being, and I love him. I believe he is the only one I really ever loved."

Mary laughed: "How can you say that, Isadora? Tell me now the absolute truth. Whom above all did you really love the best?"

"Well, to tell you the real, real truth, Mary, I don't know. I seem to love each one of them to the uttermost limits of love, and if Ted, Lohengrin, the Archangel, and Sergei stood before me, I wouldn't know which one to choose. I loved, and still love them all." She paused. "Perhaps I'm many persons in one and perhaps many others feel as I do, but won't admit it, even to themselves. And so they go on, fooling themselves all their lives, but I could never fool myself or anyone else for that matter."[72]

Singer had promised to return the next day with a check. Mary remembered "a carload of newspapermen standing two and three in front of the hotel," still hoping for the inside story of Isadora's "engagement" to Chanler. In the early evening, finally, Bugatti arrived. Isadora was sleeping:

> By this time a maid kept running up the stairs every few minutes, saying, "Another young man to see Miss Duncan." . . . In answer to a timid knock I opened the door and there stood a handsome young man, apologizing for his costume, as he just came from a job, saying Mme. Tétu had given him my address, telling him I had wanted to buy a Bugatti. I told him rather sharply that I was not Miss Duncan but if he would leave his card I would give it to her.

"Isadora, Bugatti was here while you slept," Mary said casually when Isadora awoke. They were expected for dinner with Isadora's occasional manager and impresario, Georges Hottois:

> She sprang from the couch like a tiger.
> "I don't believe you, Mary. It's some silly joke. You would have awakened me, you never would have sent him away without telling me."
> "Oh, yes I did," I said.
> "Well, then, I'll never forgive you. Good heavens, can't you understand how terribly important it is? . . . Mary, what have you done? We must find him, the first thing in the morning."
> "Isadora, I believe you are losing your mind. What can this chauffeur have to do with you?"
> "I tell you he's not a chauffeur, but a messenger of the gods. He's divine."

Soon the maid knocked again, this time with a letter for Mary. Inside was a check from an American friend, meant to buy flowers for Isadora. "Surely some kind of God was looking out for us," Mary agreed. "Now we had the price of several taxis, and tomorrow full of promise." But that night at dinner, when Hottois's "exquisite little three-year-old son came to the table," Mary saw Isadora's head fall. She grew "pale as death, trying her best to conquer her feelings."

"What's the matter with the beautiful lady?" the child asked.[73] Isadora "ran out screaming." The next morning she told Mary "that she could no longer live in a world where there were little golden-haired children of three," as Mary reported in a letter to Preston.[74] Mary had hoped to return to Paris after Singer reappeared, but Isadora warned her against it. "You may be sure, Mary," she said, "before you've gone ten miles, I shall have walked into the sea; and this time I shall take the precaution to tie an iron around my throat."[75]

Bugatti wasn't a Greek god, but a Niçois *garagiste,* French-Italian as his name confirms: Bénoit Falchetto. Neither was his car a Bugatti, but an Amilcar Grand Sport, according to the first reports from the Riviera, "Serial No. 2318M9."[76] On the morning of September 14, Isadora went to the address Falchetto had left on his card, the Helvétia Garage. Falchetto was out on a call "but would be back in the afternoon. She said she wanted to buy a car, and asked him to come to her studio at five." Singer was coming at four. Isadora's spirits had risen again, after Mary promised not to leave her. British serialization of *My Life* had begun, and Bradley had promised to deliver the balance of her advance by the end of the week.

"Now, that's right, Mary," said Isadora. "If you will only stay by me and see the thing through, just stick to me. . . ." With the money from her memoirs, they would rebuild her school: "We'll go to Russia, get the children, and we'll end in a burst of glory yet. You're grand, Mary. You're just grand." After lunch she had her hair done, saying that she wanted to look her best "for an old beau and a young one. . . . You see what a little happiness does. Stick on the job, Mary, and we'll ride to glory, I promise you."

That afternoon, while waiting for Singer at her studio, Isadora danced around the room, "more radiant every moment, as though she had some wonderful secret that she felt bursting out, but could not tell to anyone. 'Oh, Mary, Mary,' she would say every little while, and then go on dancing again." When a knock came, it wasn't Singer but Falchetto.

"Here is your Bugatti," Mary said; "I am going to the hotel."

Isadora returned about an hour later, laughing, and alone. "I've lost them both, Mary"; she cried, "I've lost Bugatti and I've lost Lohengrin! . . . It's no use. I always get caught." Falchetto wasn't just "divine" but a modern Mercury, an airplane pilot. "Of course, that settled it," Mary explained: "Here was what she was always looking for — a man not afraid of anything. She would get an aeroplane, and together they would fly to America." Singer had appeared at roughly that moment.

"I see you haven't changed," he said. It was all Isadora could do to keep both men from leaving. "She turned to the very embarrassed young man, and said, 'You are coming at nine tonight with the little racing car.' He said he would, looking very sheepishly at the hand-some stately Lohengrin, and left." Isadora then told Singer that Mary wanted to buy the young man's car: "Poor Isadora! She was rather bad at lying." But Singer had turned a corner. "Earthly love or desire had no part in this marvelous reunion," Mary wrote:

> Lohengrin told her he had been detained and must leave immedi-ately, but would come in the morning to take her to lunch and give her the check he had promised. He had not been able to attend to all these things that day. . . . His family passed at this moment to pick him up in their car. . . . He waved good-bye, saying he would stop on his way back if he felt well enough.
>
> As he drove away, she came to the hotel. "Now we will see what we will see," she said. "I don't believe he will come, or Bugatti, either."[77]

At the hotel Mary was talking with Ivan Nikolenko, Alice Spicer's friend, who still hoped to make a film of Isadora dancing. Isadora had seen the short reel Nikolenko had shot on their way to Nice. "She was perfectly satisfied with the experimental pictures," Spicer wrote, "and told Ivan though she had all her life refused to be filmed — she would let him take these pictures because she knew he was an artist. . . . They were to begin work the next day!"[78] About eight o'clock Isadora went to dinner with Mary and Nikolenko at the café across from her hotel, leaving a note for Falchetto on the door of her room: *"Suis en face Chez Henry."* She wore the red batik shawl Mary had packed be-fore leaving New York — two yards long, five feet wide, "of heavy crêpe, with a great yellow bird almost covering it, and blue Chinese asters and Chinese characters in black — a marvelous, lovely thing, the light of Isadora's life. She would go nowhere without it."[79] Mary had designed the shawl herself in New York. The fringes on either end were eighteen inches long.

"This shawl is magic, dear," Isadora told Mary. "I feel waves of elec-tricity coming from it. . . . What a red — the color of heart's blood." Normally, she wrapped it several times around her shoulders and neck — Francis Rose even painted her wearing it: "When I showed her the finished picture, in which I was experimenting with a form of cu-bism, she cried out: 'But Francis, you have cut my throat.'"[80] At dinner with Nikolenko, Mary suddenly felt ill at ease, "turning deadly white and trembling." She wrote to Preston a week later:

Isadora, terribly alarmed, begged me to tell her what was the matter. I told her I felt some terrible catastrophe has happened, that perhaps Preston had had an accident. She said, "Mary, I have never seen such a melancholy face." She asked the waiter to run quickly and get me a brandy. As we went across the street to her studio from the restaurant, I begged her not to try out the little sports auto that night as I feared a tragedy. Taking my hand, she danced across the street saying, "I would go all the quicker if I knew it would be my last ride. . . ." We went into the studio, she turned on the gramophone and began her dance, singing, "I'm in love again," and declaring it was one of the happiest days of her life. Suddenly she saw the little auto drive up and ran out, I running ahead of her, begging her at least to wear my cape as it was cold. She refused, saying she would only wear her red shawl.[81]

The Amilcar was a low, two-seat racing model, "in the general pattern of a torpedo," the left-side passenger seat staggered slightly back from the driver's on the right. Mary pleaded with Falchetto: "I don't believe you realize what a great person you are driving tonight. I beg of you to be careful. . . . I'm terribly nervous." Isadora kissed her, threw her shawl another time around her neck, and cried, *"Adieu, mes amis, je vais à la gloire!"* — Good-bye, my friends, I go to glory! It was the kind of thing she might have said anytime, in the same words, a reliable exit line for a woman fully conscious of her decrease.

As Isadora sat down, the long fringes of her shawl fell over the side of the car and caught in the spokes of the left rear wheel. Mary just had time to call out, *"Isadora, ta châle! Ramasse ta châle!"* — Isadora, your shawl! Pick up your shawl! But the car roared off, and "before she could say, 'Oh!'" with the first, sharp turn of the wheel, her neck was broken and she was dead.[82]

Epilogue

"It is only in romances that people undergo a sudden metamorphosis," Isadora declared. "In real life, even after the most terrible experiences, the main character remains exactly the same."[1] Arnold Genthe called it "a blessing," nevertheless, that there were two of her — "the woman that you are and the artist that you are."

"How stupid of you," Isadora answered. "The woman I am is the artist I am. There is no difference."

"I, for one, am grateful that there is," said Genthe.[2] But the manner of her death seemed to prove her point, so dramatically and indelibly that many believed she had staged it herself, in a spectacular suicide. "Isadora's end is *perfect*," wrote Jean Cocteau — "a kind of horror that leaves one calm."[3] French newspapers invoked the myth of Hippolytus, strangled as he rode along the Greek seacoast when the reins of his chariot caught in the branches of a fig tree. Americans, who knew and thought about Isadora differently, treated her passing with a lighter hand. "One hopes that the sky was rose-colored," wrote a reporter in Cleveland, "and that a jest was falling from her lips as the soft silk tightened around her throat."[4]

The force of the wheel as her shawl wrapped around it had pulled her out of the car, hurling her to the street "in an extraordinary manner"[5] and trapping her head between the body and the tire — Isadora's death was as quick, but not as clean as is normally imagined and described. According to local reports, she was dragged some twenty or thirty meters before the car came to a stop. Mary began to scream, as did Falchetto — Bugatti — "who lost his head," said the *Petit Niçois,* running in circles around the accident, "gesticulating" and crying, "I've killed the Madonna! I've killed the Madonna!"[6]

A crowd had already gathered on the promenade des Anglais by the time Mary could flag down another motorist, who helped her lift the rear of the Amilcar and disentangle Isadora's clothing from the wheel. "I never lost my head for a second," Mary wrote later to Preston. "I ran and got a knife, tried to cut through, then scissors. . . . Then I helped lift her into a passing car and we rode, she and I alone and the couple who owned the car, I holding her poor head . . . trying to get her to breathe, never realizing she was already dead, just we two among strangers."[7] Isadora's death certificate, completed with Mary's help at Nice's Hôpital Saint-Roch, puts the time of death at 9:30 P.M. on September 14, 1927. The *Petit Marseillais* reported that "Dr. Auzias, who conducted the post-mortem, ascertained two breaks to the vertebral column, as well as heavy internal bleeding. Death was instantaneous and there was no suffering."[8]

That night, after Mary's pleading, the body was brought back to the studio, where the doors were padlocked and seals set by order of the police, who remained guarding the building. Isadora's Russian travel documents had been found among her effects — her body would not be released until morning, after the Soviet consul arrived from Marseilles and gave his permission. The news had already flashed around the world. ARRIVING BY FIRST TRAIN TO BRING ISADORA FOR INCINERATION IN PARIS, Raymond cabled bluntly.[9] Paris Singer, "stricken," came from Cap Ferrat to take charge of local arrangements and reassure Isadora's friends, in person and by telegram: SHE DIED PAINLESSLY MARY AND I WATCHING HER.[10]

Over the next day, while her friends on the Riviera crowded the studio to pay their respects, Isadora's body lay in a scarlet robe and billowing black cape on her divan, surrounded by flowers and burning incense and covered with a thin white veil: "She seemed to be sleeping. . . . The whole studio studded with candles looked like an ancient shrine to beauty."[11] Among the signatures in the guest book — Cocteau, Picabia, Grand Duke Boris of Russia — "many were written with a trembling hand."[12]

On September 16 Raymond arrived with Victor Seroff, who had

heard about the accident from his landlady in Paris, and who spent most of the day alone in a café, away from "weeping and wailing" women. Following a simple musical service — "no words, no rites"[13] — the body was placed in an oak coffin. Three sprays of fleurs-de-lis lay on Isadora's breast, one each from Elizabeth, Augustin, and Raymond, along with roses that Mary dropped into the casket in the name of "her dearest friends across the sea — Mary Fanton Roberts, Ruth Mitchell . . . Mercedes de Acosta . . . Edward Steichen . . . and a little bunch of roses from her school. . . . Then they solemnly closed it and soldered it fast."[14] It had been raining all day, and as the train carrying Isadora's remains left Nice for Paris, "a perfect hurricane" blew up, "a torrential storm" noted by all the newspapers.[15] Singer was too upset to make the trip.

In Paris a tug-of-war broke out between Isadora's family and her friends for control of the obsequies. Lisa Duncan led the party who welcomed the coffin at Gare Saint-Lazare. Irma cabled from Moscow, asking that the funeral be delayed until she could get there, a request that Raymond, now in charge, had no intention of granting. For two days the coffin lay at his studio in Auteuil, draped in purple velvet and massed in flowers — "roses of every color," said the *New York Times,* "rare orchids, camellias and flowers of all seasons. On a table near the body between burning tapers was a photograph of the artist holding her two children in her arms."[16] Pictures taken at the bier show Raymond in his customary white robes and Elizabeth, arrived from Salzburg, a contrast in solid black. She had fainted on hearing the news of Isadora's death, but rallied to tell reporters, "No person reveals the discrepancy between life and art better than Isadora. In art she reached a supreme height, but in life she was a helpless child."[17] There wasn't time for Augustin to come from New York.

"Despite Raymond who wanted to give our glorious darling a second-class funeral," Allan Ross Macdougall reported, "Desti, [Cécile] Sartoris, [Ralph] Lawton and I saw that she had all the beautiful flowers that she loved and immortal music to wing her flight away from this drab earth."[18] The funeral procession to Père-Lachaise on September 19, under a leaden sky, coincided with an American Legion parade on the Champs-Elysées marking the tenth anniversary of America's involvement in World War I. DUNCAN CORTEGE HARDLY NOTICED IN DAY'S FURORE, read the next day's headlines in the United States. FEW ATTEND ISADORA DUNCAN'S RITES AS COMPATRIOTS PARADE.[19] Had American reporters continued to the cemetery — they didn't — a different scene would have met their eyes. A crowd estimated at as high as 10,000 people had gathered at Père-Lachaise, "perched on the tombs," in one report, "tearing up the pathways, panting, out of breath . . . among them simple working men and women, carrying their children in their arms and telling them a beautiful tale."[20] In the crematorium, as at Nice, there were no funeral rites, only music: Liszt's *Funérailles,* the *Ave Maria,* and Beethoven's *In Questa Tomba Oscura,* sung by the baritone Garcia Marsellac.

More than a thousand people had jammed into the crematory chapel. Outside, Bernadine Szold stood with Janet Flanner and "a throng of students from the Left Bank, artists of Montparnasse and Montmartre, cripples and beggars and apaches and great ladies, and small tradespeople, all mixed together in common mourning, and everywhere you heard her name 'ISADORA.'"[21] As the doors of the furnace opened to receive the body, the service concluded with Bach's "Air on the G String."

"[Isadora] always told me her soul would never leave until it mounted on the strains of that lovely thing," Mary wrote to Preston, "and so we all felt that second [that] it left."[22] The crowd outside fell silent as "a thin, fine gray cylinder of smoke [rose] very straight and very high" from the crematorium chimney, finally turning white, wavering, then "disappearing into the mist. And there was a murmur through all that immense throng," Szold remembered: "'Ah, there goes Isadora, adieu, adieu.'"[23] Her ashes were placed in the columbarium beneath her children's, and not far from those of her mother. In her hometown, the *San Francisco Call & Post* ran her picture on the front page, above the caption: RETURNS TO MORTAL DUST.[24]

Sources and Acknowledgments

All research about Isadora Duncan must begin with her own, incomplete autobiography, *My Life*, first published in the United States in December 1927, just three months after her death. I have used the most recent edition (Liveright, 1995) except where excisions or errors have been made in reprinting the original text. Isadora's way with capitalization and punctuation has also demanded the occasional clarification, and, where noted, I have sometimes combined passages from *My Life* to correct her own casual chronology of events. I have retained her spelling of both English and foreign words.

When I began this work, only three full biographies of Isadora Duncan existed in English (and none of them were in print): Allan Ross Macdougall's *Isadora: A Revolutionary in Art and Love* (1960); Victor Seroff's *Real Isadora* (1971); and Fredrika Blair's *Isadora: Portrait of the Artist as a Woman* (1986), certainly the most thorough of the three. Early published sources include Sewell Stokes's *Isadora: An Intimate Portrait*, Mary Desti's *Untold Story: The Life of Isadora Duncan, 1921–1927*, and Irma Duncan and Allan Ross Macdougall's *Isadora Duncan's Russian Days and Her Last Years in France*, all of which appeared within two years of Isadora's death. Apart from these, among secondary sources, mention must be made of Irma Duncan's autobiography, *Duncan Dancer* (1966); Cynthia Splatt's *Isadora Duncan and*

Gordon Craig: The Prose & Poetry of Action (1988) and Dorée Duncan, Carol Pratl, and Cynthia Splatt's *Life Into Art: Isadora Duncan and Her World* (1993), both of which contain original Duncan family materials otherwise unavailable to researchers; and of *"Your Isadora": The Love Story of Isadora Duncan and Gordon Craig* (1974), edited by Francis Steegmuller and published from the Craig-Duncan Collection by the New York Public Library. Other published sources dealing directly with Isadora's life and the lives of her family, students, colleagues, and friends are listed individually in the source key and, where applicable, in the notes.

In 1958 Irma Duncan Rogers donated her large Isadora Duncan archive to the New York Public Library, where, with Macdougall's papers and Isadora's letters to Gordon Craig, it remains a centerpiece of the Dance Collection at the Library for the Performing Arts at Lincoln Center. Other public repositories of Duncan material are in the Theatre Collection (Mary Fanton Roberts Papers) at the Museum of the City of New York; the Mary Desti Collection on Isadora Duncan at the University of California at Irvine, as well as a smaller group of Desti papers (with the Preston Sturges archive) at UCLA; the Isadora Duncan Collection at the San Francisco Performing Arts Library and Museum; the Harry Ransom Humanities Research Center at the University of Texas at Austin; the Beinecke Rare Book and Manuscript Library at Yale University; the Isadora Duncan Collection at York University's Scott Library in Toronto; the University of Georgia's Georgia Museum of Art at Athens; the Bibliothèque Nationale in Paris; the Deutsches Tanzarchiv at Cologne (where the records and papers of the Elizabeth Duncan School are now also kept); the Bakhrushin Theatre Museum in Moscow and the Russian State Museum of Theatre in St. Petersburg; and Kathleen Quinlan's Anna Duncan Archive at Stockholm's Dansmuseet. Mary Duncan papers and archives are still held privately. A catalog of the Howard Holtzman Collection of Duncan material has been published, but the collection is not yet open to research.

Since Isadora's death in 1927, Duncan scholars, specialists, and enthusiasts have never ceased to report and publish the results of their work — the New York Public Library's Dance Collection currently lists some nine hundred separate items on Isadora in addition to the three major collections mentioned above. This book, which attempts to synthesize the available material in a single biographical narrative, stands on the shoulders of all who worked before me. In this regard, I want to mention specially Kay Bardsley, Lillian Loewenthal, Julia Levien, Lori Belilove, Nesta Macdonald, Ann Daly, Jeanne Bresciani, Dr. Adela Roatcap, Gordon McVay, Gedeon Dienes, Fredrika Blair Hastings, Lee Freeson, Kathleen Quinlan, Hannelore Schick, Franklin Rosemont, Francis Steegmuller, Dorée Duncan-Seligmann, Carol Pratl, Cynthia Splatt, Elizabeth Kendall, Deborah Jowitt, and Millicent Dillon. Some of these people I know personally and others not, but I'm confident in saying this book could not have been written without their help. All errors of fact and interpretation are my own.

Among archivists and librarians I want to thank particularly Madeleine Nichols, Monica Moseley, Charles Perrier, and Karen Nickerson of the Dance Collection at Lincoln Center; Marty Jacobs and Marguerite Lavin at the Museum of the City of New York, Saundra Taylor, Nancy Shawcross, Elizabeth Fuller, Erik Näslund, Marga Allansson, Elena Danielson, Eric Pumroy, Eunice C. MacGill, Ryan Carpenter, Ron Scherl, Kirsten Tanaka, Patricia Miller, Alfred Mueller, Kathryn Miller Haines, Steve R. Drew, Deanna Kastler, David Rodger, Teresa S. Defibaugh, Gudrun Foettinger, Cathy Henderson, Beverly Faison, and Gunnar M. Berg. My particular gratitude to Doree Duncan-Seligmann for permission to reprint photographs from the Duncan Collection.

Others who helped in large ways and small are Hortense Kooluris, Victoria T. Fischman, Robert Spoo, the late George Seldes, Marian Seldes, Nikita A. and Natalya Tolstoï, Tatyana Tolstaya, Stanley Joseph, Julie Harris, Nat Des Marais, Mrs. Russell C. Barnes, Richard Torrence, Sandy Sturges, Tim Scholl, Kevin Moss, Shain Stodt, Barbara Solomon, Lyle Almond, Judith Danoff, Edvard Radzinsky, Lynn Franklin, Louisa Young, Helen Sheehy, the late Roddy McDowall, Vitaly Chernetsky, George Becker, William Breeze, Edmund White, Mrs. Robert E. Flynn, Donald Norsic, Leigh Feldman, Mark van der Linde, Helen Zalomova, Yevgeny Nagornykh, Dmitri Macedonsky, Martin Sherman, Marianne Williamson, Bruce E. Hall, the late Alastair Forbes, Barbara Victor, Carl Rollyson, Carol Easton, Al Pischl, Barbara Feldon, Marie Waldron, J. C. Connell, and Charles Timbrell.

Among friends: Carol Allen, Drusilla Walsh, Carol Kitzmiller, Chad Nagle, David Neiweem and Alan Parshley, Maggi Hayes, Ed and Betty Levin, Nancy Stearns Bercaw and Allan Nicholls, Christopher Mierzejewski, Dwight Garner, Genevieve Lyons, Grant Menzies, William Luce, Jane Gunther, Lisa DiMona, Jeremy Wren, Laura Miller, Lisa Cohen, Marlene E. Koenig, Jeff Martin, Greg King, Penny Wilson,

Kevin Treloar, Mike Shaw, Steven West, James Mackenzie, Teresa Carpenter, the late Charles Debuire, Isabel Huggan, Gloria Vanderbilt, Helen Gurley Brown, Jack Austin, Mrs. Edward J. Wynkoop, Pamela Polston, Paula Routly, Reverend Walter Miller, Paul Hance, Paul Pilcher, the late Dr. Peter Hendrickson, Tim Palmer, Vicky Rosenwald, Reverend Peter Grandell, Victoria Boothby, Beth Davey, Meg Wynn Owen, Michael Murphy, Brooke Gladstone, Veronica Richel, and Blaine Bragg. To any and all I may have inadvertently overlooked, my apologies.

Finally, my deepest thanks to all my family; to Claudia Hannah, Matt Hannah and Antje Rickert; to Fran Bradfield, Candace Metz-Longinette-Gahring, Eleanor Lanahan, Katherine Layton, and Edward Pattillo; to Ray Roberts, who gave me the idea; Rafe Sagalyn, who whipped it into shape; to the late Carolyn Brunton; and to my intrepid editorial teams on both sides of the Atlantic: Richard Beswick, Donna Coonan, Annie Cook, Steve Lamont, Karen Auerbach, Jennifer Brennan, and Mary Tondorf-Dick, whose patience, guidance, and fortitude are apparent to me, at least, in every chapter, page, and line.

Special thanks to Todd Fuhrman, whose way with an iced coffee is sorely missed. And, of course, to John.

Abbreviations

ID	ISADORA DUNCAN
EGC	EDWARD GORDON CRAIG
EAC	EDWARD ANTHONY CRAIG, *Gordon Craig: The Story of His Life* (New York: Knopf, 1968)
MFR	MARY FANTON ROBERTS
SE	SERGEI ESENIN
City Museum	Museum of the City of New York
DC	Dance Collection, New York Public Library for the Performing Arts
CD	Craig-Duncan Collection
AD	Anna Duncan, *In the Footsteps of Isadora (I Isadoras fotspår)* (Stockholm: Dansmuseet, 1995)
AOD	Isadora Duncan, *The Art of the Dance,* edited by Sheldon Cheney (New York: Theatre Arts, 1928)
DD	Irma Duncan, *Duncan Dancer* (Middletown, Conn.: Wesleyan University Press, 1966)
Desti	Mary Desti, *The Untold Story: The Life of Isadora Duncan, 1921–1927* (New York: Horace Liveright, 1929)
Dumesnil	Maurice Dumesnil, *An Amazing Journey: Isadora Duncan in South America* (New York: Washburn, 1932)
IED	Frank-Manuel Peter, *Isadora und Elizabeth Duncan in Deutschland* (Cologne: Wienand Verlag, 2000)
IDRD	Irma Duncan and Allan Ross Macdougall, *Isadora Duncan's Russian Days and Her Last Years in France* (New York: Covici-Friede, 1929)
Index	Edward Gordon Craig, *Index to the Story of My Days* (New York: Viking, 1957)
Loewenthal	Lillian Loewenthal, *The Search for Isadora: The Legend and Legacy of Isadora Duncan* (Pennington, New Jersey: Princeton Book Co., 1993)
Macdougall	Allan Ross Macdougall, *Isadora: A Revolutionary in Art and Love* (New York: Thomas Nelson and Sons, 1960)
McVay	Gordon McVay, *Isadora and Esenin* (Ann Arbor: Ardis, 1980)
ML	Isadora Duncan, *My Life* (New York: Boni and Liveright, 1927)
Rosemont	Franklin Rosemont, ed., *Isadora Speaks: Writings and Speeches of Isadora Duncan* (Chicago: Charles H. Kerr, 1994)
Schneider	Ilya Ilyitch Schneider, *Isadora Duncan: The Russian Years,* translated by David Magarshack (New York: Harcourt, Brace and World, 1969)
Seroff	Victor Seroff, *The Real Isadora* (New York: The Dial Press, 1971)
Splatt	Cynthia Splatt, *Isadora Duncan and Gordon Craig: The Prose and Poetry of Action* (San Francisco: The Book Club of California, 1988)
Steegmuller	Francis Steegmuller, ed., *"Your Isadora": The Love Story of Isadora Duncan and Gordon Craig* (New York: Random House and The New York Public Library, 1974)
Stokes	Sewell Stokes, *Isadora Duncan: An Intimate Portrait* (London: Brentano, 1928)
Sturges	Preston Sturges, *Preston Sturges,* adapted and edited by Sandy Sturges (New York: Touchstone, 1990)

Notes

Preface

[1] Reynaldo Hahn, "La Musique," March 29, 1913, in Loewenthal, 140.

[2] *New York Telegraph,* May 10, 1915, DC.

[3] *IDRD,* 168.

[4] Janet Flanner, "Isadora," *The New Yorker,* January 1, 1927.

[5] John Dos Passos, *The Big Money* (Boston: Houghton Mifflin, 1960), 139.

[6] Abram Lerner and Bartlett Cowdrey, Abraham Walkowitz oral history interview, Smithsonian Institution, December 8 and 22, 1958.

[7] Shaemas O'Sheel, "Isadora," *The New Republic,* October 26, 1927.

[8] Robert Edmond Jones, "The Gloves of Isadora," *Theater Arts* 31, October 1947.

Chapter 1: A Baby Bolshevik

[1] CD 23 (January 15, 1905).

[2] Seroff, 18. The book referred to is Pasquale Villari, *Life and Times of Girolamo Savonarola* (1888).

[3] Augustin Duncan interview with Margaret Lloyd, *Christian Science Monitor,* February 16, 1946. See also Margherita Duncan to Irma Duncan, July 29, 1949, Irma Duncan Collection, folder 31, DC.

[4] *ML,* 10. Walter Sorell (quoting Isadora), *Dance in Its Time* (New York: Columbia University Press, 1986), 321.

[5] ID, untitled ms. (Moscow 1921), in *IDRD,* 229–30.

[6] ID, "I See America Dancing," *New York Herald Tribune,* October 2, 1927, DC. The essay was printed with alterations in *AOD,* 47–50, and also inserted into *ML,* 339–43. Different drafts exist in DC and elsewhere.

[7] Augustin Duncan, *New York Herald Tribune,* May 2, 1937, DC. See also Adela Spindler Roatcap, *Raymond Duncan: Printer . . . Expatriate . . . Eccentric Artist* (San Francisco: Book Club of California, 1991), 1. For both the Gray and Duncan families, I have relied chiefly on the Isadora Duncan Collection at the San Francisco Performing Arts Library and Museum (SF PALM). The collection is "artificial" and always growing, containing original family materials, press accounts, programs, unpublished biographies and memoirs, photographs, etc. It includes Harry Mulford's "Notes and Items Relating to Joseph Charles Duncan," Russell Hartley's collection of Isadora Duncan materials, as well as original research material for Lois Rather's *Lovely Isadora* (Oakland, Calif.: The Rather Press, 1976); Judd Boynton's *Florence Treadwell and Berkeley* (oral history transcript), tape-recorded interview conducted by Suzanne B. Riess, Regional Oral History Office, Bancroft Library, University of California, Berkeley, 1978; and *Dance at the Temple of the Wings, the Boynton-Quitzow Family in Berkeley* (oral history transcript), tape-recorded interview conducted 1972 by Suzanne Riess and Margaretta Mitchell for the Regional Oral History Office, Bancroft Library, University of California, Berkeley, 1973. See also Adela Spindler Roatcap, "Joseph Charles Duncan, Journalist, Art Dealer, Poet, Banker," in *The Argonaut: Journal of the San Francisco Historical Society* 6, no. 1 (Summer 1995), and "On to the Golden Commonwealth, Colonel Thomas Gray & Maggie O'Gorman," *The Argonaut* 10, no. 1 (Spring 1999).

[8] *ML,* 19.

[9]Ibid., 15.

[10]*San Francisco Evening Bulletin,* October 8, 1877, SF PALM.

[11]Raymond Duncan in the *New York Herald Tribune,* April 21, 1948. In addition to the sources cited above, I've used the vivid account of Joseph Duncan's life in the *San Francisco Examiner* ("Californian Who Went Down with the Mohegan"), November 13, 1898, published just a month after Duncan's death.

[12]*Chestertown Telegraph,* January 26, 1827, quoted in Robert G. Bailey to Harry Mulford, December 13, 1974, SF PALM.

[13]Loose notes in Mulford collection, SF PALM (Box 1, Joseph Charles Duncan).

[14]Published in the *Sangamo (Illinois) Journal,* November 12, 1841, SF PALM.

[15]Tom Cole, *A Short History of San Francisco* (San Francisco: Don't Call It Frisco Press, 1988), 44–45. Cole's classic volume provides a quick and lively view of the city's rambunctious history.

[16]Ibid., 49.

[17]Mark Twain, *Roughing It,* with a foreword by Shelley Fisher Fishkin, introduction by George Plimpton, afterword by Henry B. Wonham (New York: Oxford University Press, 1996), 420.

[18]Rather Collection, SF PALM.

[19]Raymond Duncan, *Pages from My Press* (Paris: self-printed, 1947); also loose notes, SF PALM.

[20]Samuel Dickson, "Isadora Duncan," ms. of radio address at the Museum of the City of San Francisco; see also Macdougall, 26.

[21]It isn't known whether Elmira Hill divorced Joseph Duncan or died and left him a widower. The 1906 earthquake and fire took most such records with it.

[22]Florence Treadwell Boynton, quoted in Paul Hertelendy, "New Light, Old Legend: Isadora's Early Years," *Oakland Tribune,* December 18, 1977.

[23]ML, 9.

[24]ID, "Notes for a speech preceding the Liszt-Scriabin program," Kamerny Theatre, Moscow, September 21, 1924, in IDRD, 269. See also George Seldes, "What Love Meant to Isadora Duncan," *The Mentor,* February 1930. A report in the *San Francisco Chronicle* (February 29, 1880) remarks that, at the time of his arrest, "if Duncan were bailed out he could not walk half the length of Kearny Street alive."

[25]ML, 9.

[26]Blair, 6; Rather, *Lovely Isadora,* 20. See also Paul Hertelendy, "Isadora's Childhood: Clearing Away the Clouds," in *Dance Magazine,* July 1977, 48–50. All the Duncan children were baptized at the same time, apparently at the insistence of the Gray family, in the wake of the Pioneer scandal. Isadora's godfather was her grown half brother, William Duncan.

[27]*San Francisco Chronicle,* October 9, 1877.

[28]*San Francisco Examiner,* November 13, 1898.

[29]Benjamin E. Lloyd, *Lights and Shades in San Francisco* (San Francisco: A. L. Bancroft, 1876), 88.

[30]*San Francisco Examiner,* November 13, 1898.

[31]Peter Fanning, *Great Crimes of the West* (self-printed, 1929), 150.

[32]*San Francisco Chronicle,* October 9, 1877.

[33]Fanning, *Great Crimes of the West,* 150–53, SF PALM.

[34]See the *Sacramento Daily Record-Union,* July 27, 1882, SF PALM: "The case against J. C. Duncan of the defunct Pioneer Bank was dismissed today, owing to the failure of important evidence relied upon by the prosecution."

[35]*San Francisco Examiner,* November 13, 1898.

[36]Roatcap, "Joseph Charles Duncan," 33.

[37]*San Francisco Examiner,* November 13, 1898. The wreck of the *Mohegan* remains one of the most popular sites for divers off the coast of Cornwall. The victims were buried in a mass grave.

[38]ML, 10.

[39]Boynton-Quitzow family oral history, SF PALM.

[40]ML, 15–17.

[41]Boynton-Quitzow family oral history, SF PALM.

[42]ML, 17.

[43]"Notes for a speech preceding the Liszt-Scriabin program."

[44]*Christian Science Monitor,* February 16, 1946.

[45]Hertelendy, "Isadora's Childhood."

[46]"Notes for a speech preceding the Liszt-Scriabin program."

[47]Irma Duncan Rogers to Francis Steegmuller, September 10, 1974, Irma Duncan Collection, folders 115–16, DC.

[48]Quoted in Millicent Dillon, "Looking for Isadora: A Lecture," transcript at SF PALM.

[49]In Margaretta K. Mitchell, "Dance for Life: ID and Her California Dance Legacy at the Temple of the Wings," ms. at SF PALM, edited in *Encore: The Archives for the Performing Arts Quarterly* 2, no. 4 (Autumn 1985).

[50]From Gertrude Stein, *The Making of Americans,* quoted in Elizabeth Sprigge to Allan Ross Macdougall, August 23, 1955, in Macdougall Collection, folder 44, DC.

[51]*Oakland Tribune,* December 18, 1977.

[52]Robert Ingersoll, "Art and Morality," *North American Review,* March 1888.

[53]"Notes for a speech preceding the Liszt-Scriabin program."

[54]*ML,* 12.

[55]ID, "Fragments and Thoughts," in *AOD,* 128–29. Sheldon Cheney identifies this as "the earliest existing fragment of ID's writings."

[56]Isadora's memories are rarely reliable on the subject of age, though she told roughly this same story to a Dutch reporter as early as April 1905 (clipping in Isadora Duncan Collection, folder 19, Scott Library, York University, Toronto): "I became a dance instructor at the age of 11 years. We were afraid that nobody would trust me because I was so young . . . and so I put my hair up, put on a long dress and looked like a mature lady of 16 years." On the other hand, in notes for her autobiography, Isadora claimed that she was "a girl of 15" when she left San Francisco in 1895 (ID to Paul Kennaday, May 12, 1925, in Macdougall Collection, folder 4, DC). The three years she shaved off at the start of her career stayed off; for publicity purposes, her birth date was sometimes given as 1880 and even 1884.

[57]*ML,* 14.

[58]Ibid., 11.

[59]"Notes for a speech preceding the Liszt-Scriabin program."

Chapter 2: "I Dreamed of a Different Dance"

[1]*ML,* 213.

[2]ID, "Fragments and Thoughts," in *AOD,* 128.

[3]*ML,* 14.

[4]ID, "Depth," in *AOD,* 99.

[5]See also her essay "Dancing in Relation to Religion and Love," in *AOD,* 121–27.

[6]*IDRD,* 5–6. On American Hellenism, see especially Deborah Jowitt, *Time and the Dancing Image* (New York: William Morrow, 1988), 80–81; on Isadora, chapter 2, "The Search for Motion."

[7]The words are taken from a poem of Joseph Duncan, "Intaglio: Lines on a Beautiful Greek Antique," first published in Bret Harte's *Outcroppings* (1865) and reprinted in *AOD,* 144.

[8]Kenneth Starr, *Americans and the California Dream, 1850–1915* (New York: Oxford University Press, 1973), chapter 12, "An American Mediterranean."

[9]*ML,* 19.

[10]See Ann Louise Wagner, *Adversaries of Dance: From Puritans to the Present* (Urbana: University of Illinois Press, 1997), 19, 366, and Lynne Conner, *Spreading the Gospel of Modern Dance: Newspaper Dance Criticism in the United States, 1850–1934* (Pittsburgh: University of Pittsburgh Press, 1997), *passim.*

[11]John Martin, *Introduction to the Dance* (New York: W. W. Norton & Co., 1939), 225.

[12]ID, "I See America Dancing," in *AOD,* 48–49.

[13]ID, "The Dance of the Future," in *AOD,* 56, 58. See also Deborah Jowitt, "The Impact of Greek Art on the Style and Persona of Isadora Duncan," Society of Dance History Scholars, *Proceedings,* 10th annual conference (1987), 195–201.

[14]*ML,* 14.

[15]ID, "The Great Source," in *AOD*. See also Allan Ross Macdougall, "Isadora Duncan and the Artists," in Paul Magriel, ed., *Isadora Duncan* (New York: Henry Holt, 1947), 35.

[16]*IDRD*, 168.

[17]ID, "I See America Dancing." "Beethoven created the dance in mighty rhythm. Wagner in sculptural form. Nietzsche in spirit. Nietzsche was the first dancing philosopher." Elsewhere, Isadora included Whitman and Rousseau among her "great precursors."

[18]Quoted in Dillon, "Looking for Isadora: A Lecture."

[19]ID, "The Great Source," 102.

[20]See Troy Kinney and Margaret West Kinney, *The Dance: Its Place in Art and Life* (New York: F. A. Stokes Co., 1914), chapter 11, "The Romantic Revolution": "Let it not be supposed that her ideal contemplated an imitation of natural actions, or had any relation to realism. *Natural qualities, not actions,* she proposed to *interpret, not imitate, by means of natural movements.* . . . From this it does not follow that uncultivated movements would be acceptable by the terms of the proposition. To raise an arm is a natural movement, hence acceptable to this code. To learn to raise it gracefully, a Duncanite would need to put in just as much time and thought as a ballet student, standards of grace being equal. It does, however, follow that any gravity-defying step would be unacceptable by the terms of the proposition. Without special training it cannot be executed, badly or at all; which, from the Duncan point of view, would throw it into the class of unnatural movements."

[21]*ML*, 175.

[22]*Christian Science Monitor,* February 16, 1946.

[23]*ML*, 21.

[24]*Christian Science Monitor,* February 16, 1946.

[25]M. R. Werner, *To Whom It May Concern: The Story of Victor Ilyitch Seroff* (New York: Cape and Smith, 1931), 260. In an unidentified clipping (Amsterdam, April 1905), Isadora remarks: "I persisted in asking my mother to let me attend ballet school. I learned diligently, but more and more I disliked the stiff and awkward forms and lifeless ballet movements" (Isadora Duncan Collection, folder 19, Scott Library, York University). In 1903, when she appeared at the Théâtre Sarah Bernhardt in Paris, she let it be said in program notes (DC) that she had studied ballet for five years.

[26]ID program notes (1905), quoted in Splatt, 16.

[27]Mulford collection, SF PALM.

[28]Quoted in Macdougall, 28.

[29]Florence Jacoby Arnstein, quoted in Dillon, "Looking for Isadora: A Lecture," also in Millicent Dillon, *After Egypt: Isadora Duncan and Mary Cassatt, A Dual Biography* (New York: Dutton, 1990), 164.

[30]Hertelendy, "Isadora's Childhood." Here the name is given as *Massbaum.*

[31]*New York Herald Tribune,* April 21, 1948.

[32]Referenced to "San Francisco Clippings," SF PALM, in Ann Daly, *Done Into Dance: Isadora Duncan in America* (Bloomington: Indiana University Press, 1995), 69.

[33]Elizabeth Duncan, "Autobiographical Note," at Deutsches Tanz-Archiv, Cologne, and in *IED*, 123 ff.

[34]Like Isadora, Raymond Duncan identified their Irish grandmother as being "key" to the development of the family ethic. "It was she who gave me the lesson of my life," Raymond declared: "She said, 'Raymond, you must never do what everybody does'" (quoted in Daly, *Done Into Dance,* 224 n. 47).

[35]See Constance Rourke, *Troupers of the Gold Coast, or the Rise of Lotta Crabtree* (New York: Harcourt, Brace & Co., 1928), and Misha Berson, *The San Francisco Stage, Part I: From Goldrush to Golden Spike, 1849–1869* (San Francisco: SF PALM Library and Museum Series, no. 2, Fall 1989).

[36]Stokes, 32.

[37]*Christian Science Monitor,* February 16, 1946.

[38]*New York Herald Tribune,* April 21, 1948.

[39]ID reports without further comment that Elizabeth "was brought up by our grandmother" and only "afterward came to live with us" (*ML*, 14). The Alameda County census in 1880 lists the Duncans at 764 Fourth Street in Oakland, but includes only "Dora (30), Gussie [Augustin] (7), Raymond (5) and Dora [Isadora] (3)," along with their "servant, Mary Ward (40)."

[40]News-clipping files on all the Duncans are at DC and SF PALM.

[41]Hertelendy, "Isadora's Childhood," quoting Augustin's daughter by Margherita Sargent, Andrea Duncan Ellis.

[42]Boynton-Quitzow family oral history, SF PALM.

[43]Blair, 19. See also Dorée Duncan, Carol Pratl, and Cynthia Splatt, eds., *Life into Art: Isadora Duncan and Her World*, text by Cynthia Splatt (New York: Norton: 1993), 26–27: "In fact [Duncan] seems to have maintained contact with the family over the years. . . . The house at 1365 8th Street in Oakland was [also] bought for them by their father." Isadora's half brothers and sisters doubted that she had seen him as seldom as she claimed.

[44]Elizabeth told the Associated Press at the time of Isadora's death: "Even when a child, Isadora grasped the slightest suggestion or remark about dancing with the comprehension of genius" ("Sister Collapses at News," dateline Vienna, September 16, 1927).

[45]*ML*, 22.

[46]*Cleveland Leader,* March 19, 1916.

[47]*San Francisco Chronicle,* September 2, 1894.

[48]From ID program notes, 1898, DC; in Walter Terry, *Isadora Duncan: Her Art, Her Life, Her Legacy* (New York: Dodd, Mead & Co. 1963), 19–20.

[49]ID quoted in *St. Louis Sunday Gazette,* December 26, 1902.

[50]See Elizabeth's "Autobiographical Note."

[51]Sorell, *Dance in Its Time,* 300.

[52]For Delsarte, see Ted Shawn, *Every Little Movement: A Book About François Delsarte* (New York: M. Witmark and Sons, 1954); Olga Maynard, "In Homage to François Delsarte: 1811–1871," in *Dance Magazine,* August 1971, 64–65; Dillon, *After Egypt,* 164–69; Daly, *Done Into Dance,* 122–32; and Nancy Lee Chalfa Ruyter, *Reformers and Visionaries: The Americanization of the Art of Dance* (New York: Dance Horizons, 1979), *passim.*

[53]Jowitt, *Time and the Dancing Image,* 80.

[54]ID to Walter Shaw, in Macdougall, 31.

[55]Dillon, *After Egypt,* 164. Florence's daughter Sülgwynn, a dancer, remembered that "Delsarte to us meant lifting the arms and hands slowly, very slowly, and coming down in many positions. . . . All the way up and all the way down as if your hands didn't end. As if they went way beyond. And there were neck and head movements too. There might have been [a book] but I never saw it. . . . Well, it just came, that's all, it was like eating" (Boynton-Quitzow oral history, SF PALM).

[56]Ibid., 167.

[57]ID in *The Director* (Portland, Me.), "Emotional Expression," March 1898, DC.

[58]CD 23 (January 15, 1905).

[59]See Margaret Thompson Drewal, "Isis and Isadora," Society of Dance History Scholars, *Proceedings,* 10th annual conference (1987), 185–94.

[60]Francis Galton, "Human Faculty," quoted in *The Darwin Papers* 1, no. 13 (Millennium Issue 2000).

[61]Kazin quoted in Robert Coe, *Dance in America* (New York: Dutton, 1985), 123.

[62]See Judy Levine, "Nineteenth-Century Scientism as an Organizer of Belief: The Role of Evolutionism in the Philosophy of Isadora Duncan," Society of Dance History Scholars, *Proceedings,* 10th annual conference (1987), 119–26.

[63]ID address to Berlin Press Club, 1903, DC, in Rosemont, 33.

[64]ID, "The Dance of the Future."

[65]Coe, *Dance in America,* 122; Misha Berson, *The San Francisco Stage, Part II, From Golden Spike to Great Earthquake, 1869–1906* (San Francisco: SF PALM Library and Museum Series, no. 4, February 1992), 109–14.

[66]ID, "I See America Dancing."

[67]ID, "Fragments and Thoughts," 135.

[68]Coe, *Dance in America,* 122.

[69]For Isadora and Whitman, see Ruth L. Bohan, "'I Sing the Body Electric': Isadora Duncan, Walt Whitman, and the Dance," in Ezra Greenspan, ed., *The Cambridge Companion to Walt Whitman* (Cambridge and New York: Cambridge University Press, 1995), 166–93; Harriet Johnson,

"Isadora Duncan and Walt Whitman — Their Infatuation with America," *Dance Observer,* February 1949, 20–21; and Ellen Graff, "Walt Whitman and Isadora Duncan: The Construction of a Personal Mythology," Society of Dance History Scholars, *Proceedings,* 10th annual conference, 1987, 177–84.

[70]ID, "The Dance of the Future," 56.

[71]Boynton-Quitzow family oral history, SF PALM.

[72]*ML,* 25. ID and her mother apparently also borrowed money from the Treadwells and "Grandma Young," a German friend in San Francisco who had predicted that Isadora would become "another Fanny Elssler," the Romantic ballerina. "My grandfather sold some of their antiques, lovely things, to raise money for them. . . . I guess they had a lot of friends who would help them" (Sülgwynn Quitzow in Boynton-Quitzow family oral history, SF PALM). Isadora told Oszkár Beregi, her first lover, that she had sold popcorn on the street to raise money for her fare.

[73]Charles Caldwell Dobie quoted in Macdougall, 28.

[74]ID notebook (May 11, 1902), DC.

Chapter 3: Flying Eastward

[1]For the World's Columbian Exposition, see John E. Findling, *Historical Dictionary of World's Fairs and Expositions, 1851–1988* (New York: Greenwood Press, 1990), 122–32, and Steven Watson, *Strange Bedfellows: The First American Avant-Garde* (New York: Abbeville Press, 1991), 12–13.

[2]ID to Paul Kennaday, May 12, 1925, DC.

[3]See "Duncan Dance Adds to Fame," *Chicago Journal,* December 1, 1908, which confirms much of ID's story of "tramping the fashionable streets of Chicago, going from door to door while trying to sell old laces. . . . She was a timid girl [sic] and suffered keenly at the rebuffs of maids and butlers." ID is quoted here on dancing at the Roof Garden: "There's no use trying to live it down! It just will out! It *is* out!"

[4]ID to Paul Kennaday, op. cit.

[5]*ML,* 26. ID on Chicago in *ML,* 25–32.

[6]*Chicago Tribune,* November 29, 1908.

[7]*ML,* 27.

[8]*Chicago Tribune,* November 29, 1908.

[9]For Martha Holden, see Albert Parry, *Garrets and Pretenders: A History of Bohemianism in America* (New York: Covici-Friede, 1933), 182–83, 187.

[10]*ML,* 28–29.

[11]"Duncan Dance Adds to Fame."

[12]Nesta Macdonald, "Isadora Reexamined: Lesser-Known Aspects of the Great Dancer's Life, Part I," *Dance Magazine,* July 1977.

[13]"Legs in Disfavor. Why Did Some New York Women Leave the Omar Show? Was It Envy or Modesty?" undated, unidentified news clipping (New York, 1899), DC.

[14]*ML,* 29–30.

[15]Ibid., 30.

[16]Undated, unidentified news clipping, DC.

[17]*ML,* 31–32.

[18]Diana Forbes-Robertson, *My Aunt Maxine* (New York: Viking, 1964), 79. Forbes-Robertson was a daughter of the great British actor Johnston Forbes-Robertson and Gertrude Elliott, whose sister, Maxine Elliott, spent a brief but memorable season as Daly's resident ingenue in 1895, just before Isadora joined the company.

[19]ID to Paul Kennaday, op. cit.

[20]Don B. Wilmeth and Rosemary Cullen, eds., *Plays by Augustin Daly* (Cambridge: Cambridge University Press, 1984), 17.

[21]She was billed, indeed, only once, as "Sara" Duncan. ID at Daly's in *ML,* 33–41.

[22]*ML,* 34. See also Marvin Felheim, *The Theater of Augustin Daly, An Account of the Late Nineteenth Century Stage* (Cambridge: Harvard University Press, 1956), 213. *Miss Pygmalion* was written by Michel Carré *fils* in collaboration with May, who used the nom de plume of Jean Herbert. Sometimes called "Jeanne" May, she was described by the *New York Times* (November 19, 1895) as "highly esteemed in Paris as an actress, and especially as a nimble, saucy, conscienceless Pierrôt."

[23]*ML*, 35.

[24]*New York Times*, November 19, 1895.

[25]Note that the pantomime of the era was not the solo art it became, but a form of direct theatrical narrative — formal, stylized, and comically broad in its movements.

[26]*ML*, 35–36.

[27]Ibid., 34–35.

[28]*New York Times*, March 1, 1896.

[29]*ML*, 36.

[30]Daly's *Dream* reviewed in *New York Times*, April 14, 1895.

[31]*ML*, 37.

[32]*San Francisco Examiner* (ca. May 17, 1896), SF PALM; in Rather, 39.

[33]*ML*, 37.

[34]Ibid., 41.

[35]*New York Times*, September 10, 1896.

[36]*ML*, 41.

[37]*New York World*, December 16, 1900, DC.

[38]*ML*, 40–41

[39]ID quoted in *Musical America*, September 4, 1909.

[40]*ML*, 42.

[41]See the program for this concert in the Nevin collection, Center for American Music, Stephen Foster Memorial Library, University of Pittsburgh.

[42]*The Director*, October–November 1898, DC.

[43]*New York Herald*, February 20, 1898.

[44]Kay Bardsley, "The Duncans at Carnegie Hall," *Ballet Review* 19, no. 3 (Fall 1991), 85–96.

[45]ID, "Fragments and Thoughts," 129.

[46]Terry, *Isadora Duncan*, 19.

[47]Macdonald, "Isadora Reexamined."

[48]Daly, *Done Into Dance*, 71.

[49]In 1908, during ID's first American tour as a solo dancer, Henry Taylor Parker wrote in the *Boston Evening Transcript* (undated [December 1908], DC): "Whether Isadora ever studied the classical technique of the ballet is not easy to learn. . . . At least, in the nineties, when she was one of the dancing girls at Daly's Theatre, she must have learned something of the way of ordinary stage dancing. Doubtless they trained her muscles to their present perfect obedience, doubtless they gave her something of her present skill to hide all trace of mechanism; and most surely of all they taught her much to avoid."

[50]Ann Daly cites Bonfanti's immortal retort: "Isadora Duncan? . . . Isadora Donkey! That is not dancing, whatever enthusiasts may call it" Daly, *Done Into Dance*, 39.

[51]"Legs in Disfavor."

[52]"A Soulful Function," undated, unidentified clipping (1899), DC.

[53]"Emotional Expression," *New York Herald*, February 20, 1898.

[54]"The Dance and Philosophy," *New York Times*, February 16, 1898.

[55]*New York Post* (1898), DC.

[56]With his wife, actress Cissie Loftus, McCarthy also helped introduce Isadora to London society when she returned to England in 1899. It may be that they had met there the summer before: there is evidence that Isadora was also in England in July 1898.

[57]"Legs in Disfavor."

[58]Gertrude Norman, "Isadora Duncan and Her Greek Barefoot Dances," *Theatre Magazine*, ca. 1905, DC. Norman saw Isadora's *Rubáiyát* in New York in 1899.

[59]For Newport and its hostesses, see Richard O'Connor, *The Golden Summer* (New York: Putnam, 1974); Cleveland Amory, *The Last Resorts* (New York: Harper and Brothers, 1948); and Lloyd Morris, *Postscript to Yesterday* (New York: Random House, 1947), 3–33.

[60]*ML*, 43.

[61]Morris, *Postscript to Yesterday*, 16.

[62]Amory, *The Last Resorts*, 217.

[63]Irma Duncan Rogers to Allan Ross Macdougall, February 26, 1955, DC.

[64]*ML*, 43.

[65]Edith Wharton, *A Backward Glance* (New York: Appleton-Century, 1934), 321–22.

[66]A telegram at SF PALM from sculptor Gutzon Borglum, dated October 20, 1898, and presumably addressed to the Duncans, reads: ALL LOST BODIES IDENTIFIED BURIED PERSONALS HELD POWER ATTORNEY NEEDED. . . . Borglum became a friend of Isadora's in London on one of her early trips there. See Willadene Price, *Gutzon Borglum, Artist and Patriot* (New York: Rand McNally, 1961), 49, quoting Borglum's brother Auguste on a party in London: "There were many elegantly dressed ladies and gentlemen. They had come to see a talented young dancer from California named Isadora Duncan perform. I must say she was a real success. She danced barefooted with complete abandon but so beautifully that many of Gutzon's staid British guests engaged her right then and there to perform at various functions."

[67]*ML*, 44.

[68]*Broadway Magazine,* June 1899, DC.

[69]"A Soulful Function."

[70]*ML*, 46.

[71]Marie-Louise de Meeus, "A Star Danced," *The Cornhill Magazine* 72 (May 1932), 546–47.

[72]*ML*, 44–45.

[73]*New York Times,* March 18, 1899. At the start of this account, the *Times* confirmed that "the Misses Isadora and Elizabeth" Duncan had assisted their mother in the rescue; the coolheaded maid's name was not given, only that she was in the employ of a Mrs. Edgar.

[74]Ibid. See also Raymond Duncan to the *New York Sun,* February 6, 1947: "[We] were living at the Windsor, where we also had a large salon on the ground floor with a special entrance on 47th Street. During the fire Elizabeth, who had a children's dancing class at that hour, leading her thirty little girls to the 47th Street door, found it locked, and then with great calm and courage led the children through smoke and flames to the Fifth Avenue door and saved them. This fire, where we lost everything we had, was the reason of our leaving for Europe." It no doubt irritated the family in later years to see only Isadora's name mentioned in this heroic context.

[75]*New York Herald,* March 18, 1899.

[76]*ML*, 47–48.

Chapter 4: London

[1]*ML*, 49. For ID in London, see *ML*, 48–65.

[2]Ibid., 52.

[3]Ibid., 53.

[4]Ibid., 54.

[5]Ibid., 59.

[6]ID, "The Dance of the Future."

[7]For Stella Campbell, see Margot Peters, *Mrs. Pat: The Life of Mrs. Patrick Campbell* (New York: Knopf, 1984).

[8]*ML*, 60–61.

[9]W. Graham Robertson, *Time Was* (London: Hamish Hamilton, 1931), 46.

[10]Wilfrid Blunt, *England's Michelangelo: A Biography of George Frederic Watts, O. M., R. A.* (London: Hamish Hamilton, 1975), 219.

[11] Robertson, *Time Was,* 208.

[12]ID, "Fragments and Thoughts," 140.

[13]Alice Comyns Carr quoted in Nesta Macdonald, "Isadora Reexamined (Part II)," *Dance Magazine,* August 1977. Comyns Carr was a great friend of Ellen Terry (Penelope Fitzgerald, *Edward Burne-Jones* [London: Michael Joseph, 1967], 166).

[14]*The Times* (London), March 17, 1900.

[15]*The Stage* (1900), in Macdonald, "Isadora Reexamined, Part II." Copies of Benson programs in Isadora Duncan Collection, Scott Library, York University.

[16]J. C. Trewin, *Benson and the Bensonians* (London: Barrie and Rockliff, 1960), 109.

[17]*ML*, 65.

[18]John Fuller-Maitland, *A Door-Keeper of Music* (London: John Murray, 1929), 202–03. The relevant passage in Fuller-Maitland's autobiography, eternally cited by dance historians, reads: "It was luckily my place to notice her performances, and I ventured to [hint] that it would be an improvement if she would dance, not to poems (she used to announce that she would dance 'to an idyll of *Theocrates*') but to good music, and specially mentioned the waltzes of Chopin. She introduced herself to me and asked me to recommend music that she could illustrate in her art. I told her how anxious I was to have the *rubato* of Chopin carried out in the dance; and she came and went through one or two of the Chopin pieces until she could get the right elasticity of rhythm." Early reviews in New York make plain, however, that she had been working on dances from Chopin since 1898, at least; apart from his own account, published after Isadora's death, there is no evidence that Fuller-Maitland had any influence on her dancing at all. His review of Isadora's second New Gallery concert (*Times* [London], July 6, 1900), remarks that "almost all attempt to illustrate well-known stories or poems was dispensed with, and the reading, which has been felt as a wholly unnecessary and tiresome addition, was left out altogether." Fuller-Maitland was a member of the committee that sponsored Isadora at the New Gallery.

[19]Karl Federn, "Nach Fünf und Zwanzig Jahren," preface to *Der Tanz der Zukunft* (*The Dance of the Future*) (Jena, Germany: 1929), English translation in *DD*, 35.

[20]Undated, unidentified clipping (London), DC.

[21]Elizabeth Kendall, *Where She Danced: The Birth of American Art Dance* (Berkeley: University of California Press, 1979), 64–65.

[22]*New York Tribune*, May 7, 1899, DC; Macdougall, 46.

[23]Norman, "Isadora Duncan and Her Greek Barefoot Dances."

[24]Federn, "Nach Fünf und Zwanzig Jahren."

[25]Quoted in Jill Silverman, "André Levinson and Isadora Duncan," *Ballet Review* 6, no. 4 (1977–78).

[26]ID, "The Dance of the Greeks," in *AOD*, 93.

[27]*The Lady*, August 2, 1900, DC.

[28]Marie-Louise de Meeus, "A Star Danced," *The Cornhill Magazine* 72, May 1932, 545.

[29]Ella Hepworth Dixon, *"As I Knew Them": Sketches of People I Have Met on the Way* (London: Hutchinson, 1930), 168.

[30]*ML*, 62–63.

[31]ID to Grant Duff Douglas Ainslie, undated, Douglas Ainslie Papers, Harry Ransom Humanities Research Center, University of Texas, Austin.

[32]*ML*, 56–57.

[33]ID letters to Ainslie, all undated, Austin.

Chapter 5: Paris

[1]*ML*, 67–68. For ID in Paris, see *ML*, 66–93.

[2]Ibid., 105–06.

[3]Ibid., 100–01.

[4]Roatcap, *Raymond Duncan*, 11.

[5]*ML*, 66–67. See "Raymond Duncan the Executive," *Dance Magazine*, February 1930: "It is naturally useless to speculate whether or no Isadora would have been Isadora without Raymond. But the facts are that throughout her formative period it was Raymond who was continually at her side, excavating for her the conception of a return to the beautiful simplicity of ancient Greek life as he saw it and instilling in her, for inspiration, the figures of Greek statuary which he studied with greatest care."

[6]*ML*, 80. ID's dance notes in Irma Duncan Collection, folder 141, DC. She inscribes from Descartes: *"Ne cherchez pas ce qu'on a écrit et pensé avant vous, mais sachez-vous en tenir à ce que vous reconnaissez vous-même pour évident."*

[7]ID, "The Great Source," in *AOD*, 101. Also in draft, with variations, DC.

[8]For the Paris Exposition and the Loie Fuller pavilion, see Martin Battersly, *The World of Art Nouveau* (London: Arlington, 1968).

[9]*ML*, 95.

[10]Richard Kraus and Sarah Chapman, *History of the Dance in Art and Education* (New York: Prentice-Hall, 1980), 125.

[11]*ML*, 69.

[12]There are a number of biographies of Rodin in English. I have consulted Ruth Butler, *Rodin: The Shape of Genius* (New Haven: Yale University Press, 1993); Frederic V. Grunfeld, *Rodin: A Biography* (New York: Henry Holt, 1987); Anita Leslie, *Rodin, Immortal Peasant,* with an introduction by Sir John Lavery (New York: Prentice-Hall, 1937); and Denys Sutton, *Triumphant Satyr: The World of Auguste Rodin* (London: Country Life, 1966).

[13]*ML*, 90.

[14]ID to Douglas Ainslie, December 8, 1900, Austin.

[15]*ML*, 87.

[16]*New York World,* December 16, 1900.

[17]Undated, unidentified clipping, DC.

[18]Michele Sarde, *Colette* (New York: William Morrow, 1980), 135.

[19]*ML*, 70–71.

[20]Peter Quennell, *Customs and Characters: Contemporary Portraits* (London: Weidenfeld and Nicolson, 1982), 126.

[21]*ML*, 77–78.

[22]*New York Journal & Advertiser,* June 8, 1901, DC.

[23]*ML*, 71–72.

[24]Mrs. W. A. Bradley to Liliane Zeigel, March 25, 1963, Steegmuller collection, folder 72, DC.

[25]CD 112, undated (Warsaw, December 1906).

[26]*ML*, 73–74.

[27]For Winaretta Singer, see Michael de Cossart, *The Food of Love: Princesse Edmond de Polignac* (London: Hamish Hamilton, 1978); Ruth Brandon, *The Dollar Princesses* (New York: Knopf, 1980); and *A Capitalist Romance: Singer and the Sewing Machine* (Philadelphia: Lippincott, 1977).

[28]Louise Collis, *Impetuous Heart: The Story of Ethel Smyth* (London: William Kimber, 1984), 86.

[29]*ML*, 80.

[30]Ibid., 90–91.

[31]For Carrière, see Robert James Bantens, *Eugène Carrière: His Work and Influence* (Ann Arbor: UMI Research Press, 1983).

[32]*ML*, 91–92; Yorska quoted in *ML*, 92.

[33]*ML*, 74–75.

[34]Ibid., 75.

[35]Joseph Mazo, *Prime Movers: The Makers of Modern Dance in America* (Princeton, N.J.: 1977), 42.

[36]*ML*, 75.

[37]"Fragments and Thoughts," *AOD,* 142.

[38]John Martin, "Isadora Duncan," in *America Dancing: The Background and Personalities of the Modern Dance* (New York: Dodge Publishing Co., 1936), 141, 133.

[39]John Martin, "Isadora Duncan and Basic Dance," in Magriel, *Isadora Duncan.*

[40]ID, "The Philosopher's Stone of Dancing," in *AOD,* 52.

[41]ID, "The Dance in Relation to Tragedy," *Theatre Arts Monthly,* October 1927, 757, in *ML,* 76.

[42]See, for example, Anna Kisselgoff's interview with Paul Taylor in the *New York Times,* March 4, 2001: "So why is Mr. Taylor the ballet world's most popular modern-dance choreographer? Possibly because his dances have a remarkable momentum that recalls ballet's linked phrases. Yet within this continuum, there is hardly a ballet step as such, and it isn't hard for Mr. Taylor to describe what he dislikes about ballet technique. 'It's the movement from the hands and the periphery. It makes the ballet dancer look decorative, like a hollow person,' he says matter-of-factly, as if there can be no dispute."

[43]Martin, "Isadora Duncan."

[44]Irma Duncan Collection, folder 141 (ID notebook), DC.

[45]Princess der Ling, *Lotos Petals* (New York: Dodd, Mead, 1930), 246.

[46]"Poetry Rather than Millions," *New England Magazine* (Boston), June 23, 1901, DC.

[47]Der Ling, *Lotos Petals*, 240–41.

[48]Desti, 22–32. Mary was Canadian by birth, born in 1871 in Quebec City.

[49]Ibid., 26.

[50]Sturges, 21.

[51]Desti, 32. Mary added in a private memorandum: "Isadora was alcoholic always" (Mary Desti Papers, Collection 2055, Department of Special Collections, University Research Library, University of California, Los Angeles).

[52]Vincent Cronin, *Paris on the Eve: 1900–1914* (New York: St. Martin's Press, 1990), 18.

[53]Desti, 31.

[54]Der Ling, *Lotos Petals*, 249–50.

[55]ML, 86.

[56]Ibid., 94.

[57]Fuller's ms. draft, *Fifteen Years of a Dancer's Life*, DC.

[58]ML, 94.

[59]Richard Nelson Current and Marcia Ewing Current, *Loie Fuller: Goddess of Light* (Boston: Northeastern University Press, 1997), 5.

[60]Gabriele Brandstetter and Brygida Maria Ochaim, *Loïe Fuller: Tanz, Licht-Spiel, Art Nouveau* (Freiburg: Rombach, 1989), 54–57. Fuller's school was founded in 1901, three years before Isadora's.

[61]Galley sheets of excisions in *ML*, DC. ID's full description of Fuller and her girls, along with other of her comments about sex and sexuality, was published in the French edition, *Ma Vie* (Paris: Gallimard, 1928).

[62]ML, 95.

[63]Fuller's ms. draft, *Fifteen Years of a Dancer's Life*.

[64]According to Fuller, "Napoleon was born great, and so was Paulina Metternich" (ibid).

[65]Fuller never used Isadora's name in her account.

[66]Fuller's ms. draft, *Fifteen Years of a Dancer's Life*.

[67]An AP report at the time of Isadora's death informed that the imperial minister of arts and education had been present at her Hotel Bristol concert, along with Klimt: "When some days later her [dancing] unclothed in public was announced, Vienna police felt constrained to permit it, fearing to disavow the Minister of Education. Berlin and other cities in Europe then followed suit" (dateline Nice, September 15, 1927, DC).

[68]Fuller's ms. draft, *Fifteen Years of a Dancer's Life*.

[69]Unidentified clipping, May 13, 1903, DC.

[70]ML, 99.

[71]Fuller's ms. draft, *Fifteen Years of a Dancer's Life*.

[72]ML, 96–98. Despite their differences, ID attended Fuller's opening in New York in November 1909 as a guest of honor, along with "Salome" dancer Gertrude Hoffman. Fuller died in 1928, and was able to read ID's praise of her work in *ML*.

[73]For ID in Hungary, see Gedeon Dienes, "Isadora Duncan in Hungary," Society of Dance History Scholars, *Proceedings*, 10th annual conference (1987), 147–58, DC. A collection of news clippings obtained from the Orzságos Szinhaztorteneti Museum in Budapest, with accompanying English translations, is in the Macdougall Collection, folder 28, DC. A note affirms that it "seems to be complete as far as this short section of Miss Duncan's career is concerned."

[74]ML, 101.

[75]Oszkár Beregi, "Isadora," translated by András Török, in *Hungarian Quarterly* 40, no. 154 (Summer 1999).

[76]In *ML*, ID remembered that she had seen Beregi first as Romeo, and only later as Antony.

[77]Beregi, "Isadora."

[78]Uz Idôk (Budapest), April 20, 1902, DC. It may be that this story was invented for publicity purposes.

[79]Norman, "Isadora Duncan and Her Greek Barefoot Dances"; *ML*, 100.

[80]Margherita Duncan, "Isadora," in *AOD*, 23.

[81]ML, 104; ID notebook in Irma Duncan Collection, folder 141, DC. The words are in Hun-

garian, written down at Isadora's request, so that she could express her feelings to her lover in his own tongue. She did the same in Russia later with Sergei Esenin.

Chapter 6: Germany

[1]ID narrative of Budapest and Beregi in *ML*, 99–107. See also Macdougall, 69–70.

[2]*ML*, 105.

[3]Ibid., 101.

[4]Ibid., 105.

[5]Ibid., 102–03; galley proofs with excisions, DC.

[6]This was Isadora's own interpretation of Elizabeth's arrival.

[7]Beregi, "Isadora."

[8]Desti, 33.

[9]ID notebook, DC.

[10]Dienes, "Isadora Duncan in Hungary."

[11]Desti, 33.

[12]*ML*, 105–06.

[13]Beregi, "Isadora."

[14]Budapest press clippings, DC.

[15]Beregi, "Isadora."

[16]*ML*, 107.

[17]Dienes, "Isadora Duncan in Hungary."

[18]*ML*, 107.

[19]Beregi, "Isadora."

[20]Passages combined from *ML*, 108, 137, 114.

[21]Ibid., 108–09. ID wrote famously: "At that Villa in Abbazia [Opatija], there was a palm tree before our windows. . . . I used to notice its leaves trembling in the early morning breeze, and from them I created in my dance that light fluttering of the arms, hands and fingers, which has been so much abused by my imitators; for they forget to go to the original source and contemplate the movements of the palm tree, to receive them inwardly before giving them outwardly."

[22]Allan Ross Macdougall, "Isadora Duncan and the Artists," in Magriel, *Isadora Duncan*.

[23]*St. Louis Sunday Gazette*, December 26, 1902, DC.

[24]ID on Munich in *ML*, 110–11. See also Wolfgang Bode, "Isadora in München, 1902," *Gymnastik und Rhythmus* 9, no. 4 (October–December 1977).

[25]*St. Louis Sunday Gazette*, December 26, 1902, DC.

[26]Ibid.

[27]Bode, "Isadora Duncan in München."

[28]Quoted in Irma Duncan, *Isadora Duncan, Pioneer in the Art of Dance* (New York: New York Public Library, 1959).

[29]*ML*, 96, 112.

[30]Max Osborn, *Der Bunte Spiegel: Erinnerungen aus dem Kunst-, Kultur- und Geistesleben der Jahre 1890 bis 1933* (New York: Verlag Felix Krause, 1945), 169–70.

[31]*New York Times*, January 11, 1903.

[32]*San Francisco Examiner*, February 25, 1903, SF PALM.

[33]ID on Berlin 1903, *ML*, 114–15.

[34]"Wins Plaudits Far from Home," *San Francisco Call*, February 25, 1903, SF PALM.

[35]Press clippings, DC.

[36]ID, "The Dancer and Nature," in *AOD*, 66.

[37]See "Interviewing Isadora," *New York Morning Telegraph*, February 14, 1915, DC: "We women can get anything in the world we want without the vote. We doubtless wouldn't keep our own names even if we had the right of franchise. We start in life with a man's name — we marry and take another man's name. Now, Isadora belongs to me — Duncan is my father's."

[38]ID, "The Dance of the Future."

[39]"The Dance of the Future" was assembled from various of ID's notes and written in collaboration with Raymond Duncan.

[40]See *The Oxford History of Western Philosophy* (New York: Oxford University Press, 1994), 217.

[41]ID, "The Dance of the Future."

[42]ID to Doublas Ainslie, undated, Austin.

[43]Mabel Dodge Luhan, *Intimate Memories,* vol. 3, "Movers and Shakers" (New York: Harcourt, Brace & Co., 1936), 320.

[44]"Isadora Duncan, zooals zij in werkelijkheid was," interview with Marie Kist, undated, unidentified clipping (1936), Isadora Duncan Collection, folder 20, Scott Library, York University.

[45]Maria-Theresa quoted in Loewenthal, 18–19.

[46]*ML,* 123.

[47]*Le Temps* (Paris), September 16, 1927.

[48]*ML,* 116, 141.

[49]Mabel Dolmetsch, *Personal Recollections of Arnold Dolmetsch* (London: Routledge & Paul, 1958), 44–47. In another account, published after her death and sourced to an unnamed "friend," Isadora performed a whole evening of dances without music at the Sarah Bernhardt, after her orchestra walked out, at the demand of her audience: *"Isadora s'avança sur le proscenium, s'excusant de ne pouvoir danser. 'Dansez quand même!' Et elle dansa, deux heures durant, sans musique. Et elle fut prodigieuse"* (*Annales politiques et littéraires,* October 1, 1927, 322).

[50]Quoted in unidentified, undated news clipping (Paris 1903), DC.

[51]Macdougall, 75–76.

[52]Butler, *Rodin: The Shape of Genius,* 420.

[53]Kathleen, Lady Kennet (Kathleen Bruce), *Self-Portrait of an Artist* (London: John Murray, 1949), 44.

[54]Mario Amaya, "Isadora and the Sculptor," in *The Dance in Art* 7 (August 1962), 32, DC.

[55]DC. In addition, Rodin wrote: *"Miss Duncan a proprement unifié la vie en la danse. Elle est naturelle sur la scène où on l'est si rarement. Elle rend la danse sensible à la ligne et elle est simple comme l'antique qui est le synonyme de la beauté."* Also quoted in Macdougall, 76.

[56]Sutton, *Triumphant Satyr,* 103.

[57]Grunfeld, *Rodin,* 461–62 n.

[58]Unidentified news clipping, July 27, 1903, DC.

[59]Georges Delaquys quoted in Loewenthal, 130.

Chapter 7: Myth

[1]*ML,* 123. Quotes from ID about the Greek adventure are from *ML,* 115–35, unless otherwise noted.

[2]Kennet, *Self-Portrait of an Artist,* 71. See also Louisa Young, *A Great Task of Happiness: The Life of Kathleen Scott* (London: Macmillan, 1995).

[3]Interview with Raymond Duncan, *Philadelphia Daily News,* January 28, 1958, DC.

[4]Macdougall, 81–82.

[5]Luhan, *Intimate Memories,* 333.

[6]*New York World,* November 15, 1903, DC. According to an unidentified report, datelined "Paris, Dec. 12 [1903]," Isadora planned to dance in the new Olympic stadium in Athens, "when the Olympian games are next held." It is evident from her letters and other accounts that she hoped to open her school in Greece. A program survives (DC) of her *Chopin-Soirée* in Athens on November 28, 1903. See also Macdougall, 81–82.

[7]Eleusis was the site of the mystery cult of Demeter and the spiritual center of the classical world.

[8]*New York World,* November 15, 1903, DC.

[9]In Greek mythology, Hymettos belonged to Hephaestus, god of the forge, while the river that originates there, Ilissós (Ilissus), was sacred to Aphrodite. The mountain was known for its birds and honey and its spectacular view of Athens.

[10]Kennet, *Self-Portrait of an Artist,* 72–75.

[11]ID, "The Parthenon," in *AOD,* 64–65.

[12]The Greek boys' "professor" was Panajiotis Tzanneas.

[13]*ML,* 136–37.

[14]Ibid., 139–40.

[15]June Rose, *Marie Stopes and the Sexual Revolution* (London and Boston: Faber and Faber, 1992), 20.

[16]Percival Pollard in "The Regnant Wave of Sensational Dance," *New York Times*, August 23, 1908.

[17]*ML*, 141.

[18]*Jugend*, no. 13 (1904), 257. This same issue contained an item about a theater cloakroom attendant in Munich who watched Isadora one night from the wings and reported to her friends that she had no idea what the dancer was doing. "I don't know," said the bewildered girl. "When I looked in, she seemed to be catching flies."

[19]Louis Laloy, "Isadora Duncan et la danse nouvelle," in *La Revue Mondiale* 4, no. 10 (1904), 249–53, DC.

[20]Loewenthal, 131.

[21]Macdougall, 87.

[22]ID on Bayreuth in *ML*, 142–60.

[23]Paul Busching in *Die Musik* 3, no. 2, 382, in Macdougall Collection, folder 19, DC.

[24]Seroff, 63.

[25]George R. Marek, *Cosima Wagner* (New York: Harper & Row, 1981), 235, 225.

[26]Wolfgang Wagner, *ACTS: The Autobiography of Wolfgang Wagner* (London: Weidenfeld and Nicolson, 1994), 18.

[27]*ML*, 143–44.

[28]Letter from Gertrud Strobel, Richard-Wagner-Archiv, Bayreuth, to Allan Ross Macdougall, November 4, 1955, DC, enclosing excerpts from Christian Ebersberger, "Drei Generationen im Hause Wahnfried" (privately printed, Bayreuth).

[29]Marek, *Cosima Wagner,* 234.

[30]Desti, 35.

[31]*ML*, 142.

[32]Marek, *Cosima Wagner,* 229.

[33]*ML*, 145.

[34]Sturges, 29.

[35]Desti, 34. Ibid. 34–46 for Mary's narrative of Bayreuth.

[36]Ibid., 36.

[37]Seroff, 64.

[38]Sturges, 20.

[39]*ML*, 147. ID on Thode in *ML*, 148–50, 158–60.

[40]Douglas Sutherland, *Twilight of the Swans* (London: New English Library, 1974), 279.

[41]EGC to Ellen Terry, March 17, 1905, Gordon Craig miscellaneous manuscripts, gift of Fredrika Blair Hastings, DC.

[42]*ML*, 149.

[43]Desti, 39.

[44]Sturges, 31–32.

[45]Daniel Gasman, *The Scientific Origins of National Socialism* (London: Macdonald, 1971), xiii–xiv.

[46]*New York Times*, August 10, 1919 (Haeckel obituary).

[47]Heinrich Schmidt, director of the Ernst Haeckel Archive, Jena, "The Riddle of the Universe and the Dancer: Isadora Duncan and Ernst Haeckel," Macdougall Collection, folder 34, DC.

[48]*ML*, 153–54.

[49]Schmidt, "The Riddle of the Universe and the Dancer."

[50]Busching in *Die Musik*, edited in Macdougall, 93.

[51]Undated, unidentified clipping ("1908"), DC: "On the other hand, the majority [sic] of critics in Germany laughed at the maid, and at times even threatened to have her dancing in public stopped."

[52]*ML*, 158.

[53]Ibid., 156.

[54]Frederic Spots, *Bayreuth,* 109. *IED,* 153 ff.

[55]*ML,* 159–60.

[56]Ibid., 182–83.

[57]Steegmuller Collection, folder 71, DC; in Steegmuller, 354.

Chapter 8: Teddy and Topsy

[1]CD 289 ("January, 1917"). ID's love affair with Gordon Craig has been narrated many times, not just in biographies but in plays, films, dance works, and a splendid collection of their intimate letters, edited, "with a connecting text," by Francis Steegmuller as *"Your Isadora": The Love Story of Isadora Duncan and Gordon Craig* (New York: Random House and the New York Public Library, 1974). Steegmuller's book takes its title from the customary closing of Isadora's letters to Craig, which Craig sold to the NYPL in 1962, along with complementary material relating to their association: notebooks, sketches, and narrative drafts. A separate register, with an index to the letters, is available at DC. I have cited the letters by catalog number.

[2]*ML,* 183.

[3]The first line of *Book Topsy* (see note 52 below); in Steegmuller, 21.

[4]EGC to Kessler, December 13, 1904, in L. M. Newman, ed., *The Correspondence of Edward Gordon Craig and Count Harry Kessler, 1903–1937* (London: W. S. Maney & Son, 1995), 29.

[5]Craig's daybook in L. M. Newman to Francis Steegmuller, Steegmuller Collection, folder 20, DC.

[6]*ML,* 180. ID's account of their meeting drove Craig into a rage. "This cannot have been written by I.D.," he declared: "But of course she never wrote [it]. Her assistants when she was dead or her editor or publisher had it all written in so as to pad out the book to full size." That *My Life* was a forgery Craig insisted till he died. (See Steegmuller Collection, folder 46, containing photostats of Craig's annotations and ruminations on *ML.* Also Craig's correspondence with Mercedes de Acosta, Steegmuller Collection, folder 35.)

[7]For Craig's life and history, see especially EAC and Christopher Innes, *Edward Gordon Craig* (Cambridge: Cambridge University Press, 1983); for Craig and ID, see Steegmuller and Splatt; Arnold Rood, *Gordon Craig on Movement and Dance* (New York: Dance Horizons, 1977); and Irene Eyant-Confino, *Beyond the Mask: Gordon Craig, Movement and the Actor* (Carbondale, Ill.: Southern Illinois University Press, 1988).

[8]Steegmuller, 9.

[9]George Nash, *Edward Gordon Craig* (Imprint London, H. M. S. O., 1967).

[10]Steegmuller Collection, folder 22, miscellaneous, DC.

[11]Quoted in Macdougall Collection, miscellaneous notes, folder 29, DC.

[12]John Stokes, Michael Booth, and Susan Bassenett, *The Actress in Her Time* (Cambridge: Cambridge University Press, 1988), 117.

[13]Quoted in Joy Melville, "Ellen Terry," in *British Heritage,* August–September 1997.

[14]E. J. West, ed., *Shaw on Theatre* (New York: Hill and Wang, 1958), 206–07.

[15]From EGC, *Ellen Terry and Her Secret Self* (New York: E. P. Dutton, 1932), quoted in Nash, *Edward Gordon Craig,* 3.

[16]EGC to George Wolfe Plank, undated (ca. 1907), in George Plank Papers, Yale Collection of American Literature, Beinecke Rare Book and Manuscript Library, Yale University, folders 26–33 (1907–14).

[17]Steegmuller, 10.

[18]Ibid., 8–9.

[19]Ellen Terry to George Bernard Shaw, October 13, 1896, in Christopher St. John (Christabel Marshall), ed., *Ellen Terry and Bernard Shaw: A Correspondence* (New York: G. P. Putnam's Sons, 1931), 75.

[20]EAC, 99.

[21]Entry on Gordon Craig in *Chambers' Encyclopaedia,* extract in Steegmuller research files, Steegmuller Collection, folder 19, DC. I have chosen this description of Craig's work because it was written during his lifetime, after his ideas on stage design had begun to be accepted throughout Western theater.

[22]EAC, 198.

[23]EGC in *The Mask*, April 1908 (second issue).

[24]EAC, 199.

[25]Quoted in Kenneth Paul Shorey, "Edward Gordon Craig, 1872–1966," in *Ballet Review* 1, no. 5 (1966), 23–26.

[26]Steegmuller, 98.

[27]Daly, *Done Into Dance*, 136.

[28]EAC, 191–92; 189. See also Innes, *Edward Gordon Craig*, 116, and Dr. Renée Vincent, "The Influences of Isadora Duncan on the Designs of Edward Gordon Craig," in *Theatre Design & Technology* 34, no. 1 (Winter 1998), 37–48.

[29]*ML*, 183–86.

[30]See Steegmuller's correspondence with Robert Craig, September–October 1972, Steegmuller Collection, folder 56, and notes after meeting with Robert Craig, folder 58, DC. Ellen Terry added: "I considered Isadora too temperamental for your father, Bobs, and what is more no woman should fall in love with a perfectionist — ever."

[31]EGC, *The Theatre — Advancing* (Boston: Little, Brown and Co., 1919), 39.

[32]EAC, 20–21.

[33]Ibid., 83, 128–30.

[34]EGC, *Index*, 7.

[35]CD 255.

[36]Sir Bernard Miles to Francis Steegmuller, March 11, 1975, in Steegmuller Collection, "Miscellaneous" folder, DC.

[37]Nina Auerbach, *Ellen Terry, Player in Her Time* (New York: Norton, 1987), 348.

[38]Ellen Terry to George Bernard Shaw, October 13, 1896, in *Ellen Terry and Bernard Shaw*, 75.

[39]Melville, "Ellen Terry."

[40]EAC, 162.

[41]EGC to Kessler, October 18, 1903, in Newman, *The Correspondence of Edward Gordon Craig and Count Harry Kessler, 1903–1937*.

[42]Donald Oenslager, introduction to Arnold Rood, *Edward Gordon Craig, Artist of the Theater, 1872–1966: A Memorial Exhibition in the Amsterdam Gallery* (New York: New York Public Library, 1967), 6.

[43]EGC to George Plank, op. cit.

[44]Steegmuller, 14.

[45]EAC, 189.

[46]EGC, *The Theatre — Advancing*, 42.

[47]EAC, 189.

[48]*Index*, 256–59.

[49]*ML*, 181.

[50]The original of *Book Topsy* is in the Craig Collection at the Harry Ransom Humanities Research Center, University of Texas, Austin. Much of the contents are reprinted in Steegmuller (Chapter 3, "Appointments in Berlin: *Book Topsy*), 21–36. Other pages written by Craig about ID at different times are considered part of *Book Topsy* for purposes of classification, especially his addendum of 1943.

[51]See Steegmuller's correspondence with Donald Sinden, February–March 1976, in Steegmuller Collection, folder 11, DC.

[52]*Book Topsy*, in Steegmuller, 21–22.

[53]Blair, 96.

[54]Craig collection, BN; copies in Steegmuller Collection, folder 33, DC.

[55]*Index*, 262; adapted (with minor variations) from EGC, "Isadora Duncan: A BBC Radio Talk by Gordon Craig," in *The Listener*, June 5, 1952, and, with Craig's addenda, in Steegmuller, 359–63.

[56]Karl Federn, Isadora's unwitting accomplice in her escape with Craig, was at the time an almost constant presence in her life. It was Federn who had helped Isadora with her reading of Nietzsche in 1903 and who later went with her to Paris in her first attempt to conquer the public there. He was assisting her now with the plans for her new school in Grunewald, acting as aca-

demic adviser for the curriculum. Federn remembered her as "full of wit and high spirits, anxiously watched over by her suspicious mother, admired and even a bit feared by her brothers and sister."

[57]EGC, *Book Topsy,* in Steegmuller, 24–25.

[58]Donald Oenslager in Rood, *Edward Gordon Craig, Artist of the Theatre,* 6.

[59]In Steegmuller, 25–26.

[60]EAC, 193.

[61]EGC addendum to *Book Topsy* (1943), CD, in Steegmuller, 353.

[62]*Book Topsy,* in Steegmuller, 28.

[63]EGC addendum to *Book Topsy* (1943), CD, in Steegmuller, 353–54.

[64]*Book Topsy,* in Steegmuller, 28.

[65]ML, 183.

[66]EGC addendum to *Book Topsy* (1943), CD, in Steegmuller, 353.

[67]CD 1 ("December 19, '04 morning").

[68]*Book Topsy,* in Steegmuller, 29.

[69]CD 5 ("Dec. 23, 1904").

[70]CD 249.

[71]In Steegmuller, 36.

[72]CD 6.

Chapter 9: "Your Isadora"

[1]CD 7. ID on St. Petersburg in *ML,* 160–72.

[2]Sergei Diaghilev to W. A. Popert, quoted in Steegmuller, 40; in Macdougall, 101.

[3]Quoted by Archie Bell in *Cleveland News,* September 17, 1927.

[4]Diaghilev to Popert, in Macdougall, 101.

[5]Mathilde Kschessinska, *Dancing in Petersburg,* translated by Arnold Haskell (Garden City, N.Y.: Doubleday, 1961), 105. There are only so many ways to say this. MFR quotes Anna Pavlova on the same topic: "She came to Russia and brought freedom to us all" (MFR, "Isadora — The Dancer," in *Denishawn Magazine,* 1925, City Museum). John Martin: "She caused the ranks of the Imperial ballet to split asunder on her first visit to Russia and thus revitalized the whole medium of the ballet" (*New York Times,* January 8, 1928). Most convincingly, perhaps, Russian balletomane André Levinson: "All that a generation wished for or dreamed about in dance was accomplished thanks to her — or against her; never outside of her. . . . Because, by a miracle of faith, she had imprinted her seal on an entire epoch" (quoted in Jill Silverman, "André Levinson on Isadora Duncan," op. cit.). See Elizabeth Souritz, "ID's Influence on Dance in Russia," *Dance Chronicle* 18, no. 2 (1995), 281–91, and Kay Bardsley, "Isadora Duncan and the Russian Ballet," Society of Dance History Scholars, *Proceedings,* 11th annual conference (1988), 121–30.

[6]Debra Goldman, "Mothers and Fathers: A View of Isadora and Fokine," *Ballet Review* 6, no. 4 (1977–78), 33–43.

[7]Kinney and Kinney, *The Dance: Its Place in Art and Life,* 246–47.

[8]See Allan Ross Macdougall to Irma Duncan Rogers, November 20, 1955, DC.

[9]ML, 161–62.

[10]On this subject, and on all of ID's first Russian trip, see Steegmuller, 37–52 ("St. Petersburg"); Steegmuller Collection, research files, folders 1–14, DC; and Natalia Roslasleva, comp., "Isadora Duncan: Reviews and Materials Relating Primarily to Her Performances in St. Petersburg and Moscow," 1904–05, in Steegmuller research files, DC.

[11]ML, 162.

[12]CD 7.

[13]CD 8.

[14]CD 12.

[15]CD 11.

[16]CD 13.

[17]This notice was sent to newspapers all over Germany. See Hedwig Müller, "The Story of the Duncan School in Germany," in *AD,* 42.

[18]*Petersburg Gazette* (*Peterburgskaya Gazeta*), December 15, 1904, Steegmuller Collection, DC.

[19]Sorell, *Dance in Its Time*, 286–87.

[20]Prince Lieven, quoted in Macdougall, 100.

[21]Natalia Roslasleva to Francis Steegmuller, December 7, 1972, Steegmuller Collection, research files, folder 1. See also Goldman, "Mothers and Fathers: A View of Isadora and Fokine."

[22]Stefanida Dmitrievna Rudneva, untitled manuscript, [(S)*MGZM-Res. Rud S], DC.

[23]Steegmuller Collection, research files, folder 1, DC; in Steegmuller, 41–44.

[24]Ibid.; in Steegmuller, 44.

[25]Valerian Svetlov, "Isadora Duncan," in *Dancing Times*, December 1927, 327–28, 336, DC. In 1904 Svetlov was content to dismiss her as "just a new kind of Heinrich Schliemann," that is, presumably, a dazzling publicity stunt. See Steegmuller Collection, research files, folder 1, DC.

[26]Steegmuller Collection, research files, folder 1, DC; in Steegmuller, 43–44.

[27]Michel Fokine, *Fokine: Memoirs of a Ballet Master,* translated by Vitale Fokine, Anatoly Chujoy, ed. (Boston: Little, Brown and Co., 1961), 256.

[28]Lynn Garafola, *Diaghilev's Ballets Russes* (New York and Oxford: Oxford University Press, 1989), 40.

[29]ML, 172.

[30]CD 15.

[31]Natalia Roslasleva to Francis Steegmuller, November 16, 1972, quoting *Petersburg Gazette,* December 17, 1904, in Steegmuller Collection, research files, folder 1, DC.

[32]Typed extract from Margaret Wycherly, *As I Knew Them,* in Macdougall Collection, folder 37, DC. The story was told to Wycherly by Augustin Duncan's first wife, Sarah Whiteford.

[33]Splatt, 33.

[34]CD 17.

[35]ML, 164–66.

[36]Steegmuller Collection, research files, folder 1, DC; in Steegmuller, 47–48.

[37]CD 16.

[38]CD 18–19.

[39]CD 21.

[40]Steegmuller, 69.

[41]CD 26.

[42]*Index,* 267.

[43]CD 294, Elizabeth Duncan, annotated by Craig, June 15, 1907.

[44]ML, 186.

[45]Ibid., 187–88.

[46]CD 36 (March 16, 1905).

[47]Gertrude Stein, *The Autobiography of Alice B. Toklas,* in Carl Van Vechten, ed., *Selected Writings of Gertrude Stein* (New York: Vintage, 1972), 40–41.

[48]Ardée Duncan, *The Sole and the Thong* (privately printed, copy at SF PALM).

[49]Federn, "Nach Fünf und Zwanzig Jahren."

[50]CD 22.

[51]Splatt, 41–42.

[52]ID notebook (1905), DC.

[53]Steegmuller, 72, 63.

[54]EAC, 197.

[55]*Index,* 269.

[56]ID remarks that the Grunewald school was opened "with such speediness as marked everything else we did. . . . We acted exactly as though we were people in Grimms' fairy tales" (*ML,* 173).

[57]DD, 6; in *The Dance of the Future* (American edition, 1908), DC.

[58]Macdougall, 107.

[59]Interview with Maria-Theresa, undated, unidentified ("Dance Conversations," Don Oscar Becque), in Maria-Theresa clipping file, DC.

[60]Anna remembered that Isadora rejected her on sight and that she was saved by Augustin Duncan, who said, "You could not send back a child with such a smile" (*AD,* 28).

[61]"Isadora and Vanessa," Anna Duncan interview with Parker Tyler, *Ballet Review* 3, no. 1 (1969), 20–36.

[62]*Index,* 264.

[63]*DD,* 10–12.

[64]Ibid., 12–13. Craig confirmed Irma's recollection in correspondence with her, DC, and in *Index,* 270.

[65]Ibid., 13–19.

Chapter 10: Their Own Sweet Will

[1]*ML,* 173.

[2]*New York Herald,* February 20, 1898, DC.

[3]ID, "Movement Is Life," in *AOD,* 77.

[4]In a statement in 1922, ID declared: "I believe, as Jean-Jacques Rousseau did, that it is unnecessary to worry a child's brain during the first twelve years of its life. One should offer poetry, music, dancing, not book-learning, during that period. The spiritual experiences last a lifetime" (in Rosemont, 55). Rousseau had argued that most people never progress mentally past the age of twelve, and that it was therefore unnecessary to worry their brains at all.

[5]*ML,* 173.

[6]Ibid., 174.

[7]For Grunewald, see Kay Bardsley, "Isadora's First School," *Dance Research Collage* (CORD Dance Research Annual), 219–49; Loewenthal, 35–49; Müller, "The Story of the Duncan School in Germany" (also in *IED,* 88–121, as " 'Unser Tanz besteht wirklich nur aus der Schönheit der herrlichen Natur': Anna Duncans Wedegang in der Duncan-Schule"); and Amy Swanson, "Isadora Duncan: A propos de son enseignement et de sa filiation," *La recherche en danse,* no. 2, 1983, 63–74.

[8]*DD,* 18.

[9]Bardsley, "Isadora's First School," 234.

[10]Maria-Theresa, "The Truth about the Duncan Creed," in *The Dance Magazine,* June 1926.

[11]Maria-Theresa in *Music Journal* 17 (September 1959), DC.

[12]ID, "Beauty and Exercise," in *AOD,* 82.

[13]"Isadora and Vanessa," Anna Duncan interview with Parker Tyler.

[14]Deborah Jowitt, *Time and the Dancing Image,* 95.

[15]*DD,* 30.

[16]Ibid., 29.

[17]Luhan, "Movers and Shakers," in *Intimate Memories,* 347–48.

[18]*DD,* 58.

[19]"Isadora and Vanessa," Anna Duncan interview with Parker Tyler.

[20]Maria-Theresa in Bardsley, "Isadora's First School," 231.

[21]"Isadora and Vanessa," Anna Duncan interview with Parker Tyler.

[22]*DD,* 127.

[23]Maria-Theresa in Loewenthal, 48.

[24]*DD,* 54.

[25]Ibid., 27.

[26]ID to Ferdinand of Bulgaria, December 20 (1905), in Ferdinand of Bulgaria Papers, box 20, folder 5, Hoover Institution on War, Revolution and Peace, Stanford University.

[27]*DD,* 40.

[28]*Index,* 263.

[29]Max Osborn, "The First Public Performance," translated (1908) from *Nationale Zeitung* (Berlin), October 31, 1905, for American edition of *The Dance of the Future,* DC.

[30]Müller, "The Story of the Duncan School in Germany," 51.

[31]Victor Ottmann, "Isadora Duncan at Home," translated from *Der Tag* (Berlin), August 17, 1906, for American edition of *The Dance of the Future,* DC.

[32]Anna Duncan in Loewenthal, 37.

[33]Maria-Theresa in "The Classic Dance" (ca. 1930), in Maria-Theresa clipping file (*MGZR), DC.

[34]*DD*, 41–42.

[35]Seroff, 118; Macdougall 104–05.

[36]Richard Buckle, *Diaghilev* (New York: Atheneum, 1979), 97, 99. Tellingly, Rimsky-Korsakov was dismissed from the Conservatory for his "liberal" views.

[37]Seroff, 120.

[38]For an overview of the Seventh Symphony controversy, see Nancy de Wilde, "Isadora Duncan's Seventh Symphony in the Netherlands," Society of Dance History Scholars, *Proceedings,* 10th annual conference (1987), 166–76.

[39]ID, "The Dance in Relation to Tragedy," in *AOD,* 84.

[40]CD 112 (Warsaw, December 1906).

[41]CD 116 (Warsaw).

[42]*Algemeen Handelsblad* (Amsterdam), January 7, 1906; in Loewenthal, 21.

[43]Steegmuller, 65.

[44]EGC to Ellen Terry, March 17, 1905, Gordon Craig miscellaneous manuscripts, gift of Fredrika Blair, DC.

[45]Steegmuller, 67.

[46]Konstantin Stanislavsky, *My Life in Art* (New York: Theatre Arts Books, 1924), 505–06.

[47]CD 29 (February 24, 1905).

[48]CD 31.

[49]Splatt, 37.

[50]*Book Topsy,* in Austin; in Steegmuller 59–60.

[51]CD 29.

[52]CD 56 (undated, Hotel Royal, Hannover).

[53]CD 57 (undated, Hotel zur Krone, Göttingen).

[54]"Prologue" in EGC, *Isadora Duncan: Studies for Six Dance Movements,* in Magriel, *Isadora Duncan,* 65. This is the so-called *Isadora-Mappe,* first published in Leipzig by Insel-Verlag, 1906, as *Isadora Duncan: Sechs Bewegungs Studien,* DC.

[55]*Index,* 268.

[56]EAC 197–99.

[57]Ibid. 198.

[58]Steegmuller, 70.

[59]*Index,* 276.

[60]Craig devotes considerable space to Magnus in *Index,* 275–84; see also EAC, 203–06.

[61]*Index,* 278.

[62]EAC, 205–06.

[63]Ibid., 204.

[64]CD 35 (undated, Berlin, March 10–15, 1905).

[65]CD 36 (note by Craig: "March 16, 1905, at Magdeburg to me Berlin. She is in Berlin March 17").

[66]CD 37 (Brussels, March 22 or 23, 1905).

[67]EAC, 214–15.

[68]Ibid., 195–96.

[69]CD 263.

[70]EGC to Irma Duncan Rogers, May 20, 1955, in Irma Duncan Collection, folder 41, DC.

[71]Splatt, 39.

[72]CD 46 (Brussels, March 28 or 29, 1905).

[73]*DD*, 59–60.

[74]CD 46.

Chapter 11: Maternity

[1]*ML,* 188–89.

[2]CD 42 (Brussels, March 27 or 28, 1905).

[3]CD 40 (probably Brussels, 1905).

[4]CD 42.

[5]CD 43.

[6]For this and other news accounts of ID's Dutch tour, see folder 19, Isadora Duncan Collection, Scott Library, York University. Some of the contents also appear in Lillian Loewenthal, "Isadora Duncan in the Netherlands," *Dance Chronicle* 3, no. 3, (1979–80), 227–53.

[7]CD 111.

[8]*Algemeen Handelsblad,* April 14, 1905, Isadora Duncan Collection, folder 19, Scott Library, York University.

[9]Ibid., April 15, 1905, in Loewenthal, "Isadora Duncan in the Netherlands," 230.

[10]Henri Lavedan, "Miss Isadora Duncan," *L'Illustration,* February 6, 1909 (reviewing *Iphigenia*), in MFR papers, City Museum.

[11]EAC, 213.

[12]Steegmuller Collection, folder 23, DC: Craig notes in his copy of Hugo von Hofmannsthal's *Die Weisse Fächer.*

[13]CD 48 (postmarked 's Gravenhage, October 24, 1905).

[14]Steegmuller, 105–06.

[15]CD 61.

[16]Herman Heyermans, "Isadora en Kees," *Algemeen Handelsblad,* November 4, 1905, Isadora Duncan Collection, folder 19, Scott Library, York University.

[17]EAC, 212.

[18]Steegmuller, 107–08.

[19]CD 55 (probably Berlin, January 1906).

[20]Blair, 122. See also Claudia Jeschke and Gabi Vettermann, "Isadora Duncan, Berlin and Munich in 1906: Just an ordinary year in a dancer's career," *Dance Chronicle* 18, no. 2 (1995), 217–29.

[21]*DD,* 42. Reports conflict on this. See Müller, "The Story of the Duncan School in Germany," 52.

[22]Ibid., 50.

[23]For St. Denis, see Ruth St. Denis, *An Unfinished Life* (New York: Harper & Bros., 1939), and Suzanne Shelton, *Ruth St. Denis: A Biography of the Divine Dancer* (Austin: University of Texas, 1981); for Maud Allan, see Felix Cherniavsky, *The Salome Dancer: The Life and Times of Maud Allan* (Toronto: McClelland & Stewart, 1991).

[24]ID quoted in Arthur Ruhl, "Some Ladies Who Dance," *Collier's,* February 5, 1910, DC.

[25]ID to MFR, undated (Winter 1910, "Dahabeah 'Horus' — Cook's Dahabeahs on the Nile"), MFR Collection, City Museum.

[26]Quoted in Jeschke and Vettermann, "Isadora Duncan, Berlin and Munich in 1906."

[27]Ibid.

[28]*ML,* 186.

[29]CD 52 (October 30–31, 1905); CD 61 (November 5).

[30]*ML,* 186.

[31]In *AOD.*

[32]*ML,* 186–87.

[33]Craig wrote years later (CD 340): "She was at one time — for some 6 or 7 years or longer — down upon every artist who married. She would be scathing about them. . . . She would go on & on about marriage."

[34]EAC, 208.

[35]Kennet, *Self-Portrait of the Artist,* 44.

[36]Martin Shaw, *Up to Now* (London: Oxford University Press, 1929), 65–76, in Steegmuller, 383–88.

[37]Craig made the same point (CD 339): "Never is Miss Duncan in a hurry. It is one of her most marked characteristics that she does nothing hurriedly — in speech, action, in her work, or, when giving directions about it. Perfect natural ease acquired by very few."

[38]CD 58.

[39]Shaw, *Up till Now,* in Steegmuller, 385–86.

[40]Loewenthal, "Isadora Duncan in the Netherlands," 238.

[41]Shaw, *Up to Now,* in Steegmuller, 386.

[42]CD 66.

[43]Index, 287.

[44]CD 68.

[45]ML, 191, 194.

[46]Algemeen Handelsblad, n.d. (August 1906), and August 23, 1906, in Isadora Duncan Collection, folder 20, Scott Library, York University.

[47]CD 77.

[48]"Isadora Duncan, zooals zij in werkelijkheid was," interview with Marie Kist, undated, unidentified clipping (1936), Isadora Duncan Collection, folder 20, Scott Library, York University.

[49]In AOD, 74–76.

[50]ML, 190–91.

[51]CD 86.

[52] Kennet, Self-Portrait of the Artist, 64. See also Young, A Great Task of Happiness, 60–71 (chapter 5, "Isadora's Baby").

[53]ML, 192.

[54]Kennet, Self-Portrait of the Artist, 63.

[55]Ibid., 64.

[56]Lady Kennet's diary for 25 September 1906 at Cambridge University Library ("Kennet D/41").

[57]ML, 194–95.

[58]Francis Steegmuller to Irma Duncan (quoting Craig), undated (August 1974), in Irma Duncan Collection, folder 116, DC.

[59]ML, 196.

[60]CD 103.

Chapter 12: Breaking Stones

[1]DD, 61. See also New York Sun, September 8, 1908, DC.

[2]ML, 196.

[3]EGC to Ellen Terry, Gordon Craig Miscellaneous Manuscripts, DC.

[4]CD 61 (The Hague, November 6, 1905).

[5]ID, "Dancing in Relation to Religion and Love," in AOD, 121.

[6]EAC, 216.

[7]Index, 291.

[8]ML, 198–99.

[9]EAC, 216–17.

[10]ML, 200–01.

[11]Ibid., 202.

[12]EAC, 218.

[13]ML, 203–04.

[14]EAC, 220.

[15]Noccioli in William Weaver, Duse: A Biography (New York: Harcourt Brace Jovanovich, 1984), 278.

[16]EAC, 219–20; Steegmuller, 163.

[17]EAC., 220–21

[18]CD 105 ("Hotel Bristol, Varsovie, Dec. 18, 1906").

[19]Index, 292.

[20]ML, 206.

[21]CD 104 (December 16 [?], 1906).

[22]Javabode, October 30, 1906, Isadora Duncan Collection, folder 19, Scott Library, York University.

[23]Blair 137.

[24]ML, 206.

[25]CD 105 ("Dec. 18, 1906").

[26]CD, 109 ("Dec 19th [1906] After second performance —").

[27]CD 110.

[28]CD 113 ("Saturday").

[29]CD 108.

[30]CD 114.

[31]CD 111.

[32]CD 120.

[33]CD 115.

[34]CD 123 ("Wednesday night").

[35]CD 121.

[36]CD 124.

[37]EAC, 217.

[38]EGC to Ellen Terry, undated (1906), in Steegmuller, 391.

[39]Ibid., 193.

[40]ML, 206.

[41]For a feminist perspective and analysis of Isadora's collapse and recovery in 1907, see Daly, Done Into Dance, 166–68.

[42]CD 133 (Amsterdam, January 1907).

[43]Steegmuller collection, folder 44, DC.

[44]CD 145.

[45]Javabode, October 30, 1906.

[46]Telegraaf and Nieuws quoted in Loewenthal, "Isadora Duncan in the Netherlands," 247, 245.

[47]Noccioli in Weaver, Duse, 279.

[48]EAC, 222.

[49]ML, 207.

[50]Blair, 144.

[51]Weaver, Duse, 279–80.

[52]EAC, 223.

[53]Steegmuller, 195–96.

[54]Index, 297.

[55]CD 142.

[56]CD 258. See also CD 178 (June 1907).

[57]ML, 208.

[58]CD 140 (February 23, 1907).

[59]CD 141.

[60]CD 147 ("Mont Boron Palace Hotel").

[61]Postcard of Ellen Terry to EGC (March 1907), Irma Duncan Collection, folder 117, DC. Terry added that her daughter, "my poor old Edy," wasn't happy with the marriage.

[62]Index, 291.

[63]CD 144.

[64]CD 159.

[65]CD 154.

[66]CD 258.

[67]CD 158 (Amsterdam, April 1, 1907).

[68]Index, 269.

[69]CD 166 (postmarked Berlin, April 21, 1907).

[70]CD 340 (loose).

[71]CD 177 (Berlin); CD 168 (Berlin); CD 169 (Baden-Baden).

[72]CD 190 (Bad Neuenahr, July 10, 1907).

[73]CD 175 (Mannheim).

[74]Konrad Müller-Fürer, "Ich sagte irgend etwas Dummes über 'Wirklichkeit gewordene Künstlerträume,'" in IED, 51.

[75]Max Merz, "'Don't Look Back — Look Forward!' Erinnerungen an das 'Tanzkloster' und seine Bewohner," in ibid., 165.

[76]CD 187 (Baden-Baden); CD 177 (Berlin).

[77]CD 183; CD 184 (June 29, 1907).

[78]Steegmuller, 254.

[79]CD 194 (Berlin).

[80]CD 202 (Venice).

[81]CD 206 (The Hague).

[82]CD 272.

[83]CD 340.

[84]CD 253.

[85]CD 205 ("Dom-Hotel, Köln, Domplatz").

[86]EAC, 223.

[87]ML, 209.

[88]"November 20 1944 Paris," in Steegmuller Collection, research files, folder 46, DC.

[89]EAC, 224.

Chapter 13: Pim and Pure Pleasure

[1]ML, 216.

[2]CD 218 ("Hotel Adlon, Berlin" [April 2 (?), 1908]). Craig wrote on the letter: "To me in my one room . . ."

[3]CD 214 ("Address for six days, Grand Hotel d'Europe, St. Pétersbourg").

[4]CD 218.

[5]ML, 208–09.

[6]See Steegmuller Collection, folder 18, including correspondence with Dan H. Laurence, literary adviser for Shaw estate, and Shaw's letter to the *Sachliches Volksblatt* (Zwickau), March 3, 1926: "No beautiful American dancer has ever proposed marriage to me, on eugenic or any other grounds. [An] Italian journalist invented the dancer and her proposal . . . and chose me for the hero of this tale because newspapers always buy stories about me." Another account has Shaw admitting the story but denying that it was Isadora who made the proposition to him: "The story has been told about me in connexion with several famous women, particularly Isadora Duncan. But I really received the strange offer from a foreign actress whose name you wouldn't know, and which I've forgotten. But I did make that reply" (from Sewell Stokes, *Hear the Lions Roar* [London: Harold Shaylor, 1931], photocopied pages in Steegmuller Collection, folder 18). The story was already in circulation at the time of Isadora's death in 1927 (*New York News*, September 17, 1927, DC).

[7]*New York Evening Journal*, October 4, 1922, DC.

[8]ML, 211.

[9]Maurice Magnus, "Memoirs of Golden Russia," typescript ms. in Norman Douglas Collection, folder 536, General Collection, Beinecke Rare Book and Manuscript Library, Yale University. See also Wright, "Touring Russia with Isadora."

[10]ML, 211.

[11]CD 206 ("Hotel des Indes, La Haye" [October 1907]); CD 209 ("Hotel Bristol, Varsovie" [November 1907]).

[12]"Isadora Duncan, zooals zij in werkelijkheid was."

[13]Boynton-Quitzow oral history, SF PALM.

[14]CD 207.

[15]CD 209.

[16]ID quoted in John Ava Carpenter, *Gazette Times,* undated (London, July 1908), DC.

[17]*Algemeen Handelsblad* (Amsterdam), January 26, 1907, Isadora Duncan Collection, folder 20, Scott Library, York University.

[18]CD 215.

[19]Isadora quotes from *My Life in Art* in ML, 166–69. The transcription is exact, from J. J. Robbins's 1924 translation of Stanislavsky.

[20]Ibid., 170.

[21]Schneider, 31.

[22]To a colleague at the Moscow Art Theatre, Stanislavsky, a famous prude, related Isadora's effort to seduce him in incredulous tones: "You know, Duncan is a remarkable woman . . . God has endowed her with much . . . but she doesn't know herself . . . she doesn't know how to watch out for herself, she does herself harm. . . . A few days ago . . . when she was dancing, she asked me af-

terward to go with her to a restaurant! . . . Whew, you understand. I went, we got to the restaurant and Duncan insisted on a private room . . . then she ordered champagne . . . I didn't know what to think . . . suddenly she sat on the sofa, but she started to behave so oddly. . . . Well, you understand, don't you . . . so wantonly . . . you understand?" (quoted in Laurence Senelick, *Gordon Craig's Moscow Hamlet: A Reconstruction* [Westport, Conn.: Greenwood Press, 1982], 13).

[23]Ibid.

[24]Alexandre Benois, *Memoirs, Volume II,* translated by Moura Budberg (London: Chatto & Windus, 1964), 218.

[25]Pollard, "The Regnant Wave of Sensational Dance."

[26]*Musical Leader,* October 12, 1908, DC.

[27]CD 215.

[28]Seroff, 117.

[29]*ML,* 214.

[30]Schneider, 33.

[31]Felix Cherniavsky, *The Salome Dancer,* 162–63.

[32]*New York Times,* August 16, 1908.

[33]Ibid., July 12, 1908.

[34]Arthur Ruhl, "Some Ladies Who Dance," DC.

[35]CD 218.

[36]*Gazette Times,* undated (1908), op. cit.

[37]CD 220.

[38]Cherniavsky, *The Salome Dancer,* 160.

[39]For Allan in London, see Cherniavsky, *The Salome Dancer;* Cherniavsky, "Maud Allan, Part III: Two Years of Triumph, 1908–1909," in *Dance Chronicle* 7, no. 2 (1984), 119–58; and Lacy McDearmon, "Maud Allan: The Public Record," in ibid. 2, no. 2 (1978), 85–105.

[40]"Isadora Duncan Raps Maud Allan," *New York Times,* August 9, 1908.

[41]*The Academy,* May 2, 1908.

[42]Shelton, *Ruth St. Denis,* 83.

[43]St. Denis, *An Unfinished Life,* 117–18.

[44]*The Times* (London), July 7, 1908.

[45]Quoted in Steegmuller, 386.

[46]MFR, "The Dance of the Future as Created and Illustrated by Isadora Duncan," in the *Craftsman,* October 1908; reprinted in *The Dance of the Future* (American edition).

[47]CD 222 (postmarked London, August 3, 1908).

[48]Splatt, 65.

[49]CD 283.

[50]CD 222.

[51]Reprinted in *DD,* 83–85.

[52]*New York Times,* August 2, 1908.

[53]Ibid., August 9, 1908.

[54]Ibid., August 2, 1908.

[55]*DD,* 82. See also Konrad Müller-Fürer, "Ich sagte irgend etwas Dummes," 73–75: "Some of the eldest ones soon had so much experience in dealing with porters, taxi-drivers and hotel personnel, and had developed a special packing technique, that one could be envious. They were just as adept and uninhibited when they were confronted with a prince, a great artist, or a scholar."

[56]*ML,* 216.

[57]CD 282.

[58]Quoted in *Minneapolis News,* December 4, 1908, DC.

[59]Undated, unidentified news clipping (New York, 1908), DC. See also the *New York Sun,* August 21, 1908, DC.

[60]*Boston Evening Transcript,* November 28, 1908, in Olive Holmes, ed., *Motion Arrested: Dance Reviews of H. T. Parker* (Middletown, Conn.: Wesleyan University Press, 1982), 60.

[61]*New York Telegraph,* undated (August 1908), DC.

[62]*New York Sun,* August 21, 1908, DC.

[63]Macdougall, 119. An unidentified critic described Isadora as "a misguided woman capering around in a directory nightie" (quoted in Arthur Mason, "Mistress of the Dance," in *The Green Book Album*, January 1909, 139).

[64]MFR, "Isadora," lecture compiled for the Mills School, Mary Fanton Roberts Collection, City Museum.

[65]Jean Paul Lafitte, *Les danses d'Isadora Duncan; avec une préface d'Elie Faure* (Paris: Mercure de France, 1910); in Macdougall, 125.

[66]Jacob Adler speech in typescript, DC.

[67]*ML*, 219.

[68]Quoted in *New York Sun*, March 22, 1917, DC.

[69]*ML*, 218.

[70]For Damrosch, see George Martin, *The Damrosch Dynasty: America's First Family of Music* (Boston: Houghton Mifflin, 1983).

[71]Ibid., 221.

[72]*Musical America*, November 14, 1908.

[73]Program in DC.

[74]Max Eastman, "Difficulties in Worshipping Isadora Duncan," in Max Eastman mss., Lilly Library, Indiana University; revised as "Heroism Plus Heroics: Difficulties in Worshipping Isadora Duncan," in Max Eastman, *Heroes I Have Known: Twelve Who Lived Great Lives* (New York: Simon and Schuster, 1942).

Chapter 14: Daughter of Prometheus

[1]"Isadora Duncan Receives," *New York Sun*, November 15, 1908, quoted in part in *ML*, 220–22.

[2]*Chicago Tribune*, December 1, 1908.

[3]*ML*, 211–12.

[4]"Isadora Duncan," quoted in the *Kansas City Post*, January 14, 1909, DC.

[5]See *New York Times*, November 2, 1909.

[6]Gretchen (Damrosch) Finletter, *From the Top of the Stairs* (Boston: Little, Brown and Co., 1946), 213–14.

[7]Margherita Duncan, "Isadora," in *AOD*, 18.

[8]Ira Glackens, *William Glackens and the Ashcan Group* (New York: Crown, 1957), 135.

[9]Steegmuller, 396.

[10]*Cincinnati Commercial*, August 29, 1908, DC.

[11]Steegmuller, 395.

[12]Dumesnil, 180.

[13]*ML*, 226.

[14]*New York Sun*, November 15, 1908, DC.

[15]Ibid., September 20, 1908, DC.

[16]Finletter, *From the Top of the Stairs*, 215–16.

[17]Hermann Hagedorn, *Edwin Arlington Robinson: A Biography* (New York: Macmillan, 1938), 230–31.

[18]*Boston Herald*, undated clipping (1908–09), DC.

[19]*Boston Sunday Herald*, November 28, 1909.

[20]*New York Sun*, January 1, 1909, DC.

[21]Sturges, 61; on Mary and Crowley, see 75–78.

[22]*ML*, 57.

[23]Aurélien Lugné-Poë, *Sous les étoiles* (Paris: Gallimard, 1933), 239–40.

[24]*ML*, 229.

[25]Lugné-Poë, *Sous les étoiles*, 240.

[26]The *Boston Herald* of October 13, 1908, quotes Maybelle Corey to ID: "To think that you should be paying to house your school in Paris, when I have a chateau standing empty which they might as well occupy! There is a farm there, too, and there are servants with nothing to do but wait

on them." As Maybelle Gilman, Mrs. Corey had been in the Augustin Daly company with Isadora, appearing with her in *The Geisha*.

[27]*DD*, 82.

[28]Ibid., 91–92.

[29]See Anna Duncan's letters from Villegenis, undated (C08-04, "Chateau de la Salle de Marche"); November 1, 1908 (C08-05), and December 6, 1908 (C08-06), Anna Duncan Collection, Dansmuseet, Stockholm.

[30]Sturges, 39.

[31]Irma Erich-Grimme to Frau Grimme, undated ("Chateau Villegenis, Massy, Seine et Oise"), in Irma Duncan Collection, correspondence files, folder 1, DC.

[32]*DD*, 55.

[33]Ibid., 107. Merz believed that "a so-called broad education" was bad for children, especially for girls: "It has finally made its way to the female sex and, to a degree, infected their healthy instincts. . . . The development of healthy female bodies is the prime consideration of the Duncan school" (*Muenchener Neueste Nachrichten*, November 5, 1910).

[34]Irma Erich-Grimme to Frau Grimme, undated, op. cit.

[35]For the Hôtel Biron, see Francis Steegmuller, *Cocteau: A Biography* (London: Constable, 1986), 38–42.

[36]See Marinetti's 1917 "Manifesto of the Futurist Dance" in *Marinetti: Selected Writings*, ed. with introduction by R. W. Fling (Farrar, Straus & Giroux, 1971), 137–39: "There are many points of contact between Isadora's art and pictorial Impressionism, as there are between Nijinsky's art and Cézanne's constructions of volumes and forms. . . . We Futurists prefer Loie Fuller and the 'cakewalk' of the Negroes (utlization of electric light and mechanisms). One must go beyond muscular possibilities and aim in the dance for that ideal *multiplied body* of the motor that we have so long dreamed of. One must imitate the movements of machines with gestures; pay assiduous court to steering wheels, ordinary wheels, pistons, thereby preparing the fusion of man with the machine, to achieve the metallicity of the Futurist dance." During World War I, Marinetti proposed a "Dance of the Shrapnel."

[37]Poiret quoted in "The Poiret Ball," in James Laver, ed., *Memorable Balls*, illustrated by Walter Goetz (London: Derek Verschoyle, 1954), 111.

[38]Kendall, *Where She Danced*, 87.

[39]Fernand Divoire, with illustrations by Emile-Antoine Bourdelle, *Isadora Duncan, Fille de Prométhée* (Paris: Editions Muses Françaises, 1919).

[40]Loewenthal, 52.

[41]Ibid., 9.

[42]Wharton, *A Backward Glance*, 322.

[43]*New York Times*, May 23, 1909.

[44]Joseph Paul-Boncour, "L'art de la danseuse sublime," *Le Figaro*, May 22, 1909. Note that this was three days after the opening of the Ballets Russes.

[45]Richard Buckle, *Nijinsky* (New York: Simon and Schuster, 1971), 80. For Diaghilev and the Ballets Russes, see Richard Buckle, *Diaghilev*; and Garafola, *Diaghilev's Ballets Russes*.

[46]Arnold L. Haskell, *Ballet Russe: The Art of Diaghilev* (London: Weidenfeld and Nicolson, 1968), 61–62.

[47]Vera Krasovskaya, *Nijinsky*, translated from the Russian by John E. Bowlt (New York: Schirmer Books, 1979), 116.

[48]Pavlova quoted in Fernand Divoire, *Pour la danse* (Paris: Editions de la danse, 1935), 49–50.

[49]Pavlova quoted in *Musical America*, March 5, 1910.

[50]CD 242. In a speech at the Metropolitan Opera in 1917, ID complained: "I have to pay $1,000 for this house and $1,500 for the orchestra. Yet they paid $180,000 to bring to America the Russian Ballet, an organization which in its present form never would have existed if it had not been for me, and which is the end and not the beginning of an art. Forgive me for mentioning these dreadful things, but I would not make a speech at all if it were not for my school" (*Musical America*, May 12, 1917).

[51]ID did dance with Nijinsky at a luncheon in New York City in 1915–16, according to Mary Fanton Roberts (MFR, "Isadora — The Dancer"). Sir Francis Rose also mentions a party in Venice, no date given, where ID and Nijinsky danced, quoting ID: "It was more wonderful than making love with a Negro boxer on Mr. Singer's billiard-table. I arrived with many lovers, and Nijinsky was there. No one asked us to dance, we just decided to dance, so without talking about it we danced and danced and danced" (Sir Francis Rose, *Saying Life* [London: Cassell, 1961], 70).

[52]Romola Nijinsky, *Nijinsky* (New York: AMS Press, 1968), 93. See also Charles H. Morgan, *George Bellows: Painter of America* (New York: Reynal and Co., 1965), 197, quoting Emma Bellows, when her husband went to a party of Isadora's in New York: "Do you suppose this will be the night she asks him to father her next child? She does, you know." On Bellows's return: "'Did she ask you?' It was a long time before he admitted that she had."

[53]Photostat of Nijinsky's original statement at the Bibliothèque Nationale, in Steegmuller Collection, folder 34, DC.

[54]Krasovskaya, *Nijinsky*, 193.

[55]Loewenthal, 135.

[56]Jeanne Gazeau, "Isadora Duncan," in *Les Entretiens Idéalistes*, December 25, 1909.

[57]Macdougall, 127–28.

[58]There is no biography of Paris Singer. I've cited sources on Singer individually. For the Singer dynasty, see Ruth Brandon, *A Capitalist Romance*.

[59]Alva Johnston, *The Legendary Mizners* (New York: Farrar, Straus & Giroux, 1953), 42. See also letter of Alice De Lamar concerning Paris Singer in the archives of the Palm Beach Historical Society, Palm Beach, Florida.

[60]Johnston, *The Legendary Mizners*, 40–43.

[61]Sturges, 62.

[62]Nesta Macdonald, "Isadora Reexamined, Part V," in *Dance Magazine*, November 1977.

[63]*ML*, 229.

[64]Macdonald, "Isadora Reexamined, Part V."

[65]*ML*, 230.

[66]CD 340.

[67]*ML*, 234.

[68]Ibid., 235.

[69]Steegmuller, 308. Craig's account of the St. Petersburg dinner, appended in 1944, is in *Book Topsy*, Austin, and in Steegmuller, 307–10.

[70]*ML*, 236. The episode with "Miss S." is cut from the 1995 edition of *ML*.

[71]*Book Topsy*, Austin, in Steegmuller, 309–10.

[72]*ML*, 236–37.

Chapter 15: To Love in a Certain Way

[1]*ML*, 233.

[2]Seroff, 164, 139.

[3]Stokes, 141.

[4]*ML*, 233.

[5]See letter of Alice De Lamar concerning Paris Singer, op. cit., in Palm Beach Historical Society archives.

[6]Seroff, 166.

[7]Ibid., 167.

[8]Ibid., 165.

[9]Stokes, 141.

[10]*ML*, 237.

[11]For the Neuilly house, see Loewenthal, 49–58. Mrs. Loewenthal made a study of all of Isadora's residences in France.

[12]*DD*, 125.

[13]Maurice Bazalgette, "Isadora Duncan," in *Renaissance romantique* (Paris), July 1909, 50.

[14]*ML*, 261.

[15]*Palm Beach Post,* June 25, 1932 (Singer obituary). See also *Palm Beach Post,* November 17, 1977, quoting Addison Mizner: "Paris always loved pageants and parties. Why, I never understood. For although his costumes were always wonderfully done, he never seemed to enter into the gaiety but stood in the background looking on."

[16]Stokes, 143.

[17]*ML,* 254.

[18]Stokes, 144.

[19]*ML,* 237.

[20]Stokes, 154.

[21]Seroff, 169.

[22]"Isadora and Vanessa," Anna Duncan interview with Parker Tyler.

[23]Translations of Stanislavsky's letters from Paris in Natalia Roslasleva, "Isadora Duncan and Constantin Stanislavsky," *Dance Magazine* 37, no. 7 (July 1963), 40–43.

[24]Stanislavsky to Lev Sulerzhitsky, *ibid.*

[25]See ID's letter ("7. July 1909") in Irma Duncan Collection, folder 1, DC.

[26]*DD,* 102.

[27]Merz, "Don't Look Back — Look Forward!" 169.

[28]Ibid., 163.

[29]*DD,* 103.

[30]Müller, "The Story of the Duncan School in Germany," 44. The girls sometimes smuggled out letters with the help of visitors and staff, especially their governesses. Isadora herself, blaming Merz for turning Elizabeth against her, used the word *kidnapped* in interviews with the French press to describe the disappearance of her students: "*On me les a enlevées!*" (*Excelsior,* December 28, 1910, Isadora Duncan Collection, folder 19, Scott Library, York University). The same is confirmed in handwritten notes of Christine Palliès, Macdougall Collection, folder 29, DC: "*Elizabeth reprenait de force les meilleures élèves.*"

[31]*DD,* 103.

[32]Roslasleva, "Isadora Duncan and Constantin Stanislavsky."

[33]Schneider, 36.

[34]Roslasleva, "Isadora Duncan and Constantin Stanislavsky."

[35]Kay Bardsley, "Isadora's First School." See also "Isadora and Vanessa," Anna Duncan interview with Parker Tyler: "[Merz] had no trouble in persuading Elizabeth to stay in Germany and continue with a school of her own. He used every means to convince our parents how much better off we would be at that school instead of with Isadora, who even made up her lips, he told them, in front of us growing girls!"

[36]*ML,* 239–41.

[37]Ibid., 241.

[38]*New York Times,* November 17, 1909.

[39]Merz, "Don't Look Back — Look Forward!" 154. See also Temple Duncan Pearson to Irma Duncan, April 21, 1962, Irma Duncan Collection, folder 64, DC.

[40]"Isadora Duncan and the Puritocracy," *Musical America,* August 14, 1909.

[41]*Musical America,* October 30, 1909.

[42]*ML,* 241–42.

[43]*Boston Sunday Herald,* November 28, 1909.

[44]*New York Mirror,* December 12, 1909, DC.

[45]*Louisville Herald,* December 12, 1909, DC.

[46]*Musical America* reported on January 15, 1910, that Menalkas, then four, was "wonderful, chubby and vigorous" and "has never eaten meat, had the croup, been down with the measles, caught cold or worn anything more substantially protective for the cold than a knitted shirt and leather sandals."

[47]Sturges, 70.

[48]CD 129, 164 (January 1907).

[49]*ML,* 242–44.

[50]In Irma Duncan Collection, folder 64, DC.

[51]ML, 245.

[52]Macdougall, 132.

[53]ML, 246.

[54]Blair, 207–08.

[55]ML, 247.

[56]Ibid., 247–52.

[57]Stokes, 149–52.

[58]ML, 252.

[59]Kay Bardsley, "The Duncans at Carnegie Hall," 89.

[60]Caroline and Charles H. Caffin, *Dancing and Dancers of Today: The Modern Revival of Dancing as an Art* (New York: Dodd, Mead, 1912), 61–62.

[61]Bardsley, "The Duncans at Carnegie Hall," 89.

[62]Caffin, *Dancing and Dancers of Today,* 61.

[63]*New York Times,* February 11, 1911.

[64]*Brooklyn Eagle,* December 10, 1909, DC.

[65]*New York Tribune,* February 11, 1911.

[66]Henry Taylor Parker in *Boston Evening Transcript,* February 24, 1911.

[67]*Ibid.*

[68]*New York Times,* February 16, 1911.

[69]Ibid.

[70]*New York Sun,* February 16, 1911, DC.

[71]Caffin, *Dancing and Dancers of Today,* 67.

[72]*Boston Evening Transcript,* February 24, 1911.

[73]Witter Bynner to Haniel Long, March 28, 1911, in James Kraft, ed., *The Works of Witter Bynner: Selected Letters* (New York: Farrar, Straus & Giroux, 1981), 31–32.

[74]ML, 254. "Danny Deever," with words by Rudyard Kipling, was David Bispham's signature tune (his *Blue Danube,* so to speak). Bispham's memoirs, *A Quaker Singer's Recollections* (New York: Macmillan, 1920), are so discreet about his private life that even his wife is mentioned only once.

[75]*Boston Evening Transcript,* February 24, 1911.

[76]Arthur Ruhl, "Some Ladies Who Dance," DC.

[77]Undated, unidentified news clipping (1911), Mary Fanton Roberts Collection, City Museum.

[78]ML, 255. The "governess" was artist Christine Dalliès, later Isadora's boon companion and secretary, who left a truncated account of their friendship for Allan Ross Macdougall, "*1910: Comment je restais avec les enfants à Versailles pendant la tournée d'Isadora aux Etats-Unis*" (in Macdougall Collection, folder 29, DC).

[79]ID to MFR, undated (1910–11), Mary Fanton Roberts Collection, City Museum.

[80]MFR, "Isadora — The Dancer," Mary Fanton Roberts Collection, City Museum.

[81]Albert Flament in *Excelsior,* April 21, 1913, Isadora Duncan Collection, folder 19, Scott Library, York University.

[82]ID, "Notes et extraits de correspondances intimes," edited by Christine Dalliès, in *Ecrits sur la danse* (Paris: Editions du Grenier, 1927).

[83]Seroff, 177.

[84]Kennet, *Self-Portrait of an Artist,* 93.

[85]Young, *A Great Task of Happiness,* 130.

[86]DD, 109.

[87]Merz, "Don't Look Back — Look Forward!" 169.

[88]DD, 108.

[89]Letter from Anna, October 24, 1909 (C09-01), Anna Duncan Collection, Dansmuseet, Stockholm.

[90]Müller, "The Story of the Duncan School in Germany," 62–63.

[91]Seroff, 161.

[92]DD, 114–15.

[93]Young, *A Great Task of Happiness,* 130.

[94]Kennet, *Self-Portrait of an Artist,* 97–98.

[95]*ML,* 239.

[96]*Le Temps,* January 24, 1911; in Loewenthal, 139–40.

[97]Leo Stein to Gertrude Stein, undated (1911), in Edmund Fuller, ed., *Journey Into the Self* (New York: Crown, 1950), 47. Singer was apparently infatuated with Stein's future wife, Nina Auxias: "It was news to me that with Nina he was not interested but madly in love. I saw a couple of his letters — he writes to her every day . . . he plays on the pianner with her photo before him; he longs for her every minute; and if she will only say the word he will break at once with Isadora and come home on the wings of love and the wheels of an express train." Another letter of August 22, 1911 (ibid., 48), relates: "I saw S. who has finished with Isadora — he is looking very badly. Nina is looking very well. Their present plans look to permanence."

[98]Valerian Svetlov in *Peterburgskaya Gazeta,* January 9, 1913; reprinted in *Dance News,* November, 1957, DC. For Isadora and Gilbert Murray, see also *Proceedings of the American Philosophical Society* 122, no. 3 (June 9, 1978), 182–92.

[99]Splatt, 72–73.

[100]EAC, 261.

[101]Anita Loos, *A Girl Like I* (New York: Viking, 1966), 259.

[102]EGC to Irma Duncan Rogers, August 8, 1955, in Irma Duncan Collection, folder 41, DC.

[103]EGC to George Plank, undated (1911–12), in George Plank Papers, Yale Collection of American Literature, Beinecke Rare Book and Manuscript Library, Yale University.

[104]CD 340.

[105]Michel Georges-Michel, "La danseuse nue," *Gil Blas,* December 7, 1911; in Loewenthal, 141.

[106]Ibid.

[107]Maria-Theresa, "As I Saw Isadora Duncan," *The Dance Magazine,* November 1928, 49.

[108]Georges-Michel, "La danseuse nue."

[109]*ML,* 273.

[110]Ibid., 263.

[111]See Fenella Lovell to EGC (CD 302); and Crowley's "Account of a Communication made to Fra. Perdurabo . . . through the seer Ouarda," in *The Equinox* 1, no. 7. Both Mary Desti and Isadora appear as fictional characters in Crowley's novel *Moonchild,* first published in 1917 (York Beach, Me.: Samuel Weiser, Inc., 1970). See also Franklin Rosemont, "Isadora and the Magicians," in Rosemont, ed., *Surrealism & Its Popular Accomplices* (San Francisco: City Lights Books, 1980), 91–92: "Isadora's interest in this shadowy domain has not received the attention it deserves. It is worth emphasizing that these preoccupations were not at all peripheral to her other interests. . . . It would be no exaggeration, indeed, to say that her meanderings into the 'Mysteries' form an integral part of the Isadorian world view."

[112]Irma's account to end of chapter in *DD,* 118–23.

[113]Lugné-Poë, *Sous les étoiles,* 247.

Chapter 16: One Great Cry

[1]*Daily Mail* (London), October 29, 1912, DC.

[2]*New York Telegraph,* undated (Fall 1912), DC.

[3]Paris Singer to Louis Sue, undated (1912), in Donald Oenslager Collection of Edward Gordon Craig, General Collection, Beinecke Rare Book and Manuscript Library, Yale University, folder 46. See also folders 27–48 ("Correspondence concerning the Duncan Theatre").

[4]Ibid.

[5]ID to Singer, undated (1912), in Donald Oenslager Collection of Edward Gordon Craig, General Collection, Beinecke Rare Book and Manuscript Library, Yale University, folder 33.

[6]Michel Georges-Michel, "Isadora — Isadora," *Gil Blas,* September 6, 1912, Isadora Duncan Collection, folder 19, Scott Library, York University.

[7]*ML,* 256.

[8]Virginia Cowles, *1913: An End and a Beginning* (New York: Harper & Row, 1968), 175–76.

[9]Paul Poiret, *King of Fashion: The Autobiography of Paul Poiret* (Philadelphia: Lippincott, 1931), 205.

[10]Buckle, *Diaghilev,* 225–27; Garafola, *Diaghilev's Ballets Russes,* 57.

[11]*Chicago Examiner,* January 10, 1912, and *New York Morning Telegraph,* December 18, 1911, DC.

[12]Cécile Sorel, *Les belles heures de ma vie* (Monaco: Editions du Rocher, 1956), 122–23.

[13]Lugné-Poë, *Sous les étoiles,* 244.

[14]Steegmuller, *Cocteau,* 77, 72.

[15]Sylvia Salinger, April 4, 1913, in Albert S. Bennett, ed., *Just a Very Pretty Girl from the Country: Letters from Gertrude Stein's Paris* (New York: Paragon House, 1988), 76.

[16]EGC to Singer, July 30, 1912, in Donald Oenslager Collection of Edward Gordon Craig, General Collection, Beinecke Rare Book and Manuscript Library, Yale University, folder 39.

[17]EGC to Singer, undated, ibid.

[18]EGC to Irma Duncan Rogers, June 8, 1953, Irma Duncan Collection, folder 37.

[19]*ML,* 261.

[20]Poiret, *King of Fashion,* 206.

[21]"Temperaments of Artists Clash at Orientalist Ball: Trouble Arises When Enthusiastic Playwright Kisses Greek Dancer's Foot," *New York American,* November 17, 1912 (MFR Collection, City Museum): "The jealousy spread. A Hungarian with dove's eyes was over-attentive to Madame [Poiret]. . . . Berthe Bady, the actress, grew furiously jealous of Madame Vely Bey [Mary Desti]. . . . Gunsburg [the orchestra leader] slapped the face of a Russian who sat at the feet of Cécile Sorel," etc. Bataille, *"poète de la douleur moderne,"* was the author of *The Naked Woman,* a play based on Claude Debussy's abandonment of his wife.

[22]*ML,* 262.

[23]Ibid., 265.

[24]Desti, 49.

[25]*ML,* 263.

[26]ID to Georges Maurevert, undated (Summer 1913), in Macdougall Collection, folder 2, DC; and Macdougall, 142. Maurevert published the contents of Isadora's letter in August 1913 (unidentified clipping in Isadora Duncan Collection, folder 19, Scott Library, York University). See *New York World,* August 7, 1913, DC, and *New York Times,* August 10, 1913, in which the letter is said to have "started anew a discussion of the question of presentiments."

[27]"Moscow Letters from Augustin Duncan," *Equity,* March 1970, 21.

[28]Splatt, 69–71.

[29]ID to Louis Sue, undated (1913, Hotel Astoria, St. Petersburg), Isadora Duncan Miscellaneous Manuscripts (ISADORA [(S) *MGZM-Res. Dun Is - 3]), DC.

[30]*ML,* 264–65.

[31]Desti, 50–51.

[32]ID program, DC.

[33]Péladan, "Isadora Duncan et la Tragédie Grecque," unidentified clipping, March 29, 1913, Isadora Duncan Collection, folder 19, Scott Library, York University. Péladan "was a major figure in the French occult revival of 1880–1920," according to Franklin Rosemont. "A prolific playwright, poet, novelist, essayist, author of numerous volumes on the 'black arts,' he was the founder and leader of a Rosicrucian sect, the Aesthetic Rose Cross. His work is a feverish blend of magic, eroticism, a virulently decadent Catholicism, ancient mythology, Satanism, blasphemy and homeopathic medicine" (Rosemont, "Isadora and the Magicians").

[34]*DD,* 128–29.

[35]*Journal de Paris,* undated (April 1913), DC.

[36]*New York Sun,* April 21, 1913, DC.

[37]*ML,* 267–68.

[38]Ibid., 270. ID's account of her children's last days, death, and funeral in *ML,* 270–77. All quotations from ID to end of chapter are from *ML* unless otherwise noted.

[39]Albert Flament, "Une automobile tombe dans la Seine: on retire, noyés, deux des enfants de Madame Isadora Duncan," *Excelsior,* April 21, 1913, Isadora Duncan Collection, folder 24, Scott Library, York University. Cécile Sorel remembered: "Three days before the catastrophe that took her two children, she said to me: 'I am the happiest of women'" (*Les belles heures de ma vie,* 123–24).

[40]Desti, 51.

[41]The name is given in some press reports as Masserand. Preston Sturges (Sturges, 96) refers to Isadora's regular chauffeur, Marcel Bouhiron, while the *San Francisco Examiner* (April 21, 1913) calls him Morevand. Isadora had seen the *Examiner's* correspondent in Paris, Charles Henry Meltzer, on the night of the eighteenth, after her concert at the Châtelet, and said how much she looked forward to dancing in California when she returned to the United States, as originally planned, in May 1913. Through Charles Coburn, she had already booked a theater in San Francisco.

[42]*DD*, 130.

[43]All Duncan archives contain press clippings about the death of Isadora's children. The tragedy was front-page news in Europe and the United States. I've noted sources individually.

[44]*New York Times*, April 20, 1913.

[45]Unidentified news clipping, April 20, 1913, Mary Fanton Roberts Collection, City Museum.

[46]Flament, "Une automobile tombe dans la Seine."

[47]Desti, 52. Mary's narrative of the children's deaths and funeral in Desti, 52–59.

[48]Marie Sophie Amalie, Duchess in Bavaria, widow of King Francesco II of the Two Sicilies, was a sister of Empress Elisabeth of Austria — the ill-fated "Sissi" — assassinated at Geneva in 1898. In *ML* (269), Isadora foreshadows the death of her children with an unexpected visit from the queen: "With a sudden tender gesture, she took my two little ones in her arms and held them to her bosom, but when I saw those two blonde heads enshrouded in black, again I experienced that strange oppression that had so often affected me lately."

[49]CD 227 (April 19, 1913).

[50]Desti, 55.

[51]Ibid., 56.

[52]*ML*, 275. This same passage appears in the introduction, *ML*, 7–8.

[53]Mrs. Patrick Campbell to G. B. Shaw ("15th April, 1913"), in *Bernard Shaw and Mrs. Patrick Campbell* (New York: Knopf, 1952), 118–19.

[54]Desti, 56.

[55]*New York Times*, April 21, 1913.

[56]Maurice Ravel to Igor Stravinsky, in Eric White, *Stravinsky: The Composer and His Works* (London: Faber & Faber, 1966), 548.

[57]Desti, 56–57.

[58]Blair, 447; *New York Times*, April 23, 1913. The French press reported that Isadora's Renault wasn't the first automobile to fall into the Seine at the same spot on boulevard Bourdon. See also T. A. Boyd, *Professional Amateur: The Biography of Charles Franklin Kettering* (New York: Dutton, 1957), 81–82. In America, a demand for self-starting automobiles, without crank engines, "was intensified by an unfortunate accident involving the children of . . . Isadora Duncan."

[59]*New York Times*, April 21, 1913.

[60] "DIVORCE FOR A. G. DUNCAN. Brother of Dancer Wins Suit Against His Wife," *New York Tribune*, August 28, 1913: "Duncan mentioned in his suit Jay F. Brown, with whom he alleged Mrs. Duncan lived as Mrs. Brown for nearly three years, beginning in February 1910."

[61]*New York Times*, April 20, 1913. The children's names and ages were constantly mixed up in press accounts of their deaths. Usually, it was said that Patrick was the elder; Deirdre's name was given variously as "Deardree," "Doodie," "Doodle," "Doddie," and "Beatrice."

[62]*ML*, 276.

[63]*DD*, 132.

[64]Letter of Anna to her parents, Darmstadt, April 22, 1913, Anna Duncan Collection, Dansmuseet, Stockholm.

[65]EAC, 284–85.

[66]Splatt, 76.

[67]EGC to ID, undated, in "Isadora Duncan Materials in Irma Duncan Collection," [(S) *MGZMC — Res 23] folder 40, DC.

[68]CD 228 (April 21, 1913).

[69]*ML*, 276.

[70]Michel Georges-Michel, "La mort sous les fleurs: Les funerailles païennes des deux enfants d'Isadora Duncan," *Comoedia*, April 23, 1913.

[71]*New York Times,* April 23, 1913.

[72]Sorel, *Les belles heures de ma vie,* 125; in Seroff, 189–90.

[73]EGC to Count Harry Kessler, April 22, 1913, in Newman, *Correspondence,* 109. Ellen Terry dispatched a telegram to Craig, HOPE YOU HAVE SENT WORD OF GRAVE SYMPATHY POOR THING LOVE FROM ELENA AND MOTHER (CD 305), and urged him to attend the funeral. Craig's response says everything: "Why should I go to Paris? Did I ask you? . . . Why should everyone weep? and why many things? Isadora herself does not weep — and everyone writes me she commands the situation. . . . So is it needful to say I wired to her at once[?] . . . & I wrote & wrote . . . but travelled swifter than all wires all letters in person — or what we know is US. . . . What I feel & see I cannot talk about — even here" (Steegmuller, 320–21).

[74]CD 301 (Kessler to EGC, April 23, 1913); in Newman, *Correspondence,* 110–11.

[75]Sturges, 98.

[76]Desti, 57–58.

[77]*New York Times,* April 23, 1913.

[78]ID writes (*ML,* 277): "I had some definite plan to end my own life."

[79]Desti, 58–59.

Chapter 17: The Rock of Niobe

[1]Roatcap, *Raymond Duncan,* 18–20. See also "Raymond Duncan the Executive."

[2]*ML,* 280.

[3]ID to Louis Sue, May 14, 1913, in Macdougall Collection, DC; quoted in Macdougall, 140–41.

[4]*ML,* 278. A Paris wire report of May 16, 1913, declared, without elaboration, that "Isadora Duncan is lying seriously ill at Corfu" (*New York Times,* May 17, 1913).

[5]ID to Georges Maurevert (summer 1913), op. cit.; in Macdougall, 142.

[6]*Paris Herald,* August 24, 1913, DC.

[7]CD 229 (dated by EGC May 31, 1913).

[8]CD 230 (arrival postmark July 7, 1913).

[9]See various clippings in Mary Desti Collection on Isadora Duncan, MS-P 5, Department of Special Collections, University of California, Irvine, at the time of Isadora's death (September 15–16, 1927): *"La célèbre danseuse avait a cette époque scandalisé le 'Tout Paris' en suivant les cercueils de ses deux enfants vêtue de ses voiles et accomplissant sur le parcours des danses rythmiques."* Christine Dalliès's notes of her friendship with Isadora (Macdougall Collection, folder 29, DC) are vehement on this point: *"Isadora ne dansa pas devant les cerceuils."*

[10]Sturges, 97–98. See also Max Eastman, "Difficulties in Worshipping Isadora Duncan": "Certainly that element of meaningless bad luck in a life devoted with such magnificent courage to an outlawed ideal of love and motherhood must, in all who do not pretend it was the judgment of God, win her a forgiving sympathy."

[11]*New York Times,* April 29, 1913.

[12]Dillon, *After Egypt,* 54; referenced to unedited mss. of de Montesquiou in the Bibliothèque Nationale, Paris.

[13]Steegmuller, 330 (referenced to a "private collection," probably the archives of the late Dr. Arnold Rood).

[14]EAC, 285, 287.

[15]EGC to ID, May 15, 1913, in "Isadora Duncan Materials," Irma Duncan Collection, DC.

[16]CD 230, 231, 229.

[17]*ML,* 277.

[18]Ibid., 279.

[19]Blair, 230.

[20]*ML,* 279.

[21]Ibid., 282–88.

[22]Ibid., 323.

[23]"Dancer Not to Tour," unidentified clipping (August 1913), DC. The *New York Tribune* had first reported that ID would tour on June 22 (DC). Isadora's response seems to have been motivated by the August publication of her private letter to Georges Maurevert (chapter 16), relating her pre-

sentiments about the children's deaths. Maurevert had read about her touring plans and ventured to hope that the publication of her letter had moved her in this direction.

[24]*Paris Herald,* August 24, 1913.

[25]ID to Hener Skene, facsimile ms. in ID, *Ecrits sur la danse* (Paris: Editions du Grenier, 1927). The date is given here as October 1913, but none appears on the letter.

[26]CD 232.

[27]Augustin Duncan to ID, October 18, 1913, in "Isadora Duncan Materials," Irma Duncan Collection, folder 60, DC: "I do wish you would come on to Munich or Stuttgart because we have a beautiful plan if you would like it. It is unrealizable without you, and must then remain a dream."

[28]*ML,* 289–290.

[29]CD 232.

[30]EGC to Elena Meo, September 7, 1913, in Steegmuller, 329.

[31]*ML,* 290.

[32]ID narrative of Duse, *ML,* 291–98.

[33]*New York Sun,* September 8, 1908, DC.

[34]Duse's notes to ID, mostly undated, are in "Isadora Duncan Materials," Irma Duncan Collection, DC, folders 68–86.

[35]Duse to ID, undated, DC.

[36]*ML,* 296.

[37]PK interview with Agnes Gorky. See also Weaver, *Duse,* 293.

[38]*ML,* 297.

[39]Duse to Lugné-Poë, undated, in Macdougall Collection, folder 1, DC.

[40]ID to Mercedes de Acosta, in Mercedes de Acosta, *Here Lies the Heart* (New York: Reynal & Co., 1960), 51.

[41]*ML,* 297.

[42]Duse to Lugné-Poë, op. cit.

[43]*ML,* 298.

[44]Facsimile ms. in ID, *Ecrits sur la danse.*

[45]*ML,* 295.

[46]Duse to ID, undated, DC.

[47]*ML,* 298–99.

[48]Ibid., 299. For Bellevue, see Loewenthal, 58–65.

[49]A letter from Irma Duncan to *Dance Magazine,* February 12, 1967, tells of the time Isadora's secretary at Bellevue, Alicia Franck, admitted "a little red haired girl, about four years old," to the Duncan school. On seeing her, Isadora "demanded to know what that infant was doing in her school and when told by Miss Frank, she became so angry she ordered that child sent home immediately. In her anger and upset state she also nearly dismissed her secretary for disobeying orders."

[50]Of the first, senior class, only Isabelle Branche stayed with Elizabeth and Merz in Darmstadt.

[51]Anna Duncan to her father, 1914 (C 14–02), Anna Duncan Collection, Dansmuseet, Stockholm.

[52]*DD,* 144.

[53]"Isadora and Vanessa," Anna Duncan interview with Parker Tyler.

[54]Anna Duncan to her father, op. cit.

[55]*ML,* 300. All ID quotations on Bellevue are from *ML,* 299–304 unless otherwise noted.

[56]Loewenthal, 62.

[57]MFR, "Isadora — The Dancer."

[58]Elsa Lanchester, *Elsa Lanchester: Herself* (New York: St. Martin's, 1983), 28.

[59]MFR, "Isadora — The Dancer."

[60]Lanchester, *Elsa Lanchester,* 29.

[61]*Le Temps,* April 12, 1914; in Loewenthal, 62–63. See also ID's short essay "Une Visite de Rodin," Mary Fanton Roberts Collection, City Museum, in which she speaks for herself and her students: "Dear Master, like an all-powerful god, you created an epoch, and we are your creation, like your works of marble; we are your thoughts made flesh. . . . We, the students of the Dance, exist because we were born in the epoch of the Great Rodin."

[62]MFR, "Isadora — The Dancer."

[63]*ML*, 256.

[64]Gabriele D'Annunzio to ID, undated (Rome, December 1913), in "Isadora Duncan Materials," Irma Duncan Collection, DC, folder 44.

[65]*ML*, 6.

[66]Duncan, "Isadora," in *AOD*, 20.

[67]Georges Claretie, "Isadora Duncan à Bellevue et Procès de la Cigale," unidentified clipping, May 4, 1914, Isadora Duncan Collection, folder 24, Scott Library, York University.

[68]*ML*, 301.

[69]Maurice Montabré, "Les nymphes ont dansé," June 29, 1914, quoted in Loewenthal, 66.

[70]Ibid.

[71]*ML*, 304.

[72]Cronin, *Paris on the Eve*, 428.

[73]*ML*, 305.

[74]Ibid., 307–08.

[75]Ibid., 304. ID's narrative of the birth of her third child in *ML*, 305–07; all ID quotes from there unless otherwise noted.

[76]*New York Times*, July 16, 1914.

[77]Desti, 62–63.

[78]Ibid., 64.

[79]*ML*, 307. Craig's copy, in the Craig Collection at the Bibliothèque Nationale in Paris, bears his annotation next to this passage: "The crass idiocy of addressing a new life with an insult from the first!"

[80]Fernand Divoire, "Isadora Duncan," *L'Intransigeant*, September 16, 1927.

[81]*Boston Evening Transcript*, May 7, 1915, DC.

[82]Kay Bardsley, "Social Cause as Dance — Enter Isadora," *Ballet Review* 22, no. 2 (Summer 1994).

[83]Duncan, "Isadora," 21.

[84]*New York Sun*, March 7, 1917, DC.

[85]*ML*, 308–09.

[86]Ibid., 310. ID on Deauville in *ML*, 309–15.

[87]Sturges, 110.

[88]Desti, 66–67.

[89]MFR, "Isadora — The Dancer."

[90]*ML*, 313–14. ID identifies her doctor-lover only as André.

[91]Ibid., 314–15.

Chapter 18: Dionysion 1915

[1]MFR, "Isadora Duncan's School," typescript in Mary Fanton Roberts Collection, City Museum.

[2]*ML*, 316.

[3]Singer later married Joan Balsh, the nurse who supervised the wartime hospital in Oldway mansion. It's possible that his romance with Balsh had already begun. Photographs of the Isadorables and the Bellevue children at Oldway in 1914 show no sign of their host.

[4]*New York Times*, September 14, 1914.

[5]*ML*, 316.

[6]*New York Evening Mail*, November 20, 1914, DC.

[7]Virginia Cowles, 1913, 235–36.

[8]ID, "Dancing in Relation to Religion and Love."

[9]Quoted in Watson, *Strange Bedfellows*, 172.

[10]Max Eastman, *Enjoyment of Living* (New York: Harper, 1948), 420. See also William L. O'Neill, *The Last Romantic: A Life of Max Eastman* (New York: Oxford University Press, 1978), 26–29, and Thomas Bender, *New York Intellect: A History of Intellectual Life in New York City, from 1750 to the Beginnings of Our Own Time* (New York: Knopf, 1987), 228–31.

[11]Untermeyer quoted in *Becoming Modern: The Life on Mina Loy* (New York: Farrar, Straus & Giroux, 1996), 195.

[12]Floyd Dell, *Women as World Builders: Studies in Modern Feminism* (New York: Hyperion, 1976), 44–45.

[13]Floyd Dell, "Who Said That Beauty Passes Like a Dream?," *The Masses* 8, no. 12 (October 1916), reprinted in Dell, *Looking at Life* (New York: Knopf, 1924), 49.

[14]Max Eastman, "Difficulties in Worshipping Isadora Duncan," op. cit., and "Isadora Duncan Is Dead," *The Nation,* September 28, 1927, reprinted in *AOD,* 37–40.

[15]Ira Glackens, *William Glackens and the Ashcan Group* (New York: Crown, 1957), 135.

[16]Floyd Dell, *Homecoming: An Autobiography* (New York: Farrar and Rhinehart, 1933), 274–75.

[17]Arvia MacKaye Ege, *Power of the Impossible: The Life Story of Percy and Marion MacKaye* (Falmouth, Me.: Kennebec River Press, 1992), 258.

[18]Edward Steichen quotes Isadora in *Life in Photography* (Garden City, N.Y.: Doubleday, 1963), unpaginated, Chapter 6, "To Greece with the Duncan Isadorables": "She said she didn't want her dancing recorded in motion pictures but would rather have it remembered as a legend." In *Accent on Life* (Ames, Iowa: Iowa State University Press, 1964), Merle Armitage adds fuel to this fire, recounting a party at Max Eastman's, date unspecified, when Isadora purportedly remarked, "I want no visual record *whatever* to remain of my dancing. I wish to become entirely a legend. After I am gone people will ask: 'How did Isadora dance?' and no one will be able to tell how Isadora danced!" Nothing so incites the glee of anti-Duncanites as this presumed calculation, which is taken as proof that Isadora meant to obfuscate her record — an absurdity, given how hard she worked to train pupils and keep them from altering or exploiting her work. See also Daly, *Done Into Dance,* ix–x: " 'Isadora' is a product of our own personal and collective projections. And, indeed, that is the way she wanted it, from the very beginning. Duncan insisted on mythologizing herself, because she longed to be noticed and remembered. That is why she refused to be filmed, because she wanted to become a legend: an absence rendered perpetually present. The sense of longing that was so much a part of Duncan's dancing reproduces itself in our always thwarted but never-ceasing desire to see her dance, if not in the flesh or on celluloid, then at least in the mind's eye." Armitage recognized that live and filmed performance aren't the same thing: "The powerful emanation, the undeniable communication which penetrated well beyond the walls of halls and theaters, was there [in Isadora] — eluding, as does all great art, analysis via semantics."

[19]Arnold Genthe manuscript draft [(S) *MGZM-Res. Gen Ar], DC.

[20]*ML,* 327.

[21]Genthe ms. draft, DC.

[22]Arnold Genthe, *Isadora Duncan: Twenty-Four Studies* (New York: Mitchell Kennerley, 1929).

[23]*IED,* 121. The program for the Isadorables' first American concert announces: "Miss Isadora Duncan. At which Miss Duncan will present six young dancers."

[24]*New York World,* February 5, 1915.

[25]Luhan, "Movers and Shakers," 330.

[26]*New York Sun* quoted in *Literary Digest,* May 1, 1915.

[27]Lisa Duncan to Irma Duncan, undated, Irma Duncan Collection, folder 102, DC.

[28]*Musical America,* March 6, 1915.

[29]*Boston Evening Transcript,* February 4, 1915, DC.

[30]Sonya Levien, "The Art of Isadora Duncan," *Metropolitan* 42, (June 1915), DC.

[31]Henrietta Rodman, unidentified, undated clipping (*New York Tribune*), DC.

[32]*New York World,* March 5, 1915; *Musical America,* March 6, 1915.

[33]Luhan, "Movers and Shakers," 83.

[34]O'Neill, *The Last Romantic,* 29.

[35]Luhan, "Movers and Shakers," 322.

[36]Mabel Dodge to Gertrude Stein, undated (January 1915), in Patricia R. Everett, *A History of Having a Great Many Times Not Continued to Be Friends* (Albuquerque: University of New Mexico Press, 1996), 240.

[37]Defeated in his bid for reelection in 1916, Mitchel later volunteered for service in World War I, in which he reportedly died by "falling out of an airplane."

[38]Luhan, "Movers and Shakers," 324.

[39]Genthe, *As I Remember* (New York: Reynal & Hitchcock, 1936), 179.

[40]Luhan, "Movers and Shakers," 327.

[41]"No Wickedness in Ida Rogers," *New York Evening Sun,* January 12, 1915, DC: "When people learn that it is to the benefit of the State to support all children up to the age of 16 and to give rich and poor alike a simple, beautiful education, comprising great music, poetry and dancing — when people understand that love cannot be made 'legal' and that every woman has a right to children as a tree has to blossoms and fruit, perhaps some of these horrors of marriage, divorce and prostitution will cease." Ida Sniffen was also known as Ida Rogers and Ida Walters.

[42]Luhan, "Movers and Shakers," 328.

[43]Genthe, *As I Remember,* 180.

[44]Luhan, "Movers and Shakers," 331.

[45]*Musical America,* February 13, 1915.

[46]"Oh! Shame on America! Isadora Duncan Leaves Us — We Have No Appreciation of Art — Americans Are Money Worshippers, Unintelligent and Beyond Hope of Artistic Redemption," *Louisville Herald,* undated (March 1915), DC.

[47]Sylvester Rawling in *New York World,* February 26, 1915, DC.

[48]MFR, lecture compiled for the Mills School, Mary Fanton Roberts Collection, City Museum.

[49]Macdougall, 152.

[50]James Kraft, ed., *The Works of Witter Bynner: Prose Pieces* (New York: Farrar, Straus & Giroux, 1978), 138. Bynner worked on a translation of *Iphigenia* for Isadora at the Century, but she quit the scene before his version could be mounted. See ID to MFR, December 5, 1915, Mary Fanton Roberts Collection, City Museum: "I received Wytter [sic] Bynner's Iphigenia and think it Beautiful. Will you tell him as soon as I am better I will write to thank him."

[51]MFR, "Isadora — The Dancer."

[52]Margaret Wycherly, typed extract from *As I Knew Them,* in Macdougall collection, folder 37, DC.

[53]Sylvester Rawling in *New York World,* April 1, 1915, DC.

[54]Rosemont, 39–40. See also "Miss Duncan Talks Again," *New York Times,* April 10, 1915.

[55]*DD,* 152–53.

[56]Blair, 247–48. Toye was married to soprano Marguerite Namara.

[57]Ibid., 249.

[58]Sturges, 122–24.

[59]*New York Times,* April 24, 1915.

[60]*New York Tribune,* April 24, 1915.

[61]See the correspondence on this subject in the Otto H. Kahn Papers, Firestone Library, Princeton University, and Augustin Duncan to MFR, December 22, 1915: "Enclosed is a check for $43 which Mr. Singer wished me to see that you received. He is making a settlement with the 'creditors' . . . and about one hundred !!! of them have accepted and will be cleared off. The musicians and chorus prefer to wait; hoping for a settlement in full one day."

[62]*New York Telegraph,* May 10, 1915, DC.

[63]Genthe, *As I Remember,* 179.

[64]Luhan, "Movers and Shakers," 334–35.

[65]Robert Edmond Jones, "The Gloves of Isadora," *Theatre Arts* 31 (October 1947).

[66]Sturges, 127.

Chapter 19: South America

[1]ID to MFR, undated ("6.10 PM"), in Mary Fanton Roberts Papers, 1900–1956, Archives of American Art, Smithsonian Institution. A similar cable is at City Museum, from Isadora at the Regina Carlton Hotel in Rome, May 28, 1915: TOYE TURNED TRAITOR . . . ABDUCTED LISEL, and a third in Otto Kahn's papers at Princeton: TRIP DELAYED OWING ABSOLUTE PROOF TOYES COMPLETE DISHONESTY PLEASE AUDIT CENTURY ACCOUNTS DISCOVERED PLOT TOYE TAKING SCHOOL SOUTH AMERICA ISADORA DUNCAN REGINA CARLTON HOTEL. See also Desti, 68–70, for Toye. It's impossible to know the truth about the incident. Irma and Anna say nothing about it; Toye denied everything in correspondence with

James Herbert, Kahn's lawyer. See Toye's letter of June 28, 1915, to Kahn attorney James Herbert, Otto Kahn papers, Princeton: "It is a very serious matter to me that Miss Duncan should have the temerity to accuse me of misappropriation of funds and I wish to have you assured through expert accountants that my books are square to the last cent. . . . It may interest you to know that one of the chief reasons for my quitting Miss Duncan was that she owes me $625 and I could not afford to continue." Toye represented Isadora again briefly the following year for a concert in Pittsburgh.

[2]*DD,* 156.

[3]ID to MFR, December 5, 1915, Mary Fanton Roberts Collection, City Museum.

[4]McCormick may have been the "daughter of a well-known American millionaire" whom Isadora mentions in *My Life* (320): "When I approached her on the subject of helping my school, she replied, 'Yes, they may be lovely, but they do not interest me. I am only interested in the analysis of my own soul.' She had been studying for years with Dr. Jung, the disciple of the celebrated Freud" — the only time Isadora is known to have mentioned Freud's name.

[5]George Middleton, *These Things Are Mine* (New York: Macmillan, 1947), 349.

[6]*ML,* 320–21.

[7]*ML,* 321–22.

[8]*Pall Mall Gazette,* October 23, 1915, DC.

[9]ID to MFR, December 5, 1915, Mary Fanton Roberts Collection, City Museum.

[10]*ML,* 331–32.

[11]*L'Intransigeant,* September 16, 1927, DC.

[12]*New York Telegraph,* April 14, 1916, quoting "a writer of gossip" in the *Daily Sketch* (Paris), DC.

[13]*ML,* 331.

[14]Dumesnil, 20, 18.

[15]Ibid., 28, 46–47.

[16]Dumesnil on Trocadéro concerts, 33–40.

[17]Bardsley, "Social Cause as Dance — Enter Isadora."

[18]Loose notes of Irma Duncan concerning Isadora's dances, Irma Duncan Collection, folder 166, DC.

[19]*ML,* 316.

[20]Van Vechten quoted in "The New Isadora," in Magriel, *Isadora Duncan,* 30–31.

[21]Macdougall, 158.

[22]Dumesnil, 40.

[23]Also at "Les Hirondelles" was Raymond Duncan's son, Menalkas, put under Isadora's charge after his mother, Penelope Sikelianos, entered a sanatorium in Davos for treatment of tuberculosis. "With the company of one other small boy [Jean] he had recourse to nothing but boyish deviltry in that female haven," wrote Menalkas' future wife, Ardée Duncan, in her privately published pamphlet, *The Sole and the Thong.* "He made a complete nuisance of himself, and his father finally had to come and take him back to besieged Paris. His mother died in 1917, while he and his father were staying in Isadora's home at Neuilly."

[24]Dumesnil, 42–45.

[25]Ibid., 39, 47–53.

[26]All quotations to end of chapter are from Dumesnil unless specified; I have given page numbers corresponding to sections of the narrative.

[27]*ML,* 324; on South America, 323–27.

[28]Dumesnil, 112.

[29]Ibid., 24.

[30]Quoted in *San Francisco Chronicle,* March 30, 1986.

[31]From Bordeaux to New York, see Dumesnil, 54–60.

[32]ID in New York, May 1916, ibid., 60–68.

[33]*New York Times,* May 22, 1916. See also Coppelia Kahn, "Caliban at the Stadium: Shakespeare and the Making of Americans," *Massachusetts Review* 41, no. 2 (Summer 2000).

[34]Dumesnil, 62.

[35]Allan Ross Macdougall, "Isadora, A Memoir," in Macdougall Collection, folder 55, DC.

[36]Dumesnil, 63.

[37]Ibid., 63, 72. On the *Byron* to Buenos Aires, 72–99.

[38]Ibid., 92.

[39]*ML*, 324.

[40]Dumesnil, 97.

[41]ID in Buenos Aires, ibid., 100–81.

[42]*ML*, 325.

[43]Dumesnil, 153.

[44]See *New York Review,* September 16, 1916, DC.

[45]ID to Fernand Divoire, July 1916, in Macdougall Collection, folder 3, DC.

[46]Dumesnil, 146.

[47]ID to Fernand Divoire, op. cit.

[48]*DD*, 156.

[49]Interview with Maria-Theresa, undated, unidentified ("Dance Conversations," Don Oscar Becque), in Maria-Theresa clipping file, DC.

[50]Dumesnil, 207. ID in Montevideo and Rio, 185–304.

[51]Ibid., 194–95.

[52]Ibid., 246.

[53]Macdougall, 164.

[54]Transcript of unidentified news clipping (Rio de Janeiro, 1916) in Irma Duncan Collection, folder 184, DC.

[55]Dumesnil, 302.

Chapter 20: "I Tell You She Drives 'Em Mad"

[1]*ML*, 327–29. Isadora and Singer had seen each other earlier in 1916, when she passed through New York on her way to South America. Her remarks about "Wilkins" were excised from later editions of *My Life.*

[2]The printed invitation was dated November 1, 1916: "As many friends have expressed the desire to see the work which Miss Isadora Duncan presented to the wounded soldiers at the Trocadéro in Paris . . . she has decided to invite them to a private dress rehearsal at the Metropolitan Opera House." Isadora also appeared at the Pitt Theatre in Pittsburgh on October 24, 1916.

[3]MFR, lecture compiled for the Mills School, in Mary Fanton Roberts Collection, City Museum. See also *New York Herald,* November 22, 1916, DC: MISS ISADORA DUNCAN POSES WITH ONE SIDE BARE TO WAIST.

[4]Genthe, *As I Remember,* 183.

[5]Macdougall, 166.

[6]"Isadora and Vanessa," Anna Duncan interview with Parker Tyler.

[7]Max Eastman, "Difficulties in Worshipping Isadora Duncan."

[8]Quoted in Blair, 273.

[9]Macdougall, 167. ID on Havana and Palm Beach, *ML,* 329–31. See also Macdougall, 167–69, and Macdougall, "Isadora — A Memoir."

[10]Seroff, 232.

[11]Macdougall to Witter Bynner, undated ("c. 1916"), in Allan Ross Macdougall miscellaneous manuscripts [(S) *MGZM-Res Mac A], DC. According to Maurice Dumesnil, Isadora's gramophone was "a very primitive and simple talking machine; just a plain wooden box surmounted by a plate covered with ordinary green felt cloth." It had become "very dear to her." Among her records Dumesnil saw Paderewski playing Chopin, Kreisler's "'Liebeslied," Wagner's "Träume," and "a double-faced record of two tangos, 'El Bercerro' and 'El Diez y Seis'" (Dumesnil, 73).

[12]*ML,* 330.

[13]Jack Owen, *Palm Beach Scandals: An Intimate Guide (The First 100 Years),* vol. 1 (Florida: Rainbow Books, 1992), 50.

[14]Eastman, "Difficulties in Worshipping Isadora Duncan"; Genthe, *As I Remember,* 186.

[15]Seroff, 235.

[16]On a card to Mary Roberts from Palm Beach (Mary Fanton Roberts Collection, City Museum), Isadora left the astonishing inscription: "Tell Billy I shall *Marry!!*" If, indeed, against her

better judgment, she had agreed to marry Singer, it might explain why this break, of all breaks, was the last.

[17]*ML*, 334.

[18]Carl Van Vechten, *New York Times,* July 14, 1917. See also Bardsley, "Social Cause as Dance — Enter Isadora."

[19]*New York Sun,* March 7, 1917, DC.

[20]*New York Herald,* March 7, 1917, DC.

[21]Ray Stannard Baker, *Woodrow Wilson: Life and Letters: Facing War, 1915–1917* (London: Heinemann, 1938), 501–02.

[22]*ML*, 334.

[23]ID, "Moscow Impressions," in *AOD,* 109.

[24]Blair 431–32, n. 11.

[25]Carl Van Vechten, "The New Isadora," in *The Merry-Go-Round* (New York: Knopf, 1918), reprinted in Magriel, *Isadora Duncan,* 31.

[26]*ML*, 334.

[27]"Isadora Duncan's Misfortune," in Margaret Anderson, ed., *The Little Review Anthology* (New York: Hermitage House, 1953), 80–81. Another critic said that Isadora's dancing made him think of "Grant's Tomb in love."

[28]Carl Van Vechten to Gertrude Stein (erroneously dated "April 5," 1917), in *The Letters of Carl Van Vechten* (New Haven, Conn.: Yale University Press, 1987), 23–24.

[29]*New York Herald,* March 7, 1917.

[30]Eastman, "Difficulties in Worshipping Isadora Duncan."

[31]Ibid.

[32]See U.S. Military Intelligence Reports: Surveillance of Radicals in the U.S. 1917–1941 (86–893580 GUIDE: 105–33), Library of Congress.

[33]Agnes de Mille, *Portrait Gallery* (Boston: Houghton Mifflin, 1990). De Mille's essay on Isadora was first published in the *New York Times Magazine,* September 14, 1952, as "The Revolution of Isadora" and was recycled several times. It outraged every one of Isadora's friends. See Allan Ross Macdougall to Irma Duncan, December 1, 1955, Macdougall Collection, folder 15, DC: "When I went to see Knopf they told me there that they were about to contract for an Isadora biography written by — hold yourself in — Agnes de Mille! Does that curdle your blood?"

[34]Carl Van Vechten to Bruce Keller (1963), in *The Letters of Carl Van Vechten,* 24.

[35]Quoted in Edwin Ver Becke, "Den sanna historien om Isadora," in *AD,* 122.

[36]John Martin, "Isadora Duncan Danced Like a 'Puritanical Pagan,'" *New York Times Book Review,* January 8, 1928.

[37]Eastman, "Difficulties in Worshipping Isadora Duncan."

[38]Quoted in Ver Becke, "Den sanna historien om Isadora," 122.

[39]Anna Duncan letter, June 17, 1919 (C19–01), Anna Duncan Collection, Dansmuseet, Stockholm.

[40]Anna Duncan letter, October 14, 1915 (C15–02), Anna Duncan Collection, Dansmuseet, Stockholm.

[41]*DD,* 163.

[42]Irma Duncan to Genevieve Oswald, January 27, 1958, Irma Duncan Collection, folder 49, DC.

[43]Anna Duncan, "Om Isadora," in *AD,* 127.

[44]*DD,* 163.

[45]Maria-Theresa, "As I Saw Isadora Duncan," in *The Dance,* November 1928.

[46]Anna Duncan to Nadine Robertson, August 20, 1975, copy in Anna Duncan Collection, Dansmuseet, Stockholm.

[47]Loewenthal, 71–72.

[48]Genthe, *As I Remember,* 187.

[49]Seroff, 238.

[50]Swiss composer and music teacher Emile Jacque-Dalcroze had visited the Grunewald school as early as 1906, leading Elizabeth Duncan to exclaim, "My God, that man doesn't know what rhythm is!" (Merz, "Don't Look Back — Look Forward!" in *AOD,* 166.) Eurythmics, involving gym-

nastic exercises, "music visualization," and the exact coordination of motion and sound, was a spiritual descendant of Delsarte, and would sweep Europe "as an aid to mental and moral training and discipline." According to George Bernard Shaw, "the Dalcrozians walk to music, play to music, think to music, obey drill commands that would bewilder a guardsman to music . . . [and] get so clearheaded about music that they can move their several limbs each in a different meter until they become living magazines of cross-rhythms." Manifestly untrue are claims that eurythmics had any influence on Isadora's dancing. Dalcroze complained about her lack of technique; she, in turn, wrote to Gordon Craig from Paris in 1920: "We went to a performance of [*Oedipus*] at the Circus which was appalling. Everyone shouted & bawled & hundreds of Dalcrozes hopping about naked & athletes walking on their hands — Fortunately I met a friend in need who administered to me a bottle of Champagne in the entre acte — otherwise I would have died of it" (CD 240).

[51]Ted Shawn, "American Influence in the Dance," *The Modern Dance Magazine*, June–July, 1917, Mary Fanton Roberts Collection, City Museum.

[52]ID quoted in *San Francisco Examiner*, November 25, 1917, SF PALM.

[53]*ML*, 336.

[54]Genthe, *As I Remember*, 188.

[55]*DD*, 159.

[56]De Acosta, *Here Lies the Heart*, 78–81.

[57]Watson, *Strange Bedfellows*, 325–26.

[58]Calvin Tomkins, *Duchamp: A Biography* (New York: Henry Holt, 1996), 199.

[59]Watson, *Strange Bedfellows*, 137, 326.

[60]Germaine Everling, *L'Anneau de Saturne* (Paris: Fayard, 1970), 140–41. Everling added that whenever Isadora came to see them later in Paris, she and Picabia kept their young son, Lorenzo, out of sight for fear of upsetting her: "But one morning she ran into him when he came back from his walk. Knowing that he was Francis's son, she took him in her arms, her eyes filled with tears, and she said while kissing him: 'One day you'll be able to tell people that you were the only child Isadora ever kissed after she lost her own.'"

[61]*ML*, 336.

[62]Maria-Theresa to Irma Duncan, undated (April 1957), Irma Duncan Collection, folder 46, DC.

[63]*DD*, 163–64.

[64]*Town and Country*, November 10, 1919. See also Augustin Duncan clipping file, DC.

[65]Anna Duncan to Angus Duncan, undated (1975), draft in Anna Duncan Collection, Dansmuseet, Stockholm.

[66]Anna Duncan to Augustin Duncan, undated (1917, C17–01), typed copy in Anna Duncan Collection, Dansmuseet, Stockholm.

[67]*DD*, 164.

[68]Agnes de Mille, *Martha: The Life and Work of Martha Graham* (New York: Random House, 1991), 27.

[69]*DD*, 165.

Chapter 21: Sunk in Sorrow, Tossed in Joy

[1]*San Francisco Bulletin*, November 19, 1917, SF PALM.

[2]*San Francisco Examiner*, November 20, 1917, SF PALM.

[3]*ML*, 337.

[4]*San Francisco Examiner*, November 25, 1917, SF PALM.

[5]Raymond Duncan, *San Francisco* (self-published, Paris 1944).

[6]*San Francisco Examiner*, November 25, 1917, SF PALM.

[7]*San Francisco Bulletin*, November 26, 1917, SF PALM.

[8]Boynton-Quitzow oral history.

[9]Florence Treadwell Boynton memoir in Dillon, *After Egypt*, 151–53.

[10]*ML*, 337.

[11]*San Francisco Examiner* quoted in Rather, *Lovely Isadora*, 81.

[12]Harold Bauer to Margaret Anderson, January 17, 1918, in Harold Bauer Collection, Music Division, Library of Congress.

[13]Harold Bauer, "Self-Portrait of the Artist as a Young Man," *Musical Quarterly* 29, no. 2 (April 1943), 153–68.

[14]Rather, *Lovely Isadora,* 82.

[15]Blair, 279; ID holograph ms. in Irma Duncan Collection, DC.

[16]*San Francisco Examiner,* January 4, 1917, SF PALM.

[17]ID to Mason, undated, in J. Redfern Mason Papers, Bancroft Library, University of California at Berkeley.

[18]Quoted in Dillon, *After Egypt,* 154–55.

[19]ID to Mason, undated, in Mason Papers, University of California at Berkeley.

[20]*DD,* 165.

[21]Mary Desti, "Essay written on 50th anniversary [sic] of Isadora Duncan's birth," Mary Desti Collection on Isadora Duncan, MS-P 5, Department of Special Collections, University of California at Irvine.

[22]De Acosta, *Here Lies the Heart,* 80.

[23]*ML,* 345. This line was cut from later editions of *My Life.*

[24]ID to Mary Desti, undated (London 1918), Mary Desti Papers (Collection 2055), Department of Special Collections, University Research Library, University of California, Los Angeles.

[25]Young, *A Great Task of Happiness,* 178.

[26]*ML,* 346.

[27]Young, *A Great Task of Happiness,* 177–78.

[28]Stokes, *Hear the Lions Roar.*

[29]Young, *A Great Task of Happiness,* 178.

[30]Stokes, *Hear the Lions Roar.*

[31]Peter Quennell to Francis Steegmuller, January 14, 1975, in Steegmuller Collection, folder 53, DC.

[32]ID to MFR, undated (Cap Ferrat, Summer 1918), Mary Fanton Roberts Collection, City Museum.

[33]ID to Mary Desti, undated (1918), Mary Desti Papers (Collection 2055), Department of Special Collections, University Research Library, University of California, Los Angeles.

[34]ID to Mary Desti, April 16 and April 26, 1918, Mary Desti Papers (Collection 2055), Department of Special Collections, University Research Library, University of California, Los Angeles.

[35]CD 240 (postmarked December 19, 1919).

[36]*ML,* 349.

[37]Ibid., 347.

[38]For Rummel, see Charles Timbrell, "Walter Morse Rummel, Debussy's 'Prince of Virtuosos,'" *Cahiers Debussy* 11, 1987; Timbrell, "A Colourful Life: Walter Rummel Rediscovered," *International Piano Quarterly,* Summer 1999; and Omar Pound and Robert Spoo, eds., *Ezra Pound and Margaret Cravens: A Tragic Friendship, 1910–1912* (Durham: Duke University Press, 1988), Appendix 1: "Walter Morse Rummel."

[39]Quoted in James R. Briscoe, ed., *Debussy in Performance* (New Haven: Yale University Press, 1999), 103.

[40]Frances Gregg, *The Mystic Leeway,* with an account of Frances Gregg by Oliver Marlow Wilkinson; edited by Ben Jones (Ottawa: Carleton University Press, 1995), 126–27.

[41]Loewenthal, 138.

[42]*ML,* 357.

[43]Ibid., 349.

[44]ID to MFR, undated (Cap Ferrat, Summer 1918), in Mary Fanton Roberts Collection, City Museum.

[45]Oddly enough, all three of Isadora's accompanists in the years 1916–21 were not only admirers but favored students of Debussy. None of them could persuade her to rethink her attitude toward modern music. Maurice Dumesnil wrote: "Her ideas were very set, and she wasn't in the least eclectic. I hadn't realized this during our rehearsals. . . . She had an adoration for Gluck and Wagner. She appreciated Tchaikovsky and César Franck. She loved Chopin, of course. But the modern French school remained absolutely foreign to her. She didn't understand it. The genius of

Debussy failed to impress her. Her opinions were often stubborn, and she expressed them in a manner that was not only abrupt, but sometimes rude. 'Terrible . . . awful! Do you call that music? Please, play some Wagner' " (Dumesnil, 58–59).

[46] Published as "A Letter to the Pupils" in *AOD*, 107–08, original in Irma Duncan Collection, folder 4, DC. The portions of the letter relating to music also appeared in the *New York Telegraph*, October 24, 1918, DC.

[47]*ML*, 348.

[48]Ibid., 350–51.

[49]Ibid., 348.

[50]Seroff, 246.

[51]*ML*, 348.

[52]John Dos Passos, *Nineteen Nineteen* (Boston: Houghton Mifflin, 1960), 3.

[53]*ML*, 349.

[54]Unedited ms. in Macdougall Collection, folder 55 ("Isadora, A Memoir"), published as "Paris Cinemas of Yesteryear and Today," in *Films in Review*, April 1950, DC.

[55]*ML*, 349.

[56]Fernand Divoire in *L'Intransigeant,* undated (July 1919), in "Isadora Duncan Materials," Irma Duncan Collection, folder 53, DC. Divoire's correspondence with ID in folders 52–59.

[57]Sisley Huddleston, *Paris Salons, Cafés, Studios* (Philadelphia: Lippincott, 1928), 182–83.

[58]Macdougall, 175.

[59]Walter Rummel to Fernand Divoire, October 29, 1919, from Biskra, in Blair, 283.

[60]CD 237 (postmarked Rome, December 12, 1919).

[61]CD 289.

[62]Steegmuller, 347 (referenced to "private collection").

[63]CD 238 ("Saturday," December 13, 1919).

[64]*Book Topsy*, Austin, in Steegmuller, 347.

[65]EAC, 308.

[66]CD 290.

[67]Quoted from ID program, 1920, *Festival Schubert-Tschaikowsky*, Palais du Trocadéro, in *Howard Holtzman Documentation of Isadora Duncan* (catalog), DC, item 188.

[68]Loewenthal, 144.

[69]Huddleston, *Paris Salons, Cafés, Studios,* 185–86.

[70]Karl Kane, "Looking Back on Isadora," undated, unidentified clipping, DC.

[71]CD 240 (postmarked Paris, December 20, 1919).

[72]Antoine Banès, *Le Figaro,* January 27, 1921, in Loewenthal, 148.

[73]Levinson in *Comoedia-Illustré,* undated (1921 or 1923), DC.

[74]Pierre Scize, "Isadora Danse," unidentified source, April 4, 1920, Isadora Duncan Collection, folder 26, Scott Library, York University.

[75]Allan Ross Macdougall, quoting "a witty friend of mine" in "Ballets Russian and Swedish," undated (1920), in Macdougall Reserve Clipping File, DC.

[76]Loewenthal, 143.

[77]Allan Ross Macdougall, "The Dancer Speaks (Two Speeches by Isadora Duncan)," *Touchstone,* February 1921, 336–39.

[78]*IDRD*, 14.

[79]*Piedmont Chronicle,* dateline Paris, April 16, 1921, DC.

[80]Macdougall, "The Dancer Speaks."

[81]*ML*, 351.

Chapter 22: The Bad Fairy

[1]James Beasley Simpson, comp., *Simpson's Contemporary Quotations: The Most Notable Quotes since 1950* (Boston: Houghton Mifflin, 1988), entry 9048.

[2]Sol Hurok with Ruth Goode, *Impresario* (New York: Random House, 1946), 94.

[3]Kendall, *Where She Danced,* 172.

[4]Quoted in *DD,* 169.

[5]*San Francisco Examiner* (January 1918), in *DD,* 174.

[6]Undated, unidentified clipping, Anna Duncan reserve clipping file, DC.

[7]*DD,* 173; original in Irma Duncan Collection, DC.

[8]From a short biography of Raymond, unidentified, in Raymond Duncan Reserve Clipping File, DC.

[9]Irma Duncan, "A Visit with Raymond," unpublished ms. (1924) in Irma Duncan Collection, folder 142, DC.

[10]Lisa Duncan to Irma Duncan, June 7 (1923), in Irma Duncan Collection, folder 7, DC.

[11]Irma Duncan, "A Visit with Raymond."

[12]*DD,* 184–85.

[13]Anna Duncan letter, undated (March 1920, C20–02), copy in Anna Duncan Collection, Dansmuseet, Stockholm.

[14]Interview with Maria-Theresa in "Dance Conversations."

[15]*DD,* 185.

[16]*New York Times,* May 13, 1920.

[17]*DD,* 186.

[18]*ML,* 351.

[19]*DD,* 187.

[20]*ML,* 353–54.

[21]*DD,* 188–89.

[22]Joseph U. Milward, unedited manuscript, *Two Unpublished Chapters in the Life of Isadora Duncan,* 18.

[23]Anna to Augustin and Margherita Duncan, January 6, 1921, typed copy in Anna Duncan Collection (C21–02a), Dansmuseet, Stockholm.

[24]Bernardine Szold Fritz, typescript ms., in Anna Duncan Collection, Dansmuseet, Stockholm.

[25]*ML.*

[26]Penelope Niven, *Steichen: A Biography* (New York: Clarkson Potter, 1997), 316; 475. See also "Artist Only Friend of Isadora Duncan," *New York Times,* March 2, 1921.

[27]Marevna Vorobëv, *Life in Two Worlds,* translated by Benet Nash, with a preface by Ossip Zadkine (London and New York: Abelard-Schuman, 1962), 275. Vorobëv was a student of Margot Duncan (Zehle) in Paris.

[28]ID to Anna Duncan, "Hotel Britannia, Venice 1920," typescript in Anna Duncan Collection, (C20–10), Dansmuseet, Stockholm.

[29]*ML,* 352–54.

[30]Steichen, *Life in Photography.*

[31]Walter Rummel to ID, February 21, 1921, in "Isadora Duncan Materials," Irma Duncan Collection, folder 112, DC.

[32]*ML,* 354–55.

[33]*DD,* 193.

[34]Steichen, *Life in Photography.* In March 1917, when Isadora danced at the Metropolitan Opera, Billy Sunday's religious revival show arrived in New York with the slogan "It's Jesus Christ or Nothing." Sunday's nightly remonstrations against wicked cities, sinful women, and demon rum included a general proscription on "pernicious" literature, with specific reference to the "degenerate" Greeks. "Certain persons . . . have raised $100,000 in order to bring a speaker to this city to tell us strange things," Isadora told her audience. "I am the daughter of Aeschylus, Sophocles, Euripides, Tyndall, Huxley, Herbert Spencer, and Walt Whitman; and this speaker tells me that they are all in Hell. Well, I wish he would go to that Hell so that he may speak with authority."

[35]*DD,* 193.

[36]ID-Irma correspondence, September 30–October 1, 1920, in Irma Duncan Collection, folder 3, in *DD,* 194–97.

[37]See A. B. Malan, "Monkey Bite," in *Royalty Digest* 4, no. 9 (March 1995), 279–80.

[38]*DD*, 198, 203.

[39]Anna Duncan to Augustin Duncan, February 28, 1921, typed copy in Anna Duncan Collection (C21–03c), Dansmuseet, Stockholm.

[40]Augustin Duncan to Norman Harle, November 25, 1920, Irma Duncan Collection, folder 61; in *DD*, 203–04.

[41]Anna Duncan to Augustin Duncan, May 10, 1921 (C21–10), copy in Anna Duncan Collection, Dansmuseet, Stockholm.

[42]Anna Duncan to Augustin Duncan, February 28, 1921 (C21–03c), copy in Anna Duncan Collection, Dansmuseet, Stockholm.

[43]*ML*, 318–19.

[44]Anna Duncan to Augustin Duncan, February 28, 1921 (C21–03c), copy in Anna Duncan Collection, Dansmuseet, Stockholm.

[45]Anna Duncan, "Om Isadora," 128.

[46]*DD*, 202.

[47]Fernand Nozière (Guy Launay), "Un festival de danse et de musique," unidentified clipping, November 29, 1920, in Loewenthal, 145–46.

[48]See Carolyn Lanchner, ed., *Fernand Léger* (New York: Museum of Modern Art, 1998), 16 ff.

[49]Janet Flanner, "Isadora," in *The New Yorker,* January 1, 1927.

[50]Notes of Liliane Zeigel, "Is. Duncan, Visite à Mrs. [William Aspinwall] Bradley, du 25 Mars 1963," in Steegmuller Collection, folder 72, DC.

[51]Michel Georges-Michel, "Dans la Chapelle d'Isadora . . . ," *Paris-Midi,* November 26, 1920, in Loewenthal, 75.

[52]See Pierre de Massot, "Extraits d'un cahier noir, Paris 1917–1921," in Poupard-Lieussou (Yves) Correspondence and Collected Papers on Dada and Surrealism, Series IV, Pierre de Massot letters and manuscripts, 1905–1968, Getty Research Institute.

[53]Quoted from "La Fourchardière," *L'Oeuvre,* in Loewenthal, 144.

[54]Banès quoted in *The Dancing Times* (London), "Paris Notes," March 1921, 494–95, DC.

[55]Anna Duncan, "Om Isadora," 128.

[56]Walter Rummel to ID, February 21, 1921, op. cit.

[57]Debussy quoted on ID programs, 1919–20, DC.

[58]Anna Duncan, "Om Isadora," 130.

[59]Anna Duncan to ID, March 29, 1921 (C21–08c), typed copy in Anna Duncan Collection, Dansmuseet, Stockholm.

[60]*IDRD*, 11.

[61]Ibid., 12–13.

[62]Walter Rummel to Anna Duncan, April 17, 1921 (C21–09), in Anna Duncan Collection, Dansmuseet, Stockholm.

[63]Anna Duncan to Augustin Duncan, May 10, 1921 (C21–10), copy in Anna Duncan Collection, Dansmuseet, Stockholm.

[64]*Illustrated London News*, April 23, 1921.

[65]*The Times* (London), April 17, 1921.

[66]David Vaughan, *Frederick Ashton and His Ballets* (New York: Knopf, 1977), 4–5.

[67]*DD*, 204–05.

[68]ID letters to the Isadorables, postmarked London, April 6, 1921, and Brussels, April 30, 1921, in Irma Duncan Collection, folders 4 and 5, DC; edited in *DD*, 205–07.

[69]*ML*, 356.

[70]*DD*, 209.

[71]Ibid., 208.

[72]*The Times* (London), May 30, 1921; *New York Times*, May 29, 1921.

[73]Desti, 73–74.

[74]*IDRD*, 14–17.

[75]Howard L. Holtzman to Irma Duncan, September 4, 1974, in Irma Duncan Collection, folder 117, DC; original guestbook listed in *Howard Holtzman Documentation of Isadora Duncan* (catalog), item 8.

Chapter 23: Comrade Duncan

[1]Desti, 76–77.

[2]*IDRD*, 84. Irma noted in her diary on July 10, 1921, that the clairvoyant was "not especially bright" (Irma Duncan, agenda and diaries [1921–24], Irma Duncan Collection, DC).

[3]*ML*, 359.

[4]June 4, 1921, Irma Duncan, agenda and diaries (1921–24), DC.

[5]Interview with Maria-Theresa in "Dance Conversations."

[6]*DD*, 213–14.

[7]Ellen Terry, *Ellen Terry's Memoirs*, with a preface, notes, and additional biographical chapters by Edith Craig and Christopher St. John (Christabel Marshall) (New York: G. P. Putnam's Sons, 1932), 300.

[8]Ibid., 328.

[9]Ellen Terry to ID, undated (June 1921), "Isadora Duncan Materials," Irma Duncan Collection, folders 117–20, DC.

[10]*New York Times*, May 29, 1921.

[11]*DD*, 217.

[12]ID in George Seldes, "What Love Meant to Isadora Duncan," *The Mentor*, February 1930.

[13]Desti, 76–77.

[14]*DD*, 218. Irma's diary for July 10, 1921 (DC), mentions "luncheon" with the Krassins and adds: "Isadora upset them all frightfully. We were almost thrown out."

[15]Desti, 77.

[16]Schneider, 27.

[17]*IDRD*, 33. Most of the material on Russia in Macdougall is taken directly from *Isadora Duncan's Russian Days and Her Last Years in France* (*IDRD*), the book Macdougall and Irma Duncan produced together in 1929. I have used the original source where possible. Mary Desti's account is taken from Isadora's recollections, as told to Mary in Paris and Berlin, 1922–27. Other sources as cited.

[18]Schneider, 27.

[19]*DD*, 219–20.

[20]From Tallinn to Moscow in *IDRD*, 22–25; Macdougall, 185–86.

[21]Desti, 78.

[22]*IDRD*, 24.

[23]*DD*, 221.

[24]*IDRD*, 25.

[25]Desti, 78–79.

[26]*IDRD*, 28–29.

[27]Ibid., 62.

[28]Ibid., 30–35.

[29]Quoted in catalog of the Lenin Museum, Moscow. Lunacharsky had shared Lenin's exile in Zurich before and during World War I.

[30]*IDRD*, 48–49.

[31]Quoted in Natalia Roslasleva, "Prechistenka 20: The Isadora Duncan School in Moscow," in *Dance Perspectives* 16, no. 84 (Winter 1975). See also *IDRD*, 51.

[32]*IDRD*, 38.

[33]Schneider, 36.

[34]Ibid., 26.

[35]Ilya Ilyich Schneider to Maria-Theresa, July 25, 1975, in Anna Duncan Collection, Dansmuseet, Stockholm.

[36]Schneider, 26–29.

[37]See "Irma Duncan Engaged," *New York Times*, January 4, 1922. In later years Irma erased Schneider from her life and her accounts of the Duncan school in Moscow.

[38]*IDRD*, 42; Macdougall, 188. See also Irma Duncan to Selma Jeanne Cohen, November 1, 1965, Irma Duncan Collection, folder 87, DC, quoting her diary entry of July 28, 1921: "Stanislavsky is just as sweet as ever."

[39]*IDRD*, 46–47; Schneider, 36. Irma's diary reports on July 30 (DC) that "we had a lot of cognac for dinner" before Isadora left for the party at Kharitonenko's mansion and that "Isadora insulted them all."

[40]Ibid., 12.

[41]Anatoly Lunacharsky, "Our Guest" (*"Nasha gost'ia"*), *Izvestia*, August 24, 1921; *IDRD*, 48–51.

[42]*DD*, 225.

[43]Macdougall, 192.

[44]*DD*, 225.

[45]*IDRD*, 52–53.

[46]Macdougall, 193.

[47]Schneider, 42.

[48]*IDRD*, 55–56.

[49]Ibid., 64.

[50]Ibid., 67–69.

[51]Schneider, 41.

[52]Roslasleva, "Prechistenka 20," 8–9.

[53]*IDRD*, 71.

[54]Macdougall, 194.

[55]*DD*, 227.

[56]Macdougall, 195.

[57]Schneider, 49.

[58]Ibid., 51; *IDRD*, 76.

[59]*IDRD*, 78.

[60]Ibid., 79

[61]Schneider, 55.

[62]*IDRD*, 79.

[63]*The New Yorker* (Vladimir Sokoloff profile by Lillian Ross), October 21, 1961; and Mercedes de Acosta, "Isadora Duncan — An Experience. A Conversation with the Actor Sokoloff," in Mercedes de Acosta Papers, Rosenbach Library, Philadelphia.

[64]Schneider, 52–55.

[65]Yuri Annenkov quoted in Macdougall, 197.

[66]Roslasleva, "Prechistenka 20," 9.

[67]Irma Duncan to Selma Jeanne Cohen, March 22, 1976, Irma Duncan Collection, folder 119, DC.

[68]Irma had written in her diary on July 25 (DC): "Met a lot of contre-revolutionaries. There seem to be very few communists in Russia."

[69]McVay, 261, n. 16, quoting speech of V. E. Meyerhold, November 11, 1921, in *Teatral'naia Moskva*, November 15–17, 1921.

[70]ID, "Notes for a Speech Preceding the Liszt-Scriabin Program," Kamerny Theatre, Moscow, September 21, 1924, in *IDRD*, 274.

[71]*IDRD*, 92–93.

[72]Roslasleva, "Prechistenka 20," 11.

[73]Quoted in *IDRD*, 95.

[74]Christo Pakov quoted in Roslasleva, "Prechistenka 20," 10. Irma noted in her diary on November 6 (DC) that Lunacharsky, seeing Isadora's *Marche Slave*, "was crazy about it."

[75]*IDRD*, 95.

[76]Ibid., 95–96.

[77]ID to Augustin Duncan, op. cit., in *AOD*, 111.

[78]*IDRD*, 98.

[79]*DD*, 230.

[80]ID, "Art for the Masses," *Izvestia*, November 23, 1921, in McVay, 261, n. 16.

[81]*IDRD*, 99.

[82]Roslasleva, "Prechistenka 20," 12.

83Ibid., 14.

84ID, "Art for the Masses."

85McVay, 263, n. 31.

86Roslasleva, "Prechistenka 20," 11.

87Schneider, 51.

88Seroff, 288.

89The exact date of Isadora's meeting with Esenin is unknown. Irma's diary (DC) mentions him by name for the first time on November 9, 1921. On November 30 Irma writes: "Tea with Isadora's Beau Ессенин [original in Cyrillic]. He is ill." And again on December 29: "Ессенин and Mariengoff for supper." For Esenin, see Gordon McVay, *Esenin: A Life* (New York: Paragon House, 1988) and *Isadora and Esenin* (Ann Arbor, Mich.: Ardis, 1980); Frances de Graaff, *Sergej Esenin: A Biographical Sketch* (The Hague: Mouton & Co., 1966); Jessie Davies, *Isadora Duncan's Russian Husband, or Child of the Terrible Years: The Life of Sergei Esenin* (Liverpool: Antony Rowe, Ltd., 1990); and J. Davies, ed., *Esenin: A Biography in Memoirs, Letters, and Documents* (Ann Arbor, Mich.: Ardis, 1982). Other sources cited separately.

90Desti, 125.

91Ibid., 91.

92*IDRD*, 87–88. Mariengof's account in *Novel Without Lies* is also translated from the French by J. W. Bienstock, in *The Living Age* 333, no. 4318 (November 15, 1927). All Mariengof quotations in McVay are from the poet's written memoirs at the Russian State Lenin Library in Moscow.

93Schneider, 57–58.

Chapter 24: Wayward Child

1Max Eastman, *Artists in Uniform: A Study of Literature and Bureaucratism* (New York: Knopf, 1934), 56.

2Ibid., 50–51.

3Ilya Ehrenburg, *People and Life, 1891–1921* (New York: Knopf, 1962), 397.

4Nikolai Poletaev quoted in McVay, 18.

5Ibid., 13.

6SE to Alexander Kusikov, February 7, 1923 (on board the *George Washington*), in McVay, 151.

7Ehrenburg, *People and Life,* 398.

8McVay, 19.

9J. W. Bienstock, tr., "Isadora Duncan's Russian Husband," in *The Living Age,* 926–27.

10Desti, 92.

11*IDRD*, 89–90.

12Blair, 306–07.

13*IDRD*, 115.

14Ibid., 105.

15Blair, 307.

16Quoted in Seroff, 290. See also Simon Karlinsky in the *New York Times Book Review,* May 9, 1976 (in review of Gordon McVay's, *Esenin: A Life*): "There is nothing 'latent' about the 17-year-old Esenin confessing to Maria Balzamova, a young woman infatuated with him, that the great love of his life might turn out to be either a man or a woman; nor is there anything 'latent' about the love letters and poems Esenin and [poet Nikolai] Klyuev exchanged. 'Pressure of the milieu' cannot account for Esenin's recurrent close relationships with men who were either homosexual or had bisexual episodes in their lives ([Sergei] Gorodetsky, Ryurik Ivnev and Leonid Kannegiser, to name a few) or for his widely attested habit of sharing his bed with his male friends. Esenin's alternating attraction to homosexuality and his revulsion against it . . . may well have contributed to his alcoholism and his suicide. His battered and abandoned wives and mistresses seem to have been the principal victims of this poet's inability to come to terms with his bisexuality."

17McVay, 29.

18Ibid., 41.

19Ibid., 42.

[20]*Toledo Blade*, October 2, 1922, DC.

[21]Anna Nikritina to Gordon McVay, December 1, 1976, in McVay, 57–58.

[22]Ibid., 253 n. 4.

[23]Walter Duranty, *I Write as I Please* (New York: Simon & Schuster, 1935), 241–42. See also S. J. Taylor, *Stalin's Apologist: Walter Duranty, The New York Times's Man in Moscow* (New York: Oxford University Press, 1990).

[24]Eastman, *Artists in Uniform,* 56.

[25]Seroff, 294; Schneider, 61.

[26]Schneider, 61.

[27]*IDRD,* 108–09.

[28]Schneider, 88.

[29]*IDRD,* 113.

[30]Schneider, 59.

[31]Ibid., 92.

[32]Ibid., 65.

[33]McVay, 47.

[34]Bienstock, "Isadora Duncan's Russian Husband," 928.

[35]Schneider, 60.

[36]Ibid., 80, 86–88.

[37]Roslasleva, "Prechistenka 20," 14.

[38]*IDRD,* 117–18.

[39]Schneider, 83.

[40]McVay, 48.

[41]Schneider, 98.

[42]Ibid., 85. The conductor was Nikolai Malko, who left dubious memories of Isadora in his autobiography, *A Certain Art* (New York: William Morrow, 1966), 157. Malko imagined that Isadora was in love with him and quotes her saying, "If it were not Esenin, it would have been you."

[43]*IDRD,* 120.

[44]Seroff, 303. The diminutive *Sidora,* which Esenin invariably used, derives from the Russian spelling and pronunciation of Isadora's name — Аиседора, or "Eye-se-dora" — in use since her first concerts in Petersburg in 1904.

[45]Ibid., 121–22.

[46]Elizabeth Duncan to ID, April 11 (1922), "Isadora Duncan Materials," Irma Duncan Collection, folder 63, DC.

[47]*IDRD,* 122.

[48]Schneider, 87.

[49]*IDRD,* 124.

[50]McVay, 53.

[51]Ibid., 51; telegram dated April 18, 1922, original in the Central State Archive of Literature and Art, Moscow.

[52]Hurok, *Impresario,* 89.

[53]*IDRD,* 126.

[54]Seroff, 307.

[55]*IDRD,* 125.

[56]Ibid., 123.

[57]ID, "America Makes Me Sick!" in Rosemont, 129.

[58]McVay, 55.

[59]Quoted in de Graaff, *Sergej Esenin,* 95.

[60]DD, 231.

[61]McVay, 55.

[62]Schneider, 99–100.

[63]Davies, *Esenin: A Biography in Memoirs, Letters, and Documents,* 40.

[64]*IDRD,* 126–27. See also Schneider, 101–03, on Isadora's will.

Chapter 25: "How Russian! How Russian!"

[1]Desti, 105. Isadora traveled everywhere with her personal scrapbooks, photographs, and "a basketful of newspaper clippings," held together loosely by rubber bands. A year later, when Mary joined her with Esenin on the road, "this basket . . . opened and thousands of clippings formed a carpet and trail straight from Berlin to Leipzig. Bits of these clippings stuck to our hats, our shoes and our clothes, generally making themselves seen by everyone. We left traces of them all the way to Paris" (Desti, 153). The Mary Desti Collection on Isadora Duncan (University of California, Irvine) contains newspaper clippings dating from 1901 until after Isadora's death.

[2]Ibid., 104–105.

[3]Ibid., 103.

[4]Hurok, Impresario, 96.

[5]Seroff, 314.

[6]Joseph U. Milward left an unedited manuscript of his friendship with Isadora, Two Unpublished Chapters in the Life of Isadora Duncan. I have cited this source simply as Milward ms.

[7]This was a running joke with ID. See also New York Times (Walter Duranty), December 29, 1925.

[8]Milward ms., 3–7.

[9]Nicolas Nabokov, Bagázh: Memoirs of a Russian Cosmopolitan (New York: Atheneum, 1975), 123.

[10]McVay, 62.

[11]Schneider, 110.

[12]Paris Herald, February 19, 1923, DC.

[13]McVay, 67.

[14]Stokes, 173.

[15]Nabokov, Bagázh, 124.

[16]Maxim Gorky to I. A. Gruzdev, January 9, 1926, in Maksim Gorky: Selected Letters, selected, translated, and edited by Andrew Barratt and Barry P. Scherr (Oxford: Clarendon Press, 1997), 257.

[17]Gorky quoted in McVay, 66.

[18]Gorky quoted in Seroff, 317.

[19]Nabokov, Bagázh, 125–27.

[20]Desti, 105–06.

[21]Seroff, 318.

[22]Nakanune (Berlin), May 14, 1922; in McVay, 63.

[23]SE to I. I. Schneider, June 21, 1922, in Davies, Esenin, 41; also in Schneider, 114, and IDRD, 135.

[24]McVay, 77.

[25]Maxim Gorky to I. A. Gruzdev, January 9, 1926, in Maksim Gorky: Selected Letters.

[26]Seroff, 341. See also Morris R. Werner, To Whom It May Concern: The Story of Victor Ilyitch Seroff (New York: Cape and Smith, 1932).

[27]Desti, 104.

[28]Seroff, 299.

[29]IDRD, 106

[30]Seroff, 314.

[31]IDRD, 140.

[32]McVay, 74; 68.

[33]Author interview with Nikita Alexeivitch Tolstoy, St. Petersburg, October 15, 1993.

[34]IDRD, 133.

[35]Zweig quoted in Suzanne Everett, Lost Berlin (New York: Gallery Books, 1979), 68.

[36]McVay, 75.

[37]Milward ms., 10–13: "A photograph and description of the brocade was published in Harper's Bazaar and a costume for Mlle. Sorel was designed and made from this brocade by Baron de Meyer."

[38]ID to Irma Duncan, undated (1922), "Isadora Duncan Letters" in Irma Duncan Collection [(S) *MGZMC — Res 23], folder 2, DC.

[39]SE to I. I. Schneider, June 21, 1922, in de Graaff, Sergej Esenin, 97–98.

[40]SE to A. M. Sakharov, undated, in McVay, 81.

[41]SE to Anatoly Mariengof, July 9, 1922, in de Graaff, *Sergej Esenin*, 98.

[42]Milward ms., 22.

[43]Lola Kinel, *This Is My Affair* (Boston: Little, Brown, 1937). Hereinafter referred to simply as Kinel.

[44]Ibid., 235–37.

[45]Ibid., 255.

[46]Ibid., 267.

[47]Ibid., 242.

[48]Ibid., 246–47.

[49]Ibid., 249–54.

[50]Milward ms., 18.

[51]Ibid., 17.

[52]Ibid., 18.

[53]Ibid., 6.

[54]SE to Maxim Litvinov, June 29, 1922, in McVay, 79.

[55]SE to I. I. Schneider, July 13, 1922, in Schneider, 116.

[56]Author interview with George Seldes, Hartland, Vermont, August 1991.

[57]Richard Meryman, *Mank: The Wit, World, and Life of Herman Mankiewicz* (New York: William Morrow, 1978), 63.

[58]Ibid., 64.

[59]Schneider, 117.

[60]*DD*, 234.

[61]Milward ms., 24.

[62] Franz Hellens, "Le poête russe et la danseuse," in *Documents secrets* (Paris: Albin Michel, 1958), 136.

[63]Kinel, 261–62.

[64]Milward ms., 25.

[65]*IDRD*, 139.

[66]Ibid., 140–42.

[67]From SE, *The Iron Mirgorod*, in McVay, 105.

[68]Milward ms., 22.

[69]*IDRD*, 152.

[70]Typescript, DC, in Rosemont, 94.

[71]Hurok, *Impresario*, 98.

[72]Ibid., 96.

[73]*New York World*, October 2, 1922, DC.

[74]Joseph Kaye, "The Last Chapters of Isadora's Life, Part Two," *The Dance Magazine*, May 1929, 23.

[75]*New York Tribune; New York American*, October 2, 1922, DC.

[76]*New York World*, October 2, 1922, DC.

[77]Quoted in *IDRD*, 145.

[78]Hurok, *Impresario*, 100.

[79]*IDRD*, 147.

[80]*New York Tribune*, October 3, 1922, DC.

[81]*IDRD*, 148–49.

[82]Hurok, *Impresario*, 101.

[83]*New York Tribune*, October 3, 1922, DC.

[84]*New York Times*, October 3, 1922.

[85]*IDRD*, 150.

[86]*New York Times*, October 8, 1922.

[87]Kaye, "The Last Chapters of Isadora's Life, Part Two," 60.

[88]Hurok, *Impresario*, 102.

[89]*Boston Evening Transcript*, October 21, 1922, DC.

[90]Hurok, *Impresario,* 103.

[91]*Boston Evening Transcript,* October 23, 1922, DC.

[92]*IDRD,* 153.

[93]Ibid., 152.

[94]Hurok, *Impresario,* 105. Hurok added: "This act of defiance the newspapers never revealed in so many words. . . . I record it in justice both to her and to the newspapers, for it was the cue which led the press thereafter to treat her with the contempt, the disrespect, the sly innuendo which they would accord to a fan dancer." Hurok's representatives were, of course, in Boston with Isadora.

[95]Kaye, "The Last Chapters of Isadora's Life, Part Two," 61.

[96]*Boston Evening Transcript,* October 23, 1922, DC.

[97]"Mephisto's Musings," *Musical America,* November 4, 1922.

[98]*Musical America,* October 28, 1922.

[99]*Morning Oregonian,* October 23, 1922, SF PALM.

[100]Stokes, 70.

[101]*Musical America,* October 28, 1922.

[102]Kaye, "The Last Chapters of Isadora's Life, Part Two," 62.

[103]*IDRD,* 165.

[104]Ibid., 154–55.

[105]Ibid., 159.

[106]Hurok, *Impresario,* 95.

Chapter 26: Just a Wee Bit Eccentric

[1]Unidentified news clipping (Chicago, February 1923), SF PALM.

[2]*IDRD,* 158.

[3]Unidentified news clippings (Cleveland, December 12–13, 1922), SF PALM.

[4]John Unterecker, *Voyager: A Life of Hart Crane* (New York: Farrar, Straus & Giroux, 1969), 288.

[5]Hart Crane to Gorham Munson, December 12, 1922, in Brom Weber, *The Letters of Hart Crane, 1916–1932* (New York: Hermitage House, 1952), 109.

[6]*IDRD,* 160.

[7]Hurok, *Impresario,* 107.

[8]*New Republic,* November 28, 1928.

[9]*New York World,* undated (November 1922), DC.

[10]*New York Times,* November 15, 1922.

[11]Joseph Kaye, "The Last Chapters of Isadora's Life, Part Three," *The Dance Magazine,* June 1929, 30.

[12]*New York Times,* November 16, 1922.

[13]Julia Levien, interview with Elizabeth Kendall, August 24, 1976, transcript [*MGZMT 3–1656], DC.

[14]John Sloan to Robert Henri, November 25, 1922, in Bennard B. Perlman, *Revolutionaries of Realism: The Letters of John Sloan and Robert Henri* (Princeton: Princeton University Press, 1997), 282–83; transcript in Mary Fanton Roberts Collection, City Museum, with Henri's note to MFR: "We have missed seeing her but we know that she was there. This surprise we have when Isadora comes back and is still Isadora is interesting. All that she is is because she is a really free creature, free to be, but that anyone could possibly go on being free in this world of slaves seems too much for our ordinary comprehension."

[15]*IDRD,* 162.

[16]Undated, unidentified news clipping, DC.

[17]*Louisville Courier,* November 25, 1922, in Kaye, "The Last Chapters of Isadora's Life, Part Three," 31.

[18]*IDRD,* 163.

[19]Kaye, "The Last Chapters of Isadora's Life, Part Three," 30–31.

[20]Hurok, *Impresario,* 107.

[21]Ibid., 113.

[22]SE to Anatoly Mariengof, in Davies, *Esenin,* 44–45.

[23]Hurok, *Impresario,* 116.

[24]McVay, 114.

[25]Ibid., 148–49.

[26]De Graaff, *Sergej Esenin,* 100.

[27]Undated, unidentified clipping (Esenin obituary, 1925), DC.

[28]Undated clipping, *Cleveland News* (December 12–13, 1922), SF PALM.

[29]*IDRD,* 167, 170.

[30]*San Francisco Examiner,* October 16 and 25, 1922, SF PALM; quoted in Daly, *Done Into Dance,* 203.

[31]Reprinted in Rosemont, 129–36.

[32]Kaye, "The Last Chapters of Isadora's Life, Part Three," 32.

[33]Unidentified clippings, December 26–28, 1922, SF PALM.

[34]Kaye, "The Last Chapters of Isadora's Life, Part Three," 58.

[35]Margherita Duncan, "Isadora," in *AOD,* 21–22.

[36]Desti, 127.

[37]Ruth Mitchell to Joe Milward, January 7, 1923, copy in Anna Duncan Collection, Dansmuseet, Stockholm.

[38]Hurok, *Impresario,* 109–10.

[39]McVay, 140.

[40]Judith Danoff to Peter Kurth, October 10, 1992. This famous incident is told in all accounts of Isadora's last American tour. Danoff added: "The women took a sobbing Isadora into the bedroom and ministered to her wounds. . . . They asked [her] why she stayed with him. It's her answer that I think no one knows. She said she stayed with him because he looked like her two dead children." See also Hurok, *Impresario,* 110–15; McVay, 136–40; and bountiful news clippings, DC and SF PALM.

[41]Milward ms., 47–48.

[42]*New York Sun,* February 3, 1923, DC.

[43]*New York Times,* March 11, 1923.

[44]*New York Tribune,* February 3, 1923, DC.

[45]McVay, 148–49.

[46]Desti, 120. Mary's account of ID and SE in Paris and Berlin fills four chapters, 120–68.

[47]Ibid., 123.

[48]Ibid., 127.

[49]*Paris Tribune,* February 17, 1923, SF PALM.

[50]Ibid., February 19, 1922, DC.

[51]Ibid., February 28, 1923, DC.

[52]*8-Uhr Abendblatt,* February 19, 1923, in McVay, 165–66.

[53]Telegram of February 24, 1923 (from Kusikov archive), in McVay, 167.

[54]Desti, 129.

[55]Ibid., 129–37.

[56]*IDRD,* 171.

[57]Desti, 139–43.

[58]Ibid., 149–55.

[59]Ibid., 164–66.

[60]Lisa Duncan to Irma Duncan, "Mai 14" (1923), Irma Duncan Collection, folder 130, DC.

[61]Milward ms., 38.

[62]André Levinson, "Mme. Isadora Duncan au Trocadéro," *Comoedia-Illustré,* May 29, 1923; in Loewenthal, 150.

[63]Michel Georges-Michel, "Retour de Russie," unidentified news clipping, May 30, 1923, Isadora Duncan Collection, folder 28, Scott Library, York University.

[64]*IDRD,* 181.

[65]Lisa Duncan to Irma Duncan, June 7, 1923, Irma Duncan Collection, folder 7, DC.

[66]Harold Clurman, *All People Are Famous* (New York: Harcourt Brace Jovanovich, 1974), 51–52.

[67] Anna Duncan to Irma Duncan, June 11, 1923, Irma Duncan Collection, folder 7, DC.

[68] Walter Rummel to Anna Duncan, March 10, 1923 (C23–03), Anna Duncan Collection, Dansmuseet, Stockholm.

[69] Anna Duncan to Irma Duncan, June 11, 1923, DC.

[70] Lisa Duncan to Irma Duncan (May 14, 1923), DC.

[71] Emil Thorel to Anna Duncan, February 23, 1923 (C23–02c), Anna Duncan Collection, Dansmuseet, Stockholm.

[72] "Girls Repudiate Isadora Duncan," *New York Morning Telegraph,* May 29, 1923, DC.

[73] Lisa Duncan to Irma Duncan, June 7, 1923, DC.

[74] Milward ms., 51–52.

[75] *Journal d'Eclair,* June 16, 1923, in McVay, 194–95.

[76] *Toledo Blade,* June 18, 1923, DC.

[77] *IDRD,* 182.

[78] *Toledo Blade,* June 18, 1923, DC.

[79] *IDRD,* 182–85.

[80] Desti, 167–68.

Chapter 27: Genius and Kaputt

[1] Schneider, 136–38.

[2] Roslasleva, "Prechistenka 20," 16.

[3] *DD,* 262.

[4] Dorothy Thompson, *The New Russia* (New York: Henry Holt, 1928), 31.

[5] Quoted in Natalia Roslasleva to Irma Duncan, November 2, 1967, Irma Duncan Collection, folder 103, DC.

[6] Schneider, 143–44.

[7] *IDRD,* 189.

[8] Schneider, 145–48.

[9] *IDRD,* 191–92. Schneider on Litvinovo, 145–47.

[10] See Irma Duncan to Selma Jeanne Cohen, March 22, 1976, Irma Duncan Collection, folder 119, DC: "Isadora Duncan, of course, conceived and initiated the whole project but that does not detract from the fact that I, Irma Duncan, single-handedly developed, and brought said project to a successful conclusion. Every single movement and dance gesture the pupils in that school learned to make (with one exception) was demonstrated and taught them by no one else but me."

[11] Roslasleva, "Prechistenka 20," 21.

[12] Schneider, 160–61.

[13] Davies, *Esenin,* 158.

[14] McVay, 211.

[15] *IDRD,* 192.

[16] Max Eastman, "Difficulties in Worshipping Isadora Duncan."

[17] Schneider, 148–49.

[18] *IDRD,* 197.

[19] Max Eastman, "Difficulties in Worshipping Isadora Duncan."

[20] *IDRD,* 199–205.

[21] Ibid., 206.

[22] Schneider, 159.

[23] Ibid., 165–66.

[24] *IDRD,* 218.

[25] Schneider, 167.

[26] *IDRD,* 220.

[27] Schneider, 168–69.

[28] *IDRD,* 221.

[29] McVay, 213–16.

[30] Schneider, 171.

[31] Davies, *Isadora Duncan's Russian Husband,* 221.

[32]McVay, 215–16.

[33]Schneider, 176.

[34]Davies, *Isadora Duncan's Russian Husband,* 243; *IDRD,* 218.

[35]McVay, 217.

[36]*IDRD,* 225–26.

[37]*New York Times,* November 23, 1923.

[38]Ibid., November 28, 1923.

[39]Ibid., November 24, 1923. See also Taylor, *Stalin's Apologist,* 124–25.

[40]Quoted in *New York Times,* December 29, 1925.

[41]Davies, *Esenin,* 161–62.

[42]McVay, 204.

[43]*IDRD,* 263.

[44]Schneider, 180–81.

[45]ID to Augustin Duncan, undated, incomplete, Isadora Duncan Miscellaneous Manuscripts [(S) *MGZM-Res. Dun Is], DC.

[46]ID to Louis Schaffer, December 14, 1923, Isadora Duncan Miscellaneous Manuscripts, DC.

[47]Roslasleva, "Prechistenka 20," 21.

[48]Ann Daly, *Theatre Journal,* October 1990 (in review of Eden's Expressway's re-creation of *Isadora's Workers' Songs*), 369.

[49]Bardsley, "Social Cause as Dance — Enter Isadora."

[50]Daly, *Theatre Journal.*

[51]Roslasleva, "Prechistenka 20," 21.

[52]Irma Duncan to Allan Ross Macdougall, October 31, 1928, in Macdougall Collection, folder 9, DC.

[53]Schneider, 195.

[54]*IDRD,* 240.

[55]Schneider, 197.

[56]*IDRD,* 242–43.

[57]ID to Irma Duncan and I. I. Schneider, July 28, 1924, in Isadora Duncan Letters [(S) *MGZMC - Res 23], Irma Duncan Collection, DC.

[58]*IDRD,* 245.

[59]Schneider, 142.

[60]ID to Irma Duncan and I. I. Schneider, "Vyatka, August 12, 1924," Isadora Duncan Letters, Irma Duncan Collection, DC.

[61]*IDRD,* 258.

[62]ID to Allan Ross Macdougall, "Moscow, Sept. 2, 1924," in IDRD, 259–61.

[63]*IDRD,* 258.

[64]"Notes for a Speech Preceding the Liszt-Scriabin Program," in *IDRD,* 266–76.

[65]*Chicago Tribune,* October 4, 1924, DC, and author interview with George Seldes, Hartland, Vermont, October 1991.

[66]*IDRD,* 278.

Chapter 28: Love and Ideals

[1]*Chicago Tribune,* October 4, 1924, DC.

[2]Quoted in "A Russian Opinion of Isadora Duncan," *Living Age* 323, (November 15, 1924), 401.

[3]*New York Evening Post,* October 25, 1924, DC.

[4]George Seldes to Marian Seldes, November 1, 1976, in George Seldes, *Witness to a Century* (New York: Ballantine, 1987), 156–57. Marian Seldes played Isadora at the American Place Theatre in New York in January 1977, in Jeff Wanshel's *Isadora Duncan Sleeps with the Russian Navy.*

[5]*New York World,* October 5, 1924, DC.

[6]Ibid., October 6, 1924, DC.

[7]Bernard Taper, *Balanchine: A Biography* (New York: Times Books, 1984), 59.

[8]ID to Irma Duncan, October 13, 1924, in Irma Duncan Collection, folder 24, DC.

[9]*Chicago Tribune,* October 4, 1924, DC.

[10]ID letters to Irma Duncan, "End of Sept. '24" to "Dec. 16, 1924," Irma Duncan Collection, folders 20–26, DC.

[11]Quoted in *The Living Age,* 323.

[12]Quoted in Terry, *Isadora Duncan,* 76.

[13]Desti, 177–78.

[14]*DD,* 262.

[15]Allan Coe to Allan Ross Macdougall, undated, in *IDRD,* 291–92.

[16]Author interview with George Seldes, Hartland, Vermont, October 1991.

[17]*Chicago Tribune,* December 14, 1924, DC.

[18]George Seldes to Francis Steegmuller, December 9 (1973), Steegmuller Collection, folder 22, DC.

[19]*Chicago Tribune,* December 14, 1924, DC.

[20]ID to Irma Duncan, "Paris, Feb. 2, 1925," in Irma Duncan Collection, folder 27, DC.

[21]Unidentified clipping, December 31, 1924, CD.

[22]Seldes published his account of Isadora several times, first in *The Mentor,* February 1930 (as "What Love Meant to Isadora Duncan"), and later in several books of memoir and autobiography. See George Seldes, *Tell the Truth and Run* (New York: Greenberg, 1953), 108–14. Isadora's dictated chapter was called, first, "What Love Means to Different Men"; later, "What Love Means to Me"; and finally, "Love and Ideals."

[23]*Chicago Tribune,* December 14, 1925.

[24]Jean Tarvel, "Mme. Isadora Duncan, peut-elle être autorisée à revenir en France?" *Comoedia,* January 2, 1925, DC.

[25]"What Love Meant to Isadora Duncan," in *The Mentor.*

[26]See Fredrika Blair Hastings to Francis Steegmuller, January 5, 1973, in Steegmuller collection, folder 79, DC, and Blair, 374, where Levine is named along with French socialist deputy Jean Longuet, "a grandson of Karl Marx, who at length obtained permission for Isadora to return to France."

[27]ID to Irma Duncan, February 2, 1925, in Irma Duncan Collection, folder 27, DC.

[28]ID to Irma Duncan, March 30, 1925, in Irma Duncan Collection, folder 29, DC.

[29]Roatcap, *Raymond Duncan,* 24.

[30]Quoted in Raymond Duncan obituary, *New York Times,* August 17, 1966: "He was never ashamed of his antics. He once remarked that 'wonderful are the fruits of publicity.'"

[31]Roatcap, *Raymond Duncan,* 28, 30.

[32]*IDRD,* 296.

[33]ID to Irma Duncan, March 12, 1925, in Irma Duncan Collection, folder 28, DC.

[34]*IDRD,* 297.

[35]ID to Irma Duncan, March 30, 1925, in Irma Duncan Collection, folder 29, DC.

[36]ID to Mary Desti, March 24, 1925, Mary Desti Papers, UCLA.

[37]Ibid.

[38]*IDRD,* 301.

[39]ID to Mary Desti, undated, Mary Desti Papers, UCLA.

[40]Telegrams, April 18 and March 25, 1925, in Mary Desti Papers, UCLA.

[41]*IDRD,* 303–04.

[42]*New York World,* April 22, 1925, DC.

[43]John Dos Passos, "Art and Isadora," in *The Big Money* (Boston: Houghton Mifflin, 1960), 136–41.

[44]F. Scott Fitzgerald [Zelda Fitzgerald], "Auction — Model 1934," in *The Crack-Up,* 58.

[45]Quoted in Mary Blume, *Côte d'Azur: Inventing the French Riviera* (London: Thames and Hudson, 1992), 79.

[46]Nancy Milford, *Zelda: A Biography* (New York: Harper & Row, 1970), 117–18.

[47]Tony Buttitta, *The Lost Summer: A Personal Memoir of F. Scott Fitzgerald* (London: Sceptre, 1988), 146–47.

[48]Quoted in Blume, *Côte d'Azur,* 76.

[49]Pierre Loving, "Who Wrote Isadora's Book?" *The Dance Magazine,* May 1931, 58.

[50]Quoted in Blume, *Côte d'Azur,* 83.

[51]Loving, "Who Wrote Isadora's Book?" 58.

[52]Glenway Wescott, "Notes re: Ford Madox Ford and Isadora Duncan," n.d., Glenway Wescott Papers, Yale Collection of American Literature, Beinecke Rare Book and Manuscript Library.

[53]Jean Negulesco, *Things I Did and Things I Think I Did: A Hollywood Memoir* (New York: Linden Press / Simon and Schuster, 1984), 73–78.

[54]*IDRD*, 313.

[55]See *IDRD*, 306–13, for Isadora's efforts with French communists, and Henriette Sauret, "Isadora Duncan, impératrice errante," *La Revue Mondiale* (Paris), March 15, 1928, 161–71.

[56]Seroff, 375, 373.

[57]M. R. Werner, *To Whom It May Concern: The Story of Victor Ilyitch Seroff*, 245–51.

[58]CD 340 (Paris Singer to EGC, May 12, 1925).

[59]Mme. Yorska, "Isadora Duncan! What She Hopes to Achieve in the Future," *Arts & Decoration*, August 1927, 80, DC.

[60]CD 306 (Richard Wallace to EGC, "In bed — date unknown").

[61]Yorska, "Isadora Duncan!" 80.

[62]ID to André Arnyvelde, December 11, 1925, in Sauret, "Isadora Duncan, impératrice errante," 165.

[63]Harrison Kinney, *James Thurber: His Life and Times* (New York: Henry Holt, 1995), 300.

[64](James Thurber), "Morbid Suicide of Russian Poet Stuns Isadora Duncan at Nice," *Chicago Tribune* (wire service), December 30, 1925, CD.

[65]McVay, *Esenin: A Life*, 295.

[66]*IDRD*, 315.

[67]"Isadora Duncan refuse l'héritage du poète Essenine," *Paris-Midi*, November 25, 1926, Isadora Duncan Collection, folder 23, Scott Library, York University. On September 4, 1926, the *New York Times* had estimated Esenin's fortune at $10,000.

[68]Seroff, 385.

[69]ID to Irma Duncan, January 27, 1926, in *IDRD*, 316.

Chapter 29: Seraphita

[1]Minna Besser Geddes, "Isadora: The Last Year," *Dance Magazine*, January 1978, 69.

[2]Jessie Henderson in *The New Yorker Abroad*, July 18, 1926, DC. It may be that Macdougall wrote this story under a pseudonym, of which he used many as a freelance reporter in Paris: "Pierre Duhamel," "Rosita Allan," etc.

[3]Claude McKay, *A Long Way from Home* (New York: Leo Furman, 1937), 258, 290–91.

[4]Loving, "Who Wrote Isadora's Book?" 56–57.

[5]M. R. Werner, *To Whom It May Concern*, 249.

[6]Ibid., 248.

[7]Seroff, 379.

[8]Sir Francis Rose, *Saying Life: The Memoirs of Sir Francis Rose* (London: Cassell, 1961), 71.

[9]From Jean Cocteau, *La difficulté d'être*, in Robert Phelps, ed., *Professional Secrets: An Autobiography of Jean Cocteau*, translated from the French by Richard Howard (New York: Farrar, Straus & Giroux, 1970), 106–07. Rose speaks of the same incident in *Saying Life*, 75–76: "Suddenly a terrible cry rang out from one of the balconies and through the window the Captain's watch came flying into the room. Isadora, with a torn toga, then appeared on the threshold with the beginnings of a beautiful black eye. She cried out that the Captain had struck her. When one of the 'pigeons' protested at this scene and told her that her black eye was only mascara and green eye-shadow paint badly smeared, she seized a lobster covered with mayonnaise and threw it at him. Luckily, or unluckily, it missed and landed in Lady McCarthy's lap." Rose quotes Isadora: "For Christ's sake, stop those lobsters screaming" (Sir Francis Rose, "Isadora Really," *Vogue*, July 1969, 162–63).

[10]Eastman, "Difficulties in Worshipping Isadora Duncan."

[11]Desti, 195–96.

[12]Seroff, 379–80.

[13]Notes of Liliane Zeigel, "Is. Duncan, Visite à Mrs. [William Aspinwall] Bradley, du 25 Mars 1963," in Steegmuller collection, folder 72, DC.

[14]Stokes, 89–90.

[15]Rose, "Isadora Really," 162–63.

[16]ID to Irma Duncan, January 27, 1926, in Irma Duncan Collection, folder 30, DC.

[17]ID to Irma Duncan, March 30, 1925, in Irma Duncan Collection, folder 29, DC.

[18]ID to Irma Duncan, April 7, 1926, in Irma Duncan Collection, folder 31, DC.

[19]ID, "Moscow Impressions," in *AOD,* 114–15.

[20]ID to Irma Duncan, June 15, 1926, in Irma Duncan Collection, folder 32, DC.

[21]Joseph Kaye, "The Last Chapters of Isadora's Life, Part Four," *The Dance Magazine,* July 1929, 37.

[22]Werner, *To Whom It May Concern,* 252.

[23]Ibid., 254.

[24]Kay Boyle and Robert McAlmon, *Being Geniuses Together* (Garden City, N.Y.: Doubleday, 1968), 334–35.

[25]Loving, "Who Wrote Isadora's Book?" 57–58.

[26]Allan Ross Macdougall in *Arts & Decoration,* July 1926, in Macdougall Reserve Clipping File, DC.

[27]Seroff, 235.

[28]Ibid., 376.

[29]Janet Flanner, "Isadora," *The New Yorker,* January 1, 1927.

[30]Solita Solano, "The Hotel Bonaparte," in Janet Flanner–Natalia Danesi Murray Papers, container 16, Manuscript Division, Library of Congress.

[31]Toklas quoted in Axel Madsen, *The Sewing Circle: Hollywood's Greatest Secret: Female Stars Who Loved Other Women* (New York: Birch Lane Press, 1995), 71.

[32]Maria Riva quoted in Madsen, *The Sewing Circle,* 9.

[33]Quoted in Hugo Vickers, *Loving Garbo* (New York: Random House, 1994), 10.

[34]Janet Flanner to Mercedes de Acosta, 1928, in Mercedes de Acosta Papers, Rosenbach Library, Philadelphia.

[35]De Acosta, *Here Lies the Heart,* 170–73. Mercedes's account of Isadora in Paris is largely corroborated in Desti, 184–85.

[36]Photo facsimile with inscription in de Acosta, *Here Lies the Heart.*

[37]Originals in Mercedes de Acosta Papers, Rosenbach Library, Philadelphia.

[38]Seroff, 387.

[39]Milward ms., 28.

[40]Desti, 187.

[41]Rose, "Isadora Really," 103.

[42]Rose, *Saying Life,* 72–73.

[43]Michel Georges-Michel, "Isadora . . . Isadora . . . ," *Paris-Midi,* April 29, 1925, Isadora Duncan Collection, folder 28, Scott Library, York University.

[44]Seroff, 394.

[45]Steegmuller, *Cocteau,* 374.

[46]Glenway Wescott, "Notes re: Ford Madox Ford and Isadora Duncan," n.d., Glenway Wescott Papers, Yale Collection of American Literature, Beinecke Rare Book and Manuscript Library.

[47]Stokes, 25–34.

[48]Ruth Mitchell to Mary Desti, undated (1927–28), in Mary Desti Collection on Isadora Duncan, University of California, Irvine.

[49]Stokes, 16, 43.

[50]For the fate of Isadora's Neuilly house, see Blair, 386, and Loewenthal, 56–58.

[51]Seroff, 391.

[52]Undated, unidentified clipping ("Isadora Duncan May Be Able to Buy Back Home"), DC.

The account mentions as donors and members of the Neuilly committee Count Boni de Castellane, Gordon Craig, Lady Rothermere, Joseph Paul-Boncour, Charles Rappoport, Doris Stevens, and Thalia Rosales, the Argentinian dancer.

[53]De Acosta, *Here Lies the Heart,* 99.

[54]Seroff, 405, 391.

[55]Statement of Lotte Yorska, September 28, 1927, in Mary Desti Collection on Isadora Duncan, University of California at Irvine.

[56]Stokes, 18.

[57]Peggy Guggenheim, *Out of This Century: Confessions of an Art Addict,* foreword by Gore Vidal, introduction by Alfred H. Barr (New York: Universe Books, 1979), 73.

[58]Milward ms., 58–59.

[59]Statement of Lotte Yorska, September 28, 1927, in Mary Desti Collection on Isadora Duncan, University of California at Irvine.

[60]Werner, *To Whom It May Concern,* 263.

[61]ID to Dolly (Mme. Alexander) Votichenko, "Dec. 11," in Fredrika Blair miscellaneous manuscripts [(S) *MGZMB-Res. 87–214], DC.

[62]Eastman, "Difficulties in Worshipping Isadora Duncan." See also Michel Georges-Michel, "Le Suicide Manqué d'Isadora Duncan," *Le Journal,* undated clipping (January 1927), Isadora Duncan Collection, folder 30, Scott Library, York University. According to Georges-Michel, Isadora remarked on being pulled from the water, "Well, then, it is written that I shall have other adventures."

[63]Inscribed on the *Italian Mail,* January 20, 1927 ("Isadora Duncan Attempts Suicide"), CD.

[64]Werner, *To Whom It May Concern,* 263. But see Alice Spicer to Mary Desti, December 26, 1928, in Mary Desti Papers, University of California at Irvine: "This is to certify that the story of Isadora's [attempted] suicide is correct. I am perfectly willing to have you use my first name in telling the story."

[65]Stokes 55.

[66]Werner, *To Whom It May Concern,* 263.

[67]Stokes, 111.

[68]Ibid., 35–37.

[69]Ibid., 50, 103.

[70]De Acosta, *Here Lies the Heart,* 173.

[71]Seroff, 396.

[72]Mercedes de Acosta to EGC, March 18, 1928, in Steegmuller Collection, folder 35, DC.

[73]T. R. Smith to Mercedes de Acosta, September 30, 1926, in Mercedes de Acosta Papers, Rosenbach Library, Philadelphia. Smith disclosed that the firm had been interested in Isadora's book "for several years. . . . We dealt with Mary Desti who is an old friend of Isadora's [sic], but even she could not get her down to any actual date on which we might expect completion of the manuscript — a very important matter to be considered, of course, by any publisher. We had expected to cooperate with some popular magazine . . . thereby assuring Miss Duncan of a fairly large sum, ever so much larger, of course, than she could expect as an advance royalty against the book."

[74]*IDRD,* 329.

[75]Bernardine Szold Fritz, unpublished ms.

[76]Loving, "Who Wrote Isadora's Book?" 21.

[77]Seroff, 390.

[78]Loving, "Who Wrote Isadora's Book?" 58.

[79]*IDRD,* 330–32.

[80]Werner, *To Whom It May Concern,* 264.

Chapter 30: The Ride to Glory

[1]Loving, "Who Wrote Isadora's Book?" 21.

[2]*IDRD,* 340.

[3]Werner, *To Whom It May Concern,* 265.

[4]Geddes, "Isadora: The Last Year," 67–70.

[5]Loving, "Who Wrote Isadora's Book?" 56.

[6]Seroff, 375.

[7]Ibid., 410–11.

[8]Flanner, "Isadora." Duse had died in Pittsburgh in 1924 while touring the United States.

[9]Lotte Yorska, untitled, *Comoedia*, February 28, 1927.

[10]Werner, *To Whom It May Concern*, 267.

[11]Flanner, "Isadora."

[12]*ML*, 351.

[13]ID to Mercedes de Acosta, February 25, 1927, Mercedes de Acosta Papers, Rosenbach Library, Philadelphia.

[14]ID to Boni & Liveright, February 25, 1927, Mercedes de Acosta Papers, Rosenbach Library, Philadelphia.

[15]Zeigel, "Is. Duncan, Visite à Mrs. Bradley." See also *Paris Tribune* and *Le Soir* (Brussels), September 16, 1927.

[16]Eastman, "Difficulties in Worshipping Isadora Duncan."

[17]William L. Shirer, *20th Century Journey: A Memoir of a Life and the Times, Volume 1: The Start* (New York: Simon & Schuster 1976), 314–15.

[18]Ibid., 313.

[19]*Paris Tribune*, August 10, 1927, DC.

[20]Geddes, "Isadora: The Last Year."

[21]Lotte Yorska to Mary Desti, undated (1927, "Monday"), in Mary Desti Collection on Isadora Duncan, University of California at Irvine.

[22]Sturges, 187.

[23]Ibid., 225.

[24]All quotes from Mary to end of chapter are from Desti, 193–281. I have given page references corresponding to the narrative.

[25]Desti, 194–95.

[26]Mary Desti to Preston Sturges, June 3, 1927, Preston Sturges Papers, 1920–1959 (Collection 1114), Department of Special Collections, University Research Library, UCLA.

[27]Desti, 212.

[28]Ibid., 196.

[29]Seroff, 395.

[30]Desti, 204–05.

[31]Ibid., 206–07.

[32]Niven, *Steichen*, 528.

[33]*DD*, 314.

[34]Ibid., 311.

[35]Desti, 217.

[36]Kaye, "The Last Chapters of Isadora's Life, Part Four," 36.

[37]Zeigel, "Is. Duncan, Visite à Mrs. Bradley."

[38]Werner, *To Whom It May Concern*, 273.

[39]*IDRD*, 344.

[40]Middleton, *These Things Are Mine*, 350.

[41]*IDRD*, 344.

[42]Desti, 221.

[43]Seroff, 422.

[44]*IDRD*, 345–46.

[45]Szold ms.

[46]De Acosta, *Here Lies the Heart*, 188.

[47]ID to Mercedes de Acosta, Mercedes de Acosta Papers, Rosenbach Library, Philadelphia. In the third line, the word *Hard* is written above the word *Soft*, but neither is deleted.

[48]De Acosta, *Here Lies the Heart*, 189.

[49]Middleton, *These Things Are Mine*, 351–52.

[50]De Acosta, *Here Lies the Heart*, 190.

[51]Desti, 229.

[52]Ibid., 228–29.

[53]Seroff, 426.

[54]Desti, 236–37.

[55]Alice Spicer to Juliet Rublee, September 21, 1927, Gift of Paul Danz [(S) *MGZM-Res. Dun Is — 2], DC.

[56]Desti, 239.

[57]Werner, *To Whom It May Concern,* 274.

[58]Seroff, 429.

[59]Desti, 241–47.

[60]Sturges, 229.

[61]Loving, "Who Wrote Isadora's Book?" 56.

[62]Szold ms. In May 1926, at a birthday lunch in Paris, the same sort of joke was perpetrated when Isadora's pending marriage to a nonexistent "Duc de Chartres" was announced to the press (unidentified wire report, May 27, 1926, in the *Daily Oklahoman*).

[63]Loving, "Who Wrote Isadora's Book?" 58.

[64]De Acosta, *Here Lies the Heart,* 127–28.

[65]Szold ms.

[66]Glenway Wescott, *Continual Lessons: The Journals of Glenway Wescott, 1937–1955,* Robert Phelps and Jerry Rosco, eds. (New York: Farrar, Straus & Giroux, 1990), 62.

[67]AP dispatch, dateline Nice, September 14, 1927.

[68]Wescott, *Continual Lessons,* 62.

[69]*Palm Beach Post,* April 30, 1927.

[70]Zeigel, "Is. Duncan, Visite à Mrs. Bradley."

[71]Paris Singer to Preston Sturges, July 5, 1927, in Preston Sturges Papers, UCLA.

[72]Desti, 250–54.

[73]Ibid., 260–63.

[74]Mary Desti to Preston Sturges, October 3, 1927, Preston Sturges Papers, UCLA.

[75]Desti, 265.

[76]See *France de Nice et du Sud-Est,* September 15, 1927, and *Petit Niçois,* September 17, 1927, in Mary Desti Collection on Isadora Duncan, University of California at Irvine.

[77]Ibid., 265–69.

[78]Alice Spicer to Juliet Rublee, October 16, 1927, gift of Paul Danz, DC.

[79]Desti, 269–70. See also Sturges, 223–24, for the history of the shawl.

[80]Rose, *Saying Life,* 73.

[81]Mary Desti to Preston Sturges, October 3, 1927, in Preston Sturges Papers, UCLA.

[82]Desti, 271–72.

Epilogue

[1]*ML,* 3.

[2]Genthe, *As I Remember,* 198.

[3]Cocteau to Glenway Wescott, in Steegmuller, *Cocteau,* 387.

[4]*Cleveland Plain Dealer,* September 16, 1927, SF PALM.

[5]*New York Times,* September 15, 1927.

[6]*Petit Niçois,* September 15, 1927, Mary Desti Collection; *IDRD,* 353.

[7]Mary Desti to Preston Sturges, October 3, 1927, in Preston Sturges Papers, UCLA.

[8]*Petit Marseillais,* September 17, 1927, Mary Desti Collection.

[9]Telegram in Mary Desti Collection.

[10]Paris Singer to Mary Fanton Roberts, September 15, 1927, telegram in Mary Fanton Roberts Collection, City Museum.

[11]Mary Desti to Preston Sturges, October 3, 1927, Preston Sturges Papers, UCLA.

[12]*La France de Nice et du Sud-Est,* September 17, 1927, Mary Desti Collection.

[13]Ibid.

[14]Desti, 276.

[15]Ibid., 277. See also *Le Solaire* (Nice), September 17, 1927, Mary Desti Collection.

[16]*New York Times,* September 19, 1927.

[17]*Chicago Tribune,* September 17, 1927, DC.

[18]Allan Ross Macdougall to MFR, October 12, 1927, Mary Fanton Roberts Collection, City Museum.

[19]*New York Herald-Tribune,* September 20, 1927, DC.

[20]*Paris Matinale,* September 20, 1927, Mary Desti Collection.

[21]Bernardine Szold ms. in Anna Duncan Collection, Dansmuseet, Stockholm.

[22]Mary Desti to Preston Sturges, October 3, 1927, Preston Sturges Papers.

[23]Szold ms., Anna Duncan Collection, Dansmuseet, Stockholm.

[24]*San Francisco Call & Post,* September 15, 1927, DC.

Index

A

Abélard, Peter, 300
Academy, The (periodical), 228
Acis and Galatea (ballet), 154
Acosta, Mercedes de, 368–69, 377, 530,
  532–33, 534, 538, 548
  friendship with Isadora, 523–27, 543–44
actionalism, 391–92
Actor Prepares, An (Stanislavsky), 223
Adams, Maude, 26, 231
Adler, Jacob, 233–34, 330
Aeschylus, 115
Afternoon of a Faun (ballet), 286
Agamemnon, 99, 186
  Raymond copies palace of, 113, 340
Ainslie, Douglas, 65, 66–67, 72
Ala (Duncan pupil), 324
Albania, relief efforts in, 297, 303, 307, 341
Alcestis' Farewell (Duncan dance), 90
Alexander Mikhailovitch, Grand Duke, 541
Alexander, king of the Hellenes, 393, 399
"Alexander's Ragtime Band" (Berlin), 324
Alexandra, empress of Russia, 244
Alexandra, queen of England, 230, 250, 251
Algemeen Handelsblad, 185
Algren, Nelson, 35
Ali Baba and the Forty Thieves (Vaughan
  dance), 60
Allan, Maud, 189–90, 226, 227–29, 230
All-Russian Union of Writers, 515

Alma-Tadema, Lawrence, 59, 60, 61, 65
Amazing Journey, An (Dumesnil), 346–47
"Amber" (Martha Everts Holden), 37
Ambrogio di Predis, Giovanni, 61
American Red Cross poster, 367
American Relief Association (ARA), 418, 425,
  446, 491
American Weekly, 469, 471
Amsterdam *Nieuwsblad,* 185
Anderson, Margaret, 362
Anderson, Marian, 390
Andrei Vladimirovitch, Grand Duke, 156
Angel with a Viol (dance representation), 61,
  90
Anna ("Isadorable"). *See* Denzler, Anna
Anna (maid), 176
Annette (Duncan pupil), 324
Anspacher, Louis K., 498
Apollinaire, Guillaume, 245
Apollo (vs. Dionysus), 60, 67, 77, 93, 103
Arabian Nights quoted, 155
Arden, Elsie, 543
Armitage, Merle, 601n18
Armory Show (modern art), 325
Armour, Phil, 38
Arnyvelde, André, 314, 512, 530
art nouveau
  Fuller as "queen" of, 85
  German, 100
Art of the Theatre, The (Craig), 159, 186, 195
Arts & Decoration magazine, 233

Ashcan School of painting, 233, 325
Ashton, Sir Frederick, 405
Associated Press, 549
Astor, Mrs. William Backhouse Jr., 48, 49
Astor fortune, 548
As You Like It (Daly production), 45
Atkin, Gabriel, 528
Auer, Leopold, 175
Augusta Victoria, Kaiserin, 171, 189, 389
Auxias, Nina (Mrs. Leo Stein), 595n97
Ave Maria (Schubert), 329, 357, 376, 420, 470,
    489–90, 543
Axen, Gertrud von, 86

Ƀ

Bacchae, The (Euripides), 291
Bacchanal. See Tännhauser
Bacchus and Ariadne (Duncan dance), 90
Bach, Duncan interpretation of, 374
    Air on the G String, 359
    Suite in D, 271, 273
Bady, Berthe, 596n21
Baker, Josephine, 523
Bakst, Léon, 152, 156, 245, 246, 247, 511
Balanchine, George, 225, 500
Balashova, Alexandra, 419, 429
Balkan League, 341
Balkan War (1912–13), 297, 303
ballet:
    Bolshoi, 416, 417
    "death" of, 246
    Empire (London), 63
    Imperial Russian, 419, 426
    Isadora's influence on, 147–48, 154–55,
        190, 405
    Isadora's view of, 22, 24–25, 31–32, 45,
        104–05, 151, 156–57, 247–48
    out of favor, 425
Ballets Russes, 74, 147–48, 151, 190, 229, 367,
    388, 390, 500
    opens, 245, 246–48
Ballets Suédois, 388
ballroom dancing, 32, 50, 227, 324–25
Balsh, Joan, 360, 600n3
Balzac, Honoré de, 300, 518
Balzac (Rodin statue), 72
Banès, Antoine, 401
Bankhead, Tallulah, 524
Bardsley, Kay, 270
Barnard, George Gray, 234, 241, 331, 359
Barnes, Djuna, 523
Barney, Natalie, 523
Barnum, P. T., 404

Barnwell, Manya, 519
Barrie, J. M., 131
Barrymore, Ethel, 231
Bataille, Henri, 288
Bauer, Harold, 374–76, 380
Bayadère, La (ballet), 151
Bayreuth festival, 117–25, 171, 286–87
Beach, Sylvia, 523
Beardsley, Aubrey, 226, 529
Beaugnies, Jacques, 72, 73, 74
Beaumont, Count Etienne de, 519
Beaunier, André, 72, 74–75, 77, 85
Beaux-Arts academy, 233
Beckwourth, Jim, 19
Beerbohm, Max, 133
Beethoven, Ludwig van, 18, 23, 173, 190, 311,
        313, 374, 387, 391. See also Seventh
        Symphony
Belasco, David, 189
Bel Geddes, Norman, 142
Belgium Tragic, Belgium Heroic (Duncan
        dance), 382
Bell, Archie, 468, 469
Bell, Clive, 378
Bellevue (Dionysion), 311–16
    as military hospital, 319–20, 323, 385
    parody of school, 315
    school during World War I, 323–24, 328,
        330, 338, (closes) 353, (rebuilding
        planned) 365, 384, 385, 391
    sold, 387, 389
Bellows, George and Emma, 592n52
Belmont, Mrs. O. H. P., 49, 50
Bely, Andrei, 152, 175
Bénédiction de Dieu dans la Solitude, La (Liszt),
        382
Benislavskaya, Galina, 488, 489
Benois, Alexandre, 152, 156, 157, 224, 246,
        247, 511
Benson, Frank, 61
Benson, Stuart, 367
Bérault, Tristan and Isolde de, 280
Beregi, Oszkár, Isadora's affair with, 89–90, 91,
        92–95, 96–98, 121, 122, 570n72
Bergson, Henri, 314
Berkman, Alexander, 457
Berlin, Irving, 324
Berliner Tageblatt, 190
Berlin Press Club, 103
Berlioz, Hector, 387
Bernhardt, Sarah, 26, 102, 200, 245, 470, 537
    Isadora meets, 368
Bertrand, Aia, 391, 508
Besser, Minna, 536, 539

Bey, Vely, 278, 539–40
Bibesco, Princess Marthe, 73
Bible readings, 329, 330
Big Money, The (Dos Passos), 508
Billy Budd (Melville), 518
"Biomechanics," 422
Birth of Tragedy from the Spirit of Music, The (Nietszche), 103
Bispham, David, 273
Bizet, Georges, 29
Black Crook, The (dance extravaganza), 32, 46
Blacksmith, The (Duncan dance), 492
Blake, William, 208, 276
Blavatsky, Helena, 30
Bloch, Ernst, 353
Bloch, Gabrielle, 86
Bloody Sunday (1905), 148, 149
Bloomsbury group, 378
Blue Danube (Strauss), 90–91, 115–16, 185–86, 238
Blum, René, 266
Bohemian Club (Chicago), 37–38
Boissevain, Eugene, 370
Bolshevism, 361, 400, 402, 423, 489
    ban on word "God," 452
    Esenin's, denounced, 480
    fears of (Red scare), 364, 383, 388, 412, 457–59, 461–62
    Isadora and, 327, 422, 541, (defends) 403, 406, 413, (denies) 465, 477, 505, (and meaning of word) 495–96
    Old Bolsheviks, 415
    women and, 490
Bolshoi Ballet, 416, 417, 435
Bolshoi Theatre, 422, 423, 424, 425, 457
    Isadora dances at, 489, 491, 496
Bonaparte, Jérôme, 243
Bonfanti, Marie, 32, 46
Boni & Liveright, 533, 536, 538
Bonnard, Sylvestre, 452
Book Topsy (Craig), 140–45, 177
Booth, Edwin, 26
Borglum, Auguste, 572n66
Borglum, Gutzon, 331, 572n66
Boris, Grand Duke, 152
Borodin, Alexander, 246
Bosson, Dr. Emil, 265, 277, 291, 317
Boston Evening Transcript, 232, 271, 330, 460, 461
Boston Herald, 241
Boston incident, 462, 464
Boston Opera Company, 266
Botticelli, Sandro, 18, 21, 61–62
Bouhiron, Marcel, 597n41

Bourdelle, Emile-Antoine, 108, 290–91, 297, 389, 514, 530
Bourgeois, Stephan, 370, 411
Boynton, Florence Treadwell, 16, 23–29 *passim,* 222, 373–74, 376
Brackett, Charlie, 510
Bradley, Jenny, 508, 520, 537, 542, 549
Bradley, William Aspinwall, 508, 532–38 *passim,* 544, 552
Brahm, Otto, 138, 202
Brahms, Johannes, 190, 194, 373, 400, 405, 470
Branche, Isabelle ("Isadorable"), 167, 275, 599n50
Braque, Georges, 245
Bridge, The (Crane), 464
Brillant, Maurice, 247
British Architect, The (periodical), 132
British "pantos," 32
Broadway Magazine, 51
Brooklyn Academy of Music, 467, 470
Brooklyn Eagle, 367
Brooks, Louise, 367
Brooks, Romaine, 523
Brouckère, Elise and Jeanne de, 140
Broun, Heywood, 458
Brown, Jay F., 597n60
Browning, Robert, 18, 65
Bruce, Kathleen. *See* Scott, Kathleen Bruce
Bryan, William Jennings, 49
Buffalo Bill (William Cody), 71
"Bugatti." *See* Falchetto, Bénoit
Building a Character (Stanislavsky), 223
Bukharin, Nikolai, 489
Burgstahler (tenor), 123
Burne-Jones, Edward, 51, 59
Burns, Robert, 18
Busching, Paul, 118, 124
Bynner, Witter, 272–73, 322, 336, 358
Byron, George Lord, 21, 110, 327

C

Caesar and Cleopatra (Shaw), 178, 188
Caffin, Charles H., 269, 270, 272
Caillaux, Joseph and Henriette, 316
Caliban of the Golden Sands (MacKaye "civic masque"), 239, 348
"California Faun, The," 37
California Home Journal, 9
Calmette, Gaston, 286, 295–96, 299, 316
Campbell, Mrs. Patrick, 58–59, 296
Canterbury Pilgrims (MacKaye play), 264
Caplet, André, Isadora's affair with, 268–69

Carew, James, 211
Carew, Kate, 285
Carnegie Hall (New York), 44, 235, 264, 269, 324, 465–66, 470
  audience warned, 271–72
  Duncan studio in, 43, 52
  Isadorables at, 328, 390, 393
  Isadora lectures at, 45
  sold out, 390, 460
Carpeaux, Jean-Baptiste, 286
Carrière, Eugène, 77, 258, 313, 346
Caruso, Enrico, 278
Casals, Pablo, 64
Casati, Marchesa, 540–41
Cassatt, Mary, 30
Castle, Vernon and Irene, 325
Catholic Church, 10, 124, 299
  mother breaks with, 16
Catholic Encyclopedia, The, 5
Cavalieri, Lina, 247, 548–49
Century Theater experiment (New York), 335–38, 347, 353, 399
Cézanne, Paul, 591n36
Chaigneau, Thérèse, 383
Chaliapin, Fyodor, 247, 416
Champollion, Jean-François, 300
Chanel, Coco, 400
Chanler, John, 549
Chanler, Robert, 548–49, 551
Chansons de Bilitis (Louÿs), 74, 480
Chaplin, Charlie, 510, 523
Charpentier, Gustave, 117
Château Villegenis, 240, 242–43, 245
Châtelet. See Théâtre du Châtelet
Chicago Daily Forward, 491
Chicago Press Club, 35, 36
Chicago Tribune, 36, 238, 462, 503–04, 515, 539
Chicago world's fair (1893), 34, 70
Child, Julia, 371
"Child Dancing, A" (Duncan essay), 196
child labor laws, 231
children, modern thinking about, 123
Chopin, Frédéric:
  burial spot of, 300
  Isadora's use of music of, 73, 90, 152, 190, 194, 228, 233, 248, 337, 380, 511, 608n45, (experiment with) 206, (interpretation of), 47, 63, 374–75, 420, ("package") 382, 385, (popularity of) 336, 345, 354, 373, 400, (precedent for) 155, 173
  Isadorables' interpretation, 393, 405
  Sand and, 446

  See also Funeral March (Chopin); Sylphides, Les
Chopin Abend (Duncan performance), 141
Chopin Festival (Duncan program), 387
Christ and Anti-Christ (Merezhkovsky), 480
Christian baptism, 489
Christian Science, 31, 373
Claflin, Tennessee, 327
Claudel, Paul, 73, 245
Clef Club Orchestra, 324
Clemenceau, Georges, 76, 83
Cléopâtre (ballet), 246
Clurman, Harold, 478
Coburn, Charles, 263–64, 370, 371, 597n41
Cocteau, Jean, 244, 297, 314, 510, 511–12, 521
  quoted, 286, 519–20, 528
Coe, Allan, 502
Cole, Tom, 8
Colette (Duncan pupil), 324
Colette (writer), 73, 245
Collier, John, 331, 332, 333
Collier's magazine, 367
Colonne, Edouard, and Colonne Orchestra, 117, 266, 268, 290, 299
Columbus, Christopher, 34, 110
Comédie-Française, 39, 77, 245
Comintern, the, 489
Comité International du Patronage Artistique, 74
Committee for the Furtherance of Isadora Duncan's Work in America, 331
Communist Party, 414, 417, 496
  French, 512
  Women's Section, 489–90
Comoedia (periodical), 537
Comyns Carr, Alice, 572n13
Concerts Lamoureux Orchestra, 246
Confessions of a Hooligan (Esenin), 447, 455
Constantine I, king of Greece, 341–42, 393
Cook, George Cram, 338
Coolbrith, Ina Donna, 10, 19
Copeau, Jacques, 401
Copeland, George, 337, 376, 390
Coquelin, Benoît Constant, 102
Corey, Mrs. W. E. (Maybelle), 243
Corfu, Duncans in, 303–07
Cornelius, Karl, 165
costumes, 57, 61–62, 63, 86, 90, 102, 186, 257, 266
  "little white tunic," 19, 46
  lost in fire, 54, 57
  and "nudity," 46, 87–88, 119, 153, 175, 176, 238, 280, 423, 461, (dances

barefoot) 83, 87, 151–52, 155, 187, 189, 264, ("indecency" claims) 280, 462

Western dress abandoned, 109–10, 120, (returns to designer fashions) 245, 257, 271, 275, 400, 459

Coué, Emile, 242, 365

Countess Gucki, The (Daly production), 42

Covent Garden (London), 405

Crabtree, Little Lotta, 26

Craftsman, The (periodical), 233

Craig, David, 210

Craig, Edith (Edy), 130, 132, 228, 412

Craig, Edward A., 136, 180, 386
quoted, 134–38 *passim,* 143, 178, 181, 201, 202, 209, 216

Craig, Edward Henry Gordon, 221, 228, 407, 429–30, 439, 531
birth and childhood, 130–33
Duncan family hostility to, 145, 157–58
and Grunewald school, 161, 162, 163, 171
importance of own work to, 134, 184, 188
Isadora meets, 121, 125–26, 129–30, 133–35, 136–46, 379, (break with) 134, 204, 216, 219, 222, 238, 259, 278–79, (later meeting) 252–53
Isadora's finances, 183, 193, 206, 214, 222, 231, 513, 514
Isadora's letters to, 75, 145–50 *passim,* 155, 157, 159, 174, 176–78, 180–85 *passim,* 194, 195–96, 204–15 *passim,* 219, 222, 229, (after children's death) 304–05, 306, 308, 385–86, 387, (Craig rereads) 129, 146
as Isadora's manager, 179, 187, 213, 287
and Isadora's memoirs, 216, 220, 532–33
letters to Isadora, 155–56, 177, 212–15, 231, 306, 503
letters to Martin Shaw, 133, 137, 159–60, 178, 188, 230, 306, (about Duse) 203, 204, 207, 210
marriage and children of, 136, 177, 179–81, 210, (child with Isadora) 184, 194–201 *passim,* 204–06, 219, 222, 231, 236, 262, 287, 289, (children's death) 295–300 *passim,* 305–06, 308
in Russia with Isadora, 173, 175, 176
as stage designer, 132, 133, 137–38, 142, 178, 186, 200–04, 230, 338, (Duse and) 203, 204, 207, 210, (*Hamlet*) 176, 200, 231, 253, 287, 289, (opens school) 287

Übermarionetten, 133, 178, 210

PUBLICATIONS, 128
The Art of the Theatre, 159, 186, 195
autobiography (*Index to the Story of My Days*), 136, 139, 178–79, 201
Book Topsy, 140–45, 177
drawings of Isadora, 178, 192
magazine (*The Mask*), 178, 210, 213, 278

Crane, Hart, 464–65

Cravens, Margaret, 383

Criterion Theater (New York), 232, 233

Critique of Pure Reason (Kant), 101

Cronin, Vincent, 83

Crowley, Aleister, 242, 278, 280, 446

Cuba, Isadora in, 358–59

cubism, 245, 285

Curie, Marie and Pierre, 70, 71

Curley, Mayor James M., 462

D

Dada movement, 367, 369, 547

d'Agoult, Marie, 119

Dalcroze, Jaques-Emile, 367

Dalliès, Christine, 378, 393, 394, 395, 403
as Isadora's secretary, 379, 385, 594n78

Daly, Ann, 133, 571n50

Daly, Augustin, 38–43, 45–46, 231

Dames de France, Bellevue given to, 319

Damrosch, Gretchen, 238–39, 240

Damrosch, Walter, 234–35, 238, 240, 270, 271–72

Dance Idylls (Duncan program), 155, 185

Dance Magazine, The, 470

Dance of the Apprentices, Dance of the Flower Maidens (Wagner reprise), 401

Dance of the Future (Duncan essay/speech), 58, 103–05, 185, 238

Dance of Wandering, A (Duncan dance), 47

"Dancer and Nature, The" (Duncan essay), 184, 191, 220

dancing
as abstraction, 390–91
Puritan view of, 22
"skirt," 32, 60, 70, 140
theater vs. social, 32
See also ballet; ballroom dancing

Dancing in Petersburg (Kschessinska), 148

Dancing Times (Paris), 401, 501

D'Annunzio, Gabriele, 201, 314–15, 439, 503

Danse, La (Carpeaux statue), 286

Danse du Sauvage (Baker revue), 523

Darmstadt school, 308
formed, 244, 260, 275, 290, 312, 320, 331–32

Darmstadt school (*continued*)
  moved to U.S., 376, (government investi-
    gates) 364
  returns to Germany, 437, 501, 522
Darwin, Charles, and Darwinism, 31, 99, 103,
    123, 166
Davenport, Fanny, 26
David, Jacques-Louis, 267
Davidson, Jo, 543
Davis, Belle, 228
"Dazié, Mlle.," 226
Death and the Maiden (Duncan dance), 248
Debussy, Claude, 73, 268, 346, 374, 380, 402,
    596n21
  Isadora's objection to, 381, 607n45
  Nijinsky dances to, 285–86
de Caraman-Chimay, Clara Ward, 73
de Castellane, Anna Gould, 73
Decembrists, 419
de Croy, Princess Auguste, 73
Dehn, Adolph, 510
Delacroix, Eugène, 325, 345
Dell, Floyd, 326–27, 510
Delsarte, François, 28–30, 31, 47, 62, 237, 367
Delsarte System of Expression, The (Stebbins), 29
de Mérode, Cléo, 100
de Meyer, Adolf, 367, 371
De Mille, Cecil B., 371
de Mille, Agnes, 364
Denis, Maurice, 290, 389
Denishawn School of Dancing and Related
    Arts, 367, 391
Denzler, Anna ("Isadorable"), 243, 244, 313
  arrives, 161–62
  and Elizabeth/Merz regime, 168–69, 275,
    312
  and Isadora, 170, 172–73, 365, 366, 382,
    392–93, 399–400, (breaks connection
    with) 412, 479, 507
  in New York, 328, 329, 332, 370, 391
  Rummel's affair with, 389, 393–97,
    401–02, 403, 406, 453, 478–79
  takes surname of Duncan, 392
de Quincey, Thomas, 83
Descartes, René, and Cartesianism, 70, 93
Desprès, Suzanne, 401
Desti, Mary (Mary Dempsey; Mrs. Solomon
    Sturges, later Mme. Vely Bey), 96, 243,
    288, 291, 292, 359, 368, 399, 405, 406,
    413, 426, 520, 529, 596n21
  autobiography, 540–41, 553
  as companion on Isadora's travels, 120–21,
    122, 319, 411, 540 (1915 return to
    Europe) 339

and Crowley's cult, 242, 278, 280, 446
and Duncan children's death, 295–97, 298,
    300–02, (and third Duncan child)
    316–18
and Esenin, 420, 441–42, 473, 474–76,
    480
and Isadora's finances, 378–79, 403, 472,
    507–08, 539, 545, 547, 550
and Isadora's memoirs, 534
Maison Desti (cosmetics firm), 278, 320,
    341, 376–77, 540
premonition of Isadora's death, 553–54
Diaghilev, Sergei, 148, 152, 156, 266, 511
  Ballets Russes of, 74, 147, 190, (dance
    innovations) 246–47, 248, 285–86,
    (innovations banished) 500, (Pavlova)
    229, (Pavlova leaves) 271
Diamond Jubilee (England, 1897), 45
Dickens, Charles, 18
Diesel, Rudolf, 251
Dietrich, Marlene, 524
Dillon, Millicent, 30
Dionysion (school). *See* Bellevue
Dionysus, 57–58, 60, 69, 93, 112, 381, 389
Director, The (periodical), 44, 103
Direktion Vereinigter Künste (United Arts
    Management), 179, 187
Divoire, Fernand, 246, 249, 290, 342, 346,
    378, 385
  Isadora's letters to, 311, 353
  names "Isadorables," 168
Dixon, Mort, 547n
Dni (Russian daily, Berlin), 501
Dobie, Charles Caldwell, 25
Dodge, Mrs. Arthur, 49
Dodge, Mabel, 169, 331–34, 338, 347, 376
Dolly Sisters, 543
Dolmetsch, Arnold, 64, 107
Dongen, Kees van, 477
Don Quixote (ballet), 151
Doolittle, Hilda "H. D.," 380
Dorynne, Jess, 136
Dos Passos, John, 383, 508, 509
Douglas, Lord Alfred, 290
Downey, Donald, 82
Doyen (French surgeon), 251
Dream of Eugene Aram (Hood), 132
Dreiser, Theodore, 331
Dressler, Marie, 531
Dreyfus affair, 83
Drury Lane Theatre (London), 195
Dubinushka (Duncan dance), 492
Duchamp, Marcel, 325, 367
Dumas, Alexandre, 10

Dumesnil, Maurice, 343–44, 345–55, 604n11, 607n45
Duncan, Angus, 297
Duncan, Augustin "Gus" (brother) 10–11, 42, 275, 292, 359, 568n39
  blindness, 521
  in Chicago, 33, 39
  Craig meets, 140, 141, 143
  Duncan children's death, 295, 296, 298, 299, 300
  finances, 221, 507
  in Greece, 110, 112, 114, (war relief) 303
  letters to and from Isadora, 378, 391, 422, 424, 491
  as Isadora's manager, 158, 213–14, 264, 278, 280, (South America) 349, 350, (U.S.) 233, 241, 332
  and Isadorables, 312, 337, 370–71, 399, (on tour) 308, 353, 376, 390
  marries, 52, 54, 106, (marriage fails) 158, 263, 297, (remarries) 239, 313
  as performer, 26–27, 47, 263–64, 329, 330, 336, 370
  quoted on Isadora, 5, 15, 24, 25, 28
  Theatre Guild cofounded by, 27, 370
Duncan, Mrs. Augustin (Sarah Whiteford, first wife), 52, 54, 106, 112, 140, 143, 144
  marriage ends, 158, 263, 297
Duncan, Mrs. Augustin (Margherita Sargent, second wife), 239, 297, 313, 319, 332, 359, 470
Duncan, Caroline (half sister), 8
Duncan, Deirdre (daughter), 275, 286
  birth of, 198, 200, (and baby days) 212, 219, 240
  and brother Patrick, 263, 265, 276
  care of, 201, 204, 213, 243, 244, 252, 268, 274, 280–81, 305, (nurse Kist) 221, 257, (nurse Sim) 292–95
  Craig and, 198, 222, 231, 236, 287, 295–300 passim, 305, 308
  forebodings about and death of, 289–301, 303–06, 308–10, 329, 366, 412, 447, (Isadora writes about) 318, 320, 536
  Stanislavsky and, 262
Duncan, Elizabeth (Mary Elizabeth, sister), 10, 29, 33, 116, 269, 289, 359
  affair with Merz, 191, 214, 243, 244, (stillborn baby) 243
  and Craig, 140, 158, 210, 215
  as dancing teacher, 25–26, 27, 43, 52, 53, 57, 169, 312
  death of Isadora's children, 295, 299, 300

as director of Grunewald school, 158, 164, 166–72, 193, 195, 222, 240, 243, 263, (and finances) 193, 206, (forms Society for Support of) 171, 191, (struggle for control) 260–62, 275–76, 290, (as "Tante Miss") 169, 281, 312
  in Egypt, 280, 281
  forms Darmstadt school, 244, 260, 275, 290, 312, 320, 331–32, (moves it to U.S.) 364, 376, (returns it to Germany) 437, 501, 522
  in Greece, 110, 114, (war relief) 303
  Isadora out of touch with, 378, 391
  and Isadora's relationship with Beregi, 94, 96, 99
  as performer, 47, 50
Duncan, Harriet (half sister), 8
Duncan, Isadora (Angela Isadora)
  antecedents, 6–15
  biographies of, 30, 92, 358
  birth and birth date, 5, 11, 14, 567n56
  childhood years, 6, 9, 14–19
  coping with advancing age, 366, 371
  as dance student, 25–26
  death, 554
  and feminism, 99, 102–03, 327
  insensitivity, arrogance of, 282, 337, 345, (racial prejudice) 349–50, 352–53, 385
  as "Isis," 30, 280, 285
  life philosophy of, 16–17, 42, (dance representing) 249
  penury in early days, 33, 35, 40–41, 43, 55–56, 57, 63, 495
  personal appearance, 38, 236, 286, 327, 363, (dyed red hair) 320, 338, 469, 495 (later years) 371, 378, 423, 425, 444–45, 461
  politics of, 388–89, 414, 415, 417–19, 423–26, 467, 469, 505 (see also Bolshevism)
  portraits of, 101, 225, 327, 328, 356, 396, (refuses, later agrees to filming) 327–28, 545
  "shameless" behavior of, 285–86, 288, 347–49, 351, 357–58, 364, 368, 369, 378, 400
  studies and training, 25, 45–46
  suicidal thoughts, 222, 309, 377, 455, 501, 514, 516, 531–32, 552
  U.S. citizenship lost, 472
  World War I efforts, 316, 323–24, 340–46, 360–63, 373, 381, (U.S. government investigation) 364

Duncan, Isadora (*continued*)
DANCE CAREER
  ballet as viewed by, 22, 24–25, 31–32, 45,
    104–05
  and birth of modern dance, 20–33, 43,
    44–45, 78–80 (dance debut) 26
  blue stage curtains of, 105–06, 130, 323,
    335, 336
  career launched in Chicago, 33, 34–38,
    ("big break") 38–39
  costumes, *see* costumes
  critiqued, 86, 190, (compared with classi-
    cal art) 248, (England) 61, 225, (Ger-
    many) 124, 499–500, (Holland) 185,
    187–88, 208–09, (Paris) 107, 277–78,
    290, 401, (Russia) 148, 152–55,
    173–74, (South America) 352, 354,
    (Soviet Union) 425, (U.S.) 233–35,
    263, 272–73, 318–19, 324, 327, 330,
    461, (U.S. Midwest) 238, 264, (U.S.
    salon performances) 48, 51–52
  evolution of technique, 23–33, 61–64,
    78–80, 107, ("Furies") 269–70
  finances, 98, 192, 337, 350, 452, 455,
    501–03, 518–19, 521, (benefit held in
    Paris) 530–31, (Craig and) 157–59,
    179, 206, 213–14, 231, (debts) 108,
    338, 343–44, 346, 353, 354, 448–49,
    525, 534, (Esenin and) 467, 471, 473,
    476, (in Greece) 113, 114, (Isadora's
    pregnancy and) 188, 193, (Ruth
    Mitchell and) 527, 529, (school) 222,
    227, 341, 376, 491, 493, (Singer and)
    356–59, 367, 379, 513
  influence and imitators of, 148, 189–90,
    228–29, 239, 366–67, 390–91, 487
  influences on, 14, 18, 21, 23, 31, (chil-
    dren's death) 318
  lectures on dance, 45, 191–92, 240, 467,
    (lecture canceled) 469–70
  in New York, 43–47, 51, (hotel fire) 52–54,
    232
  salon performances, 48–51, 74
  speeches, 103–05, 361, 466, 591n50
  as teacher, 20, 24, 80, 81–82, 168, 170,
    (Stanislavsky's opinion) 261–62, (sued)
    188–89 (*see also* Bellevue; Isadora
    Duncan School of Dance [Grunewald];
    Isadora Duncan School [Moscow])
LOVE AFFAIRS, MARRIAGE, AND CHIL-
    DREN, 42, 103, 112, 182–83, 473, 499
  admirers, 65–67, 72, 74–78, 83–84
  Beregi (first lover), 89–90, 91, 92–95,
    96–98, 121, 122, 570n72

California affairs, 374–76
Caplet affair, 268–69
Chanler "engagement," 548–49, 550–51
Craig affair, 121, 125–26, 129–30, 133,
    136–37, 138–46, 147, (break with)
    216, 219, 259, 278–79
eroticism, 68–69, 220–22, 224–25, 254
Esenin affair and marriage, 426–27,
    428–40, 441–62, 499, 504–05, 515–16,
    540
Falchetto ("Bugatti") affair, 546–48, 551,
    552–53, 554
free love, 39
longing for children, 96, 180, 184, 187
marriage foretold, 411
Miroski affair, 38–39, 41–42, 65–66
Picabia affair, 368, 369, 547
"Pim" affair, 220–22
pregnancies and childbirth, 97–98, 188,
    190–200 *passim*, 204, 205, 262–65,
    266, 310–18 *passim*, (illness resulting
    from) 207–09, 211, (third child born,
    dies) 317–18
premonitions about and death of children,
    288–90, 292–301, 303–06, 309–20
    passim, 368, 374, 447, 514, (maternal
    feelings) 366, 369, (performances after)
    329–31, 344, 376, 382–83
Romanelli affair, 310
Rummel affair, 379–85, 389, 393–95, 397,
    401–02, 403, 405–06, 453
"Seraphita" affairs, 517–19, 526
Seroff affair, 255, 518–23 *passim*, 526–32
    passim, 535, 536, 537, 541–47 *passim*
Singer affair, 249–54, 263, 275, 280, 286,
    452–53, (quarrels) 255–59, 261,
    265–69, 274–78 *passim*, 284, 287–88,
    292, 358–60, (reconciliation) 549–53,
    (theater project) 283–84, 287, 290
  and sale of love letters or memoirs,
    503–08, 513
TRAVELS, TOURS, AND LIFE ABROAD
Cuba, 358–59
Austria-Hungary, 86–91, 95–99, (leaves
    Fuller company) 88–89, (with Greek
    boys' choir in) 115–16
Egypt, 264–65, 280–82, 285
England, 308, (London) 45, 51, 54, 55–67,
    107, 229–31, 269, (return to) 377–78,
    403–05, 406, 411–12
France, *see* Paris; Riviera, the, *below*
Germany, 95–106, 108, 148, 176–78,
    192–93, 213–14, 215, (bad publicity)
    188–91, (Bayreuth) 117–25, 171,

286–87, (buys house and operates
school) 125, 143, 145, 151, 158,
160–64, 165–73, 206, ("cult of Isadora")
99–102, (meets Craig) 139–45, 159–60,
(refuses tours) 106, 116, 117
Germany, postwar, 441–53, 474–76, 495,
496 (tour collapses) 501–03
Greece, "pilgrimage" to, 109–15, (buys
property, builds house) 113–15, (World
War I and postwar) 341–42, 393,
395–99
Isadora loses statehood, 448
Italy, 200, 201–04, 215, 262–63, 278,
308–11, (World War I and postwar)
340–41, 395
Low Countries, 184–88, 191–200 passim,
206, 207–09, 220
as "Maggie O'Gorman," 55
North Africa, 385
Paris, 68–85, 106–08, 117, 173, 233, 242
(lives in) 172, 244–46, 269, 274–75,
(Paris police) 279–80, 473, 478, (studio in Neuilly) 245–46, 257–58, 274,
284, 308, 378, (theater planned for)
280, 283–84, 287, 292, 313, (World
War I) 342–46, 378–83, (postwar)
384–89, 473, 476–80, 512–14, 520–27,
529–32, 537
Riviera, the, 381–83, 506–12, 514, 519,
521, 527–29, 534–35
Russia, 143, 145, 147–55, 173–76, 221,
222–26, 227, 253, 288–89, (Poland as
part of) 204–07 (see also Soviet Union,
below)
Scandinavia, 193, 194, 213
South America, 345–46, 348–55, 356
Soviet Union, 406–07, 411–27, 428–40,
480, 482–96 (automobile accident)
493, (command performance) 422,
(and secret police) 485–87
Switzerland, 341, 343, 345
war relief efforts, 303–07
U.S. TOURS
prewar, 230, 231–35, 236–41, 263–64,
270–74
during war, 323–25, 327–39, 347–48,
356–58, 360–70, 371, 372–76
postwar, 456–63, 464–72, (detained by
Customs) 458–60, (performances
canceled) 465, 469–70
WRITINGS
autobiographical sketch, 25
autobiography/memoirs, see My Life
(Isadora Duncan)

"A Child Dancing," 196
The Dance of the Future, 58, 103–05, 185
"The Dancer and Nature," 184, 220
essay on La Bacchanale, 400
letters to Craig, see Craig, Edward Henry
Gordon
"The Parthenon," 115
poems and letter to de Acosta, 526, 527,
543–44
Duncan, Joseph (half brother), 8
Duncan, Joseph Charles (father), 7–15, 19, 27,
51, 65, 495
Pioneer Bank scandal, 11–13
Duncan, Mrs. Joseph Charles (Elmira Hill, first
wife), 8, 10
Duncan, Mrs. Joseph Charles (Mary Dora
Gray, second wife; Isadora's mother), 6,
10, 11, 13–19 passim, 27, 52, 54, 83,
391, 495, 540
at Bayreuth, 122
as chaperon, 33, 38, 65, 74, 75, 84–91
passim, (disapproval of Isadora's affairs)
42, 94, 96, 99, 145, 158
and care of grandchild, 204, 213
as dancing teacher, 26
in Greece, 110, 114
Isadora estranged from, 222, 308, 372
as pianist, 18, 21, 25, 43, 47, 50, 53, 78, 82
returns to U.S., 221–22, (brought back to
Paris) 392, 411, (dies) 436–37
Duncan, Mrs. Joseph Charles (Mary, third
wife), 14
Duncan, Joseph Moulder (grandfather), 8
Duncan, Menalkas (nephew), 159, 264,
603n23
Duncan, Mrs. Menalkas (Ardée), 603n23
Duncan, Patrick Augustus, 268, 274, 276, 277,
280, 286, 426, 447
birth of, 265, 266
forebodings about and death of, 289–301,
303–06, 308–10, 318, 320, 329, 366,
540, (Isadora writes about) 536
Duncan, Raymond (brother), 11, 16, 27, 33,
43, 52, 54
death of Isadora's children, 297, 299, 301
in England, 56, 57, 58
entourage of, 264–65, 297, 341, 391–92
in Greece, 109–14, 125, 158–59, (aban-
dons Western clothing) 84, 109–10,
264, 297, (designs temple) 113, 340,
(marries) 114, (war relief) 297,
303–04, 306, 307, (World War I) 341
and Isadora's finances, 114, 502, 546
as Isadora's manager, 106

Duncan, Raymond (*continued*)
  and Isadorables, 392
  as painter, 114, 506
  in Paris, 67, 68, 69, 75, 78, 82, (leaves) 84,
    (returns) 106, 158–59, 193, 477, 528
  as performer, 47, 64, 264
  quoted, 7, 25, 568n34
  as vegetarian, 55, 112, 392, 521
Duncan, Mrs. Raymond (Penelope Sikelianos),
  114, 158, 159, 193, 264, 307, 391, 452,
  603n23
Duncan, Rosa (half sister), 14
Duncan, Temple (niece), 106–07, 120,
  122–23, 140, 195, 196, 264, 298
  as pupil, 160, 168, 172, 263, 290
Duncan, William (half brother), 8, 566n26
Duncan, William Lorenzo (uncle), 8, 12
Duncan Dancer (Duncan, Irma), 243, 454
Duncan traveling program, 26–27
Dunclings. *See* Isadora Duncan School
  (Moscow)
Duranty, Walter, 432–33, 489, 490
Durrant, Theodore, 228
Duse, Eleonora, 66, 178, 242, 262, 314, 537
  Craig designs set for, 200–04, 207, 209–10
  Isadora meets, 194, 201–03, 308–10, 311
Dying Swan, The (ballet), 154, 229, 271

E

Eagels, Jeanne, 231
Eastman, Crystal, 510
Eastman, Max, 326, 331, 365, 370, 428, 486,
  510, 520, 601n18
  Lisa and, 370, 479
  quoted on Isadora, 235, 327, 358, 363–64,
    433, 485, 531, 538
Ebersberger, Christian, 119
Echo and Narcissus (Duncan program), 308
Ecole des Beaux-Arts, 296
Eddis, Anita, 228
Edward VII, king of England, 57, 64, 227–28,
  230–31, 250, 251
Egeria myth, 224
Ehrenburg, Ilya, 429
Eight, The (painters), 233
8-Uhr Abendblatt (Berlin), 474
Eisler, Hans, 478
Elektra (Sophocles), 178, 264
Elgar, Edward, 373
El Greco, 363
Elisabeth, empress of Austria, 597n48
Ellen Terry and Her Secret Self (Craig), 131
Elliott, Gertrude, 570n18

Elliott, Maxine, 510, 570n18
Ellis, Havelock, 326
Elssler, Fanny, 45, 570n72
Elton, Sam, 228
Emerson, Ralph Waldo, 21
Empire Ballet (London), 63
Enfance du Christ (Berlioz), 387
England. *See* Duncan, Isadora: TRAVELS,
  TOURS, AND LIFE ABROAD
entretiens idéalistes, Les (Gazeau), 248
Erich-Grimme, Irma ("Isadorable"), 329, 370,
  391, 397
  autobiography of, 243, 454, (extracts
    from) 162–64, 243, 394, 398
  as companion for Deirdre, 276, 280–81,
    292
  and Elizabeth/Merz regime, 275, 312
  at Grunewald, 167, 168, 169, 170
  and Isadora, 170, 182, 244, 282, (after
    children's death) 298, (denigrates
    Isadora's influence) 483, (Isadora's
    resentment) 337, 371, 398, ("mutiny"
    against) 341, 366
  Isadora's letters to, 381–82, 507, 521
  public performances, 171, 173, 332, 393,
    405
  in Russia, 313
  in Soviet Union, 411–24 *passim*, 433,
    436–37, 439–40, 453, 479, 485, 487,
    488, (meets, marries Schneider)
    416–17, 437, (takes lead) 481–82, 484,
    495, 521, 542
  takes surname of Duncan, 365, 392
  at Villegenis, 243
Erika ("Isadorable"), 164, 168, 275, 312, 329,
  366, 382, 391
  leaves troupe, 370, 392, 406
Ernst-Ludwig, grand duke of Hesse, 244
Esenin, Sergei, 410, 426–27, 428–40, 441–62,
  466, 467–69, 470–80, 482, 495, 503,
  504–05, 520, 540
  leaves Isadora, 483–91
  remarriage, 516
  suicide of, 515–16, 521
Espionage Act (U.S., 1917), 363
Estournelles de Constant, Paul d', 266
Etude in D sharp Minor (Scriabin), 420
Eugene Onegin (Tchaikovsky), 417
eugenics, 244
Eunice (ballet), 154
Euripides, 186, 278
Europe, James Reese, 324
Everling, Germaine, 369
Excelsior (periodical), 294

F

Fair, Charles, 36
Fairbanks, Douglas, 510, 523
Falchetto, Bénoit ("Bugatti"), 546–48, 551,
    552–53, 554
Falck, Edward, 329, 335
Farwell, Arthur, 348
fashion design, 245, 271, 285, 400
Fauchois, René, 345, 346
Faure, Elie, 233
Fauré, Gabriel, 73, 76, 247
Federal Bureau of Investigation, 457
Federn, Karl, 61, 63, 142, 159, 580–81n56
Fellowes, Daisy, 73
feminism, 10, 99, 102–03, 326–27
Ferdinand, king of Bulgaria, 171
Festival of Music and Dance (Duncan program),
    386–87
Figaro, Le, 246, 286, 296, 316, 401, 406
Fish, Mrs. Stuyvesant (Mamie), 49–50
Fiske, Lillian, 510
Fitzgerald, Edward, 48
Fitzgerald, F. Scott and Zelda, 508–09
*Five Brahms Waltzes in the Manner of Isadora
    Duncan* (ballet), 405
Flanner, Janet ("Genêt," "Hippolyta"), 523–24,
    537–38
Flaubert, Gustave, 75
Fleming, Ike, 36
Florinsky, Count, 415
flu epidemic (1918), 383
Flynn, Elizabeth Gurley, 325
Fokine, Michel, 147, 148, 152, 154, 175, 246,
    247
Folies-Bergère, 70, 84
Forbes-Robertson, Diana, 570n18
Forbes-Robertson, Johnston, 58, 570n18
Ford, Ford Madox, 543
Ford, Simeon, 323
Ford's Theater (Washington), 26
Forrest, Edwin, 26
Fortuny, Mario, 266, 271
Four Hundred, the, 49–50
France, Anatole, 71
France
    first Soviet citizens in, 454
    Isadora in, *see* Duncan, Isadora: TRAVELS,
        TOURS, AND LIFE ABROAD
    Isadora as symbol in, 99, 290
    World War I begins, 316–17
Franck, Alicia, 599n49
Franck, César, 318, 608n45
Franz Ferdinand, Archduke, assassinated, 315

Franz Joseph, emperor of Austria, 99
Frederick the Great, king of Prussia, 166
free love, 39, 326, 363, 364, 490
French Legion of Honor, 107
Freud, Sigmund, 326, 603n4
Froebel, Friedrich, 166
Froelich, Bianca, 226
Frohman, Charles, 227, 229, 230, 231–32,
    233, 234, 340
fuoco, Il (D'Annunzio), 201
Fuller, Loie, 70–71, 84–88, 101, 173, 271,
    591n36
Fuller-Maitland, John, 60–61, 229
Funérailles, Les (Liszt), 382
Funeral March (Chopin), 289, 291, 385
Funeral March (Liszt), 420
futurism, 245, 285, 591n36

G

Gabriel, Jacques-Ange, 244
Gaité-Lyrique theater (Montparnasse), 242,
    246, 248, 249, 252, 257, 262, 269
Galsworthy, John, 230
Galton, Francis, 31
Garbo, Greta, 524
garconne, La (Margueritte), 480
Garros, Roland "Ace," 379
Gates of Hell, The (Rodin statue), 72
Gazeau, Jeanne, 248
Geisha, The (Daly production), 42, 43
Geisha and the Knight, The (Japanese produc-
    tion), 71
Geltser, Ekaterina, 416, 419
Genée, Adeline, 227
Genthe, Arnold, 335, 338, 357, 358, 359, 366,
    368
    portraits by, 327–28, 356, 367
George I, king of the Hellenes, 114
Georges-Michel, Michel, 279, 280, 284, 286,
    401
Germany
    "cult of Isadora" in, 99–102
    Isadora in, *see* Duncan, Isadora: TRAVELS,
        TOURS, AND LIFE ABROAD
    postwar inflation in, 449
    public education in, 166, 172
    World War I, 316–17, 360, (anti-German
        feeling) 340, 365, (postwar) 384
Gervex, Henri, 257
Gibbons, Floyd, 543
Gibson, May, 136, 231
Gibson Girl, 326
Gide, André, 245

Giselle (ballet), 156
Gish, Lillian, 77
Gish sisters, 367
Giuletti, Cesare, 353, 354
Glackens, William, 233
Glaspell, Susan, 338
Gleichen, Countesses Valda and Feodora, 60
Gleizes, Albert and Juliet, 369
Gluck, Christoph Willibald von, 43, 63, 99,
        186, 239, 290, 308, 608n45
    Orfeo, 78, 174, 185, 269, 270, 299
Godowsky, Leopold, 379
Godwin, Edward William, 130, 131, 132
Goethe, Johann, 101
Gogol, Nikolai, 472
Goldman, Emma, 326, 457
Goncourt, Edmond de, 73, 77
Gordon, Lady, 130
Gorky, Maxim, 431, 438, 445, 446, 447, 462
Gould, Jay, 73
Graham, Lillie. *See* Singer, Mrs. Paris (first
        wife)
Graham, Martha, 367, 478
Grandjouan, Jules, 280
Grandmothers, The (Wescott), 533
Grand Theater (New York), 330
Grand Theatre (Geneva), 345
Grant, Ulysses S., 7
Gray, Ellen, Elizabeth, and Augusta (aunts), 7
Gray, Mary Dora. *See* Duncan, Mrs. Joseph
        Charles (second wife)
Gray, Colonel Thomas (grandfather), 6–7, 8,
        12, 13, 372
Gray, Mrs. Thomas (Maggie Gorman, grand-
        mother), 7
Greece
    Isadora in, *see* Duncan, Isadora: TRAVELS,
        TOURS, AND LIFE ABROAD
    Raymond in, *see* Duncan, Raymond
    war relief in Corfu, 303–07
    in World War I, 341
Greek boys' choir, 115–16
Greek ideal, 20–22, 23, 58, 74, 111, 237,
        278
    in costumes and everyday clothing, 25, 30,
        57, 63, 109–10, 155, (abandoned) 271
    Craig shares, 134
    in dance, 32, 45, 47, 67, (Berlin success)
        102, (Isadora's version) 230, 335
    Greek chorus, 64, 115, 283, 314
    "Greek Dancing" at Paris Opéra, 72
    Nietzsche analyzes, 103
Greenwich Village (New York), 326–27, 331,
        363

Greffulhe, Countess Elisabeth, 73–74, 287
Gregg, Frances, 380
Grein, J. T., 404
Gretel (later Margot; "Isadorable"), 275, 329,
        366, 370, 382, 391, 393, 405, 411
    dances as Isadorable, 168, 312, (breaks
        connection with Isadora) 479
    illness and death of, 397, 401, 406, 412,
        506, 513
Greuze, Jean-Baptiste, 248
Griffith, D. W., 367
Grosvenor Gallery founded, 59
Grosz, Sándor, 88, 89, 90, 94, 96, 97, 98, 100,
        106, 116–17
Group Theatre (New York), 478
Grunewald school. *See* Isadora Duncan School
        of Dance
Guggenheim, Peggy, 530
Guilbert, Yvette, 245, 247, 266, 543
Guitry, Sacha, 319
Guy Mannering (Scott), 42

H

Haarlem Municipal Orchestra, 188, 194
Haeckel, Ernst, 123–24, 265
Hall, Mrs. Bolton, 49
Hallé, Edward Charles, 59, 60, 65, 66, 72
Hall of Nobles (St. Petersburg), 150, 152, 154
Hamlet (Stanislavsky-Craig production), 176,
        200, 231, 253, 287, 289
Hammond, Lorimer, 473
Hänsel und Gretel (Humperdinck opera), 165
Hapgood, Hutchins, 326, 338
Happier Age of Gold, The (Duncan program),
        51
Harle, Norman, 399
Harlem Renaissance, 468
Harrington, Sarah, 479
Harris, Frank, 508
Harris, William, 233
Harry's New York Bar (Paris), 537
Harte, Bret, 10
Hartley, Marsden, 326
Harvard Lampoon, 238
Harvard University, Socialist
        Club at, 326
Hayes, Rutherford B., 85
Haywood, "Big Bill," 325
Hearst newspapers, 465, 469
Heinrich VII of Reuss, Princess, 171
Helena, Princess Christian of Schleswig-
        Holstein, 60
Hellens, Franz, 447, 454, 455–56

Héloise, 300
Henri, Robert, 233, 331, 466
Henry V (Benson production), 61
Herbert, James, 603n1
Here Lies the Heart (de Acosta), 524–25, 532, 544
Herrand, Marcel, 528, 529
Heyermans, Herman, 187–88
Hoffman, Gertrude, 226, 575n72
Hofmannsthal, Hugo von, 138
Holden, Martha Everts ("Amber"), 37
Holland, Isadora in, 185–87, 191, 195–99, 206, 207–09
homosexuality, 75, 76, 220–21, 258, 307, 341, 358, 415, 445, 448, 450–51, 526, 528, 530
Hood, Thomas, 132
Hoover, Herbert, 418
Hoover, J. Edgar, 457, 458
Horace, 90
Hôtel Biron (Paris), shut down, 244–45
Hottois, Georges, 551
Huddleston, Sisley, 385, 387
Humboldt, Wilhelm von, 101
Humperdinck, Engelbert, 123, 165, 189
Humphrey, Doris, 367
Hungarian National Theater, 89, 97
Hungarian Royal Opera, 90
Hunt, William Holman, 59, 60, 61
Hurok, Sol, 390, 393, 399, 438, 456–63 *passim*, 465–72 *passim*
Hutton, Eleanor, 550
Hygienic Exhibition, First International (1911), 276
Hymn to the Heroes of Hungary (Duncan dance), 90

I

Ibañez, Blasco, 508, 510
Ibsen, Henrik, 137, 203, 278
If I Were King (McCarthy), 48
Illustrated London News, 404
imaginists, 428, 431, 447, 489
impressionism, 60, 591n36
Index to the Story of My Days (Craig), 136, 139, 178–79, 201
Industrial Workers of the World, 325
Ingersoll, Robert, 16, 166
Ingram, Rex, 509, 511
Ingres, Jean-Dominique, 325
Internationale, L', 444, 480
  Duncan dance, 423, 424
Intimate Memories (Dodge), 332

Intolerance (Griffith film), 367
Intransigeant, L' (periodical), 342
Iphigenia (Duncan dance), 99, 174, 186, 225, 230, 246, 279, 337, 373, 402
Irma ("Isadorable"). *See* Erich-Grimme, Irma
Iron Mirgorod, The (Esenin), 472
Irvine, St. John, 370
Irving, Henry, 26, 66, 130, 131, 132, 190
  death of, 188, 195
"Isadorables," 168–73
  Anna, *see* Denzler, Anna
  Augustin and, *see* Duncan, Augustin
  costumes for, 214, 257
  critiqued, 230, 277, 279–80, 391
  Erika, *see* Erika
  first performances, 225, 246
  German performances banned, 189
  Irma, *see* Erich-Grimme, Irma
  Isabelle, *see* Branche, Isabelle
  Isadora's letter to, 381–82
  Lisa, *see* Milker, Elisabeth
  "mutiny" of, 340–41, 353, 366, 369–71, 376, 390–91, 398, 405–06, (break connection with Isadora) 412, 479, 507
  named, 290
  and school funding, 222
  in struggle for control of school, 244, 261–62, 275–76, 290, (move to Belle-vue) 312–14
  Theresa, *see* Kruger, Theresa
  at Villegenis, 240, 242–43, 245
  in World War I (New York), 320, 323–24, 328–34, 337–38, (at Carnegie Hall) 328, 390, 393, (detained at Ellis Island) 324, 328, (return to Europe) 339, 340–41, 343, 345, 353, (return to New York) 359, 363, 370, 381, 391, (take name of Duncan) 365, 392, (under contract) 365, 371, 398, 399
  post–World War I, 389, 390–407
Isadora Duncan Dancers, 376
Isadora Duncan School of Dance (Grunewald), 165–73, 206, 311, 313
  Elizabeth as director, *see* Duncan, Elizabeth
  finances, 222, 231, 242–43, 244, (society formed for support of) 171, 191
  house purchased, 125, 143, 145, 165, (sold) 449
  lectures about, 240
  operation of, 151, 158, 160–64, 165–73, 206, (closed) 227, 241–42, (reopening planned) 270

Isadora Duncan School of Dance (*continued*)
  struggle for control of, 244, 260–62,
    275–76, 290
  See also Bellevue; Darmstadt school
Isadora Duncan School (Moscow), 420–23,
    424–26, 435, 437, 466, 477, 488
  financing for, 491, 493, 494, 495, 512, 518,
    522
  first students at, 492
  New York tour planned, 438
  taken over by Schneiders, 481–83, 521
"I See America Dancing" (1927 broadside), 22,
    565n6
Isidore of Seville, Saint, 5
Isis, Isadora known as, 30, 280, 285
Isis Unveiled (Blavatsky), 30
Italian Mail (newspaper), 531
Italy
  Isadora in, *see* Duncan, Isadora: TRAVELS,
    TOURS, AND LIFE ABROAD
  in World War I, 341
Ivan III (the Great), 419
Izryadnova, Anna, 431
Izvestia, 417, 423, 424, 425, 479, 482

J

James, Henry, 51, 60
Jamois, Marguerite, 511
Jászai, Mari, 90
Javabode (Amsterdam newspaper), 205
Jean (only male Duncan pupil), 313, 314, 324,
    330, 353
Jeanne (Isadora's dresser), 413, 415, 416, 419,
    420, 450, 451, 473
Jehanne d'Arc (de Acosta play), 523
John Ferguson (Irvine play), 370
Johnston, Alva, 251
Jones, Robert Edmond, 142, 326, 338–29
Journal d'Eclair, 480
Journey to Athens (Winckelmann), 56
Joyce, James, 522
Joyce, Nora, 523
Jozan, Edouard, 509
Jugend (periodical), 101, 117
Julius Caesar (Hungarian production), 90
Jung, Carl, 603n4

K

Kahn, Otto, 335, 357, 603n1
Kalinin, Mrs. Mikhail, 496
Kaltenborn, Hans von, 367
Kamerny Theatre (Moscow), 495, 496

Kant, Immanuel, 101, 166, 258
Karl Theater (Vienna), 194
Karsavina, Tamara, 247
Kaulbach, F. A. von, 101, 225
Kaye, Joseph, 470, 522
Kazin, Alfred, 31
Keats, John, 18, 21, 65, 170
Keene, Laura "the Duchess," 26
Kendall, Elizabeth, 62, 245, 390
Kessler, Count Harry, 129, 138, 139, 142, 178,
    188, 300, 445
Kharitonenko, Pavel, 417
Khayyám, Omar, 48
kindergarten movement, 166
Kinel, Lola, 450–52, 454
Kirkpatrick, John, 12
Kisselgoff, Anna, 574n42
Kist, Marie, 196, 206, 221
Klamath Indians, 265
Klimt, Gustav, 87, 226
Klyuev, Nikolai, 434, 440, 613n16
Kollontai, Alexandra, 490
Kölnischer Zeitung, 189
Konenkov, Sergei, 489
Königskinder (Humperdinck opera), 165
Krassin, Leonid, 402, 412, 413, 420, 488
Kreisler, Fritz, 367
Kroll's New Royal Opera House (Berlin), 101,
    171, 173, 186
Kruger, Theresa ("Isadorable"), 275, 312, 313,
    329, 332, 382, 391, 393, 405, 406, 412,
    507
  arrives, 161
  in Elizabeth/Merz regime, 262, 275, 312
  falls in love, marries, 370, 411
  and Isadora, 173, 280, (as teacher) 168,
    170
  and "mutiny," 353, 366, 393, 405, 406
  Steichen and, 396–97
Kschessinska, Mathilde, 148, 156, 414
Kun, Béla, 420
Kusikov, Alexander, 447–48, 473, 474, 475

L

Ladies' Home Journal, 324
Lady, The (periodical), 64
Lady Evelyn (Singer's yacht), 250, 252
Laemmle, Carl, 510
Lafont, Hermann, 175
Lalo, Pierre, 277–78
Laloy, Louis, 117
Lanchester, Elsa, 313, 314
Lang, Andrew, 51, 60

Langtry, Lillie, 26
Lanner, Katti, 45, 63
Lansing, Robert, 361
Laurencin, Marie, 511
Lawton, Ralph, 451
Leaves of Grass (Whitman), 534
Lebrun, Charles, 267
Lees, Dorothy Neville, 210
Lees, Isaiah, 12–13
Le Gallienne, Eva, 523, 541, 543
Le Gallienne, Gwen, 510
Le Gallienne, Richard, 510, 511
Léger, Fernand, 400
Lehr, Harry, 50
Leib, Mani, 471
Lenin, Vladimir Ilyich, 415, 419, 421, 423,
     457, 486, 490
   death of, 495, 496
"Lenten" (Lyceum) matinees, 44, 47, 48
lesbianism, 74, 76, 368, 480, 523, 524, 528, 541
Lessing Theatre (Berlin), 138
Levien, Julia, 466
Levien, Sonya, 330
Levine, Isaac Don, 506
Levinson, André, 64, 388, 477, 478, 581n5
Le Warne, Benjamin (uncle), 12
Lewisohn Stadium (New York), 348
Liberty Leading the People (Delacroix painting),
     345
Liberty Theater (New York), 370, 371
Liebestod (Wagner), 271, 401, 543
Lieven, Prince Peter, 151
Lightner, "Lizzie" (aunt), 145. *See also* Gray,
     Elizabeth
Lincoln, Abraham, 7, 9, 26, 234
Lind, Jenny, 29
Lindbergh, Charles A., 539
Ling, Princess der, 81, 82
Lippmann, Walter, 326, 331, 332, 334
Lisa, Liesel ("Isadorable"). *See* Milker, Elisa-
     beth
Lisle, Rouget de, 344
Liszt, Franz, 10, 90, 119, 379, 382, 420, 528,
     548
Little Jesse James (musical comedy), 499
Little Review (periodical), 362
Litvinov, Ivy, 414, 425
Litvinov, Maxim, 453
Liveright, Horace, 507
Loeser, Charles, 210
Loftus, Cissie, 571n56
"Lohengrin." *See* Singer, Paris
Lohengrin legend, 252, 253
London *Daily Herald*, 418

London *Daily Mail*, 283
London Symphony Orchestra, 402
London *Times*, 60, 229, 293–94, 385, 404
Longfellow, Henry Wadsworth, 28
Loos, Anita, 510, 543
"lost generation," 509
Loubet, Emile, 80
Louis XIV staircase, 267
Louisville Courier, 467
Louÿs, Pierre de, 74, 480
Loving, Pierre, 510, 518, 523, 533
Lucile of Paris (fashions), 271, 400
Ludwig I, king of Bavaria, 10
Ludwig II, king of Bavaria, 121
Lugné-Poë, Aurélien, 242, 259, 282, 286, 310,
     401
Lully, Jean-Baptiste, 64
Lunacharsky, Anatoly Vassilievitch, 403, 415,
     417–24 *passim*, 437, 438, 477, 491, 522
Lusitania (British liner), 264
   torpedoed, 340
Lydig, Rita de Acosta, 524
Lyuboschitz, Pierre, 420

M

McAlmon, Robert, 522
McBans, the (jugglers), 228
McCarthy, Justin Huntly, 48
McCormick, Edith Rockefeller, 341
McCoy, Charles "Kid," 359
Macdougall, Allan Ross, 248, 358–59, 384,
     402, 495, 512, 523
   on Esenin, 447, 490
   and Isadora's finances, 502, 507
   and Isadora's memoirs, 533, 534, 543
McKay, Claude, 468, 518
MacKaye, Arvia, 327
MacKaye, Percy, 237, 239, 241, 264, 327, 348
MacKaye, Steele, 29, 237
MacLeish, Archibald, 510
McVey, Gordon, 429
Madeleine, Mlle. (French dancer), 116
Madison Square Garden (New York), 358, 359,
     362
Maeterlinck, Maurice, 75, 314
Magnus, Maurice, 179, 187, 221, 385
Malko, Nikolai, 614n42
Mamontov, Savva, 176
Manchester, duchess of. *See* Yznaga, Consuelo
Mankiewicz, Herman ("Mank"), 453–54
Mankiewicz, Sara, 453–54
Mannes, David, 510
Manning, Bishop William T., 470

Manship, Paul, 331
Marais, Henriette, 250
Marche Funèbre (Chopin), 385, 389, 391, 531
Marche Héröique (Schubert), 315
Marche Lorraine (Duncan dance), 363
Marche Militaire (Duncan dance), 263, 327
Marche Slave (Tchaikovsky), 362, 412, 423, 485–86
Marcus Aurelius, 42
Mare Nostrum (Ibañez), 510
Margot ("Isadorable"). *See* Gretel
Margueritte, Victor, 480
Maria Pavlovna, Grand Duchess, 152
Marie, queen of Romania, 71
Mariengof, Anatoly, 426, 429–34 *passim,* 438–40 *passim,* 449, 467, 468, 483–84
Marin, John, 326
Marinetti, F. T., 245
"Marseillaise, La," 339, 342
Marseillaise (Duncan dance), 343, 344–45, 346, 352, 357, 360, 371, 373
Marshall, Christabel, 228
Marshall Field's department store, 36, 377
Marta (pupil at Grunewald), 160
Martin, John, 22, 79, 80, 232, 581n5
Marwig, Carl, 46
Marx, Harpo, 510
Marx, Karl, 256
Maryinsky Theatre (St. Petersburg), 147, 148, 151, 156, 225, 436
Mask, The (Craig's magazine), 178, 210, 213, 278
Mason, Redfern, 372–73, 374, 375–76, 391
Massborn, Jay, 25, 27
Masses, The (periodical), 235, 326, 327, 363
Mata Hari, 190, 226, 364, 465
Matisse, Henri, 244
Maupassant, Guy de, 75
Maurevert, Georges, 106, 266, 290, 507, 508, 598–99n23
Mauriac, François, 73
Maurois, André, 73
Max, Edouard de, 244
Maxwell, Elsa, 368
May, Jane, 40, 41
Meditations (Marcus Aurelius), 42
Meg Merrilies, or the Witch of Ellangowan (Daly production), 42
Meichik, Mark, 493
Meistersinger, Die (Wagner opera), 271
Mélos, Constantine, 342
Meltzer, Charles Henry, 597n41
Melville, Herman, 518
Mendelssohn, Felix, 18, 36, 41, 43, 228
Mendelssohn, Giulietta, 171, 190

Mendelssohn, Robert, 190
Mendelssohn family, 194, 201
Meo, Elena ("Nelly"), 136, 179–81, 182, 196, 212, 231, 287, 305, 308, 386
Merchant of Venice, The (Japanese production), 71
Mercure de France (periodical), 117
Meredith, George, 51
Merezhkovsky, Dmitri, 480
Merz, Max, 214, 243, 308
and Duncan Schools, 191, 244, 260–61, 262, 263, 275–76, 290, 312, 320, 471
Messager, André, 73
Method acting, 79, 223–24
Metropolitan Opera, 226, 235, 263, 334, 335, 344, 356–57, 360
Metternich, Princess Paulina, 86, 87–88
Meunier, Mario, 291, 378
Meyerhold, V. E., 422, 425, 431
Middleton, George, 341, 543, 544
Midsummer Night's Dream, A
Benson production, 61
Daly production, 41–42
Mila (Duncan pupil), 324
Miles, Sir Bernard, 136
Milker, Elisabeth ("Lisa"; "Isadorable"), 168, 313, 332, 382, 391, 397, 543
arrives, 160–61
under Elisabeth/Merz regime, 274, 312
Genthe photograph of, 367
on Isadora, 329, 478
and Max Eastman, 411–12, 479
and "mutiny," 366, 393, 405, 406, (breaks connection with Isadora) 411–12, 479
as nightclub dancer, 477, 500, 540
takes Duncan surname, 392
Millay, Edna St. Vincent, 326, 370, 518
Miller, Marilyn, 543
Miloslavskaya, Maria, 455
Milward, Joe, 471, 477, 527
on Esenin, 442–43, 472, 479
as Isadora's agent, 448, 450, 452–56 *passim,* 530–31
mimodramas, 25, 28
Minter, Mary Miles, 543
Mirbeau, Octave, 76, 245, 247
Miroir de Jésus (Caplet), 268
Miroski, Ivan, 38, 39, 41, 42, 65–66
Miss Pygmalion (pantomime), 39–41
Mistinguette, 509
Mitchel, Mayor John Purroy, 332–34, 357
Mitchell, Ruth ("Aunty Ruthy"), 399, 413, 471, 507, 527, 528–29
Mizner, Addison, 360, 593n15

Mocchi, Walter, 344, 350, 351, 353, 355
Modern Art, International Exhibition of, 325
Modjeska, Helena, 26
Mohegan (steamship), 14, 51
Molière, Jean Baptiste, 75
Moment Musicale (Schubert), 238
monism, 123, 265
Montesquiou, Count Robert de, 73, 305, 319
Montessori, Maria, 166
Monteverdi, Claudio, 64
Montez, Lola, 10, 26
Moody, William Vaughn, 237, 241
Mordkin, Mikhail, 271, 500
Morris, William, 65
Morrison, Jim, 429
Morse, Leila, 380
Morse, Samuel F. B., 379
Morverand, Paul, 292, 293, 294, 297
Moscow Art Theatre, 79, 175, 176, 222, 224,
    259, 287, 289, 422, 435
Mounet-Sully, Jean, 77, 279, 286, 290, 291
Mouvet, Maurice, 357
Much Ado About Nothing
    Craig production, 137
    Daly production, 42
Müller-Fürer, Konrad, 214, 243
Munich Künstlerhaus, 100, 101
Murphy, Gerald and Sara, 509, 510
Murray, Gilbert, 278
Musical America magazine, 235, 334, 461
Musik, Die (periodical), 124
My Life (Isadora Duncan) 23, 24, 43, 88–89,
    92, 97, 307, 309, 513, 525, 536–38
    authorship of, 532–34
    on children and death of children, 274,
        306, 309, 536
    on Craig, 129, 134–35, 140, (Craig's reac-
        tion to) 216, 220, 532–33
    extracts from, 85, 98, 112, 268, 504
    finished, 535, 549
    omissions from, 45, 85n, 280
    Russian journey, 148, 149, 204
    serial rights sold, 543, 544, 552
My Life and Loves (Harris), 508
My Life in Art (Stanislavsky), 175–76
Mysovskaya, Maria ("Moussy"), 492

N

Nabokov, Nicolas, 444, 445
Nación, La (Buenos Aires), 352
Namara, Marguerite, 329, 510
Napoleon Bonaparte, painting of coronation
    of, 267

Natural History of Creation (Haeckel), 123
Nazimova, Alla, 523
Nazi view of biology, 123
Negro dance, 133, 325, 591n36
Negulesco, Jean, 510–11
Neuilly studio, 245–46, 257–58
Nevada, Emma, 84
Nevin, Ethelbert, 43–44, 47
Newman, Ernest, 404
Newport society, 48–50
New Republic, The (periodical), 326, 465
"New Woman," 326
New Russia, The (Thompson), 482
New Yorker, The (magazine), 251, 523, 537
New York Evening Mail, 324
New York Evening Post, 499
New York Herald, 45, 46, 54, 165
New York Mail, 391
New York Mirror, 264
New York Morning Telegraph, 576n37
New York Post, 47
New York Sun, 236–37, 240, 272, 291, 319,
    329, 333, 360
New York Symphony, 234, 270, 328
New York Telegraph, 232, 338
New York Times, 22, 40, 43, 47, 53, 79, 189,
    232, 246, 263, 271, 337, 348, 392, 393,
    432, 460, 466
    on Duncan children's death, 297–98,
        299
    first dance critic, 232
    Isadora interviewed by, 228, 230
    on modern art, 325
New York Tribune, 271, 330, 459, 460
New York World, 73, 111, 112, 328, 334–35, 508
Nicholas II, tsar of Russia, 150, 152, 156, 257,
    412, 493–94
    abdicates, 361
Nickson, Ruth, 534–35
Nicolson, Harold, 76
Nietzsche, Friedrich, 15, 23, 103–04, 166,
    177, 532
Nieuws van der Dag, 194, 208–09
Nijinsky, Vaslav, 247–48, 266, 285–86, 290,
    473, 514, 591n36
Nike of Samothrace, 248, 263
Nikolenko, Ivan, 545, 553
Nikritina, Anna, 431, 432
Nineteen Nineteen (Dos Passos), 383
Niobe myth, 304, 305
Niobe myth, 304, 305
Noailles, Anna de, 247
Nobel Peace Prize, 266
Noccioli, Guido, 203–04, 209
Normand, Mabel, 367

Norton, "Emperor," 9
Norton, Louise, 369
Noufflard, Charles, 72, 74, 77–78
Novel Without Lies (Mariengof), 426–27
Nude Descending a Staircase (Duchamp), 325

O

Oakland's Shell Academy for Girls, 26
Oakland Tribune, 12
Oberon (Weber), 41
Oedipus Rex
    French production, 77
    New York production, 336, 337
Oelrichs, Mrs. Hermann (Tessie), 49
Old Glory (Duncan dance), 373
Olga Alexandrovna, Grand Duchess, 151
Olympic Games, 577n6
O'Neill, Eugene, 338
O'Neill, James, 26
On the Eve (Russian emigré publication), 444
Oppenheimer, E., 510
Orchestra Hall (Chicago), 238
Orchidée, 86
Orcier's Baths, 542
Orfeo ed Euridice (Gluck opera), 78, 174, 185, 269
Orphée (Cocteau), 510, 511–12
Orpheus (Duncan dance), 90, 269–70, 271, 277, 400
Orpheus legend, 63–64
Osborn, Max, 102, 171
Osbourne, Lloyd, 237
O'Sheel, Shaemas, 4
Otojiro, Kawakami, 71, 84, 88
Otway, Thomas, 138
Ovid, 90
Oxford Book of Carols, The, 192

P

Pabst, G. W., 367
Paderewski, Ignaz, 47, 63, 604n11
Pageant of the Paterson Strike (1913), 338
Palace Theatre (London), 227–28
Palm Beach Story, The (Sturges film), 550
Pan and Echo (Duncan dance), 63, 90, 107
Pandora's Box (Pabst film), 367
Paris
    Isadora in, *see* Duncan, Isadora: TRAVELS, TOURS, AND LIFE ABROAD
    in World War I, 316–17,
    (postwar) 384–85

Paris Commune, 29
Paris Exposition (1900), 70, 72, 107
Paris Herald, 304, 307
Paris Opéra, 69, 71, 107, 246, 286
    Jean joins, 353
    refuses performance, 279
Paris Peace Conference (Versailles, 1919), 384, 388
Paris Revue Nègre, 523
Paris Tribune, 473
Parker, Dorothy, 329
Parker, Henry Taylor (HTP), 232, 271, 272, 273, 318, 330, 460, 461, 571n49
Parsifal (Wagner opera), 271, 287, 382, 399–400, 401
"Parthenon, The" (Duncan essay), 115
Pasdeloup Orchestra, 542
Paterson strike (1913), 325, 338
Pathétique (Duncan dance), 343–44, 392, 423, 460, 461, 465, 499
Patton, William, 12
Paul-Boncour, Joseph, 246, 266
Pavlova, Anna, 154, 156, 221, 247, 357, 500, 511, 581n5
    Hurok and, 390, 438
    Isadora compared with, 271, 373
Pavlovna, Grand Duchess Maria, 400
Péguy, Charles, 245
Péladan, Joséphin Sar, 290
Pelléas et Mélisande (Maeterlinck), 75
People's Institute (New York), 331
Perch, Howard ("Punch"), 540
Père-Lachaise cemetery, 300–01
Peterkin, Daisy ("Mlle. Dazié"), 226
Peter Pan (Barrie), 166
Petersburg Gazette, 151, 152, 155
Petersburg Philharmonic orchestra, 175
Petipa, Marius, 151
Philadelphia, concerts in, 238
Picabia, Francis, 367–68, 369, 547
Picabia, Germaine, 547
Picabia, Lorenzo, 606n60
Picasso, Pablo, 245, 248, 510, 511, 519
Pickford, Mary, 510
Pierné, Gabriel, 266
"Pim." *See* van Goor, Willem Noothoven
Pinero, Arthur Wing, 201
Pioneer Bank scandal, 11–13, 566n26
Plamondon, Rodolphe, 290
Plato, 112, 248, 256, 307
Podvoysky, Nikolai, 418–19, 426
Poe, Edgar Allan, 149, 494
Poème de l'extase (Scriabin), 174

poetry and Bible readings, 47, 65, 83, 90, 263, 290, 329, 330
Poincaré, Raymond, 448
Poiret, Paul, 245, 271, 275, 288, 400
   Olympian Ball of, 285
   studio designs by, 246, 257–58, 291, 311, 313, 385
Poland, journey to, 204–07
Poland Tragic, Poland Heroic (Duncan dance), 382, 385
Polignac, Prince Edmond de, 76, 252
Polignac, Princess de (Winaretta Singer), 73, 76, 250
Pompadour, Mme. de, 311
Poole, Abram, 524
populism, 49
Post, Marjorie Merriweather, 550
Pound, Ezra, 380
Povitsky, Lev, 483
Prairie Flower, The (magazine), 8
Pravda, 489
Pre-Raphaelite movement, 59, 60, 61, 62, 63
Primavera (Botticelli), 18, 21
   Duncan representation of, 61–62, 90
"primitive" art, 233
Prohibition, 457, 467, 470
Prometheus, 20
   Isadora as "daughter of," 246
Proust, Marcel, 51, 72, 73, 245
Provincetown Players, 338
Prussian Academy of Arts, 101
Psyche myth, 143
Puccini, Giacomo, 276
Pulszky, Romola de, 248
Purcell Operatic Society, 137
Puritanism, 22, 235, 463, 466
Pygmalion (Shaw), 58
Pygmalion and Galatea (Duncan dance), 96

Q

Quack, M.D. (Fuller production), 85
Quitzow, Sülgwynn, 569n55, 570n72

R

Rabinovitch, Max, 470
Rachel, Mademoiselle (French actress), 29
Radha (St. Denis dance), 190
Radiguet, Raymond, 510
Radziwill, Princess Dominique, 73
Raikh, Zinaida, 431
Rakoczy March (Liszt), 90
Rakovsky, Christian, 522

Rappoport, Charles, 477, 522, 543
Ravel, Maurice, 73, 297, 374
Ravicz, Joseph, 221
Rawlings, Sylvester, 334–35, 336
Ray, Man, 73
Real Isadora, The (Seroff), 520
Rédemption (Duncan dance), 318–19, 343, 543
Red International, 489
Red scare. See Bolshevism
Red Stadium (Moscow), 494, 495
Reed, John, 326, 331
Reformation, the, 22
Rehan, Ada, 38, 39
Reid, Mrs. Whitelaw, 49
Reinach, Theodore, 401
Reinhardt, Max, 178, 188
Reiss, Winold, 367, 370, 392
Réjane, Mme. (actress), 245, 381
Rémy, Marcel, 228
Renaissance art and music, 62, 64
rhythmic gymnastics, 28
Richmond, William, 61
Riddle of the Universe, The (Haeckel), 123
Rilke, Rainer Maria, 244
Rimsky-Korsakov, Nikolai, 174
Riva, Maria, 524
Roberts, Mary Fanton, 233, 237, 313, 314, 335, 357, 378
   establishes aid committee, 331
   Isadora's letters to, 274, 341, 342, 604n16
Roberts, W. Carman ("Billy"), 233, 237
Robertson, Wolford Graham, 59, 60
Robeson, Paul, 370
Robinson, Edwin Arlington, 237, 241
Rodin, Auguste, 109, 244, 247, 310, 314, 344, 528
   Isadora quoted on, 76–77, 366, 372
   works shown at Paris Exposition, 71–72, 107–08
Rodman, Henrietta, 330
Rogers, Robert Cameron, 44n
Rolland, Romain, 431
Romanelli, Romano, 310
Romanov family, 152, 156, 361, 541
   slaughter of, 413, 493–94
Rose, Sir Francis, 519–20, 521, 527, 553
Rosetti, Dante Gabriel, 65
Rosicrucian sect, 596n33
Rosmersholm (Ibsen), 200, 201, 202, 203–04, 207, 209–10
Rousseau, Jean-Jacques, 70, 166, 167
Royal Academy, "secession" from, 59
Royal Ballet (London), 405

Royal family (English), 314
Royal family (Greek), 341
Rubáiyát of Omar Khayyám, The, 48, 81
Rubinstein, Beryl, 390
Rude, François, 344
Ruhl, Arthur, 273
Rummel, Frank, 502, 514
Rummel, Walter Morse, 379–85, 389, 393–97,
    400–06 *passim,* 453, 478–79, 502
Rumnev, Alexander, 425–26
Russell, Henry, 266
Russia, Isadora in. *See* Duncan, Isadora: TRAV-
    ELS, TOURS, AND LIFE ABROAD
Russian House of Arts (Berlin), 444
Russian Revolution
    1905, 148–49, 207
    1917, 361–62, 388, 400, 418, 436, 447,
        496, (fourth anniversary) 422
Russian workers' songs, 492

S

Sacchetto, Rita, 86
Sacco-Vanzetti case, 539
St. Denis, Ruth, 189–90, 226, 228–29, 271,
    367, 373, 376
St. John, Christopher, 228
St. Louis Sunday Gazette, 100–01
Saint-Marceaux, Meg de, 73
St. Petersburg Conservatory, 174
Saint-Saëns, Camille, 247
"Salomania," 226–29
Salome (Strauss opera), 226
Salvati, Renato, 350
Salvini, Tomasso, 204
Sand, George, 446
Sand, Robert, 124
San Francisco Art Association, 10
San Francisco Bulletin, 373
San Francisco Call, 102
San Francisco Chronicle, 12, 28
San Francisco earthquake, 6, 221, 328,
    373
San Francisco Examiner, 13, 372, 375
San Francisco *Morning Globe, Evening Globe,
    Mirror,* 9
Sarah Bernhardt Theatre (Paris), 106, 108,
    577n49
Sargent, John Singer, 59
Sargent, Margherita. *See* Duncan, Mrs.
    Augustin (second wife)
Sartoris, Cècile (Séverine), 407, 530, 542
Savonarola, Girolamo, 5
Scey-Montbéliard, Prince de, 76

Schaffer, Louis, 491
Schliemann, Heinrich, 21
Schloss, Jacob, 46, 51
Schneider, Ilya Ilyich, 224, 416–21, 424–30
    passim, 433–37, 440, 446, 449, 453,
    454, 481–95 *passim,* 499
School for Scandal, A (Daly production), 42
Schopenhauer, Arthur, 101
Schott, Walter, 313
Schubert, Franz, 194, 238, 263, 315, 330, 373,
    381, 387, 392, 400, 543. See also *Ave
    Maria*
Schumann, Robert, 155, 163
Scize, Pierre, 388
Scott, Kathleen Bruce, 108, 231, 265, 377, 378
    with Isadora at Deirdre's birth, 196,
        197–98
    joins Isadora on travels, 109, 114, 192,
        274–75, 276–77, 320
Scott, Peter, 274, 275, 277
Scott, Captain Robert Falcon, 231, 274
Scott, Sir Walter, 42
Scriabin, Alexander, 174, 420–21, 477, 546
Sea King's Daughter, The (pantomime), 161
Second Mrs. Tanqueray, The (Pinero), 66, 201
Seldes, George, 499–500, 503–04, 505–06
Seldes, Marian, 500
Selfridge, Gordon, 36, 376, 377, 413
Seraphita (Balzac), 518
Sergei Alexandrovitch, Grand Duke, 175
Seroff, Victor, 268, 383, 438, 442, 445, 446,
    512–13
    Isadora's affair with, 255, 518–35 *passim,*
        536, 537, 541–46 *passim*
Sert, Misia, 247
Seven German Dances (Schubert), 194
Seventh Symphony (Beethoven), 174, 233, 235,
    246, 373, 392, 470
    as "profanation," 117, 175, 263
Seymour, Lynn, 405
Shakespeare, William, 18, 26, 83, 90, 131,
    137, 331
    commemorated, 348
Shank, Mayor Lew, 466
Shaw, George Bernard, 29, 58, 131, 133, 178,
    220, 296, 380, 606n50
    Isadora meets, 378
Shaw, Martin, 192–93, 194, 229
    Craig's letters to, *see* Craig, Edward Henry
        Gordon
Shaw, Walter, 510, 511, 513, 518–19, 528, 529
Shawn, Ted, 367
Shebuyev, Nicolai Georgievitch, 152–54, 175
Shelley, Percy Bysshe, 18, 21, 83, 134

Shirer, William L., 539

Sibelius, Jean, 487

Sides, Alfredo, 530

Sikelianos, Angelos, 84

Sikelianos, Penelope. *See* Duncan, Mrs. Raymond

Sim, Annie, 292–93, 294, 295, 299, 301

Simonson, Lee, 142

Simplicissimus (German satirical weekly), 100

Sinden, Topsy, 140

Singer, Isaac Merritt, 73, 76, 249, 250

Singer, Mrs. Isaac Merritt (Isabella Boyer, second wife), 250

Singer, Isabella (Duchess Decazes), 73

Singer, Paris, 278, 316, 317, 320, 323, 439, 452, 503, 534

  divorce and remarriage, 360

  Isadora meets, 249–54, 263, 280, 286, 452–53, (quarrels) 255–59, 261, 265–69, 274–78 *passim*, 284, 287–88, 292, 358–60, (reconciliation) 549–53

  Isadora's child born, 265, (death of children) 294–96, 300, 302, 306–07

  and Isadora's finances, 338, 356–59, 367, 379, 472, 473, 513

  and theater plans, 280, 283–84, 286–87, 289, 290, 311, 313–14

Singer, Mrs. Paris (Lillie Graham, first wife), 250, 251

Singer, Mrs. Paris (Joan Balsh, second wife), 360, 453, 600n3

Singer, Winaretta (Paris's sister). *See* Polignac, Princess de

Singer, Winaretta (Paris's daughter), 251, 252

Skene, Hener, 265, 280, 281, 284, 288, 292, 308, 310, 311, 313, 375

"skirt" dancing, 32, 60, 70, 140

Sleeping Beauty (ballet), 151

Sloan, John, 233, 326, 327, 466

Slovo (periodical), 156

Smith, Joe, 83

Smith, Joseph, 10

Smith, T. R. "Tommy," 533

Smyth, Ethel, 73

Sniffen, Ida, 333

Socialist Club (Harvard), 326

Socialist International, 522

Socialist Party, 207, 326

Society for the Prevention of Cruelty to Children (St. Petersburg), 150, 155

Society for the Support and Maintenance of the Dance School of Isadora Duncan, 171, 191

Sokoloff, Vladimir, 421

Solano, Solita, 523–24

Sonata Pathétique (Beethoven), 311

Sophocles, 178, 336, 348, 447

Sorel, Cécile, 245, 286, 378, 448–49, 453, 455, 543, 596n21, 597n39

  quoted on Isadora, 299–300

Sorell, Walter, 151

South America

  Duncan tour, 344, 345–46, 348–55

  Toye plans "Isadorables" tour in, 340–41

Soviet Trade Commission, 402

Soviet Union, 384, 388, 393, 404, 444, 448, 458, 500, 541

  ballet and Duncan school funding, 481, 494

  and Duncan school, 482

  famine in, 418, 421

  Isadora in, *see* Duncan, Isadora: TRAVELS, TOURS, AND LIFE ABROAD

  Isadora's letter to, 521–22

  marriage in, 438, 439

  New Economic Policy (NEP), 421, 424, 425

  secret police (Cheka), 485–87

  tightens grip on artists, 515

Spaeth, Sigmund, 391

Spanish-American War, 42

Specter of the Rose, The (ballet), 286

Spencer, Herbert, 166, 327

Spewack, Sam, 500

Spicer, Alice, 531, 545, 553

Spirescu, Oscar, 357

Spirit of a Nation Drawn into War, The (Duncan program), 360

Spirit of St. Louis, The (airplane), 539

Stalin, Joseph, 431, 489

Stanislavsky, Konstantin, 416, 422, 435

  and Craig, 176, 231, 253

  and Isadora, 175–76, 222, 225, 234, 253, 259–60, 261–62, 289, 417

  and Method acting, 79, 223–24

Startsev, Ivan, 430

State Higher Theater Workshop (Soviet Union), 422

Stebbins, Genevieve, 29, 30

Steffens, Lincoln, 326

Steichen, Clara, 395

Steichen, Edward, 367, 395, 396–97, 541–42, 601n18

Stein, Gertrude, 16, 19, 158, 286, 331, 363, 506, 509, 519, 523, 595n97

Stein, Leo, 278

Steiner, Rudolf, 380

Stern, Isaac, 390

Stieglitz, Alfred, 367
stock market crash (1929), 549
Stokes, Sewell, 528–29, 530, 532
Stopes, Marie, 116
Strauss, Richard, 226
Strauss waltzes, 43, 46, 90–91, 115–16, 186,
190, 228, 238
Stravinsky, Igor, 510
strike, Paterson (1913), 325, 338
Sturges, Preston, 82–83, 84, 121, 251, 377,
539–40, 549, 551, 553–54
quoted on Duncans, 120, 122–23, 242,
243, 264, 300, 305, 320, 337, 339,
548
Sturges, Solomon, 84, 120, 242, 540
Sturges, Mrs. Solomon. See Desti, Mary
Sue, Louis, 246, 283–84, 289, 303, 306, 311,
313
Sullivan, Mark, 44
Sunday, Reverend Billy, 462
Suppliants (Aeschylus), 115
Susanna (Duncan pupil), 162
Suzanne (Duncan pupil), 324
Svetlov, Valerian, 153
Swan Lake (ballet), 151
Sweet, Blanche, 367
Swinburne, Algernon, 51
Switzerland, Isadorables in, 359, 365
Sykes, Captain, 276–77
Sylphides, Les (ballet), 154, 175, 246
Symphonie zu Dantes Divina Commedia (Liszt),
548
Szold, Bernardine, 533, 543, 548, 549

T

Taft, Lorado, 384
Tägliche Rundschau (periodical), 172
Talleyrand-Périgord, Charles-Maurice de,
300
Tannhäuser (Wagner opera), 117–19, 120, 124,
382
Bacchanal (Duncan dance), 118, 271, 273,
279, 400, 401, 478
Taylor, Paul, 574n42
Tchaikovsky, Peter Ilyich, 151, 362, 373, 387,
417, 425, 462, 608n45. See also Pathé-
tique (Duncan dance)
Tchelitchew, Pavel, 519
Telegraaf, De (Amsterdam), 208
Telyakovsky, Vladimir, 225
Temps, Le (Paris), 277, 314
Ten Broeck, Helen, 108
Terry, Alice, 510

Terry, Ellen, 26, 66, 184, 188, 314, 331,
572n13
Craig as son of, 130–33, 137, 196, 207,
230, 231
golden jubilee of, 195
granddaughter Deirdre, 198, 200, 296,
308, 412
Isadora meets, 229–30
remarries, 211
Terry, Walter, 45
Thackeray, William Makepeace, 18
Thalheimer, Abe, 233
Thaulow, Fritz, 108
Thaw, Harry, 81
Theater des Westens (Berlin), 191
Théâtre de l'Oeuvre (Paris), 242, 401
Théâtre des Champs Elysées, 290, 389, 401
Théâtre du Beau, Le, plans for, 280, 283–84,
287, 289, 290, 292, 313
Théâtre du Châtelet (Paris), 245, 269, 279,
280, 290, 291
Théâtre Galéries (Brussels), 453
Theatre Guild, 27, 370
Théâtre-Lyrique (Montparnasse). See Gaité-
Lyrique
Théâtre Mogador (Paris), 542–43
Theresa ("Isadorable"). See Kruger, Theresa
Thibaud, Jacques, 347
This Is My Affair (Kinel), 450
Thode, Heinrich, 121–22, 125, 189
Thode, Mrs. Heinrich (Daniela Wagner), 121
Thompson, Dorothy, 482, 499
Thurber, James, 515
Thus Spake Zarathustra (Nietszche), 103
Tiller Girls, 446
Time Was (Robertson), 59
Toklas, Alice B., 524
Tolstoy, Alexei, 445, 447
Tolstoy, Leo, 278, 516
Tolstoy, Natalya, 447
Tolstoy, Nikita, 447
Tolstoy, Sofia, 516
Torrence, Ridgely, 237
Touchstone, The (periodical), 233, 237
Toye, Frederick, 337, 340–41
Treadwell, Florence. See Boynton, Florence
Treadwell
Tresca, Carlo, 325
Tristan und Isolde (Wagner opera), 215, 271,
378, 382, 543
Trocadéro (Paris), 246, 290, 315
wartime performances at, 343–45, 359,
(postwar) 386–87, 454, 477, 478, 480
Trotsky, Leon, 418, 457, 485, 486

Twain, Mark, 9
Twelfth Night (Daly production), 42

U

Udine, Jean d', 107
Ukrainian Chorus, 400
Ultima Hora (Buenos Aires), 352
United Arts Management (Direktion
    Vereinigter Künste), 179, 187
Universal Exposition (Paris, 1900), 70, 72
Untermeyer, Louis, 218, 326
Untold Story, The (Desti), 540–41
Up to Now (Shaw), 192
Ustinov, George, 439
Uzès, Duchess d', 74

V

Vail, Lawrence, 530
Vala (Duncan pupil), 324
Valencia, Tórtola, 226
Valentino, Rudolph, 510
Valls, Ernesto, 348, 349, 350
Valse Triste (Sibelius), 487
Vanderbilt, Mrs. Frederick W., 49
Vanderlip, Frank, 338
Van Goor, Willem Noothoven, 220–21, 222,
    238
Vanity Fair magazine, 367, 396
Van Vechten, Carl, 263, 271, 272, 273, 345,
    360, 362, 363, 364
Van Vlissingen, Mrs. Arend, 48
Varèse, Edgard, 367, 369
Variety magazine, 233
Vashentseva, Yulia, 425, 435
Vaughan, Kate, 60
vegetarianism, 55, 112, 167, 521
Venice Preserved (Otway), 138
Venizélos, Eleuthérios, 341–42, 393, 397,
    399
Verlaine, Paul, 73
Vetlugin, Vladimir, 455, 471
Victoria, princess of Wales, 60
Victoria, queen of England, 45, 60, 244, 330
Victoria of Saxe-Meiningen, 171
Vieux-Colombier (Paris), 401
Vikings (Ibsen), 137
Village. See Greenwich Village
Villari, Pasquale, 565n2
Vision of Salomé (Allan dance), 190, 227–29
Vladimir Alexandrovitch, Grand Duke, 152
Vogue magazine, 329
Volpin, Valentin, 431

von Bülow, Hans, 119
Votichenko, Dolly, 405–06, 531

W

Wagner, Cosima, 118, 119–20, 121, 123, 124,
    125, 189, 475
Wagner, Richard, 23, 117, 118–20, 121, 125,
    234, 235, 266, 278, 532, 608n45
  Duncan dances to music of, 190, 271,
    272, 388, 399–400, 401, 478, (South
    American fiasco) 352, 353, ("tedious")
    461
Wagner, Siegfried, 99, 118
Wagner, Wolfgang, 118
Wagner (Bayreuth) festival, 117–25, 171,
    286–87
Wallace, Richard, 514
Waltz Evening (Duncan program), 194
Waltz in A-flat (Brahms), 470
Ward, Mary (servant), 16, 568n39
Wardell, Charles (Charles Kelly), 131
Warsaw Philharmonic orchestra, 205
Warshavianka (Duncan dance), 492
Washington, George and Martha, miniatures
    of, 10
Watts, George F., 51, 59, 60, 61, 66, 130,
    131
Weber, Carl Maria von, 41
Weidman, Charles, 367
Wendt, William de, 369
Wescott, Glenway, 510, 528, 533, 548, 549
Wharton, Edith, 50–51, 246
Wheeler, Monroe, 510
Whistler, James, 51
White, Stanford, 81
Whiteford, Sarah. See Duncan, Mrs. Augustin
    (first wife)
Whitman, Walt, 22, 166, 177, 326, 327,
    534
  Isadora as "spiritual daughter" of, 18, 32,
    103, 221, 235, 255, 364
  quoted, 222, 460
Whitney, Gertrude Vanderbilt, 357
Wickman, Anna, 510
Wiesenthal sisters, 190
Wilde, Oscar, 26, 65, 75, 132, 226, 300, 341
Wilhelm II, German kaiser, 99, 317, 341–42,
    389
Wilson, Woodrow, 360, 361, 384, 523
Winckelmann, Johann, 21, 56
Wind Fire (Steichen portrait), 396
Windsor Hotel fire, 52–54, 57, 73, 232
Winged Victory. See Nike of Samothrace

Wolff, Albert, 542
woman suffrage, 29, 102, 457, 530
Women as World Builders (Dell), 326–27
Woodhull, Victoria, 327
Woolf, Virginia, 378
Workers' Moscow, The (periodical), 421
World's Columbian Exposition (Chicago, 1893), 34, 70
World War I, 268, 285
  begins, 315–17
  ends, 383–84
  U.S. enters, 360–64
World War II, 521
Württemberg, king and queen of, 123
Wycherly, Margaret, 336
Wyndham, George and Sibell, 59

Y

Yacco, Sada, 71, 85
Yakoleva (Lunacharsky's deputy), 491

Yakulov, George, 426, 429
Yalta Conference, 488–89
Yeats, John Butler, 239–40
Yorska, Lotte, 77, 513–14, 529, 530–31, 537, 539
Young Intellectuals, 326
Ysaÿe, Eugène, 63, 367, 369, 374, 453
Yvette (Duncan pupil), 324
Yznaga, Consuelo, duchess of Manchester, 227, 230, 231

Z

Zehme, Dr. and Mrs., 194
Zelle, Margarete. See Mata Hari
Zetkin, Klara, 489
Ziegfeld, Florenz, 227
Ziegfeld's Follies, 232
Zimin Theatre (Moscow), 424, 425, 426
Zinoviev, "Zino," 493
Zweig, Stefan, 447